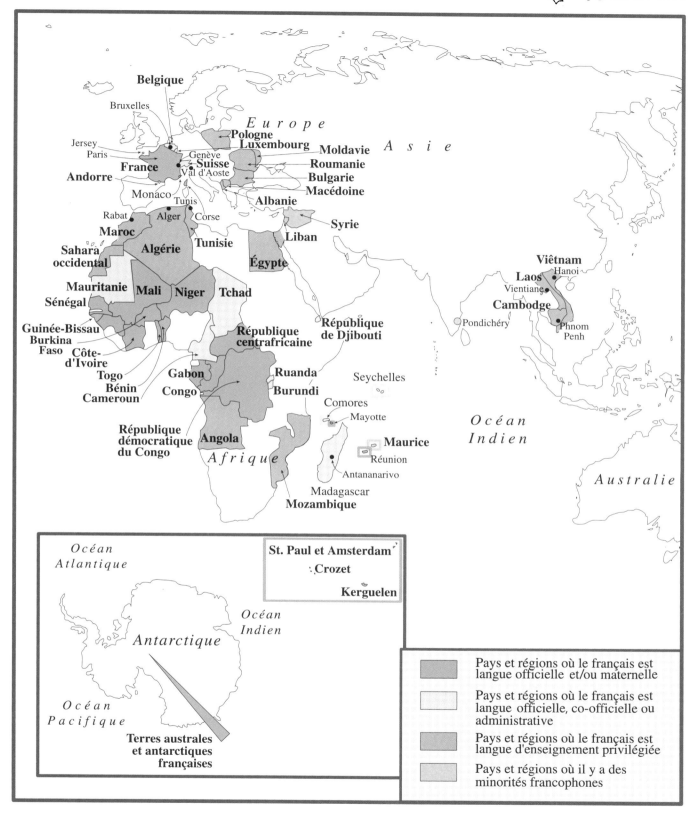

Bruxelles
*E u r o p e*
*A s i e*
Belgique
Pologne
Luxembourg
Moldavie
Jersey
Paris
Genève
Roumanie
Suisse
France
Val d'Aoste
Bulgarie
Macédoine
Andorre
Monaco
Albanie
Tunis
Syrie
Rabat
Alger
Corse
Liban
Maroc
Algérie
Égypte
Sahara
occidental
Tunisie
Viêtnam
Hanoi
Laos
Mauritanie
Mali
Niger
Tchad
Vientiane
Sénégal
Cambodge
Guinée-Bissau
République
centrafricaine
République
de Djibouti
Pondichéry
Phnom
Penh
Burkina
Faso
Côte-
d'Ivoire
Togo
Gabon
Ruanda
Seychelles
*Océan
Indien*
Bénin
Cameroun
Congo
Burundi
Comores
Mayotte
République
démocratique
du Congo
Angola
Maurice
*Afrique*
Réunion
Antananarivo
*Australie*
Madagascar
Mozambique

*Océan
Atlantique*

St. Paul et Amsterdam
Crozet
Kerguelen

*Océan
Indien*

*Antarctique*

*Océan
Pacifique*

Terres australes
et antarctiques
françaises

Pays et régions où le français est
langue officielle et/ou maternelle

Pays et régions où le français est
langue officielle, co-officielle ou
administrative

Pays et régions où le français est
langue d'enseignement privilégiée

Pays et régions où il y a des
minorités francophones

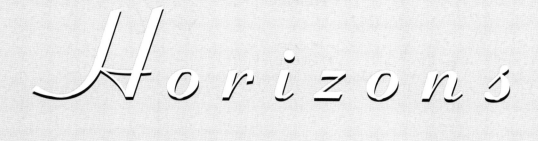

# Horizons

## THIRD EDITION

**Joan H. Manley**
*University of Texas—El Paso*

**Stuart Smith**
*Austin Community College*

**John T. McMinn**
*Austin Community College*

**Marc A. Prévost**
*Austin Community College*

THOMSON
™
HEINLE

Australia   Canada   Mexico   Singapore   Spain   United Kingdom   United States

Horizons
Third Edition
Manley | Smith | McMinn | Prévost

Publisher: Janet Dracksdorf
Acquisitions Editor: Lara Semones
Senior Production Project Manager: Esther Marshall
Development Editor: Mayanne Wright
Assistant Editor: Arlinda Shtuni
Marketing Manager: Lindsey Richardson
Marketing Assistant: Rachel Bairstow
Advertising Project Manager: Stacey Purviance
Manufacturing Manager: Marcia Locke
Compositor: Pre-Press Company, Inc.

Project Management: Pre-Press Company, Inc. & Sev Champeny
Photo Manager: Sheri Blaney
Photo Reseacher: Linda Finigan
Interior Designer: Brian Salisbury
Cover Designer: Diane Levy
Cover Printer: Coral Graphics
Printer: CTPS

Cover image: © Robert Harding Picture Library Ltd./Alamy Images

Printed in China
3  4  5  08  07  06

For more information about our products, contact us at:
**Thomson Learning Academic Resource Center**
**1-800-423-0563**
For permission to use material from this text or product, submit a request online at **http://www.thomsonrights.com.**
Any additional questions about permissions can be submitted by email to **thomsonrights@thomson.com.**

Library of Congress Control Number:  2004116034

Student Edition: ISBN 1-4130-0534-9
Annotated Instructor's Edition: ISBN 1-4130-0530-6

**Thomson Higher Education**
**25 Thomson Place**
**Boston, MA 02210-1202**
**USA**

Credits appear on page 492, which constitute a continuation of the copyright page.

**Asia (including India)**
Thomson Learning
5 Shenton Way
#01-01 UIC Building
Singapore 068808

**Australia/New Zealand**
Thomson Learning Australia
102 Dodds Street
Southbank, Victoria 3006
Australia

**Canada**
Thomson Nelson
1120 Birchmount Road
Toronto, Ontario M1K 5G4
Canada

**UK/Europe/Middle East/Africa**
Thomson Learning
High Holborn House
50–51 Bedford Road
London WC1R 4LR
United Kingdom

**Latin America**
Thomson Learning
Seneca, 53
Colonia Polanco
11560 Mexico
D.F. Mexico

**Spain (including Portugal)**
Thomson Paraninfo
Calle Magallanes, 25
28015 Madrid, Spain

# Table des matières

# Preface

## Do you have a gift for languages?

Have you ever heard people say that they know someone who has a gift for languages? What does that mean? Are some people born with a special ability to learn languages? How do you know if you have a gift for languages? If you understood the sentence you just read, then you have a gift for languages. After all, you have already learned to speak and understand at least one language well—English. Everybody is born with a natural ability to learn languages, but some individuals seem to learn languages more quickly than others do. This is because, over time, we develop different learning styles.

The process individuals use to learn languages depends a great deal on their personality. As with any other process, such as learning a new computer program or writing a composition for English class, individuals can attain similar results, although they approach the task differently. Some language learners like to plan each step before beginning. Others prefer to jump in as soon as they know enough to get started, and continue from there using a hit-or-miss method. Some language learners like to understand in detail why a language works the way it does before they try to use it, whereas others are ready to try speaking as soon as they know only the most basic rules, making educated guesses about how to express themselves.

Both methods have advantages and disadvantages. Some people become so bogged down in details that they lose sight of their main purpose—communication. Others pay so little attention to details that what they say is unintelligible. No matter what sort of learner you are, the most important part of the language-learning process is to constantly try to use the language to express yourself. Always alternate study of vocabulary and structures with attempts to communicate.

Since you now know that you have a gift for languages, you might think of the following pages as a user's manual that suggests how to use your language-learning capacity to learn French efficiently. Some of the learning techniques will work for you, others may not fit your learning style. Read through the following three sections before beginning your French studies, and refer to them later to develop the language-learning process that works best for you.

- **Goals and expectations:** How much French should you expect to learn in your first year of study and how much time and effort will be required of you?

- **Motivation:** How do you motivate yourself to study and practice the language?

- **Learning techniques:** What are some study tips that will facilitate learning French?

## Goals and Expectations

### Who can learn a language?

Many people believe that, as an adult, you cannot learn a language as well as you might have when you were a child. It is true that children are good language learners, but there is no reason why adults cannot learn to speak a language with near-native fluency. Children learn languages well because they can adapt very easily and they do it willingly. Being able to adapt is very important in language learning. Children are not afraid to try something new, and they are not easily embarrassed if things do not turn out as they expect. Adults, on the other hand, are often afraid of doing something wrong or looking ridiculous. Don't be afraid to experiment, using what you already know to guess at how to express yourself in French. It does no harm if you try to say something and you do not get the expected response. Just try again.

By the time people become adults, they generally learn by analyzing, rather than by doing. They have also grown so accustomed to their own way of doing things that they are reluctant to change. Similarly, adult language learners often feel that the way English works is the natural way. They try to force the language they are learning into the same mold. In fact, languages work in a variety of ways, all equally natural. Learn to accept that the French way of doing things is just as natural and valid as the English way.

Another difference in the way that children and adults learn languages is that children spend a lot more time focused on what they are doing. When children learn languages, they spend almost every hour they are awake for several years doing nothing but learning the language. Learning to communicate is their principal objective in life. Most adults, on the other hand, spend just a few hours a week studying a new language, and during this time they are often distracted by many other aspects of their lives. In a classroom setting where small children have contact with a foreign language for just a few hours per week, children do not learn better than adults. In fact, adults have several advantages over children, such as their ability to organize and their longer attention spans. Your ability to develop fluency in French depends mainly on three things: the amount of time you spend with the language, how focused you are, and how willing you are to try to communicate using it.

### How well will you speak after a year?

Those of you who are new to foreign language study probably have a variety of ideas about what you will be doing in this course. People who become frustrated in foreign language study generally do so because they start off with the wrong expectations. Some people begin a foreign language course with a negative attitude, thinking that it is impossible to really learn a language without going to a country where it is spoken. Although it is indeed usually easier to learn French in a French-speaking region, you can learn to speak French very fluently here as well. Once again, it is a question of spending time with the language, while focusing on how to communicate with it.

There are also some students who begin foreign language classes with expectations that are too high, thinking that they will begin speaking French with complete fluency nearly overnight. Learning a language takes time. Even after two years of concentrated study, it is reasonable to have achieved only basic fluency. If you set a goal for yourself to have every-day conversation skills after your second year of study, and if you work hard toward this goal, you will be able to function in most everyday conversation settings; however, you will still frequently have to look for words, you will probably still speak in short simple sentences, and you will often have to use circumlocution to get your meaning across. In *Horizons,* you will learn how to function in the most common situations in which you are likely to find yourself in a francophone region. To illustrate how much you will learn during the first few weeks of study, take out a sheet of paper, and list, in English, the first eight questions you would probably ask in the following situation: Before the first day of class, you sit down next to a student you have never seen before and you begin to chat.

In this situation, students generally ask questions like the following:

- How are you doing?
- What's your name?
- What are you studying?
- Where are you from?
- Where do you live? / Do you live on campus?
- Do you like it there?
- Do you work? Where?
- When are you graduating?

This is the extent of the conversation that you have with many people you will meet, and you will be able to do this in French after only a few weeks.

## How much time and effort must you invest to be a successful language learner?

There are three P's involved in learning a language: patience, practice, and persistence. We have already said that success in learning a foreign language depends on how much time you spend studying and practicing it. You might wonder how time-consuming French class will be. The amount of time re-quired depends on your study skills and attention span. However, nobody can be successful without devoting many hours to studying and using the language. Generally, to make steady progress at the rate that material is presented in most college or university classes, you should expect to spend two to three hours on the language outside of class, for every hour that you are in class.

## What is involved in learning to express yourself in another language?

Students studying a foreign language for the first time may have false expectations about what is involved in learning to speak another language. Many people think that you just substitute a French word for the equivalent word in English. Most of the time, you cannot translate word for word from one language to another. For example, if a French speaker substituted the equivalent English word for each French word in the following sentence, it would create a very un-usual sentence.

**Nous ne l'avons pas encore fait.**

*\*We not it have not still done.*

You might be able to figure out that this sentence means, "We haven't done it yet," but sometimes translating word for word can give a completely wrong meaning. For example, if you translate the following sentence word for word, you would think that it has the first meaning that follows it, whereas it really has the second. This is because the indirect object pronoun **vous** (*[to] you*) precedes the verb in French.

**Je voudrais vous parler demain, s'il vous plaît.**

*\*I would like you to speak tomorrow, if it you pleases.*

*I would like to speak to you tomorrow, please.*

You probably noticed in this last example that one word in English may be translated by several words in French and vice versa (**voudrais** = *would like,* **vous** = *to you,* **parler** = *to speak,* **s'il vous plaît** = *please*).

Differences in languages are not due simply to a lack of one-to-one correspondence between words and structures. Cultural differences also strongly affect how we communicate. Culture and language are so interrelated that it is impossible to learn a language fluently without becoming famil-iar with the culture(s) where it is spoken. For example, in French, a cultural difference that affects the spoken language is that French society is not as informal as ours. Adults gen-erally do not call each other by their first names, and the words for *sir* and *madam* are used much more frequently than in English. For example, it is normal to say **Bonjour, monsieur** (*Hello, sir*), whereas English speakers say *Hello.*

Cultural differences affect the spoken language and also nonverbal communication. For instance, when the French speak to each other, they generally stand closer than we do. When we are talking to a French-speaker, we may feel that our space is invaded and back away. The French interpret this as standoffishness. As you can see, learning to communicate in French entails a lot more than substituting French words for English words in a sentence.

## Does practice make perfect?

Your goal in learning French should not be to say everything perfectly. If you set this goal for yourself, you will probably be afraid to open your mouth, fearing mistakes. Your goal should be to communicate clearly, but you should expect to make mistakes when speaking. If you make a mistake that impedes communication, those you are speaking to will ask for clarification or repeat what you have said to be sure of what you mean. Listen carefully to how they express themselves, and make adjustments the next time you need to convey a similar message.

Although perfection is not the goal of language learners, practice is vital to success. (Remember the three P's of language learning: patience, practice, and persistence.) You can learn every vocabulary word and rule in the book, but unless you practice regularly, listening to French and attempting to speak it, you will not learn the language. Practicing a language is just as necessary for success as practicing a sport or a musical instrument. Imagine that you are a football player or pianist. You might know every play in the book, or you might understand music theory completely, but unless you practice, you will never be able to perform. It is important to learn the rules of French, but you must also practice it regularly.

## What do you do if foreign languages make you panic?

Most individuals feel nervous when they have to speak to strangers. This is true when you speak your own language, and it's even truer when speaking a foreign language. There is no reason to be nervous, yet fear of looking ridiculous is often difficult to control. It is normal to experience some anxiety in class. If you suffer extreme anxiety in language class—to such a degree that it impedes your ability to concentrate—it is best to recognize that you fear having to perform in class. Go see your instructor and discuss your anxiety. In order to conquer it, you must acknowledge it.

## Motivation

### How can learning a foreign language help you?

Learning a foreign language should be fun. After all, you will spend a lot of class time chatting with classmates, which most of us find enjoyable. However, learning French takes time and effort. No matter how much you enjoy it, there will be times when you need to motivate yourself to study or practice. You can use motivation techniques for practicing a language similar to those musicians or athletes use to practice an instrument or a sport.

Many musicians and athletes have a personal goal. They imagine themselves playing a great concert at Carnegie Hall or winning a big game, receiving applause and praise. Similarly, each time you start to practice French, imagine yourself speaking French fluently with a beautiful accent. In this mental image, you might be a diplomat, or you might be talking to the waiter at a French restaurant, impressing your friends.

Some people who practice an instrument or a sport do so for personal growth. Many people feel that learning a new language helps them discover a new side of their personality. By learning to appreciate another culture, you learn to understand your own better. You also come to know yourself better and you broaden your horizons.

Of course, a lot of people are motivated to practice an instrument or a sport because they make their living from it. This is good motivation for learning a language too. In today's international economy, the best jobs are going more and more to those who speak more than one language, and who have an understanding of other cultures. Many jobs in the travel industry, in communications, in government, and in companies dealing in international trade and business require proficiency in another language.

### How can you learn to enjoy studying?

As with any accomplishment, learning a foreign language requires a lot of work. You will enjoy it more if you think of it as a hobby or a pastime and as an opportunity to develop a skill. Here are some training techniques that can help you learn a new language.

- Get into a routine. Devote a particular time of day to studying French. It is best to find a time when you are fresh and free of distractions, so you can concentrate on what you are doing. If you study at the same time every day, getting started will become habitual, and you will have won half the battle. Once you are settled working and learning, it becomes fun.
- Make sure that the place where you study is inviting and that you enjoy being there.
- Study frequently for short periods of time, rather than having marathon sessions. After about two hours of study, the ability of the brain to retain information is greatly reduced. You tend to remember what you learn at the beginning of each study session and at the end. What you study in the middle tends to become blurred. To illustrate this, read the following words one time, then turn the page and see how many you remember.

   dog, house, sofa, cat, rooster, room, telephone, mouse, book, pencil, television

Most people can remember the first word and the last. The longer the list, the harder it is to remember the words in the middle. The same is true with studying. Study smaller "chunks" of material more frequently, and set reasonable goals for yourself. Don't try to learn it all at once.

- Study with a classmate or a friend. It is much easier to practice talking with someone else, and it is easier to spend more time working with the language if you are interacting with another person. Also, by studying with classmates, you will feel more comfortable speaking in front of them, which eliminates some of the embarrassment some adults feel when trying to pronounce foreign words in front of the whole class.

- Play games with the language. It is fun to learn how to say things in a new language. For instance, ask yourself how you would say things you hear on the radio or television in French. If you do know how to say something in French that you hear, your knowledge will become more certain. If you don't know how to say something in French, that's normal if you are a beginner. When you finally learn the word or expression you were wondering about, you will remember it more easily, because you have already thought about it.

- Surround yourself by French. Rent French movies or watch DVDs of American movies in the French-language track, listen to French music, and read French comic books and magazines. Magazines with a lot of pictures are the best, because the pictures give you clues to the meaning of unfamiliar words. You probably will not understand very much at first in movies and songs, but they will motivate you to learn more. They teach you about cultural differences, and they help give you a sense of good pronunciation.

- Don't let yourself get frustrated. If you are frustrated each time you sit down to study, ask yourself why. First of all, make sure that you are not studying when you are too tired or hungry. Also, make sure that you clearly understand your assignment and its purpose. Learn to distinguish a language-learning problem from a problem understanding instructions. If you are confused about what you are to do or why, see your instructor during office hours or contact another student. (This is another reason to study with a classmate!)

# Learning Techniques

## How can you spend your study time most efficiently?

Individuals organize material differently as they learn it. Some people learn better by seeing something; others learn better by hearing it. The following are some study tips for how to go about learning French. You may find that some of these methods work for you and others do not. Be creative in practicing your French, using a variety of study techniques.

## General study tips

- Learn not to translate word for word. Learn to read and listen to whole sentences at a time.

- Keep a log of your study time in a small spiral notebook. This will help you learn to study more efficiently. Each time you sit down to study new material, write down the time you begin. When you finish, write down the time you stop, and two or three sentences summarizing what you studied. Students often feel frustrated that they spend a lot of time studying, but they do not retain much. By keeping a log, you will know exactly how much time you spend on French. Writing one or two sentences summarizing what you studied helps you check your retention.

- Alternate speaking, listening, reading, and writing activities. By changing tasks frequently, you will be able to study longer without losing your concentration.

## Vocabulary-learning techniques

- Use your senses. Pronounce words aloud as you study them. Close your eyes as you pronounce the word and picture the thing or activity represented by nouns or verbs.

- Use flashcards. When possible, draw a simple picture instead of the English word. Also, write a sentence using the word on the card, trying to remember it each time you look at the card. Use different colored inks to help you visualize the meaning of words. For example, when studying colors, write them on the flashcard in that color. When learning food items, write the words for red foods, such as strawberries and tomatoes, in red, the words for green foods in green, etc. Write words that can be associated with shapes, such as tall, short, big, small, round, or square, with letters having similar shapes.

- Learn useful common phrases such as "What time is it?" or "How are you?" as a whole.

- Label household items in French on masking tape.

- Tape lists of vocabulary in places where you spend time doing routine tasks.

- Study vocabulary in manageable "chunks." Each morning, write out a list of 20 new words and carry it in your pocket. A few times during the day, spend two minutes trying to remember the words on the list. Take out the list and review the words you forgot for two minutes. By the end of the day, you will have spent just a few minutes and you will have learned the 20 words.

- Learn 10 useful phrases every day.
- If you know a French speaker, ask him or her to record the vocabulary words you want to learn on a cassette so you can play them at home, while you jog, or in your car.
- Make tests for yourself. At the end of a study session, write the English words or phrases on a sheet of paper. Put the sheet of paper away for a few hours. Later, take it out and see how many of the French equivalents of these words or phrases you remember.
- Group words in logical categories. For example, learn words for fruits together, words for animals together, sports-related vocabulary together, etc.
- Make flashcards with antonyms on each side such as hot/cold, near/far, to go to sleep/to wake up, etc.
- Use related English words to help you remember the French. For example, the French word for *to begin* is **commencer.** Associate it with *to commence.* Be creative in finding associations. For example, the word for *open* is **ouvert.** You can associate it with *overture,* which is the opening part of a musical piece, or an *overt* action, which is one that is done in the open. Write related English words on flashcards.
- Learn to say **"Comment dit-on... ?"** (*"How do you say . . . ?"*) when you do not know a word or phrase.
- Remember that we cannot say everything even in our own language. If you do not know a word, try to think of another way to say what you want. Use circumlocution. For example, if you do not know how to say "to drive," say "to take the car" instead.

## Grammar-learning techniques

- Play teacher. Try to guess what your instructor would ask you to do if he or she were giving a quiz the next day.
- Do the **Pour vérifier** self-checks in the margins next to explanations of structures.
- Use color coding to help you remember grammatical information. For example, all nouns in French are categorized either as masculine or feminine, and you must memorize in which category each noun belongs. When you make the flashcards, write feminine nouns on pink cards or with pink ink and use blue for masculine nouns. Use an eye-catching color on flashcards to indicate points you want to remember, such as irregular plurals or verbs that take **être** in the **passé composé.**

- If you like to use lists to study, organize them so that they help you remember information about words. For example, to remember noun gender, write masculine words in a column on the left and feminine words in a column on the right. If you can visualize where the word is on the list, you can remember its gender.
- Learn to accept ambiguity. Sometimes, as soon as you learn a new rule, you find out that it doesn't always work the way you expect it to.

## Pronunciation-learning techniques

- Repeat everything you hear in French under your breath or in your head, even if you have no idea what it means. This will not only help your pronunciation, it will help your listening comprehension and your ability to learn vocabulary. For instance, if you keep repeating an unfamiliar word you hear in your head, when you finally find out what it means, you will remember it very easily.
- Read French words aloud as you study.
- Listen to the CDs that go with the book and the *Cahier d'activités orales* (Lab Manual) several times. It is impossible to concentrate both on meaning and pronunciation the first time you listen to them. Listen to them at least once focusing on pronunciation only.
- Make tapes of yourself and compare them to those of native speakers.
- Exaggerate as you practice at home. Any pronunciation that is not English will seem like exaggeration. Psychologically, it is very difficult to listen to yourself speaking another language. Pretend you are a French actor playing a role as you practice pronunciation.

## Using the *Text Audio CDs* and the *Lab Audio CDs*

There are two distinct CDs that go with each chapter of the **Horizons** program: the *Text Audio CD* and the *Lab Audio CD.* The activities on the *Text Audio CDs* correspond to the listening sections marked with an audio icon in the textbook. These CDs are provided so that you can review material covered in class on your own, or prepare for the next day's class. The activities corresponding to the *Lab Audio CDs* are found in the *Cahier,* in the *Activités orales* section. These activities give you extra practice listening to and pronouncing French. When you are preparing to do a listening activity in the textbook or the *Activités orales* section of the *Cahier,* it is important to make sure that you have the right CD.

In order to get maximum benefit from the CDs, approach listening activities with the right attitude. It takes time, patience, and practice to understand French spoken at a normal conversational speed. Do not be surprised if you find it difficult at first. Relax and listen to passages more than once. You will understand a little more each time. Remember that you will not understand everything and that, for some exercises, you are only expected to understand enough to answer specific questions. Read through exercises prior to starting the CD, so that you know what to listen for.

If you find you do not have enough time to process and respond to a question before the next one, take advantage of the pause or stop button on your CD player to give yourself more time. Most importantly, be patient and remember that you can always listen again.

Be willing to listen to the CDs several times. It is important to listen to them at least one separate time focusing solely on pronunciation. Practice, patience, and persistence pay!

We hope that the preceding suggestions on how to go about learning French will serve you well, helping you to become a successful language learner. Good luck with your French studies, and most of all, enjoy yourself!

## Acknowledgments

We are grateful to a great many people for helping us transform our collective classroom experience into this text.

Principal among these are: Lara Semones for the opportunity to work with Thomson Heinle and for her guidance; the Development Editor, Mayanne Wright; Esther Marshall with the help of Sev Champeny and the PrePress Company service, for their support and hard work down the home stretch. Our thanks also go to the other people and freelancers: copyeditor, Jackie Rebisz; native reader, Valérie Simondet; proofreaders, Christian Hiltenbrand and Dianne Harwood; interior designer, Brian Salisbury and cover designer, Diane Levy.

We would particularly like to thank our reviewers of the current and previous editions:

Diane Fagin Adler, *North Carolina State University*

Lynne Barnes, *Colorado State University*

Patricia Brand, *University of Colorado, Boulder*

Lawrence Busenbark, *University of Oregon*

Glenda Carl, *Southwestern University*

Brigette Cross, *Marquette University*

Nadine DeVito, *University of Chicago*

Béatrice Dupuy, *Louisiana State University*

Bonnie Fonseca-Greber, *Bowling Green State University*

Janette Funaro, *Johnson County Community College*

Angela Elsey, *University of California, Santa Cruz*

Marie-France Étienne, *Hobart & William Smith College*

Al Ford, *California State University, Northridge*

Barbara Galbraith, *Wright State University*

Kirsten Halling, *Wright State University*

Carol Hofmann, *University of Southern California*

Andrea Javel, *Boston College*

Catherine Jolivet, *University of Louisiana*

Denise Jones, *Southwestern Louisiana University*

Alice Kornovich, *Loyola University, New Orleans*

June Legge, *Clayton State University*

Marie Léticée, *University of Central Florida*

Jane Lindebaugh, *York College*

Kathy Lorenz, *University of Cincinnati*

Roy Luna, *Miami Dade Community College, Wolfson*

Carole Maccotta, *University of North Carolina, Chapel Hill*

Marie-Laure Marceaux, *University of Northern Colorado*

Chantal Maréchal, *Virginia Commonwealth University*

Heather MacLean, *Kent State University*

Mari O'Brien, *Wright State University*

Jean-Louis Picherit, *University of Wyoming*

Leslee Poultons, *University of Wisconsin*

Joanna Radin, *University of Colorado*

Jocelyn Rapinac, *Tufts University*

Molly Recchia, *Western Michigan University*

Kittye Robbins-Herring, *Mississippi State University*

Dianne Sears, *University of Massachusetts-Amherst*

Larry Schehr, *North Carolina State University*

Michael Schwartz, *East Carolina University*

Leslie Sconduto, *Armstrong State College*

Alex Silverman, *School for International Training*

Laurie Sauble-Otto, *University of Northern Colorado*

Yvonne Stebbins, *Sinclair Community College*

Katheryn Stewart, *Oakland Community College*

Robert M. Terry, *University of Richmond*

Suzanne Toczyski, *Sonoma State University*

Louise Wills, *Harvard University*

C.W. Vance, *University of North Carolina, Charlotte*

May Waggoner, *University of Louisiana at Lafayette*

A special thanks to both Jims, Laura, Andrew, Annick, Daniel, and Joel.

Last, but obviously not least, we thank each other for the tolerance, mutual encouragement, and strengthened bonds of friendship such an endeavor requires.

Merci mille fois!

**Nature morte**
**RAOUL DUFY**
**(1877–1953)**

1934
Evergreen House
Foundation/The Johns
Hopkins University

Vivid colorful scenes depicting the pleasures and luxuries of his time
are typical of Dufy's work.

# Le monde francophone

# On commence!

# Le monde francophone

## Bienvenue dans le monde francophone!

Spoken in 44 countries, French plays an important role in international business and diplomacy. It is one of the official languages of the United Nations.

### Connaissez-vous...

**NOTE**
Boldfaced words are glossed at the bottom of the page. Try to guess their meaning from the context before looking at the glosses.

la cuisine et le vin français: le pâté, la quiche, la soupe à l'oignon, le bœuf bourguignon, le coq au vin, **les escargots**, le champagne, le beaujolais?

la mode et les parfums français: Cartier, Chanel, Dior, Hermès, Vuitton, Christian Lacroix, Jean-Paul Gaultier, Yves Saint Laurent?

la littérature francophone: Colette, Jules Verne, Voltaire, Alexandre Dumas, Jean-Paul Sartre, George Sand, Léopold Senghor, Albert Camus, Victor Hugo, Molière?

le cinéma français: Louis Malle, François Truffaut, Euzhan Palcy, Claude Chabrol, François Ozon, Catherine Deneuve, Gérard Depardieu, Juliette Binoche, Daniel Auteuil, Audrey Tautou?

---

**Bienvenue dans le monde francophone!** *Welcome to the French-speaking world!*
**Connaissez-vous... ?** *Are you familiar with . . . ?*   **les escargots** *snails*

les peintres et les sculpteurs: Pierre Auguste Renoir, Camille Claudel, Auguste Rodin?

la musique de Claude Debussy, d'Édith Piaf, de Jacques Brel? la musique **cadienne**? la musique zouk?

la science et la technologie françaises: Pierre et Marie Curie, Descartes, Louis Pasteur, **la fusée** Ariane, le TGV?

les produits français: Bic, Danone, Yoplait, Michelin, Thomson, Lancôme, Perrier, Renault?

Test your knowledge of the francophone world. Before you look at the map inside the front cover, see how many of these questions you can answer.

1. In how many countries is French spoken: about 5, about 25, about 40, or about 100?
2. There are several places in the Americas where French is spoken. Name two.
3. In which three of these places in the Caribbean is French an important language: the Dominican Republic, Haiti, Guadeloupe, the Virgin Islands, the Bahamas, Martinique, the Cayman Islands?
4. True or false? French is not spoken in any areas of the South Pacific.
5. True or false? Some people in Laos, Cambodia, and Vietnam speak French.
6. True or false? The existence of French-speaking people in the Americas, Africa, Asia, and the Pacific is largely due to the history of French colonialism.
7. French is spoken in several other countries of Europe besides France. Name two.
8. French is spoken in many countries in Africa. Are most of them found in the north, west, east, or south?
9. French developed from a Latin base, whereas English developed from a Germanic base. However, English was greatly influenced by French largely due to what historical event?
10. Where in South America is French spoken?

---

**cadienne** *Cajun*    **la fusée** *the rocket*

# Greeting people

## Les formules de politesse

*Use these expressions to greet adult strangers and those to whom you show respect.*

— Bonjour, madame.
— Bonjour, monsieur. Je suis Hélène Cauvin. Et vous, comment vous appelez-vous?
— Je m'appelle Jean-Marc Bertin.

— Bonsoir, mademoiselle.
— Bonsoir, monsieur. **Comment allez-vous?**
— **Je vais très bien, merci.** Et vous?
— **Assez** bien.

*Use these expressions to say how you are doing.*

Comment allez-vous?

Je vais très bien. Et vous?

Assez bien. / **Pas mal.**

Pas très bien.

**Comment allez-vous?** *How are you?*    **Je vais très bien, merci.** *I'm doing very well, thank you.*    **Assez** *Fairly, Rather*
**Pas mal.** *Not badly.*

**Prononciation**

CD 1-4   *Les consonnes muettes et la liaison*

---

In French, consonants at the end of words are often silent. The letter **h** is always silent, as it is in some English words such as *hour* and *honest*. As you hear these greetings, note which consonants are not pronounced.

> — Bonjour, monsieur. Je m'appelle Paul Richard. Et vous, comment vous appelez-vous?
> — Je m'appelle Henri Dulac.
> — Comment allez-vous?
> — Très bien, et vous, monsieur?
> — Très bien, merci.

The consonants **c, r, f,** and **l** (CaReFuL) are the only consonants that are generally pronounced at the end of a word. The final **r** of **monsieur,** however, is not pronounced.

Marc            bonjour            actif            Chantal

If a consonant at the end of a word is followed by a word beginning with a vowel sound (**a, e, i, o, u, y**) or mute **h,** the final consonant sound is often pronounced and is linked to the beginning of the next word. This linking is called **liaison.** In liaison, a single **s** is pronounced like a **z.**

Comment vous ͜z͜ appelez-vous?        Comment ͜t͜ allez-vous?

---

**A. Prononcez bien.** Copy these sentences, crossing out the consonants that should not be pronounced and marking where liaison would occur.

> **Exemple**    Comment ͜allez-vous, monsieur?

1. Je suis Chantal Hubert.
2. Bonjour, madame. Comment allez-vous?
3. Très bien, monsieur. Comment vous appelez-vous?
4. Je m'appelle Henri Dufour. Et vous?

Now go back and reorder the four sentences to create a logical conversation to read with a partner.

**B. Que dit-on?** Complétez les conversations.

1.    2.    3.

**C. Bonsoir!** Imagine that you are at a formal reception. Greet three people, exchange names, and find out how they are doing. Be sure to shake hands.

>Note
*culturelle*

When people greet one another in France, they usually shake hands or exchange brief kisses on the cheek called *bises*. What do people do when they greet each other in your region?

## Les salutations familières

*To greet or exchange names with classmates, friends, family members, or children, say:*

**VOCABULAIRE SUPPLÉMENTAIRE**

**Comment t'appelles-tu? / Comment tu t'appelles?** *What's your name?* (familiar)
**Comment vas-tu?** *How are you?* (familiar)
**Ciao!** *Bye!* (familiar)
**Salut!** *Hi! Bye!* (familiar)
**Bon week-end!** *Have a good weekend!*
**Bonne journée!** *Have a good day!*

CD 1-5

— Salut, Jean-Pierre. **Ça va?**
— Salut, Micheline. **Ça va.** Et toi, **comment ça va?**
— Pas mal.

— Bonjour, je m'appelle Anne-Marie. Et toi, tu t'appelles comment?
— Moi, je m'appelle Robert.

*Here are several ways to say good-bye in either formal or familiar situations.*

CD 1-6

| | |
|---|---|
| Au revoir. | *Good-bye.* |
| À tout à l'heure. | *See you in a little while.* |
| À bientôt. | *See you soon.* |
| À demain. | *See you tomorrow.* |

## Prononciation

CD 1-7

*Les voyelles **a, e, i, o, u***

When you pronounce vowels in English, your tongue or lips move as you say them, so that the position of your mouth is not the same at the end of a vowel as at the beginning. In French, you hold your tongue and mouth firmly in one place while pronouncing vowels. This gives vowels a tenser sound. Practice saying these sounds.

| | | | | | | |
|---|---|---|---|---|---|---|
| **a** [a]: | *à* | *ça* | *va* | m*a*dame | m*a*l | *a*ssez |
| **e** [ə]: | j*e* | n*e* | qu*e* | d*e* | d*e*main | d*e*voirs |
| **i** [i]: | qu*i*che | *i*déal | Par*i*s | M*i*cheline | s*i*x | merc*i* |
| **o** [ɔ]: | v*o*tre | n*o*tre | Hect*o*r | p*o*rt | f*o*rt | *o*ptimiste |
| **u** [y]: | t*u* | sal*u*t | L*u*c | s*u*per | d*u* | *u*niversité |

The vowel **o** has two pronunciations, [ɔ] or [o], and the vowel **e** has three pronunciations, [ə], [e], or [ɛ]. You will learn more about this in ***Chapitre 3.*** Final unaccented **e** is not generally pronounced, unless it is the only vowel in a word, as in **je.**

| | | | | |
|---|---|---|---|---|
| Franc*e* | madam*e* | appell*e* | un*e* | Ann*e* |

---

**Ça va?** *How's it going?*  **Ça va.** *It's going fine.*  **Comment ça va?** *How's it going?*

**A. Dans quelle situation?** Would you be more likely to hear these phrases in situation **A** or **B?**

A

B

**1.** Bonsoir, madame.
**2.** Salut, Thomas.
**3.** Très bien, merci. Et vous?
**4.** Tu t'appelles comment?

**5.** Ça va?
**6.** Comment allez-vous?
**7.** Ça va. Et toi?
**8.** Comment vous appelez-vous?

Now, go back and indicate how one might respond to each of the phrases above.

**B. Conversations.** Act out the following conversations with a partner. Then act them out again, making the suggested changes that follow.

**1.** — Comment ça va, André(e)?
  — Pas mal. Et toi, René(e)?
  — Ça va.
  — Bon, à demain!
  — À demain!

  **a.** André(e) is not having a very good day.
  **b.** The two friends plan to see each other later today.
  **c.** The conversation is between two business associates, **Christian(e) Sankara** and **François(e) Mazet.**

**2.** — Bonjour, monsieur. Je suis Cécilia Pastini. Et vous, comment vous appelez-vous?
  — Bonjour, madame. Je m'appelle André Cardin.

  **a.** The woman is young and unmarried.
  **b.** The conversation is between two students, Denis(e) and Adrien(ne).

**C. Que disent-ils?** Imagine what these people are saying. Prepare brief exchanges with a partner.

# Counting and telling time

## Les chiffres de zéro à trente

**Comptez** de zéro à trente, **s'il vous plaît!**

| | | | | | |
|---|---|---|---|---|---|
| **0** | zéro | | | | |
| **1** | un | **11** | onze | **21** | vingt et un |
| **2** | deux | **12** | douze | **22** | vingt-deux |
| **3** | trois | **13** | treize | **23** | vingt-trois |
| **4** | quatre | **14** | quatorze | **24** | vingt-quatre |
| **5** | cinq | **15** | quinze | **25** | vingt-cinq |
| **6** | six | **16** | seize | **26** | vingt-six |
| **7** | sept | **17** | dix-sept | **27** | vingt-sept |
| **8** | huit | **18** | dix-huit | **28** | vingt-huit |
| **9** | neuf | **19** | dix-neuf | **29** | vingt-neuf |
| **10** | dix | **20** | vingt | **30** | trente |

$2 + 2 = 4$     **Combien** font deux et deux?
Deux et deux font quatre.

$10 - 3 = 7$     **Combien** font dix moins trois?
Dix moins trois font sept.

 ## Prononciation

CD 1-8   *Les chiffres et les voyelles nasales*

Although final consonants are generally silent in French, they are pronounced in the following numbers when counting. In **sept,** the **p** is silent, but the final **t** is pronounced. The final **x** in **six** and **dix** is pronounced like the *s* in *so.*

cinq      six      se**p**t      huit      neuf      dix

Many numbers also contain nasal vowels. In French, when a vowel is followed by the letter **m** or **n** in the same syllable, the **m** or **n** is silent and the vowel is nasal. Use the words below as models of how to pronounce each of the three nasal sounds. The letter combinations that are grouped together are all pronounced alike.

| | | | | |
|---|---|---|---|---|
| [ɛ̃]: **in / im / ain / aim / un / um** | cinq | quinze | vingt | un |
| [ɑ̃]: **en / em / an / am** | trente | Henri | Jean | comment |
| [ɔ̃]: **on / om** | onze | bonjour | bonsoir | Simon |

---

**Comptez** *Count*   **de** *from*   **à** *to*   **s'il vous plaît** *please*   **Combien** *How much, How many*

**A. C'est logique!** Complétez avec les chiffres logiques.

1. 1, 3, 5, ?, 9, 11, ?, 15, 17, ?
2. 2, 4, ?, 8, 10, ?, 14, ?, 18, 20
3. 0, 5, 10, ?, 20, ?, 30
4. 3, 6, ?, 12, 15, 18, ?

5. 20, 19, 18, ?, 16, 15, ?
6. 10, 11, 12, ?, 14, 15, ?
7. 11, 13, 15, ?, 19, 21, 23, 25, ?
8. 0, 10, 20, ?

**B. Messages secrets.** You will hear a series of numbers read by your instructor. Write the letter corresponding to each number and you will discover a secret message. When you hear **zéro,** start another word (**un autre mot**).

**Exemple**    VOUS ENTENDEZ *(YOU HEAR):* 8, 30, 29, 9, 30, 6, 10, 0, 12, 18, 0, 15, 18
VOUS ÉCRIVEZ *(YOU WRITE):* **Bonjour, ça va?**

| **0** | un autre mot | | | | | | | | | | |
|---|---|---|---|---|---|---|---|---|---|---|---|
| **1** | é | **6** | u | **11** | f | **16** | ô | **21** | l | **26** | p |
| **2** | q | **7** | z | **12** | ç | **17** | t | **22** | w | **27** | y |
| **3** | c | **8** | b | **13** | g | **18** | a | **23** | à | **28** | è |
| **4** | i | **9** | j | **14** | x | **19** | s | **24** | m | **29** | n |
| **5** | d | **10** | r | **15** | v | **20** | h | **25** | e | **30** | o |

**C. Combien font… ?**

1. $2 + 3 =$
2. $1 + 6 =$
3. $9 + 4 =$
4. $14 + 16 =$
5. $10 + 9 =$

6. $28 - 17 =$
7. $18 - 12 =$
8. $13 - 5 =$
9. $24 - 9 =$

**D. En taxi.** You've taken a taxi in a francophone country. Tell the driver the address of your destination.

**Exemple**    28, rue du Dragon
**Vingt-huit rue du Dragon, s'il vous plaît.**

1. 27, boulevard Diderot
2. 11, rue Petit
3. 16, place Saint-Denis
4. 25, rue d'Angleterre

5. 15, rue Sébastopol
6. 12, rue Garibaldi
7. 30, boulevard Gabriel
8. 7, rue du Temple

**E. Populations.** Guess the populations of these francophone countries. Your instructor will give you cues by saying **plus que ça** *(more than that)* or **moins que ça** *(less than that),* until you guess the correct number.

| | | |
|---|---|---|
| 1. | la Suisse | 4 millions |
| 2. | le Sénégal | 19 millions |
| 3. | la Côte d'Ivoire | 18 millions |
| 4. | la Belgique | 11 millions |
| 5. | la République centrafricaine | 5 millions |
| 6. | le Canada | 10 millions |
| 7. | le Maroc | 31 millions |
| 8. | Madagascar | 32 millions |
| 9. | le Togo | 7 millions |
| 10. | le Burkina Faso | 12 millions |

Traditionally, the French workday followed a particular pattern: breakfast in the early morning, work, a two-hour break for lunch, then work in the afternoon and into the evening. Most people went home for lunch to eat and be with their family. As France has become more urban, however, *la journée continue*, or a nine-to-five schedule, has become a way of life. There is a shorter lunch break, and people have lunch at work or in a nearby restaurant, fast-food chain, or café. How does this compare to a typical workday in your area?

**NOTES DE VOCABULAIRE**

**1. Heures** has an **-s** except with **une heure.**
**2.** There is an **e** at the end of **demi(e)** when it is used with the word **heure,** but not with **midi** and **minuit.**
**3.** Some people use **douze heures** for **midi.**
**4.** One may also tell time by telling the minutes after the hour, instead of using **et quart, et demie,** and **moins...** For example, one hears **Il est trois heures quinze** or **Il est cinq heures trente-cinq.**
**5.** Although *at* may be dropped in English, **à** cannot be omitted in French: *(At) What time is French class?* **À quelle heure est le cours de français?**

## L'heure

Quelle heure est-il **maintenant?**

Il est une heure.  Il est une heure dix.  Il est une heure et quart.  Il est une heure et demie.

Il est deux heures moins vingt-cinq.  Il est deux heures moins le quart.  Il est deux heures moins cinq.  Il est deux heures.

Il est midi.  Il est midi et demi.  Il est minuit.  Il est minuit et demi.

*The French do not use A.M. and P.M. to distinguish morning from afternoon and evening. Instead, they use:*

du matin *(after midnight until noon)*  Il est huit heures **du matin.**
de l'après-midi *(after noon until 6 P.M.)*  Il est une heure **de l'après-midi.**
du soir *(6 P.M. until midnight)*  Il est neuf heures **du soir.**

*Do not use these expressions with **midi** or **minuit.***

*Use **à** to ask or tell **at** what time something takes place.*

**Le cours de français est** à quelle heure?

 Le cours de français **commence** à une heure.

 Le cours de français **finit** à deux heures moins dix.

---

**maintenant** *now*   **Le cours de français** *(The) French class*   **est** *is*   **commence** *begins*   **finit** *finishes, ends*

*To say that you do something **from** a certain time **to** another, use **de... à.** Use **avant** to say **before** and **après** to say **after.***

Avant dix heures, **je suis à la maison.**

Après dix heures, **je ne suis pas** à la maison. Je suis **en cours** de dix heures à deux heures.

**Je travaille** de deux heures à sept heures.

Après sept heures, **je ne travaille pas.**

**NOTE DE VOCABULAIRE**

Notice that you use two words, **ne... pas,** to say what someone does *not* do. They are usually placed around the verb in a sentence. You will learn more about this in ***Chapitre 1.***

# Prononciation

CD 1-9 *L'heure et la liaison*

The pronunciation of some numbers changes in liaison with the word **heures.**

| | |
|---|---|
| deux | Il est deux ⌣ᶻ heures dix. |
| trois | Il est trois ⌣ᶻ heures et quart. |
| six | Il est six ⌣ᶻ heures et demie. |
| huit | Il est huit ⌣ᵗ heures. |
| neuf | Il est neuf ⌣ᵛ heures. |
| dix | Il est dix ⌣ᶻ heures moins cinq. |

**A. En français!** Complete these expressions to tell the time in French.

**Exemple**  *4:30 A.M.*
Il est quatre heures **et demie du matin.**

1. *5:10 A.M.*  Il est cinq heures...
2. *5:15 A.M.*  Il est cinq heures...
3. *3:20 P.M.*  Il est trois heures...
4. *3:30 P.M.*  Il est trois heures...
5. *7:35 P.M.*  Il est huit heures...
6. *7:45 P.M.*  Il est huit heures...
7. *7:50 P.M.*  Il est huit heures...
8. *8:00 P.M.*  Il est...
9. *12:00 A.M.*  Il est...
10. *12:00 P.M.*  Il est...

---

**je suis à la maison** *I'm at home*   **je ne suis pas** *I'm not*   **en cours** *in class*   **Je travaille** *I work*   **je ne travaille pas** *I do not work*

## B. Quelle heure est-il?

**Exemple**
— Quelle heure est-il?
— Il est une heure de l'après-midi.

1.    2.    3.

4.    5.

6. 7.

## C. Quand? Complete these sentences so that they are true for you the first day of the week you have your French class.

**Exemple** Je suis à la maison **avant** **sept heures et demie.**
                      *before*        *[time]*

1. Je suis à la maison _____ _____.
                        *before*   *[time]*

2. Le cours de français commence _____ _____.
                                    *at*     *[time]*

3. Le cours de français finit _____ _____.
                          *at*    *[time]*

4. Je suis en cours _____ _____ _____ _____.
                 *from*   *[time]*    *to*   *[time]*

5. Je travaille _____ _____ _____ _____. (Je ne travaille pas.)
            *from*   *[time]*    *to*   *[time]*

6. Je suis à la maison _____ _____.
                        *after*   *[time]*

## D. Il est quelle heure? Write the times you hear dictated. Notice how the word **heure(s)** is abbreviated in French.

**Exemple** VOUS ENTENDEZ *(YOU HEAR):* Il est dix heures et quart.
                    VOUS ÉCRIVEZ *(YOU WRITE):* **10h15**

**E. Fuseaux horaires.** You are working for an international corporation in Louisiana, and you have to telephone clients in other francophone places around the globe. Using the time zone comparison chart, tell what time it is in each place.

| Louisiane | Québec | Guyane française | Côte d'Ivoire | France | Madagascar |
|---|---|---|---|---|---|
| APRÈS-MIDI——————————————— SOIR——————————————— | | | | | |
| 12h00 | 1h00 | 3h00 | 6h00 | 7h00 | 9h00 |

> **Exemple**   En Louisiane, il est midi dix.
> Au Québec, **il est une heure dix.**
> En Guyane française, **il est trois heures dix.**

1. En Louisiane, il est une heure et quart.
   Au Québec,...
   En Côte d'Ivoire,...
   En France,...

2. En Louisiane, il est deux heures et demie.
   En Guyane française,...
   En France,...
   À Madagascar,...

3. En Louisiane, il est quatre heures moins vingt.
   Au Québec,...
   En Côte d'Ivoire,...
   À Madagascar,...

4. En Louisiane, il est cinq heures moins le quart.
   En Guyane française,...
   En Côte d'Ivoire,...
   En France,...

5. En Louisiane, il est six heures.
   En Guyane française,...
   En France,...
   À Madagascar,...

**F. À la télé.** A friend wants to watch these shows this morning on TV5, the international French TV station. Tell him from what time to what time each one is on. The first one has been done for you.

> **Exemple**   TV5, Le Journal live **est de quatre heures à quatre heures et quart.**

| TV5, Le Journal live | 4h00–4h15 |
|---|---|
| TV5, L'invité | 4h15–4h30 |
| Reflets sud | 5h–6h |
| TV5 Infos | 6h–6h05 |
| JTA | 6h05–6h20 |
| Télématin | 6h20–7h30 |
| Journal Radio Canada | 7h30–8h |
| Les Zap | 8h30–9h |
| Zig Zag Café | 11h05–12h |

# Talking about yourself and your schedule

**NOTES DE GRAMMAIRE**

**1.** The words **je, ne,** and **de** change to **j', n',** and **d'** before vowels or a mute **h.** Similarly, **parce que** *(because)* changes to **parce qu'.** This is called elision. You will learn more about it in *Chapitre 1.*
**2.** Many adjectives in French add an **-e** when describing females. You will learn more about this in *Chapitre 1.*

## Un autoportrait

*Use these expressions to talk about yourself. Include the ending in parentheses if you are female.*

| | |
|---|---|
| Je suis... | étudiant(e). |
| Je ne suis pas... | professeur. |
| | américain(e). |
| | canadien(ne). |
| | **de** Chicago. |
| | **d'ici.** |

| | |
|---|---|
| **J'habite...** | à Toronto. |
| Je n'habite pas... | avec **un ami / une amie.** |
| | avec deux amis / deux amies. |
| | avec **un camarade de chambre / une camarade de chambre.** |
| | avec **un colocataire / une colocataire.** |
| | **seul(e).** |
| | avec ma famille. |

Je suis de Montréal, mais je suis étudiante à Paris maintenant. Je parle anglais et français.

| | |
|---|---|
| Je travaille... | **beaucoup.** |
| Je ne travaille pas... | à l'université. |
| | **pour** IBM. |

| | |
|---|---|
| **Je parle...** | anglais. |
| Je ne parle pas... | français. |
| | espagnol. |
| | beaucoup en cours. |

| | |
|---|---|
| **Je pense que** le français est... | assez **facile.** |
| | **un peu** difficile. |
| | intéressant. |
| | super! |
| | assez cool! |

CD 1-10

*In the following conversation, two people meet at a Canadian-American cultural event in Montréal.*

— **Vous êtes** canadien?
— Oui, je suis d'ici. Et vous, vous êtes canadienne **aussi?**
— Non, je suis de Cleveland.
— **Mais** vous parlez très bien français! Vous habitez ici maintenant?
— Oui, **parce que** je suis étudiante à l'université. Et vous, vous travaillez ici?
— Non, je suis étudiant aussi.

---

**de (d')** *from*   **ici** *here*   **J'habite** *I live*   **un ami** *a friend (male)*   **une amie** *a friend (female)*
**un camarade de chambre** *a roommate (male)*   **une camarade de chambre** *a roommate (female)*
**un colocataire** *a housemate (male)*   **une colocataire** *a housemate (female)*   **seul(e)** *alone*   **beaucoup** *a lot*   **pour** *for*
**Je parle** *I speak, I talk*   **Je pense que** *I think that*   **facile** *easy*   **un peu** *a little*   **Vous êtes** *You are (formal)*   **aussi** *also, too*
**Mais** *But*   **parce que** *because*

**A. Moi, je...** Choose the words in parentheses so that each sentence describes you.

1. (Je suis / Je ne suis pas) étudiant(e).
2. (Je suis / Je ne suis pas) en cours maintenant.
3. (Je suis / Je ne suis pas) de Los Angeles.
4. (Je suis / Je ne suis pas) canadien(ne).
5. (J'habite / Je n'habite pas) à Minneapolis.
6. (J'habite / Je n'habite pas) avec ma famille maintenant.
7. (Je travaille / Je ne travaille pas) à l'université.
8. (Je parle / Je ne parle pas) très bien français.

**B. Nationalités.** Some international students from different French-speaking countries are talking about themselves. Can you find the sentences from each column that go together?

**Exemple**   **Je suis française. Je suis de France. J'habite à Paris.**

| | | |
|---|---|---|
| Je suis français. | Je suis de Belgique. | J'habite à Alger. |
| Je suis algérienne. | Je suis du Canada. | J'habite à Genève. |
| Je suis canadien. | Je suis d'Algérie. | J'habite à Paris. |
| Je suis belge. | Je suis de Côte d'Ivoire. | J'habite à Québec. |
| Je suis ivoirienne. | Je suis de Suisse. | J'habite à Abidjan. |
| Je suis suisse. | Je suis de France. | J'habite à Bruxelles. |

**C. Descriptions.** Change the words in italics so that each statement is true for you. If a statement already is true, read it as it is.

1. Je m'appelle *Chris Jones.*
2. Je suis de *Toronto.*
3. Je suis *canadien(ne).*
4. Maintenant, j'habite à *Chapel Hill.*
5. Je suis étudiant(e) à *l'université de Caroline du Nord.*
6. J'habite *avec un(e) camarade de chambre.*
7. Je parle *un peu* français.
8. Je parle *anglais et espagnol.*
9. Je pense que le français est *très facile.*

**D. Et vous?** Répondez aux questions suivantes.

1. Comment vous appelez-vous?
2. Comment allez-vous?
3. Vous êtes étudiant(e)?
4. Vous travaillez aussi?
5. Vous êtes américain(e)?
6. Vous êtes d'ici?
7. Vous habitez à Denver maintenant?
8. Vous parlez espagnol?

**E. Conversation.** With a partner, read aloud the conversation at the bottom of the previous page, paying particular attention to the pronunciation. Then act it out, changing it to make it true for you. Afterward, switch roles and do it again.

**VOCABULAIRE SUPPLÉMENTAIRE**

**pendant la semaine** *during the week*
**tous les jours (sauf)** *every day (except)*

**NOTES DE VOCABULAIRE**

**1.** Days of the week are not capitalized in French.
**2.** Use **du matin / de l'après-midi / du soir** only for indicating *A.M.* and *P.M.* when telling time. Use **le matin / l'après-midi / le soir** to say *in the morning / afternoon / evening* in other cases.
**3.** Use **de... à...** rather than **du... au...** to say *from . . . to . . .* with days of the week when talking about one particular week.
**4.** Most French universities run on a system of **trimestres**, rather than **semestres**.

# Les jours de la semaine et votre emploi du temps

*To ask and tell the day of the week, say:*

— **C'est quel jour aujourd'hui?**
— C'est lundi.

| lundi | mardi | mercredi | jeudi | vendredi | samedi | dimanche |
|-------|-------|----------|-------|----------|--------|----------|
| (17) | 18 | 19 | 20 | 21 | 22 | 23 |
| 24 | 25 | 26 | 27 | 28 | 29 | 30 |

*Do not translate the word **on** to say that you do something on a certain day. To say that you do something **every** Monday (or another day), use **le** with the day of the week.*

Je travaille **lundi.**     *I work on Monday.* (this Monday)
Je travaille **le lundi.**     *I work on Mondays.* (every Monday)

*To say **from** what day **to** what day you do something every week, use **du... au...***

Je travaille **du** lundi **au** vendredi.     *I work Mondays to Fridays.* (every week)

*Use **le matin, l'après-midi,** or **le soir** to say you do something **in the morning, in the afternoon,** or **in the evening,** and **le week-end** to say **on the weekend.***

**Le matin,** je suis en cours.     *In the morning, I'm in class.*
**L'après-midi,** je travaille.     *In the afternoon, I work.*
**Le soir** et **le week-end,** je suis     *In the evening and on the weekend,*
    à la maison.     *I'm at home.*

CD 1-11    *Two friends are talking about their schedule this semester.*

— **Tu es** en cours quels jours **ce semestre?**
— Je suis en cours le lundi, le mercredi et le vendredi.
— Tu travailles aussi?
— Oui, je travaille le mardi matin, le jeudi matin et le week-end.

**A. Ciao!** Say good-bye to a friend whom you will see again in two days.

    **Exemple**    Aujourd'hui, c'est lundi. **Au revoir! À mercredi!**

Aujourd'hui c'est...

1. dimanche        4. jeudi
2. mercredi        5. vendredi
3. samedi        6. mardi

---

**Les jours de la semaine** *The days of the week*    **votre emploi du temps** *your schedule*
**C'est quel jour aujourd'hui?** *It's what day today?*    **Tu es... ?** *You are . . . ? (familiar)*    **ce semestre** *this semester*

## B. C'est quel jour?

1. Aujourd'hui, c'est...
2. Demain, c'est...
3. Après demain, c'est...
4. Après le week-end, c'est...
5. Avant le week-end, c'est...
6. Les jours du week-end sont...
7. Les jours du cours de français sont...
8. Je suis en cours...
9. Je travaille...
10. Je suis souvent *(often)* à la maison...

## C. Quand? Change the words in italics so that each statement is true. If a statement is already true, read it as it is.

1. Je suis à l'université *du lundi au vendredi.*
2. Je travaille *le mardi matin, le jeudi matin et le week-end. Le mardi,* je travaille de *huit heures* à *midi.* [Je ne travaille pas.]
3. Aujourd'hui, c'est *lundi* et maintenant il est *huit heures vingt.*
4. Aujourd'hui, je suis en cours de *dix heures et demie* à *quatre heures.*
5. Je suis souvent *(often)* à la maison *le week-end.*
6. Je suis rarement *(rarely)* à la maison *le vendredi soir.*

## D. Votre emploi du temps. On a sheet of paper, copy the schedule below twice, changing it to describe your schedule on one copy and leaving the other one blank. You and your partner take turns describing your schedules to each other. On your second (blank) schedule, fill in your partner's schedule as he/she describes it to you.

**Exemple**    **Le lundi, je suis en cours de dix heures à une heure. Je travaille de deux heures à quatre heures. Je suis à la maison après cinq heures. Le mardi...**

## E. Conversation. With a partner, read aloud the conversation on the previous page, paying particular attention to the pronunciation. Then act it out, changing it to make it true for you. Switch roles and do it again.

# Communicating in class

## En cours

Le professeur **dit aux** étudiants:

### EN COURS

Ouvrez votre livre à la page 23.

Fermez votre livre.

Écoutez la question.

Répondez à la question.

Allez au tableau.

Écrivez la réponse en phrases complètes.

Prenez une feuille de papier et un crayon ou un stylo.

**Faites** l'exercice A à la page 21.

Donnez-moi votre feuille de papier.

### À LA MAISON

Lisez la page 17 et **apprenez** les mots de vocabulaire.

Préparez l'examen pour le **prochain** cours.

Faites **les devoirs** dans le cahier et écoutez le CD.

---

**dit aux** *says to the*   **Faites** *Do*   **apprenez** *learn*   **prochain(e)** *next*   **les devoirs** *the homework*

# Prononciation

*Les voyelles groupées*

Practice the pronunciation of the following vowel combinations. Notice that the combination **eu** has two different sounds, depending on whether it is followed by a pronounced consonant in the same syllable.

- a + u / e + u / o + u

| | | | | |
|---|---|---|---|---|
| **au, eau** [o]: | au | aussi | beaucoup | tableau |
| **eu** [ø]: | deux | peu | jeudi | monsieur |
| **eu** [œ]: | heure | neuf | professeur | seul(e) |
| **ou** [u]: | vous | douze | jour | pour |

- a + i / e + i / o + i / u + i

| | | | | |
|---|---|---|---|---|
| **ai** [ɛ]: | français | je vais | je sais | vrai |
| **ei** [ɛ]: | treize | seize | beige | neige |
| **oi** [wa]: | moi | toi | trois | au revoir |
| **ui** [ɥi]: | huit | minuit | aujourd'hui | suis |

**A. Où?** Is your professor telling you to do these things **en cours** or **à la maison?**

1. Fermez votre livre.
2. Apprenez les mots de vocabulaire.
3. Écoutez et répondez, s'il vous plaît.
4. Allez au tableau.
5. Prenez une feuille de papier.
6. Lisez les pages 12, 13 et 14.
7. Faites les devoirs dans le cahier.
8. Ouvrez votre livre à la page 23.

**B. En cours.** In groups, make up commands your instructor might give you by matching items from the two columns. Which group can come up with the most?

| | |
|---|---|
| Fermez... | ... les devoirs. |
| Allez... | ... les mots de vocabulaire. |
| Lisez... | ... le CD. |
| Apprenez... | ... l'exercice A. |
| Comptez... | ... de 0 à 30. |
| Écoutez... | ... au tableau. |
| Prenez... | ... une feuille de papier. |
| Écrivez... | ... la phrase. |
| Faites... | ... votre livre. |

**C. C'est logique?** How many logical ways can you complete these commands?

1. Écrivez...
2. Lisez...
3. Apprenez...
4. Prenez...
5. Faites...
6. Écoutez...

# Des expressions utiles et l'alphabet

*When you hear new words, it may be helpful to see how they are spelled. You can ask:*

| | |
|---|---|
| Ça s'écrit comment? | *How is that written?* |
| Ça s'écrit avec un accent ou sans accent? | *Is that written with an accent or without an accent?* |
| Ça s'écrit avec un **s** ou deux **s** en français / en anglais? | *Is that written with one **s** or two in French / in English?* |
| Ça s'écrit... | |

**NOTE D'ORTHOGRAPHE**

The **cédille** occurs only on the letter **c** and causes it to be pronounced /s/. The accent marks occur only on vowels. They do not indicate stress. They may be used to indicate a difference in pronunciation (**é** versus **è**), to differentiate two words (**ou** [*or*] versus **où** [*where*]), or for historical reasons. You will learn more about **é** versus **è** and the use of the **cédille** in **Chapitre 2.** Learn the accents as part of the spelling of a new word.

| | | | | | | | |
|---|---|---|---|---|---|---|---|
| **a** | a | **i** | i | **q** | ku | **y** | i grec |
| **b** | bé | **j** | ji | **r** | erre | **z** | zède |
| **c** | cé | **k** | ka | **s** | esse | | |
| **d** | dé | **l** | elle | **t** | té | **é** = e accent aigu | |
| **e** | e | **m** | emme | **u** | u | **è** = e accent grave | |
| **f** | effe | **n** | enne | **v** | vé | **â** = a accent circonflexe | |
| **g** | gé | **o** | o | **w** | double vé | **ï** = i tréma | |
| **h** | hache | **p** | pé | **x** | iks | **ç** = c cédille | |

*You may also need to use these expressions.*

| | |
|---|---|
| Comment? Répétez, s'il vous plaît. | *What? Please repeat.* |
| — Vous comprenez? | — *Do you understand?* |
| — Oui, je comprends. | — *Yes, I understand.* |
| Non, je ne comprends pas. | *No, I don't understand.* |
| — Comment dit-on *a pen* en français? | — *How does one say **a pen** in French?* |
| — On dit **un stylo.** | — *One says **un stylo.*** |
| — Qu'est-ce que ça veut dire **votre?** | — *What does **votre** mean?* |
| — Ça veut dire *your.* | — *It means **your.*** |
| — Je ne sais pas. | — *I don't know.* |
| — Merci (bien). | — *Thanks.* |
| — De rien. | — *You're welcome.* |
| — Pardon. / Excusez-moi. | — *Excuse me.* |

**NOTES DE VOCABULAIRE**

**1.** There are several ways to say *You're welcome.*
**De rien.**
**Il n'y a pas de quoi.**
**Je vous en prie.** (formal)
**Je t'en prie.** (familiar)
**2. Pardon** and **excusez-moi** are not always interchangeable. Generally, use **pardon** to pass through a crowd or get someone's attention. Use **excusez-moi** (**excuse-moi** [informal]) if you want to excuse something you have done.

**A. Dans l'ordre logique.** Put the sentences of the following conversations in the logical order.

1. — Ça veut dire *pen.*
   — Non, qu'est-ce que ça veut dire?
   — Vous comprenez le mot **stylo?**

2. — Je ne sais pas.
   — Comment dit-on *hi* en français?
   — On dit **salut.**

3. — Comment? Répétez s'il vous plaît.
   — Qu'est-ce que ça veut dire **bientôt?**
   — Je ne sais pas.
   — Qu'est-ce que ça veut dire **bientôt?**

4. — Ça s'écrit B-E-A-U-C-O-U-P.
   — Comment dit-on *a lot* en français?
   — On dit **beaucoup.**
   — Ça s'écrit comment?

**B. Réponses.** Look back at the expressions above and below the alphabet box on the preceding page. What would you say in the following situations?

1. You understood the question, but you don't know the answer.
2. You want to know how to say *giraffe* in French.
3. You want to know if *giraffe* is written with one or two *f*'s in French.
4. You want to know what the word **fou** means in English.
5. You need to pass through a group of students.
6. You stepped on someone's foot.

**C. La francophonie.** Say what letter is missing at the beginning of the following names of francophone places. Can you locate each place on the map inside the front cover?

**Exemple** \_\_uébec
          **Q**

1. \_\_rance
2. \_\_lgérie
3. \_\_ôte d'Ivoire
4. \_\_aïti
5. \_\_ahiti
6. \_\_uadeloupe
7. \_\_aroc
8. \_\_elgique
9. \_\_énégal
10. \_\_ouisiane
11. \_\_uanda
12. \_\_uinée

Jemma el Fna, Marrakech, Maroc

**D. Ça s'écrit comment?** Here are some French words that are similar to their English equivalents but spelled slightly differently. Explain to a French friend how to spell them in English. Your friend already knows not to use accents.

**Exemples** indépendance    **En anglais, *independence,* ça s'écrit avec un *e.***
          appartement    **En anglais, *apartment,* ça s'écrit avec un *p* et**
                          **sans *e.***

1. littérature
2. activité
3. chocolat
4. symptôme
5. criminel

6. dîner
7. environnement
8. moderne
9. hôpital

**E. Présentations.** Introduce yourself to a classmate, who will ask you to spell your last name.

**Exemple**
    — **Bonjour, je suis Paul Wyndel.**
    — **Wyndel? Ça s'écrit comment?**
    — **W-Y-N-D-E-L. Et toi, tu t'appelles comment?**
    — **Je m'appelle Lynn Phan.**
    — **Phan? Ça s'écrit comment?**
    — **P-H-A-N.**

## L'heure officielle

**In** official schedules and sometimes in conversations, the French use the 24-hour clock rather than the conversational manner of telling time, which you have already learned. With the 24-hour clock, you continue counting 13 to 24, instead of beginning with 1 to 12 o'clock again during the P.M. hours.

When using the 24-hour clock, state the hour and the number of minutes after the hour with a number, instead of using **midi, minuit, et quart, et demie,** or **moins le quart.** You will need the numbers **quarante** *(forty)* and **cinquante** *(fifty)*.

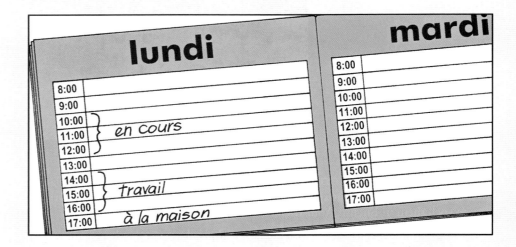

douze heures trente
= midi et demi

treize heures quinze
= une heure et quart
de l'après-midi

treize heures quarante-cinq
= deux heures moins le quart
de l'après-midi

**Au restaurant.** From what time to what time are these restaurants open?

**Exemple**    L'Européen **est ouvert** *(is open)* **de onze heures à une heure du matin.**

**L'EUROPÉEN**
*La brasserie très parisienne*
plateaux de fruits de mer
huîtres, coquillages
cuisine traditionnelle
ouvert de 11h à 1h du matin
**face à la Gare de Lyon**
→ consultez l'Annuaire Électronique
**01 43 43 99 70**
21 bis, boulevard Diderot **75012 PARIS**

*Le Laumière*
Ouvert tous les jours de 12h à 14h30 et de 19h à 22h30

Spécialités de poissons
Crustacés en vivier - Fruits de mer
Cuisine traditionnelle
Repas d'affaires
Plats du jour midi et soir

4, rue Petit 75019 PARIS
→ consultez l'Annuaire Électronique
**01 42 02 46 71**

**Restaurant** *Chez Babette*
3 restaurants *à votre service* de 12h à 15h, 19h à 23h
fermé le samedi midi et le dimanche
**dans le 17ème**
**BABETTE VILLIERS** 75, av. de Villiers___ **01 47 63 86 45**
**BABETTE LE FOUR A PAIN**
19, r. Guy Moquet_____ **01 42 29 07 30**
**dans le 18ème**
**BABETTE** 41, r. Championnet _____ **01 42 64 71 80**

**La Chope d'Alsace**

Spécialités alsaciennes
*Toute l'année de midi à 2 heures du matin*

4, carrefour de l'Odéon **75006 PARIS**
**01 43 26 67 76**
→ consultez l'Annuaire Électronique

## À discuter

1. Is the 24-hour clock used in your country? In what circumstances?
2. Does using the 24-hour clock make things clearer or less clear to you? Why?

visit http://horizons.heinle.com

## Greeting people

| | |
|---|---|
| À bientôt. | *See you soon.* |
| À demain. | *See you tomorrow.* |
| À tout à l'heure. | *See you in a little while.* |
| Au revoir. | *Good-bye.* |
| Bonjour. | *Hello.,Good morning.* |
| Bonsoir. | *Good evening.* |
| Comment allez-vous? | *How are you?* (formal) |
| Je vais très bien. | *I'm doing very well.* |
| Assez bien. | *Fairly well.* |
| Pas mal. | *Not badly.* |
| Pas très bien. | *Not very well.* |
| Comment ça va? / Ça va? | *How's it going?* (familiar) |
| Ça va. | *It's going fine.* |
| Comment vous appelez-vous? | *What's your name?* (formal) |
| Tu t'appelles comment? | *What's your name?* (familiar) |
| Je m'appelle... | *My name is . . .* |
| Je suis... | *I'm . . .* |
| et | *and* |
| Et toi? | *And you?* (familiar) |
| Et vous? | *And you?* (formal) |
| madame | *Mrs., madam* |
| mademoiselle | *Miss* |
| merci | *thank you, thanks* |
| moi | *me* |
| monsieur | *Mr., sir* |
| Salut! | *Hi!* |

## Counting and telling time

| | |
|---|---|
| un chiffre | *a number, a numeral* |
| Combien font... et... ? | *How much is . . . plus . . . ?* |
| ... et... font... | *. . . plus . . . equals . . .* |
| Combien font... moins... ? | *How much is . . . minus . . . ?* |
| ... moins... font... | *. . . minus . . . equals . . .* |
| Comptez de... à... | *Count from . . . to . . .* |
| s'il vous plaît | *please* (formal) |
| l'heure | *the time* |
| une heure | *an hour* |
| Quelle heure est-il maintenant? | *What time is it now?* |
| Il est une heure / deux heures. | *It's one o'clock / two o'clock.* |
| et quart / et demi(e) | *a quarter past / half past* |
| moins le quart | *a quarter till* |
| midi | *noon* |
| minuit | *midnight* |
| À quelle heure? | *At what time?* |
| à... heure(s) | *at . . . o'clock* |
| du matin | *in the morning* |
| de l'après-midi | *in the afternoon* |
| du soir | *in the evening* |
| Je (ne) suis (pas) à la maison. | *I'm (not) at home.* |
| Je (ne) suis (pas) en cours. | *I'm (not) in class.* |
| Je (ne) travaille (pas)... | *I (don't) work . . .* |
| avant | *before* |
| après | *after* |
| de... à... | *from . . . to . . .* |
| maintenant | *now* |
| Le cours de français est à quelle heure? | *What time is French class?* |
| Le cours de français commence / finit à... | *French class starts / finishes at . . .* |

*Pour les chiffres de zéro à trente, voir la page 10.*

*Vocabulaire*

## Talking about yourself and your schedule

| | |
|---|---|
| C'est quel jour aujourd'hui? | What day is today? |
| C'est lundi / mardi / mercredi / jeudi / vendredi / samedi / dimanche. | It's Monday / Tuesday / Wednesday / Thursday / Friday / Saturday / Sunday. |
| les jours de la semaine | the days of the week |
| votre emploi du temps | your schedule |
| Je suis en cours / à la maison... | I am in class / at home . . . |
| le lundi | on Mondays |
| le matin, l'après-midi, le soir | in the morning, in the afternoon, in the evening |
| le week-end | weekends / on the weekend |
| du lundi au vendredi | from Monday to Friday (every week) |
| Tu es... ? / Vous êtes... ? | Are you . . . ? |
| Je suis / Je ne suis pas... | I am / I am not . . . |
| américain(e) | American |
| canadien(ne) | Canadian |
| de (d')... (+ city) | from . . . (+ city) |
| d'ici | from here |
| étudiant(e) | a student |
| professeur | a professor |
| Vous habitez... ? | Do you live . . . ? |
| J'habite / Je n'habite pas... | I live / I do not live . . . |
| à... (+ city) | in . . . (+ city) |
| avec ma famille | with my family |
| avec un(e) ami(e) | with a friend |
| avec un(e) camarade de chambre | with a roommate |
| avec un(e) colocataire | with a housemate |
| seul(e) | alone |
| Vous parlez... ? | Do you speak . . . ? |
| Je parle / Je ne parle pas... | I speak / I do not speak . . . |
| anglais | English |
| espagnol | Spanish |
| français | French |
| beaucoup en cours | a lot in class |
| Je pense que... | I think that . . . |
| le français est... | French is . . . |
| un peu difficile | a little difficult / hard |
| assez facile | fairly easy |
| intéressant | interesting |
| super | great |
| assez cool | pretty cool |
| Vous travaillez...? / Tu travailles... ? | Do you work . . . ? |
| Je travaille / Je ne travaille pas... | I work / I do not work . . . |
| pour | for |
| à l'université | at the university |
| aussi | also |
| un autoportrait | a self-portrait |
| ce semestre | this semester |
| ici | here |
| mais | but |
| non | no |
| oui | yes |
| parce que | because |

## Communicating in class

| | |
|---|---|
| Comment? Répétez, s'il vous plaît. | What? Please repeat. |
| Vous comprenez? | Do you understand? |
| Oui, je comprends. / Non, je ne comprends pas. | Yes, I understand. / No, I don't understand. |
| Comment dit-on... en français / en anglais? | How does one say . . . in French / in English? |
| On dit... | One says . . . |
| Qu'est-ce que ça veut dire? | What does that mean? |
| Ça veut dire... | That means . . . |
| Je ne sais pas. | I don't know. |
| Ça s'écrit comment? | How is that written? |
| Ça s'écrit... | That's written . . . |
| avec | with |
| ou | or |
| sans | without |
| un accent | an accent |
| Merci (bien). | Thank you. / Thanks. |
| De rien. | You're welcome. |
| Pardon. / Excusez-moi. | Excuse me. |
| Le professeur dit aux étudiants... | The professor says to the students . . . |
| en cours | in class |
| Ouvrez votre livre à la page 23. | Open your book to page 23. |
| Fermez votre livre. | Close your book. |
| Écoutez la question. | Listen to the question. |
| Répondez à la question. | Answer the question. |
| Allez au tableau. | Go to the board. |
| Écrivez la réponse en phrases complètes. | Write the answer in complete sentences. |
| Prenez une feuille de papier et un crayon ou un stylo. | Take out a piece of paper and a pencil or a pen. |
| Faites l'exercice A à la page 21. | Do exercise A on page 21. |
| Donnez-moi votre feuille de papier. | Give me your piece of paper. |
| à la maison | at home |
| Lisez la page 17. | Read page 17. |
| Apprenez les mots de vocabulaire. | Learn the vocabulary words. |
| Préparez l'examen pour le prochain cours. | Prepare for the exam for the next class. |
| Faites les devoirs dans le cahier et écoutez le CD. | Do the homework in the workbook and listen to the CD. |

*Pour l'alphabet, voir la page 22.*

This is a view of Cannes, a resort town on the **Côte d'Azur,** as seen from a window of Picasso's 19th-century villa, **La Californie.** The same view is the subject of many of Picasso's paintings from this period.

# Sur la Côte d'Azur

**LA FRANCE (LA RÉPUBLIQUE FRANÇAISE)**
**SUPERFICIE:** 543 965 kilomètres carrés
**NOMBRE D' HABITANTS:** 59 490 000 (les Français)
**CAPITALE:** Paris
**INDUSTRIES PRINCIPALES:** aéronautique, agriculture, industries manufacturières, secteur des services, technologie, tourisme

# À l'université

 Video activities are on pages 212-215.

Quelles régions françaises **connaissez-vous?**
Regardez les photos, lisez les descriptions et identifiez la région:

- **les Pays-de-la-Loire / le Centre**
- **la Côte d'Azur / la Provence**
- **l'Alsace**
- **la Bretagne**

Dans cette région le long de la Loire, **il y a** plus de 120 **châteaux. Parmi** les plus **connus** sont Chambord, Chenonceau, Blois, Amboise, Cheverny et Sully-sur-Loire.

**Nommée** pour la couleur de l'eau et du ciel, cette région **se trouve** le long de la mer Méditerranée. C'est *the Riviera* en anglais.

---

**connaissez-vous?** *do you know?*    **il y a** *there is, there are*    **châteaux** *castles*    **Parmi** *Among*    **connus** *known*    **Nommée** *Named*
**de l'eau** *of the water*    **du ciel** *of the sky*    **se trouve** *is located*

Historiquement et géographiquement **liée à la Grande-Bretagne,** cette région **maintient** l'esprit religieux et indépendant de ses **ancêtres** celtes. Les dolmens et les menhirs **reflètent** les traditions de ses anciens habitants.

**Jadis** une partie de **l'Allemagne,** cette région **montre** des influences allemandes et françaises dans sa culture.

---

**liée à la Grande-Bretagne** *connected to Great Britain*    **maintient** *maintains*    **ancêtres** *ancestors*    **reflètent** *reflect*
**Jadis** *Formerly*    **l'Allemagne** *Germany*    **montre** *shows*

# Identifying people and describing appearance

**NOTE DE VOCABULAIRE**

Use **c'est** *(he/she/it/this is)* to identify people and things and **il est** *(he/it is)* or **elle est** *(she/it is)* when describing them. Notice that adjectives have a different form depending on whether a man or a woman is being described. You will learn more about this later in this chapter.

## Les gens à l'université

**Ce sont mes amis**, David et Annette. Ils sont étudiants à l'université de Nice. Ils sont dans **le même** cours de littérature.

**C'est** David, **un jeune homme** français.
Il est étudiant.
Il est de Nice.

C'est Annette, **une jeune femme** américaine.
Elle est étudiante.
Elle est de Los Angeles.

C'est Jean, **le frère de** David.
Il n'est pas étudiant.
Il travaille.

C'est Yvette, **la sœur jumelle d'**Annette.
Elle n'est pas étudiante.
Elle travaille.

Yvette et Annette ne sont pas françaises. Elles sont américaines. Annette est à Nice **pour étudier.** Yvette est en France pour **voir sa** sœur et pour visiter la France.

**Comment est** David?

Il est petit.
Il n'est pas grand, **comme** Jean.
David est **mince** mais Jean est un peu gros.

Comment est Annette?

Elle est petite, comme David.
Elle n'est pas grande.
Elle est mince.
Elle n'est pas grosse.

David est jeune et **beau.**
Il n'est pas vieux ou **laid.**
Il est **célibataire.**
Il n'est pas marié, fiancé ou divorcé.

Elle est jeune et belle.
Elle n'est pas vieille ou laide.
Elle est célibataire.
Elle n'est pas mariée, fiancée ou divorcée.

---

**Les gens** *People*   **Ce sont...** *They/These are . . .*   **mes ami(e)s** *my friends*   **le même** *the same*   **C'est...** *He/She/It/This is . . .*   **un jeune homme** *a young man*   **une jeune femme** *a young woman*   **le frère de** *the brother of*   **la sœur de** *the sister of*   **jumeau (jumelle)** *twin*   **pour** *for, in order to*   **étudier** *to study*   **voir** *to see*   **sa** *his/her/its*   **Comment est... ?** *What is . . . like?*   **comme** *like*   **mince** *thin*   **beau (belle)** *handsome, beautiful*   **laid(e)** *ugly*   **célibataire** *single*

CD 1-13

David et Annette **font connaissance la première semaine des cours.**

DAVID:     Salut! Je suis David Cauvin. **Nous sommes** dans le même cours de littérature, non?
ANNETTE:   Oui, c'est ça. **Alors**, bonjour! Moi, je m'appelle Annette Clark. Tu es d'ici?
DAVID:     Oui, je suis de Nice. Et toi, tu es **d'où**?
ANNETTE:   Je suis de Los Angeles, mais j'habite ici maintenant parce que je suis étudiante à l'université.

---

## A. Identification. Qui est-ce? *(Who is it?)*

| C'est... | David | Yvette | |
|---|---|---|---|
| Ce sont... | David et Annette | Annette et Yvette | David et Jean |

1. Il est étudiant.
2. C'est le frère de Jean.
3. Elles sont de Los Angeles.
4. C'est la sœur jumelle d'Annette.
5. Elle est à Nice pour voir la France.
6. Ce sont des jeunes femmes.
7. Ils sont français.
8. Ils sont dans le même cours de littérature.

## B. C'est vrai? Regardez les illustrations de David et d'Annette à la page précédente. Décidez si ce que *(what)* vous entendez est vrai *(true)* ou faux *(false)*.

**Exemples**   VOUS ENTENDEZ:   Annette est très grande.   David n'est pas laid.
          VOUS DITES:   **C'est faux.**   **C'est vrai.**

## C. Après les cours. Vous êtes dans un café et vous pensez reconnaître *(to recognize)* un(e) camarade de classe. Préparez une conversation avec les questions suivantes.

1. Tu es étudiant(e) à *(name of your college),* non?
2. Tu es en cours de français *(days of your French course)* à *(time of your French course)?*
3. Le professeur, c'est un homme ou une femme?
4. Le professeur, c'est *(name of your professor)?*
5. Nous sommes dans le même cours, non?

## D. Conversation. Avec un(e) partenaire, relisez à haute voix *(aloud)* la conversation entre David et Annette en haut de la page *(at the top of the page)*. Ensuite, changez la conversation pour décrire *(to describe)* votre propre *(own)* situation.

---

**font connaissance (faire connaissance** *to meet)*   **la première semaine des cours** *the first week of classes*
**Nous sommes** *We are*   **Alors** *So, Then, Thus*   **d'où** *from where*

These self-check questions are provided throughout the book. Read the entire explanation before trying to answer the questions.

**1.** What two expressions are used to identify who someone is? What are the negative forms of these expressions?

**2.** When describing someone with an adjective, how do you say *he is? she is? they are* for a group of all females? *they are* for a group of all males or for a mixed group? What are the negative forms of these expressions?

**3.** What is the base form of an adjective? What do you usually do to make it feminine? masculine plural? feminine plural?

**4.** What is the feminine form of **gros? canadien? beau? vieux?**

**5.** Is there a difference in pronunciation between **petit** and **petite?**

# Identifying and describing people

*C'est* et *il/elle est* et *les adjectifs*

To *identify* people, use **c'est** and **ce sont.** Note their negative forms.

| | | | |
|---|---|---|---|
| **C'est** (+ noun) | *He is* *She is* *It is* *This is* | **Ce n'est pas** (+ noun) | *He isn't* *She isn't* *It isn't* *This isn't* |
| **Ce sont** (+ noun) | *They are* *These are* | **Ce ne sont pas** (+ noun) | *They aren't* *These aren't* |

To *describe* people with adjectives, use **il est, elle est, ils sont,** and **elles sont.** Use **ils** for a group of males or a mixed group and **elles** for a group of all females. Note their negative forms.

| | | | | | |
|---|---|---|---|---|---|
| **Il est** **Elle est** | (+ adjective) | *He is* *She is* | **Il n'est pas** **Elle n'est pas** | (+ adjective) | *He isn't* *She isn't* |
| **Ils sont** **Elles sont** | (+ adjective) | *They are* *They are* | **Ils ne sont pas** **Elles ne sont pas** | (+ adjective) | *They aren't* *They aren't* |

In French, adjective forms vary depending on whether they describe a male or a female, and whether they describe one person or more than one.

The masculine singular form of the adjective is used as the base form. To change the form to feminine, add an **e** to the masculine form, unless it already ends in an *unaccented* **e.** If it ends in an *accented* **é,** add another **e** to form the feminine. Add an **s** to make an adjective plural, unless it already ends in an **s** or **x.**

| MASCULINE | | FEMININE | |
|---|---|---|---|
| *singular* | *plural* | *singular* | *plural* |
| petit | petit**s** | petit**e** | petit**es** |
| jeune | jeune**s** | jeune | jeune**s** |
| marié | marié**s** | marié**e** | marié**es** |
| français | français | français**e** | français**es** |

Some adjectives, such as **gros** and **canadien,** double their final consonant before adding the **e** for agreement with feminine nouns.

| MASCULINE | | FEMININE | |
|---|---|---|---|
| *singular* | *plural* | *singular* | *plural* |
| gros | gros | gros**se** | gros**ses** |
| canadien | canadien**s** | canadien**ne** | canadien**nes** |

The adjectives **beau, jumeau,** and **vieux** are irregular.

| MASCULINE | | FEMININE | |
|---|---|---|---|
| *singular* | *plural* | *singular* | *plural* |
| beau | beaux | belle | belles |
| jumeau | jumeaux | jumelle | jumelles |
| vieux | vieux | vieille | vieilles |

# Prononciation

### *Il est* + *adjectif* / *Elle est* + *adjectif*

Since most final consonants are silent, you will not hear or say the final consonant of masculine adjective forms, unless they end in **c, r, f,** or **l.** When the **e** is added to make the feminine form, the consonant is no longer final and is pronounced.

    petit / petite                   français / française

The final **s** of plurals is not pronounced, nor is a consonant that immediately precedes it, unless it is **c, r, f,** or **l.**

    Ilſ sont petitſ.              Elleſ sont petiteſ.

Be careful to pronounce the vowels in **il/ils** and **elle/elles** distinctly. The letter **i** in French is pronounced similarly to the double *ee* in the English words *see* and *feed,* but it is said more quickly and the tongue is held more tensely. The letter **e** in **elle/elles** is pronounced somewhat like the *e* in the English word *bet.*

    Il est grand. Ils sont beaux.     Elle est grande. Elles sont belles.

---

**A. Claude qui?** Écoutez les phrases. C'est la phrase **a** pour Claude Bellon ou la phrase **b** pour Claude Lacoste?

1. **a.** Claude est grand.

        **b.** Claude est grande.
2. **a.** Claude n'est pas petit.
        **b.** Claude n'est pas petite.
3. **a.** Claude est français.
        **b.** Claude est française.
4. **a.** Claude n'est pas canadien.
        **b.** Claude n'est pas canadienne.
5. **a.** Claude n'est pas gros.
        **b.** Claude n'est pas grosse.

**a.** Claude Bellon                                     **b.** Claude Lacoste

**B. Comment sont-ils?** Décrivez David et Annette comme dans l'exemple.

    **Exemple**     David n'est pas marié.
                   **Il est célibataire.**

1. David n'est pas gros.               4. Annette n'est pas mariée.
2. David n'est pas vieux.             5. Annette n'est pas laide.
3. David n'est pas laid.               6. Annette n'est pas vieille.

**C. Gens célèbres.** Répondez logiquement.

    **Exemple**     Tom Cruise est grand?
                   **Non, il n'est pas grand. Il est petit.**

1. Rosie O'Donnell est mince?       5. Julia Roberts est laide?
2. Cameron Diaz est grosse?        6. Shaquille O'Neal est petit?
3. Brad Pitt est célibataire?        7. Jennifer Lopez est vieille?
4. Woody Allen est beau?           8. Will Smith est vieux?

## Stratégies et Lecture

*Using cognates and familiar words to read for the gist*

Cognates are words that look the same or similar in two languages and have the same meaning. Take advantage of cognates to help you read French more easily. There are some patterns in cognates. What three patterns do you see here? What do the last two words in each column mean?

| | | |
|---|---|---|
| soudainement *suddenly* | obligé *obliged* | hôpital *hospital* |
| décidément *decidedly* | décidé *decided* | île *isle, island* |
| complètement *???* | compliqué *???* | honnête *???* |
| généralement *???* | sauvé *???* | forêt *???* |

Recognizing words you have already learned in different forms will also help you read. Use the phrases you already know on the left to guess the meaning of those on the right.

Comment dit-on *pen* en français?      Qu'est-ce que tu dis?

Je ne sais pas la réponse.      Yvette ne sait pas quoi répondre.

You will run across many unknown words in reading French, but this should not prevent you from understanding. Be flexible, changing forms of words or word order if necessary, and skip over little words that may not be needed to get the message.

**A. Avant de lire.** Can you state the general idea of the following sentences? Do not try to read them word by word; rather, focus on the words that you can understand.

Yvette hésite un moment avant de répondre.

C'est juste à ce moment qu'Annette arrive.

Annette sauve la pauvre Yvette.

David voit Annette et Yvette et s'exclame: «Je vois double!»

**B. Mots apparentés.** Before reading the following text, *Qui est-ce?*, skim through it and list the cognates you see. You should find about twenty.

CD 1-15

## Qui est-ce?

*Yvette Clark is visiting her twin sister, Annette, a student at the University of Nice. As she waits for her sister in front of the **musée des Beaux-Arts,** a young man approaches. Since she does not speak French very well, Yvette is unsure what to say when he speaks to her.*

— Salut, Annette! Ça va?

Yvette hésite un moment avant de répondre.

— Non, non... euh, ça va, mais... euh... je regrette... je ne suis pas Annette. Je suis Yvette.
— Qu'est-ce que tu dis, Annette?

Yvette pense en elle-même: «*He thinks I'm Annette. How do I tell him . . . ?*»

— Non, non, répond Yvette. Vous ne comprenez pas. Je ne suis pas Annette.
— Comment ça, tu n'es pas Annette?

Décidément, ce jeune homme ne comprend rien! Yvette insiste encore une fois.

— Je ne suis pas Annette. Vous ne comprenez pas! Écoutez! Je ne suis pas Annette! Je ne suis pas étudiante.
— Mais qu'est-ce que tu dis? demande David. Tu es malade? C'est moi, David. Nous sommes dans le même cours de littérature.

Yvette pense: «*I'm never going to get this guy to understand. He's so sure I'm Annette.*»

C'est juste à ce moment qu'Annette arrive. La pauvre Yvette est sauvée.

— Salut, Yvette! Bonjour, David!

David, très surpris de voir les deux sœurs jumelles, s'exclame:

— Mais, ce n'est pas possible! Je vois double! Maintenant je comprends. C'est ta sœur jumelle, Annette.
— Mon pauvre David! Voilà, je te présente ma sœur, Yvette.
— Bonjour, Yvette. Désolé pour la confusion, mais quelle ressemblance!

---

## A. Avez-vous compris? Qui parle: **David, Yvette** ou **Annette?**

1. Vous ne comprenez pas. Je ne suis pas Annette.
2. Mais nous sommes dans le même cours de littérature.
3. Je ne suis pas étudiante à l'université de Nice.
4. Je ne parle pas très bien français.
5. Je te présente ma sœur.

## B. D'abord... Which happens first, **a** or **b**?

1. **a.** David dit bonjour à Yvette.
   **b.** Yvette arrive au musée des Beaux-Arts.

2. **a.** David dit: «Bonjour, Annette.»
   **b.** Yvette pense: «Il ne comprend pas.»

3. **a.** Yvette hésite à répondre parce qu'elle ne parle pas très bien français.
   **b.** Yvette répond: «Non, non, vous ne comprenez pas.»

4. **a.** David comprend qu'Annette et Yvette sont des sœurs jumelles.
   **b.** Annette arrive.

5. **a.** David dit: «Désolé *(Sorry)* pour la confusion.»
   **b.** David comprend la situation.

# Describing personality

**VOCABULAIRE SUPPLÉMENTAIRE**

| | |
|---|---|
| excentrique | sérieux (sérieuse) |
| matérialiste | têtu(e) *stubborn* |
| énergique | brillant(e) |
| (dés)organisé(e) | imaginatif *(imaginative)* |
| sociable | honnête *honest* |

## Les personnalités

Je suis très... Je suis **plutôt...** Je suis assez... Je suis un peu...
Je **ne** suis **pas (du tout)**...

optimiste, idéaliste / pessimiste, réaliste

timide / extraverti(e)

**sympathique** (sympa), **gentil(le),** agréable / méchant(e), désagréable

intelligent(e), intellectuel(le) / **bête**

amusant(e), intéressant(e) / ennuyeux (ennuyeuse)

**dynamique,** sportif (sportive) / paresseux (paresseuse)

*What are you like, compared to your best friend?*

> Je suis **plus** dynamique **que mon meilleur ami (ma meilleure amie).**
> Je suis **aussi** sportif (sportive) **que** mon meilleur ami (ma meilleure amie).
> Je suis **moins** bête **que** mon meilleur ami (ma meilleure amie).

CD 1-16

Une **nouvelle** amie, Marie-Louise, parle avec David.

MARIE-LOUISE: **Tes amis** et toi, vous êtes étudiants, non?
DAVID: Oui, nous sommes étudiants à l'université de Nice.
MARIE-LOUISE: Vous êtes plutôt intellectuels, alors?
DAVID: Mes amis sont assez intellectuels, mais moi, je ne suis pas très intellectuel. Et toi? Tu es étudiante aussi?
MARIE-LOUISE: Non, **les études, ce n'est pas mon truc.**
DAVID: Et le sport? **Tu aimes** le sport?
MARIE-LOUISE: Oui, j'aime bien le sport. Je suis très sportive. J'aime beaucoup le tennis, mais je n'aime pas beaucoup **le football.**

---

plutôt *rather*   ne... pas du tout *not at all*   sympathique *nice*   gentil(le) *nice*   bête *stupid, dumb*   dynamique *active*   plus... que *more . . . than*
mon meilleur ami (ma meilleure amie) *my best friend*   aussi... que *as . . . as*   moins... que *less . . . than*   nouveau (nouvelle) *new*
Tes amis *Your friends*   les études *studies, going to school*   ce n'est pas mon truc *it's not my thing*   Tu aimes *You like*   le football *soccer*

## A. Ils sont comment? Complétez les phrases.

**Exemple**  Ben Afflek est (plus, moins, aussi) grand que Tom Cruise.
**Ben Afflek est plus grand que Tom Cruise.**

1. Ben Affleck est (plus, moins, aussi) beau que Tom Cruise.
2. Jay Leno est (plus, moins, aussi) amusant que David Letterman.
3. Tiger Woods est (plus, moins, aussi) sportif que Sammy Sosa.
4. Julia Roberts est (plus, moins, aussi) belle que Demi Moore.
5. Katie Couric est (plus, moins, aussi) intelligente que Oprah Winfrey.
6. Les Républicains sont (plus, moins, aussi) idéalistes que les Démocrates.

## B. Comment sont-ils? Complétez les phrases.

1. Moi, *je suis / je ne suis pas* très extraverti(e).
2. *Je suis / Je ne suis pas* pessimiste.
3. Mon meilleur ami *est / n'est pas* bête.
4. *Il est / Il n'est pas* américain.
5. Mes amis *sont / ne sont pas* sportifs.
6. *Ils sont / Ils ne sont pas* paresseux.
7. Ma famille et moi, *nous sommes / nous ne sommes pas* très dynamiques.
8. *Nous sommes / Nous ne sommes pas* gentils.
9. Et vous, *(name your professor)*, vous êtes / vous n'êtes pas très méchant(e)!

## C. Et vous? Comment êtes-vous?

très    plutôt    assez    un peu    ne… pas du tout

**Exemple**  optimistic
**Je suis très / plutôt / assez / un peu optimiste.**
**Je ne suis pas (du tout) optimiste.**

| | |
|---|---|
| 1. idealistic | 5. shy |
| 2. mean | 6. boring |
| 3. lazy | 7. athletic |
| 4. intellectual | 8. married |

## D. Réponses. Quelle est la réponse logique?

1. Tu es étudiant(e)?
2. Tu aimes le sport?
3. Tes amis et toi, vous êtes sportifs?
4. Tes amis et toi, vous êtes intellectuels?
5. Tes amis sont extravertis?
6. Tes amis sont dynamiques?

a. Oui, nous sommes très sportifs.
b. Oui, nous sommes assez intellectuels.
c. Oui, je suis étudiant(e).
d. Non, ils sont plutôt paresseux.
e. Oui, j'aime beaucoup le football et le tennis.
f. Non, ils sont plutôt timides.

## E. Conversation. Avec un(e) partenaire, relisez à haute voix *(aloud)* la conversation entre Marie-Louise et David à la page précédente. Ensuite, changez la conversation pour décrire *(to describe)* votre propre *(own)* situation.

**1.** What pronoun would you use to address a child? two children? a salesclerk?

**2.** How do you say *I* in French? *We? He? She? They?*

**3.** What is an infinitive? How do you say *to be?*

**4.** What form of **être** do you use with each of the subject pronouns?

**5.** What do you place before a conjugated verb to negate it? What do you place after it? What happens to **ne** when it is followed by a vowel sound?

**6.** What is elision?

**7.** What are five patterns of adjective agreement? What is the feminine form of **gros?** **gentil?** of **beau?** of **nouveau?**

# Describing people

*Les pronoms sujets, le verbe **être**, la négation et d'autres adjectifs*

Below are the subject pronouns in French. Notice that there are two ways to say *you.* Use **tu** to talk to a friend, a family member, a classmate, or a child. Use **vous** when you are addressing an adult stranger or someone to whom you should show respect. Always use **vous** when talking to more than one person.

| | | | |
|---|---|---|---|
| **je** | *I* | **nous** | *we* |
| **tu** | *you* (singular familiar) | **vous** | *you* (singular formal, all plurals) |
| **il** | *he, it* (masculine) | **ils** | *they* (masculine or a mixed group) |
| **elle** | *she, it* (feminine) | **elles** | *they* (feminine) |

You have seen all of the forms of the verb **être** *(to be).* The word **être** is the infinitive, the form of the verb you would find in a dictionary. The conjugation chart shows the forms you use with the different subject pronouns or names of people.

| ÊTRE *(to be)* | | | | |
|---|---|---|---|---|
| je **suis** | *I am* | nous **sommes** | *we are* |
| tu **es** | *you are* | vous **êtes** | *you are* |
| il/elle **est** | *he/she/it is* | ils/elles **sont** | *they are* |
| David **est** | *David is* | David et Jean **sont** | *David and Jean are* |

To negate a conjugated verb, place **ne** before and **pas** after it. **Ne** changes to **n'** before a vowel or mute **h.** Generally, a final unaccented **e** in single-syllable words like **je, ne,** or **que** must be dropped when the next word begins with a vowel or mute **h.** This is called elision. The pronouns **tu** and **elle** never elide.

| | |
|---|---|
| Elles ne sont pas mariées. | *They aren't married.* |
| Le professeur n'est pas grand. | *The professor's not tall.* |
| Je n'habite pas ici. | *I don't live here.* |

Remember that adjectives agree in gender (masculine, feminine) and number (singular, plural) with what they describe. Review the forms of adjectives on page 34. Note the patterns of these common adjective endings when **-e** is added for the feminine form.

| MASCULINE | FEMININE | MASCULINE | | FEMININE | |
|---|---|---|---|---|---|
| | | *singular* | *plural* | *singular* | *plural* |
| -eux | -euse | paresseux | paresseux | paresseuse | paresseuses |
| -en | -enne | canadien | canadiens | canadienne | canadiennes |
| -if | -ive | sportif | sportifs | sportive | sportives |
| -el | -elle | intellectuel | intellectuels | intellectuelle | intellectuelles |
| -er | -ère | premier | premiers | première | premières |

Like **gros, gentil** doubles the final consonant before adding **-e** for the feminine form (**gros→grosse**).

The adjective **nouveau** follows the same pattern as **beau** and **jumeau.**

| MASCULINE | | FEMININE | |
|---|---|---|---|
| *singular* | *plural* | *singular* | *plural* |
| nouveau | nouveaux | nouvelle | nouvelles |
| beau | beaux | belle | belles |

**A. Tu ou vous?** Demandez à ces personnes si elles sont fatiguées *(tired)*.

> **Exemple**    your sister: **Tu es fatiguée?**
> your boss: **Vous êtes fatigué(e)?**

1. your roommate
2. your classmate
3. your parents
4. a salesclerk
5. two friends
6. an elderly neighbor

**B. Au contraire!** Complétez les descriptions avec le verbe **être**. Donnez le négatif si nécessaire.

> **Exemple**    Les étudiants du cours de français... (bêtes, dynamiques, intelligents)
> **Les étudiants du cours de français ne sont pas bêtes. Ils sont dynamiques. Ils sont intelligents.**

1. Moi, en classe, je... (extraverti[e], dynamique, timide, un peu paresseux [paresseuse])
2. En général, mes professeurs... (intéressants, intellectuels, bêtes, ennuyeux, intelligents)
3. Les autres *(other)* étudiants du cours de français... (intéressants, extravertis, ennuyeux, désagréables, agréables)
4. Mes amis et moi, nous... (sportifs, intellectuels, paresseux, sympathiques)

**C. Comment sont-ils?** Dites si chaque adjectif donné décrit la personne indiquée. Faites attention à la forme de l'adjectif!

> **Exemple**    Annette ... beau, laid.
> **Annette est belle. Elle n'est pas laide.**

Annette...
intellectuel, dynamique,
paresseux, gros

Annette et Yvette...
américain, français,
gentil, méchant, beau

David et Jean...
laid, beau, vieux, jeune

Moi, je...
dynamique, paresseux,
ennuyeux, sportif

**D. Descriptions.** Décrivez ces personnes. Faites attention à la forme de l'adjectif!

1. votre meilleur ami
2. votre meilleure amie
3. vos *(your)* amis et vous
4. vous
5. les étudiants du cours de français
6. les étudiantes du cours de français

| elles<br>nous<br>il<br>je<br>elle<br>ils | (ne / n') | suis<br>est<br>sommes<br>sont | (pas) | sportif<br>sympathique<br>ennuyeux<br>amusant<br>marié<br>timide<br>extraverti<br>??? |
|---|---|---|---|---|

**Pour vérifier**

**1.** What are three ways of asking a question that can be answered with **oui** or **non?** What happens to your intonation in each case?

**2.** What happens to **est-ce que** before a vowel sound?

# Asking what someone is like

*Les questions*

There are several ways of asking a question that will be answered **oui** or **non**.

- You can ask a question with rising intonation, that is by raising the pitch of your voice at the end. A statement normally has falling intonation.

STATEMENT:   Tu es extravertie.
*You are outgoing.*

QUESTION:   Tu es extravertie?
*Are you outgoing?*

- You can also ask a question by adding **est-ce que** to the beginning of a statement and using rising intonation.

STATEMENT:   Tu es sportif.
*You are athletic.*

QUESTION:   Est-ce que tu es sportif?
*Are you athletic?*

- If you are presuming that someone will probably answer **oui** to a question, you can use either **n'est-ce pas?** *(isn't that right?)* or **non?** at the end of a question with rising intonation.

STATEMENT:   Il est marié.
*He's married.*

QUESTION:   Il est marié, n'est-ce pas?
Il est marié, non?
*He's married, isn't he?*

Due to elision, **est-ce que** becomes **est-ce qu'** before vowel sounds.

— Est-ce qu'il est d'ici?     — Est-ce qu'elles sont canadiennes?
— Non, il est d'Atlanta.     — Non, elles sont d'ici.

**A. C'est une question?** Listen to your instructor make some statements and ask some questions about your class and university. If you hear a statement, don't write anything on your paper. If you hear a question, answer it with **oui** or **non** on your paper.

**B. Et toi?** Demandez à un(e) camarade de classe comment il/elle est. Faites attention à la forme de l'adjectif!

**Exemple**    sportif ou intellectuel
    **— Est-ce que tu es sportif (sportive) ou intellectuel(le)?**
    **— Je suis plutôt sportif (sportive) / plutôt intellectuel(le) /**
    **les deux** *(both).*

1. idéaliste ou réaliste
2. timide ou extraverti
3. gentil ou méchant
4. intelligent ou bête
5. amusant ou ennuyeux
6. dynamique ou paresseux
7. optimiste ou pessimiste
8. marié, célibataire, fiancé ou divorcé

Maintenant, présentez votre partenaire à la classe en suivant l'exemple.

**Exemple**    **C'est Mario. Il est intellectuel...**

**C. Et le professeur?** Posez ces questions à votre professeur. Utilisez **est-ce que**, **n'est-ce pas** ou **non**.

> **Exemple**    Vous êtes marié(e)?
> **Est-ce que vous êtes marié(e)?**
> **Vous êtes marié(e), n'est-ce pas / non?**

1. Vous êtes américain(e)?
2. Le français est facile pour vous?
3. Les examens de français sont difficiles?
4. Votre premier cours commence à huit heures?
5. Vous êtes à l'université le lundi matin?
6. Vous êtes en cours à trois heures?

**D. Encore des questions!** David pose des questions à Annette. Qu'est-ce qu'il dit? Formez des questions logiques avec le verbe **être**.

> **Exemple**    **Est-ce que tu es plus jeune que moi?**

| Est-ce que | tes amis... nous... tu... ta sœur... | américaine de Los Angeles étudiante d'ici dans le même cours plus extravertis que toi plus jeune que moi en cours à une heure aussi intelligente que toi |
|---|---|---|

**E. Entretien.** Interviewez votre partenaire.

1. Est-ce que tu es américain(e)? Ta famille et toi, vous êtes d'ici? Est-ce que vous êtes plutôt idéalistes ou plutôt réalistes?
2. Est-ce que les études sont faciles ou difficiles pour toi? Est-ce que les professeurs ici sont intéressants ou ennuyeux? Ton meilleur ami (Ta meilleure amie) est étudiant(e) aussi? Tes amis et toi, est-ce que vous êtes intellectuels? Est-ce que tes amis sont intelligents ou bêtes? Ils sont amusants ou ennuyeux?
3. Est-ce que tu aimes le sport? Tu es plutôt sportif (sportive)? Est-ce que tu es dynamique ou plutôt paresseux (paresseuse)?

# Describing the university area

## Le campus et le quartier

**Qu'est-ce qu'il y a sur** votre campus?

Sur le campus, **il y a**...

des salles *(f)* de classe *(f)*

un amphithéâtre

une bibliothèque

des résidences *(f)*

un stade avec des matchs *(m)* de football américain

une librairie

un parking

**Dans le quartier universitaire, près de** l'université, il y a...

beaucoup de grands bâtiments *(m)* modernes avec des **bureaux** *(m)*

des maisons *(f)*

un parc avec beaucoup d'arbres *(m)*

des concerts *(m)* de rock *(m)* / de jazz *(m)* / de musique *(f)* populaire / de musique classique

### VOCABULAIRE SUPPLÉMENTAIRE
**un arrêt d'autobus** *a bus stop*
**un centre administratif** *an administration building*
**un centre d'étudiants** *a student center*
**une infirmerie** *a health center*
**un court de tennis** *a tennis court*
**une fontaine** *a fountain*
**un gymnase** *a gym*
**un laboratoire** *a lab*
**une piscine** *a pool*

---

**Qu'est-ce qu'il y a... ?** *What is there . . . ?*   **sur** *on*   **il y a** *there is, there are*   **Dans** *In*   **le quartier** *the neighborhood*
**universitaire** *university (adj.)*   **près de** *near*   **un bureau** *an office*

une boîte de nuit

un théâtre

un cinéma avec des films **étrangers** et des films américains

un club de gym

CD 1-17

Annette et un ami parlent du campus et du quartier.

MICHEL: Comment est **ton** université? Tu aimes le campus?
ANNETTE: Oui, il est très agréable. Les vieux bâtiments sont très **jolis.**
MICHEL: Qu'est-ce qu'il y a sur le campus?
ANNETTE: Il y a une grande bibliothèque et beaucoup d'arbres, mais **il n'y a pas assez de** parkings.
MICHEL: Qu'est-ce qu'il y a dans le quartier?
ANNETTE: Il y a de jolies maisons, des cafés, deux ou trois **bons** restaurants et beaucoup de **mauvais** fast-foods.

### A. Chez nous. Décrivez votre université.

1. Le campus ici est *grand / petit / joli / laid / ???.*
2. Sur le campus il y a *plus de nouveaux bâtiments / plus de vieux bâtiments.*
3. La bibliothèque universitaire est *grande / petite / agréable / ???.*
4. *Il y a / Il n'y a pas* assez de résidences sur le campus.
5. *Il y a / Il n'y a pas* beaucoup d'arbres sur le campus.
6. Le restaurant universitaire, c'est un *bon / mauvais* restaurant. *(Il n'y a pas de restaurant sur le campus.)*
7. *Il y a / Il n'y a pas* assez de parkings.
8. Le week-end, il y a souvent *(often) des matchs de football américain / des concerts / des films / ???.*
9. Dans le quartier près de l'université, il y a *des restaurants / des cafés / des fast-foods / un joli parc / ???.*
10. *Barnes & Noble / BookPeople / ???* est une bonne librairie dans le quartier.

### B. Qu'est-ce qu'il y a? Complétez ces phrases pour décrire votre quartier universitaire.

1. Sur le campus, il y a...
2. Dans le quartier universitaire, il y a...

### C. Conversation. Avec un(e) partenaire, relisez la conversation entre Michel et Annette ci-dessus *(above)*. Ensuite, changez la conversation pour décrire votre propre université.

---

**étranger (étrangère)** *foreign*   **ton (ta, tes)** *your*   **joli(e)** *pretty*   **il n'y a pas** *there isn't, there aren't*   **assez de** *enough*
**bon(ne)** *good*   **mauvais(e)** *bad*

**Pour vérifier**

**1.** What are the two forms of the word for *a*? When do you use each? How do you say *some*?

**2.** How do you say *there is? there are? there isn't? there aren't?*

**3.** In what three circumstances do you use **de (d')** instead of **un, une,** or **des?** What is an exception to replacing **un, une,** or **des** with **de (d')** in a negative sentence?

## Saying what there is

*Le genre, l'article indéfini et l'expression **il y a***

All nouns in French have a gender (masculine or feminine). The categorization of most nouns as masculine or feminine cannot be guessed, unless they represent people.

The short word **un** *(a, an),* **une** *(a, an),* or **des** *(some)* before a noun is called the indefinite article. Use **un** with masculine singular nouns, **une** with feminine singular nouns, and **des** with all plural nouns.

To make a noun plural, add an **s** to the end of it. Do not add an **s,** however, if the noun already ends in an **s, x,** or **z.** Nouns that end in **eau (bureau)** form their plural in **-x (bureaux).**

|  | SINGULAR | PLURAL |
|---|---|---|
| MASCULINE | un théâtre | des théâtres |
| FEMININE | une bibliothèque | des bibliothèques |

Always learn a new noun as a unit with the article **(un, une)** in order to remember its gender!

To say *there is* or *there are* in French, use the expression **il y a (un, une, des... ).** To say *there isn't* or *there aren't,* use **il n'y a pas (de...).**

**Un, une,** and **des** change to **de (d')** in the following cases.

- After negated verbs, except after the verb **être.**

| | |
|---|---|
| Il y a **un** stade. | Il n'y a pas **de** stade. |
| Il y a **des** matchs de football. | Il n' y pas **de** matchs de football. |
| Écrivez **des** phrases complètes. | N'écrivez pas **de** phrases complètes. |

But not after **être:**

| | |
|---|---|
| C'est **un** bon restaurant. | Ce n'est pas **un** bon restaurant. |

- After expressions of quantity, such as **combien, beaucoup,** and **assez.**

| | |
|---|---|
| Il y a **des** cinémas. | Il y a beaucoup **de** cinémas. |
| Il y a **un** parking. | Il y a assez **de** parkings. |

- Directly before a plural adjective.

| | |
|---|---|
| Il y a **des** bâtiments modernes. | Il y a **de** nouveaux bâtiments. |

## Prononciation
CD 1-18

*L'article indéfini*

Be careful to pronounce **un** and **une** differently. Use the very tight sound **u** with lips rounded, as in **tu,** to say **une.** To pronounce the **u** sound, position your mouth to pronounce a French **i** with your tongue held high in your mouth. Then, round your lips. The vowel sound of **un** is nasal. Pronounce the **n** in **un** only when there is **liaison** with a following noun beginning with a vowel sound.

| | |
|---|---|
| **une** résidence | **un** bâtiment |
| **une** amie | **un** ami |

**A. Scènes.** Complétez ces questions avec **un, une** ou **des**. Après, posez les questions à votre partenaire.

1. C'est _____ bibliothèque
   ou _____ restaurant?
   Ce sont _____ étudiants
   ou _____ professeurs?

2. C'est _____ cinéma
   ou _____ salle de classe?
   Ce sont _____ femmes
   ou _____ hommes?

3. C'est _____ concert
   ou _____ film?
   C'est _____ concert de
   jazz ou de musique classique?

4. C'est _____ librairie
   ou _____ boîte de nuit?
   Ce sont _____ gens timides
   ou _____ gens extravertis?

**B. Qu'est-ce qu'il y a?** Est-ce qu'il y a les choses *(things)* indiquées entre parenthèses dans chaque endroit *(each place)?*

    **Exemple**    à l'université (une bibliothèque, une boîte de nuit)
               **À l'université, il y a une bibliothèque. Il n'y a pas de boîte de nuit.**

1. dans la salle de classe (un professeur, des matchs de football, des étudiants, des livres, des arbres, un tableau)
2. dans le quartier universitaire (des maisons, un cinéma, des films étrangers, un théâtre, des concerts, un restaurant, des boîtes de nuit)

**C. Qu'est-ce qu'il y a?** Relisez la *Note culturelle* à la page 44. Sur le campus d'une université française, est-ce qu'il y a probablement ces choses?

    **Exemples**    un restaurant universitaire        des matchs de football
              **Oui, il y a un restaurant**        **Non, il n'y a pas de matchs**
              **universitaire.**                 **de football.**

1. des amphithéâtres
2. un stade
3. des bureaux de profs
4. une bibliothèque
5. des résidences
6. des salles de classe
7. une boîte de nuit
8. des matchs de football américain

**D. Est-ce qu'il y a... ?** Complétez ces questions avec **un, une, des** ou **de (d')**. Après, posez-les à votre partenaire.

    **Exemple**    — Ici à l'université, est-ce qu'il y a **des** concerts de rock?
               **— Oui, il y a des concerts de rock. /**
               **Non, il n'y a pas de concerts de rock.**

Ici à l'université, est-ce qu'il y a...

1. ... beaucoup _____ vieux bâtiments?
2. ... _____ grands amphithéâtres?
3. ... _____ salles de classe modernes?
4. ... _____ grande bibliothèque?
5. ... assez _____ parkings?
6. ... _____ grand stade?
7. ... _____ théâtre?
8. ... _____ librairie?
9. ... _____ jolis arbres?
10. ... _____ concerts de jazz?

**1.** Do you use **c'est** and **ce sont** or **il/elle est** and **ils/elles sont** to identify *who* or *what* someone or something is? to say *where* someone or something is? to say *what* someone or something *is like* using an adjective?

**2.** Are most adjectives placed before or after the noun they describe? Which adjectives are placed before the noun they describe?

**3.** What are the alternate masculine singular forms of **beau, nouveau,** and **vieux**? When are they used?

# Identifying and describing people and things

*C'est ou **il/elle est** et la place de l'adjectif*

Since all nouns in French are either masculine or feminine, there is no neuter *it*. Use **il est, elle est, ils sont,** and **elles sont** with *an adjective to describe* things, just as you do with people.

— Comment est Annette? — Comment est la bibliothèque?
— **Elle est** grande. — **Elle est** grande.

Use **il/elle est** and **ils/elles sont** to state someone's profession, nationality, or religion. Note that you do not use any equivalent for the English word *a* and you do not capitalize nationalities or religions.

Elle est étudiante. Elle est américaine. Il est catholique.

Also use **il est, elle est, ils sont,** and **elles sont** with *a preposition of place to say where* someone or something is.

Où est David? *Where's David?*
**Il est** au café. *He's at a café.*
Où est le café? *Where's the café?*
**Il est** près de l'université. *It's near the university.*

Use **c'est** and **ce sont** with *a noun to identify or describe* someone or something.

Ce n'est pas Annette. *She's not Annette.*
C'est Yvette. *She's Yvette.*
C'est une femme intéressante. *She's an interesting woman.*
Ce n'est pas un parc. *It's not a park.*
C'est un grand campus. *It's a big campus.*
Ce ne sont pas mes amis. *They're not my friends.*
Ce sont mes frères. *They're my brothers.*

Remember to use **il y a** to say what *there is/are*.

**Il y a** un parc dans le quartier. *There is a park in the neighborhood.*

In French, unlike in English, most adjectives *follow* the nouns they describe.

Il y a **des résidences *modernes*** sur le campus.

Only a few adjectives go before the noun. They include:

| | | | | |
|---|---|---|---|---|
| beau (belle) | jeune | bon (bonne) | grand(e) | autre *(other)* |
| joli(e) | vieux (vieille) | mauvais(e) | petit(e) | même |
| | nouveau (nouvelle) | gentil(le) | gros(se) | seul(e) *(only)* |

The adjectives **beau, nouveau,** and **vieux** have alternate masculine singular forms, **bel, nouvel,** and **vieil,** that are used before nouns beginning with a vowel sound.

| MASCULINE SINGULAR (PLUS CONSONANT SOUND) | MASCULINE SINGULAR (PLUS VOWEL SOUND) | FEMININE |
|---|---|---|
| un beau quartier | un bel ami | une belle amie |
| un nouveau quartier | un nouvel ami | une nouvelle amie |
| un vieux quartier | un vieil ami | une vieille amie |

**A. Qu'est-ce que c'est?** Identifiez ces personnes ou ces choses. Après, décrivez-les avec l'adjectif le plus logique.

**Exemples**  café (grand / petit)
**C'est un café.**
**Il est petit.**

 étudiantes (sympa / méchant)
**Ce sont des étudiantes.**
**Elles sont sympas (sympathiques).**

**1.**
maisons (nouveau / vieux)

**2.**
amphithéâtre (grand / petit)

**3.**
maison (grand / petit)

**4.**
femme (sportif / paresseux)

**5.**
parc (joli / laid)

**6.**
salle de classe (moderne / vieux)

**B. Descriptions.** Faites des phrases comme dans l'exemple.

**Exemple** **C'est un jeune homme. Il est dynamique.**
**Il n'est pas paresseux. Il est sportif. Il est beau.**

un jeune homme, dynamique, paresseux, sportif, beau

**1.**  des hommes, étudiants, jeunes, sympathiques

**2.**  Yvette, française, en France, étudiante, à l'université, à la maison

**C. Compliments.** Faites des compliments. Écrivez la forme correcte de l'adjectif logique dans la phrase pour faire un compliment.

**Exemple** C'est une _____ femme _____ . (intelligent / bête)
**C'est une femme intelligente.**

**1.** C'est un _____ restaurant _____. (bon / mauvais)
**2.** Ce sont des _____ étudiants _____. (sympa / méchant)
**3.** C'est un _____ campus _____. (beau / laid)
**4.** C'est un _____ professeur _____. (intéressant / ennuyeux)
**5.** C'est une _____ femme _____. (joli / laid)
**6.** C'est un _____ homme _____. (beau / laid)
**7.** Ce sont des _____ étudiantes _____. (dynamique / paresseux)
**8.** C'est une _____ résidence _____. (nouveau / vieux)
**9.** C'est une _____ salle de classe _____. (agréable / désagréable)
**10.** C'est une _____ famille _____. (gentil / méchant)

# Talking about your studies

## L'université et les cours

Est-ce que vous aimez l'université?

| J'aime beaucoup... | J'aime assez... | Je n'aime pas (du tout)... | Je préfère... |
|---|---|---|---|
| l'université | le campus | les cours | **les boums** *(f)* / |
| les professeurs | la bibliothèque | les devoirs *(m)* | **les fêtes** *(f)* |
| les étudiants | les salles de classe | les examens *(m)* | le sport |
| | le laboratoire | | les matchs de |
| | de langues / | | football |
| | d'informatique | | américain / |
| | | | de basket *(m)* |

Qu'est-ce que vous étudiez?

J'étudie la philosophie.              Je n'étudie pas la littérature.

LES LANGUES *(f)*
**l'allemand** *(m)*
l'anglais *(m)*
l'espagnol *(m)*
le français

LES SCIENCES HUMAINES *(f)*
l'histoire *(f)*
la psychologie
**les sciences politiques** *(f)*

LES BEAUX-ARTS *(m)*
le théâtre
la musique

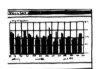

LES COURS DE COMMERCE
**la comptabilité**
le marketing

LES COURS TECHNIQUES
les mathématiques
  (les maths) *(f)*
**l'informatique** *(f)*

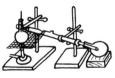

LES SCIENCES
la biologie
**la chimie**
la physique

J'aime beaucoup le cours de...
Il est facile / difficile / intéressant.

CD 1-19

David et Annette parlent de **leurs** études.

DAVID:      Qu'est-ce que tu étudies ce semestre?
ANNETTE:   J'étudie le français et la littérature classique. Et toi?
DAVID:      J'étudie la philosophie et la littérature classique, comme toi.
ANNETTE:   Comment sont tes cours?
DAVID:      J'aime beaucoup le cours de philosophie. Il est très intéressant. Je n'aime pas du tout le cours de littérature parce que le prof est ennuyeux.

---

**une boum** *a party*   **une fête** *a party*   **l'allemand** *(m) German*   **les sciences politiques** *(f) government, political science*
**les beaux-arts** *(m) fine arts*   **la comptabilité** *accounting*   **l'informatique** *(f) computer science*   **la chimie** *chemistry*   **leur(s)** *their*

**A. Préférences.** Interviewez votre partenaire sur ses préférences.

**Exemple**    le français / les mathématiques
   **— Est-ce que tu préfères le français ou les mathématiques?**
   **— Je préfère le français.**

1. la littérature / les sciences
2. les cours de commerce / les langues
3. les cours à huit heures du matin / les cours à deux heures de l'après-midi
4. les matchs de football américain / les matchs de basket
5. les cours dans les grands amphithéâtres / les cours dans les petites salles de classe / les cours dans le laboratoire de langues
6. les examens / les fêtes

**B. Et vous?** Changez les phrases pour parler de vous.

1. J'étudie *le français, la biologie et les mathématiques.*
2. À l'université, j'aime *les étudiants.*
3. À l'université, je n'aime pas *les matchs de football américain.*
4. Je préfère les cours à *dix heures du matin.*
5. J'aime le cours de *français.* Il est intéressant.
6. Je n'aime pas le cours de *marketing.* Il est ennuyeux.

**C. Entretien.** Interviewez votre partenaire.

1. Qu'est-ce que tu étudies ce semestre?
2. Quels cours est-ce que tu préfères?
3. Pour toi, la chimie est plus facile ou plus difficile que la biologie?
4. Les maths sont plus intéressantes ou moins intéressantes que l'informatique?
5. L'histoire est plus ennuyeuse ou moins ennuyeuse que les sciences politiques?
6. La philosophie est plus intéressante ou moins intéressante que la littérature?

**D. Conversation.** Avec un(e) partenaire, relisez à haute voix la conversation entre David et Annette à la page précédente. Ensuite, changez la conversation pour décrire vos cours ce semestre.

La cour de la Sorbonne

**Pour vérifier**

**1.** What are the four forms of the word for *the* in French? When do you use each?

**2.** Besides meaning *the,* what are two other uses of the definite article in French?

**3.** When is the **s** of the plural form **les** pronounced?

# Identifying people and things

*L'article défini*

The short words **le, la, l', les** *(the)* before nouns are called definite articles.

le campus        la bibliothèque        l'université        les cours

The form of the definite article you use depends on the noun's gender, whether it starts with a consonant or vowel sound, and whether it is singular or plural.

|  | SINGULAR BEFORE CONSONANT SOUND | SINGULAR BEFORE VOWEL SOUND | PLURAL |
|---|---|---|---|
| MASCULINE | **le** livre | **l'**homme | **les** livres, **les** hommes |
| FEMININE | **la** librairie | **l'**étudiante | **les** librairies, **les** étudiantes |

Use the definite article before nouns:

- To specify items, as when using *the* in English.
  Apprenez **les** mots de vocabulaire.   *Learn **the** vocabulary words.*

- To say what you like, dislike, or prefer.
  Je n'aime pas **les** devoirs.                 *I don't like homework.*

- To talk about something as a general category or an abstract noun.
  **Les** langues sont faciles pour moi.   *Languages are easy for me.*

In the last two cases, there is no article in English.

#  Prononciation

CD 1-20  *La voyelle **e** et l'article défini*

As you know, a final unaccented **e** is usually not pronounced, unless it is the only vowel, as in **le.**

grand**e**        histoir**e**        langu**e**        bibliothèqu**e**        j'aim**e**

Otherwise, an unaccented **e** can have three different pronunciations, depending on what follows it.

- In short words like **le** or **je,** or when **e** is followed by a single consonant within a word, pronounce it as in:

  j**e**        n**e**        l**e**        r**e**garde        d**e**voirs

- When, as in **les, e** is followed by an unpronounced consonant at the end of a word, pronounce it as in:

  l**es**        m**es**        parl**ez**        aim**ez**        étudi**ez**

- In words like **elle,** where **e** is followed by two consonants within a word, or by a single pronounced consonant at the end of a word, pronounce it as in:

  int**e**llectu**el**        b**e**lle        qu**el**        **e**spagnol        bask**et**

Since the final **s** of plural nouns is not pronounced, you must pronounce the article correctly to differentiate singular and plural nouns. Listen carefully as you repeat each of the following nouns. Notice the **z** sound of a final **s** in liaison.

| le livre | la science | l'étudiant | l'étudiante |
| les livres | les sciences | les ‿z étudiants | les ‿z étudiantes |

**A. Parlez bien.** Listen as David talks about university life. In each sentence, you will hear the singular or plural form of one of the following nouns. Indicate which form you hear by writing the article on your paper.

1. le professeur — les professeurs
2. le cours — les cours
3. l'étudiant — les étudiants
4. l'examen — les examens
5. le livre — les livres
6. l'exercice — les exercices
7. le campus — les campus
8. la bibliothèque — les bibliothèques

**B. Vos cours.** Est-ce que vous étudiez les matières suivantes *(following subjects)?*

Exemple  **Oui, j'étudie la chimie.**
**Non, je n'étudie pas la chimie.**

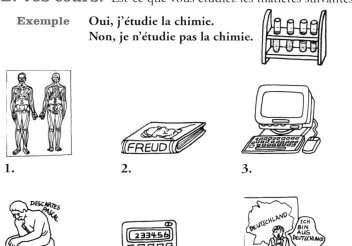

1.   2.   3.

4.   5.   6.   7.

**C. Et vous?** Complétez les phrases pour parler de vos cours et de votre université.

1. J'étudie...
2. J'aime beaucoup...
3. J'aime assez...
4. Je n'aime pas beaucoup...
5. Je n'aime pas du tout...
6. Je ne comprends pas...
7. Je comprends bien...
8. Je pense que le cours de... est...

**D. Entretien.** Complétez les questions suivantes avec l'article défini (**le, la, l', les**) ou l'article indéfini (**un, une, des**). Après, posez ces questions à votre partenaire.

1. Est-ce que tu aimes _____ université?
2. Est-ce que tu es à _____ bibliothèque avant le cours de français?
3. Est-ce que tu aimes _____ cours de français?
4. Est-ce qu'il y a _____ étudiants étrangers dans _____ classe?
5. Est-ce qu'il y a _____ examen aujourd'hui?
6. Est-ce que tu comprends bien _____ français?
7. Est-ce que tu travailles dans _____ restaurant?
8. Est-ce que tu travailles ici à _____ université?

## Reprise

*Talking about the university and your studies*

In ***Chapitre 1,*** you practiced talking about your classes and identifying and describing the people, places, and things found at and around a university. Now you have a chance to review what you have learned.

**A. Qui est-ce?** Complétez les descriptions de ces célébrités francophones avec **c'est, il est** ou **elle est.**

Juliette Binoche

Jacob Desvarieux

_____ Juliette Binoche.
_____ une femme.
_____ très belle.
_____ actrice.
_____ française.

_____ Jacob Desvarieux.
_____ un homme.
_____ intéressant.
_____ musicien.
_____ de Guadeloupe.

Maintenant, identifiez un(e) camarade de classe et parlez un peu de lui *(him)* ou d'elle.

**B. Interview.** Formez des questions logiques avec le verbe **être.** Interviewez votre partenaire avec les questions.

> **Exemple**  Est-ce que tu / en cours le lundi?
> — **Est-ce que tu es en cours le lundi?**
> — **Oui, je suis en cours le lundi. / Non, je ne suis pas en cours le lundi.**

1. Est-ce que le cours de français / très facile?
2. Est-ce que le prof / méchant?
3. Est-ce que tu / timide en cours?
4. Est-ce que les devoirs / intéressants?
5. Est-ce que les examens / difficiles?
6. Est-ce que tu / dynamique en classe?
7. Est-ce que les autres étudiants / intelligents?
8. Tes amis et toi, est-ce que vous / intellectuels?
9. Tes amis et toi, est-ce que vous / sportifs?

**C. Descriptions.** Identifiez et décrivez les personnes et les objets suivants avec les adjectifs donnés.

**Exemple**    maison (laid, petit)
**C'est une petite maison laide.**

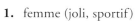

**1.** femme (joli, sportif)    **2.** homme (sympa, vieux)    **3.** homme (beau, sportif)

**4.** restaurant (mauvais, désagréable)    **5.** femme (intelligent, jeune)    **6.** boîte de nuit (grand, populaire)

**D. Entretien.** Complétez les questions suivantes avec l'article défini **(le, la, l', les),** l'article indéfini **(un, une, des)** ou avec **de (d').** Après, posez ces questions à votre partenaire.

**1.** Est-ce qu'il y a beaucoup _____ vieux bâtiments sur le campus? Est-ce que tu aimes _____ vieux bâtiments? Est-ce qu'il y a beaucoup _____ arbres sur le campus? Est-ce qu'il y a assez _____ parkings?

**2.** Est-ce que tu aimes _____ sport? Est-ce qu'il y a _____ matchs de football américain à l'université? Est-ce que tu aimes _____ matchs de football américain? Tu préfères _____ football américain, _____ basket ou _____ tennis?

**3.** Est-ce qu'il y a _____ cinémas près de l'université? Est-ce qu'il y a _____ cinéma ici où on passe *(they show)* _____ films étrangers? Est-ce que tu aimes _____ films étrangers? Est-ce que tu préfères _____ films étrangers ou _____ films américains?

**E. Vos cours.** Avec un(e) partenaire, préparez la conversation suivante. Ensuite, changez de rôles.

Ask your partner:

- what he/she is studying this semester
- what his/her course(s) is (are) like
- if he/she likes the university
- what the students and professors are like
- what the campus is like
- what there is on campus and in the neighborhood

## Lecture: *L'accent grave*

Jacques Prévert (1900–1977) was one of the most popular French poets of the twentieth century. The following conversation between a teacher and a student is from the collection of poems, ***Paroles,*** published in 1949. The student's name is Hamlet. What was Shakespeare's Hamlet famous for saying?

### *L'accent grave*

**Le professeur**
**Élève** Hamlet!

**L'élève Hamlet** *(sursautant)*
... **Hein**... **Quoi**... Pardon... **Qu'est-ce qui se passe**... Qu'est-ce qu'il y a... Qu'est-ce que c'est?...

**Le professeur** *(mécontent)*
**Vous ne pouvez pas répondre** "présent" comme **tout le monde?** Pas possible, vous êtes encore dans **les nuages.**

**Élève Hamlet**
Être ou ne pas être dans les nuages!

**Le professeur**
**Suffit. Pas tant de manières.** Et conjuguez-moi le verbe être, comme tout le monde, c'est tout ce que je vous demande.

**Élève Hamlet**
To be...

**Le professeur**
En français, s'il vous plaît, comme tout le monde.

**Élève Hamlet**
Bien, monsieur. *(Il conjugue:)*
Je suis ou je ne suis pas
Tu es ou tu n'es pas
Il est ou il n'est pas
Nous sommes ou nous ne sommes pas...

**Le professeur** *(excessivement mécontent)*
Mais **c'est vous qui n'y êtes pas,** mon pauvre ami!

**Élève Hamlet**
C'est exact, monsieur le professeur,
Je suis "où" je ne suis pas
Et, **dans le fond,** hein, à la réflexion,
Être "où" ne pas être
C'est **peut-être** aussi la question.

---

**un(e) élève** *a student, a pupil*   **sursautant** *looking up startled*   **Hein** *Huh*   **Quoi** *What*
**Qu'est-ce qui se passe?** *What's going on?*   **mécontent(e)** *displeased*   **Vous ne pouvez pas répondre...** *Can't you answer...*
**tout le monde** *everyone*   **les nuages** *the clouds*   **Suffit.** *Enough.*   **Pas tant de manières.** *Don't make such a fuss.*
**c'est vous qui n'y êtes pas** *you're the one that's not with it*   **dans le fond** *really, basically*   **peut-être** *perhaps*

# Compréhension

1. Dans quel cours sont-ils? À votre avis *(In your opinion)*, les élèves sont très jeunes, assez jeunes ou ils ne sont pas jeunes? Pourquoi pensez-vous ça?

2. Qu'est-ce que ça veut dire, **ou?** Et **où?** Qu'est-ce que ça veut dire **être ou ne pas être?** Et **être où ne pas être?**

3. Comment est l'élève Hamlet? Attentif ou inattentif? Conformiste ou rebelle? Bon ou mauvais? Intelligent ou bête? Intellectuel?

4. Comment est le professeur? Patient ou impatient? Intéressant ou ennuyeux? Sympathique ou méchant?

5. Comment est la lecture *(the reading)?* Intéressante ou ennuyeuse? Amusante? Facile ou difficile à comprendre?

# Composition

**A. Organisez-vous.** You will be writing a short description of yourself and your studies. When you write in French, use and combine what you know and avoid translating from English. It is very difficult to translate correctly. First organize your thoughts by completing these sentences in French.

1. Je m'appelle...
2. Je suis de (d')...
3. J'habite...
4. Du point de vue physique, je suis...
5. Du point de vue personnalité, je suis...
6. Je suis étudiant(e) à...
7. Sur le campus, il y a... mais il n'y a pas...
8. Dans le quartier universitaire, il y a... mais il n'y a pas...
9. En général, j'aime / je n'aime pas l'université parce que...
10. J'étudie...
11. J'aime / Je n'aime pas...

> If you have access to SYSTÈME-D software, you will find the following phrases, vocabulary, grammar, and dictionary aids there.
>
> ---
>
> **Phrases:** Introducing; Describing people
> **Vocabulary:** Studies, courses; Personality
> **Grammar:** Definite articles; Indefinite article; Nouns after **c'est, il est;** Comparison with **que**
> **Dictionary:** The verb **être**

**B. Rédaction: autoportrait.** Write a short paragraph introducing yourself. Use the sentences you completed in *A. Organisez-vous* to guide you. Link sentences with words like **et, mais,** or **parce que** to make your paragraph flow better.

> Exemple   **Je m'appelle Daniel Reyna. Je suis de San Antonio mais maintenant j'habite à Austin...**

**C. Présentations.** After you have completed *B. Rédaction: autoportrait,* exchange papers with a classmate. Read each other's composition, then go around the room and introduce your partner to several classmates, telling them a few things that you learned about him or her. You will need to use the following verb forms to describe him or her: **il (elle) s'appelle, il (elle) étudie, il (elle) aime, il (elle) habite.**

**D. Comparaisons.** Now that you know your partner from *C. Présentations* better, work together to prepare at least five sentences comparing yourselves to each other and take turns reading them to the class.

> Exemple   ALEX:   **Monique est plus sportive que moi.**
> MONIQUE:   **Alex est moins dynamique que moi.**

# COMPARAISONS *culturelles*

## Les études

**How** similar (**semblable**) is the French education system to the education system in your area? Read these descriptions of secondary schools and universities in France and compare them to schools in your region, by saying one of the following.

**C'est très semblable ici. / C'est assez semblable ici. / C'est très différent ici.**

1. Students in high school (**le lycée**) already have a "major." They pursue their diploma, **le baccalauréat,** in a chosen field, such as **le bac littéraire, scientifique, économique, technologique,** or **professionnel.**
2. At the end of their secondary studies, French students must pass a series of difficult national exams covering all the material they have studied in order to receive the **baccalauréat (le bac).** The results of the exam are so important that the day of the exam is sometimes referred to as **le Jour J** *(D-Day).* On average, over 600,000 students take the exam each year.
3. The failure rate of the **baccalauréat** in recent years has been a little over 20%. If students do not pass, they cannot go on to the university, unless they repeat the last year at the **lycée** and successfully retest.
4. University students enter directly into field-specific courses (including law and medical school).

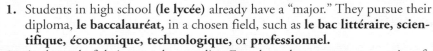

5. In France, most older universities do not have campuses. The **facultés** have buildings in various areas of town where their classes meet. They are often older buildings in the center of town. Some more modern universities, however, do have a campus that is more similar to that found at universities in the United States and Canada.
6. Traditionally, most university classes in France took place in huge lecture halls in a lecture format. Grades were based almost entirely on one or two exams. Recently, there has been a movement toward smaller classes, working in groups, and more frequent assignments.

7. Students generally only pay the equivalent of about $300 per year to attend French universities, because the government pays over $6,000 per student.
8. Most French students live at home with their parents and attend the university in their region.
9. There are few student activities; extracurricular events and sports are not generally a part of the university.
10. If you want to continue your education after receiving the **baccalauréat,** you have a wide range of choices:

**Une université:**

Two-year degrees:
**un DEUG (diplôme d'études universitaires générales);**
**un DEUST (diplôme d'études universitaires scientifiques et techniques)**
Three-year degree: **une licence**
Four-year degree: **une maîtrise**
Seven–eight-year degree: **un doctorat**
Five–eleven-year degrees: **un diplôme de médecine, de chirurgie dentaire ou de pharmacie**

**Un institut universitaire de technologie (IUT):**

Two-year degree: **un DUT (diplôme universitaire de technologie)**

**Un lycée:**

Two-year certificate: **un BTS (brevet de technicien supérieur)**
Two years of preparatory school: **Classes préparatoires aux grandes écoles**

**Une grande école (GE):**

Five–six-year degree: **un diplôme d'ingénieur, de sciences, d'économie, de commerce ou de lettres**

**Une école spécialisée:**

Two–five-year degree: **un diplôme d'art**
Three–five-year degrees: **un diplôme de travail social ou de commerce**
Six-year degree: **un diplôme d'architecte**

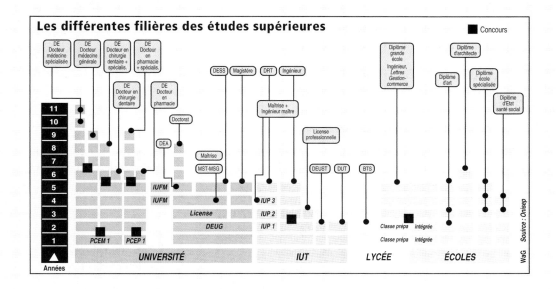

Les différentes filières des études supérieures

## À discuter

1. What would be the advantages and disadvantages of a system in which students must pass a cumulative exam in order to receive a secondary education diploma? Should requirements for graduation from high school be changed here?
2. How do you think students feel about taking the **baccalauréat** exam? What percentage fail the test? Do you think this has a positive or a negative effect on secondary education in France? Why?
3. Should higher education be almost free in the United States as in France? What would be the advantages and disadvantages?

**visit http://horizons.heinle.com**

**Note.** If you are interested in studying in a francophone country, see the **Branchez-vous** section on 220.

# Résumé de grammaire

## Subject pronouns, the verb *être*, and *il y a*

Conjugate verbs by changing their forms to correspond to each of the subject pronouns. Here is the conjugation of **être** *(to be)*.

Je **suis** timide.
Tu **es** étudiant?
Le professeur **est** sympa.
Nous **sommes** d'ici.
Vous **êtes** français?
Ils **sont** en cours.

| ÊTRE (*to be*) | | | | | |
|---|---|---|---|---|---|
| je **suis** | *I am* | | nous **sommes** | *we are* |
| tu **es** | *you are* | | vous **êtes** | *you are* |
| il/elle **est** | *he/she/it is* | | ils/elles **sont** | *they are* |

To negate a verb, place **ne** before it and **pas** after. **Ne** elides to **n'** before vowels or silent **h.**

Je **ne** suis **pas** optimiste.
Tu **n'**es **pas** bête!

Use **il est/elle est** and **ils sont/elles sont** with *adjectives or prepositional phrases* to describe people or things. Use **c'est** and **ce sont** instead of **il est/elle est** and **ils sont/elles sont** to say *he/she/it is* or *they are* when identifying or describing someone *with a noun*.

**Il est** sympathique.
**Ce sont** mes amis.
**C'est un** bon ami.

Use **il est/elle est** and **ils sont/elles sont** without the indefinite article to state professions, nationalities, or religions.

**Ils sont** étudiants.
**Il est** professeur.

Use **il y a** instead of **être** to say *there is, there are, is there* or *are there*. Its negated form is **il n'y a pas.**

—**Il y a** un examen demain?
—Non, **il n'y a pas** d'examen.

## Nouns and articles

Nouns in French are classified by gender as either masculine or feminine. The definite and indefinite articles have different forms, depending on a noun's gender and whether it is singular or plural.

| DEFINITE ARTICLE (*the*) | | |
|---|---|---|
| | *Singular* | *Plural* |
| MASCULINE | **le** cours, **l'**examen | **les** cours, **les** examens |
| FEMININE | **la** classe, **l'**étudiante | **les** classes, **les** étudiantes |

**Le** and **la** elide to **l'** before vowel sounds.

Où sont **les** étudiants?
Ils sont à **la** bibliothèque.
J'étudie **l'**anglais.

Besides translating the word *the*, the definite article is also used where there is no article in English . . .

- to say what you like or prefer
- to make generalized statements

J'aime **la** musique classique.
**Les** concerts de rock sont amusants.

| INDEFINITE ARTICLE (*a, an, some*) | | |
|---|---|---|
| | *Singular* | *Plural* |
| MASCULINE | **un** cours, **un** examen | **des** cours, **des** examens |
| FEMININE | **une** classe, **une** étudiante | **des** classes, **des** étudiantes |

Il y a **des** restaurants près d'ici?
*Chez Pierre* est **un** bon restaurant.
Tu as **une** amie américaine.

The indefinite article changes to **de** (**d'** before vowel sounds) . . .

- after negated verbs (except after **être**)
- after expressions of quantity like **beaucoup** or **assez**
- directly before plural adjectives

Il **n'**y a **pas de** librairie ici.
(Ce **n'est pas une** librairie.)
Il y a **beaucoup de** devoirs et **d'**examens.
Ce sont **de bons** amis.

## Adjectives

Adjectives have masculine and feminine, singular and plural forms, which correspond to the nouns they describe. Add an **e** to the masculine form of most adjectives to form the feminine, unless it already ends in an *unaccented* **e.** Add an **s** to make an adjective plural, unless it already ends in **s** or **x.**

| MASCULINE | | FEMININE | |
|---|---|---|---|
| *Singular* | *Plural* | *Singular* | *Plural* |
| joli | jolis | jolie | jolies |
| divorcé | divorcés | divorcée | divorcées |
| français | français | française | françaises |
| bête | bêtes | bête | bêtes |

Le parc est **joli.** / La maison est **jolie.**
Il est **divorcé.** / Elle est **divorcée.**
Mes amis sont **français.** / Mes amies sont **françaises.**
Il n'est pas **bête.** / Elle n'est pas **bête.**

The following adjective endings have consonant changes before adding the **e** for the feminine form. The adjectives **bon(ne), gros(se),** and **gentil(le)** also double their final consonants.

| | MASCULINE | | FEMININE | |
|---|---|---|---|---|
| | *Singular* | *Plural* | *Singular* | *Plural* |
| -eux / -euse: | ennuyeux | ennuyeux | ennuyeuse | ennuyeuses |
| -en / -enne: | canadien | canadiens | canadienne | canadiennes |
| -if / -ive: | sportif | sportifs | sportive | sportives |
| -el / -elle: | intellectuel | intellectuels | intellectuelle | intellectuelles |
| -er / -ère: | étranger | étrangers | étrangère | étrangères |

Le film est **ennuyeux.** / La fête est **ennuyeuse.**
David est **sportif.** / Yvette est **sportive.**
Ils sont **intellectuels.** / Elles sont **intellectuelles.**

Adjectives generally are placed after nouns they describe.

The following adjectives go before nouns.

| | | | | |
|---|---|---|---|---|
| beau (belle) | jeune | bon (bonne) | grand(e) | autre |
| joli(e) | vieux (vieille) | mauvais(e) | petit(e) | même |
| | nouveau (nouvelle) | gentil(le) | gros(se) | seul(e) |

C'est un **cours intéressant** mais il y a beaucoup d'**examens difficiles.**

Sur le campus il y a beaucoup de **nouveaux bâtiments** et une **grande bibliothèque.**

The adjectives **beau, nouveau,** and **vieux** have irregular forms. The alternate singular forms **bel, nouvel,** and **vieil** are used before masculine singular nouns beginning with a vowel sound.

| MASCULINE | | FEMININE | |
|---|---|---|---|
| *Singular* | *Plural* | *Singular* | *Plural* |
| beau (bel) | beaux | belle | belles |
| nouveau (nouvel) | nouveaux | nouvelle | nouvelles |
| vieux (vieil) | vieux | vieille | vieilles |

un **beau** parc / un **bel** homme / une **belle** femme
un **nouveau** film / un **nouvel** ami / une **nouvelle** amie
un **vieux** bâtiment / un **vieil** homme / une **vieille** femme

## Questions

Questions that are answered with **oui** or **non** have rising intonation. You may just use rising intonation or you may begin the question with **est-ce que,** which elides to **est-ce qu'** before vowel sounds.

Le professeur est bon?
**Est-ce qu'**il est sympa?

If you expect the answer to a question to be **oui,** use **n'est-ce pas?** or **non?** to translate tag questions like *right?, isn't he?, can't you?,* or *won't they?* in English.

Tu étudies le français, **n'est-ce pas?**
Nous sommes dans le même cours, **non?**

# Vocabulaire

## COMPÉTENCE 1

### Identifying people and describing appearance

**NOMS MASCULINS**

| | |
|---|---|
| mes amis | my friends |
| un cours de littérature | a literature class |
| un frère | a brother |
| les gens | people |
| un (jeune) homme | a (young) man |

**NOMS FÉMININS**

| | |
|---|---|
| mes amies | my friends |
| une (jeune) femme | a (young) woman |
| la France | France |
| une semaine | a week |
| une sœur | a sister |
| l'université | the university |

**ADJECTIFS**

| | |
|---|---|
| américain(e) | American |
| beau (belle) | handsome, pretty |
| célibataire | single |
| divorcé(e) | divorced |
| fiancé(e) | engaged |
| français(e) | French |
| grand(e) | tall, big |
| gros(se) | fat |
| jeune | young |
| jumeau (jumelle) | twin |
| laid(e) | ugly |
| marié(e) | married |
| même | same |
| mince | thin |
| petit(e) | short, small |
| premier (première) | first |
| vieux (vieille) | old |

**EXPRESSIONS VERBALES**

| | |
|---|---|
| C'est... | He/She/This/It is . . . |
| Ce sont... | They/These are . . . |
| Ce n'est pas... | He/She/It/This is not . . . |
| Ce ne sont pas... | They/These are not . . . |
| Comment est... ? | What is . . . like? |
| Il/Elle est... | He/She/It is . . . |
| Ils/Elles sont... | They are . . . |
| Il/Elle n'est pas... | He/She/It is not . . . |
| Ils/Elles ne sont pas... | They are not . . . |
| faire connaissance | to meet |
| Nous sommes... | We are . . . |
| (pour) étudier | (in order) to study |
| (pour) visiter | (in order) to visit |
| (pour) voir | (in order) to see |
| Tu es... | You are . . . |

**DIVERS**

| | |
|---|---|
| à | to, at, in |
| alors | so, then, thus |
| comme | like, as, for |
| dans | in |
| de | of, from, about |
| d'où | from where |
| non? | right? |
| sa | his, her, its |

## COMPÉTENCE 2

### Describing personality

**NOMS MASCULINS**

| | |
|---|---|
| tes amis | your friends |
| le football | soccer |
| mon meilleur ami | my best friend |
| le sport | sports |
| le tennis | tennis |

**NOMS FÉMININS**

| | |
|---|---|
| tes amies | your friends |
| les études | studies, going to school |
| ma meilleure amie | my best friend |
| la personnalité | personality |

**ADJECTIFS**

| | |
|---|---|
| agréable | pleasant |
| amusant(e) | fun, amusing |
| bête | stupid, dumb |
| désagréable | unpleasant |
| dynamique | active |
| ennuyeux (ennuyeuse) | boring |
| extraverti(e) | extroverted, outgoing |
| gentil (gentille) | nice |
| idéaliste | idealistic |
| intellectuel(le) | intellectual |
| intelligent(e) | intelligent |
| intéressant(e) | interesting |
| méchant(e) | mean |
| nouveau (nouvelle) | new |
| optimiste | optimistic |
| paresseux (paresseuse) | lazy |
| pessimiste | pessimistic |
| réaliste | realistic |
| sportif (sportive) | athletic |
| sympathique (sympa) | nice |
| timide | timid, shy |

**EXPRESSIONS VERBALES**

| | |
|---|---|
| être | to be |
| je suis... | I am . . . |
| tu es... | you are . . . |
| il est... | he/it is . . . |
| elle est... | she/it is . . . |
| nous sommes... | we are . . . |
| vous êtes... | you are . . . |
| ils/elles sont... | they are . . . |
| j'aime / je n'aime pas | I like / I don't like |
| tu aimes | you like |

**DIVERS**

| | |
|---|---|
| assez | rather |
| aussi... que | as . . . as |
| Ce n'est pas mon truc. | That's not my thing. |
| Est-ce que... | (particle used in questions) |
| moins... que | less . . . than |
| ne... pas | not |
| ne... pas du tout | not at all |
| n'est-ce pas? | right? |
| plus... que | more . . . than |
| plutôt | rather |
| un peu | a little |

## Describing the university area

**NOMS MASCULINS**

| | |
|---|---|
| un amphithéâtre | a lecture hall |
| un arbre | a tree |
| un bâtiment | a building |
| un bureau | an office |
| un café | a café |
| un campus | a campus |
| un cinéma | a movie theater |
| un club de gym | a gym, a fitness club |
| un concert (de jazz, de rock, de musique populaire, de musique classique) | a (jazz, rock, pop music, classical music) concert |
| un fast-food | a fast-food restaurant |
| un film | a movie, a film |
| un match de football américain | a football game |
| un parc | a park |
| un parking | a parking lot |
| un quartier (universitaire) | a (university) neighborhood |
| un restaurant | a restaurant |
| un stade | a stadium |
| un théâtre | a theater (for live performances) |

**NOMS FÉMININS**

| | |
|---|---|
| une bibliothèque | a library |
| une boîte de nuit | a nightclub |
| une classe | a class |
| une librairie | a bookstore |
| une maison | a house |
| une résidence | a dormitory |
| une salle de classe | a classroom |

**ADJECTIFS**

| | |
|---|---|
| autre | other |
| bon(ne) | good |
| catholique | catholic |
| étranger (étrangère) | foreign |
| joli(e) | pretty |
| mauvais(e) | bad |
| moderne | modern |
| populaire | popular |
| seul(e) | only |
| universitaire | university |

**EXPRESSIONS VERBALES**

| | |
|---|---|
| Comment est… ? | What is . . . like? |
| Comment sont… ? | What are . . . like? |
| Il y a… | There is, There are . . . |
| Il n'y a pas (de)… | There isn't, There aren't . . . |
| Où est… ? | Where is . . . ? |
| Qu'est-ce qu'il y a… ? | What is there . . . ? |

**DIVERS**

| | |
|---|---|
| assez (de) | enough (of) |
| beaucoup (de) | a lot (of) |
| dans | in |
| des | some |
| près de | near |
| sur | on |
| ton | your |
| un(e) | a, an |

## Talking about your studies

**NOMS MASCULINS**

| | |
|---|---|
| l'allemand | German |
| l'anglais | English |
| le basket | basketball |
| les beaux-arts | the fine arts |
| un cours de commerce | a business course |
| un cours technique | a technical course |
| les devoirs | homework |
| l'espagnol | Spanish |
| un examen | an exam |
| le français | French |
| un laboratoire de langues / d'informatique | a language / computer lab |
| le marketing | marketing |
| le théâtre | theater, drama |

**NOMS FÉMININS**

| | |
|---|---|
| la biologie | biology |
| une boum | a party |
| la chimie | chemistry |
| la comptabilité | accounting |
| une fête | a party |
| l'histoire | history |
| l'informatique | computer science |
| une langue | a language |
| la littérature classique | classical literature |
| les mathématiques (les maths) | mathematics (math) |
| la musique | music |
| la philosophie | philosophy |
| la physique | physics |
| la psychologie | psychology |
| les sciences (humaines) | the (social) sciences |
| les sciences politiques | political science, government |

**EXPRESSIONS VERBALES**

| | |
|---|---|
| Est-ce que vous aimez… ? | Do you like . . . ? |
| J'aime beaucoup / assez… | I like a lot / somewhat . . . |
| Je n'aime pas (du tout)… | I don't like (at all) . . . |
| Je préfère… | I prefer . . . |
| Qu'est-ce que vous étudiez/tu étudies? | What are you studying?, What do you study? |
| J'étudie… | I study . . . |
| Je n'étudie pas… | I don't study . . . |

**DIVERS**

| | |
|---|---|
| leur(s) | their |

## Nature morte aux grenades
**HENRI MATISSE**
**(1869–1954)**

1947
Nice, Musée Matisse
Giraudon/Art Resource, New York
© 1998 Succession H. Matisse/Artists Rights Society
(ARS), New York

Nice was the subject of many of Matisse's paintings. He painted indoor scenes as well as outdoor scenes of the city he loved. This still life focuses on the contrast between the brilliant Mediterranean light and the shadowed interior of a room.

## Santon
**NICE, FRANCE**

**PHOTOGRAPH: BERYL GOLDBERG, 1993**

**Santon** means *little saint*. **Santons** are placed in Christmas manger scenes in the Provence region.

## Sur la Côte d'Azur

**NICE**
**NOMBRE D'HABITANTS:** 329 800 (avec ses agglomérations *[metropolitan region]:* 949 200) (les Niçois)
**DÉPARTEMENT:** Alpes-Maritimes
**RÉGION:** Provence-Alpes-Côte d'Azur
**INDUSTRIES PRINCIPALES:** tourisme, agriculture [fruits, primeurs *(produce)*, fleurs *(flowers)*, riz *(rice)*, vin *(wine)*]
**PLATS RÉGIONAUX:** bouillabaisse, salade niçoise

# Après les cours

**COMPÉTENCE**

Video activities are on pages 212–215.

Imaginez que vous êtes un(e) touriste à Nice et faites une liste de ces activités dans l'ordre de vos préférences.

Faire une promenade le long de la mer sur la Promenade des Anglais.

Voir la mer Méditerranée et la Baie des Anges.

Visiter le quartier médiéval du Vieux Nice.

Visiter les ruines romaines à Nice-Cimiez.

Voir les peintures d'Henri Matisse au musée Matisse.

Aller au Carnaval de Nice.

Aller dans les boutiques, les restaurants et les cafés de la rue Masséna.

# Saying what you like to do

> **Note**
*culturelle*

Le passe-temps le plus populaire en France, c'est regarder la télé. En moyenne *(average)*, les Français regardent la télé deux heures et demie par jour. Quels sont les passe-temps les plus populaires dans votre région?

**NOTES DE VOCABULAIRE**

1. To say what you *like*, use **j'aime.** To say what you *would like*, or *want*, use **je voudrais.**
2. There are many ways to say *an e-mail:* **un mail, un e-mail, un email, un mel, un mèl, un mél, un courriel, un courrier électronique.**

## Les passe-temps

— Qu'est-ce que vous aimez **faire** après les cours?
— J'aime...          — Je n'aime pas...          — Je préfère...

— Qu'est-ce que **vous voudriez** faire aujourd'hui après les cours?
— **Je voudrais...**

### SORTIR AVEC DES AMIS

**aller** au cinéma
(aller) voir un film

aller au café
(aller) **prendre un verre**

aller en boîte
(aller) danser

dîner au restaurant

faire du sport
jouer au tennis / au basket /
au football / au volley

faire du jogging

### RESTER À LA MAISON

écouter la radio / de la
musique / la chaîne hi-fi

regarder la télé(vision) /
une vidéo / un DVD
jouer à des jeux vidéo *(m)*

**bricoler**

dormir

lire

travailler sur l'ordinateur
surfer le Net
écrire **des mails** *(m)*

---

**faire** *to do*   **vous voudriez** *you would like*   **Je voudrais** *I would like*   **sortir** *to go out*   **aller** *to go*
**prendre un verre** *to have a drink*   **rester** *to stay, to remain*   **bricoler** *to do handiwork*   **un mail** *an e-mail*

jouer de la guitare / **de la batterie** / du piano

parler au téléphone

inviter des amis à la maison

CD 1-21

David invite Annette à sortir.

DAVID: Tu es **libre ce soir?** Tu voudrais faire **quelque chose?**
ANNETTE: Je voudrais bien. Où est-ce que tu voudrais aller?
DAVID: Je ne sais pas. Tu voudrais aller en boîte?
ANNETTE: Non, **pas vraiment.** Je préfère aller au cinéma.
DAVID: Bon, **d'accord! On va** prendre un verre avant?
ANNETTE: **Pourquoi pas? Vers** quelle heure?
DAVID: Vers sept heures, sept heures et demie... au café La Martinique?
ANNETTE: D'accord. Alors, **à plus tard.**
DAVID: Au revoir, Annette. À ce soir!

## A. Qu'est-ce que vous aimez faire? Complétez les phrases.

1. Après les cours, j'aime... mais je n'aime pas...
2. Aujourd'hui après les cours, je voudrais...
3. Le samedi matin, j'aime...
4. Le samedi soir, j'aime...
5. Le dimanche, je préfère...
6. Ce week-end, je voudrais...
7. À la maison, j'aime...
8. Je n'aime pas du tout...

## B. Invitations. Invitez votre partenaire à faire les choses suivantes.

**Exemple**  (demain) jouer au tennis
—Tu es libre demain? Tu voudrais jouer au tennis avec moi?
—Oui, je voudrais bien. / Pas vraiment. Je préfère aller au cinéma.
—Vers quelle heure?
—Vers deux heures.
—Bon, d'accord. Alors, à demain.
—À demain. Au revoir!

1. (ce soir) dîner au restaurant
2. (vendredi soir) aller voir un film
3. (aujourd'hui après les cours) faire les devoirs
4. (demain après-midi) aller prendre un verre

**VOCABULAIRE SUPPLÉMENTAIRE**

**aller à l'église / au temple / à la mosquée / à la synagogue** *to go to church (Catholic) / to temple or church (Protestant) / to mosque / to synagogue*
**aller au lac / à la montagne / au parc / à la plage** *to go to the lake / to the mountains / to the park / to the beach*
**courir** *to run*
**dessiner** *to draw*
**faire de la muscu** *to do bodybuilding*
**faire de l'exercice / de l'aérobic / de la gymnastique**
**faire du shopping** *to go shopping*
**faire la cuisine** *to cook*
**jardiner** *to garden*
**jouer à des jeux d'ordinateur** *to play computer games*
**jouer au billard / aux cartes / au disc-golf / au frisbee** *to play pool / cards / disc golf / frisbee*
**marcher** *to walk*
**nager** *to swim*
**peindre** *to paint*
**promener le chien** *to walk the dog*
**voyager** *to travel*
*For additional pastimes, see* **Chapitre 5.**

---

**de la batterie** *drums*    **libre** *free*    **ce soir** *this evening*    **quelque chose** *something*    **pas vraiment** *not really*    **d'accord** *okay*
**On va... ?** *Shall we go . . . ?*    **Pourquoi pas?** *Why not?*    **Vers** *About, Around, Toward*    **à plus tard** *see you later*

**1.** What do you call the basic form of the verb that you find listed in the dictionary?

**2.** What are the four possible endings for infinitives in French?

**3.** When you have a sequence of more than one verb, which one is conjugated? Which ones are in the infinitive?

**VOCABULAIRE SUPPLÉMENTAIRE**

jouer...

    **de la clarinette**

    **du clavier** *keyboard*

    **du cor d'harmonie** *French horn*

    **de la flûte**

    **de la guitare électrique**

    **du hautbois** *oboe*

    **des orgues** *organ*

    **du piccolo**

    **de la trompette**

    **du tuba**

    **du violon**

    **du violoncelle** *cello*

# Saying what you like to do

## *L'infinitif*

To name an activity in French, use the verb in the infinitive. The infinitive is the basic form of the verb that you find listed in the dictionary. French infinitives are single words ending in **-er, -ir, -oir,** or **-re,** like **jouer** *(to play),* **dormir** *(to sleep),* **voir** *(to see),* or **être** *(to be).* In French, whenever there are two or more verbs together in a clause, the first verb is conjugated, but verbs that immediately follow are in the infinitive.

— Qu'est-ce que tu **aimes faire?**

— J'**aime jouer** au football américain.

— Est-ce que tu **voudrais sortir?**

— Je **préfère rester** à la maison.

Use **jouer** *au* to talk about playing most sports using balls or pucks. Many other sports use **faire** *du / de la / de l'.*

jouer **au** base-ball    jouer **au** golf    faire **du** jogging

Use **jouer** *du / de la / des* to talk about playing most musical instruments.

jouer **du** piano    jouer **de la** guitare

As with **un, une,** and **des; du, de la,** and **de l'** change to **de (d')** after a negative expression.

— Tu joues **de la** guitare?

— Non, je ne joue pas **de** guitare.

— Tu fais **du** jogging le week-end?

— Non, je ne fais pas **de** jogging.

# Prononciation

CD 1-22

## *La consonne **r** et l'infinitif*

The consonant **r** is one of the few (CaReFuL) consonants that are often pronounced at the end of words. The final **r** of infinitives ending in **-er,** however, is not pronounced. The **-er** ending is pronounced [e], like the **é** in **café.**

parler    inviter    danser    aller

regarder    jouer    écouter    dîner

The **r** in infinitives ending in **-ir, -oir,** or **-re** is pronounced. To pronounce a French **r,** hold the back of your tongue firmly arched upward in the back of your mouth and pronounce a vocalized English *h* sound in your throat.

Pronounce the **-ir** verb ending as [iʀ], unless the verb ends in **-oir** [waʀ].

sortir    dormir    voir

The infinitive ending of **-re** verbs is pronounced [ʀ] when preceded by a vowel and [ʀə] when preceded by a consonant.

faire    lire    être    prendre

**A. Préférences.** Demandez à votre partenaire quelle activité il/elle préfère.

> **Exemple**    lire / faire les devoirs
> — **Tu préfères lire ou faire les devoirs?**
> — **Je préfère lire.**

1. faire du jogging / dormir
2. sortir avec des amis / inviter des amis à la maison
3. prendre un verre au café / dîner au restaurant
4. jouer au tennis / regarder un match de tennis à la télé
5. regarder la télé / aller au cinéma
6. être à la maison / être en cours
7. parler à un ami au téléphone / inviter un ami à la maison
8. surfer le Net / écrire des mails

**NOTE DE VOCABULAIRE**

To say you don't like either activity, use **ne... ni... ni...** (*neither . . . nor . . .* ): **Je *n'*aime *ni* lire *ni* faire les devoirs.** To say that you like *both* activities, use **J'aime *les deux*.**

**B. Chacun ses goûts.** Est-ce que vous aimez ces activités?

**J'aime beaucoup...**     **J'aime assez...**     **Je n'aime pas beaucoup...**
**Je n'aime pas du tout...**

> **Exemple**    **J'aime assez bricoler.**

2.      3.      4.

5.      6.      7.

**C. Entretien.** Interviewez votre partenaire.

1. Qu'est-ce que tu aimes faire après les cours? Qu'est-ce que tu voudrais faire aujourd'hui après les cours?
2. Est-ce que tu aimes rester à la maison le week-end? Qu'est-ce que tu aimes faire le week-end? Qu'est-ce que tu voudrais faire ce week-end?
3. Est-ce que tu aimes travailler sur l'ordinateur? Tu aimes surfer le Net?
4. Est-ce que tu voudrais aller au cinéma ce week-end? Quel film est-ce que tu voudrais voir? Tu préfères aller voir un film au cinéma ou regarder une vidéo à la maison?
5. Quel sport est-ce que tu préfères, le tennis, le golf ou le basket? Est-ce que tu préfères faire du sport ou regarder des matchs à la télévision?

## Stratégies et Compréhension auditive

*Listening for specific information*

It takes time and practice to understand a foreign language when you hear it. However, using listening strategies can help you learn to understand spoken French more quickly.

Often, you do not need to comprehend everything you hear. Practice listening for specific details, such as times, places, or prices. Do not worry about understanding every word.

CD 1-23

**A. Quand?** Écoutez ces trois scènes. Indiquez le jour et l'heure choisis *(chosen)*.

SCÈNE A: LE JOUR _____
L'HEURE _____

SCÈNE B: LE JOUR _____
L'HEURE _____

SCÈNE C: LE JOUR _____
L'HEURE _____

CD 1-24

**B. Qu'est-ce qu'elles font?** Annette invite Yvette à sortir. Pour les trois scènes, indiquez ce qu'Yvette préfère faire.

SCÈNE A: _____

SCÈNE B: _____

SCÈNE C: _____

## On sort ensemble?

CD 1-25

David, Yvette, and Annette run into two of David's friends. Listen to their conversation. Do not try to understand every word. The first time, listen only for the leisure activities they mention. Each time you hear one mentioned, write it down.

**A. Vous comprenez?** Écoutez une seconde fois *(time)* la conversation entre David et ses amis et répondez à ces questions.

1. Est-ce que Thomas et Gisèle sont des amis d'Annette?
2. Faites une liste de trois choses que Thomas et Gisèle découvrent *(discover)* au sujet d'Annette et d'Yvette *(about Annette and Yvette)*.

**B. Tu voudrais sortir?** Invitez votre partenaire à faire les choses suivantes.
Utilisez *B. Invitations* à la page 69 comme modèle.

voir un film

jouer au foot

faire du vélo

faire du jogging

# Saying how you spend your free time

**>Note**
*culturelle*

La majorité des Français se livrent à *(participate in)* une activité sportive régulière. Le sport le plus populaire, c'est le football. Quels sont les sports les plus populaires dans votre région?

## Le week-end

Comment est-ce que vous aimez **passer le temps?** Qu'est-ce que **vous faites d'habitude** le samedi?

| **toujours** | **souvent** | **quelquefois** | **rarement** | **ne... jamais** |
|---|---|---|---|---|
| *always* | *often* | *sometimes* | *rarely* | *never* |

Le samedi, je passe **presque** toujours **la matinée** à la maison.

Je reste au lit **jusqu'à** 10 heures.

Je mange quelque chose.

Je prépare les cours. (J'étudie.)

Le soir, je ne reste jamais à la maison.

L'après-midi, j'aime faire du sport.

Je nage souvent.

Quelquefois je joue au foot(ball).

**Je vais** presque toujours au cinéma.

Est-ce que vous aimez faire du sport? de la musique? Est-ce que vous jouez... ?

| **très bien** | **assez bien** | **comme ci comme ça** *so-so* | **assez mal** | **très mal** |
|---|---|---|---|---|
| *very well* | *fairly well* | | *fairly badly* | *very badly* |

Je joue très bien au hockey.

Je joue du piano comme ci comme ça.

Je chante assez mal.

Je joue **mieux** au basket **qu'**au hockey. **Quand** je joue au basket, **je gagne** presque toujours!

---

**passer le temps** *to spend time*   **vous faites** (**faire** *to do, to make*)   **d'habitude** *usually, generally*   **presque** *almost*
**la matinée** *the morning*   **jusqu'à** *until*   **Je vais** (**aller** *to go*)   **mieux** (**que**) *better (than)*   **Quand** *When*
**je gagne** (**gagner** *to win*)

CD 1-26

Annette et David parlent de leurs activités *(f)* du week-end.

ANNETTE: Qu'est-ce que **tu fais** d'habitude le week-end?
DAVID: Le samedi matin je reste au lit, le samedi après-midi je joue au tennis et le soir j'aime sortir. Et toi?
ANNETTE: Le matin je prépare mes cours, l'après-midi j'aime **faire du shopping** et le soir, moi aussi, **je sors.**
DAVID: Alors, tu es libre samedi soir? Tu voudrais sortir? Il y a un bon film au cinéclub **à la fac.** C'est un vieux classique de Truffaut.
ANNETTE: Oui, oui, je voudrais bien.
DAVID: Le film commence à huit heures. Je **passe chez toi** vers sept heures?
ANNETTE: D'accord! À samedi, alors.

**A. Passe-temps.** Complétez ces phrases pour parler de vous.

1. Le samedi matin, je passe *presque toujours / souvent / rarement* la matinée à la maison. *(Je ne passe jamais la matinée à la maison.)*

2. Le samedi matin, je reste au lit jusqu'à *sept heures / dix heures / ???.*

3. D'habitude, le samedi matin, je mange quelque chose *à la maison / dans un fast-food / au café / ???. (Je ne mange pas le samedi matin.)*

4. D'habitude je prépare les cours *à la maison / à la bibliothèque / chez un(e) ami(e) / au café / ???.*

5. Comme *(For)* exercice, je préfère *faire du sport / faire du jogging / nager / ???. (Je n'aime pas faire de l'exercice.)*

6. Quand je joue *au tennis / au hockey / ???,* je gagne *toujours / souvent / rarement. (Je n'aime pas faire du sport.)*

7. Le samedi soir, le plus souvent *je reste à la maison / je travaille / j'invite des amis à la maison / je préfère sortir.*

8. Je vais plus souvent au cinéma *seul(e) / avec des amis / avec mon meilleur ami / avec ma meilleure amie / avec ma famille / ???.*

9. Je chante *très bien / assez bien / comme ci comme ça / ???.*

10. Je danse *très bien / assez bien / comme ci comme ça / ???.*

11. Je chante *mieux / aussi bien / moins bien* que je danse.

12. Je *joue du piano / de la guitare / de la batterie / ???. (Je ne joue pas d'un instrument de musique.)*

**B. Conversation.** Avec un(e) partenaire, relisez à haute voix la conversation entre Annette et David en haut de la page *(at the top of the page).* Ensuite, changez la conversation pour décrire vos activités du week-end et pour inviter votre partenaire à faire quelque chose que vous voudriez faire.

---

**tu fais (faire** *to do, to make)* **faire du shopping** *to go shopping* **je sors (sortir** *to go out)* **à la fac** *at the university*
**passer** *to pass (by)* **chez toi** *your house* **(chez...** = *to / at / in / by the house of . . . )*

**1.** How do you determine the stem of an **-er** verb? What endings do you add to it?

**2.** When do you drop the final **e** of words like **je, ne,** and **le?**

**3.** Where do you generally place adverbs such as **bien?** Which three of the adverbs given are exceptions?

**4.** Which **-er** verb endings are silent? Which ones are pronounced?

## Telling what you do, how often, and how well

*Les verbes en **-er** et les adverbes*

Regular verbs are groups of verbs that follow a predictable pattern of conjugation. The largest group of regular verbs have infinitives ending in **-er.** Most verbs ending in **-er** that you have learned, *except* **aller,** are conjugated in the present tense by dropping the **-er** and adding the following endings.

| PARLER *(to speak, to talk)* | |
|---|---|
| je parl**e** | nous parl**ons** |
| tu parl**es** | vous parl**ez** |
| il/elle parl**e** | ils/elles parl**ent** |

The present tense can be expressed in three ways in English. Express all three of the following English structures by a single verb in French.

*I work.*
*I am working.* } Je travaille.
*I do work.*

*He studies.*
*He is studying.* } Il étudie.
*He does study.*

Here are the regular **-er** verbs that you have seen so far.

| | | | |
|---|---|---|---|
| aimer | *to like, to love* | jouer | *to play* |
| bricoler | *to do handiwork* | manger | *to eat* |
| chanter | *to sing* | nager | *to swim* |
| commencer | *to begin, to start* | parler | *to speak, to talk* |
| compter | *to count* | passer | *to pass (by), to spend (time)* |
| danser | *to dance* | penser | *to think* |
| dîner | *to have dinner* | préférer | *to prefer* |
| donner | *to give* | préparer | *to prepare* |
| écouter | *to listen (to)* | regarder | *to look (at), to watch* |
| étudier | *to study* | répéter | *to repeat* |
| fermer | *to close* | rester | *to stay, to remain* |
| habiter | *to live* | surfer | *to surf* |
| inviter | *to invite* | travailler | *to work, to study* |

Remember that words such as **je, le, que,** and **ne** make elision before a vowel sound.

**j'**aime / je **n'**aime pas          **j'**habite / je **n'**habite pas

Adverbs such as **bien, souvent, rarement,** and **beaucoup** tell how well, how often, or how much you do something. In French, these adverbs generally follow directly after the conjugated verb. However, **quelquefois** and **d'habitude** are often placed at the beginning or end of the clause and **comme ci comme ça** is placed at the end.

Thomas regarde **souvent** la télé.          *Thomas **often** watches T.V.*
**Quelquefois,** je joue **bien** du piano.          ***Sometimes,** I play the piano **well.***
**D'habitude,** je travaille le week-end.          ***Usually,** I work weekends.*
Je joue au tennis **comme ci comme ça.**          *I play tennis **so-so.***

**Ne... jamais** *(never)* follows the same placement rule as **ne... pas.**

Je **ne** joue **jamais** au golf.          *I **never** play golf.*

# Prononciation

**CD 1-27**

*Les verbes en -er*

All the present tense endings of **-er** verbs, except for the **nous (-ons)** and **vous (-ez)** forms, are silent.

je rest~~e~~    tu rest~~es~~    il rest~~e~~    elle rest~~e~~    ils rest~~ent~~    elles rest~~ent~~

Rely on context to distinguish between **il** and **ils,** or **elle** and **elles.** You will hear a difference only with verbs beginning with a vowel sound.

il travaill~~e~~ — il~~s~~ travaill~~ent~~    il aim~~e~~ — ils <sup>z</sup> aim~~ent~~

The **-ons** ending of the **nous** form rhymes with the **bon** of **bonjour,** and the **-ez** of the **vous** form rhymes with **les** and sounds like the **-er** ending of the infinitive. There is liaison between the **s** of **nous** and **vous** and verbs beginning with vowel sounds.

nou~~s~~ parlons    vou~~s~~ parlez    nous <sup>z</sup> étudions    vous <sup>z</sup> étudiez

---

**A. Activités.** Complétez les phrases de la première colonne avec un choix logique de la deuxième colonne.

1. Le samedi soir, j'...
2. Et toi, qu'est-ce que tu...
3. Tes amis et toi, est-ce que vous...
4. Mes amis et moi, nous...
5. Les étudiants...
6. Mais mon meilleur ami...

   a. invitez souvent des amis à la maison?
   b. aimes faire?
   c. aime sortir avec des amis.
   d. préférons aller danser.
   e. aiment mieux sortir que travailler.
   f. préfère rester à la maison.

**B. Opinions.** Comment est le/la colocataire idéal(e)?

> **Exemple**    travailler beaucoup
> **Il/Elle travaille beaucoup.**
> **Il/Elle ne travaille pas beaucoup.**

1. aimer beaucoup aller en boîte
2. parler souvent au téléphone
3. bricoler bien
4. passer beaucoup de temps à la maison
5. inviter souvent des amis à la maison
6. regarder toujours la télé le week-end
7. chanter beaucoup et mal
8. écouter toujours de la musique rap

**C. Et toi?** Interviewez un(e) partenaire avec les verbes de l'exercice précédent.

> **Exemple**    — **Est-ce que tu travailles beaucoup?**
> — **Oui, je travaille beaucoup. / Non, je ne travaille pas beaucoup.**

Après, parlez de votre partenaire à la classe.

> **Exemple**    **Il/Elle travaille beaucoup et...**

**D. Le samedi.** Est-ce que vous faites toujours, souvent... ces choses le samedi?

| | | |
|---|---|---|
| **(presque) toujours** | **quelquefois** | **ne... jamais** |
| **souvent** | **rarement** | |

**Exemple**   le samedi matin: passer la matinée à la maison
**Le samedi matin, je passe toujours (souvent... ) la matinée à la maison. / Je ne passe jamais la matinée à la maison.**

1. le samedi matin:
    rester à la maison
    manger à la maison
    travailler
    étudier

2. le samedi après-midi:
    nager
    jouer au foot
    regarder la télé
    surfer le Net

3. le samedi soir:
    dîner au restaurant
    manger dans un fast-food
    inviter des amis à la maison
    danser en boîte

Maintenant, demandez à votre professeur s'il/si elle fait souvent les choses indiquées.

**Exemple**   le samedi matin: passer la matinée à la maison
**Le samedi matin, est-ce que vous passez souvent la matinée à la maison?**

**E. C'est vrai?** Formez des phrases pour décrire *(to describe)* votre classe.

**Exemple**   je / parler beaucoup en cours
**Je parle beaucoup en cours.**
**Je ne parle pas beaucoup en cours.**

1. le professeur / parler quelquefois anglais en cours
2. les étudiants / commencer à parler très bien français
3. nous / travailler beaucoup en cours
4. je / aimer dormir en cours
5. les étudiants / travailler quelquefois ensemble *(together)*
6. nous / aimer travailler ensemble
7. je / écouter toujours les CD
8. les étudiants / manger quelquefois en cours

**F. Talents.** Dites si ces personnes font ces choses bien ou mal.

> **Exemple** **Ma sœur joue très bien (assez mal) de la guitare.**
> **Ma sœur ne joue pas de guitare.**
> **Je n'ai pas de sœur.** *(I don't have a sister.)*

**très bien**         **comme ci comme ça**         **très mal**

  **assez bien**                                **assez mal**

**Exemple**  Ma sœur...
  Moi, je...

**1.** Mon meilleur ami (Ma meilleure amie)...
  Mon frère...

**2.** Mes parents...
  Moi, je...

**3.** Moi, je...
  Mon ami _____
  *(name a friend)*...

**4.** Mes ami(e)s _____
  et _____ *(name two friends)*...
  Mes amis et moi, nous...

**G. Entretien.** Interviewez votre partenaire.

1. Tu es musicien(ne)? Est-ce que tu danses bien ou mal? Est-ce que tu chantes bien? Tu préfères écouter la radio ou regarder la télé? Est-ce que tu regardes la télé quand tu manges? Tu écoutes de la musique quand tu étudies?
2. Est-ce que tu es sportif (sportive)? Est-ce que tu aimes le sport? Quel sport est-ce que tu préfères, le football américain, le basket, le golf ou le base-ball? Est-ce que tu joues au tennis? au golf? au volley? (Est-ce que tu gagnes souvent?)
3. Est-ce que tu restes souvent à la maison le week-end? Est-ce que tu bricoles quelquefois le week-end? Est-ce que tu prépares les cours à la maison? Est-ce que tu préfères bricoler ou préparer les cours?

**H. Qu'est-ce qui se passe?**
Décrivez la scène chez la famille Li
ce week-end. Dites au moins cinq choses.

Étienne   Monsieur Li   Madame Li

Audrey   Louise   Dominique   Georges   Antoine et le chien

**Pour vérifier**

**1.** In verbs like **préférer,** which forms have a spelling change in the stem in the present tense? What is the change? Which forms have stems like the infinitive?

**2.** What is special about the **nous** form of a verb with an infinitive ending in **-ger?** in **-cer?**

## Telling what you do

*Quelques verbes à changements orthographiques*

A few **-er** verbs have spelling changes in their stems in the present tense.

- When the next-to-last syllable of an infinitive has an **e** or **é,** this letter often changes to **è** in all forms except **nous** and **vous.** The stem for the **nous** and **vous** forms is like the infinitive.

| PRÉFÉRER *(to prefer)* | | RÉPÉTER *(to repeat)* | |
|---|---|---|---|
| je préf**è**re | nous préférons | je rép**è**te | nous répétons |
| tu préf**è**res | vous préférez | tu rép**è**tes | vous répétez |
| il/elle préf**è**re | ils/elles préf**è**rent | il/elle rép**è**te | ils/elles rép**è**tent |

- Verbs ending in **-cer** and **-ger** also have spelling changes. With verbs ending in **-ger,** like **manger, nager,** and **voyager** *(to travel),* you must insert an **e** before the **-ons** ending in the **nous** form. With verbs ending in **-cer,** like **commencer,** the **c** changes to a **ç** before the **-ons** ending in the **nous** form.

| VOYAGER *(to travel)* | | COMMENCER *(to start, to begin)* | |
|---|---|---|---|
| je voyage | nous voyag**e**ons | je commence | nous commen**ç**ons |
| tu voyages | vous voyagez | tu commences | vous commencez |
| il/elle voyage | ils/elles voyagent | il/elle commence | ils/elles commencent |

CD 1-28

## Prononciation

*Les verbes à changements orthographiques*

Spelling changes occur in verbs to reflect pronunciation. The letter **é** (**e accent aigu**) sounds like the vowel of **les.**

— Vous préférez passer la matinée à la maison?
— Non, nous préférons passer la matinée au café.

The letter **è** (**e accent grave**) often occurs in the final syllable of words ending in a silent **e** (**Michèle**) and sounds similar to the *e* in the English word *let.*

Je préfère aller à la bibliothèque avec Michèle.

In French, **c** and **g** are pronounced soft (the **c** like an **s** and the **g** like a French **j**) before an **e, i,** or **y.** They are pronounced hard (the **c** like a **k** and the **g** similar to the *g* in the English word *go*) before an **a, o, u,** or a consonant.

Soft **g:** Georges, Gérard, Gilbert      Hard **g:** Gabrielle, Hugo, Guillaume
Soft **c:** Cécile, Maurice      Hard **c:** Catherine, Colette

The letter **ç** is used to indicate that a **c** is soft before **a, o,** or **u.** In verb endings, use **ç** to keep **c** soft before **o,** and introduce an **e** to keep **g** soft before **o.**

commen**ç**ons     **ç**a va     fran**ç**ais     mang**e**ons     voy**age**ons     nag**e**ons

**A. Qui est-ce?** Complétez les noms de ces gens célèbres. Prononcez leurs noms. Qui sont-ils?

1. Gabrielle
2. Guillaume
3. Hubert
4. George
5. Charles
6. Guy

a. de Gaulle
b. de Maupassant
c. Sand
d. de Givenchy
e. Roy
f. le Conquérant

**B. Ça s'écrit comment?** Dans les mots suivants, la lettre **c** est prononcée [s]. Lesquels de ces mots requièrent *(require)* une cédille?

1. mena**c**e / mena**c**ant
2. fa**c**ade / fa**c**ile
3. Ni**c**e / ni**c**ois
4. fa**c**e / fa**c**on

5. Fran**c**e / fran**c**ais
6. proven**c**al / Proven**c**e
7. pronun**c**iation / pronon**c**ons
8. **c**ela / **c**a

**C. Préférences.** Complétez ces questions avec le verbe indiqué et interviewez votre partenaire.

1. Avec qui *(With whom)* est-ce que tu _____ (préférer) sortir?
2. Quel jour est-ce qu'il/elle _____ (préférer) sortir?
3. Vous _____ (manger) souvent ensemble *(together)*?
4. Est-ce que vous _____ (préférer) dîner ensemble à la maison ou au restaurant?
5. En général, est-ce que les étudiants _____ (préférer) dîner au restaurant ou étudier à la bibliothèque?
6. Tu _____ (aimer) le sport? Tu _____ (nager) bien?
7. Ton meilleur ami et toi, vous _____ (nager) souvent ensemble?
8. Ta famille et toi, vous _____ (voyager) souvent ensemble?

**D. Et vous?** Pour chaque paire d'activités, indiquez l'activité que chacun *(each one)* préfère et dites s'il/si elle la fait bien ou mal.

**NOTE DE VOCABULAIRE**

To say that someone likes *neither* of the activities, use **ne... ni... ni...: Je n'aime *ni* danser *ni* chanter.** To say that someone likes *both*, use **les deux: J'aime *les deux*.**

> **Exemple**    Moi, je **préfère danser. Je danse très bien.**

Moi, je...
Mon meilleur ami (Ma meilleure amie)...

Mes amis...
Ma famille et moi, nous...

Mes amis...
Mon meilleur ami (Ma meilleure amie) et moi...

# Asking about someone's day

**>Note**
*culturelle*

Les Français ont tendance à tenir à *(tend to value)* la discrétion. En France, sauf à des amis intimes, il est bon d'éviter *(to avoid)* les questions indiscrètes (religion, convictions politiques, argent *[money]*). Dans votre région, est-ce qu'on parle facilement de choses personnelles?

**NOTE DE VOCABULAIRE**

The adjective **tout** is placed before a noun's article. It means *the whole* or *all* before singular nouns (**toute la journée**) and *all* or *every* before plural nouns (**tous les jours**). It has four forms: **tout** *(masc. sing.)*, **toute** *(fem. sing.)*, **tous** *(masc. plur.)*, and **toutes** *(fem. plur.)*

## La journée

— Quand est-ce que vous êtes à l'université?
— Je suis à l'université...    le lundi, le mardi... de dix heures à quatre heures
le matin, l'après-midi, le soir
**tous les jours, sauf** le week-end
**toute la journée**

— Où est-ce que vous **déjeunez** d'habitude?
— Je déjeune...    chez moi / chez des amis / chez...
au restaurant universitaire
au café Trianon / dans un fast-food
???

— Qu'est-ce que vous aimez faire après les cours?
— J'aime...    aller au parc
**rentrer** à la maison
dormir
???

— **Avec qui** est-ce que vous **aimez mieux** sortir?
— J'aime mieux sortir...    avec mon ami(e)...
avec **mon petit ami (ma petite amie)**
avec **mon mari (ma femme)**
???

— **Pourquoi** est-ce que vous préférez sortir avec... ?
— Parce qu'il/elle est...    amusant(e), sexy, riche, beau (belle)...
Parce qu'ils/elles sont...    sympas, intéressant(e)s, dynamiques...

— Quand est-ce que vous préférez sortir **ensemble?**
— Nous préférons sortir...    le vendredi soir
le samedi après-midi
???

CD 1-29

Jean **demande** à Annette comment elle passe une journée typique.

JEAN:    Quand est-ce que tu es en cours ce semestre?
ANNETTE:    Je suis en cours tous les jours, sauf le week-end. Le lundi, par exemple, je suis en cours de midi à trois heures. Le matin, je prépare mes cours à la bibliothèque.
JEAN:    Et après les cours, qu'est-ce que tu fais en général?
ANNETTE:    Après les cours, je rentre à la maison. Je travaille ou **je dors** un peu.
JEAN:    Et le soir?
ANNETTE:    Le soir, je reste à la maison et j'étudie ou je surfe le Net.

---

**tous les jours** *every day*    **sauf** *except*    **toute la journée** *all day*    **déjeuner** *to eat lunch*    **rentrer** *to return, to go back (home)*    **Avec qui** *With whom*    **aimer mieux** *to like better, to prefer*    **mon petit ami (ma petite amie)** *my boyfriend (my girlfriend)*    **mon mari (ma femme)** *my husband (my wife)*    **Pourquoi** *Why*    **ensemble** *together*    **demander** *to ask*    **je dors (dormir** *to sleep)*

**A. Précisions.** Demain David déjeune avec des amis au café Le Trapèze. Quelle est la réponse logique pour chaque question?

1. Quand est-ce que nous déjeunons ensemble?
2. À quelle heure?
3. Qui déjeune avec nous?
4. Pourquoi est-ce que tu n'invites pas Thomas?
5. Où est-ce que nous déjeunons?
6. Qu'est-ce que tu voudrais faire après?

a. Au café Le Trapèze.
b. Gisèle et Bruno.
c. Demain.
d. Aller jouer au tennis.
e. Parce qu'il travaille demain.
f. À midi.

**B. C'est vrai?** Lisez chaque phrase et dites si **c'est vrai** ou **ce n'est pas vrai** pour vous et votre cours de français.

1. Je suis à l'université tous les jours, sauf le dimanche.
2. Nous sommes en cours de français le matin, tous les jours sauf le week-end.
3. Le cours de français est de dix heures à onze heures.
4. Les autres étudiants et moi passons beaucoup de temps ensemble après les cours.
5. Nous déjeunons souvent ensemble.
6. Le samedi, je travaille toute la journée pour préparer le cours de français.
7. J'aime mieux aller en cours de français que de sortir avec des amis.

Maintenant, corrigez les phrases qui ne sont pas vraies.

**C. Entretien.** Interviewez votre partenaire.

1. Quels jours est-ce que tu es à l'université? De quelle heure à quelle heure est-ce que tu es en cours? Est-ce que tu restes à l'université toute la journée? À quelle heure est-ce que tu rentres?
2. Quand est-ce que tu prépares les cours? Où est-ce que tu aimes mieux faire les devoirs: chez toi ou à la bibliothèque? Avec qui est-ce que tu préfères étudier?
3. Où est-ce que tu aimes mieux déjeuner? À quelle heure? Est-ce que tu déjeunes souvent chez toi? Où est-ce que tu préfères manger le soir? Est-ce que tu dînes plus souvent chez toi ou au restaurant? Est-ce que tu manges souvent dans un fast-food? Qu'est-ce que tu préfères: les hamburgers, la pizza ou les tacos?
4. Qu'est-ce que tu aimes faire le week-end? Où est-ce que tu aimes mieux aller avec des amis: au cinéma ou en boîte? Avec qui est-ce que tu préfères sortir? Quand est-ce que vous aimez mieux sortir?

**D. Conversation.** Avec un(e) partenaire, relisez à haute voix la conversation entre Annette et Jean à la page précédente. Ensuite, changez la conversation pour décrire votre situation. Changez de rôles.

LE TRAPEZE

# LE TRAPEZE

**SALON DE THÉ • SNACK • BAR • GLACIER**
**17, Bd Delfino 06000 NICE**
☎ 04 93 26 48 38

## PIZZAS

(Sauf le samedi)     euros

**MARGUERITE:** . . . . . . . . . . . . . . . . . . . **5,00**
Tomate, fromage.

**NAPOLITAINE:** . . . . . . . . . . . . . . . . . . **5,20**
Tomate, fromage, anchois, olives.

**POIVRONS:** . . . . . . . . . . . . . . . . . . . . **5,80**
Tomate, fromage, champignons, poivrons.

**REINE:** . . . . . . . . . . . . . . . . . . . . . . . . **5,80**
Tomate, fromage, olives, champignons, jambon.

**CALZONE:** . . . . . . . . . . . . . . . . . . . . . **6,00**
Tomate, champignons, œuf, crème fraîche.

*Service continu de midi à 2h du matin*

**Pour vérifier**

**1.** How do you form an information question?

**2.** Which word becomes **qu'** before a vowel, **qui** or **que?**

**3.** When are the three times you do not use **est-ce que?**

**4.** How do you say *Who is this/that? What is this/that?*

## Asking for information

*Les mots interrogatifs*

You have learned to ask questions with **est-ce que.** To ask for information such as *what, when,* or *why,* add the appropriate question word before **est-ce que.**

| | |
|---|---|
| **où** *where* | **Où est-ce que** vous étudiez? |
| **que (qu')** *what* | **Qu'est-ce que** vous étudiez? |
| **pourquoi** *why* | **Pourquoi est-ce que** vous étudiez le français? |
| **quand** *when* | **Quand est-ce que** vous préparez les cours? |
| **qui** *who* | **Avec qui est-ce que** vous préparez les cours? |
| **comment** *how* | **Comment est-ce que** vous passez la journée? |
| **à quelle heure** *at what time* | **À quelle heure est-ce que** vous êtes en cours? |
| **quel(s) jour(s)** *(on) what / which day(s)* | **Quels jours est-ce que** vous êtes en cours? |

Note that **que** makes elision before a vowel sound, but **qui** does not.

**Qu'**est-ce que vous aimez faire le soir?     Avec **qui** est-ce que vous aimez sortir?

Do not use **est-ce que** with **qui** when it is the subject of the verb, or with **où** or **comment** when they are followed by **être.**

Qui mange?     Où est Thomas?     Comment est l'université?

Use **Qui est-ce?** to ask *who* someone is. Use **Qu'est-ce que c'est?** to ask *what* something is.

— Qui est-ce?                    — Qu'est-ce que c'est?
— C'est Jean.                    — C'est un livre.

## Prononciation

CD 1-30

*Les lettres **qu** et la prononciation du mot **quand** en liaison*

In French, **qu** is usually pronounced as in the word **quiche.** It is generally only pronounced with the *w* sound heard in the English word *quite* when it is followed by **oi,** as in **pourquoi.**

qui     que     quand     quelle heure     pourquoi

Note that **d** in liaison is pronounced as a **t.**

Quand _t_ est-ce que tu travailles?

**Où est-ce que vous aimez déjeuner?**

**A. Invitations.** Des amis décident de déjeuner ensemble. Complétez les questions avec le mot convenable.

| Qui | Que (Qu') | Quand |
|-----|-----------|-------|
| Où | Pourquoi | À quelle heure |

— Tu voudrais déjeuner avec nous?
— __1__?
— Aujourd'hui.
— Je voudrais bien. __2__?
— Vers midi.
— __3__ est-ce que tu voudrais manger?
— Chez moi.
— __4__ est-ce que tu prépares?
— Une pizza.
— __5__ est-ce que tu invites?
— Jean-Luc et toi.
— __6__ est-ce que tu voudrais faire après?
— Aller au cinéma.
— __7__?
— Parce que je voudrais voir le nouveau film avec Audrey Tautou.

**B. Beaucoup de questions.** Formez des questions comme indiqué. Ensuite, posez-les à un(e) camarade de classe.

1. _____ est-ce que tu étudies? *(What? Where?)*
2. _____ est-ce que tu prépares les cours? *(When? With whom? Where?)*
3. _____ est-ce que tu aimes mieux déjeuner? *(At what time? With whom? Where?)*
4. _____ est-ce que tu dînes d'habitude le samedi soir? *(Where? With whom? At what time?)*

**C. Un jeu.** In teams, think of an appropriate question to elicit the answer in each box, using a question word (**qui, que...** ) based on the boldfaced word(s). Teams take turns selecting an item. A correct response earns the team the indicated points.

| | A | B | C | D |
|---|---|---|---|---|
| 5 points | Ça va **bien,** merci. | Je m'appelle **Annette Clark.** | Il est **5 heures.** | Aujourd'hui, c'est **lundi.** |
| 10 points | C'est **Yvette.** | C'est **un parc.** | David est **sympa.** | Annette est **à la maison.** |
| 15 points | Yvette aime **la musique.** | Thomas travaille **toute la journée.** | David aime sortir **avec Annette.** | Je rentre **à une heure.** |
| 20 points | **Annette et David** étudient les maths. | Nous aimons mieux **aller au cinéma.** | **Parce que** le prof est très intéressant. | Annette parle **bien** français. |

**1.** How would you invert the question **Il est ici?**

**2.** Do you ever use **est-ce que** and inversion in the same question?

**3.** When do you insert a **-t-** between a verb and an inverted subject pronoun?

**4.** Generally, can you invert nouns, or only pronouns? What do you do if the subject of the question is a noun? How would you invert the question: **Le prof déjeune à midi?**

**5.** What is the inverted form of **il y a?** of **c'est?**

**6.** How would you invert **Où est-ce que vous déjeunez?**

# Asking questions

## *Les questions par inversion*

You can ask a question using rising intonation or **est-ce que.** You can also use inversion; that is, you can invert the subject pronoun and the verb. Add a hyphen when the subject and verb are inverted.

> Est-ce que tu travailles le lundi? = **Travailles-tu le lundi?**

- Inversion is the equivalent of **est-ce que.** Never use both inversion and **est-ce que** in the same question.

  **Est-ce que tu joues** de la guitare? *OR* **Joues-tu** de la guitare?

- You do not normally use inversion with **je.**
- When the inverted subject is **il** or **elle** and *the verb ends in a vowel,* place a **-t-** between the verb and the pronoun. Do not add **-t-** if the verb ends in a consonant.

  | | |
  |---|---|
  | Parle-**t**-il anglais? | Est-il d'ici? |
  | Travaille-**t**-elle ici? | Est-elle d'ici? |

- Invert the *conjugated* verb and *the subject pronoun.* Do not invert a following infinitive.

  Aimes-tu aller au cinéma?   Voudriez-vous aller danser?

- If the subject of the question is a *noun,* rather than a *pronoun,* state the noun first, then supply a matching pronoun for inversion. Be sure to choose the form (**il, elle, ils, elles**) that matches the subject noun.

  | | |
  |---|---|
  | Le prof est-**il** français? | Marie parle-t-**elle** français? |
  | Les cours sont-**ils** difficiles? | Danielle et Antoinette étudient-**elles** ici? |

- The inverted form of **il y a** is **y a-t-il. C'est** becomes **est-ce.**

  **Y a-t-il** un café dans le quartier?   **Est-ce** un bon café?

- To ask information questions, place the question word before the inverted verb. **Qu'est-ce que** becomes **que (qu')** when using inversion.

  **Où** voudrais-tu aller?   **Que** voudrais-tu faire?   **Qu'**aimes-tu faire?

# Prononciation

CD 1-31

## *L'inversion et la liaison*

When the subject is **il, elle, ils,** or **elles,** there is liaison between the verb and its pronoun in inversion.

  Yvette est‿*t* elle américaine?   David et Thomas parlent‿*t* ils anglais?

**A. Prononcez bien!** D'abord *(First),* répétez ces questions après votre professeur. Ensuite, posez-les à un(e) camarade de classe. Faites attention à la prononciation!

Gisèle, où est-elle ce soir? Est-elle seule? Prépare-t-elle les cours? Thomas et Gisèle aiment-ils la musique? Dansent-ils bien? Et toi? Aimes-tu danser? Écoutes-tu souvent de la musique? Écoutons-nous de la musique française en cours quelquefois? Tes amis et toi, aimez-vous aller en boîte ensemble? Aimez-vous mieux aller au cinéma? Y a-t-il un bon cinéma dans le quartier universitaire?

Thomas       Gisèle

**B. Notre classe.** Utilisez l'inversion pour poser ces questions à un(e) camarade de classe.

**Exemple**   Est-ce que tu aimes tes cours ce semestre / trimestre?
— **Aimes-tu tes cours ce semestre?**
— **Oui, ils sont intéressants. /**
   **Non, je n'aime pas beaucoup mes cours ce semestre.**

1. Est-ce que le cours de français est facile ou difficile?
2. Est-ce que tu écoutes le CD tous les jours?
3. Est-ce que les étudiants aiment le cours?
4. Pourquoi est-ce qu'ils aiment le cours?
5. Est-ce que les examens sont faciles?
6. Est-ce que tu voudrais préparer le cours avec moi ce week-end?
7. Qu'est-ce que tu aimes faire le week-end?
8. Qu'est-ce que tu voudrais faire ce week-end?

**C. Entretien.** Changez ces phrases pour parler de vous. Après, posez une question logique à un(e) camarade de classe. Utilisez l'inversion.

**Exemple**   Je travaille *le matin*. Et toi?...
   **Je travaille le soir. Et toi? Quand travailles-tu?**

1. Je suis en cours *le lundi, le mercredi et le jeudi*. Et toi?...
2. Je prépare les cours *chez moi*. Et toi?...
3. Je prépare les cours *avec des amis*. Et toi?...
4. Je préfère étudier *le français*. Et toi?...
5. Je préfère étudier *le français parce que le cours est intéressant*. Et toi?...

**D. Le samedi.** Voilà un samedi typique pour Edgar, l'ami de David. Posez cinq questions à un(e) camarade de classe sur ce qu'Edgar fait *(on what Edgar does)* le samedi. Utilisez un mot interrogatif dans chaque question. Dites **il fait** pour *he does,* si nécessaire.

| qui | que | où | quand | pourquoi | comment |
|-----|-----|-----|-------|----------|---------|

**ses copains** *(his friends)*

# Going to the café

> Note
*culturelle*

Au café et au restaurant, l'expression service compris *(tip included)* indique que le service est inclus *(included)* dans les prix. Selon un sondage récent, 17% des Français donnent aussi un pourboire *(tip)* supplémentaire, tandis que 26% ne donnent jamais de pourboire. Et vous? Laissez-vous toujours un pourboire ou uniquement si *(if)* c'est mérité?

## Au café

Vous êtes au café. Qu'est-ce que vous allez prendre?

Je voudrais...              Pour moi...              Je vais prendre...

un expresso

un café au lait

un thé au citron

une eau
minérale

un jus de fruit ou
un jus d'orange

un coca

un Orangina

un verre de vin rouge ou
un verre de vin blanc

une bière

**un demi**

un sandwich
au jambon

un sandwich au
fromage

des frites

CD 1-32

David et Annette **commandent une boisson** au café.

| | |
|---|---|
| DAVID: | **Je n'ai pas très faim,** mais **j'ai soif.** Je vais prendre un demi. Et toi? |
| ANNETTE: | Moi, je voudrais un chocolat **chaud.** |
| DAVID: | Monsieur, s'il vous plaît. |
| LE GARÇON: | Bonjour, monsieur, mademoiselle. Vous désirez? |
| DAVID: | Pour moi, un demi. Et pour mademoiselle, un chocolat chaud. |
| LE GARÇON: | Très bien. |

**NOTE DE VOCABULAIRE**

To say *I'm hungry / I'm not hungry*, say **J'ai faim / Je n'ai pas faim** *(I have hunger / I don't have hunger)*. To say *I'm thirsty / I'm not thirsty*, say **J'ai soif / Je n'ai pas soif** *(I have thirst / I don't have thirst)*. **J'ai** rhymes with **je vais.** You will learn more about these expressions in a later chapter.

---

**un demi** *a draft beer*   **commander** *to order*   **une boisson** *a drink, a beverage*
**Je n'ai pas très faim (J'ai faim)** *I am not very hungry (I'm hungry)*   **j'ai soif** *I'm thirsty*   **chaud(e)** *hot*   **un garçon** *a waiter*

Après, David et Annette **paient.**

DAVID:             Ça fait combien, monsieur?
LE GARÇON:   Ça fait sept euros cinquante.
DAVID:             **Voilà** dix euros.
LE GARÇON:   Et **voici** votre **monnaie.** Merci bien.

>Note
*culturelle*

En 2002, le franc a disparu *(disappeared).* La monnaie d'usage en France est l'euro, comme dans tous les pays membres de l'Union moné- taire européenne (UME). L'euro est divisé en 100 centimes.

Le mot *argent* veut dire *money* en français, mais on entend *(one hears)* aussi des termes d'argot *(slang)* tels que: un radis *(a radish)*, une balle *(a bullet)* ou du blé *(wheat)* pour parler de l'ar- gent. En anglais, est-ce qu'il y a une expression en argot qu'on utilise pour dire *a dollar?*

### A. À votre santé. Quelle boisson est meilleure pour la santé *(health)?*

1. un café au lait / un jus d'orange
2. un Orangina / une eau minérale
3. un jus de fruit / un expresso
4. un thé / une bière
5. une eau minérale / un demi
6. un chocolat chaud / un jus d'orange

### B. Préférences. Offrez les choses suivantes à un(e) camarade de classe.

Exemple     — **Tu voudrais une eau minérale ou un coca?**
                   — **Je voudrais une eau minérale / un coca.**

      1.

2.       3.

4.       5.

### C. J'aime... Est-ce que vous aimez les choses indiquées dans l'exercice précédent? Utilisez **le, la, l'** ou **les** pour indiquer ce que vous aimez ou ce que vous n'aimez pas.

Exemple     **J'aime bien l'eau minérale. Je n'aime pas du tout le coca.**

### D. Conversation. Avec deux autres étudiants, relisez à haute voix la conversa- tion entre David et Annette qui commence à la page précédente. Le/La troisième étudiant(e) va jouer le rôle du serveur/de la serveuse *(server)*. Ensuite, changez la conversation pour commander ce que *(what)* vous voudriez. Changez de roles.

---

**ils paient (**payer *to pay)*     **Voilà / Voici** *There is, There are / Here is, Here are*     **la monnaie** *change*

**1.** How do you say **30? 40? 50? 60? 70? 80? 90?**

**2.** When do you use **et** with numbers? Do you use **et** with 81 and 91?

**3.** How do you say *one hundred?* Do you translate the word *one?*

**4.** What is the official currency of France?

## Paying the bill

*Les chiffres de trente à cent et l'argent*

— Un café au lait, c'est combien?
— 3,50 € (trois euros cinquante).

| | | | | |
|---|---|---|---|---|
| **30** | trente | | **70** | soixante-dix |
| **31** | trente et un | | **71** | soixante et onze |
| **32** | trente-deux | | **72** | soixante-douze |
| **33** | trente-trois... | | **73** | soixante-treize... |
| **40** | quarante | | **80** | quatre-vingts |
| **41** | quarante et un | | **81** | quatre-vingt-un |
| **42** | quarante-deux | | **82** | quatre-vingt-deux |
| **43** | quarante-trois... | | **83** | quatre-vingt-trois... |
| **50** | cinquante | | **90** | quatre-vingt-dix |
| **51** | cinquante et un | | **91** | quatre-vingt-onze |
| **52** | cinquante-deux | | **92** | quatre-vingt-douze |
| **53** | cinquante-trois... | | **93** | quatre-vingt-treize... |
| **60** | soixante | | **100** | cent |
| **61** | soixante et un | | | |
| **62** | soixante-deux | | | |
| **63** | soixante-trois... | | | |

France uses the **euro**, the common currency of most of the European Union, of which France is a part. A **euro** is divided into 100 cents or **centimes**. € is the symbol for the euro.

 ## Prononciation

CD 1-33

*Les chiffres*

Some French numbers are pronounced differently, depending on what follows them.

| | | | | | |
|---|---|---|---|---|---|
| deux | deux cafés | deux $^z$ euros | huit $^t$ | huit cafés | huit $^t$ euros |
| trois | trois cafés | trois $^z$ euros | dix $^s$ | dix cafés | dix $^z$ euros |
| six $^s$ | six cafés | six $^z$ euros | | | |

**A. Prononcez bien.** Commandez ces boissons.

| **Exemples** | trois demis | **Trois demis, s'il vous plaît.** |
| | trois expressos | **Trois expressos, s'il vous plaît.** |

deux demis      trois demis      six demis      huit demis      dix demis
deux expressos   trois expressos   six expressos   huit expressos   dix expressos

Maintenant, lisez ces prix *(prices)*. N'oubliez pas *(Don't forget)* de faire la liaison avec le mot euro si *(if)* nécessaire.

 1 €    11 €    2 €    12 €    3 €    13 €    6 €    16 €    10 €    20 €
61 €   71 €   82 €   92 €   63 €   73 €   86 €   96 €   100 €

**B. Prix indicatifs.** Combien coûte chaque chose?

| **Exemple** | une baguette | **C'est 70 centimes.** |

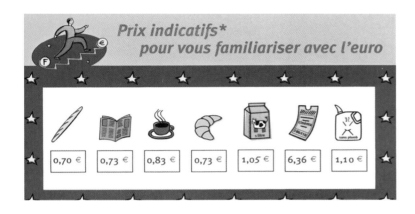

1. un journal         3. un croissant         5. un billet de cinéma
2. un expresso        4. un litre de lait      6. un litre d'essence

**C. Votre monnaie.** Vous êtes au café et vous payez pour vos amis et vous. Suivez l'exemple.

**Exemple**    6,85 € (10 €)
— **C'est combien, monsieur?**
— **Six euros quatre-vingt-cinq, mademoiselle.**
— **Voilà dix euros.**
— **Et voici votre monnaie.**

1. 12,98 € (15 €)    3. 23,68 € (30 €)    5. 36,75 € (40 €)    7. 2,50 € (5 €)
2. 32,45 € (40 €)    4. 14,88 € (15 €)    6. 7,75 € (10 €)    8. 16,80 € (20 €)

**D. Ça fait combien?** Écrivez les prix *(prices)* que vous entendez.

**Exemple**    VOUS ENTENDEZ:   C'est dix euros cinquante.
VOUS ÉCRIVEZ:    **10,50 €**

**E. Au café.** Préparez une conversation basée sur cette situation. Après, présentez la conversation à la classe.

In groups of three, prepare a scene in which you meet a friend at a café. One classmate plays the waitperson and takes your orders. The two customers order, then decide what they would like to do after leaving the café. Finally, they call the waitperson back and pay the bill.

## Reprise

*Talking about how you spend your time*

In **Chapitre 2,** you practiced saying what you like to do, asking about and telling how people spend their time, and ordering food and drink in a café. Now you have a chance to review what you learned.

**A. Passe-temps préférés.** Demandez à votre partenaire quelle activité il/elle préfère. Pour répondre *neither . . . nor . . . ,* dites **ne... ni... ni...** comme dans l'exemple. Si vous aimez les deux *(both),* dites **J'aime les deux.**

**Exemple**  — **Est-ce que tu préfères inviter des amis à la maison ou parler au téléphone?**
— **Je préfère parler au téléphone. / Je n'aime ni inviter des amis à la maison ni parler au téléphone. / J'aime les deux.**

**1.**     **2.**     **3.**     **4.**     **5.**

**B. Qu'est-ce qu'ils font?** Est-ce que ces personnes font les choses indiquées? Si oui *(If so),* est-ce qu'ils les font souvent, rarement, bien... ?

**Exemple**    mon meilleur ami (ma meilleure amie) / jouer au tennis
     **Mon meilleur ami (Ma meilleure amie) joue assez bien au tennis.**
     **Mon meilleur ami (Ma meilleure amie) ne joue jamais au tennis.**

| | | | | |
|---|---|---|---|---|
| **toujours** | **souvent** | **quelquefois** | **rarement** | **ne... jamais** |
| **beaucoup** | | **assez** | **(un) peu** | **ne... pas du tout** |
| **très bien** | **assez bien** | **comme ci comme ça** | | **assez mal** |
| | | **très mal** | | |

**1.** moi, je / jouer au golf
**2.** mon meilleur ami (ma meilleure amie) / aimer le sport
**3.** nous / jouer au volley
**4.** je / manger à la maison

**5.** ma famille et moi / dîner ensemble
**6.** nous / manger au restaurant
**7.** mes amis / aimer voyager
**8.** nous / voyager ensemble

**C. Au café.** Complétez les phrases.

**1.** Quand j'ai très soif, j'aime prendre...
**2.** Le matin, j'aime prendre...
**3.** Maintenant, je voudrais...
**4.** Avec un hamburger, j'aime prendre...
**5.** Quand je dîne au restaurant, j'aime prendre... comme *(as a)* boisson.

**D. C'est combien?** Demandez à votre partenaire les prix des choses indiquées.

    **Exemple**    un café express
                  — **Un café express, c'est combien?**
                  — **C'est deux euros quarante-cinq.**

| | | |
|---|---|---|
| **1.** un lait chaud | **4.** un double express | **7.** un Irish Coffee |
| **2.** un cappuccino | **5.** un vin chaud | **8.** un chocolat |
| **3.** un café décaféiné | **6.** un café au lait | **9.** un croissant |

**L'heure du thé**

**Prix Service Compris (15%)**

| | | | |
|---|---|---|---|
| Café express | 2,45 | Thé à la menthe | 3,50 |
| Double express | 4,10 | Thé au fruit de la passion | 3,50 |
| Café au lait | 3,40 | Thé à la framboise | 3,50 |
| Infusion | 3,50 | Cappuccino | 4,30 |
| *(Tilleul, verveine, menthe, tilleul-* | | Croissants | 1,60 |
| *menthe, verveine-menthe, camomille)* | | Confiture pot | 1,40 |
| Lait chaud | 2,90 | Tartines beurrées | 2,80 |
| Café décaféiné | 2,60 | Viandox | 3,40 |
| Double express avec pot de lait | 3,60 | Viandox avec vin | 3,80 |
| Chocolat | 3,50 | Grog au rhum | 6,10 |
| Café ou chocolat viennois | 4,30 | Vin chaud | 3,75 |
| Thé (avec lait ou citron) | 3,50 | Irish Coffee | 7,80 |

**E. Questions.** Complétez la conversation comme indiqué. Utilisez **est-ce que** pour poser les questions.

— Je voudrais sortir ce soir.
— _____?
       *What would you like to do?*

— Je voudrais aller voir le film *Star Time.*
— _____?
   *Why would you like to see Star Time?*

— Parce qu'il y a beaucoup d'action. Et toi? _____?
                                       *Would you like to see Star Time too?*

— Oui, beaucoup!
— _____
  *Are you free this evening?*          *Would you like to go to the movies with me?*

— Bon, d'accord. _____?
          *What time does the movie start?*

— Vers 9 heures. Je passe chez toi vers 8 heures?
— D'accord.

Maintenant, recommencez la conversation. Utilisez l'inversion pour poser les questions.

**F. Invitations.** Avec un(e) partenaire, préparez une conversation basée sur cette situation. Après, présentez la conversation à la classe.

Ask your partner what he/she likes to do on the weekend. Ask for some details such as when, where, with whom, and why. Make plans to do something together and decide on a place and time.

## Lecture: Aux Trois Obus

### AUX TROIS OBUS
120, rue Michel-Ange
Paris

#### NOS SALADES

| | |
|---|---|
| SALADE VERTE | 2,60 |
| SALADE NIÇOISE | 7,00 |
| (Tomate, œuf, thon, olives, salade, anchois, riz, poivron) | |
| SALADE 3 OBUS | 7,00 |
| (Salade, choux-fleur, foies de volaille, jambon, œuf dur) | |
| SALADE POULET | 7,00 |
| (Émincé de poulet, maïs, riz, tomates, poivron, salade) | |

| | |
|---|---|
| SALADE MIXTE | 5,00 |
| (Tomates, œuf dur, salade) | |
| SALADE CHEF | 7,00 |
| (Tomates, pommes à l'huile, jambon, gruyère, salade, œuf dur) | |
| SALADE DE CRUDITÉS | 6,00 |
| (Concombres, tomates, carottes, choux) | |

#### BUFFET CHAUD

| | |
|---|---|
| ŒUFS AU PLAT NATURE (3 œufs) | 4,00 |
| ŒUFS PLAT JAMBON (3 œufs) | 4,50 |
| OMELETTE NATURE | 4,00 |
| OMELETTE JAMBON | 4,50 |
| OMELETTE FROMAGE | 4,50 |
| OMELETTE MIXTE (jambon, fromage) | 6,50 |
| OMELETTE PARMENTIER | 4,50 |

| | |
|---|---|
| CROQUE-MONSIEUR | 4,00 |
| CROQUE-MADAME | 4,80 |
| HOT-DOG | 4,00 |
| FRANCFORTS FRITES | 5,00 |
| ASSIETTE DE FRITES | 2,60 |

| | |
|---|---|
| MOULES MARINIERES | 7,00 € |
| FRISEE AUX LARDONS | 7,00 € |
| ROTI DE BOEUF PUREE | 7,50 € |
| CASSOULET AU CONFIT | 11,00 € |
| ST JACQUES PROVENCALE | 14,00 € |

#### NOS SANDWICHES

| | |
|---|---|
| JAMBON DE PARIS | 2,20 |
| SAUCISSON SEC | 2,20 |
| SAUCISSON A L'AIL | 2,20 |
| RILLETTES | 2,20 |
| MIXTE (jambon, gruyère) | 3,50 |
| SANDWICH CRUDITÉS | 3,50 |

| | |
|---|---|
| JAMBON DE PAYS | 4,00 |
| PÂTÉ | 2,20 |
| TERRINE DU CHEF | 4,00 |
| CLUB SANDWICH | 6,00 |
| (Pain de mie, poulet, jambon, tomates, œuf, laitue, mayonnaise) | |
| JAMBON A L'OS | 4,00 |
| GRUYÈRE, CAMEMBERT | 2,20 |

Suppl. Pain mie 0,50   Campagne 0,80

#### FROMAGES

| | |
|---|---|
| Camembert | 2,60 |
| Roquefort | 3,00 |
| Brie | 3,00 |
| Cantal | 3,00 |
| Chèvre | 3,00 |

| | |
|---|---|
| Gruyère | 3,00 |
| Assiette de fromages | 5,00 |

**PRIX SERVICE COMPRIS (15%)**

Les chèques sont acceptés sur présentation d'une pièce d'identité.

La direction n'est pas responsable des objets oubliés dans l'établissement.

By using cognates and your ability to make intelligent guesses, you should be able to find several choices to order from this Parisian café menu. The following exercise will guide you.

**Vous savez déjà...** What you already know about cafés and restaurants will help you determine the following information.

1. Under **Buffet chaud,** what would **une omelette jambon** be? **une omelette fromage? une omelette nature?**
2. What you see at the bottom of the menu indicates that checks are accepted under one condition. What is usually the condition for accepting checks?
3. At the bottom of the menu, you see that the management claims it is not responsible for something. For what does management usually claim not to be responsible?

# Compréhension

**A. Mots apparentés.** Lisez le menu. Utilisez les mots apparentés *(cognates)* pour identifier:

1. Two kinds of sandwiches.
2. Three or four items used in the salads.
3. Two or three items you could order from the **buffet chaud.**

**B. Lisez bien.** Lisez le menu et répondez à ces questions.

1. C'est combien pour une salade verte? pour une salade niçoise? pour une salade de crudités? pour une omelette jambon?
2. Le service est compris? Les chèques sont acceptés?

**C. Bon appétit!** Faites une liste de toutes les choses que vous pouvez *(can)* identifier sur ce menu. Après, commandez quelque chose.

If you have access to SYSTÈME-D software, you will find the following phrases, vocabulary, grammar, and dictionary aids there.

**Phrases:** Greetings; Introducing; Attracting attention; Asking for information; Inviting; Leaving
**Vocabulary:** Drinks; Time expressions; Time of day; Leisure; Sports; Numbers; Money
**Dictionary:** The verb **préférer**

# Composition

**A. Organisez-vous.** You are going to prepare a scene in which two friends meet, talk, and order at a café. Before you begin, make sure you remember how to do these things in French.

- How do you greet a friend?
- How do you call the waitperson over and order a drink?
- How do you talk about what you do on the weekend?
- How do you ask what your companion likes to do and say what you like or do not like to do?
- How do you invite a friend to do something?
- How do you pay the bill?
- How do you say good-bye?

**B. Rédaction.** Using your answers from *A. Organisez-vous,* write a scene in which two college students meet at a café. They greet each other, order a drink, and start to chat about what they have in common. Remember to add details, such as when they like to do some things or why they do not like to do other things. They finally make plans to do something later, they get the bill, and they pay.

**C. Scène: Au café.** Compare the conversation you prepared in *B. Rédaction* with that of two classmates and prepare a scene together to act out for the class.

## Le café et le fast-food

**Le** café en France est presque une institution sociale. Il y a des cafés **partout.** Les gens aiment aller au café pour...

prendre un café

déjeuner

passer du temps avec des amis

passer une heure tranquille

Dans un café-tabac, **on peut aussi acheter** des cigarettes, des **timbres,** des cartes téléphoniques et des cartes postales.

Il y a une grande variété de cafés.

Il y a des cafés élégants comme Les Deux Magots à Paris, fréquenté **autrefois** par des artistes et des écrivains **tels que** Cocteau et Hemingway.

Certains cafés servent une clientèle particulière: touristes, étudiants, travailleurs, **cadres.**

Il y a aussi **le café du coin** ou du village.

---

**partout** *everywhere*   **on peut aussi acheter** *one can also buy*   **timbres** *stamps*   **autrefois** *formerly*   **tels que** *such as*
**cadres** *business executives*   **le café du coin** *the neighborhood café*

Voilà **quelques renseignements utiles.**

**Au bar, les prix sont plus bas.**

Si vous préférez être à la terrasse, les prix sont souvent plus **élevés.** Les chaises font face à la rue parce qu'un des plaisirs du café, c'est de regarder **les passants.**

**Malgré la renommée** du café, il y a de moins en moins de cafés en France et de plus en plus de fast-foods comme McDonald's (Macdo) et Quick.

## À discuter

1. Vous visitez la France. Préférez-vous déjeuner dans un fast-food ou dans un café? Pourquoi?

2. En France, il y a de plus en plus de fast-foods et de moins en moins de cafés. Pourquoi?
   a. Le service dans un fast-food est plus rapide.
   b. Les Français pensent que les hamburgers sont meilleurs que les sandwichs.
   c. Les choses américaines sont très à la mode *(in fashion)*.

3. En France, le service est presque toujours compris *(included)*. Aimez-vous cette idée? Pourquoi?
   a. Non, parce que c'est plus cher *(expensive)*.
   b. Oui, parce que c'est plus simple. (Je n'aime pas faire de calculs.)
   c. Non, ça influence la qualité du service.

4. Pourquoi est-ce que le café est plus populaire en France qu'ici? Qu'est-ce qu'on aime *(does one like)* faire au café? Est-ce que ces activités sont plus populaires en France qu'ici? Ici, où est-ce qu'on va *(one goes)* pour faire ces choses?

---

**quelques renseignements utiles** *some useful information*   **les prix** *prices*   **bas** *low*   **élevés** *high*
**les passants** *passers-by*   **Malgré la renommée** *In spite of the fame*

# Résumé de grammaire

## The infinitive, -er verbs, and adverbs

Qu'est-ce que tu aimes **faire** le soir? J'aime **rester** à la maison et **lire** ou **sortir** pour **aller voir** un film.

The first verb in a clause is conjugated. Verbs after the first verb are in the infinitive, or base form of the verb. French infinitives end in **-er, -ir, -oir,** or **-re.**

**écouter** *to listen to*    **dormir** *to sleep*    **voir** *to see*    **lire** *to read*

Regular -er verbs have the following pattern of conjugation in the present tense.

| PARLER (*to speak*) | |
|---|---|
| je parl**e** | nous parl**ons** |
| tu parl**es** | vous parl**ez** |
| il/elle parl**e** | ils/elles parl**ent** |

Mes amis **aiment** sortir mais moi j'**aime** rester à la maison.

Nous voyag**e**ons souvent ensemble. Nous commen**ç**ons l'examen.

With verbs ending in **-ger,** insert an **e** before the **-ons** ending in the **nous** form. With verbs ending in **-cer,** the **c** changes to a **ç** before the **-ons** ending in the **nous** form.

If the next-to-last syllable of an **-er** infinitive has an **e** or an **é,** this letter often changes to an **è** in all forms except **nous** and **vous.**

Après les cours, je **préfère** rentrer à la maison. Mais le vendredi après-midi, mes amis et moi **préférons** aller prendre un verre.

| PRÉFÉRER (*to prefer*) | |
|---|---|
| je préf**è**re | nous préférons |
| tu préf**è**res | vous préférez |
| il/elle préf**è**re | ils/elles préf**è**rent |

The present tense in French is the equivalent of three present tenses in English.

Je parle français.
$\begin{cases} \text{\textit{I speak French.}} \\ \text{\textit{I am speaking French.}} \\ \text{\textit{I do speak French.}} \end{cases}$

Je danse **souvent** le week-end.
Je joue **bien** au tennis.
Je vais au cinéma **quelquefois.**
Je joue du piano **comme ci comme ça.**
Je **ne** travaille **jamais** le samedi.

Adverbs that tell how much, how often, or how well you do something are placed immediately after the verb. However, **quelquefois** and **d'habitude** are normally placed at the beginning or end of the clause and **comme ci comme ça** is placed at the end. **Ne... jamais** surrounds the conjugated verb.

# Information questions and inversion

To ask information questions, place the appropriate question word (**où, qui, etc.**) before **est-ce que.**

| | |
|---|---|
| **Où** est-ce que tu travailles? | *(Where . . . ?)* |
| **Avec qui** est-ce que tu déjeunes? | *(With whom . . . ?)* |
| **Pourquoi** est-ce que tu es ici? | *(Why . . . ?)* |
| **Qu'**est-ce que tu voudrais? | *(What . . . ?)* |
| **Quand** est-ce que tu déjeunes? | *(When . . . ?)* |
| **À quelle heure** est-ce que tu dînes? | *([At] What time . . . ?)* |
| **Quels jours** est-ce que tu es en cours? | *(What / Which days . . . ?)* |
| **Comment** est-ce que tu aimes passer la matinée? | *(How . . . ?)* |

Je suis en cours le mardi et le jeudi. Et toi? **Quand est-ce que** tu es en cours?

You can also form questions by inverting the verb and its subject pronoun. Remember that:

Où **travaillez-vous?**
À quelle heure **êtes-vous** en cours?

- You do not normally use inversion with **je.**
- If the subject of the verb is a noun, state the noun, then invert the verb with the corresponding pronoun.

Les cours sont-**ils** difficiles?

- When the inverted subject is **il** or **elle** and the verb ends in a vowel, place a -**t**- between the verb and the pronoun.

Marie parle-**t**-elle français?
Marie est-elle d'ici?

- The inverted forms of **il y a** and **c'est** are **y a-t-il** and **est-ce.**

**Y a-t-il** un café dans le quartier?
**Est-ce** un bon café?

# The numbers from 30 to 100 and money

The **euro** is the official currency of France. A euro is composed of 100 **centimes.** Read prices as:

10 € 10 = dix euros dix

— C'est combien, un expresso?
— C'est **deux euros quarante.**

The numbers from 30 to 100 are based on:

30 trente
40 quarante
50 cinquante
60 soixante
70 soixante-dix
80 quatre-vingts
90 quatre-vingt-dix
100 cent

## Saying what you like to do

**Vocabulaire**

**EXPRESSIONS VERBALES**

| | |
|---|---|
| **J'aime...** | *I like . . .* |
| **Je préfère...** | *I prefer . . .* |
| **Je voudrais (bien)...** | *I would like . . .* |
| **aller en boîte / au café / au cinéma** | *to go to a club / to the café / to the movies* |
| **bricoler** | *to do handiwork* |
| **danser** | *to dance* |
| **dîner au restaurant** | *to have dinner in a restaurant* |
| **dormir** | *to sleep* |
| **écouter la radio / la chaîne hi-fi / de la musique** | *to listen to the radio / the stereo / music* |
| **écrire des mails** | *to write e-mails* |
| **faire** | *to do, to make* |
| **faire du jogging** | *to jog, to go jogging* |
| **faire du sport** | *to play sports* |
| **faire quelque chose** | *to do something* |
| **inviter des amis à la maison** | *to invite friends to the house* |
| **jouer à des jeux vidéo** | *to play video games* |
| **jouer au base-ball / au basket / au football / au football américain / au golf / au tennis / au volley** | *to play baseball / basketball / soccer / football / golf / tennis / volleyball* |
| **jouer du piano / de la batterie / de la guitare** | *to play piano / drums / guitar* |
| **lire** | *to read* |
| **parler au téléphone** | *to talk on the phone* |
| **prendre un verre** | *to have a drink* |
| **regarder la télé(vision)** | *to watch TV* |
| **regarder une vidéo / un DVD** | *to watch a video / a DVD* |
| **rester à la maison** | *to stay home* |
| **sortir avec des ami(e)s** | *to go out with friends* |
| **surfer le Net** | *to surf the Net* |
| **travailler sur l'ordinateur** | *to work on the computer* |
| **voir un film** | *to see a movie* |
| **On va... ?** | *Shall we go . . . ?* |
| **Qu'est-ce que vous aimez faire?** | *What do you like to do?* |
| **Qu'est-ce que vous voudriez faire?** | *What would you like to do?* |
| **Tu voudrais... ?** | *Would you like . . . ?* |

**DIVERS**

| | |
|---|---|
| **À ce soir!** | *See you tonight! / See you this evening!* |
| **À plus tard!** | *See you later!* |
| **après les cours** | *after class* |
| **D'accord!** | *Okay!* |
| **un passe-temps** | *a pastime* |
| **Pourquoi pas?** | *Why not?* |
| **quelque chose** | *something* |
| **Tu es libre ce soir?** | *Are you free this evening?* |
| **vers** | *about, around, toward* |
| **vraiment** | *really, truly* |

## Saying how you spend your free time

**NOMS MASCULINS**

| | |
|---|---|
| **le cinéclub** | *the cinema club* |
| **un classique** | *a classic* |

**NOMS FÉMININS**

| | |
|---|---|
| **une activité** | *an activity* |
| **la fac** | *the university, the campus* |

**EXPRESSIONS VERBALES**

| | |
|---|---|
| **Qu'est-ce que vous faites?** | *What are you doing? / What do you do?* |
| **Qu'est-ce que tu fais?** | *What are you doing? / What do you do?* |
| **chanter** | *to sing* |
| **commencer** | *to begin, to start* |
| **faire de la musique** | *to play music* |
| **faire du shopping** | *to go shopping* |
| **gagner** | *to win* |
| **jouer au hockey** | *to play hockey* |
| **manger** | *to eat* |
| **nager** | *to swim* |
| **passer chez...** | *to go by . . . 's house* |
| **passer le temps / la matinée** | *to spend one's time / the morning* |
| **préférer** | *to prefer* |
| **préparer les cours** | *to prepare for class, to study* |
| **répéter** | *to repeat* |
| **rester au lit** | *to stay in bed* |
| **je sors** | *I am going out, I go out* |
| **je vais** | *I am going, I go* |
| **voyager** | *to travel* |

**ADVERBES**

| | |
|---|---|
| **(très / assez) bien** | *(very / fairly) well* |
| **comme ci comme ça** | *so-so* |
| **d'habitude** | *usually* |
| **jusqu'à** | *until* |
| **(très / assez) mal** | *(very / fairly) badly* |
| **mieux (que)** | *better (than)* |
| **ne... jamais** | *never* |
| **presque** | *almost* |
| **quand** | *when* |
| **quelquefois** | *sometimes* |
| **rarement** | *rarely* |
| **souvent** | *often* |
| **toujours** | *always* |

**DIVERS**

| | |
|---|---|
| **chez...** | *to / at / in / by . . . 's house* |
| **le samedi matin / après-midi / soir** | *(on) Saturday mornings / afternoons / evenings* |
| **le week-end** | *the weekend, weekends, on the weekend* |

### Asking about someone's day

**NOMS MASCULINS**

| | |
|---|---|
| l'après-midi | the afternoon |
| un fast-food | a fast-food restaurant |
| un jour | a day |
| mon mari | my husband |
| le matin | the morning |
| un parc | a park |
| mon petit ami | my boyfriend |
| le soir | the evening |

**NOMS FÉMININS**

| | |
|---|---|
| ma femme | my wife |
| la journée | the day |
| ma petite amie | my girlfriend |

**EXPRESSIONS VERBALES**

| | |
|---|---|
| aimer mieux | to like better, to prefer |
| aller au parc | to go to the park |
| déjeuner | to have lunch, to eat lunch |
| demander | to ask (for) |
| je dors | I am sleeping, I sleep |
| manger dans un fast-food | to eat in a fast-food restaurant |
| rentrer | to return, to go back (home) |

**EXPRESSIONS ADVERBIALES**

| | |
|---|---|
| l'après-midi | in the afternoon, afternoons |
| de... heures à... heures | from . . . o'clock to . . . o'clock |
| ensemble | together |
| le matin | in the morning, mornings |
| le soir | in the evening, evenings |
| tous les jours | every day |
| toute la journée | all day |

**EXPRESSIONS INTERROGATIVES**

| | |
|---|---|
| à quelle heure | at what time |
| avec qui | with whom |
| comment | how |
| où | where |
| pourquoi (parce que) | why (because) |
| quand | when |
| quel(s) jour(s) | what / which day(s) |
| que (qu'est-ce que) | what |
| Qu'est-ce que c'est? | What is that/this/it?, What are these/they? |
| qui | who(m) |
| Qui est-ce? | Who is he/she/it/ that/this?, Who are they? |

**DIVERS**

| | |
|---|---|
| en général | in general |
| par exemple | for example |
| riche | rich |
| sauf | except |
| sexy | sexy |
| typique | typical |

### Going to the café

**NOMS MASCULINS**

| | |
|---|---|
| l'argent | money, silver |
| un café (au lait) | a coffee (with milk) |
| un centime | a centime, a cent |
| un chocolat (chaud) | a (hot) chocolate |
| un coca | a Coke, a cola |
| un demi | a draft beer |
| un euro | a euro |
| un expresso | an espresso |
| un garçon | a waiter |
| un jus de fruit / d'orange | a fruit / an orange juice |
| un Orangina | an Orangina |
| un sandwich au fromage / au jambon | a cheese / ham sandwich |
| un thé (au citron) | a tea (with lemon) |
| un verre de vin blanc / rouge | a glass of white / red wine |

**NOMS FÉMININS**

| | |
|---|---|
| une bière | a beer |
| une boisson | a drink, a beverage |
| une eau minérale | a mineral water |
| des frites | some fries |
| la monnaie | change |

**CHIFFRES**

| | |
|---|---|
| quarante, quarante et un... | forty, forty-one . . . |
| cinquante, cinquante et un... | fifty, fifty-one . . . |
| soixante, soixante et un... | sixty, sixty-one . . . |
| soixante-dix, soixante et onze... | seventy, seventy-one . . . |
| quatre-vingts, quatre-vingt-un... | eighty, eighty-one . . . |
| quatre-vingt-dix, quatre-vingt-onze... | ninety, ninety-one . . . |
| cent | one hundred |

**DIVERS**

| | |
|---|---|
| Ça fait combien? | How much is it? |
| Ça fait... euros. | That makes . . . euros. |
| C'est combien? | How much is it? |
| chaud(e) | hot |
| commander | to order (food and drink) |
| J'ai faim. / Je n'ai pas faim. | I'm hungry. / I'm not hungry. |
| J'ai soif. / Je n'ai pas soif. | I'm thirsty. / I'm not thirsty. |
| payer | to pay |
| Qu'est-ce que vous allez prendre? | What are you going to have? |
| Vous désirez? | What would you like? |
| Je vais prendre... | I'm going to have . . . |
| Je voudrais... | I would like . . . |
| Pour moi... s'il vous plaît. | For me . . . please. |
| voici | here is, here are |
| voilà | there is, there are |
| votre (vos) | your |

**Derrière le marché Bonsecours**
**WILLIAM RAPHAEL**
**(1833–1914)**

1866
National Gallery of Canada

Lieu de rencontre *(Meeting place)* entre les gens de la ville et les agriculteurs de la campagne depuis son inauguration en 1847 jusqu'à sa fermeture en 1963, le marché Bonsecours est un symbole de la vigueur de la vie *(life)* à Montréal. Aujourd'hui siège *(seat)* du Conseil des métiers d'art *(art professions)* du Québec, ce bel édifice a été l'Hôtel de ville pendant *(was the City Hall for)* 25 ans et site d'expositions et de conférences.

# En Amérique:
# Au Québec

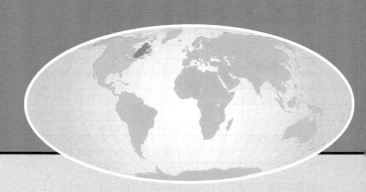

**LE QUÉBEC**
**SUPERFICIE:** 1 450 680 kilomètres carrés
**NOMBRE D'HABITANTS:** 7 529 000 (les Québécois)
**CAPITALE:** Québec
**INDUSTRIES PRINCIPALES:** agriculture, exploitation forestière, exploitation minière, hydroélectricité, technologie, tourisme

# Un nouvel appartement

**COMPÉTENCE**

 Video activities are on pages 212–215.

# En Amérique: Le Canada et le Québec

En Amérique, **on** parle français!

En Amérique du Sud, la Guyane française est francophone. Aux États-Unis, il y a des communautés francophones en Louisiane, **bien sûr**, et dans **plusieurs états** de la **Nouvelle-Angleterre**. On parle français dans plusieurs îles caraïbes: la Martinique, la Guadeloupe, Saint-Martin et Haïti. **Tout** le Canada est considéré officiellement bilingue (français / anglais) et 82% de la population de la province de Québec parle français!

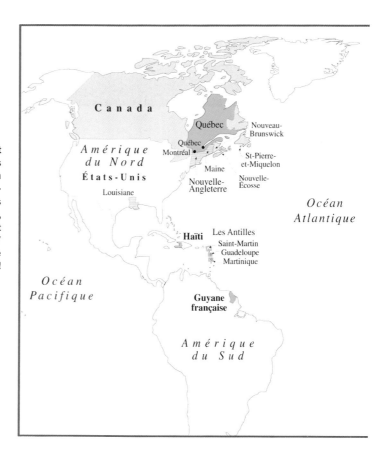

Sur le plan politique, le Canada est une confédération démocratique parlementaire composée de dix provinces et trois territoires. Sur le plan social, c'est une mosaïque de populations de diverses origines ethniques et culturelles: **les Amérindiens**, les Britanniques, les Français et **bien d'autres**.

**on** *one, people, they*    **bien sûr** *of course*    **plusieurs états** *several states*    **la Nouvelle-Angleterre** *New England*    **Tout** *All*    **les Amérindiens** *Native Americans* **bien d'autres** *many others*

Le Québec est la province francophone la plus importante du Canada. **Grâce à** son histoire, à sa langue et à **ses coutumes,** le Québec est, **à bien des égards**, une société distincte à l'intérieur du Canada. **La ville** de Québec est la capitale de la province. Fondée en 1608, c'est la plus vieille ville du Canada et la seule ville fortifiée en Amérique du Nord.

Montréal, grand centre culturel et commercial, est la plus grande ville du Québec et la **deuxième** ville francophone du monde, après Paris.

Plus vaste que l'Alaska, le Québec est la plus grande des provinces canadiennes et la deuxième en population. Le Québec est très riche et **produit** 25% du **revenu national brut** du Canada. Les forêts couvrent une grande partie du Québec et jouent un rôle important dans l'économie. L'exploitation forestière est une industrie importante.

**Grâce à** *Due to*    **ses coutumes** *its customs*    **à bien des égards** *in many regards*    **La ville** *The city*    **deuxième** *second (largest)*    **produit** *produces* **revenu national brut (R.N.B.)** *gross national product (GNP)*

# Talking about where you live

## Le logement

J'habite...

dans un appartement
dans une maison
dans **une chambre** à la
résidence universitaire

Il/Elle est...

grand(e) / petit(e)
moderne / vieux (vieille)
joli(e) / laid(e)
**(trop) cher (chère)**
confortable

Il/Elle **se trouve...**

sur le campus
**(tout) près de** l'université
(assez, très) **loin de** l'université

au centre-ville (dans un grand **immeuble**)　　en ville　　en banlieue　　à la campagne

**Le loyer** est de... **par mois.**

| 500$ | 650$ | 1 200$ |
|---|---|---|
| cinq cents dollars | six cent cinquante dollars | mille deux cents dollars |

**Je n'ai pas** de loyer!

Chez moi, il y a six **pièces** (f).

**VOCABULAIRE SUPPLÉMENTAIRE**

**une caravane** a travel trailer
**la cave** the cellar
**un duplex** a split-level apartment
**un emprunt-logement** a home loan
**le garage** the garage
**le jardin** the yard, the garden
**un mobile-home** a mobile home
**la lingerie** the laundry room
**la salle de séjour** the family room, the den

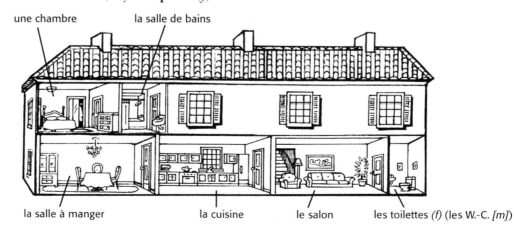

une chambre　　la salle de bains

la salle à manger　　la cuisine　　le salon　　les toilettes (f) (les W.-C. [m])

---

**le logement** lodging, housing　**une chambre** a bedroom　**trop** too　**cher (chère)** expensive
**se trouver** to be found, to be located　**(tout) près (de)** (very) near　**loin (de)** far (from)
**un immeuble** an apartment building　**Le loyer** The rent　**par mois** per month　**Je n'ai pas** I don't have
**une pièce** a room

Robert, un jeune Américain, **va** étudier à l'université Laval, au Québec.
Il parle au téléphone à son ami Thomas, avec qui il pense habiter.

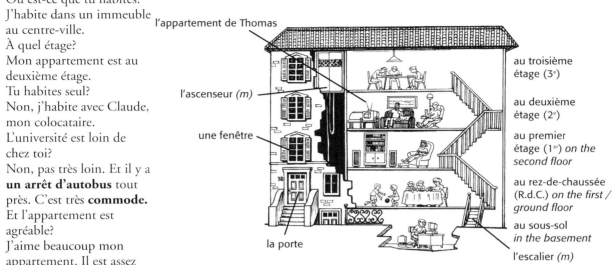

ROBERT: Où est-ce que tu habites?
THOMAS: J'habite dans un immeuble au centre-ville.
ROBERT: À quel étage?
THOMAS: Mon appartement est au deuxième étage.
ROBERT: Tu habites seul?
THOMAS: Non, j'habite avec Claude, mon colocataire.
ROBERT: L'université est loin de chez toi?
THOMAS: Non, pas très loin. Et il y a **un arrêt d'autobus** tout près. C'est très **commode.**
ROBERT: Et l'appartement est agréable?
THOMAS: J'aime beaucoup mon appartement. Il est assez grand et pas trop cher.

l'appartement de Thomas

l'ascenseur (m)

une fenêtre

la porte

au troisième étage (3ᵉ)

au deuxième étage (2ᵉ)

au premier étage (1ᵉʳ) *on the second floor*

au rez-de-chaussée (R.d.C.) *on the first / ground floor*

au sous-sol *in the basement*

l'escalier (m)

**A. Et vous?** Complétez les phrases avec les mots en italique qui vous correspondent le mieux.

1. J'habite dans *un appartement / une maison / une chambre.*
2. Il/Elle est *sur le campus / (tout) près de l'université / loin de l'université.*
3. Il/Elle se trouve *au centre-ville / en ville / en banlieue / à la campagne.*
4. Il/Elle est *joli(e) / grand(e) / moderne / confortable / ???.*
5. Il/Elle *est / n'est pas* trop cher (chère).
6. Le loyer est *plus / moins* de cinq cents dollars par mois.
7. Chez moi, il y a *une / deux / trois / quatre / ???* chambre(s).
8. Je passe beaucoup de temps dans *la cuisine / le salon / ma chambre / ???.*
9. Ma chambre se trouve *au rez-de-chaussée / au premier étage / ???.*

> **Note**
> *culturelle*

Dans les hôtels et les autres immeubles au Québec et en France, faites attention! Le premier étage est l'étage au-dessus du *(above the)* rez-de-chaussée. C'est-à-dire que le rez-de-chaussée est *the first floor / ground floor* et le premier étage est *the second floor.* À quel étage habitez-vous?

**B. Entretien.** Interviewez votre partenaire.

1. Est-ce que tu habites dans une maison, dans un appartement ou dans une chambre à la résidence universitaire? Comment est la maison / la chambre / l'appartement? Est-ce qu'il est cher / elle est chère?
2. Tu habites près de l'université, loin de l'université ou sur le campus? Est-ce que c'est commode? Est-ce qu'il y a un arrêt d'autobus tout près?
3. Préfères-tu habiter au centre-ville, en ville, en banlieue ou à la campagne? Tu préfères habiter seul(e) ou avec un(e) camarade de chambre ou un(e) colocataire? Préfères-tu habiter au rez-de-chaussée ou au premier étage?
4. Quelles pièces y a-t-il chez toi? Dans quelle pièce aimes-tu passer beaucoup de temps? faire tes devoirs? manger? regarder la télé?

**C. Conversation.** Avec un(e) partenaire, relisez à haute voix la conversation entre Robert et Thomas en haut de la page. Ensuite, changez la conversation pour décrire votre propre situation.

---

**va (aller** *to go)* **un arrêt d'autobus** *a bus stop* **commode** *convenient*

**1.** Before which two of these numbers do you never put **un: cent, mille, million?**

**2.** How do you say 1,503? 12,612?

**3.** How do you say *first? fifth?* How do you say *on the* with a floor?

**VOCABULAIRE SUPPLÉMENTAIRE**
**un milliard** *one billion*
**deux milliards** *two billion*

# Giving prices and other numerical information

*Les chiffres au-dessus de 100 et les nombres ordinaux*

To talk about rent and other numerical information in French, you need to know how to say numbers over 100.

| | | | |
|---|---|---|---|
| **100** | cent | **1 000** | mille |
| **101** | cent un | **1 001** | mille un |
| **102** | cent deux | **1 352** | mille trois cent cinquante-deux |
| **199** | cent quatre-vingt-dix-neuf | **2 000** | deux mille |
| **200** | deux cents | **1 000 000** | un million |
| **201** | deux cent un | **2 234 692** | deux millions deux cent trente-quatre mille six cent quatre-vingt-douze |
| **999** | neuf cent quatre-vingt-dix-neuf | | |

Note the following about numbers:

- **Cent** means *one hundred* and **mille** means *one thousand*. Do not put **un** before them. On the other hand, you do say **un million.**

- **Cent** has an **s** in numbers like **deux cents** and **trois cents** only when no other number follows the word **cent**. For example, there is no **s** in **deux cent un**. Never add an **s** to **mille**, even in numbers like **deux mille** and **trois mille**.

- There is no hyphen between **cent, mille,** or **un million** and another number.

- In France and in Quebec, commas are used to denote decimals, and periods (or a space) are used after thousands, millions, etc. Read a decimal as **virgule** (**1,5 = un virgule cinq**).

| USA | FRANCE / QUEBEC |
|---|---|
| 1.5 | 1,5 |
| 1,000 | 1.000 *or* 1 000 |

Use **À quel étage?** to ask *On what floor?* To say *on the* with a floor, use **au.** When counting floors, use the ordinal numbers and remember that in a French-speaking country, you start with the ground floor (**le rez-de-chaussée**).

— **À quel étage habitez-vous?** — *What floor do you live on?*
— **J'habite au troisième étage.** — *I live on the fourth floor.*

In French, to convert cardinal numbers *(two, three, four . . . )* to ordinal numbers *(second, third, fourth . . . )*, add the suffix **-ième.** Drop a final **-e** from cardinal numbers before adding **-ième.**

**deux → deuxième**     **quatre → quatrième**     **mille → millième**

These numbers are irregular:

**premier (première)**     **cinquième**     **neuvième**

**A. Le loyer.** Quel est le loyer?

**Exemple**     900$     **Le loyer est de neuf cents dollars par mois.**

| | | | | | | | |
|---|---|---|---|---|---|---|---|
| **1.** | 860$ | **4.** | 1 100$ | **7.** | 1 540$ | **10.** | 2 435$ |
| **2.** | 1 325$ | **5.** | 675$ | **8.** | 750$ | **11.** | 3 295$ |
| **3.** | 410$ | **6.** | 885$ | **9.** | 660$ | **12.** | 1 345$ |

**B. Et vous?** Décrivez l'endroit *(place)* où vous habitez en changeant les chiffres et les mots en italique.

1. La population de la ville où j'habite maintenant est de *150 000* / ??? habitants.
2. Il y a plus de *35 000* / ??? étudiants à notre *(our)* université.
3. Mon loyer est de *400$* / ??? par mois. *(Je n'ai pas de loyer.)*
4. Ma chambre est au *deuxième étage* / ???.
5. Je préfère habiter au *deuxième étage* / ???.
6. Maintenant, nous sommes au *troisième étage* / ???.
7. Le bureau du prof est *au rez-de-chaussée* / *au premier étage* / ???

**C. Statistiques.** Lisez ces statistiques sur l'université Laval, le Québec et le Canada. Devinez *(Guess)* quels chiffres correspondent à quelle description. Votre professeur dira *(will say)* **plus que ça** ou **moins que ça** jusqu'à ce que vous deviniez juste.

| | | | |
|---|---|---|---|
| 1. | la population du Canada | **a.** | 644 700 |
| 2. | le nombre de francophones au Canada | **b.** | 7 529 100 |
| 3. | la population de la province de Québec | **c.** | 32 026 600 |
| 4. | la population de la ville de Québec | **d.** | 222 |
| 5. | la population de la ville de Montréal | **e.** | 37 100 |
| 6. | le nombre d'étudiants à l'université Laval | **f.** | 3 263 800 |
| 7. | le loyer par mois dans les résidences à l'université Laval en dollars canadiens | **g.** | 9 178 100 |

**D. Chez Thomas.** Regardez l'illustration et répondez aux questions.

1. Il y a un ascenseur dans l'immeuble où habite Thomas?
2. Il y a un escalier?
3. À quel étage habite le monsieur qui travaille sur l'ordinateur?
4. À quel étage habitent Thomas et son colocataire?
5. À quel étage habite la jeune femme qui écoute de la musique?
6. Où habitent les enfants?

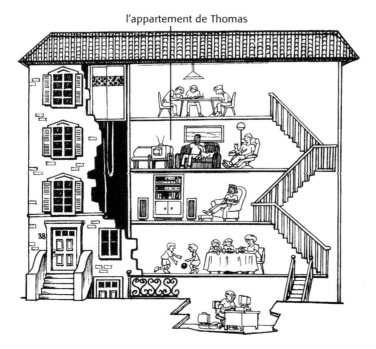

l'appartement de Thomas

## Stratégies et Lecture
*Guessing meaning from context*

You can often guess the meaning of unknown words from context. Read this passage in its entirety, then guess the meaning of the boldfaced words.

Arrivé à l'immeuble de Thomas, Robert **entre,** il **monte** l'escalier et il **sonne** à la porte de l'appartement de son ami. Une jeune femme ouvre la porte. Après un instant, elle **referme** la porte.

Some words may have different meanings in different contexts. For example, the word **bien** can mean *well* or it can also be used for emphasis, instead of **très** *(very).* Read the following sentences and use the context to decide if **bien** means *well* or *very.*

Je comprends bien.
C'est bien compliqué.
Le prénom Claude est utilisé aussi bien pour une femme que pour un homme.

**A. Selon le contexte.** The boldfaced word in each of the following sentences can have a different meaning, depending on the context. Can you guess the different meanings?

Bravo! **Encore! Encore!**

Ça, c'est **encore** plus compliqué.

Je suis au premier étage, alors je monte **encore** un étage pour aller au deuxième?

**B. Vous savez déjà...** You already know the boldfaced word or words in sentence **a.** Guess the meaning of the boldfaced words in sentence **b,** using the context.

1. **a. Ouvrez** votre livre, **lisez** le paragraphe et **fermez** le livre.
   **b.** Robert **ouvre** la lettre de Thomas, **lit** les instructions et **referme** la lettre.
2. **a. Prenez** une feuille de papier.
   **b.** Elle **prend** la lettre.
3. **a. Donnez**-moi un café, s'il vous plaît.
   **b.** Thomas **donne** l'adresse de l'appartement à Robert.

# Un nouvel appartement

CD 1-35

Robert, un jeune américain de Louisiane, arrive devant l'immeuble où habitent Thomas et son colocataire Claude.

Robert ouvre la lettre de Thomas, consulte les instructions et vérifie l'adresse. Il lit: *«Mon appartement se trouve 38, rue Dauphine. C'est un grand immeuble avec une porte bleue. J'habite au deuxième étage.»* «Oui, c'est bien là», pense-t-il. Il descend de la voiture, entre dans l'immeuble et monte l'escalier.

Il sonne à la porte de l'appartement. Quelques instants après, une jolie jeune femme lui ouvre la porte.

— Euh... Bonjour, mademoiselle, je suis Robert. C'est bien ici que Claude et Thomas habitent?

— Claude, c'est moi. Mais...

Robert, très surpris, l'interrompt et s'exclame:

— Claude, c'est vous? Euh... Mais vous êtes une femme!

— Eh oui, monsieur, je suis bien une femme! répond la jeune femme.

— Euh... je veux dire que... C'est que, vous comprenez, en anglais, Claude, c'est un prénom masculin, dit Robert.

— En français, monsieur, le prénom Claude est utilisé aussi bien pour une femme que pour un homme, répond la jeune femme.

— Ah, je comprends! Excusez-moi, mademoiselle. Je suis confus. Alors, vous êtes Claude. Moi, je suis Robert, Robert Martin. Est-ce que Thomas est ici?

— Thomas? dit-elle d'un air surpris.

— Eh oui, Thomas, mon ami. Il habite ici avec vous, n'est-ce pas?

— Mais certainement pas, monsieur! dit-elle d'un ton énervé.

Quand elle essaie de fermer la porte, Robert s'exclame:

— Un instant, s'il vous plaît, mademoiselle. Regardez! Voici l'adresse que mon ami m'a donnée.

Elle prend la lettre, lit les instructions et commence à comprendre.

— Oui, monsieur, c'est bien ici le 38, rue Dauphine, mais vous êtes au premier étage et votre ami habite au deuxième étage.

— Au premier étage? Ah! Oui, je comprends maintenant. *First floor,* c'est le rez de-chaussée et *second floor,* c'est le premier étage. Alors, je monte encore un étage pour trouver l'appartement de mon ami?

— Oui, monsieur, c'est bien ça. Au revoir, et bienvenue au Québec!

— Au revoir, mademoiselle, et merci.

## A. Vrai ou faux?

1. Robert arrive au 38, rue Dauphine, l'adresse de son ami Thomas.
2. Il monte directement au deuxième étage.
3. Il sonne et Claude, la jeune femme qui habite avec Thomas, ouvre la porte.
4. Claude est un prénom masculin et aussi un prénom féminin en français.
5. En France et au Québec, le *first floor,* c'est le rez-de-chaussée et le *second floor,* c'est le premier étage.

## B. Voilà pourquoi. Complétez le paragraphe pour expliquer la confusion de Robert.

homme  premier  premier  deuxième  deuxième  Thomas  Thomas

Robert entre dans l'immeuble pour trouver l'appartement de ___1___. Thomas habite au ___2___ étage avec Claude, un ami. Robert monte au ___3___ étage et sonne. Une jeune femme ouvre la porte. C'est Claude, mais elle n'habite pas avec Thomas. Robert ne comprend pas; il pense que la jeune femme habite avec ___4___. Voilà le problème: Robert est au ___5___ étage et Thomas et Claude habitent au ___6___ étage. C'est un autre Claude, un jeune ___7___, pas une jeune femme, qui habite avec Thomas.

# Talking about your possessions

**VOCABULAIRE SUPPLÉMENTAIRE**
**un réfrigérateur (un frigo)**
**une cuisinière** *a stove*
**un (four à) micro-ondes** *a microwave (oven)*
**un lave-vaisselle** *a dishwasher*
**un magnétoscope** *a VCR*
**une moto** *a motorcycle*
**une radio cassette K7** *a boombox*
**une table basse** *a coffee table*

## Les effets personnels

Qu'est-ce qu'il y a chez vous? **Avez-vous** beaucoup de **choses**?

Oui, **j'ai...**

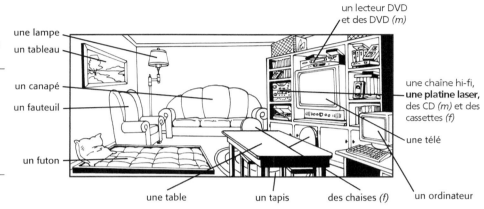

un lecteur DVD et des DVD *(m)*
une chaîne hi-fi, **une platine laser,** des CD *(m)* et des cassettes *(f)*
une télé
un ordinateur
une lampe
un tableau
un canapé
un fauteuil
un futon
une table
un tapis
des chaises *(f)*

Avez-vous aussi... ?

beaucoup de vêtements *(m)*     une voiture     un vélo     une plante     un chat     un chien

Chez Thomas **tout** est en ordre et bien **rangé.** Qu'est-ce qu'il y a... ?

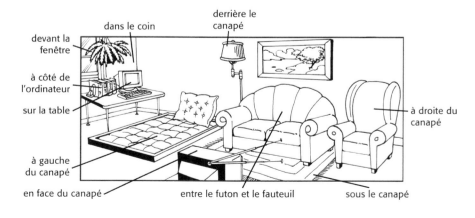

derrière le canapé
dans le coin
devant la fenêtre
à côté de l'ordinateur
sur la table
à gauche du canapé
en face du canapé
entre le futon et le fauteuil
à droite du canapé
sous le canapé

---

**vous avez (avoir** *to have*)     **une chose** *a thing*     **j'ai (avoir** *to have*)     **une platine laser** *a CD player*     **tout** *everything, all*
**rangé(e)** *arranged, put away, straightened up*

Avant d'arriver au Québec, Robert **cherche** un appartement. Il téléphone à Thomas.

CD 1-36

THOMAS: Tu cherches un appartement ici à Québec? Écoute, tu sais, moi, je **partage** un appartement avec mon ami Claude. **Nous avons** trois chambres; tu voudrais habiter avec nous?

ROBERT: **Peut-être.** Comment est **ton** appartement?

THOMAS: Il est assez grand et confortable, mais pas trop cher. Tu aimes les animaux?

ROBERT: Oui, pourquoi? **Tu as** des animaux?

THOMAS: **Claude a** un chien et un chat. Ils sont quelquefois **embêtants** et ils aiment dormir un peu **partout.**

ROBERT: Pas de problème. J'aime bien les animaux. Vous **fumez?**

THOMAS: Non, je ne fume pas et Claude **non plus.**

ROBERT: Bon, moi non plus. Alors ça va.

**A. Tu as... ?** Demandez à votre partenaire s'il/si elle a ces choses.

Exemple
— **Tu as une voiture?**
— **Oui, j'ai une voiture. / Non, je n'ai pas de voiture.**

1.     2.     3.     4.

5.     6.     7.     8.

**B. Qu'est-ce que c'est?** Regardez l'illustration du salon de Thomas en bas de la page précédente. Qu'est-ce qu'il y a dans chaque endroit *(place)?*

Exemple    sur la table
**Les livres sont sur la table.**

1. devant la fenêtre
2. en face du canapé
3. derrière le canapé
4. à droite des livres
5. à côté de l'ordinateur
6. dans le coin
7. à gauche de l'ordinateur
8. à droite du futon
9. entre le fauteuil et le futon
10. sous le canapé

**C. Conversation.** Avec un(e) partenaire, relisez à haute voix la conversation entre Robert et Thomas en haut de la page. Ensuite, imaginez que votre partenaire va habiter *(is going to live)* chez vous et changez la conversation pour décrire votre propre situation.

---

**chercher** *to look for*   **partager** *to share*   **Nous avons** (**avoir** *to have*)   **Peut-être** *Maybe, Perhaps*   **ton, ta, tes** *your (familiar)*
**Tu as** (**avoir** *to have*)   **Claude a** (**avoir** *to have*)   **embêtant(e)** *annoying*   **partout** *everywhere*   **fumer** *to smoke*
**non plus** *neither*

**1.** What does **avoir** mean? What are its forms? Why might one confuse the **tu** and **ils/elles** forms of **avoir** (to have) with those of **être** (to be)?

**2.** What does the indefinite article (**un, une, des**) change to after expressions of quantity such as **combien** or **beaucoup**? When else does this occur?

**3.** Which of these nouns would have a plural ending with **-x** instead of **-s**: **un hôpital, un animal, un tableau, un bureau, une table, un canapé?**

# Saying what you have
*Le verbe **avoir***

To say what someone has, use the verb **avoir.** Its conjugation is irregular.

| AVOIR *(to have)* | |
| --- | --- |
| j' **ai** | nous͜ᶻ **avons** |
| tu **as** | vous͜ᶻ **avez** |
| il/elle **a** | ils/elles͜ᶻ **ont** |

Remember that **un, une,** and **des** change to **de (d')** in most negative sentences and after expressions of quantity, such as **beaucoup** and **assez.** This change also occurs after the word **combien** (*how much, how many*).

| AFFIRMATIVE | NEGATIVE | AFTER AN EXPRESSION OF QUANTITY |
| --- | --- | --- |
| J'ai **des** chats. | Je n'ai pas **de** chats. | Combien **de** chats as-tu? |
| J'ai **une** plante. | Je n'ai pas **de** plantes. | J'ai beaucoup **de** plantes. |

**Un, une,** and **des** do not change after the verb **être** in negative sentences.

Ce sont **des** chats.          Ce ne sont pas **des** chats.

Although the plural of most nouns and adjectives is formed by adding **-s,** words ending in **eau, au,** or **eu** usually form their plural with **-x.** Words ending in **al** often change this ending to **-aux** in the plural.

un tableau    des tableau**x**    un bureau    des bureau**x**    un animal    des anim**aux**

CD 1-37

# Prononciation
*Avoir et Être*

Be careful to pronounce the forms of the verbs **avoir** and **être** distinctly. Open your mouth wide to pronounce the vowel **a** in **tu as** and **il/elle a.** Contrast this with the vowel sound in **es** and **est.** Pronounce **ils sont** with an **s** sound, and the liaison in **ils ont** with a **z** sound.

être: Tu es professeur.          avoir: Tu as beaucoup de cours.
Elle est professeur.                    Elle a beaucoup de cours.
Ils sont professeurs.                   Ils ͜ᶻ ont beaucoup de cours.

**A. Avoir ou être?** Entendez-vous le verbe **être,** comme dans la question **a,** ou le verbe **avoir,** comme dans la question **b?**

> **Exemple**     **a.** Tu es extraverti(e)?     **b.** Tu as beaucoup d'amis?
> VOUS ENTENDEZ:  tu as
> VOUS RÉPONDEZ:  **b**

**1. a.** Est-ce que tu es marié(e)?          **b.** Est-ce que tu as des animaux?
**2. a.** Ton appartement, il est comment?     **b.** Il a combien de chambres?
**3. a.** Ton immeuble, il est grand?          **b.** Il a combien d'étages?
**4. a.** Tes parents, ils sont d'ici?          **b.** Ils ont une grande maison?
**5. a.** Tes parents, ils sont intellectuels?   **b.** Ils ont beaucoup de livres?

Maintenant, posez ces questions à un(e) partenaire.

**B. Qu'est-ce qu'ils ont?** Complétez ces phrases selon le modèle.

**Exemple**  Moi, je (j')... (un chat, un chien).
**Moi, j'ai un chat. Je n'ai pas de chien.**

1. Chez moi, je (j')... (une chaîne hi-fi, des CD de musique française, un ordinateur, des plantes, une platine laser, beaucoup de DVD).
2. Mon meilleur ami (Ma meilleure amie)... (un chien, un chat, beaucoup de vêtements, une voiture, un vélo).
3. Dans le cours de français, nous... (beaucoup de devoirs, beaucoup d'examens, cours le lundi, cours le mardi, un examen aujourd'hui).
4. Généralement, les étudiants à l'université... (un vélo, une voiture, beaucoup de temps libre, 25 heures de cours par semaine)

**C. Chez Thomas et Claude.** Robert et ses amis parlent de ce qu'ils ont dans l'appartement. Qu'est-ce que Robert dit?

**Exemple**  **Nous avons des tableaux.**

Nous...

**1.** Thomas et Claude...

**2.** Claude...

**3.** Je (J')...

**4.** Thomas, est-ce que tu... ?

**5.** Claude et toi, est-ce que vous... ?

Maintenant, demandez à un(e) partenaire combien de ces choses il/elle a.

**Exemple**  **— Combien de tableaux est-ce que tu as?**
**— J'ai beaucoup de tableaux. / Je n'ai pas de tableaux.**

**D. Oui ou non?** Vous cherchez un nouveau logement et vous parlez à d'autres étudiants qui voudraient partager leur *(their)* appartement / maison. Complétez leurs phrases avec la forme correcte du verbe **avoir.** Ensuite, dites si vous voudriez habiter avec ces personnes. Répondez **oui, non** ou **peut-être.**

1. J'_____ un très bel appartement et le loyer n'est pas trop cher.
2. Tu aimes les animaux? J'_____ trois colocataires et ils _____ neuf chats et trois petits chiens.
3. Nous _____ une grande maison près de l'université. Les chambres _____ beaucoup de fenêtres et une belle vue *(view).*
4. Mon colocataire _____ beaucoup d'amis qui fument dans l'appartement.
5. Tu _____ une voiture? Mon immeuble n'_____ pas de parking mais il est près de tout. Moi, j'_____ un vélo.
6. J'_____ un appartement. Il est au cinquième étage mais nous _____ deux nouveaux ascenseurs.
7. L'immeuble n'_____ pas assez d'eau chaude, mais le loyer est seulement *(only)* de deux cents dollars par mois et j'_____ un très joli appartement.

**Pour vérifier**

**1.** How do you say *on? under? facing? next to?*

**2.** What does the preposition **de** mean? With which two forms of the definite article does it combine to form **du** and **des?**

# Saying where something is
*Quelques prépositions*

You can use the following prepositions to tell where something or someone is.

| | |
|---|---|
| **sur** *on* | **à côté (de)** *next to, beside* |
| **sous** *under* | **à droite (de)** *to the right (of)* |
| **entre** *between* | **à gauche (de)** *to the left (of)* |
| **dans** *in* | **en face (de)** *across (from), facing* |
| **devant** *in front of* | **près (de)** *near* |
| **derrière** *behind* | **loin (de)** *far (from)* |
| | **dans le coin (de)** *in the corner (of)* |

When used by itself, the preposition **de** means *of, from,* or *about.* It is also used with some of the prepositions above. When **de** is followed by a definite article and a noun, it combines with the masculine singular **le** and the plural **les** to form the contractions **du** and **des.** It does not change when followed by **la** or **l'**.

| CONTRACTIONS WITH *DE* | | | |
|---|---|---|---|
| de + le | → | du | J'habite près **du** centre-ville. |
| de + la | → | de la | La salle de classe est près **de la** bibliothèque. |
| de + l' | → | de l' | Mon appartement est près **de l'**université. |
| de + les | → | des | Il n'y a pas de parking près **des** résidences. |

CD 1-38

# Prononciation
*De, du, des*

Be careful to pronounce **de, du,** and **des** distinctly.

- As you know, the **e** in words like **de, le,** and **ne** is pronounced with the lips slightly puckered. The tongue is held firm in the lower part of the mouth.
- The **u** in **du,** as in **tu,** is pronounced with the tongue arched firmly near the roof of the mouth, as when pronouncing the French vowel **i** in **il,** but with the lips puckered.
- The vowel in **des** is a sharp sound like the **é** in **café,** pronounced with the corners of the lips spread.

**A. Dans la salle de classe.** Choisissez les mots en italique qui décrivent le mieux votre cours de français.

1. Le professeur *est / n'est pas* dans la salle de classe maintenant.
2. D'habitude, le professeur est *devant / derrière* les étudiants.
3. Le professeur *est / n'est pas* en face de moi maintenant.
4. Moi, je suis *près / loin* de la porte.
5. La porte est *à gauche de / à droite de / devant / derrière* nous.
6. *Je suis / Je ne suis pas* entre le professeur et la porte.
7. *Je suis / Je ne suis pas* dans le coin de la salle de classe.
8. Le tableau est *devant les étudiants / derrière les étudiants / à côté des étudiants.*

**B. C'est où?** Une amie de Thomas décrit *(is describing)* le salon chez elle. Complétez ses phrases avec la forme convenable de la préposition **de (de, du, de la, de l', des).** Ensuite *(Then)*, regardez l'illustration et dites si les phrases sont vraies ou fausses. Corrigez les phrases fausses.

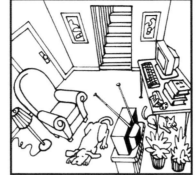

1. Sur la table, les livres sont à gauche _____ ordinateur.
2. L'ordinateur est à côté _____ mes livres.
3. La télé est en face _____ fauteuil.
4. L'escalier est à gauche _____ table.
5. La télé est à côté _____ plantes.
6. La lampe est à côté _____ fauteuil.
7. Le chien est à gauche _____ télé.
8. La porte est en face _____ escalier.

**C. Descriptions.** Faites des phrases pour décrire le salon dans ***B. C'est où?***

> Exemple    les livres / la table
> **Les livres sont sur la table.**

1. le chat / la table
2. la télé / le fauteuil
3. les plantes / la télé
4. le chien / le fauteuil et la télé
5. le chien / le fauteuil
6. la table / le salon
7. la porte / le fauteuil
8. les livres / l'ordinateur
9. l'ordinateur / la table
10. l'escalier / les tableaux

**D. À vendre.** Avec un(e) partenaire, préparez au moins huit phrases décrivant cette maison.

> Exemple    **Quand vous entrez** *(enter)* **dans la maison, les toilettes sont à gauche de la porte et le bureau est à droite. Derrière les toilettes il y a…**

au rez-de-chaussée

au premier étage

**E. Qui est-ce?** Utilisez trois prépositions pour dire où se trouve un(e) camarade de classe. Lisez votre description et un(e) autre étudiant(e) va identifier *(is going to identify)* la personne décrite.

> Exemple    — **Elle est près de la fenêtre. Elle est à droite de Paul et elle est derrière Catherine.**
> — **C'est Julie?**
> — **Oui.**

# Describing your room

## Les meubles et les couleurs

Thomas **montre** les chambres à Robert.

Voilà ta chambre. Tu as...

un placard
une affiche
des rideaux *(m)*
une commode
un bureau
un tapis
un lit
une étagère

C'est une chambre agréable. **Les murs** sont beiges et le tapis et les rideaux sont bleus. **La couverture** est bleue, rouge et verte. **J'espère** que **ça te plaît!**

Voilà **ma** chambre.
Ma chambre est toujours **propre** et en ordre.
Tout est **à sa place.**
Mes murs sont blancs et mon tapis est jaune.

Voilà la chambre de Claude.
**Sa** chambre est souvent un peu **sale** et en désordre. Il **laisse** tout **par terre.**
Sa couverture est noire, marron et grise.

Et vous? Comment est votre chambre? De quelle couleur *(f)* est votre tapis? De quelle couleur sont vos murs?

Voici des adjectifs pour indiquer la couleur de quelque chose.

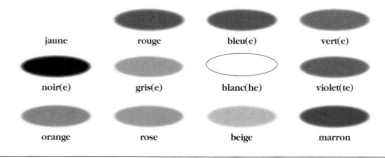

jaune        rouge        bleu(e)        vert(e)

noir(e)        gris(e)        blanc(he)        violet(te)

orange        rose        beige        marron

**NOTES DE VOCABULAIRE**

**1.** Note that **laisser** means *to leave* in the sense of leaving something somewhere, but not in the sense of leaving a place.
**2.** The formal version of **ça te plaît** is **ça vous plaît.**

**NOTE DE GRAMMAIRE**

As adjectives, the words for colors follow the noun they describe and must agree with it in gender and number: **des chaises bleues. Orange** and **marron** are exceptions. They are invariable and never change form. All colors are invariable when followed by adjectives such as **clair** *(light)*, **foncé** *(dark)*, or **vif** *(bright)*: **Ma voiture est bleu clair.**

**VOCABULAIRE SUPPLÉMENTAIRE**

**bleu clair** *light blue*
**bleu foncé** *dark blue*
**bleu vif** *bright blue*
**écossais(e)** *plaid*
**à fleurs** *floral*
**imprimé(e)** *print*
**rayé(e)** *striped*
**uni(e)** *solid-colored*

**Les meubles** *Furniture, Furnishings*    **montrer** *to show*    **un mur** *a wall*    **une couverture** *a blanket, a cover*    **espérer** *(conjugated like* **préférer***) to hope*    **ça te plaît** *you like it*    **mon, ma, mes** *my*    **propre** *clean*    **à sa place** *in its place*    **son, sa, ses** *his, her, its*    **sale** *dirty*    **laisser** *to leave*    **par terre** *on the floor, on the ground*

CD 1-39

Thomas montre les chambres à Robert.

THOMAS: Voici la chambre de Claude à côté de la cuisine. Sa chambre est toujours en désordre. Il laisse ses vêtements partout.

ROBERT: C'est ta chambre en face de la chambre de Claude?

THOMAS: Oui, **comme tu vois,** je préfère avoir tout bien rangé et **chaque** chose à sa place.

ROBERT: Et ça, c'est ma chambre **au bout du couloir?**

THOMAS: Oui, **viens voir...** Tu as un lit, une commode et une grande fenêtre avec **une** belle **vue.** J'espère que ça te plaît.

ROBERT: Oui, ça me plaît beaucoup!

THOMAS: Les murs sont beiges. Tu préfères une autre couleur?

ROBERT: Non, **justement,** le beige, c'est ma couleur **préférée.**

THOMAS: Moi, je préfère le vert.

---

**A. Chez vous?** Indiquez ce qui est vrai chez vous.

| (presque) toujours | | souvent | | quelquefois |
|---|---|---|---|---|
| | rarement | | ne... jamais | |

**Exemple** Ma chambre est en ordre.
**Ma chambre est presque toujours en ordre. /**
**Ma chambre n'est jamais en ordre.**

1. Ma chambre est propre.
2. Ma chambre est en désordre.
3. Mes livres sont sur l'étagère.
4. Ma chambre est sale.
5. Mes vêtements sont par terre.
6. Mes livres sont sur le lit.
7. Je laisse mes vêtements partout.
8. Mes livres sont sur le bureau.
9. Mes vêtements sont dans le placard ou dans la commode.

**B. Les couleurs.** Complétez les phases suivantes avec le nom d'une couleur.

1. Je préfère les vêtements...
2. J'ai beaucoup de vêtements...
3. Je préfère avoir des murs...
4. Les murs de ma chambre sont...
5. La couverture de mon lit est...
6. Je préfère les voitures...
7. Ma voiture est...
8. Je préfère les meubles...
9. Chez moi, le canapé est...
10. Ma couleur préférée, c'est le...

**C. Conversation.** Avec un(e) partenaire, relisez la conversation entre Robert et Thomas en haut de la page. Ensuite, imaginez que votre partenaire va habiter *(is going to live)* chez vous et changez la conversation pour décrire votre propre maison / appartement.

---

**comme tu vois** *as you see* **chaque** *each* **au bout de** *at the end of* **le couloir** *the hallway, the corridor*
**viens voir** *come see* **une vue** *a view* **justement** *as a matter of fact, precisely, exactly* **préféré(e)** *favorite*

**1.** How do you say *my?* How do you say *your* (familiar)? What are the forms of each word?

**2.** When do you use **mon, ton,** and **son,** instead of **ma, ta,** and **sa** before a feminine noun?

**3.** Does French have different words for *his, her,* and *its?* How do you say *his house* and *her house* in French? How do you say *his dog* and *her dog?*

**4.** How do you say *John's friend* and *Mary's car* in French?

**5.** With which two forms of the definite article does **de** combine to form the contractions **du** and **des?**

# Identifying your belongings

*Les adjectifs possessifs* **mon, ton** *et* **son**

In French, the possessive adjectives **mon/ma/mes** *(my)*, **ton/ta/tes** *(your* [familiar]*)*, and **son/sa/ses** *(his, her, its)* agree in gender and number with the noun they precede. Note, however, that the masculine form is used before feminine nouns that begin with a vowel sound.

|  | **MASCULINE SINGULAR** | **FEMININE SINGULAR** *(plus consonant sound)* | **FEMININE SINGULAR** *(plus vowel sound)* | **PLURAL** |
|---|---|---|---|---|
| *my* | **mon** livre | **ma** cassette | **mon** amie | **mes** vêtements |
| *your* | **ton** livre | **ta** cassette | **ton** amie | **tes** vêtements |
| *his/her/its* | **son** livre | **sa** cassette | **son** amie | **ses** vêtements |

— C'est **ton** livre?
— Oui, c'est **mon** livre et ce sont **mes** cassettes aussi.
— C'est le livre de Thomas?
— Oui, c'est **son** livre et ce sont **ses** cassettes aussi.

The use of the forms **son/sa/ses** *(his, her, its)* depends on the gender and number of the object possessed, not the person who owns it. **Son/sa/ses** can all mean *his, her,* or *its.*

C'est **son** fauteuil.        C'est **son** fauteuil        Et c'est **son** fauteuil aussi.

In English, possession and relationship can be indicated by *'s.* In French, you need to use a phrase with the word **de.**

Voilà la chambre **de** Thomas.    *There is Thomas's room.*
C'est le chien **de** Claude.        *That's Claude's dog.*

Remember that **de** contracts with the articles **le** and **les** to form the contractions **du** and **des.** It does not change when followed by **la** or **l'.**

le livre **du** professeur        les livres **des** professeurs
la porte **de l'**appartement        la porte **de la** cuisine

**A. Compliments.** Faites un compliment à un ami avec l'adjectif le plus logique.

**Exemple**    sœur (méchante, sympa)
        **Ta sœur est sympa.**

1. amis (intéressants, ennuyeux)
2. chien (bête, très intelligent)
3. vêtements (beaux, laids)
4. chaîne hi-fi (vieille, excellente)
5. voiture (laide, belle)
6. appartement (grand, petit)
7. chambre (agréable, désagréable)
8. chat (sympa, embêtant)

Maintenant, décrivez vos amis et vos affaires.

**Exemple**    **Ma sœur est jolie et très intelligente. / Je n'ai pas de sœur.**

**B. De quelle couleur?** Demandez à votre partenaire de quelle couleur sont ces choses. Utilisez **ton, ta** ou **tes.**

> **Exemple** — **De quelle couleur est ta voiture?**
> — **Ma voiture est grise. / Je n'ai pas de voiture.**

| voiture | canapé | fauteuil préféré | vêtements préférés |
|---------|--------|------------------|--------------------|
| chambre | vélo | tapis | rideaux | ordinateur |

Maintenant, décrivez les affaires *(belongings)* de votre partenaire à la classe.

> **Exemple** **Sa voiture est grise. / Il/Elle n'a pas de voiture.**

**C. C'est à moi!** Deux colocataires ne veulent plus *(no longer want)* habiter ensemble. Un locataire change d'appartement et il voudrait tout prendre avec lui *(him)* mais l'autre locataire n'est pas d'accord. Jouez les rôles avec un(e) partenaire.

> **Exemple** la plante — **Bon, je prends** *(I'm taking)* **ma plante.**
> — **Ah non, ce n'est pas ta plante. C'est ma plante!**

1. le bureau
2. le canapé
3. les tableaux
4. la table
5. la commode
6. l'étagère
7. la platine laser
8. les CD
9. les affiches

**D. La chambre de qui?** Complétez chaque phrase avec **son, sa** ou **ses.** Ensuite, regardez les illustrations et dites si la phrase décrit la chambre de Thomas ou la chambre de Claude.

> **Exemple** _____Sa_____ chambre est en ordre.
> **La chambre de Thomas est en ordre.**

la chambre de Thomas

1. _____ tapis est jaune.
2. _____ couverture est verte.
3. _____ murs sont blancs.
4. _____ rideaux sont gris.
5. _____ vélo est rouge.
6. Il n'y a pas d'affiches dans _____ chambre.
7. Beaucoup de _____ affaires sont par terre.
8. Il y a un livre rouge sous _____ bureau.
9. _____ chambre est propre.
10. _____ chambre est un peu sale.

la chambre de Claude

**E. Comparaisons.** Regardez bien les illustrations de l'activité **D. La chambre de qui?** Fermez votre livre et travaillez en groupe pour comparer de mémoire la chambre de Thomas et la chambre de Claude. Le groupe qui trouve le plus grand nombre de comparaisons correctes gagne.

> **Exemples** **Les murs de Thomas sont blancs mais les murs de Claude sont gris.**
> **Le bureau de Thomas est devant sa fenêtre et le bureau de Claude est devant une fenêtre aussi...**

## Indicating to whom something belongs

*Les adjectifs possessifs **notre, votre** et **leur***

You learned to use **mon/ma/mes, ton/ta/tes,** and **son/sa/ses** to indicate possession. The possessive adjectives for *our, your* (formal or plural), and *their* have only two forms, singular (**notre, votre,** and **leur**) and plural (**nos, vos,** and **leurs**).

|  | MASCULINE SINGULAR | FEMININE SINGULAR (plus consonant sound) | FEMININE SINGULAR (plus vowel sound) | PLURAL |
|---|---|---|---|---|
| *my* | **mon** lit | **ma** chambre | **mon** amie | **mes** livres |
| *your* (fam.) | **ton** lit | **ta** chambre | **ton** amie | **tes** livres |
| *his/her/its* | **son** lit | **sa** chambre | **son** amie | **ses** livres |
| *our* | **notre** lit | **notre** chambre | **notre** amie | **nos** livres |
| *your* (form./pl.) | **votre** lit | **votre** chambre | **votre** amie | **vos** livres |
| *their* | **leur** lit | **leur** chambre | **leur** amie | **leurs** livres |

## Prononciation

CD 1-40

*La voyelle **o** de **notre/votre** et de **nos/vos***

Compare the **o** sounds in **notre/votre** and **nos/vos.** The lips are puckered to make both of these sounds and the tongue is held firm, but the **o** in **nos/vos** is pronounced with the back of the tongue arched higher in the mouth than for the **o** in **notre** and **votre.** The letter **o** is pronounced with the sound of **nos** when it is the last sound in a syllable, when it is followed by an **s,** or when it is written **ô.** Otherwise, it is pronounced with the more open sound of **notre.**

notre chien / nos chiens          votre chat / vos chats

**A. Chez nous.** D'abord, complétez les questions suivantes avec **votre** ou **vos.** Ensuite, imaginez que deux amis voudraient persuader un troisième ami de partager leur appartement. Comment répondent-ils aux questions? Utilisez **notre** ou **nos** dans les réponses.

> **Exemple** — __Votre__ quartier est joli?
> — **Oui, notre quartier est très joli.**

1. _____ appartement est très cher?
2. _____ chiens sont méchants?
3. _____ cuisine est grande?
4. _____ parents passent beaucoup de temps à l'appartement?
5. _____ appartement a beaucoup de fenêtres?
6. Comment est la vue de _____ appartement?

**B. Préférences.** Aimez-vous ces choses? Utilisez **leur/leurs** ou **son/sa/ses** dans vos réponses.

**Exemples**     les vieux films avec Fred Astaire et Ginger Rogers
**J'aime bien leurs films.**

les vieux films d'Alfred Hitchcock
**Je n'aime pas beaucoup ses films.**

1. les films de Steven Spielberg     **4.** la musique de Jennifer Lopez
2. les vieux films avec les «Three Stooges»    **5.** les CD des Dixie Chicks
3. la musique des Beatles     **6.** les CD de Sting

**C. L'université Laval.** Comparez votre université avec l'université Laval en complétant les phases avec **notre/nos** ou **leur/leurs.**

**Exemple**     Fondée en 1852, l'université Laval est la première université francophone en Amérique.
**Leur** université est plus vieille que **notre** université. /
**Notre** université est plus vieille que **leur** université.

1. Il y a approximativement 37 000 étudiants à l'université Laval. _____ université est plus grande que _____ université.
2. Les frais de scolarité *(tuition)* sont de 1 800$ canadiens (= 1 430$ américains) par an *(per year)* pour les Québécois et de 3 000$ (= 2 385$ américains) par an pour les Canadiens des autres provinces. _____ université est plus chère que _____ université.
3. Le semestre d'automne commence le 1ᵉʳ septembre à l'université Laval. _____ cours commencent avant _____ cours.
4. Il y a 10 000 places pour les voitures dans les parkings de l'université Laval. _____ parkings sont plus grands que _____ parkings.
5. Il y a 2 400 chambres dans les résidences universitaires. _____ université a plus de chambres que _____ université.
6. Le loyer d'une chambre dans une résidence universitaire est de 222$ canadiens (= 176$ américains) par mois. _____ résidences sont plus chères que _____ résidences.
7. L'université Laval est située à Québec, une ville de 645 000 habitants. _____ ville est plus grande que _____ ville.

**D. Vrai ou faux?** Complétez les phrases suivantes avec la forme correcte du verbe **avoir** dans le premier blanc et l'adjectif possessif correspondant dans le deuxième. Ensuite dites si la phrase est **vraie** ou **fausse** pour vous. Corrigez les phrases fausses.

**Exemple**     Mon colocataire et moi **avons** deux salles de bains.
**Notre** appartement est assez grand.
**Faux. J'habite seul(e) et j'ai une salle de bains.**
**Mon appartement est très petit.**

1. Mon colocataire et moi _____ des voisins *(neighbors)* sympas. Nous passons beaucoup de temps chez _____ voisins.
2. Mes voisins _____ beaucoup de jolies plantes dans _____ jardin.
3. Nous _____ beaucoup d'arbres dans _____ quartier.
4. J'_____ trois grandes fenêtres dans _____ chambre.
5. Mes parents _____ une maison à la campagne. _____ maison a trois salles de bains.
6. Mon meilleur ami _____ un joli appartement. _____ appartement est près d'ici.
7. Mes parents _____ deux chiens. _____ chiens sont très intelligents.
8. Nous _____ une piscine *(pool)* chez nous. _____ amis passent beaucoup de temps chez nous.

# Giving your address and phone number

## Des renseignements

> Note
*culturelle*

Avant d'entrer à l'université au Québec, tout étudiant doit faire deux ans *(years)* d'études gratuites *(free of charge)* dans un collège d'enseignement général et professionnel, l'équivalent québécois d'un *community college*. Quels sont les avantages d'étudier dans un *community college* avant d'aller à l'université? Est-ce que les études dans un *community college* devraient *(should)* être gratuites ici?

---

**NOTES DE VOCABULAIRE**

**1.** In an e-mail address, say **arobase** for @ and **point** for *dot*.

**2.** You generally use **demander** to say *to ask*, but use **poser une question** for *to ask a question*.

Pour **s'inscrire** à l'université, Robert **doit** donner les **renseignements suivants.**

| | |
|---|---|
| Quel est votre nom? | Martin. |
| Quel est votre prénom? | Robert. |
| Quelle est votre adresse? | C'est le 215, Ursline St. |
| Quelle est votre (adresse) mail? | RobMart@airmail.net |
| Quel est votre numéro de téléphone? | C'est le (337) 988-1284. |
| Dans quel pays habitez-vous? | Les États-Unis. |
| Quel état? (Quelle province?) | La Louisiane. |
| Quelle ville? | Lafayette. |
| Quelle est votre nationalité? | Américaine. |

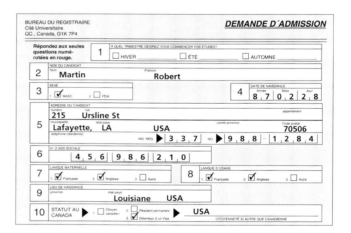

CD 1-41

Robert parle de son appartement et son ami Alain lui **pose des questions.**

| | |
|---|---|
| ALAIN: | Quelle est ton adresse? |
| ROBERT: | C'est le 38, **rue** Dauphine. |
| ALAIN: | Et c'est quel appartement? |
| ROBERT: | C'est l'appartement numéro 231. |
| ALAIN: | Et le code postal? |
| ROBERT: | G1K 7X2. |
| ALAIN: | Quel est ton numéro de téléphone? |
| ROBERT: | C'est le 692-2691. |
| ALAIN: | Et comment est le quartier? |
| ROBERT: | Il est agréable et près de tout. |
| ALAIN: | L'appartement n'est pas trop cher? C'est combien, le loyer? |
| ROBERT: | Je partage mon appartement avec deux amis, Thomas et Claude. C'est 825 dollars par mois, partagés entre nous trois. Alors pour moi, ça fait 275 dollars. |

---

**s'inscrire** *to register*   **il doit (devoir** *must, to have to)*   **les renseignements** *(m) information*   **suivant(e)** *following*
**poser une question** *to ask a question*   **une rue** *a street*

NOTE DE VOCABULAIRE

In French, the province is **le Québec** and the city, **Québec**.

**A. Et Thomas?** Quels renseignements est-ce que Thomas donne?

> **Exemple**    Bertrand
> **C'est son nom.**

1. Thomas
2. Québec
3. le Québec
4. le Canada
5. le 38, rue Dauphine

6. G1K 7X2
7. le 692-2691
8. Thomas1@homemail.com
9. 825$ par mois

**B. Et vous?** Répondez aux questions suivantes.

1. Quel est votre nom? Quel est votre prénom?
2. Quelle est votre adresse?
3. Vous habitez dans quelle ville?
4. Quel est votre numéro de téléphone?
5. Quelle est votre (adresse) mail?
6. Quelle est votre nationalité?

**C. Un abonnement.** Vous vendez des abonnements *(are selling subscriptions)* pour la revue *Brune*. Demandez les renseignements nécessaires pour compléter le formulaire d'abonnement pour un(e) camarade de classe.

> **Exemple**    — **Quel est ton nom?**
> — **Mon nom? C'est Sodji.**
> — **Quel est ton prénom? ...**

BULLETIN D'ABONNEMENT

Je désire m'abonner pour un an (4 numéros) à BRUNE.

TARIFS (par avion, sauf France)

| | |
|---|---|
| 7 000 F CFA . . . Afrique Zone CFA | 20 € . .France |
| 10 000 F CFA . . Afrique Hors Zone CFA | 30 € . .CEE |
| 40 $. . . . . . . . . . USA-Canada | 25 € . .Dom-Tom |

Règlement exclusivement par mandat international libellé en euros. France et Dom-Tom: paiement par chèque ou mandat-lettre à l'ordre de BRUNE.

Découper et retourner ce formulaire d'abonnement accompagné de votre règlement à:

BRUNE - SERVICE ABONNEMENTS
10, rue Charles-Divry - 75014 PARIS - FRANCE

NOM..............................................

PRÉNOM ......................................

ADRESSE ....................................

.....................................................

CODE POSTAL ............................

VILLE ...........................................

PAYS ...........................................

**D. Conversation.** Avec un(e) partenaire, relisez à haute voix la conversation entre Robert et son ami à la page précédente. Ensuite, changez la conversation pour décrire votre propre situation.

**1.** When do you use **quel** to say *what?* When do you use **qu'est-ce que** or **que?** What are the four forms of **quel?**

**2.** How do you say *this, that, these,* and *those?* When do you use the alternate masculine form **cet?** What suffixes can you add when you need to distinguish *this* from *that* or *these* from *those?*

## Telling which one
### Les adjectifs *quel* et *ce*

Use **quel** to say *which* before a noun. Also use it to say *what* when:

- *what* is followed by *is* or *are*

  *Quelle est votre adresse?*
  *Quelles sont tes villes préférées?*

- *what* is followed directly by a noun

  Dans *quel appartement* habitez-vous?

**Quel** agrees with the gender and number of the noun it modifies.

|          | MASCULINE | FEMININE |
|----------|-----------|----------|
| **SINGULAR** | quel | quelle |
| **PLURAL**   | quels | quelles |

**Quel** est votre numéro de téléphone?    **Quels** sont vos quartiers préférés?
**Quelle** est votre adresse?    **Quelles** sont vos villes préférées?

Remember to use **qu'est-ce que** or **que** to say *what* when it is the object of the verb. They are followed by a subject and a verb.

**Qu'est-ce que** Robert aime faire?    **Que** voudrais-tu faire ce soir?

To point out which item or person you are talking about, use the adjective **ce** (**cet**)/**cette**/**ces** to say both *this/these* and *that/those.* The masculine **ce** becomes **cet** before masculine singular nouns beginning with a vowel sound. Use **ces** with all plural nouns.

|          | SINGULAR | PLURAL |
|----------|----------|--------|
| **MASCULINE (plus consonant sound)** | ce canapé | ces canapés |
| **MASCULINE (plus vowel sound)**     | cet appartement | ces appartements |
| **FEMININE**                         | cette maison | ces maisons |

If you need to distinguish *this* from *that,* you can add the suffixes **-ci** and **-là** to the noun.

Tu préfères **cette** voiture**-ci** ou **cette** voiture**-là?**
*Do you prefer this car or that car?*

CD 1-42

## Prononciation
### La voyelle *e* de *ce/cet/cette/ces*

You already know that a final **e** is usually not pronounced in French, except in short words like **je.** As you notice in **ce/cet/cette/ces,** unaccented **e** has three different pronunciations, depending on what follows it.

In short words like **ce** and **que,** or when **e** is followed by a single consonant within a word, pronounce it as in:

je      ne      le      regarde      vendredi

When, as in **ces, e** is followed by an unpronounced consonant at the end of a word, pronounce it as in:

les      mes      parlez      manger      premier

In words like **cette** and **cet,** where **e** is followed by two consonants within a word, or a single pronounced consonant at the end of a word, pronounce it as in:

quel      cher      belle      elle      cherche

**A. Renseignements.** Formez des questions pour obtenir ces renseignements d'un(e) camarade de classe.

Exemple     numéro de téléphone
    — **Quel est ton numéro de téléphone?**
    — **C'est le quatre cent quarante-quatre, vingt-deux, soixante-quinze.**

nom       prénom       adresse       code postal       ???
numéro de téléphone       nationalité       adresse mail       couleur préférée

**B. Comparaisons.** Utilisez **ce, cet, cette** ou **ces** pour faire des comparaisons.

Exemple     cours     **Ce cours-ci est difficile, mais ce cours-là est facile.**

Exemple   cours     **1.** jeune homme     **2.** jeune femme     **3.** étudiant

**4.** chiens     **5.** maison     **6.** appartement     **7.** vêtements

**C. Préférences.** Demandez à votre partenaire quelles sont ses préférences. Après, donnez votre réaction à sa réponse en utilisant **ce, cet, cette** ou **ces.** (*If you aren't familiar with what he/she names, say* **Je ne connais pas…** )

Exemple     restaurant     — **Quel restaurant est-ce que tu aimes beaucoup?**
    — **J'aime beaucoup Pizza Nizza.**
    — **Moi aussi, j'aime beaucoup ce restaurant. /**
    **Moi, je n'aime pas ce restaurant. /**
    **Je ne connais pas ce restaurant.**

**1.** librairie       **4.** vidéo
**2.** café       **5.** sports
**3.** CD       **6.** voitures

**D. Entretien.** Complétez les questions suivantes avec la forme convenable de **quel** ou avec **qu'est-ce que.** Ensuite, posez les questions à votre partenaire.

**1.** _____ il y a dans ta chambre?
**2.** Dans _____ pièce est-ce que tu passes le plus de temps?
**3.** _____ tu voudrais acheter *(to buy)* pour ton salon ou pour ta chambre?
**4.** Dans _____ rue est-ce que tu habites?
**5.** Ta chambre est à _____ étage?
**6.** De _____ couleur sont les murs de ta chambre?
**7.** _____ tu voudrais changer chez toi?

## Reprise
*Saying where you live and what you have*

In *Chapitre 3,* you learned to talk about your belongings and where you live. Now you have a chance to review what you learned.

### A. Quelques questions.
Vous cherchez un(e) colocataire et un(e) autre étudiant(e) vous pose les questions suivantes. D'abord, complétez les questions avec **de, d', du, de la, de l'** ou **des.** Ensuite, posez les questions à votre partenaire.

1. Est-ce que tu habites près ou loin _____ centre-ville?
2. Tu habites près _____ université?
3. Y a-t-il un arrêt d'autobus près _____ chez toi?
4. Qu'est-ce qu'il y a en face _____ chez toi?
5. Est-ce que ta chambre est près _____ cuisine?
6. Dans ta chambre, qu'est-ce qu'il y a en face _____ lit?
7. Dans le salon, qu'est-ce qu'il y a en face _____ télé?

### B. Une maison.
Utilisez une préposition pour décrire où les choses suivantes se trouvent l'une par rapport à l'autre *(in relationship to each other)* dans la maison. Suivez l'exemple.

> **Exemple**    le salon / les toilettes
> **Le salon est à gauche des toilettes.**

1. le salon / la cuisine et les toilettes
2. la salle de bains / la chambre
3. le canapé / le salon
4. la lampe / le fauteuil
5. le fauteuil / l'escalier
6. la salle à manger / la cuisine
7. la table / la salle à manger
8. la table / le tapis

Maintenant, travaillez avec un(e) partenaire pour continuer la description de la maison.

> **Exemple**    **C'est une grande maison. Il y a un escalier. Le salon est au rez-de-chaussée. Dans le salon, il y a...**

### C. Qu'est-ce que vous avez?
Complétez les phrases suivantes avec le verbe **avoir** dans le premier blanc et un adjectif possessif dans le deuxième.

> **Exemple**    J'**ai** un portable *(cell phone).* **Mon** numéro de téléphone, c'est le 825-5479.

1. J'_____ un appartement au centre-ville. _____ adresse, c'est le 202, rue Cisneros.
2. Nous _____ beaucoup de restaurants dans _____ quartier.

**3.** Mes parents _____ une maison en banlieue. _____ jardin (*yard*) est très joli.

**4.** Mon meilleur ami (Ma meilleure amie) _____ un grand appartement très élégant. _____ loyer est de plus de mille dollars par mois.

**5.** J'_____ un appartement dans un quartier très agréable. _____ rue est très jolie.

**6.** Mon meilleur ami (Ma meilleure amie) _____ une belle voiture. _____ voiture est bleue.

**7.** À l'université, nous n'_____ pas beaucoup de parkings pour _____ voitures.

Maintenant, changez les phrases pour décrire votre situation ou celle de (*that of*) vos amis.

**D. C'est combien?** Vous cherchez du mobilier (*furnishings*) dans les annonces classées (*classified ads*) au Québec. Donnez le prix de chaque objet comme dans l'exemple. Utilisez **ce, cet, cette** ou **ces.**

> **Exemple**
>
> > MOBILIER CUISINE:
> > table, 6 chaises 450$.
> > Tél: 678-2665.
>
> **Cette table et ces chaises coûtent** (*cost*) **quatre cent cinquante dollars.**

**1.** TABLE SALLE À MANGER, laquée noire, 6 chaises laquées noires. Très propres. 1.150$. Tél: 760-7883.

**2.** MOBILIER salon fleuri (fauteuil, canapé) 550$. Tél: 842-5835.

**3.** TÉLÉ 48", Sony, état neuf 700$. Tél: 881-9896.

**4.** LIT D'EAU "king" complet: base, lit en pin, matelas anti-vagues, éléments chauffants. Le tout en très bon état, 150$. Tél: 653-5216.

**5.** TABLE D'ORDINATEUR: blanche, 3 tiroirs, en bon état, 115$. Tél: 832-7175.

**6.** FAUTEUIL en cuir noir. Excellente condition. 495$. Tél: 542-7060.

**E. Colocataire recherché.** Vous cherchez un nouveau logement au Québec dans les annonces classées (*classified ads*). Pour chaque annonce, faites deux ou trois phrases décrivant l'appartement / la maison ou le/la colocataire recherché(e).

> **Exemple**
>
> > COLOCATAIRE RECHERCHÉ 20–35 ans, non-fumeur, pour partager grande maison de ville, secteur paisible et recherché, près de tout, 260$/mois tout compris. Tél: 472-3472
>
> **Il/Elle cherche un(e) colocataire qui ne fume pas. La maison est grande et près de tout. Le loyer est de 260$ par mois.**

**1.** RECHERCHE FEMME OU HOMME avec emploi entre 20 et 35 ans, pour partager maison campagne, 5 minutes de la ville, très tranquille, 200$/mois. Tél: 875-3428.

**2.** RECHERCHE PERSONNE non-fumeuse pour partager appartement, 2ᵉ étage, 2 ch. Près autobus et parc, idéal pour étudiant(e), libre 15 oct. $300, 595-9065.

**3.** COLOCATAIRES RECHERCHÉS pour maison: 4 sdb / 2 salons / foyer / cuisine équipée. 450$. Tél: 680-4493.

Rue résidentielle au Québec

### Lecture: *Les couleurs et leurs effets sur la nature humaine*

You are going to read an article by an interior decorator in Quebec about how colors can change your moods. Before you begin to read, think about how different colors make you feel by doing the following activity.

**Associations.** Quelle couleur associez-vous le plus aux choses suivantes?

1. la passion
2. la dépression
3. la concentration
4. l'énergie
5. la relaxation
6. la pureté
7. l'appétit
8. l'irritation

### *Les couleurs et leurs effets sur la nature humaine*

Les couleurs changent nos **humeurs** et par conséquent reflètent notre personnalité. **Pour mieux vous faire connaître** les effets qu'ont les couleurs sur la nature humaine, nous avons préparé un guide qui va vous aider à choisir les couleurs pour votre maison ou appartement.

**Les couleurs chaudes: le rouge et le jaune.**
Le rouge stimule le métabolisme, le rythme cardiaque et la température corporelle. Le rouge est **perçu comme** une couleur agressive, **forte**, vitale et passionnante. **Puisque** c'est une couleur qui stimule l'appétit, le rouge est souvent utilisé pour les salles à manger et les restaurants.

Le jaune stimule la mémoire, le mouvement, la coordination et le système digestif. Le jaune et le rouge sont considérés comme «énergiques». Mais **faites attention,** le jaune dans une chambre de bébé **peut rendre** l'enfant irritable.

**Les couleurs froides: le bleu et le vert.**
Le bleu encourage la concentration. Le rythme cardiaque et la respiration **ralentissent**. La température du **corps baisse**. Cette couleur est très recommandée dans un bureau.

Le vert augmente la relaxation. Le corps et **l'esprit se détendent** dans une atmosphère verte. Le vert diminue l'anxiété, **la peur** et **les cauchemars.** Le vert encourage le sentiment de bien-être. Il est **donc parfait** pour une chambre à coucher.

**Les couleurs neutres: le blanc, le gris et le noir.**
Le blanc stimule les fonctions vitales, par conséquent **le sommeil** n'est pas aussi **bénéfique** dans une chambre blanche. Le blanc est aussi associé à la pureté et à l'honnêteté.

Le gris incite à la dépression et à l'indifférence. Il est préférable de l'utiliser comme accent plutôt que couleur dominante dans votre décor.

Le noir est une couleur distincte, audacieuse et classique. Le noir est un fond idéal **pour faire ressortir** les autres couleurs, mais il peut être **étouffant** en trop grande quantité.

---

**humeurs** *moods*  **Pour mieux vous faire connaître** *To inform you better about*  **perçu comme** *perceived as*  **forte** *strong*  **Puisque** *Since*  **faites attention** *be careful*  **peut rendre** *can make*  **froides** *cold*  **ralentissent** *slow down*  **corps** *body*  **baisse** *lowers*  **l'esprit** *the mind*  **se détendent** *relax*  **la peur** *fear*  **les cauchemars** *nightmares*  **donc** *therefore*  **parfait** *perfect*  **le sommeil** *sleep*  **bénéfique** *beneficial*  **pour faire ressortir** *to make stand out*  **étouffant** *stifling*

## Compréhension

Complétez les phrases suivantes avec les couleurs appropriées d'après la lecture *Les couleurs et leurs effets sur la nature humaine*.

1. Si vous désirez manger moins, évitez *(avoid)* le _____ pour décorer votre salle à manger.
2. Pour mieux vous concentrer, étudiez dans une pièce _____.
3. Si votre bébé pleure *(cries)* beaucoup, utilisez le _____ dans sa chambre et évitez le _____.
4. Si vous désirez mieux dormir, les murs _____ ne sont pas recommandés dans votre chambre.
5. Si vous souffrez de dépression, évitez le _____ dans votre décor.
6. Si vous avez souvent froid *(feel cold)* chez vous, utilisez le _____ et évitez le _____.

## Composition

**A. Organisez-vous.** Organizing your thoughts before you begin a writing assignment can greatly simplify your task. Imagine that you are responding to a roommate ad in Quebec. What would you want to know about the apartment and its occupant? Jot down as many words and phrases in French as you can under each heading, using a separate piece of paper.

| location | rooms and furnishings | roommate's personality |
| --- | --- | --- |
| | | |

**B. Rédaction: Une lettre.** You are moving to Quebec and respond to an ad for a roommate in the newspaper. Write a letter in which you introduce yourself and tell the sort of place you are looking for. Then, write three paragraphs asking about the apartment's location, the rooms and furnishings, and what the roommate is like. Begin the letter with **Cher monsieur / Chère madame / Chère mademoiselle.** End the letter with **En attendant votre réponse,** and sign your name.

If you have access to SYSTÈME-D software, you will find the following phrases, vocabulary, grammar, and dictionary aids there.

**Phrases:** Writing a letter; Introducing; Describing people; Asking for information
**Vocabulary:** House; Rooms; Furniture; Kitchen; Living room; Bedroom; Personality; Numbers; Direction and distance; Money
**Grammar:** Possessive adjectives; Demonstrative adjectives; Interrogative adjectives
**Dictionary:** The verb **avoir**

**C. Une réponse.** Exchange the letters you wrote in the preceding activity with a classmate and write a response describing yourself and the place where you live or an imaginary place where you would like to live.

**D. Colocataires.** You and the student with whom you exchanged letters in the previous activity have decided to become housemates. Choose one of your places and prepare a conversation in which the new housemate asks for information, such as the address, telephone number, rent, etc.

## Le Québec et la Révolution tranquille

Jacques Cartier

**En** 1534, Jacques Cartier, explorateur français, prend possession du Canada au nom de la France. **Pendant** les 17ᵉ et 18ᵉ **siècles** les Français et les Anglais se battent pour le contrôle du Canada. En 1763, la France est obligée de céder ses territoires canadiens aux Anglais. Pendant **200 ans**, les Québécois **vivent** sous la domination de la minorité anglophone.

Dans **les années 60,** les Québécois francophones commencent à **lutter** pour la préservation de la francophonie face à la majorité anglophone du Canada. **Cette lutte** pour la protection de leur identité culturelle **est connue** aujourd'hui sous le nom de *la Révolution tranquille.* **Vers la fin** des années soixante un mouvement séparatiste qui voudrait voir un Québec libre émerge. Le résultat en est la formation en 1968 d'un parti politique, le Parti québécois, qui **prend la tête** du mouvement pour la protection de l'identité québécoise et pour un Québec libre.

Voilà **quelques étapes** importantes dans la préservation de la langue et de la culture francophone au Québec.

**1977** Au Québec, les enfants d'immigrés sont obligés d'aller dans des **écoles** francophones. L'emploi du français est obligatoire dans toutes les transactions commerciales ou gouvernementales.

**1980** Au Québec, 40% des Québécois votent «oui» à un référendum pour un Québec indépendant.

**1982** Le bilinguisme **devient** obligatoire **à tous les niveaux** du gouvernement fédéral dans toutes les provinces canadiennes. Tout le Canada devient officiellement bilingue.

---

**Pendant** *During*   **siècles** *centuries*   **200 ans** *200 years*   **vivent** *live*   **les années 60** *the 60s*   **lutter** *to struggle*
**Cette lutte** *This struggle*   **est connue** *is known*   **Vers la fin** *Toward the end*   **prend la tête** *takes the lead*
**quelques étapes** *a few stages*   **écoles** *schools*   **devient** *becomes*   **à tous les niveaux** *at all levels*

**1987** Le gouvernement canadien donne au Québec le statut de «société distincte». Ce statut donne au Québec **le droit d'**annuler toute décision du gouvernement canadien qui menace la préservation de la culture francophone.

**1988** Au Québec, l'usage de l'anglais dans **l'affichage public** est **interdit**.

**1996** Au Québec, 49% des Québécois votent «oui» à un référendum pour un Québec indépendant.

**1998** La Cour suprême du Canada affirme que le Québec **ne peut pas** procéder unilatéralement à la sécession. La sécession unilatérale est inconstitutionnelle. Mais si une majorité **se montrait** en faveur de la sécession, le reste du Canada **aurait** alors l'obligation constitutionnelle de **négocier** les conditions de la sécession.

## À discuter

1. On appelle *(One calls)* les États-Unis un *melting pot* mais le Canada une mosaïque. Pourquoi?
2. Pensez-vous que la situation des Québécois francophones serait meilleure *(would be better)* dans un Québec indépendant?
3. Pensez-vous que ce qui se passe *(what is happening)* au Québec pourrait un jour avoir lieu *(could one day take place)* en Louisiane avec les francophones ou en Floride avec les Hispano-Américains?

visit http://horizons.heinle.com

---

**le droit de** *the right to*    **l'affichage public** *public signs*    **interdit** *forbidden*    **ne peut pas** *cannot*    **se montrait** *showed itself*
**aurait** *would have*    **négocier** *to negotiate*

# Résumé de grammaire

un million = *one million*
cent = *one hundred*
mille = *one thousand*

| | |
|---|---|
| 300 | trois cents |
| 301 | trois cent un |
| 3.000 | trois mille |
| 3.100.000 | trois millions cent mille |

## Numbers above 100

- Use **un** in **un million,** but not before the words **cent** and **mille.**
- Write **s** in the word **millions** in all numbers **deux millions** or greater and in the word **cent** in exact multiples of 100. Do not use **s** on the end of the word **mille** in any number, or **cent** when another number follows it.
- There is no hyphen between the words **cent, mille,** or **million** and another number.
- Use commas to denote decimals, and spaces or periods to set off numbers in the thousands, millions, etc.

Ma rue, c'est la première (deuxième, troisième, quatrième, cinquième, sixième, septième, huitième, neuvième, dixième, onzième… ) rue à droite.

## Ordinal numbers

Use **premier (première)** to say *first*. To form the other ordinal numbers *(second, third, fourth . . . )*, add the suffix **-ième** to the cardinal numbers **(deux, trois, quatre… ).** Drop the final **-e** of cardinal numbers before adding **-ième.** Note the spelling changes in **cinquième** *(fifth)* and **neuvième** *(ninth).*

— J'**ai** un appartement. Et toi? Tu **as** une maison?
— Ma famille **a** une petite maison. J'habite chez mes parents.
— Vous **avez** combien de chambres?
— Nous **avons** deux chambres. Mes parents **ont** la plus grande chambre et moi la plus petite.

## *Avoir*

The verb **avoir** *(to have)* is irregular.

| | |
|---|---|
| j'**ai** | nous **avons** |
| tu **as** | vous **avez** |
| il/elle **a** | ils/elles **ont** |

— Tu as **des** chats, non?
— Non, ce ne sont pas **des** chats. J'ai des chiens.
— Combien **de** chiens as-tu?
— Quatre.
— Tu n'as pas **de** problèmes avec tes colocataires?
— Non, je n'ai pas **de** colocataire.

un tableau → des tableaux
un bureau → des bureaux
un animal → des animaux

## *Un, une, des* → *de (d')*

**Un, une,** and **des** change to **de (d')** after…

- most negated verbs, except **être.**
- quantity expressions like **combien, beaucoup,** and **assez.**

## Plurals ending with *-x*

In the plural, most words ending in **eau, au,** or **eu** have **-x** rather than **-s,** and the ending **-al** becomes **-aux.**

## Prepositions

When used alone, the preposition **de** means *of, from,* or *about.* **De** is also used in some of the following prepositions.

Je rentre **de** l'université à cinq heures.
Ma résidence est **près d'**ici, **derrière** la bibliothèque et **à côté de** la librairie.

| | |
|---|---|
| **sur** *on* | **à côté (de)** *next to, beside* |
| **sous** *under* | **à droite / gauche (de)** *to the right / left (of)* |
| **entre** *between* | **en face (de)** *across (from), facing* |
| **dans** *in* | **près (de)** *near* |
| **devant** *in front of* | **loin (de)** *far (from)* |
| **derrière** *behind* | **dans le coin (de)** *in the corner (of)* |

De contracts with the articles **le** and **les,** but not with **la** or **l'**.

| CONTRACTION: | | | NO CONTRACTION: | | |
|---|---|---|---|---|---|
| de + le | → | du | de + la | → | de la |
| de + les | → | des | de + l' | → | de l' |

Je n'aime pas habiter à la résidence parce qu'elle est loin **du** parking et ma chambre est en face **des** ascenseurs, à côté **de l'**escalier et loin **de la** salle de bains!

## Possession

**De** is used instead of *'s* to indicate possession. Remember the contractions **de + le → du** and **de + les → des.**

| le bureau du professeur | *the professor's office* |
|---|---|
| la voiture de ma mère | *my mother's car* |

The possessive adjectives also indicate possession.

| | MASCULINE SINGULAR | FEMININE SINGULAR *(+ consonant sound)* | FEMININE SINGULAR *(+ vowel sound)* | PLURAL |
|---|---|---|---|---|
| *my* | **mon** vélo | **ma** voiture | **mon** adresse | **mes** meubles |
| *your* (fam.) | **ton** vélo | **ta** voiture | **ton** adresse | **tes** meubles |
| *his/her/its* | **son** vélo | **sa** voiture | **son** adresse | **ses** meubles |
| *our* | **notre** vélo | **notre** voiture | **notre** adresse | **nos** meubles |
| *your* (form./pl.) | **votre** vélo | **votre** voiture | **votre** adresse | **vos** meubles |
| *their* | **leur** vélo | **leur** voiture | **leur** adresse | **leurs** meubles |

— C'est ta voiture?
— Non, c'est la voiture **de** mon amie.

— C'est la porte **de la** salle de bains?
— Non, c'est la porte **du** placard.

— Tu habites encore chez **tes** parents?
— Non, j'habite chez **mon** frère.
— Où est **sa** maison?
— Pas loin de chez **nos** parents.
— Dans quelle rue est la maison de **vos** parents?
— **Leur** maison est dans la rue Martin.

Use the forms **mon, ton,** and **son** rather than **ma, ta,** and **sa** before feminine nouns beginning with vowel sounds.

The use of the forms **son/sa/ses** *(his, her, its)* depends on the gender and number of the object possessed, not the person who owns it. **Son/sa/ses** can all mean *his, her,* or *its*.

**Mon** amie s'appelle Monique.

son quartier = *his/her/its neighborhood*
sa porte = *his/her/its door*
ses murs = *his/her/its walls*

## *Quel/quelle/quels/quelles* and *ce (cet)/cette/ces*

Use **quel/quelle/quels/quelles** to say *which* or *what* directly before a noun or the verbs **est** and **sont.** It agrees with the gender and number of the noun it modifies.

| | MASCULINE | FEMININE |
|---|---|---|
| SINGULAR | quel état | quelle ville |
| PLURAL | quels états | quelles villes |

— Dans **quelle** ville habites-tu?
— J'habite à Sherbrooke.
— **Quelle** est ton adresse?
— C'est le 1202, rue Galt.
— **Quel** est ton numéro de téléphone?
— C'est le (819) 569-1208.

Use the demonstrative adjective **ce (cet)/cette/ces** to say both *this/these* and *that/those.* The masculine **ce** becomes **cet** before masculine singular nouns beginning with a vowel sound.

| | SINGULAR | PLURAL |
|---|---|---|
| **MASCULINE** (+ consonant sound) | ce chien | ces chiens |
| **MASCULINE** (+ vowel sound) | cet animal | ces animaux |
| **FEMININE** | cette étagère | ces étagères |

— Tu habites dans **cette** rue?
— Oui, j'aime beaucoup **ce** quartier.
— Ton appartement est dans **cet** immeuble**-ci** ou dans **cet** immeuble**-là**?
— Mon appartement est derrière **ces** arbres.

If you need to distinguish *this* from *that,* you can add the suffixes **-ci** and **-là** to the noun.

# COMPÉTENCE 1

### NOMS MASCULINS

| | |
|---|---|
| un appartement | an apartment |
| un arrêt d'autobus | a bus stop |
| un ascenseur | an elevator |
| le centre-ville | downtown |
| un dollar | a dollar |
| un escalier | stairs, a staircase |
| un étage | a floor |
| un immeuble | an apartment building |
| le logement | lodging, housing |
| le loyer | the rent |
| le rez-de-chaussée | the ground floor |
| le salon | the living room |
| le sous-sol | the basement |
| les W.-C. | the restroom, toilet |

### NOMS FÉMININS

| | |
|---|---|
| la banlieue | the suburbs |
| la campagne | the country |
| la chambre | the bedroom |
| la cuisine | the kitchen |
| une fenêtre | a window |
| une maison | a house |
| une pièce | a room |
| une porte | a door |
| la salle à manger | the dining room |
| la salle de bains | the bathroom |
| les toilettes | the restroom, the toilet |
| une ville | the city |

### ADJECTIFS

| | |
|---|---|
| cher (chère) | expensive |
| commode | convenient |
| confortable | comfortable |

### DIVERS

| | |
|---|---|
| à la campagne | in the country |
| à la résidence universitaire | in the university dorm |
| À quel étage? | On what floor? |
| au rez-de-chaussée | on the ground floor |
| au premier (deuxième... ) étage | on the second (third . . . ) floor |
| au centre-ville | downtown |
| cent | a/one hundred |
| en banlieue | in the suburbs |
| en ville | in town |
| Il/Elle se trouve... | It is located . . . |
| Je n'ai pas de... | I don't have . . . |
| loin (de) | far (from) |
| mille | a/one thousand |
| un million (de) | a/one million |
| par mois | per month |
| (tout) près (de) | (very) near |
| trop | too (much) |
| va | is going, goes |

*Pour les nombres ordinaux, voir la page 108.*

# COMPÉTENCE 2

### NOMS MASCULINS

| | |
|---|---|
| un animal (pl des animaux) | an animal |
| un canapé | a couch |
| un CD | a CD |
| un chat | a cat |
| un chien | a dog |
| des effets personnels | personal belongings |
| un fauteuil | an armchair |
| un futon | a futon |
| un lecteur DVD | a DVD player |
| un ordinateur | a computer |
| un tableau | a painting |
| un tapis | a rug |
| un vélo | a bicycle |
| des vêtements | clothes |

### NOMS FÉMININS

| | |
|---|---|
| une cassette | a cassette |
| une chaîne hi-fi | a stereo |
| une chaise | a chair |
| une chose | a thing |
| une lampe | a lamp |
| une plante | a plant |
| une platine laser | a CD player |
| une table | a table |
| une télé | a TV |
| une voiture | a car |

### PRÉPOSITIONS

| | |
|---|---|
| à côté (de) | next to, beside |
| à droite (de) | to the right (of) |
| à gauche (de) | to the left (of) |
| dans | in |
| dans le coin (de) | in the corner (of) |
| de | of, from, about |
| derrière | behind |
| devant | in front of |
| en face (de) | across from, facing |
| entre | between |
| sous | under |
| sur | on |

### VERBES

| | |
|---|---|
| arriver | to arrive |
| avoir | to have |
| chercher | to look for |
| fumer | to smoke |
| partager | to share |
| téléphoner (à) | to phone |

### DIVERS

| | |
|---|---|
| combien (de) | how many, how much |
| embêtant(e) | annoying |
| en ordre | in order |
| non plus | neither |
| partout | everywhere |
| Pas de problème. | No problem. |
| peut-être | maybe, perhaps |
| rangé(e) | arranged, put away |
| ton, ta, tes | your (fam.) |
| tout | everything, all |

## Describing your room

### NOMS MASCULINS

| | |
|---|---|
| un adjectif | an adjective |
| un bureau | a desk |
| un couloir | a hall, a corridor |
| un lit | a bed |
| des meubles | furniture, furnishings |
| un mur | a wall |
| un placard | a closet |
| des rideaux | curtains |

### NOMS FÉMININS

| | |
|---|---|
| une affiche | a poster |
| une commode | a dresser, a chest of drawers |
| une couleur | a color |
| une couverture | a cover, a blanket |
| une étagère | a bookcase, a shelf |
| une vue | a view |

### ADJECTIFS POSSESSIFS

| | |
|---|---|
| mon/ma/mes | my |
| ton/ta/tes | your |
| son/sa/ses | his, her, its |
| notre/nos | our |
| votre/vos | your |
| leur/leurs | their |

### EXPRESSIONS VERBALES

| | |
|---|---|
| Ça te plaît. / Ça me plaît. | You like it. / I like it. |
| comme tu vois | as you see |
| espérer | to hope |
| indiquer | to indicate |
| laisser | to leave |
| montrer | to show |
| Viens voir! | Come see! |

### LES COULEURS

| | |
|---|---|
| De quelle couleur est... ? | What color is . . . ? |
| De quelle couleur sont... ? | What color are . . . ? |
| beige | beige |
| blanc(he) | white |
| bleu(e) | blue |
| gris(e) | gray |
| jaune | yellow |
| marron | brown |
| noir(e) | black |
| orange | orange |
| rose | pink |
| rouge | red |
| vert(e) | green |
| violet(te) | purple |

### DIVERS

| | |
|---|---|
| à sa place | in its place |
| au bout (de) | at the end (of) |
| chaque | each |
| en désordre | in disorder |
| justement | as a matter of fact, precisely, exactly |
| par terre | on the floor, on the ground |
| préféré(e) | favorite |
| propre | clean |
| sale | dirty |

## Giving your address and phone number

### NOMS MASCULINS

| | |
|---|---|
| un code postal | a zip code |
| un état | a state |
| les États-Unis | the United States |
| un nom | a name, a noun |
| un numéro de téléphone | a telephone number |
| un pays | a country |
| un prénom | a first name |
| des renseignements | information |

### NOMS FÉMININS

| | |
|---|---|
| une adresse (mail) | an (e-mail) address |
| une nationalité | a nationality |
| une province | a province |
| une rue | a street |

### DIVERS

| | |
|---|---|
| ce (cet)/cette | this, that |
| ces | these, those |
| il/elle doit... | he/she must... |
| partagé(e) | shared, divided |
| poser une question | to ask a question |
| quel/quelle/quels/quelles | which, what |
| s'inscrire | to register |
| suivant(e) | following |

## La Dispersion des Acadiens

**HENRI BEAU**
**(1865–1949)**
1900
Musée Acadien de
L'université de Moncton, Canada

Au 17ᵉ siècle *(century)*, beaucoup de Français viennent s'établir en Cadie (plus tard l'Acadie), aujourd'hui la Nouvelle-Écosse, le Nouveau-Brunswick et l'Île-du-Prince-Édouard. En 1713, les Anglais prennent contrôle de l'Acadie et en 1755, ils commencent à expulser les Français de *(throw the French out of)* l'Acadie. On appelle cette expulsion «le Grand Dérangement». Les Cadiens *(Cajuns)* d'aujourd'hui sont les descendants des Acadiens expulsés du Canada par les Anglais.

Influencés par la splendeur mystérieuse du Mardi gras, beaucoup de peintres et sculpteurs en Louisiane francophone utilisent des couleurs iridescentes pour créer *(to create)* des mythologies et des fantaisies.

## En Amérique: En Louisiane

**HANLEY-GUENO**
**(CA. 1989–1991)**

Lafayette, Louisiana
© Philip Gould/CORBIS

**LA LOUISIANE**
**SUPERFICIE:** 128 595 kilomètres carrés
**NOMBRE D'HABITANTS:** 4 506 000 (les Louisianais) (Environ *[About]* 250 000 parlent français, cadien *(cajun)* ou créole à la maison.)
**CAPITALE:** Baton Rouge
**INDUSTRIES PRINCIPALES:** secteur des services, commerce, finance, industries manufacturières et chimiques, exploitation minière, construction, élevage *(livestock)*, pêche *(fishing)*, agriculture, ressources naturelles (pétrole et gaz naturel)

**COMPÉTENCE**

 Video activities are on pages 212-215.

Les francophones en Louisiane ne sont pas tous **originaires d'une seule** culture. Leurs origines sont **nombreuses** et variées. Les plus grands groupes culturels sont les Créoles et les Cadiens.

**À quoi pensez-vous** quand vous pensez à la Louisiane francophone? Pensez-vous à la tradition créole? à sa fameuse cuisine? à sa musique zydeco? à La Nouvelle-Orléans avec son **Vieux Carré** et son célèbre Mardi gras?

La Nouvelle-Orléans est célèbre pour son Vieux Carré.

Le Mardi gras à La Nouvelle-Orléans est **connu** dans **le monde entier.**

Ou alors, pensez-vous à la culture cadienne, avec son histoire et ses traditions uniques, sa cuisine et sa musique fascinantes?

Le Village Acadien **met en scène la vie quotidienne** des Acadiens dans **le passé.**

La Nouvelle-Orléans

Lafayette

La région **cadienne**, l'Acadiana, **comprend 22 paroisses** dans **la partie sud de** la Louisiane. La Nouvelle-Orléans est **au cœur** de la région créole. Lafayette est **au cœur de la** région cadienne.

---

**originaires d'une seule** *descendants of a single*   **nombreuses** *numerous*   **À quoi pensez-vous?** *What do you think about?*
**le Vieux Carré** *the French Quarter*   **connu** *known*   **le monde entier** *the entire world*   **met en scène la vie quotidienne**
*presents daily life*   **Acadiens** *Cajuns*   **le passé** *the past*   **cadienne** *cajun*   **comprend** *includes*   **une paroisse** *a parish*
(equivalent to a county)   **la partie sud** *the southern part*   **au cœur de** *in the heart of*

Le folklore et les traditions francophones de la Louisiane sont très appréciés dans le monde entier, en particulier sa cuisine, sa musique et ses danses.

**Connaissez-vous** la cuisine cadienne? la cuisine créole? Aimez-vous le boudin, l'andouille, le jambalaya, **les écrevisses?**

Les traditions cadiennes sont très appréciées.

Aimez-vous la musique cadienne? le zydeco? le swamp-pop? **Laissez les bons temps rouler!**

---

**Connaissez-vous... ?** *Do you know . . . ?*   **les écrevisses** *crawfish*   **Laissez les bons temps rouler!** *Let the good times roll!* (regional)

# Describing your family

## Ma famille

Robert et ses amis **ont l'intention de** passer une semaine de **vacances** chez **le père** de Robert à Lafayette. Robert parle de sa famille.

Voici ma famille.

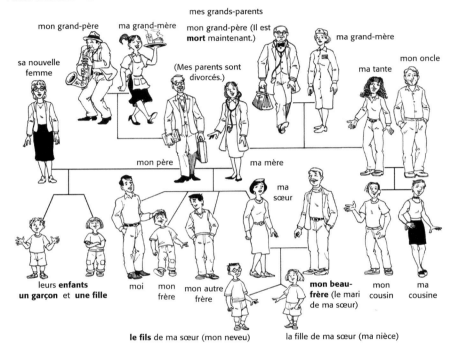

**VOCABULAIRE SUPPLÉMENTAIRE**

**adopté(e)** *adopted*
**des beaux-parents** *stepparents, in-laws*
**l'aîné (l'aînée)** *the oldest child*
**le cadet (la cadette)** *the middle child, the younger child (of two)*
**le benjamin (la benjamine)** *the youngest child (of more than two)*
**un demi-frère (une demi-sœur)** *a stepbrother, a half-brother (a stepsister, a half-sister)*
**un ex-mari (une ex-femme)** *an ex-husband (an ex-wife)*
**un fils unique (une fille unique)** *an only child*
**des petits-enfants (un petit-fils, une petite-fille)** *grandchildren (a grandson, a granddaughter)*

Mon père s'appelle Luke.
Il **a environ 50 ans** *(m)*.
Il **a l'air** *(m)* **encore** jeune.
Il est **de taille moyenne.**
Il **a les cheveux courts** et gris.

Il **a les yeux** *(m)* marron.
Il a **une barbe** grise et une moustache.
Il **porte des lunettes** *(f)*.

Et vous? Comment êtes-vous?

J'ai les yeux **noirs** / marron / verts / bleus / gris.
J'ai les cheveux courts / **mi-longs** / longs et noirs / **bruns** / **châtains** / blonds / gris / blancs / **roux.**

---

**avoir l'intention de** *to intend to*    **les vacances** *(f) vacation*    **le père** *the father*    **mort(e)** *dead*    **des enfants** *children*
**un garçon** *a boy*    **une fille** *a daughter, a girl*    **un beau-frère (une belle-sœur)** *a brother-in-law (a sister-in-law)*
**un fils** *a son*    **avoir... ans** *to be . . . years old*    **environ** *about*    **avoir l'air...** *to look, to seem . . .*    **encore** *still*
**de taille moyenne** *of medium height*    **avoir les cheveux...** *to have . . . hair*    **court(e)** *short*    **avoir les yeux...** *to have . . . eyes*
**une barbe** *a beard*    **porter** *to wear*    **des lunettes** *(f) glasses*    **noirs** *(with eyes) very dark brown*
**mi-longs** *(with hair) shoulder-length*    **bruns** *(with hair) medium brown*    **châtains** *(with hair) light to medium brown*
**roux** *(with hair) red*

Robert parle de sa famille avec Thomas.

THOMAS: Vous êtes combien dans ta famille?
ROBERT: Nous sommes sept: mon père, **ma belle-mère,** ma mère, mes deux frères, ma sœur et moi. Ma sœur est mariée et elle habite à La Nouvelle-Orléans.
THOMAS: Elle est plus jeune ou **plus âgée que** toi? Quel âge a-t-elle?
ROBERT: Elle a 28 ans.
THOMAS: Comment s'appelle-t-elle?
ROBERT: Elle s'appelle Sarah.

---

## A. La famille. Donnez l'équivalent féminin.

Exemple    le frère    **la sœur**

1. le père
2. l'oncle
3. le neveu
4. le mari
5. le fils
6. le cousin
7. le grand-père
8. le garçon
9. le beau-père
10. le beau-frère

## B. Généalogie. Complétez les phrases.

Exemple    Les parents de mon père, ce sont **mes grands-parents.**

1. Le mari de ma tante, c'est _____.
2. Le fils de ma sœur, c'est _____. Sa fille, c'est _____.
3. Les enfants de mon oncle, ce sont _____.
4. La fille de mon oncle, c'est _____ et son fils, c'est _____.
5. La femme de mon oncle, c'est _____.

## C. Mon meilleur ami. Faites des phrases pour décrire votre meilleur ami.

Exemple    Il s'appelle *Philippe / Chuong / ???.*
           **Il s'appelle Emmitt.**

1. Il s'appelle *Philippe / Chuong / ???.*
2. Il est *grand / petit / de taille moyenne.*
3. Il a *18 / 25 / 38 / 45 / ???* ans.
4. Il a les cheveux *longs / mi-longs / courts* et *blonds / noirs / ???.*
5. Il a les yeux *marron / gris / ???.*
6. Il a l'air *intellectuel / sportif / jeune / bête / ???.*

## D. Et vous? Refaites les phrases de **C. Mon meilleur ami** pour faire une description de vous-même *(yourself)*.

Exemple    **Je m'appelle Nancy.**

## E. Conversation. Avec un(e) partenaire, relisez à haute voix la conversation entre Robert et Thomas en haut de la page. Ensuite, changez la conversation pour parler de votre famille. D'abord *(First)*, dites combien vous êtes dans votre famille. Ensuite *(Then)*, décrivez un membre de votre famille.

---

**une belle-mère (un beau-père)** *a stepmother, a mother-in-law (a stepfather, a father-in-law)*    **plus âgé(e) que** *older than*

## NOTES DE VOCABULAIRE

**1.** Use the definite article **les** when talking about someone's hair and eyes. **Les cheveux** and **les yeux** are both masculine plural, so always follow them with an adjective in the masculine plural form. **Ma sœur a les cheveux bruns et les yeux verts.**

**2.** Brown eyes can be **noirs** *(dark brown)* or **marron** *(light to medium brown).* Brown hair can be **bruns** *(dark or medium brown)* or **châtains** *(light to medium brown).* The words **brun, roux,** and **châtain** are mainly used to describe someone's hair.

**3.** You can say that someone is *blond* or *a blond, brunette* or *a brunette,* or *red-headed* or *a red-head,* using **blond(e), brun(e),** or **roux (rousse). Elle est rousse mais son frère est blond.** *She's a red-head, but her brother's a blond.*

**4.** To say you are *very hot / cold / hungry...* use **très. J'ai très chaud.**

## VOCABULAIRE SUPPLÉMENTAIRE

**avoir un tatoo / un piercing**
**avoir un bouc** *to have a goatee*
**avoir des favoris** *(m) to have sideburns*
**être chauve** *to be bald*
**Il/Elle a la tête rasée.** *He/She shaves his/her head.*

# Describing feelings and appearance

## *Les expressions avec avoir*

The following expressions use **avoir** to describe someone or say how they feel.

| | | | |
|---|---|---|---|
| avoir... ans | *to be . . . years old* | avoir faim | *to be hungry* |
| avoir l'air | *to look, to seem* | avoir soif | *to be thirsty* |
| avoir une barbe / | *to have a beard /* | avoir froid | *to be cold* |
| une moustache / | *a mustache /* | avoir chaud | *to be hot* |
| des lunettes | *glasses* | avoir raison | *to be right* |
| avoir les yeux noirs / | *to have dark brown /* | avoir tort | *to be wrong* |
| verts... | *green . . . eyes* | avoir peur (de) | *to be afraid (of)* |
| avoir les cheveux | *to have long /* | avoir sommeil | *to be sleepy* |
| longs / roux... | *red . . . hair* | | |

— Mon fils a peur des chiens.    — *My son is afraid of dogs.*
— Quel âge a-t-il? Il a l'air très jeune.    — *How old is he? He looks very young.*
— Tu as raison. Il a quatre ans.    — *You're right. He's four.*

The French equivalents of the English verbs *to need, to feel like,* and *to intend* are also expressions with **avoir. Avoir l'intention de** is followed by an infinitive. **Avoir besoin de** and **avoir envie de** can be followed by an infinitive or by a noun.

| | |
|---|---|
| avoir l'intention de (d') | *to intend* |
| avoir besoin de (d') | *to need* |
| avoir envie de (d') | *to feel like* |

Mon frère a l'intention de sortir ce soir.
*My brother intends to go out tonight.*

J'ai besoin de la voiture. J'ai besoin d'aller en cours.
*I need the car. I need to go to class.*

Tu as envie de manger? Tu as envie d'un sandwich?
*You feel like eating? You feel like a sandwich?*

**A. Comment est-il?** Répondez aux questions pour faire une description du meilleur ami de Robert.

Antoine, 20 ans

1. Comment s'appelle-t-il?
2. Quel âge-a-t-il?
3. Il a les cheveux de quelle couleur? Il a les cheveux longs ou courts? Il a les yeux de quelle couleur?
4. Il a une barbe ou une moustache? Il porte des lunettes? Il a l'air content *(happy)*?

**B. Descriptions.** Changez la description d'Antoine de l'exercice *A. Comment est-il?* pour parler de votre meilleur(e) ami(e).

Exemple    **Mon meilleur ami (Ma meilleure amie) s'appelle Pat. Il/Elle a 25 ans. Il/Elle a les cheveux...**

**C. Les activités de Robert.** Quelles sont les activités que Robert a probablement envie de faire? Quelles sont les activités qu'il a probablement besoin de faire?

**Exemples** faire les devoirs **Il a besoin de faire les devoirs.**
regarder la télé **Il a envie de regarder la télé.**

**1.** aller au cinéma **3.** aller travailler **5.** sortir avec des amis
**2.** aller prendre un verre **4.** préparer les cours **6.** aller en cours

**D. Et toi?** Demandez à votre partenaire s'il/si elle a l'intention de faire les activités mentionnées dans l'exercice précédent demain.

**Exemple** faire les devoirs
— **As-tu l'intention de faire les devoirs demain?**
— **Non, je n'ai pas l'intention de faire les devoirs demain.**

**E. Moi, j'ai...** Utilisez une expression avec **avoir** selon le contexte.

**Exemple** Je voudrais aller prendre un verre.
**J'ai soif.**

**sommeil   faim   soif   froid   chaud   tort   peur   raison**

**1.** Brrrr... Fermez la fenêtre. **4.** J'ai envie de manger quelque chose.
**2.** Aïe! C'est un serpent! **5.** Je voudrais un coca.
**3.** Voilà. Ma réponse est correcte. **6.** J'ai besoin de dormir.

**F. Qu'est-ce qu'ils ont?** Aujourd'hui la nièce de Robert fête ses cinq ans *(is celebrating her fifth birthday).* Que dit sa mère? Utilisez une expression avec **avoir.**

**1.** Ma fille... aujourd'hui. **2.** Ses amis... **3.** Mon frère... **4.** Mes cousins...

**5.** Mon mari et moi, nous... **6.** Moi, j'... **7.** Le chien de mon fils... **8.** Tu... de faire ça au chien!

**G. Entretien.** Interviewez votre partenaire.

**1.** Vous êtes combien dans ta famille? Tu as des frères ou des sœurs? Combien de neveux as-tu? Combien de nièces?
**2.** Comment s'appelle ta mère? Quel âge a-t-elle?
**3.** Tu as des enfants? Voudrais-tu avoir des enfants un jour *(one day)?* Préfères-tu avoir une fille ou un garçon?
**4.** Tu as l'intention de voir ta famille ce week-end? Qu'est-ce que tu as envie de faire ce week-end? Qu'est-ce que tu as besoin de faire? Où as-tu l'intention de dîner samedi soir? Qu'est-ce que tu as l'intention de faire dimanche soir?
**5.** Où aimes-tu dîner quand tu as très faim? Tu as faim maintenant? Tu as soif? Est-ce que tu as l'intention de manger quelque chose après le cours? As-tu sommeil maintenant? As-tu l'intention de dormir après le cours?

## Stratégies et Compréhension auditive

*Asking for clarification*

When you do not understand something, it is useful to be able to ask for clarification. You already know three ways to do this: by asking for something to be repeated, by asking what a word means, or by asking how a word is spelled.

> Comment? Répétez, s'il vous plaît.
> Je ne comprends pas. Qu'est-ce que ça veut dire **belle-sœur?**
> Ça s'écrit comment?

**A. Je ne comprends pas.** Listen to three conversations. In each, which
CD 1-44 method is used to ask for clarification: **a, b,** or **c?**

a. asking for something to be repeated **(Comment? Répétez, s'il vous plaît.)**
b. asking the meaning of a word **(Qu'est-ce que ça veut dire?)**
c. asking the spelling of a word **(Ça s'écrit comment?)**

**B. Comment?** Listen to these three other scenes, in which one of the speakers is
CD 1-45 having difficulty understanding. In each case, what could he or she say to ask for clarification?

# La famille de Robert

Robert is describing his family to a friend who is studying French. Use what you know and your ability to guess logically to help you understand what he says. The first time, listen only for the number of times his friend asks for clarification.

**A. La famille de Robert.** Écoutez encore une fois *(again)* la description de la famille de Robert et complétez l'arbre généalogique *(family tree)* avec les prénoms des membres de sa famille.

**B. C'est qui?** Écoutez encore une fois la description de la famille de Robert et répondez aux questions.

1. Qui habite à Lafayette?
2. Qui habite à Atlanta?
3. Qui habite à La Nouvelle-Orléans?
4. Qui est marié?
5. Qui est divorcé?
6. Comment dit-on **pédiatre** en anglais?
7. Dans la famille de Robert, qui est pédiatre?
8. Quelle est la profession du père de Robert?

# Saying where you go in your free time

## Le temps libre

À Lafayette, **on s'amuse bien!** Et chez vous? Où est-ce qu'**on va** pour passer **son temps libre?**

On aime beaucoup les activités culturelles et **de temps en temps** on va...

au musée pour voir
**une exposition**

au théâtre pour voir
**une pièce**

à un concert ou à un festival de musique

On aime aussi les activités **de plein air** et on va souvent...

au parc pour jouer
au frisbee

à la piscine pour nager

à la plage pour **prendre un bain de soleil**

Pour **retrouver** des amis, on va...

au bar

en boîte

à l'église

Pour faire du shopping, on va...

Et pour **acheter** des livres, on va...

dans les petits magasins

au centre commercial

à la librairie

---

**on s'amuse bien** *one has a good time*    **on va** *one goes*    **son temps libre** *one's free time*
**de temps en temps** *from time to time*    **une exposition** *an exhibit*    **une pièce** *a play*    **de plein air** *outdoor*
**prendre un bain de soleil** *to sunbathe*    **retrouver** *to meet*    **acheter** *to buy*

CD 1-47

Robert et Claude parlent de leurs projets *(m)* pour ce soir.

CLAUDE: **On sort** ce soir?

ROBERT: D'accord. **On va** au cinéma?

CLAUDE: Ah, non, je préfère **connaître** un peu la région. **On dit que** la cuisine **cadienne** est extra! **Allons plutôt** au restaurant.

ROBERT: D'accord. Allons dîner au restaurant Préjean. C'est un très bon restaurant où **on sert** les spécialités de la région et il y a un orchestre cadien. **Ça te dit?**

CLAUDE: Oui, bonne idée. Allons au restaurant et après allons écouter de la musique zydeco.

ROBERT: Pas de problème. **On peut** toujours **trouver** des concerts ici!

**A. Où va-t-on pour...** Demandez à un(e) camarade de classe où on va pour faire les choses suivantes.

> **Exemple** lire
> — **Où est-ce qu'on va pour lire?**
> — **On va à la bibliothèque.**

1. dîner
2. voir une pièce
3. retrouver des amis
4. prendre un verre
5. faire du shopping
6. nager
7. voir une exposition
8. prendre un bain de soleil
9. acheter des livres

> au restaurant    au café    au parc    ???    à la plage
> au musée    au centre commercial    à la librairie
> à la piscine    à l'église    au théâtre    à la bibliothèque

**B. Entretien.** Interviewez votre partenaire.

1. Où aimes-tu retrouver tes amis? Où aimez-vous aller ensemble?
2. Dans quel restaurant aimes-tu manger? Ce restaurant est près de l'université? Il est cher?
3. Dans quel magasin aimes-tu acheter des vêtements? Ce magasin est au centre commercial? C'est un magasin cher?
4. Est-ce qu'il y a beaucoup de théâtres dans le quartier universitaire? beaucoup de musées? beaucoup de concerts? Préfères-tu aller à un concert ou au théâtre? Préfères-tu aller voir une pièce ou aller voir un film?

**C. Conversation.** Avec un(e) partenaire, relisez à haute voix la conversation entre Robert et Claude en haut de la page. Ensuite, imaginez que vous êtes chez un(e) ami(e) qui habite dans une autre ville et que vous allez sortir ensemble. Choisissez une sorte de cuisine (mexicaine, italienne, française, japonaise, chinoise…) et un genre de musique (du rock, du jazz, du hip-hop, du country, du pop, de la musique classique…) populaire dans votre région.

---

**On sort... ?** *How about going out . . . ?*    **On va... ?** *How about going . . . ?*    **connaître** *to know, to get to know*
**On dit que** *They say that*    **cadien(ne)** *Cajun*    **Allons...** *Let's go . . .*    **plutôt** *instead, rather*    **on sert** *they serve* (**servir** *to serve*)
**Ça te dit?** *How does that sound to you?*    **On peut** *One can* (**pouvoir** *can, may, to be able*)    **trouver** *to find*

**1.** What are the forms of **aller?**

**2.** With which forms of the definite article does **à** contract? What are the contracted forms? With which forms does it not contract? How do you say *to the café? to the library? to the university? to the students?*

**3.** What does the word **y** mean?

**4.** Where do you place **y** in a sentence where there is a verb followed by an infinitive? Where do you place it otherwise?

**5.** What happens to words like **je** and **ne** before **y?**

# Saying where you are going

*Le verbe **aller,** la préposition **à** et le pronom **y***

To talk about going places, use the irregular verb **aller** *(to go).*

| ALLER *(to go)* | |
|---|---|
| je **vais** | nous z **allons** |
| tu **vas** | vous z **allez** |
| il/elle **va** | ils/elles **vont** |

Use the preposition **à** *(to, at, in)* to say where you are going. When **à** falls before **le** or **les,** the two words contract to **au** and **aux.**

| CONTRACTIONS WITH À | | |
|---|---|---|
| à + le | → au | Je vais **au** cinéma. |
| à + la | → à la | Je vais **à la** librairie. |
| à + l' | → à l' | Claude va **à l'**université. |
| à + les | → aux | Robert va **aux** festivals de musique de la région. |

The pronoun **y** *(there)* is often used to avoid repeating the name of the place where one is going. **Y** is treated as a vowel sound and elision and liaison occur before it.

Je vais **au parc.**      Nous allons **au centre commercial.**
J'**y** vais avec mes cousins.      Nous z **y** allons à trois heures.

**Y** is generally placed *immediately* before the verb. It goes before the infinitive if there is one. If not, it goes before the conjugated verb.

— Il voudrait aller **au cinéma?**      — Ils vont **au musée?**
— Oui, il voudrait **y** aller.      — Oui, ils **y** vont.

In the negative, **y** remains *immediately* before the conjugated verb or the infinitive.

— Tu **y** vas?      — Tu voudrais **y** aller?
— Non, je n'**y** vais pas.      — Non, je ne voudrais pas **y** aller.

Whenever you use the verb **aller** to talk about going somewhere and don't name the place you are going, you must use **y** even when the word *there* would not be stated in English.

On y va? *Shall we go (there)?*      J'y vais. *I'm going (there).*

 CD 1-48

# Prononciation

*Les lettres **a, au** et **ai***

- Pronounce **a** or **à** with the mouth wide open as in the word *father,* but with the tongue slightly higher and closer to the front of the mouth.

  Ton ami va à Paris.      Tu vas à Paris avec ta camarade?

- Pronounce **au** like the **o** in **nos.**

  Laure va au restaurant?      Les autres y vont aussi?

- Pronounce the **ai** of **je vais** like the **ais** of **français.** Be sure to distinguish this sound from the **a** of **tu vas** or **il va.**

  Je vais au café.      Tu n'y vas jamais?

**A. J'aime beaucoup!** Est-ce que vous aimez aller à ces endroits *(places)*?

> **Exemple**     le cinéma
> **J'aime assez aller**       J'aime beaucoup aller...     Je n'aime pas beaucoup aller...
> **au cinéma.**              J'aime assez aller...        Je n'aime pas du tout aller...

**1.** l'église      **4.** le théâtre      **7.** l'université le week-end
**2.** la piscine     **5.** la bibliothèque     **8.** les festivals de musique de la région
**3.** le musée      **6.** la plage       **9.** les matchs de basket de notre équipe *(team)*

**B. On y va souvent?** Ces personnes vont-elles souvent, quelquefois, rarement ou jamais aux endroits indiqués?

> **Exemple**     Moi, je... (le musée)
> **Moi, je vais rarement au musée. / Je ne vais jamais au musée.**

**1.** Moi, je... (l'université, la plage, le théâtre, le cinéma, l'opéra)
**2.** Mes parents... (le cinéma, Paris, le parc, le centre commercial)
**3.** Mon meilleur ami (Ma meilleure amie)... (l'église, la piscine, le bar, le musée)
**4.** Mes amis et moi, nous... (les matchs de football américain de notre équipe *(team)*, la bibliothèque, les festivals de musique de la région)

**C. On sort.** Robert parle de ses amis et de sa famille. Où vont-ils?

> **Exemple**     Moi, je **vais à la piscine.**

**1.** Thomas et moi...     **2.** Mon oncle et ma     **3.** Thomas...
                     tante...

**4.** Claude et son frère...     **5.** Mon père...     **6.** Le chien de ma sœur...

**D. Et toi?** Demandez à votre partenaire s'il/si elle va quelquefois à chacun *(each one)* des endroits *(places)* illustrés dans **C. On sort.** Votre partenaire va répondre en utilisant le pronom **y.**

> **Exemple**     — **Est-ce que tu vas à la piscine quelquefois?**
>                  — **Oui, j'y vais souvent (de temps en temps, rarement... ).**

**E. Entretien.** Interviewez votre partenaire.

**1.** Où aimes-tu passer ton temps libre? Tu préfères sortir ou rester à la maison le week-end? Tu aimes les activités culturelles? Tu vas souvent au théâtre? au musée? Tu préfères aller voir un concert ou aller voir une exposition?
**2.** Avec quel membre de ta famille préfères-tu passer ton temps libre? Où aimez-vous aller ensemble?
**3.** Tu aimes les activités de plein air? Tu préfères les activités culturelles ou les activités de plein air? Tu vas souvent au parc? Tu vas souvent à la piscine? Tu préfères aller à la piscine ou à la plage? Tu aimes nager et prendre des bains de soleil? Tu nages bien?

**Pour vérifier**

**1.** What are the three possible uses of the pronoun **on?** What form of the verb do you use with **on?**

**2.** How do you form the imperative? What is it used for?

**3.** With which verbs do you drop the final **-s** in the **tu** form of the imperative?

**4.** Which two verbs have irregular command forms? What are the forms? How would you say to a friend: *Be on time! Be good! Let's be calm! Have confidence! Let's have patience!*

# Suggesting activities

*Le pronom sujet **on** et l'impératif*

Use **on** as the subject of a sentence when you are referring to people in general *(one, people, they)*. Consider the difference between these sentences.

| | |
|---|---|
| Tes parents? Ils parlent français? | *Your parents? Do they speak French?* (specific people) |
| À Paris, **on** parle français. | *In Paris, they speak French.* (general group) |

The pronoun **on** is also often used instead of **nous** to say *we.* **On** takes the same form of the verb as **il** and **elle,** regardless of its translation in English.

| | |
|---|---|
| Claude et moi, **on** aime sortir le samedi. | *Claude and I, we like to go out on Saturdays.* |

You can propose doing something with someone *(How about . . . ? Shall we . . . ?)* by asking a question with **on.**

| | |
|---|---|
| **On** va au cinéma? | *How about going to the movies?* |
| Qu'est-ce qu'**on** fait ce soir? | *What shall we do this evening?* |

The imperative (command form) can also be used to make suggestions, as well as to tell someone else to do something. Use the imperative as follows.

- To make suggestions with *Let's . . .* , use the **nous** form of the verb, without the pronoun **nous.**

| | |
|---|---|
| **Allons** au cinéma! | *Let's go to the movies!* |
| Ne **restons** pas à la maison! | *Let's not stay home!* |

- To give instructions, or to tell someone to do something, use either the **vous** form of the verb or the **tu** form of the verb, as appropriate, without the pronoun. In **tu** form commands, drop the final **-s** of **-er** verbs and of **aller.** However, as you learn other verbs that do not end in **-er,** do not drop the **-s** in the commands.

| | | |
|---|---|---|
| **Allez** à la bibliothèque! | **Va** à la bibliothèque! | *Go to the library!* |
| Ne **mangez** pas ça! | Ne **mange** pas ça! | *Don't eat that!* |

The verbs **être** and **avoir** have irregular command forms.

| **ÊTRE** *(be . . . )* | |
|---|---|
| **Sois** sage! | *Be good!* |
| **Soyons** calmes! | *Let's be calm!* |
| **Soyez** à l'heure! | *Be on time!* |

| **AVOIR** *(have . . . )* | |
|---|---|
| **Aie** confiance! | *Have confidence!* |
| **Ayons** de la patience! | *Let's have patience!* |
| **Ayez** confiance! | *Have confidence!* |

**A. Où?** Est-ce qu'on fait plus souvent les choses suivantes **en Louisiane** ou **au Québec?**

> **Exemple**  écouter de la musique zydeco
> **On écoute plus souvent de la musique zydeco en Louisiane.**

1. aller à des festivals de neige *(snow)*
2. fêter *(to celebrate)* Mardi gras
3. fêter le 4 juillet *(July)*
4. écouter de la musique québécoise
5. manger des po-boys
6. aller à des festivals de danse cadienne

**B. Tes amis et toi?** Posez ces questions à votre partenaire. Il/Elle va répondre en utilisant le pronom **on.**

> **Exemple**  **— Tes amis et toi, vous préférez aller à quel restaurant?**
> **— On préfère aller au restaurant Vermilionville.**

Tes amis et toi...

1. Quand aimez-vous sortir ensemble?
2. Où aimez-vous aller ensemble?
3. À quel restaurant allez-vous le plus souvent?
4. Où allez-vous pour retrouver des amis?
5. Vous allez souvent au parc ensemble?
6. Vous jouez au frisbee ensemble?

**C. On... ?** Un(e) ami(e) vous invite *(invites you)* à faire ces choses. Répondez à ses suggestions selon vos goûts *(according to your tastes).*

> **Exemple**  **— On va au cinéma?**
> **— D'accord. Allons au cinéma.**
> **Non, n'allons pas au cinéma.**

1.   2.   3.   4.

**D. Pour réussir.** Donnez des conseils à un groupe de nouveaux étudiants. Utilisez l'impératif.

> **Exemple**  préparer les examens avec d'autres étudiants
> **Préparez les examens avec d'autres étudiants.**
> **Ne préparez pas les examens avec d'autres étudiants.**

1. aller à tous les cours
2. être à l'heure
3. avoir confiance
4. regarder les examens des autres
5. aller en boîte tous les soirs
6. avoir peur de parler au prof

Maintenant donnez les mêmes conseils à un(e) ami(e).

> **Exemple**  préparer les examens avec d'autres étudiants
> **Prépare les examens avec d'autres étudiants.**
> **Ne prépare pas les examens avec d'autres étudiants.**

# Saying what you are going to do

## Le week-end prochain

**NOTES DE VOCABULAIRE**

**1.** Use **visiter** to say that you visit a place. Use **aller voir** *(to go see)* to say that you visit a person.
**2.** **Quitter** means *to leave* and must be followed by a direct object. That is, you must state the person or place you are leaving. **(Je quitte l'université à 3 heures.)** **Partir** means *to leave* in the sense of *to depart*. **(Je vais bientôt partir.)**

Robert va passer le week-end prochain à La Nouvelle-Orléans. Et vous? Qu'est-ce que vous allez faire?

Je vais... / Je ne vais pas...

**quitter** la maison **tôt**

**partir** pour le week-end

visiter une autre ville

faire un tour de la ville

aller **boire** quelque chose au café

rentrer **tard**

CD 1-49

Robert et Thomas **font des projets** pour le week-end prochain.

THOMAS: Qu'est-ce qu'on fait ce week-end?
ROBERT: J'ai beaucoup de projets pour ce week-end. Jeudi matin, on va partir très tôt pour La Nouvelle-Orléans. **D'abord,** on va visiter la ville. **Ensuite,** on va **aller voir** ma sœur. On va passer **la soirée** chez elle. Vendredi on va faire un tour du **Vieux Carré.** On va rentrer à Lafayette assez tard.
THOMAS: Et samedi?
ROBERT: À midi, on va déjeuner au restaurant Prudhomme. C'est un restaurant célèbre pour sa cuisine régionale. **Et puis,** le soir, on va aller à Eunice, une petite ville pas loin de Lafayette. Il y a une soirée de musique et de folklore cadiens tous les samedis.
THOMAS: **Génial!**

---

**Le week-end prochain** *Next weekend*   **quitter** *to leave*   **tôt** *early*   **partir** *to leave*   **boire** *to drink*   **tard** *late*
**faire des projets** *to make plans*   **D'abord** *First*   **Ensuite** *Next*   **aller voir** *to go see, to visit (a person)*   **la soirée** *the evening*
**le Vieux Carré** *the French Quarter*   **Et puis** *And then*   **Génial!** *Great!*

**A. Le week-end prochain.** Est-ce que vous allez faire les choses suivantes samedi prochain?

> **Exemple**  rester à la maison
> **Je vais rester à la maison. / Je ne vais pas rester à la maison.**

1. quitter la maison tôt
2. partir pour la journée
3. faire un tour de la ville
4. visiter une autre ville
5. aller voir des amis
6. retrouver des amis en ville
7. aller boire quelque chose
8. dîner au restaurant
9. rentrer tard
10. inviter des amis à la maison
11. regarder une vidéo
12. passer la soirée à la maison

**B. Entretien.** Interviewez votre partenaire.

1. D'habitude, à quelle heure est-ce que tu quittes la maison le lundi? le mardi?
   À quelle heure est-ce que tu rentres?
2. Quelle ville est-ce que tu aimes visiter? Qu'est-ce que tu aimes faire dans cette ville?
3. Est-ce que tu voudrais partir pour le week-end? (Où est-ce que tu voudrais aller?)
4. Vas-tu souvent au café? Qu'est-ce que tu aimes boire quand tu as très soif?
   Et quand tu as froid? Et quand tu as chaud?
5. En général, quels jours est-ce que tu passes la journée à la maison? Et la soirée?
   Est-ce que tu passes toute la journée chez toi de temps en temps?

**C. Conversation.** Avec un(e) partenaire, relisez à haute voix la conversation entre Robert et Thomas en bas de la page précédente. Ensuite, imaginez qu'un(e) ami(e) passe le week-end chez vous et que vous allez visiter une autre ville. Décidez quelle ville vous allez visiter et parlez de vos projets.

À La Nouvelle-Orléans

**1.** How do you say what you are going to do? How do you say what you are not going to do? How would you say *I'm going to stay home? I'm not going to work today? I'm going to go to the mall?*

**2.** Where do you place the pronoun **y** in the immediate future?

**3.** What is the immediate future form of **il y a?** How do you negate it?

# Saying what you are going to do

*Le futur immédiat*

To talk about what you *are going to do*, use a form of the verb **aller** followed by an infinitive.

> — Qu'est-ce que tu **vas faire** demain?    — *What are you going to do tomorrow?*
> — Je **vais travailler**.    — *I'm going to work.*

In the negative, put the **ne... pas** around the conjugated form of **aller**. Place the pronoun **y,** when needed, *immediately* before the infinitive.

> Ma sœur va rester à la maison mais je **ne vais pas y rester.**

**Il y a** becomes **il va y avoir** when you want to say *there is going to be / there are going to be.*

> **Il va y avoir** un festival de musique ce week-end.
> **Il ne va pas y avoir** de problèmes.

Here are some expressions you can use to tell when you are going to do something.

| | |
|---|---|
| **maintenant** *now* | **plus tard** *later* |
| **aujourd'hui** *today* | **demain** *tomorrow* |
| **ce matin** *this morning* | **demain matin** *tomorrow morning* |
| **cet après-midi** *this afternoon* | **demain après-midi** *tomorrow afternoon* |
| **ce soir** *tonight* | **demain soir** *tomorrow evening* |
| **lundi** *Monday* | **lundi prochain** *next Monday* |
| **ce week-end** *this weekend* | **le week-end prochain** *next weekend* |
| **cette semaine** *this week* | **la semaine prochaine** *next week* |
| **ce mois-ci** *this month* | **le mois prochain** *next month* |
| **cette année** *this year* | **l'année prochaine** *next year* |

**A. Qu'est-ce qu'ils vont faire?** Est-ce que ces personnes vont probablement faire ces choses samedi prochain?

> **Exemple**    Moi, je... (passer la journée à la maison, quitter la maison tôt)
> **Moi, je ne vais pas passer la journée à la maison. Je vais quitter la maison tôt.**

1. Moi, je... (passer la journée à la maison, quitter la maison tôt, aller travailler, partir pour le week-end, rester au lit, aller voir des amis)
2. Les étudiants du cours de français... (préparer les cours ensemble, être en cours, sortir ensemble, faire les devoirs)
3. Mon meilleur ami (Ma meilleure amie)... (préparer les cours, beaucoup travailler, aller à Paris, passer le week-end à la maison)
4. Mes amis et moi... (sortir ensemble, faire un tour de la ville, visiter une autre ville, aller boire quelque chose, rentrer tard)

**B. Et ensuite?** Qu'est-ce que ces gens vont faire d'abord et qu'est-ce qu'ils vont faire ensuite?

> **Exemple**    nous: manger / préparer le dîner
> **D'abord, nous allons préparer le dîner et ensuite, nous allons manger.**

1. nous: travailler tout l'après-midi / aller prendre un verre
2. moi, je: dormir / rentrer à la maison
3. mon frère: retrouver sa petite amie en ville / dîner au restaurant avec elle
4. vous: dîner au restaurant / sortir danser
5. mes amis: préparer le dîner / aller au supermarché *(supermarket)*

**C. Projets.** Demandez à un(e) camarade de classe ce qu'il/elle va faire aux moments indiqués.

> **Exemple**  ce soir  — **David, qu'est-ce que tu vas faire ce soir?**
> — **Je vais travailler ce soir.**

**1.** plus tard, après les cours

**2.** demain matin

**3.** demain soir

**4.** le week-end prochain

**5.** la semaine prochaine

**6.** l'année prochaine

> rentrer à la maison    ???    préparer les cours    travailler
> sortir    manger    aller au cinéma    être en cours    aller...
> partir pour le week-end    dormir    aller voir des amis

**D. Leurs projets.** De retour au *(Back in)* Québec, Thomas parle à Robert de leurs projets pour le lendemain *(the next day)*. Qu'est-ce que Thomas dit?

> **Exemple**    Moi, je **vais rester au lit.**

Moi, je...

**1.** Claude...

**2.** Toi et moi, est-ce que nous... ?

**3.** Ta petite amie et toi, est-ce que vous... ?

**4.** Tu... avec Claude?

**5.** Nos amis...

**6.** Nos autres amis...

**7.** Mes amis et moi, on...

**8.** Claude et son ami...

**E. Entretien.** Interviewez votre partenaire.

**1.** Qu'est-ce que tu vas faire après le cours de français aujourd'hui? À quelle heure est-ce que tu vas rentrer à la maison? Qu'est-ce que tu vas faire ensuite?

**2.** À quelle heure est-ce que tu vas quitter la maison demain? Où est-ce que tu vas passer la journée? Qu'est-ce que tu vas faire?

**3.** Ce week-end, est-ce que tu vas partir pour le week-end? Est-ce que tu vas aller voir tes parents? Est-ce que tu vas travailler? Tu vas sortir avec des amis?

**Pour vérifier**

**1.** Do you generally use cardinal or ordinal numbers to give dates in French? What is the exception?

**2.** In what two ways can the year 1789 be expressed in French? How do you say the year 2008?

**3.** What are these dates in French: 15/3/1951 and 11/1/2010?

**VOCABULAIRE SUPPLÉMENTAIRE**
**LES FÊTES**
**un anniversaire de mariage** *a wedding anniversary*
**la fête des Mères / Pères**
**la fête nationale** *Independence Day*
**Hanoukka** *(f)*
**le jour d'Action de Grâce** *Thanksgiving*
**le (réveillon du) jour de l'an** *New Year's (Eve)*
**Noël** *(m) Christmas*
**Pâques** *(f) Easter*
**la pâque juive** *Passover*
**le ramadan**
**la Saint-Valentin**
**Yom Kippour**
**Bon anniversaire!** *Happy Birthday!*
**Bonne année!** *Happy New Year!*
**Joyeux Noël!** *Merry Christmas!*

# Saying when you are going to do something
*Les dates*

You often need to give dates to say when you are going to do something.

Je vais partir en vacances le 30 décembre.

In French, dates are expressed using **le** and cardinal numbers (**deux, trois…** ), rather than ordinal numbers (**deuxième, troisième…** ), except to say *the first* of the month. For *the first*, use **le premier** (**1ᵉʳ**). To ask the date, say **Quelle est la date?**

— Quelle est la date aujourd'hui?
— Quelle est la date de votre fête *(holiday)* préférée?

— C'est le premier…     le deux…     le trois…     le quatre…

| janvier | mars | mai | juillet | septembre | novembre |
|---------|------|-----|---------|-----------|----------|
| février | avril | juin | août | octobre | décembre |

There are two ways of expressing the years 1100–1999 in French. Years starting at 2000 are only expressed using the word **mille.**

1999: mille neuf cent quatre-vingt-dix-neuf / dix-neuf cent quatre-vingt-dix-neuf
2006: deux mille six

Note that the day goes before the month in French.

14/8/1957 = le quatorze août 1957

Use **en** to say *in* what month or year.

— Ton anniversaire *(birthday)*, c'est **en** quel mois?
— C'est **en** novembre.

— **En** quelle année vas-tu finir tes études?
— **En** 2008.

**A. C'est en quel mois?** Quel mois associez-vous avec… ?

**1.** le début *(beginning)* de l'année? la fin *(end)* de l'année?
**2.** le début de l'année scolaire? le début de ce semestre / trimestre?
**3.** la fin de ce semestre / trimestre?
**4.** la fête nationale américaine? canadienne? française?
**5.** la fête des Mères? la fête des Pères?
**6.** le jour d'Action de Grâce *(Thanksgiving)*?

**B. Votre anniversaire.** Vos camarades de classe devineront *(will guess)* la date de votre anniversaire. Répondez **avant** ou **après** jusqu'à ce qu'ils devinent juste *(right)*.

> Exemple      — **Ton anniversaire, c'est en mars?**
> — **Après.**
> — **C'est en mai?**
> — **Oui.**
> — **C'est le quinze mai?**
> — **Avant…**

**C. Encore des dates.** Quelle est la date... ?

1. aujourd'hui
2. demain
3. du prochain cours de français
4. de la fête nationale américaine / canadienne
5. de Noël
6. de *Halloween*
7. du jour de l'an *(New Year's Day)*
8. de la fête nationale française

**D. Dates importantes.** Lisez à haute voix ces dates importantes.

**Exemple**  4/7/1776  (le début de la Révolution américaine)
**le quatre juillet mille sept cent soixante-seize (dix-sept cent soixante-seize)**

1. 1/11/1718 (Bienville fonde La Nouvelle-Orléans.)
2. 14/7/1789 (le début de la Révolution française)
3. 30/4/1812 (La Louisiane devient *[becomes]* un état des États-Unis.)
4. 11/11/1918 (le jour de l'Armistice)
5. 6/6/1944 (le jour du débarquement en Normandie)

**E. À quelle date?** Dites à quelle date chacun va faire les choses indiquées.

**Exemple**    Robert / rentrer chez son père...
**Robert va rentrer chez son père le 25 décembre.**

1. Beaucoup d'Américains / faire un pique-nique...

2. Les Français / célébrer leur fête nationale...

3. Beaucoup de couples / dîner au restaurant...

4. On / sortir avec des amis...

5. Thomas / aller voir sa famille...

6. Moi, je / fêter *(to celebrate)* mon anniversaire...

**F. Entretien.** Interviewez votre partenaire.

1. Quelle est la date aujourd'hui? Quelle est la date de ton anniversaire? Qu'est-ce que tu vas probablement faire ce jour-là?
2. Quelle est la date du dernier *(last)* jour du cours de français? Qu'est-ce que tu vas faire après ton dernier cours ce semestre / trimestre? Vas-tu partir en vacances après la fin *(end)* du semestre / trimestre? Que vas-tu faire? Est-ce que tu vas continuer à étudier ici l'année prochaine?

# Planning how to get there

> Note
*culturelle*

Le sud *(south)* de la Louisiane est recouvert *(covered)* d'eau. Les Acadiens arrivant du Canada en 1764 apprennent vite *(quickly learn)* à s'adapter à cette région et à s'épanouir *(to flourish)* dans les bayous et les marais *(swamps)*. En raison de *(Because of)* l'inaccessibilité de leur région, les Acadiens restent isolés et conservent largement leur héritage français. Toutefois *(However)*, depuis le 19e siècle et l'arrivée de meilleurs moyens de transport et de communication, la culture cadienne se trouve envahie par le monde anglophone *(finds itself invaded by the English-speaking world)*. Que savez-vous de *(What do you know about)* l'histoire des groupes ethniques et culturels de votre région?

**NOTES DE VOCABULAIRE**

**1. Un car** runs between cities and **un bus** runs within cities. *A tour bus* is also called **un car.** *A school bus* is **un car scolaire.**
**2.** Although traditionally it is considered correct to say **à vélo / à moto / à vélomoteur,** most people say **en vélo / en moto / en vélomoteur.**

**VOCABULAIRE SUPPLÉMENTAIRE**

**à / en moto(cyclette)** *(f) by motorcycle*
**à / en vélomoteur** *(m) by moped*

## Les moyens de transport

Robert et ses amis vont aller à La Nouvelle-Orléans en voiture. Et vous? Comment préférez-vous voyager?

Pour visiter une autre ville je préfère y aller...

en avion *(m)*

en train *(m)*

en bateau *(m)*

en car / autocar *(m)*

Il y a d'autres possibilités pour aller en ville. Comment **venez-vous** en cours?

**Je viens** en cours...

à pied *(m)*

à / en vélo *(m)*

en taxi *(m)*

en voiture *(f)*

en métro *(m)*

en bus / autobus *(m)*

CD 1-50

Robert parle à Thomas du voyage à La Nouvelle-Orléans.

ROBERT: Écoute, demain matin on va partir à La Nouvelle-Orléans. Tout est **prêt?**
THOMAS: Oui. On y va en car?
ROBERT: Non, on va **louer** une voiture, c'est plus commode.
THOMAS: C'est loin? **Ça prend combien de temps pour y aller?**
ROBERT: Ça prend environ deux heures et demie en voiture, **pas plus.**
THOMAS: Et **on revient** quand?
ROBERT: On revient vendredi soir.

---

**Les moyens** *(m)* **de transport** *means of transportation*    **vous venez** (**venir** *to come*)    **Je viens** (**venir** *to come*)
**prêt(e)** *ready*    **louer** *to rent*    **Ça prend combien de temps pour y aller?** *How long does it take to get there?*
**pas plus** *no more*    **on revient** (**revenir** *to come back*)

**A. Moyens de transport.** Complétez les phrases pour parler de vous.

1. Pour faire un long voyage, je préfère prendre *le train / l'avion / le bateau / le car / la voiture.*
2. Je n'aime pas beaucoup voyager *en train / en avion / en bateau / en car / en voiture.*
3. Je préfère aller en ville *à pied / en vélo / en taxi / en voiture / en métro / en bus / ???.*
4. Je n'aime pas beaucoup aller en ville *à pied / en vélo / en taxi / en voiture / en métro / en bus / ???.*
5. D'habitude, je viens en cours *à pied / en vélo / en taxi / en voiture / en métro / en bus / ???.*
6. Après les cours, je rentre chez moi *à pied / en vélo / en taxi / en voiture / en métro / en bus, ???.*
7. Pour aller voir mes parents, j'y vais *à pied / en voiture / en métro / en avion / ???.*

**B. On y va comment?** Dites où chacun va et comment.

> **Exemple    Ils vont à La Nouvelle-Orléans en voiture.**

Ils…

**1.** Je…

**2.** Ils…

**3.** Vous…

**4.** Nous…

**5.** Elle…

**C. Entretien.** Interviewez votre partenaire.

1. Tu préfères prendre l'avion, le train ou l'autocar pour faire un long voyage?
2. Quelle autre ville est-ce que tu visites souvent? Comment est-ce que tu y vas? (en voiture? en train? en avion?) Ça prend combien de temps pour y aller?
3. Tu voyages souvent en avion? Tu as peur de prendre l'avion? Pour aller à l'aéroport de chez toi, ça prend combien de temps? Qu'est-ce que tu aimes faire pendant *(during)* les longs voyages en avion? (dormir? lire? parler? travailler sur l'ordinateur?)
4. Quels jours est-ce que tu viens en cours? Comment viens-tu en cours d'habitude?

**D. Conversation.** Avec un(e) partenaire, relisez à haute voix la conversation entre Robert et Thomas en bas de la page précédente. Ensuite, changez la conversation pour parler d'un voyage que vous allez faire ensemble pour visiter une autre ville. Parlez de comment vous allez voyager et de combien de temps ça va prendre pour y aller.

**1.** What are the forms of **venir**? of **prendre**? What two verbs are conjugated like **venir**? like **prendre**? What verb do you use to say you are having something to eat or drink? When is **apprendre** followed by **à**?

**2.** In what forms of the verbs **venir** and **prendre** are the vowels nasal? **Je viens / tu viens / il vient** rhyme with what word? **Je prends / tu prends / il prend** rhyme with what word? How do you pronounce the **ils/elles viennent** form? the **ils/elles prennent** form?

**NOTES DE VOCABULAIRE**

**1.** Use **en** with **aller, venir,** or **voyager** to say you are traveling *by* a means of transportation. Use **prendre** to say what means of transportation you are *taking*. In this case, you can generally use the same article with the noun that you would in English: *I take the bus, a cab, the train...* **Je prends *le* bus, *un* taxi, *le* train...**
**2.** To say what courses someone is taking, you use the irregular verb **suivre** *(to follow)*, not **prendre**. See the *Appendix* for the conjugation of the verb **suivre**.

# Deciding how to get there and come back
*Les verbes **prendre** et **venir** et les moyens de transport*

The conjugations of **prendre** *(to take)* and **venir** *(to come)* are irregular.

| PRENDRE *(to take)* | | VENIR *(to come)* | |
|---|---|---|---|
| je **prends** | nous **prenons** | je **viens** | nous **venons** |
| tu **prends** | vous **prenez** | tu **viens** | vous **venez** |
| il/elle/on **prend** | ils/elles **prennent** | il/elle/on **vient** | ils/elles **viennent** |

Je **viens** en cours à pied mais mon frère **prend** l'autobus.

You can use **prendre** to say that you are *taking* a particular means of transportation. You can also use **aller, venir,** or **voyager** and the preposition **en** to say that you are *going, coming,* or *traveling by* a particular means of transportation. To say *on foot,* use **à pied.**

Je **prends** mon vélo.　　　Je **prends** l'avion.　　　Je **viens** en cours à pied.
J'y **vais** en vélo.　　　Je **voyage** en avion.

You can also use **prendre** as *to have* when talking about having something to eat or drink.

Je **prends** un sandwich et une eau minérale.

**Revenir** *(to come back)* and **devenir** *(to become)* are conjugated like **venir.**

Elle **revient** tard.　　　*She comes back late.*
Il **devient** impatient.　　　*He is becoming impatient.*

**Comprendre** *(to understand)* and **apprendre** *(to learn)* are conjugated like **prendre.** When **apprendre** is followed by an infinitive, the infinitive is preceded by **à.**

Tu **comprends** le français, non? Moi, **j'apprends à** parler français.
Ma sœur **apprend** le français aussi.

CD 1-51

# Prononciation
*Les verbes **prendre** et **venir***

In the **je, tu,** and **il/elle/on** forms of the verb **venir,** the **e** in the vowel combination **ie** has the nasal sound [ɛ̃]. The consonants after **ie** are all silent. All three forms rhyme with the word **bien.** In the **ils/elles viennent** form, however, the **ie** is not nasal and the **nn** is pronounced.

**je viens**　　　**tu viens**　　　**il vient**　　　**ils viennent**　　　**elles viennent**

Similarly, the **e** in the **je, tu,** and **il/elle/on** forms of the verb **prendre** have the nasal sound [ɑ̃] and the consonants after the vowel are silent. All three forms rhyme with the word **quand.** In the **ils/elles prennent** form, however, the **e** is not nasal. It is pronounced like the **è** in **mère** and the **nn** is pronounced.

**je prends**　　　**tu prends**　　　**il prend**　　　**ils prennent**　　　**elles prennent**

The **e** in the **nous** and **vous** forms of both verbs is pronounced like the **e** in **je.**

**nous venons**　　　**vous venez**　　　**nous prenons**　　　**vous prenez**

**A. Que faites-vous?** Est-ce que ces personnes font les choses indiquées?

> **Exemple** Moi, je... (prendre l'autobus pour venir en cours)
> **Moi, je ne prends pas l'autobus pour venir en cours.**

1. Moi, je... (venir en cours à pied, prendre un café avant le cours de français, comprendre toujours en cours, apprendre le vocabulaire avant de commencer le chapitre)
2. Nous... (venir en cours de français tous les jours, prendre beaucoup de notes en cours, apprendre l'espagnol, comprendre mieux le français tous les jours)
3. Le professeur... (prendre un café en cours, comprendre d'autres langues que le français, apprendre une autre langue, revenir à l'université le week-end)
4. En général ici, les étudiants... (prendre leur voiture pour venir en cours, venir en cours en autobus, comprendre une deuxième langue, apprendre beaucoup)

**B. Qu'est-ce qu'on fait?** Conjuguez les verbes qui sont entre parenthèses et posez les questions à votre partenaire.

1. Quels jours est-ce que tu (venir) en cours? Est-ce que tu (venir) toujours en cours? Est-ce que tu (prendre) le bus pour venir en cours?
2. Est-ce que les autres étudiants du cours de français (venir) toujours en cours? Est-ce qu'ils (comprendre) bien le français?
3. Est-ce que le cours de français (devenir) plus difficile? Est-ce que tu (prendre) beaucoup de notes en cours?
4. Est-ce que le professeur de français (venir) toujours en cours à l'heure?
5. Est-ce que le prof (devenir) impatient(e) quand les étudiants ne préparent pas bien le cours? Est-ce que tu (apprendre) bien le vocabulaire?
6. Est-ce que tu (avoir) l'intention de revenir à cette université l'année prochaine? Est-ce que tu (avoir) l'intention de devenir prof après tes études?

**C. La santé.** Votre ami voudrait améliorer sa santé *(to improve his health)*. Donnez-lui des conseils. Utilisez l'impératif.

> **Exemple** Je prends un coca ou un jus d'orange?
> **Prends un jus d'orange!**

1. Je prends une bière ou une eau minérale?
2. Je prends un café ou un jus de fruit?
3. Je viens en cours en voiture ou en vélo?
4. Je prends une salade ou des frites?
5. Je vais au parc ou je reste à la maison?
6. Je vais au parc en voiture ou à pied?
7. Je prends un bain de soleil ou je nage?

Faire du sport, c'est bon pour la santé.

**D. Une sortie.** Avec un(e) partenaire, préparez une conversation basée sur cette situation pour présenter à la classe.

Vous demandez à un(e) ami(e) s'il/si elle a envie de faire quelque chose avec vous. Parlez de quand vous allez y aller et de quel moyen de transport vous allez prendre.

## Reprise

*Talking about your family and free time*

In **Chapitre 4,** you learned to describe your family, say where you go and how you get there, invite or tell someone to do something, and talk about your plans for the near future. Now you have a chance to practice what you learned.

Didier Landry    Anne Landry
Christine    Éric

Philippe et Marie Broussard

**A. Descriptions.** Vous allez passer un mois chez cette famille francophone à Lafayette. La mère décrit chaque personne de la famille. Complétez ses descriptions d'une façon logique.

Mes parents habitent chez nous. Mon _____ a soixante-quinze ans. Il a une _____ mais il n'a pas de barbe. Il a besoin de _____ pour lire. Ma _____ a soixante-douze _____. Les deux ont les _____ gris. Mon _____ et moi, nous _____ quarante-sept _____. Nous _____ deux enfants, un _____ et une _____. Notre fils a les cheveux _____ comme nous, mais notre _____ a les cheveux _____.

**B. Qu'est-ce qu'on fait?** Vous voulez profiter au maximum de *(to make the most of)* votre visite à Lafayette. Répondez aux suggestions de la famille chez qui vous habitez. Utilisez l'impératif.

> **Exemple**    Alors, on parle anglais ou français?
> **Parlons français!**

1. On reste à la maison aujourd'hui ou on va en ville?
2. On prend un coca au McDonald ou on prend un café dans un petit café du quartier?
3. On mange un hamburger ou on mange dans un restaurant créole?
4. On visite le musée ou on rentre à la maison?
5. On va voir un film américain ou on va voir un film français?
6. On écoute un CD de Tracy Chapman ou on écoute un CD de musique cadienne?
7. On loue une vidéo en français ou en anglais?

Maintenant, dites à une amie de faire ces mêmes choses.

> **Exemple**    **Ne parle pas anglais. Parle français.**

**C. Chez les Landry.** Les Landry sont à la maison. Complétez les phrases suivantes pour décrire la situation des membres de la famille. Utilisez une expression avec **avoir.**

> **Exemple**    Les Broussard vont boire quelque chose parce qu'ils **ont soif.**

1. Madame Broussard voudrait manger quelque chose aussi parce qu'elle _____.
2. Éric voudrait mettre un pull *(to put on a sweater)* parce qu'il _____.
3. Christine voudrait enlever *(to take off)* son pull parce qu'elle _____.
4. Monsieur Broussard voudrait faire la sieste *(to take a nap)* parce qu'il _____.
5. Anne _____ d'étudier parce qu'elle a un examen demain.

**D. Comment vont-ils en ville?** Anne Landry parle des projets de sa famille pour aujourd'hui. Complétez ces phrases avec la forme convenable du verbe **prendre.**

> **Exemple** Papa **prend** le bus pour aller acheter des livres.

1. Didier _____ sa voiture pour aller voir un film.
2. Les enfants _____ le bus pour aller nager.
3. Moi, je _____ ma voiture pour aller faire du shopping.
4. Mes parents _____ un taxi pour aller voir une exposition.
5. Mon mari et moi _____ la voiture pour aller dîner ensemble.

Maintenant, dites où chacun va et comment il y va.

> **Exemple** **Papa va à la librairie. Il y va en bus.**

la librairie    le musée    le centre commercial    le restaurant
le cinéma    la piscine

**E. Des visites.** Presque tous les membres de sa famille viennent voir Didier à Lafayette cette année. Didier parle avec sa mère au téléphone pour savoir quand chacun vient. Qu'est-ce qu'ils disent?

> **Exemple** 8/8 (mes cousins)
> — **Quand est-ce que mes cousins viennent?**
> — **Le huit août.**

1. 1/1 (ma sœur)
2. 15/6 (tu)
3. 17/9 (mon oncle)
4. 15/3 (mes frères)

Maintenant, Didier parle de ce que tous les membres de sa famille vont faire aux dates indiquées. Complétez ses phrases logiquement au futur immédiat.

passer du temps en famille / avec des amis / seul(e)...
sortir avec des amis    inviter des amis à la maison
faire une fête *(to have a party)*    dîner au restaurant    ???
aller voir un défilé *(parade)*    aller danser    rester à la maison

> **Exemple** 12/25 (mes enfants)
> **Le vingt-cinq décembre, mes enfants vont passer du temps en famille.**

1. (14/2) ma femme et moi
2. (4/7) mes enfants
3. (31/12) ma tante

Maintenant, demandez à votre partenaire ce qu'il/elle va probablement faire aux dates indiquées.

> **Exemple** — **Qu'est-ce que tu vas probablement faire le vingt-cinq décembre?**
> — **Je vais passer du temps en famille.**
> **Je ne vais rien faire de spécial.**

# LECTURE ET COMPOSITION

## Lecture: *Cœur des Cajuns*

Music is an integral part of life on the bayou. You are going to read the lyrics to the song ***Cœur des Cajuns** (Heart of the Cajuns)* by Bruce Daigrepont, in which he sees Cajun music as the expression of both the **joie de vivre** *(joy of living)* and the **chagrin de cœur** *(heartache)* of the Cajun people. Before reading the lyrics, do this exercise to make your reading easier.

**Familles de mots.** Servez-vous des mots donnés pour déterminer le sens des mots en caractères gras.

danser: *to dance*  → **une danse:** *a* _____
chanter: *to sing*  → **une chanson:** *a* _____
prier: *to pray*  → **une prière:** *a* _____
valser: *to waltz*  → **une valse:** *a* _____
vivre: *to live*  → **une vie:** *a* _____

---

### CŒUR DES CAJUNS

La joie de vivre, c'est dans l'accordéon,
La joie de vivre, c'est dans les belles chansons.
La musique c'est une tradition
Et c'est dans les cœurs de tous les Cajuns.

Chagrin de cœur, c'est dans l'accordéon,
Chagrin de cœur, c'est dans les belles chansons.
La musique c'est une tradition
Et c'est dans les cœurs de tous les Cajuns.

Dansez ensemble les vieux et les jeunes.
Priez ensemble les vieux et les jeunes.
La tradition c'est **pour tout quelques-uns**
Et c'est dans les cœurs de tous les Cajuns.

Un **'tit** bébé dans **les bras** de sa maman,
**Aprévalser** dans les bras de sa maman.
Il va apprendre la tradition
Et c'est dans les cœurs de tous les Cajuns.

La joie de vivre, c'est dans l'accordéon,
La joie de vivre, c'est dans les belles chansons.
La musique c'est une tradition
Et c'est dans les cœurs de tous les Cajuns.

Chagrin de cœur, c'est dans l'accordéon,
Chagrin de cœur, c'est dans les belles chansons.
La musique c'est une tradition
Et c'est dans les cœurs de tous les Cajuns.

**by Bruce Daigrepont**
**(Bayou Pon Pon, ASCAP-Happy Valley Music, BMI)**
**from *Cœur Des Cajuns* on Rounder Records (#6026)**

---

**pour tout quelques-uns** *for everyone* (regional)   **'tit =** *petit*   **les bras** *the arms*   **Aprévalser** *Waltzing* (regional)

## Compréhension

**Cœur des Cajuns.** Lisez *Cœur des Cajuns* et complétez ces phrases.

1. La musique est une expression de la joie de vivre et aussi du _____.
2. La musique est une tradition qui se trouve dans les _____ de tous les Cajuns.
3. _____ est un instrument de musique populaire.
4. Les vieux et les jeunes vont danser, valser et _____ ensemble.

## Composition

**A. Organisez-vous.** Vous allez écrire une description de votre famille. D'abord, faites une liste de tous les membres de votre famille et écrivez tous les mots que vous associez à chacun.

> **Exemple** **mon frère (grand, beau, les yeux marron, les cheveux châtains, 26 ans, aime parler, étudiant, habite à Seattle... ); ma mère (petite, les cheveux noirs... )**

**B. Rédaction: La famille.** Écrivez une description détaillée de votre famille. Si vous êtes marié(e) ou divorcé(e), parlez de votre (ex-)mari / (ex-)femme, de vos enfants et de vos animaux. Sinon *(Otherwise)*, parlez de vos parents, de vos frères et sœurs et de vos animaux.

**C. Questions.** Échangez votre rédaction avec un(e) camarade de classe. En lisant *(While reading)* sa rédaction, préparez cinq questions sur des aspects de sa famille dont *(about which)* il/elle ne parle pas.

**D. Entretien.** Posez les questions préparées dans *C. Questions* à votre partenaire.

**E. Sa famille.** Décrivez la famille de votre partenaire à la classe.

> **Exemple** **Dans sa famille, ils sont sept: sa mère, ses deux frères et ses trois sœurs. Ses frères et sœurs habitent avec sa mère. Sa mère s'appelle...**

**F. Une seconde fois.** Récrivez votre rédaction en répondant aux questions posées dans *D. Entretien.*

If you have access to SYSTÈME-D software, you will find the following phrases, vocabulary, grammar, and dictionary aids there.

**Phrases:** Describing people; Asking for information
**Vocabulary:** Family members; Personality; Hair colors; Animals
**Grammar:** Adjective position; Contractions with **à**; Possessive adjectives
**Dictionary:** The verb **aller**

## La francophonie en Louisiane et ses origines

**La** majorité des Créoles en Louisiane aujourd'hui sont d'origine française, d'origine africaine, d'origine européenne ou d'origine mixte.

En 1682, la France prend possession de la Louisiane et en 1718 La Nouvelle-Orléans est **fondée**. Certains Créoles sont les descendants des premiers **colons** français et européens. Ces colons **faisaient souvent partie de** l'aristocratie ou de **la haute bourgeoisie**.

D'autres Créoles sont les descendants d'immigrés français **venus** en Louisiane pour **échapper** aux campagnes militaires de Napoléon.

**Encore d'autres** Créoles sont les descendants **des esclaves** ou des immigrés des îles caraïbes. En 1791, plus de 10 000 Créoles arrivent de Saint-Domingue (aujourd'hui Haïti) **pendant** la Révolte des Esclaves. En 1809, 5 700 Créoles arrivent de Saint-Domingue pendant la révolution.

**Par contre,** la majorité des Cadiens sont les descendants des Acadiens, **expulsés** du Canada **par** les Anglais **au 18ᵉ siècle.** (Le mot *cajun* **est dérivé du mot** *acadien*.)

En 1604, les Français fondent l'Acadie, aujourd'hui la Nouvelle-Écosse, le Nouveau-Brunswick et l'Île-du-Prince-Édouard.

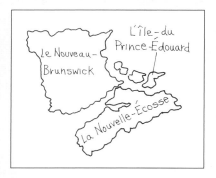

En 1713, les Anglais prennent possession de l'Acadie. En 1755, ils commencent à expulser les Français. Entre 1764 et 1785, **des vagues d'**Acadiens arrivent en Louisiane. **Il leur a fallu plus de trente ans pour trouver une patrie!**

---

**fondée** *founded*   **des colons** *colonists*   **faisaient souvent partie de** *were often part of*
**la haute bourgeoisie** *the upper middle class*   **venus** *who came*   **échapper** *to escape*   **Encore d'autres** *Still other*
**des esclaves** *slaves*   **pendant** *during*   **Par contre** *On the other hand*   **expulsés** *thrown out*   **par** *by*
**au 18ᵉ siècle** *in the 18th century*   **est dérivé du mot** *is derived from the word*   **des vagues de** *waves of*
**Il leur a fallu plus de trente ans pour trouver une patrie!** *It took them over 30 years to find a homeland!*

**En raison de** l'inaccessibilité de la région, les francophones en Louisiane restent **isolés** pendant plus de 200 ans. Ils conservent leurs héritages, leurs langues et leurs cultures.

**Vers la fin du 19ᵉ siècle,** le contact avec **le monde** extérieur est **facilité** et des vagues d'anglophones arrivent dans la région. Pendant un certain temps, la culture francophone de la Louisiane, **entourée par** la culture anglophone, est **sur le point d'être perdue.** En 1916, l'état de Louisiane **exige que la scolarité soit faite** en anglais et l'anglais devient la langue prédominante chez les jeunes. L'usage du français en Louisiane **diminue.**

Après un certain temps, un mouvement pour le développement et la protection de la langue et de la culture françaises **surgit.** En 1968, l'état **établit** CODOFIL, le Conseil pour le Développement du Français en Louisiane. L'assemblée législative **crée** la région d'Acadiana. Un amendement est **ajouté** à la Constitution de l'état pour encourager la préservation de la culture française en Louisiane et les écoles commencent à établir des programmes d'immersion en français.

Pendant plus de 200 ans, les langues et les cultures des francophones restent dominantes dans **le sud** de la Louisiane.

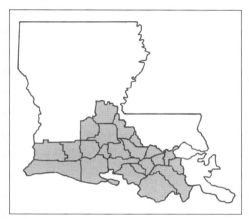

En 1971, l'assemblée législative crée la région d'Acadiana, comprenant 22 paroisses francophones.

## À discuter

1. La Louisiane a créé une agence pour la défense de la langue et de la culture d'une minorité. Que pensez-vous de cette action?

2. L'Acadiana a une culture unique. En quoi est-ce que cette région de la Louisiane diffère du reste des états du sud des États-Unis?

3. Tandis qu'un *(Whereas a)* grand nombre des habitants du sud des États-Unis ont un héritage religieux protestant fondamentaliste, les Cadiens sont issus *(come from)* d'une tradition catholique. Comment est-ce que cette différence de tradition religieuse se manifeste *(is reflected)* dans d'autres différences culturelles?

4. Dans certaines écoles élémentaires *(elementary schools)* en Louisiane, il y a des programmes d'immersion en français. À votre avis *(In your opinion)*, à quel âge est-ce qu'on devrait *(should)* commencer à étudier une autre langue? Est-il plus important d'étudier une autre langue si on est d'une famille d'une autre tradition linguistique?

visit http://horizons.heinle.com

---

**En raison de** *Because of*    **isolés** *isolated*    **Vers la fin du 19ᵉ siècle** *Towards the end of the 19th century*
**le monde** *the world*    **facilité** *facilitated*    **entourée par** *surrounded by*    **sur le point d'être perdue** *on the verge of being lost*
**exige que la scolarité soit faite** *requires that education be done*    **diminue** *diminishes*    **surgit** *surges, arises*
**établit** *establishes*    **crée** *creates*    **ajouté** *added*    **le sud** *the south*

# Résumé de grammaire

## Expressions with *avoir*

The following expressions use **avoir** to describe someone or say how someone feels.

Note the use of the definite article with **avoir les yeux / les cheveux.**

Ma tante s'appelle Sylvie. Elle **a 34 ans.** Elle **a les cheveux longs et châtains** et **les yeux noirs.** Elle **a des lunettes.** Elle **a l'air** intellectuel.

| | |
|---|---|
| avoir... ans | avoir l'air |
| avoir faim | avoir soif |
| avoir froid | avoir chaud |
| avoir raison | avoir tort |
| avoir peur (de) | avoir sommeil |
| avoir les yeux... | avoir les cheveux... |
| avoir une barbe / une moustache / des lunettes | |

— J'ai faim. Je vais aller au restaurant. Qu'est-ce que tu **as l'intention de** faire?
— Je ne sais pas. J'**ai besoin de** travailler, mais j'**ai envie de** sortir.

Use **avoir besoin de** (+ noun or infinitive) for *to need,* **avoir envie de** (+ noun or infinitive) for *to feel like,* and **avoir l'intention de** (+ infinitive) for *to intend to.*

## The verb *aller,* the preposition *à,* and the pronoun *y*

The verb **aller** *(to go)* is irregular.

— Où **vas**-tu?
— Je **vais** au cinéma. Mes parents y **vont** aussi, mais ma sœur n'y **va** pas. Et toi?
— Philippe et moi **allons** au café.

| ALLER *(to go)* | |
|---|---|
| je **vais** | nous ᶻ **allons** |
| tu **vas** | vous ᶻ **allez** |
| il/elle **va** | ils/elles **vont** |

Use the preposition **à** *(to, at, in)* to say where you are going. When **à** falls before **le** or **les,** the two words contract to **au** and **aux.**

J'aime aller **au** centre commercial, mais j'aime mieux aller **à la** librairie.
Aimes-tu aller **aux** festivals de musique de la région?

Use the pronoun **y** to mean *there,* even when *there* is only implied in English. Place it *immediately* before the infinitive if there is one. Otherwise, place it *immediately* before the conjugated verb. Treat **y** as a vowel for purposes of elision and liaison.

— Je vais à l'université. Tu voudrais **y** aller avec moi?
— Non, je n'**y** vais pas aujourd'hui.

## The subject pronoun *on* and command forms (*l'impératif*)

Use **on** as the subject of a sentence to refer to people in general *(one, people, they),* or instead of **nous** to say *we.* **On** takes the same verb form as **il/elle,** no matter what the translation in English.

**On parle** français en Louisiane.

You can invite someone to do something with you by asking a question with **on** *(Shall we . . . ? / How about . . . ?).* You can also invite someone using *Let's . . .* To say *Let's . . . ,* use the **nous** form of the appropriate verb without the pronoun **nous.**

— **On sort** ce soir?
— D'accord. **Allons** au cinéma.
— Non, **n'allons pas** au cinéma. **Dînons** plutôt au restaurant.

To tell someone to do something, use the **tu** or **vous** form of the verb, as appropriate, without the pronoun **tu** or **vous.** In **tu** form commands, drop the final **s** of **-er** verbs and **aller.**

**Va** au restaurant Préjean et **mange** les spécialités de la maison.
**Mangez** bien. **Ne mangez pas** de dessert.

Avoir and être have irregular command forms.

| ÊTRE (be . . . ) | AVOIR (have . . . ) |
|---|---|
| sois | aie |
| soyons | ayons |
| soyez | ayez |

Sois à l'heure pour tes cours.
N'aie pas peur — aie confiance!
Soyons calmes!
Ayez de la patience!

## The immediate future (Le futur immédiat)

To talk about what someone *is going to do*, use a conjugated form of the verb **aller** followed by an infinitive. To say what someone is *not* going to do, place **ne... pas** around the conjugated form of **aller. Il y a** becomes **il va y avoir** in the immediate future.

— Qu'est-ce que tu **vas faire** ce soir? Tu **vas sortir?**
— Non, je **ne vais pas sortir.** Je **vais rester** à la maison. **Il va y avoir** un festival de films à la télé.

## Dates

To tell the date, use **le** and the cardinal numbers (**deux, trois, quatre...** ) except for *the first* (**le premier**). The day goes before the month: 30/9/2007.

You can express the years 1100–1999 in two ways. Years from 2000 on are only expressed using the word **mille.**

Use **en** to say in what year or month.

— Quelle est la date aujourd'hui? C'est **le 30 septembre?**
— Non, c'est **le premier octobre.**
1910 **mille neuf cent dix /
dix-neuf cent dix**
2010 **deux mille dix**

Mon anniversaire, c'est **en** mars.
Je vais finir mes études **en** 2009.

## The verbs *prendre* and *venir* and means of transportation

**Prendre** *(to take)* and **venir** *(to come)* are irregular.

| PRENDRE (to take) | | VENIR (to come) | |
|---|---|---|---|
| je **prends** | nous **prenons** | je **viens** | nous **venons** |
| tu **prends** | vous **prenez** | tu **viens** | vous **venez** |
| il/elle/on **prend** | ils/elles **prennent** | il/elle/on **vient** | ils/elles **viennent** |

— **Venez**-vous à l'université en voiture?
— Non, je ne **viens** pas en cours en voiture. Je **prends** mon vélo. **Prenez**-vous votre voiture?

**Prendre** means *to take.* You can also use it as *to have* when talking about having something to eat or drink. **Comprendre** *(to understand)* and **apprendre** *(to learn)* are conjugated like **prendre.**

Le matin, il **prend** un café et un croissant.
Tu **comprends?**
Nous **apprenons** beaucoup dans ce cours.

**Revenir** *(to come back)* and **devenir** *(to become)* are conjugated like **venir.**

Les fils **reviennent** tard et le père **devient** impatient.

Use the preposition **en** to say *by* what means you are traveling with verbs like **aller, venir,** and **voyager.** When using **prendre** to say what means of transportation you are taking, you can often use the same article with the noun that you would in English.

D'habitude, ils **voyagent en avion** mais aujourd'hui ils **prennent le train.**

# Vocabulaire

## Describing your family

### LA FAMILLE

| | |
|---|---|
| un beau-frère / une belle-sœur | a brother-in-law / a sister-in-law |
| un beau-père / une belle-mère | a stepfather, a father-in-law / a stepmother, a mother-in-law |
| un(e) cousin(e) | a cousin |
| un(e) enfant | a child |
| un fils / une fille | a son / a daughter |
| un frère / une sœur | a brother / a sister |
| un garçon / une fille | a boy / a girl |
| des grands-parents / un grand-père / une grand-mère | grandparents / a grandfather / a grandmother |
| un mari / une femme | a husband / a wife |
| un neveu (pl des neveux) / une nièce | a nephew / a niece |
| un oncle / une tante | an uncle / an aunt |
| des parents / un père / une mère | parents / a father / a mother |

### NOMS FÉMININS

| | |
|---|---|
| une barbe | a beard |
| des lunettes | glasses |
| une moustache | a mustache |
| des vacances | vacation |

### ADJECTIFS

| | |
|---|---|
| âgé(e) | old |
| blond(e) | blond(e) |
| brun(e) | brown (with hair) |
| châtain | light / medium brown (with hair) |
| court(e) | short |
| long(ue) | long |
| mi-longs | shoulder-length (with hair) |
| mort(e) | dead |
| noir(e) | black, very dark brown (with eyes) |
| roux (rousse) | red (with hair) |

### EXPRESSIONS VERBALES

| | |
|---|---|
| avoir besoin de | to need |
| avoir chaud / froid | to be hot / cold |
| avoir envie de | to feel like, to want |
| avoir faim / soif | to be hungry / thirsty |
| avoir l'air… | to look . . . , to seem . . . |
| avoir les cheveux / les yeux… | to have . . . hair / eyes |
| avoir l'intention de | to intend to |
| avoir peur (de) | to be afraid (of) |
| avoir raison / tort | to be right / wrong |
| avoir sommeil | to be sleepy |
| Comment s'appelle-t-il/elle? | What is his/her name? |
| Il/Elle s'appelle… | His/Her name is . . . |
| porter | to wear, to carry |
| Quel âge a… ? | How old is . . . ? |
| avoir… ans | to be . . . years old |
| Vous êtes combien dans votre famille? | How many people are there in your family? |
| Nous sommes… | There are . . . of us. |

### DIVERS

| | |
|---|---|
| de taille moyenne | of medium height |
| encore | still |
| environ | about |
| La Nouvelle-Orléans | New Orleans |

## Saying where you go in your free time

### NOMS MASCULINS

| | |
|---|---|
| un bar | a bar |
| un centre commercial | a shopping mall |
| un concert | a concert |
| un festival | a festival |
| un magasin | a store |
| un musée | a museum |
| un orchestre | an orchestra, a band |
| un parc | a park |
| des projets | plans |
| le temps libre | free time |
| un théâtre | a theater |

### NOMS FÉMININS

| | |
|---|---|
| une activité (de plein air) | an (outdoor) activity |
| la cuisine | cooking, cuisine |
| une église | a church |
| une exposition | an exhibit |
| une librairie | a bookstore |
| la musique zydeco | zydeco music |
| une pièce | a play |
| une piscine | a swimming pool |
| une plage | a beach |
| une région | a region |
| une spécialité | a specialty |

### EXPRESSIONS VERBALES

| | |
|---|---|
| acheter | to buy |
| aie, ayons, ayez | have, let's have, have |
| aller (à) | to go (to) |
| avoir confiance | to have confidence |
| avoir de la patience | to have patience |
| connaître | to know, to get to know, to be acquainted / familiar with |
| jouer au frisbee | to play frisbee |
| pouvoir | can, may, to be able |
| prendre un bain de soleil | to sunbathe |
| retrouver | to meet |
| servir | to serve |
| sois, soyons, soyez | be, let's be, be |
| trouver | to find |

### DIVERS

| | |
|---|---|
| à l'heure | on time |
| bonne idée | good idea |
| cadien(ne) | Cajun |
| calme | calm |
| Ça te dit? | How does that sound? |
| culturel(le) | cultural |
| de temps en temps | from time to time |
| extra | great |
| on | one, people, they, we |
| On… ? | Shall we . . . ?, How about . . . ? |
| on dit que | they say that |
| on s'amuse bien | one has a good time |
| plutôt | rather, instead |
| pour | in order to |
| sage | good, well-behaved |
| y | there |

## Saying what you are going to do

**NOMS MASCULINS**

| | |
|---|---|
| un anniversaire | *a birthday* |
| le folklore | *folklore* |

**NOMS FÉMININS**

| | |
|---|---|
| une fête | *a holiday, a party* |
| la soirée | *the evening* |

**EXPRESSIONS VERBALES**

| | |
|---|---|
| aller voir | *to go see, to visit (a person)* |
| boire | *to drink* |
| faire des projets | *to make plans* |
| faire un tour | *to take a tour, to go for a ride* |
| partir | *to go away, to leave* |
| quitter | *to leave* |
| rentrer | *to return, to go back (home)* |
| visiter | *to visit (a place)* |

**LES DATES**

| | |
|---|---|
| En quelle année? | *In what year?* |
| En quel mois? | *In what month?* |
| Quelle est la date? | *What is the date?* |
| C'est le premier (deux, trois...) | *It's the first (second, third . . . ) of* |
| janvier / février / mars / avril / mai / juin / juillet / août / septembre / octobre / novembre / décembre | *January / February / March / April / May / June / July / August / September / October / November / December* |

**EXPRESSIONS ADVERBIALES**

| | |
|---|---|
| ce matin | *this morning* |
| ce mois-ci | *this month* |
| ce soir | *tonight, this evening* |
| ce week-end | *this weekend* |
| cet après-midi | *this afternoon* |
| cette année | *this year* |
| cette semaine | *this week* |
| d'abord | *first* |
| demain matin / après-midi / soir | *tomorrow morning / afternoon / evening* |
| ensuite | *then, next* |
| l'année prochaine | *next year* |
| la semaine prochaine | *next week* |
| le mois prochain | *next month* |
| le week-end prochain | *next weekend* |
| lundi (mardi) prochain | *next Monday (Tuesday)* |
| plus tard | *later* |
| puis | *then* |
| tard | *late* |
| tôt | *early* |

**DIVERS**

| | |
|---|---|
| célèbre | *famous* |
| génial(e) (*m.pl.* **géniaux**) | *great* |
| régional(e) (*m.pl.* **régionaux**) | *regional* |
| le Vieux Carré | *the French Quarter* |

## Planning how to get there

**NOMS MASCULINS**

| | |
|---|---|
| un (auto)bus | *a bus* |
| un (auto)car | *a bus* |
| un avion | *a plane* |
| un bateau | *a boat* |
| le métro | *the subway* |
| un moyen de transport | *a means of transportation* |
| un taxi | *a cab, a taxi* |
| un train | *a train* |
| un vélo | *a bike* |
| un voyage | *a trip* |

**NOM FÉMININ**

| | |
|---|---|
| une possibilité | *a possibility* |

**EXPRESSIONS VERBALES**

| | |
|---|---|
| aller à pied / en (à) vélo / en (auto)car / en (auto)bus / en avion / en bateau / en métro / en taxi / en train / en voiture | *to go on foot / by bike / by bus / by bus / by plane / by boat / by subway / by taxi / by train / by car* |
| apprendre | *to learn* |
| comprendre | *to understand* |
| devenir | *to become* |
| louer | *to rent* |
| prendre | *to take* |
| revenir | *to come back* |
| venir | *to come* |

**DIVERS**

| | |
|---|---|
| Ça prend combien de temps? | *How long does it take?* |
| Ça prend... | *It takes . . .* |
| impatient(e) | *impatient* |
| pas plus | *no more* |
| prêt(e) | *ready* |

## La Tour Eiffel
### ROBERT DELAUNAY
### (1885–1941)

1910–1911
Basel Kunstmuseum
Giraudon/Art Resource, New York

Entre 1909 et 1911, Delaunay a peint *(painted)* une série de trente tableaux cubistes de la tour Eiffel. Pour Delaunay, la tour Eiffel symbolisait la modernité. Dans ses tableaux de la tour Eiffel, il a exploré les effets de la lumière *(light)* et sa distortion des formes et des couleurs.

# À Paris

**LA FRANCE (LA RÉPUBLIQUE FRANÇAISE)**
**SUPERFICIE:** 543 965 kilomètres carrés
**NOMBRE D'HABITANTS:** 59 490 000 (les Français)
**CAPITALE:** Paris
**INDUSTRIES PRINCIPALES:** aéronautique, agriculture, industries manufacturières, secteur des services, technologie, tourisme

COMPÉTENCE

# La France

La France a une grande diversité géographique. Il y a...

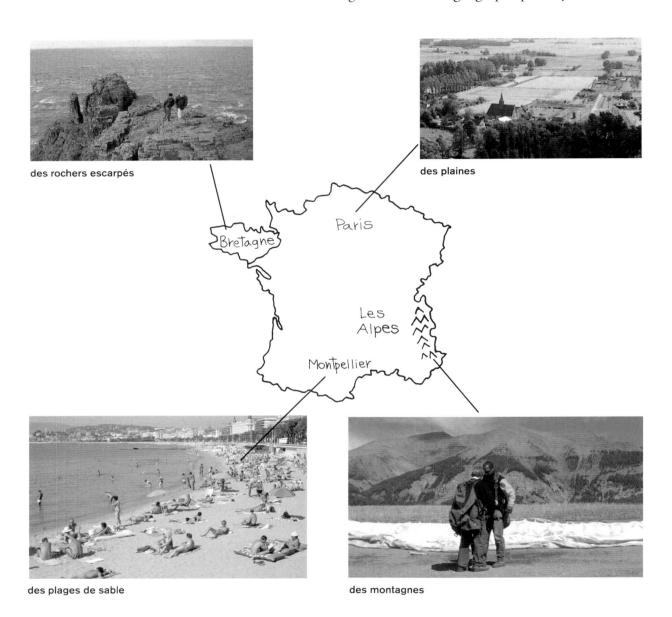

des rochers escarpés

des plaines

Bretagne

Paris

Les Alpes

Montpellier

des plages de sable

des montagnes

## À deviner

Est-ce que vous connaissez un peu la France? Lisez les renseignements donnés à la page 174 et regardez la carte de la France à **la fin** du livre. Ensuite, répondez à ces questions. (Si vous ne **savez** pas, **devinez**!)

1. La France a **à peu près la** même **superficie** que...
   **a.** l'Alaska          **b.** le Texas          **c.** la Louisiane
2. Regardez la carte de la France. **À cause de** sa forme, on appelle la France...
   **a.** le Pentagone          **b.** l'Octogone          **c.** l'Hexagone
3. Nommez les huit pays et les quatre masses d'eau qui bordent la France.
4. Nommez cinq **chaînes et massifs montagneux** qui se trouvent en France. **Lequel** ne forme pas de frontière entre la France et un autre pays?
5. Nommez sept **fleuves** ou rivières en France. Lequel **traverse** Paris?
6. Paris est la capitale de la France. Nommez deux autres villes importantes.
7. La France est un centre important de commerce, d'industrie et de technologie. L'agriculture est aussi très importante et _____ de la population française habite à la campagne.
   **a.** 25%          **b.** 50%          **c.** 75%

La belle France

**la fin** *the end*    **savez** *know*    **devinez** *guess*    **à peu près** *about*    **la superficie** *the area*    **À cause de** *Because of*
**chaînes et massifs montagneux** *mountain ranges*    **Lequel** *Which one*    **fleuves** *rivers*    **traverse** *crosses*

# Deciding what to wear and buying clothes

## VOCABULAIRE SUPPLÉMENTAIRE

**D'AUTRES VÊTEMENTS**

**un blouson** *a windbreaker, a jacket*
**une écharpe** *a winter scarf*
**un foulard** *a dress scarf*
**des gants** *(m) gloves*
**un gilet** *a vest, a cardigan*
**des hauts talons** *(m) high heels*
**un sweat** *a sweatshirt*
**un tailleur** *a woman's suit*
**une veste** *a sports coat*

**DES BIJOUX** *(m) JEWELRY*

**une bague** *a ring*
**des boucles d'oreille** *(f) earrings*
**un bracelet**
**un collier** *a necklace*

**DES SOUS-VÊTEMENTS** *UNDERWEAR*

**une chemise de nuit** *a nightgown*
**un collant** *pantyhose*
**une combinaison** *a slip*
**une culotte** *panties*
**un pyjama** *pajamas*
**un slip** *briefs*
**un soutien-gorge** *a bra*

## NOTE DE VOCABULAIRE

**Porter** means *to carry* or *to wear* and **mettre** *to put (on)*. They can both be used to say what one *wears* in general, but use **porter** to say what someone *is wearing* at a given moment.

Je **porte / mets** souvent une cravate.
*I often **wear** a tie.*

Je **porte** une cravate aujourd'hui.
*I'm **wearing** a tie today.*

The forms of **mettre** are:

| | |
|---|---|
| je **mets** | nous **mettons** |
| tu **mets** | vous **mettez** |
| il/elle/on **met** | ils/elles **mettent** |

## Les vêtements

Paris est sans doute le centre **mondial** de **la haute couture.** Et vous? Est-ce que **la mode** est importante pour vous?

Qu'est-ce que vous **mettez** pour aller en cours? pour sortir le soir?

Je mets souvent...          Je mets **parfois...**

un jean          un short          un pantalon et          une jupe
                                   une ceinture

un pull          un polo ou          une chemise et          un chemisier
                 un tee-shirt        une cravate

un survêtement     une robe     un costume     des chaussures (*f*), des
                                               chaussettes (*f*), des bottes (*f*),
                                               des sandales (*f*) ou des baskets (*f*)

un anorak     un imperméable     un manteau     un maillot de bain ou un bikini
                                                et un chapeau ou une casquette

Portez-vous quelquefois... ?

un parapluie     un sac ou          une montre          des lunettes (*f*)
                 un portefeuille                        de soleil

**mondial(e)** *world (adj)*     **la haute couture** *designer fashion*     **la mode** *fashion*     **mettez** (**mettre** *to put, to put on*)
**parfois** *sometimes*

CD 1-52

Alice Pérez, **femme d'affaires** américaine **travaillant** à Paris, cherche un nouveau maillot de bain. Elle entre dans un magasin.

| | |
|---|---|
| LA VENDEUSE: | Bonjour, madame. **Je peux vous aider?** |
| ALICE: | Je cherche un maillot de bain. |
| LA VENDEUSE: | **Quelle taille faites-vous?** |
| ALICE: | **Je fais du** 42. |
| LA VENDEUSE: | Nous avons ces maillots-ci. Ils sont très jolis et ils sont **en solde.** |
| ALICE: | J'aime bien ce maillot noir. **Je peux l'essayer?** |
| LA VENDEUSE: | Bien sûr, madame. **La cabine d'essayage** est **par ici.** |

Alice sort de la cabine d'essayage.

| | |
|---|---|
| LA VENDEUSE: | Alors, **qu'en pensez-vous?** |
| ALICE: | **Il me plaît** beaucoup. Il **coûte** combien? |
| LA VENDEUSE: | **Voyons,** c'est 65 euros. |
| ALICE: | C'est bien. Alors, je **le** prends. |

**>Note**
*culturelle*

Notez que les tailles en France ne sont pas les mêmes qu'aux USA.

| Robes et chemisiers | | Chemises hommes | |
|---|---|---|---|
| USA | FRANCE | USA | FRANCE |
| 8 | 38 | 15 | 38 |
| 10 | 40 | 15 $\frac{1}{2}$ | 39 |
| 12 | 42 | 16 | 40 |
| 14 | 44 | 16 $\frac{1}{2}$ | 41 |
| 16 | 46 | 17 | 42 |

**A. Et vous?** Regardez les illustrations à la page précédente. Dites si vous mettez souvent chaque chose.

**Exemples**    **Je mets souvent un jean.**
**Je mets rarement un short.**

**Je mets souvent un pantalon mais parfois je ne mets pas de ceinture.**
**Je ne mets jamais de jupe.**

**B. Préférences.** Complétez les phrases suivantes pour exprimer vos préférences.

1. Je préfère acheter mes vêtements *en solde / dans les meilleurs magasins / dans un magasin de seconde main (de vêtements d'occasion* [second hand]*) / ???.*
2. Si quelque chose me plaît, je préfère l'essayer *dans le magasin / à la maison.*
3. Pour sortir le soir, je mets souvent *un jean / un pantalon / ???.*
4. Quand je voyage en voiture, je mets souvent *un jean / ???.*
5. Pour aller à la plage, je mets *un short / ???.*
6. Pour aller en cours, je mets *un pantalon / ???.*
7. Quand je suis chez moi, je mets souvent *un jean / ???.*
8. Je ne mets presque jamais *de short / ???.*

**C. Conversation.** Avec un(e) partenaire, relisez la conversation entre Alice et la vendeuse en haut de la page. Ensuite, changez la conversation pour acheter un jean, un anorak ou un manteau. Après, changez de rôles et jouez le rôle du vendeur / de la vendeuse pour votre partenaire.

---

**une femme d'affaires (un homme d'affaires)** *a businesswoman (a businessman)*    **travaillant** *working*    **une vendeuse**
**(un vendeur)** *a salesclerk*    **Je peux vous aider?** *Can I help you?*    **Quelle taille faites-vous?** *What size do you wear?*
**Je fais du...** *I wear size . . .*    **en solde** *on sale*    **Je peux l'essayer? (essayer)** *Can I try it on? (to try, to try on)*
**La cabine d'essayage** *The fitting room*    **par ici** *this way*    **qu'en pensez-vous?** *what do you think about it?*
**Il me plaît. (plaire)** *I like it. / It pleases me. (to please)*    **coûter** *to cost*    **Voyons** *Let's see*    **le (la, l')** *it*

**1.** How do you say the direct object pronouns *him, her, it,* and *them* in French?

**2.** Where do you place the direct object pronoun when there is an infinitive? Where do you place it otherwise? Where do you place it in a negative sentence?

# Avoiding repetition

*Les pronoms **le, la, l'** et **les***

Use the direct object pronouns **le, la, l'**, and **les** to replace a person, animal, or thing that is the direct object of the verb. Use **le** *(him, it)* to replace masculine singular nouns and **la** *(her, it)* to replace feminine singular nouns. **Les** *(Them)* replaces all plural nouns. **Le** and **la** become **l'** when the following word begins with a vowel or silent **h**.

|  | BEFORE A CONSONANT SOUND | BEFORE A VOWEL OR SILENT H |
|---|---|---|
| *him, it (masculine)* | le | l' |
| *her, it (feminine)* | la | l' |
| *them* | les | les |

— Tu prends ce maillot?     — *Are you taking this bathing suit?*
— Oui, je **le** prends.     — *Yes, I'm taking **it.***

— Tu achètes cette chemise?     — *Are you buying this shirt?*
— Oui, je **l'**achète.     — *Yes, I'm buying **it.***

— Tu achètes ces bottes?     — *Are you buying these boots?*
— Oui, je **les** achète.     — *Yes, I'm buying **them.***

Like **y,** these pronouns are generally placed *immediately* before the verb. They go before the infinitive if there is one. If not, they go before the conjugated verb. In the negative, the pronoun remains *immediately* before the conjugated verb or the infinitive.

— Tu aimes cette chemise? Tu vas acheter cette chemise?
— Oui, je **l'**aime bien. Je vais **l'**acheter.

— Tu aimes ces bottes? Tu vas acheter ces bottes?
— Non, je ne **les** aime pas. Je ne vais pas **les** acheter.

**A. Au magasin de vêtements.** Beaucoup de personnes sont au magasin de vêtements. Complétez ce que chacun dit avec le pronom convenable **(le, la, l', les)**.

1. J'aime ce maillot de bain. Je peux _____ essayer?
2. J'aime ces bottes. Je _____ prends.
3. Je n'aime pas ce bikini. Je ne _____ prends pas.
4. Comment trouves-tu cette robe? Voudrais-tu _____ essayer?
5. Je n'aime pas cet anorak. Je ne vais pas _____ prendre.
6. Regarde cette belle chemise! Je _____ trouve super!
7. Tu aimes ces lunettes? Tu vas _____ acheter?

**B. À Paris.** Dites si vous reconnaissez *(recognize)* ces sites parisiens. Utilisez **Je reconnais...** *(I recognize . . . )* et le pronom convenable **(le, la, l', les)**.

     **Exemple**     Cette avenue?
                          **Oui, je la reconnais. C'est les Champs-Élysées.**
                          **Non, je ne la reconnais pas.**

**Exemple**    Cette avenue?

**1.** Cette cathédrale?

**2.** Ce musée?

**3.** Cette tour?

**4.** Cette place?

**5.** Ce fleuve *(river)*?

**C. Intentions.** Un(e) ami(e) voudrait savoir ce que vous allez faire avec les choses suivantes. Répondez en utilisant un pronom complément d'objet direct (**le, la, l', les**) et un verbe logique. Jouez les deux rôles avec un(e) partenaire.

| manger | regarder |
|--------|----------|
| lire | boire |
| écouter | mettre |
| acheter | |

**Exemple**    ce CD
   — **Qu'est-ce que tu vas faire avec ce CD?**
   — **Je vais l'écouter.**

**1.** ces vêtements
**2.** ce DVD
**3.** ce sandwich
**4.** ce vin
**5.** cette chemise
**6.** ce livre
**7.** ces bottes
**8.** cette eau minérale
**9.** ces frites

**D. Préférences.** Un ami vous pose des questions. Répondez à ses questions, en remplaçant les mots en italique par le pronom convenable.

**Exemple**    — J'invite souvent *mes amis* à la maison. Et toi?
   — **Moi aussi, je les invite souvent à la maison.**
   **Moi non, je ne les invite pas souvent à la maison.**

**1.** Je regarde souvent *la télé* le week-end. Et toi?
**2.** J'invite souvent *mes parents* à la maison. Et toi?
**3.** Je trouve *mon quartier* très agréable. Et toi?
**4.** Je trouve *mes cours* plutôt difficiles. Et toi?
**5.** Ce soir, je vais préparer *le prochain examen de français.* Et toi?
**6.** Ce week-end, je vais voir *mes parents.* Et toi?
**7.** Samedi soir, je vais faire *mes devoirs.* Et toi?
**8.** Dimanche, je vais regarder *la télé.* Et toi?

**E. Entretien.** Interviewez votre partenaire. Utilisez un pronom complément d'objet direct pour remplacer les mots en italique dans vos réponses.

**1.** Vas-tu voir *tes parents* ce week-end? Invites-tu souvent *tes amis* chez toi? Où est-ce que tu préfères retrouver *tes amis?*
**2.** Chez toi, dans quelle pièce est-ce que tu préfères regarder *la télé?* écouter *la chaîne hi-fi?* faire *tes devoirs?* passer *ton temps libre?*
**3.** Est-ce que tu achètes *tes vêtements* au centre commercial? Dans quel magasin est-ce que tu achètes *tes vêtements* le plus souvent?

## Stratégies et Lecture

*Using the sequence of events to make logical guesses*

You can often guess the meaning of unfamiliar verbs in a narrative by imagining what the logical order of actions would be. For example, if you take the bus, you usually wait for the bus first, and you have to get on the bus before you get off. Learn to read a whole paragraph, rather than one word at a time. Notice that the prefix **re-** means that an action in a sequence is done again, as in English *(do* and *redo, read* and *reread)*. Use the sequence of events in this passage to guess the meaning of the boldfaced words.

> Cathy ouvre une enveloppe. Elle **sort** une feuille de papier de l'enveloppe. Elle **lit** les instructions sur la feuille mais elle ne comprend pas. Alors, elle **relit** les instructions et elle **remet** la feuille de papier dans l'enveloppe.
>
> Cathy **attend** l'autobus devant son appartement. Quand il arrive, elle **monte** dedans, et elle **descend** quand elle arrive à sa destination. Elle entre dans un café et commande un coca. Elle **boit** son coca, **paie l'addition** et **repart.**
>
> Elle entre dans une station de métro et elle achète un ticket **au guichet,** mais elle ne **prend** pas le métro.
>
> Elle **s'arrête** devant un magasin de vêtements où elle admire une jolie robe bleue dans **la vitrine.** Elle entre dans le magasin et demande **le prix** de la robe.

Prepositions can indicate relationships between actions. **Pour** means *in order to* when it is followed by a verb. **Sans,** meaning *without,* can also be followed by an infinitive. What do these sentences mean?

> Cathy demande l'addition au serveur. Elle quitte le café **sans boire** son coca. Elle entre dans le magasin de vêtements **pour demander** le prix d'une robe mais elle quitte le magasin **sans essayer** la robe.

---

**A. Dans l'ordre logique.** Mettez les activités suivantes de Cathy dans l'ordre logique. La première et la dernière *(last)* sont indiquées.

_____ Elle va vers la porte.

_____ Elle lit les instructions sur la feuille de papier.

__1__ Cathy voit une enveloppe sur la table.

_____ Elle sort une feuille de papier de l'enveloppe.

_____ Elle prend l'enveloppe.

_____ Elle ouvre l'enveloppe.

__8__ Elle ouvre la porte et elle sort.

_____ Elle remet la feuille dans l'enveloppe.

**B. Quel verbe?** Complétez ces phrases logiquement.

1. Cathy quitte l'appartement sans... (boire son café, ouvrir la porte).
2. Elle prend l'autobus pour... (rester à la maison, aller en ville).
3. Elle retrouve des amis pour... (passer le week-end seule, aller au cinéma).
4. Elle va au guichet pour... (acheter des tickets, boire une bière).
5. Après, elle va au café avec des amis pour... (boire quelque chose, danser).
6. Elle rentre à la maison sans... (quitter le café, prendre l'autobus).

## Qu'est-ce qu'elle fait?

Seule dans son appartement, Cathy Pérez a l'air un peu agitée. Elle prend l'enveloppe qui se trouve sur la table et en sort une feuille de papier. Elle lit les instructions et remet la feuille dans l'enveloppe. Elle met une robe, un chapeau et des lunettes de soleil. Elle met l'enveloppe dans son sac et quitte son appartement.

Cathy entre dans un café où elle commande un coca et ensuite, elle demande l'addition. Quand l'addition arrive, elle la prend et paie le garçon. Elle ouvre l'enveloppe, relit les instructions, met l'addition dans l'enveloppe et quitte le café sans boire son coca. C'est bien bizarre! Pourquoi a-t-elle l'air si agitée?

Ensuite, Cathy va à la station de métro. Elle entre dans la station et sans regarder le plan, va au guichet et demande un ticket. Quand on lui donne son ticket, elle le met dans l'enveloppe, remonte l'escalier et quitte la station de métro. Pourquoi achète-t-elle un ticket sans prendre le métro? Tout cela est fort bizarre!

Elle continue sa route jusqu'à ce qu'elle arrive devant un magasin de vêtements. Elle regarde une robe bleue qui se trouve dans la vitrine. Elle entre dans le magasin et demande le prix de la robe. Elle marque le prix de la robe sur une feuille de papier et met la feuille de papier dans l'enveloppe. Ensuite, elle sort du magasin sans même demander d'essayer la robe!

Elle va au coin de la rue pour attendre l'autobus. Quand il arrive, elle monte dans l'autobus et elle descend à l'université. Elle semble plus calme maintenant. Qu'est-ce qui se passe? Pourquoi a-t-elle fait tout ça?

---

### A. Comprenez-vous? Est-ce que Cathy fait ces choses?

1. Cathy ouvre une enveloppe, en sort une feuille de papier et lit des instructions.
2. Elle quitte son appartement et va directement à l'université en autobus.
3. Au café, elle retrouve une amie et elles commandent un café au lait.
4. Elle achète un ticket de métro mais elle ne prend pas le métro.

### B. Maintenant... c'est à vous! Est-ce que vous trouvez les actions de Cathy plutôt bizarres? Qu'est-ce qu'elle fait? Imaginez une explication.

Est-ce qu'elle...
est agent de police ou détective privé?
souffre d'amnésie?
travaille pour la CIA?
est espionne comme James Bond?
collectionne des souvenirs de Paris?
fait un exercice pour son cours de français?

Réponse:
Il y a une explication simple et logique! Cathy suit *(is taking)* un cours de français pour étrangers à Paris. Ses devoirs, dans l'enveloppe, consistent à prouver au professeur qu'elle est capable de commander quelque chose à boire au café et d'acheter des vêtements et un ticket de métro. Elle doit rapporter *(must bring back)* l'addition, le ticket de métro et le prix de la robe de la robe dans la vitrine à son professeur.

# Discussing the weather and what to do

**VOCABULAIRE SUPPLÉMENTAIRE**
**Il fait bon.** *The weather's nice.*
**Il fait humide.** *It's humid.*
**Il fait sec.** *It's dry.*
**Il y a des nuages.** *It's cloudy.*
**Il y a du brouillard.** *It's foggy.*
**Il y a du verglas.** *It's icy.*
**Il y a un orage.** *There's a storm.*
**Il y a des éclairs.** *There's lightning.*
**Il y a du tonnerre.** *There's thunder.*
**Le ciel est couvert.** *The sky is overcast.*

## Le temps et les projets

Quelquefois les projets **dépendent du temps qu'il fait.**

Et chez vous? **Quel temps fait-il** aujourd'hui?

Il fait froid.   Il fait frais.   Il fait chaud.   Il fait beau.   Il fait mauvais.

Il fait du soleil.   Il fait du vent.   Il pleut.   Il neige.

Quelle **saison** préférez-vous? Qu'est-ce que vous faites **pendant** cette saison?

Je préfère **l'été** *(m).* En été...      Je préfère l'automne *(m).* En automne...

je vais à la plage.
je fais du bateau et
    du ski nautique.

je reste à la maison.
**je ne fais rien.**

Je préfère **l'hiver** *(m).* En hiver...      Je préfère **le printemps.** Au printemps...

je vais à la montagne.
je fais du ski.

je vais au parc.
je fais des
    promenades *(f).*

CD 1-54

C'est vendredi après-midi et Alice Pérez et sa fille, Cathy, parlent de leurs projets pour le week-end.

ALICE:   **S'il** fait beau demain, je vais faire une promenade au jardin du Luxembourg. J'ai besoin de faire de l'exercice. Et toi, qu'est-ce que tu as l'intention de faire?
CATHY:   S'il fait beau, j'ai envie de faire du jogging.
ALICE:   Et s'il fait mauvais?
CATHY:   S'il fait mauvais, je vais rester à la maison et louer un DVD.

---

**dépendre de** *to depend on*   **le temps qu'il fait** *what the weather is like*   **Quel temps fait-il?** *What is the weather like?*
**la saison** *the season*   **pendant** *during, for*   **l'été** *(m) summer*   **Je ne fais rien. (ne... rien)** *I do nothing. (nothing)*
**l'hiver** *(m) winter*   **le printemps** *spring*   **S'il (si)** *If it (if)*

## A. Et chez vous? Chez vous, en quelle saison fait-il le temps indiqué?

**Exemple**    Il neige.
**Ici, il neige souvent (quelquefois) en hiver.**
**Ici, il ne neige jamais.**

**1.** Il fait frais.          **4.** Il fait très beau.          **7.** Il fait du soleil.
**2.** Il fait du vent.        **5.** Il fait froid.              **8.** Il pleut.
**3.** Il fait mauvais.        **6.** Il fait chaud.              **9.** Il neige.

## B. Quel temps fait-il? Utilisez deux expressions pour décrire le temps pour chaque saison. Dites aussi quels vêtements on met d'habitude.

**Exemple**    en automne
**Ici, en automne, il fait frais et il fait du vent. On met souvent un jean et un pull.**

**1.** en hiver
**2.** en été
**3.** en automne
**4.** au printemps

## C. Et vous? Complétez les phrases.

**1.** Quand il fait beau, j'aime...
**2.** S'il fait beau ce week-end, j'ai l'intention de...
**3.** Quand il pleut, je préfère...
**4.** Quand il fait chaud, j'aime...
**5.** Quand il neige, j'aime...
**6.** Au printemps, j'aime...
**7.** Je ne fais rien quand...
**8.** À la montagne, j'aime...
**9.** À la plage, j'aime...
**10.** Aujourd'hui, il fait... et j'ai envie de...

## D. Entretien. Posez ces questions à votre partenaire.

**1.** Aimes-tu l'été? Aimes-tu nager? Préfères-tu faire du bateau ou faire du ski nautique? Aimes-tu aller à la plage? Que mets-tu quand tu vas à la plage?
**2.** Aimes-tu l'hiver? Aimes-tu aller à la montagne? Préfères-tu faire des promenades ou faire du ski? Que mets-tu pour faire une promenade en juillet? Et en décembre?
**3.** Qu'est-ce que tu aimes faire quand il fait chaud? Et quand il fait froid? Et quand il neige? Quand est-ce que tu ne fais rien?
**4.** Quelle saison préfères-tu? Qu'est-ce que tu aimes faire pendant cette saison?
**5.** Quel temps fait-il aujourd'hui? Qu'est-ce que tu as envie de faire? Qu'est-ce que tu vas faire après les cours?

## E. Conversation. Avec un(e) partenaire, relisez la conversation entre Alice et Cathy en bas de la page précédente. Ensuite, changez la conversation pour parler de vos projets pour le week-end.

**Pour vérifier**

**1.** How do you say *to make* or *to do* in French? What are the forms of the verb **faire?** How is the **vous** form of this verb different from the usual **vous** form of a verb?

**2.** How do you say that you are doing *nothing?*

**3.** How do you say *What is the weather like? The weather is nice? It is raining? It is snowing?*

**4.** How do you say *What is the weather going to be like? It is going to be nice? It is going to rain? It is going to snow?*

**5.** How do you say *I like snow? I like rain?*

**NOTE DE PRONONCIATION**

The **ai** in **fais, fait** and **faites** rhymes with the **ai** in **français** and **française**, but the **ai** of **faisons** rhymes with the **e** in **je.**

# Talking about the weather and what you do

*Le verbe* **faire,** *l'expression* **ne... rien** *et les expressions pour décrire le temps*

To say *to make* or *to do,* use the irregular verb **faire.**

| FAIRE (to make, to do) | |
|---|---|
| je **fais** | nous **faisons** |
| tu **fais** | vous **faites** |
| il/elle/on **fait** | ils/elles **font** |

— Qu'est-ce que tu fais ce soir?
— Je reste à la maison. Je fais mes devoirs.

— Qu'est-ce que Papa fait dans la cuisine?
— Il fait des sandwichs.

To say that you do *nothing* or you do *not* do *anything,* use **ne... rien.** This expression can be the subject or object of the verb, or the object of a preposition.

**Rien n'**est en solde.    Je **ne** fais **rien.**    Il **ne** parle de **rien.**

When negating an infinitive, place both parts of the negative expression before it.

Je préfère **ne pas** sortir ce soir. Je voudrais **ne rien** faire.

**Faire** is also used in many, but not all, weather expressions. To tell what the weather is going to be like, you also need the infinitives **pleuvoir** *(to rain)* and **neiger** *(to snow).*

| | |
|---|---|
| Quel temps fait-il? | Quel temps va-t-il faire? |
| Il fait beau / mauvais / chaud... | Il va faire beau / mauvais / chaud... |
| Il pleut. | Il va pleuvoir. |
| Il neige. | Il va neiger. |

You may also want to use these words when talking about the weather.

la neige *the snow*    la pluie *the rain*

**A. Qu'est-ce qu'on fait?** Dites ou demandez si ces personnes font les choses indiquées.

1. Moi, je... (faire beaucoup de choses seul[e], faire souvent des bêtises *[stupid things]*)
2. Mon meilleur ami (Ma meilleure amie)... (faire beaucoup de choses pour moi, faire beaucoup de choses le week-end)
3. En cours, nous... (faire beaucoup d'exercices oraux, faire beaucoup d'exercices ensemble)
4. Mes parents... (faire beaucoup de choses le week-end, faire beaucoup de choses avec moi)
5. *[au professeur]* Est-ce que vous... (faire quelque chose d'intéressant après le cours de français, faire quelque chose avec vos amis ce week-end, faire souvent du sport)

**B. Quel temps fait-il?** Quel temps fait-il aujourd'hui dans ces régions françaises? Utilisez au moins deux expressions pour chaque photo.

Dans les Alpes

En Normandie

En Guadeloupe

**C. Quel temps va-t-il faire?** Vous travaillez dans une agence de voyages. Des clients vont visiter les endroits indiqués dans l'exercice précédent et ils voudraient savoir quel temps il va faire. Jouez les rôles avec un(e) partenaire.

> **Exemple**    — **Quel temps va-t-il faire dans les Alpes?**
>               — **Il va...**

**D. Que font-il?** Est-ce que les personnes suivantes font quelque chose ensemble ce week-end ou est-ce qu'elles ne font rien ensemble?

> **Exemple**    Moi, je... (avec mes parents)
>                 **Moi, je ne fais rien avec mes parents ce week-end.**
>                 **Moi, je vais manger chez mes parents ce dimanche.**

1. Mon (Ma) meilleur(e) ami(e)... (avec moi)
2. Mes parents... (avec moi)
3. Mes parents et moi... (avec mes grands-parents)
4. Moi, je... (avec d'autres étudiants de notre classe)
5. Mon (Ma) camarade de chambre (colocataire)... (avec moi)

**E. Entretien.** Interviewez votre partenaire.

1. Est-ce que tu fais beaucoup de choses le week-end? Qu'est-ce que tu aimes faire le vendredi soir? le samedi soir? Qu'est-ce que tu fais d'habitude le dimanche matin? Quand est-ce que tu ne fais rien?
2. Quel temps va-t-il faire ce week-end? Qu'est-ce que tu as envie de faire s'il fait beau? Qu'est-ce que tu as l'intention de faire s'il fait mauvais? Qu'est-ce que tu as besoin de faire? Est-ce que tu préfères ne rien faire?
3. Ton meilleur ami (Ta meilleure amie) et toi, quand est-ce que vous aimez sortir ensemble? Qu'est-ce que vous faites souvent ensemble?

**F. Qu'est-ce que vous allez faire?** Un(e) ami(e) passe le week-end chez vous. Vous parlez de ce que vous allez faire. Préparez la scène avec un(e) autre étudiant(e). Décidez ce que vous allez faire s'il fait beau et s'il fait mauvais.

**1.** How do you say *to go camping? to ride a bike? to do housework? to do laundry?*

**2.** In the expressions with **faire,** which articles change to **de (d')** in a negative sentence? Which do not?

**VOCABULAIRE SUPPLÉMENTAIRE**

**aller à la chasse** *to go hunting*
**aller à la pêche** *to go fishing*
**faire de l'alpinisme** *to go mountain climbing*
**faire de la varappe / de l'escalade** *to go rock climbing*
**faire du patin (à glace)** *to go (ice-)skating*
**faire de la marche à pied** *to go walking*
**faire du cheval** *to go horseback riding*
**faire de la musculation** *to do weight training*
**faire la fête** *to party*
**faire une randonnée (des randonnées)** *to go for a hike (hiking)*
**faire du roller** *to go rollerblading*
**faire sa toilette** *to get cleaned up, to get ready*

# Talking about activities

*Les expressions avec* **faire**

The verb **faire** can have a variety of meanings in idiomatic expressions.

| LE SPORT ET LES DISTRACTIONS | LE MÉNAGE ET LES COURSES |
|---|---|
| faire de l'exercice | faire le ménage *(to do housework)* |
| faire du bateau | faire des courses *(to run errands)* |
| faire du camping | faire du jardinage *(to garden)* |
| faire du jogging | faire du shopping |
| faire du ski (nautique) | faire la cuisine *(to cook)* |
| faire du sport (du tennis, du hockey... ) | faire la lessive *(to do laundry)* |
| faire du vélo | faire la vaisselle *(to do the dishes)* |
| faire une promenade | |
| faire un voyage *(to take a trip)* | |

The **un, une, des, du, de la,** and **de l'** in the expressions with **faire** become **de (d')** when the verb is negated. The definite article (**le, la, l', les**) does not change.

|  | Je fais **du** jogging. | Je ne fais pas **de** jogging. |
|---|---|---|
| BUT | Nous faisons **la** cuisine. | Nous ne faisons pas **la** cuisine. |

**A. On en a besoin ou envie?** Commencez ces phrases logiquement avec **J'ai envie de...** ou **J'ai besoin de...**

| **Exemples** | faire des devoirs | **J'ai besoin de faire des devoirs.** |
|---|---|---|
| | faire un voyage | **J'ai envie de faire un voyage.** |

1. faire des courses
2. faire du bateau
3. faire la lessive
4. faire de l'exercice
5. faire le ménage
6. faire la cuisine
7. faire du shopping
8. rester à la maison et ne rien faire

**Avez-vous envie de faire du camping?**

**B. Préférences.** Sur une feuille de papier, écrivez les activités suivantes dans l'ordre de vos préférences. Votre partenaire va vous poser des questions pour determiner l'ordre des activités sur votre feuille de papier.

faire du jogging / faire du camping / faire du shopping / faire la cuisine / faire du vélo / ne rien faire

| **Exemple** | — **Préfères-tu faire du jogging ou ne rien faire?** |
|---|---|
| | — **Je préfère ne rien faire.** |
| | — **Préfères-tu faire du jogging ou faire la cuisine?...** |

## C. Que font-ils?

Éric, le fils d'Alice, parle avec sa mère des projets de la famille pour aujourd'hui. Complétez ses phrases avec une expression avec **faire**.

1. Maman, est-ce que tu... ce matin?

2. Michel et toi, vous... cet après-midi.

3. Papa...

4. Papa et toi, vous...

5. Cathy et moi, nous...

6. Moi, je...

## D. Dans ma famille.

Qui dans votre famille fait les choses suivantes?

**Exemple**  faire du jogging
**Moi, je fais du jogging.**
**Nous faisons tous du jogging.**
**On ne fait pas de jogging dans ma famille.**

1. faire souvent du shopping
2. faire la cuisine
3. faire le ménage
4. faire du sport
5. faire beaucoup de promenades
6. faire souvent de l'exercice
7. faire du ski
8. faire du jardinage

## E. Conseils.

Donnez des conseils à un ami. Utilisez l'impératif.

> faire le ménage   louer une vidéo   faire du shopping
> ???   rester à la maison   faire du vélo   faire une promenade
> faire la cuisine   faire la lessive   faire tes devoirs   ne rien faire

**Exemple**  — La vaisselle est sale.
**— Eh bien, fais la vaisselle!**

1. J'ai faim.
2. Tous mes vêtements sont sales.
3. J'ai envie de faire de l'exercice.
4. J'ai besoin d'acheter de nouveaux vêtements.
5. Mon appartement est très sale.
6. Je n'ai pas envie de sortir ce soir.
7. J'ai beaucoup de devoirs à faire ce soir!
8. Je voudrais voir un film mais je n'ai pas envie d'aller au cinéma.

# Saying what you did

## Le week-end dernier

Alice parle de ses activités de **samedi dernier.** Et vous?

**Où est-ce que vous êtes allé(e)?**    **Qu'est-ce que vous avez fait?**

Samedi matin...

je ne suis pas sortie,
je suis restée chez moi.

J'ai dormi jusqu'à 10 heures.

J'ai **pris** mon **petit déjeuner.**

Samedi après-midi...

je suis allée en ville.

Je n'ai pas travaillé.

J'ai déjeuné au restaurant
et j'ai bien mangé.

Samedi soir...

je suis sortie.

J'ai vu un film au cinéma.

J'ai retrouvé un ami au café.

je suis rentrée.

J'ai lu le journal.

Je n'ai rien fait.

---

**samedi dernier** *last Saturday*    **Où est-ce que vous êtes allé(e)?** *Where did you go?*
**Qu'est-ce que vous avez fait?** *What did you do?*    **prendre son petit déjeuner** *to have one's breakfast*

CD 1-55

C'est lundi et Cathy parle avec un ami des activités du week-end dernier.

CATHY: Tu as passé un bon week-end?
EDGAR: Oui, génial. Samedi matin, j'ai préparé les cours et samedi après-midi, j'ai joué au foot avec des amis.
CATHY: Qu'est-ce que tu as fait samedi soir?
EDGAR: Je suis sorti. Je suis allé en boîte et j'ai beaucoup dansé.
CATHY: Et **hier?**
EDGAR: Hier matin, j'ai fait une promenade sur les Champs-Élysées où j'ai pris un café. Hier soir, je suis resté à la maison et j'ai regardé la télé.

**A. Activités logiques.** Formez des phrases logiques. Complétez les phrases de la première colonne avec un choix logique de la deuxième colonne.

1. Je suis resté(e) au lit et...          j'ai pris un verre.
2. J'ai retrouvé des amis au café où...    j'ai dormi.
3. J'ai dîné au restaurant où...           j'ai beaucoup dansé.
4. Je suis allé(e) au cinéma où...         je n'ai pas gagné.
5. Je suis allé(e) en boîte où...          j'ai vu un film étranger.
6. J'ai joué au tennis avec une amie mais... j'ai très bien mangé.
7. Je suis allé(e) au parc où...           j'ai fait une promenade.

**B. Et vous?** Complétez les phrases pour indiquer comment vous avez passé la journée d'hier.

1. J'ai dormi jusqu'à *8 heures / 10 heures / ???.*
2. J'ai pris le petit déjeuner *chez moi / au café / chez une amie / ???. [Je n'ai pas pris de petit déjeuner.]*
3. J'ai lu *le journal / un livre / ???. [Je n'ai rien lu.]*
4. *Je suis allé(e) / Je ne suis pas allé(e)* en cours.
5. J'ai déjeuné *chez moi / chez des amis / au restaurant / ???. [Je n'ai pas déjeuné.]*
6. *J'ai travaillé. / Je n'ai pas travaillé.*
7. J'ai dîné *chez moi / chez mes parents / dans un fast-food / ???. [Je n'ai pas dîné.]*
8. J'ai *beaucoup / peu* mangé. *[Je n'ai pas mangé.]*
9. Le soir, *je suis resté(e) chez moi / je suis sorti(e) / je n'ai rien fait / ???.*

**C. Conversation.** Avec un(e) partenaire, relisez à haute voix la conversation entre Cathy et Edgar en haut de la page. Ensuite, imaginez que c'est lundi matin et changez la conversation pour parler de votre week-end passé.

*Note: You may not know how to say everything you did. Pick two or three things that you know how to say or ask your instructor for help.*

---

**hier** *yesterday*

**1.** The **passé composé** always has two parts. What are they called?

**2.** How do you form the past participle of most **-er** and **-ir** verbs? Which verbs that you know have irregular past participles?

**3.** How do you negate verbs in the **passé composé?**

**4.** In the **passé composé,** where do you place adverbs like **souvent** or **bien?**

**5.** What are the three possible English translations of **j'ai mangé?**

**NOTE DE GRAMMAIRE**

Some verbs expressing *going, coming,* and *staying,* such as **aller, sortir, rentrer,** and **rester,** have **être,** not **avoir,** as their auxiliary verb. You will learn about them in the next **Compétence.** For now, remember to use **je suis allé(e), je suis sorti(e), je suis resté(e),** and **je suis rentré(e)** if you want to say *I went, I went out, I stayed,* and *I returned.* (If you are a female, add an extra **-e** to the past participle of these verbs, just as you do with adjectives.)

# Saying what you did

*Le passé composé avec avoir*

To say what someone did or what happened in the past, put the verb in the **passé composé.** The **passé composé** is always composed of two parts, the auxiliary verb and the past participle. The auxiliary verb, usually **avoir,** is conjugated to agree with the subject. Note how the past participle is formed for **-er** or **-ir** verbs.

| PARLER → PARLÉ | |
|---|---|
| j'**ai parlé** | nous **avons parlé** |
| tu **as parlé** | vous **avez parlé** |
| il/elle/on **a parlé** | ils/elles **ont parlé** |

| DORMIR → DORMI | |
|---|---|
| j'**ai dormi** | nous **avons dormi** |
| tu **as dormi** | vous **avez dormi** |
| il/elle/on **a dormi** | ils/elles **ont dormi** |

Many irregular verbs have irregular past participles that must be memorized.

| avoir | j'ai eu, tu as eu... | être | j'ai été, tu as été... |
|---|---|---|---|
| il y a | il y a eu | faire | j'ai fait, tu as fait... |
| boire | j'ai bu, tu as bu... | écrire | j'ai écrit, tu as écrit... |
| lire | j'ai lu, tu as lu... | mettre | j'ai mis, tu as mis... |
| pleuvoir | il a plu | prendre | j'ai pris, tu as pris... |
| voir | j'ai vu, tu as vu... | apprendre | j'ai appris, tu as appris... |
| | | comprendre | j'ai compris, tu as compris... |

To talk about the weather in the **passé composé,** use these expressions.

> Quel temps a-t-il fait?
> Il a fait beau / chaud / du soleil...
> Il a plu.
> Il a neigé.

Place **ne... pas, ne... jamais,** and **ne... rien** around the auxiliary verb.

— Est-ce que tu as travaillé hier?
— Non, je **n'**ai **pas** travaillé. Je **n'**ai **rien** fait.

Adverbs indicating how often (**toujours, souvent...** ) and how well (**bien, mal, assez bien...** ) are usually placed between the auxiliary verb and the past participle.

J'ai **bien** mangé.          Ils ont **toujours** travaillé le week-end.

The **passé composé** can be translated in a variety of ways in English.

*I took the bus.*
*I have taken the bus.*     J'ai pris l'autobus.
*I did take the bus.*

**A. Et vous?** Avez-vous fait ces choses hier?

**Exemple**  quitter la maison tôt
**J'ai quitté la maison tôt hier.**
**Je n'ai pas quitté la maison tôt hier.**

**1.** passer la journée chez moi
**2.** être malade *(sick)*
**3.** prendre le petit déjeuner
**4.** lire le journal
**5.** faire mes devoirs de français

**6.** mettre un jean et un tee-shirt
**7.** travailler
**8.** voir ma famille
**9.** préparer les cours
**10.** faire du sport

**B. Un peu d'histoire.** Quels Français célèbres de la colonne de gauche ont fait chacune des choses de la colonne de droite? Si vous n'êtes pas certain(e), devinez *(guess).*

**Exemples**  **Pascal a étudié les mathématiques.**
**Berlioz et Ravel ont composé des symphonies.**

| | |
|---|---|
| Pascal... | participer à la construction de la statue de la Liberté |
| Berlioz et Ravel... | faire le premier film |
| Pierre et Marie Curie... | faire des sculptures |
| Les frères Lumière... | composer des symphonies |
| Charles de Gaulle... | étudier les mathématiques |
| Gustave Eiffel... | faire des voyages sous-marins |
| Coco Chanel... | lancer *(to launch, to start)* un style élégant et simple |
| Jacques Cousteau... | pour la mode féminine |
| Auguste Rodin et | faire des travaux sur les effets de la radioactivité |
| Camille Claudel... | être président de la République française pendant |
| | les années cinquante et soixante |

**C. La journée de Cathy.** Voilà les activités de Cathy, la fille d'Alice, le week-end dernier. Est-ce qu'elle a fait les choses suivantes?

**Exemple**  Samedi matin, Cathy... (quitter la maison très tôt)
**Samedi matin, Cathy n'a pas quitté la maison très tôt.**

Samedi matin, Cathy (travailler, faire du jogging, dormir, déjeuner au café)

Samedi après-midi, elle (mettre son maillot de bain, visiter un musée, faire du ski nautique, lire un livre)

Samedi soir, Cathy et ses amis (passer la soirée au café, boire quelque chose, parler jusqu'à deux heures du matin)

**D. Et toi?** Demandez à votre partenaire s'il/si elle a fait chacune *(each)* des choses de l'exercice précédent le week-end dernier.

**Exemples**  — **Tu as quitté la maison très tôt samedi matin?**
— **Oui, j'ai quitté la maison à sept heures.**

— **Tes amis et toi, vous avez passé la soirée au café samedi soir?**
— **Non, on n'a pas passé la soirée ensemble.**

Après, décrivez la journée de votre partenaire à la classe.

**Exemple**  **Rachel a quitté la maison à sept heures samedi matin...**
**Rachel et ses amis n'ont pas passé la soirée ensemble.**

**E. Entre amis.** Demandez à votre partenaire s'il/si elle a fait ces choses avec son meilleur ami (sa meilleure amie) cette semaine.

> Exemple    déjeuner ensemble
> **— Est-ce que vous avez déjeuné ensemble?**
> **— Oui, nous avons déjeuné ensemble lundi.**
> **Non, nous n'avons pas déjeuné ensemble.**

1. dîner ensemble
2. voir un film ensemble
3. faire une promenade ensemble
4. faire du sport ensemble
5. préparer les cours ensemble
6. faire du shopping ensemble
7. être ensemble toute la journée
8. louer une vidéo ensemble

**F. Devinez!** Dites à votre partenaire combien des choses suivantes vous avez faites samedi dernier et votre partenaire va deviner lesquelles *(guess which ones).*

| | | | | |
|---|---|---|---|---|
| **faire des devoirs** | **travailler** | **jouer au basket** | **écrire des mails** | **boire un café** |
| **mettre un jean** | **passer la journée à la maison** | **louer un DVD** | **danser** | **regarder la télé** |
| **dormir tard** | **dîner au restaurant** | **faire la lessive** | | **lire le journal** |
| **prendre un verre avec des amis** | **faire une promenade** | | **faire le ménage** | |

> Exemple    **— Samedi dernier, j'ai fait cinq choses de la liste.**
> **— Tu as écrit des mails, non?**
> **— Oui, j'ai écrit des mails. (Non, je n'ai pas écrit de mails.)**
> **— Tu as dormi tard?...**

**G. Qu'est-ce qu'ils ont fait?** Alice parle des activités récentes de sa famille. Complétez ses phrases.

> Exemple    Hier, j'**ai lu.**

Exemple  Hier, j'...

1. À Deauville, toute la famille...

2. Vendredi dernier, Vincent et moi...

3. À Chamonix, les enfants...

4. Hier, Vincent...

5. Ce matin, Vincent et Éric...

**H. Quel temps a-t-il fait?** Pour chaque dessin de l'activité précédente, dites le temps qu'il a fait ce jour-là.

> Exemple    **Hier, il a fait mauvais. Il a plu.**

**I. À Paris.** Il y a beaucoup de choses à faire à Paris. Les touristes qui ont pris ces photos ont visité Paris la semaine dernière. Imaginez ce qu'ils ont probablement fait à chaque endroit *(place)*.

**Exemple** **Ils ont visité le Quartier latin. Ils ont fait une promenade.**

acheter    lire    ???    regarder    visiter
???    boire    faire une promenade    ???    voir    parler

Le Quartier latin

Le musée d'Orsay

Les Champs-Élysées

Le Forum des Halles

**1.** How do you say that you did something *yesterday?*
*for two hours? last week? last year? three years*
*ago? a few days ago? a long time ago?*

**2.** What do **déjà** and **ne... pas encore** mean? Where
do you place them with a verb in the **passé**
**composé?**

**NOTE DE VOCABULAIRE**

You can say **il y a une semaine** for *a week ago,* but
people also say **il y a huit jours.** One also hears **il y**
**a quinze jours** for **il y a deux semaines.**

# Telling when you did something

*Les expressions qui désignent le passé*

The following expressions are useful when talking about the past.

| | |
|---|---|
| hier (matin, après-midi) | *yesterday (morning, afternoon)* |
| hier soir | *last night, yesterday evening* |
| lundi (mardi... ) dernier | *last Monday (Tuesday . . . )* |
| le week-end dernier | *last weekend* |
| la semaine dernière | *last week* |
| le mois dernier | *last month* |
| l'année dernière | *last year* |
| la dernière fois | *the last time* |
| récemment | *recently* |
| Pendant combien de temps? | *For how long?* |
| pendant deux heures (longtemps) | *for two hours (a long time)* |
| Il y a combien de temps? | *How long ago?* |
| il y a quelques secondes (cinq minutes, trois jours, cinq ans) | *a few seconds (five minutes, three days, five years) ago* |

Note that you use the word **an** *(m),* instead of **année** *(f),* to say *year* after a number.

To talk about the past, it is also useful to know the expressions **déjà** *(already)* and **ne...**
**pas encore** *(not yet).* **Déjà** is placed between the auxiliary verb and the past participle.
**Ne... pas encore** goes around the auxiliary verb.

| | |
|---|---|
| Tu as **déjà** vu ce film? | *Have you **already** seen this movie?* |
| Non, je **n'**ai **pas encore** vu ce film. | *No, I have**n't** seen this movie **yet**.* |

**A. Et vous?** Indiquez la dernière fois que vous avez fait les choses suivantes.

**Exemple**    dîner au restaurant
**J'ai dîné au restaurant vendredi dernier.**
**Je n'ai pas dîné au restaurant récemment.**

1. voir un bon film
2. visiter un musée
3. faire du shopping
4. lire un bon livre
5. mettre une robe / un costume
6. être chez vos parents
7. jouer au volley
8. dormir toute la journée

**B. Quand?** Voilà le calendrier d'Alice. Quand est-ce qu'elle a fait les choses in-diquées? Aujourd'hui, c'est le 14 novembre.

**il y a un mois      il y a six semaines      le mois dernier**

**hier      le week-end dernier      mardi dernier**

**la semaine dernière      il y a une semaine**

> **Exemple**    Alice a beaucoup travaillé **le mois dernier.**

**1.** Elle a dîné chez une amie...
**2.** Elle a visité le Louvre...
**3.** Elle a passé le week-end à Deauville...
**4.** Elle a fait du shopping...
**5.** Elle a passé *(took)* un examen...
**6.** Elle a préparé l'examen...

**C. Entre amis.** Complétez les phrases avec quelque chose que vous avez fait récemment. Demandez à un(e) camarade de classe s'il/si elle a déjà fait la même chose. Il/Elle va répondre avec **déjà** ou **ne... pas encore.**

> **Exemple**    — J'ai visité la ville de **Chicago récemment. Et toi, est-ce que tu as déjà visité Chicago?**
> — **Oui, j'ai déjà visité Chicago.**
> **Non, je n'ai pas encore visité Chicago.**

**1.** J'ai vu le film... récemment.
**2.** J'ai visité la ville de... récemment.
**3.** J'ai mangé au restaurant... récemment.
**4.** J'ai loué le DVD... récemment.

**D. Entretien.** Interviewez votre partenaire.

**1.** Quel temps a-t-il fait le week-end dernier? Quels vêtements est-ce que tu as mis? Est-ce que tu as travaillé? Est-ce que tu as fait du sport? Jusqu'à quelle heure est-ce que tu as dormi samedi matin? Est-ce que tu as fait le ménage? la lessive? la vaisselle? des courses? Qu'est-ce que tu as fait dimanche?
**2.** Est-ce que tu as été malade *(sick)* récemment? Il y a combien de temps? Pendant combien de jours? Est-ce que tu as beaucoup dormi? Est-ce que tu as regardé la télé? Est-ce que tu as lu?
**3.** Quel film est-ce que tu as vu récemment? Est-ce que tu as aimé ce film? Quel film récent est-ce que tu n'as pas aimé?
**4.** Est-ce que tu as eu un accident de voiture récemment? Il y a combien de temps?

# Telling where you went

>Note
*culturelle*

D'après une enquête *(survey)* récente, 48% des Français sont partis en week-end au moins une fois l'année précédente, 26% l'ont fait au moins quatre fois et 13% au moins dix fois. 84% sont allés voir leur famille ou des amis et 40% sont allés à la campagne. Combien de fois êtes-vous parti(e) en week-end l'année dernière? Où êtes-vous allé(e)?

**NOTE DE VOCABULAIRE**

Use **des parents** to say *relatives* and **mes parents** to say *my parents.*

## Je suis parti(e) en week-end

La dernière fois que vous êtes parti(e) en week-end, où est-ce que vous êtes allé(e)? Qu'est-ce que vous avez fait?

| | | | |
|---|---|---|---|
| Je suis allé(e) | à Denver.<br>à New York.<br>??? | **J'y suis allé(e)** | en avion.<br>en train.<br>en autocar.<br>en voiture **(de location).** |
| Je suis parti(e) | le vendredi après-midi.<br>le samedi matin.<br>??? | Je suis arrivé(e) | le vendredi soir.<br>le samedi après-midi.<br>??? |
| **Je suis descendu(e)** | à l'hôtel.<br>dans un camping. | Je suis resté(e) | **une nuit.**<br>trois jours.<br>le week-end. |
| Je suis resté(e) | chez des amis.<br>chez **des parents.** | | |
| Je suis allé(e) | à la plage.<br>à un concert.<br>dans un club. | Je suis rentré(e) | le dimanche soir.<br>le lundi matin. |

CD 1-56

Alice et son amie Claire parlent d'un voyage qu'Alice a fait.

CLAIRE: Qu'est-ce que tu as fait le week-end dernier?
ALICE: J'ai pris le train pour aller à Deauville.
CLAIRE: Quand est-ce que tu es partie?
ALICE: Je suis partie samedi matin et je suis rentrée hier soir.
CLAIRE: Tu as trouvé un bon hôtel?
ALICE: Je suis descendue dans un petit hôtel confortable, pas trop loin de la plage.
CLAIRE: **Quelle chance!** Moi aussi, j'ai envie de visiter Deauville.

**A. En week-end.** Décrivez la dernière fois que vous êtes parti(e) en week-end.

1. Je suis allé(e) à (Chicago, ???).
2. J'y suis allé(e) (en avion, ???).
3. Je suis parti(e) (le vendredi soir, ???).
4. Je suis arrivé(e) (une heure, ???) plus tard.
5. Je suis descendu(e) (à l'hôtel, ???).
6. Je suis resté(e) (deux jours, ???).
7. Je suis allé(e) (en ville, ???).
8. Je suis rentré(e) (le lundi, ???).

---

**J'y suis allé(e)** *I went there* **de location** *rental* **Je suis descendu(e) (descendre [de / dans / à])** *I stayed (to descend, to come down, to get off/out [of], to stay [at])* **une nuit** *one night* **des parents** *relatives* **Quelle chance!** *What luck!*

**B. Un tour de Paris.** Alice et sa famille adorent visiter Paris et la région parisienne. Regardez les photos et complétez les phrases avec une expression de la colonne de droite.

1. Vincent est allé à la Sainte-Chapelle pour...
2. Les enfants sont allés à Versailles pour...
3. Ils sont allés à Notre-Dame pour...
4. Ils sont allés au musée d'Orsay pour...
5. Ils sont allés au café sur les Champs-Élysées pour...
6. Alice est allée au bois de Boulogne pour...

voir une nouvelle exposition.
faire une promenade.
prendre un café.
voir son architecture gothique.
admirer les vitraux *(stained-glass windows)*.
visiter le château de Versailles.

La Sainte-Chapelle

Le château de Versailles

Le musée d'Orsay

Notre-Dame

Le bois de Boulogne

Les Champs-Élysées

**C. Conversation.** Avec un(e) partenaire, relisez à haute voix la conversation entre Alice et Claire à la page précédente. Ensuite, changez la conversation pour parler de la dernière fois que vous êtes parti(e) pour le week-end. Après, changez de rôles et parlez du dernier voyage de votre partenaire.

**1.** Which verbs have **être** as the auxiliary in the **passé composé?**

**2.** What do you have to remember to do with the past participle of these verbs?

**3.** Where do you place the direct object pronouns and **y** in the **passé composé?**

**NOTE DE GRAMMAIRE**

When **on** means *we*, its verb may either be left in the masculine singular form (**On est sorti.**) or it may agree (**On est sorti[e]s**). Either form is considered correct.

# Telling where you went

*Le passé composé avec **être***

A few verbs have **être** as their auxiliary verb in the **passé composé.** The past participle of these verbs must agree with the subject in number and gender.

| ALLER → ALLÉ | | SORTIR → SORTI | |
|---|---|---|---|
| je **suis allé(e)** | nous **sommes allé(e)s** | je **suis sorti(e)** | nous **sommes sorti(e)s** |
| tu **es allé(e)** | vous **êtes allé(e)(s)** | tu **es sorti(e)** | vous **êtes sorti(e)(s)** |
| il **est allé** | ils **sont allés** | il **est sorti** | ils **sont sortis** |
| elle **est allée** | elles **sont allées** | elle **est sortie** | elles **sont sorties** |
| on **est allé(e)(s)** | | on **est sorti(e)(s)** | |

Here are some verbs that have **être** as their auxiliary verb.

| aller | je suis allé(e) | *I went* |
|---|---|---|
| venir | je suis venu(e) | *I came* |
| arriver | je suis arrivé(e) | *I arrived* |
| rester | je suis resté(e) | *I stayed, I remained* |
| entrer (dans) | je suis entré(e) (dans) | *I entered, I went in* |
| sortir (de) | je suis sorti(e) (de) | *I went/came out (of)* |
| partir (de) | je suis parti(e) (de) | *I left* |
| rentrer | je suis rentré(e) | *I came home, I returned* |
| retourner | je suis retourné(e) | *I returned, I went back* |
| revenir | je suis revenu(e) | *I came back* |
| monter (dans) | je suis monté(e) (dans) | *I went up, I got on / in* |
| descendre (de / dans / à) | je suis descendu(e) (de / dans / à) | *I came down, I got out / off (of), I stayed (at)* |
| devenir | je suis devenu(e) | *I became* |
| naître | je suis né(e) | *I was born* |
| mourir | il/elle est mort(e) | *he/she died* |

**Rentrer** means *to return / go back home* (or to the place you are staying). Use **retourner** for *to return* in most other cases. **Partir** means *to leave* as in *to go away*. It is the opposite of **arriver. Sortir** means *to leave* as in *to go out*. It is the opposite of **entrer** and **rentrer. Quitter** also means *to leave*. It takes **avoir** as its auxiliary verb and must have a direct object: **Elle a quitté la maison tôt.**

In the **passé composé,** direct object pronouns and **y** are placed *immediately* before the auxiliary verb.

| Je **l'**ai fait. | Je ne **l'**ai pas fait. |
|---|---|
| J'**y** suis allé(e). | Je n'**y** suis pas allé(e). |

You know that the past participle agrees with the subject when the auxiliary verb is **être,** but not when it is **avoir.** When **avoir** is the auxiliary verb, the past participle agrees with the *direct object* of the verb, but only *when the object precedes the verb* in the sentence, as it does when you use the direct object pronouns **le, la, l',** and **les.**

| Vincent a regardé **la télé.** | Vincent **l'**a regardé**e.** |
|---|---|

CD 1-57

# Prononciation

*Les verbes auxiliaires **avoir** et **être***

As you practice when to use **avoir** and when to use **être** to form the **passé composé,** be careful to pronounce the forms of these auxiliary verbs distinctly.

tu as parlé / tu es parti(e)      il a parlé / il est parti      ils ͡z ont parlé / ils sont partis

**A. Qu'est-ce que vous avez fait?** Parlez de la dernière fois que vous avez mangé au restaurant avec un(e) ami(e) ou avec des amis.

> **Exemple**    je / sortir (avec qui?)
> **Je suis sorti(e) avec Thomas et Karima.**

1. je / sortir (avec qui?)
2. je / partir de la maison (à quelle heure?)
3. nous / aller (à quel restaurant?)
4. nous / arriver au restaurant (vers quelle heure?)
5. nous / rester au restaurant (combien de temps?)
6. après le repas *(meal),* nous / aller (où?)
7. je / rentrer (vers quelle heure?)
8. le lendemain *(the next day)* je / rester au lit (jusqu'à quelle heure?)

**B. À Deauville.** Est-ce que les Pérez ont fait les choses suivantes le week-end dernier?

> **Exemple**    samedi matin: rester à la maison
> **Non, ils ne sont pas restés à la maison.**

samedi matin: partir pour le week-end, aller à Nice, visiter Deauville, y aller en voiture, prendre le train, partir après huit heures

samedi après-midi: rester chez des amis, descendre à l'hôtel, prendre l'autobus pour aller à l'hôtel, y aller en taxi, mettre tous leurs bagages dans le taxi, arriver à l'hôtel avant midi

dimanche matin: rester à l'hôtel, sortir avant neuf heures, faire du shopping, aller à la plage, mettre leur maillot de bain, louer un bateau

dimanche soir: rentrer à la maison, revenir en taxi, arriver à la maison avant minuit, laisser tous leurs bagages à l'hôtel

**C. Tu es partie en week-end?** Imaginez que vous êtes l'ami(e) d'Alice Pérez de l'exercice précédent. Posez des questions comme dans l'exemple à votre partenaire qui va jouer le rôle d'Alice.

> **Exemple**    où / aller
> **— Où est-ce que tu es allée?**
> **— Je suis allée à Deauville.**

1. quand / partir
2. avec qui / voyager
3. comment / y aller
4. quand / arriver
5. où / descendre
6. combien de temps / rester
7. que / faire
8. quand / rentrer

Maintenant, posez les mêmes questions à votre partenaire sur la dernière fois qu'il/elle est parti(e) en weekend.

**D. Entretien.** Interviewez votre partenaire.

1. Est-ce que tu as quitté la maison tôt samedi dernier ou est-ce que tu es resté(e) chez toi samedi matin? Jusqu'à quelle heure est-ce que tu es resté(e) au lit? Est-ce que tu as déjeuné au café samedi ou dimanche?
2. Est-ce que tu es allé(e) au cinéma le week-end dernier? Est-ce que tu as dîné au restaurant? Est-ce que tu es sorti(e) avec des amis samedi soir ou est-ce que tu as passé la soirée à la maison?
3. Est-ce que tu es venu(e) en cours tous les jours la semaine dernière? Est-ce que tu es allé(e) à la bibliothèque hier? À quelle heure est-ce que tu es arrivé(e) en cours aujourd'hui? Est-ce que tu es venu(e) en autobus, en voiture ou à pied?

## Reprise
*Talking about activities and making plans*

Dans le ***Chapitre 5***, vous avez appris à parler des vêtements, du temps, de vos sorties et de vos activités préférées. Vous avez parlé d'où vous êtes allé(e) et de ce que vous avez fait récemment. Maintenant vous allez réviser ce que vous avez appris.

**A. Vos activités.** Comment passez-vous votre temps? Répondez aux questions en remplaçant les mots en italique par le pronom convenable: **le, la, l'** ou **les.**

1. Est-ce que vous retrouvez souvent *vos camarades de classe* après les cours? Est-ce que vous faites souvent *les devoirs* ensemble? Est-ce que vous avez préparé *le cours* ensemble hier soir? Est-ce que vous allez préparer *le prochain examen de français* ensemble?

2. Est-ce que vous prenez *votre petit déjeuner* à la maison d'habitude? Est-ce que vous avez pris *le petit déjeuner* chez vous hier? Préférez-vous prendre *le petit déjeuner* chez vous, au restaurant, au café ou dans un fast-food?

3. Est-ce que vous invitez souvent *vos amis* chez vous? Est-ce que vous aimez regarder *la télé* ensemble? Est-ce que vous allez regarder *la télé* ce soir?

**B. Quel temps fait-il?** Donnez deux expressions pour décrire le temps dans chaque illustration. Ensuite, dites quels vêtements on met et ce qu'on porte dans ces circonstances.

Exemple

**Il pleut et il fait mauvais. On met un imperméable et des bottes ou on porte un parapluie.**

**1.**      **2.**      **3.**

**C. Qui fait ça?** Est-ce que ces gens font souvent les choses indiquées?

Exemple

Mes amis **font souvent du jogging.**
Mes amis **ne font pas souvent de jogging.**

**1.** Le week-end, mes parents...     **2.** Mon meilleur ami (Ma meilleure amie)...     **3.** Mes amis et moi...

**4.** Ma mère...   **5.** Moi, je...   **6.** Mon père...

**D. Récemment.** Dites quand ces personnes ont fait les choses indiquées récemment.

> **Exemple**   je / passer toute la journée à la maison
> **J'ai passé toute la journée à la maison il y a trois jours.**
> **Je n'ai pas passé toute la journée à la maison récemment.**
> **Je n'ai jamais passé toute la journée à la maison.**

**1.** je / rester au lit jusqu'à midi
**2.** je / travailler
**3.** je / rentrer tard
**4.** je / aller au cinéma
**5.** je / sortir avec des amis
**6.** mes amis et moi / sortir ensemble
**7.** nous / manger ensemble
**8.** nous / rentrer tard
**9.** mon meilleur ami (ma meilleure amie) / téléphoner
**10.** il (elle) / dîner avec moi
**11.** les autres étudiants du cours de français / préparer le cours ensemble
**12.** les autres étudiants du cours de français / sortir ensemble

**E. Entretien.** Interviewez votre partenaire.

**1.** Est-ce que tu es sorti(e) avec des amis récemment? Quand est-ce que tu es sorti(e) avec des amis? Quels vêtements est-ce que tu as mis? Où est-ce que vous êtes allés ensemble? Qu'est-ce que vous avez fait? Est-ce que vous êtes rentrés tard?
**2.** D'habitude, est-ce que tu quittes la maison tôt ou tard le matin pendant la semaine? Est-ce que tu as quitté la maison tôt ce matin? À quelle heure est-ce que tu es arrivé(e) à ton premier cours? Jusqu'à quelle heure vas-tu rester ici? Est-ce que tu vas rentrer chez toi tôt ou tard aujourd'hui? À quelle heure est-ce que tu es rentré(e) hier?
**3.** Est-ce que tu es parti(e) en week-end récemment? La dernière fois que tu es parti(e) en week-end, où est-ce que tu es allé(e)? Quand est-ce que tu es parti(e)? Est-ce que tu as pris ta voiture? Où est-ce que tu es descendu(e)? Combien de temps est-ce que tu es resté(e)? Qu'est-ce que tu as fait? Quand est-ce que tu es rentré(e)?

**F. En week-end.** Pensez à une ville où vous avez passé un week-end magnifique. Parlez de ce week-end en donnant les renseignements suivants.

- où vous êtes allé(e)
- quand vous êtes parti(e)
- avec qui vous y êtes allé(e)
- si vous avez pris l'avion ou votre voiture
- combien de temps vous y avez passé
- où vous êtes descendu(e)
- ce que *(what)* vous y avez fait
- si vous avez l'intention d'y retourner bientôt

## Lecture: *L'emploi du temps des Français*

Vous allez lire une enquête / un sondage *(survey)* sur la journée typique des Français. L'exercice suivant vous aidera *(will help you)* à lire avec plus de facilité.

**En contexte.** Utilisez le contexte pour deviner le sens des mots en italique.

1. Les Français modernes sont toujours *pressés*. On n'a jamais assez de temps.
2. Beaucoup de gens ne *consacrent* pas assez de temps à *s'occuper d'eux-mêmes*. Ils ne dorment pas assez et ils mangent mal et trop rapidement.
3. Le *sommeil* prend le plus de temps sur une journée. Les hommes actifs dorment en moyenne huit heures et trente minutes par jour.
4. On prend moins de *repas* ensemble et on mange plus souvent dans des fast-foods.
5. Les femmes *s'occupent* plus des enfants que les hommes, qui consacrent peu de temps aux *soins aux enfants*.

### L'emploi du temps des Français

L'homme et la femme modernes sont des individus pressés. 80% des Français estiment qu'ils ne consacrent pas assez de temps sur une journée à leurs amis, 74% à leur famille, 69% à s'occuper d'eux-mêmes, 38% à leur vie professionnelle. Le tableau à gauche présente les résultats d'une enquête récente sur l'emploi du temps des Français (en heures et en minutes).

| | Hommes | | Femmes | |
|---|---|---|---|---|
| | **Actifs** | **Inactifs** | **Actives** | **Inactives** |
| *Temps physiologique, dont* | *11h22* | *12h39* | *11h35* | *12h37* |
| - Sommeil | 8h30 | 9h34 | 8h37 | 9h32 |
| - Toilette | 42 | 46 | 49 | 53 |
| - Repas | 2h16 | 2h18 | 2h09 | 2h12 |
| *Temps professionnel et de formation, dont* | *6h22* | *1h32* | *5h01* | *59* |
| - Travail professionnel | 5h42 | 13 | 4h28 | 5 |
| - Transport domicile-travail | 37 | 9 | 30 | 5 |
| - Études | 1 | 1h07 | 0 | 47 |
| *Temps domestique, dont* | *1h59* | *2h55* | *3h48* | *4h47* |
| - Ménage, cuisine, lessive, courses | 1h04 | 1h35 | 3h06 | 3h58 |
| - Soins aux enfants et adultes | 11 | 6 | 27 | 26 |
| - Bricolage | 30 | 36 | 4 | 5 |
| - Jardinage, soins aux animaux | 14 | 38 | 11 | 18 |
| *Temps de loisirs, dont* | *2h57* | *5h06* | *2h19* | *3h57* |
| - Télévision | 1h47 | 2h44 | 1h24 | 2h28 |
| - **Lecture** | 16 | 36 | 17 | 30 |
| - Promenade | 15 | 32 | 14 | 22 |
| - Jeux | 12 | 30 | 6 | 15 |
| - Sport | 10 | 15 | 5 | 5 |
| *Temps de sociabilité (hors repas), dont* | *47* | *1h10* | *43* | *1h04* |
| - Conversations, téléphone, **courrier** | 13 | 20 | 16 | 22 |
| - Visites, réceptions | 26 | 36 | 22 | 33 |
| *Transport (hors domicile-travail)* | *33* | *38* | *34* | *35* |

---

**actifs** *working* **dont** *out of which* **toilette** *getting ready, getting cleaned up* **lecture** *reading* **hors** *outside of* **courrier** *mail*

## Compréhension

1. À qui et à quoi *(what)* est-ce que les Français voudraient consacrer plus de temps?
2. Est-ce que les Français passent plus de temps à dormir ou à travailler? à étudier ou à faire le ménage? à faire du jardinage ou à lire? à faire des promenades ou à faire du sport? Pendant combien de temps est-ce que les Français ont fait chacune *(each one)* de ces activités hier s'ils ont travaillé? S'ils n'ont pas travaillé? Et les Françaises?
3. Quelles sont les différences les plus importantes entre les emplois du temps des hommes et ceux *(those)* des femmes? Entre les personnes actives et inactives?
4. En quoi est-ce que l'emploi du temps d'un étudiant diffère de l'emploi du temps des gens actifs ou inactifs? En quoi est-ce que l'emploi du temps des gens de votre région diffère de celui des *(that of the)* Français?

## Composition

**A. Organisez-vous.** Vous allez décrire un voyage imaginaire à Paris. Regardez ces photos et les photos des pages 195, 199 et 224–225 et faites une liste des choses à faire dans trois endroits différents.

> Exemple    au Quartier latin
> **parler avec des étudiants, faire une promenade...**

**Le musée Picasso**

**Le centre Georges Pompidou**

**B. Rédaction: Une semaine à Paris.** Vous avez passé une semaine à Paris. Décrivez votre semaine. Parlez des choses suivantes:

- à quelle heure vous êtes parti(e) d'ici
- à quelle heure vous êtes arrivé(e) à Paris
- dans quelle sorte d'hôtel vous êtes descendu(e)
- combien de temps vous avez passé à l'hôtel
- ce que *(what)* vous avez fait lundi, mardi...
- ce que vous avez beaucoup aimé
- si vous avez l'intention d'y retourner et quand

If you have access to SYSTÈME-D software, you will find the following phrases, vocabulary, grammar, and dictionary aids there.

**Phrases:** Telling time; Linking ideas; Sequencing events
**Vocabulary:** Leisure; Sports; City
**Grammar:** Compound past tense; Locative pronoun **y**
**Dictionary:** The verb **faire**

**C. Ressemblances.** Échangez votre description avec un(e) camarade de classe. Comparez votre semaine à Paris avec celle de votre partenaire et décrivez-les aux autres étudiants.

## Les loisirs des Français

**Si** on **met à part les repas**, qui représentent un temps libre «obligatoire», la télévision occupe **de loin** la plus grande partie du temps de loisir des Français. Ils sont exposés aux médias en moyenne environ 6h30 par jour, dont 3h38 pour la télévision et 1h57 pour la radio. Mais le temps qu'ils consacrent **à chacun à titre exclusif** est très inférieur; **on peut** écouter par exemple la radio ou regarder la télévision tout en faisant la cuisine ou le ménage, **voire** en travaillant. Les Français regardent la télévision à titre principal en moyenne 2h07 par jour. Ils **n'**écoutent la radio **que** 4 minutes, ce qui signifie qu'ils l'écoutent presque toujours à titre secondaire, en même temps qu'ils pratiquent une autre activité, considérée comme principale.

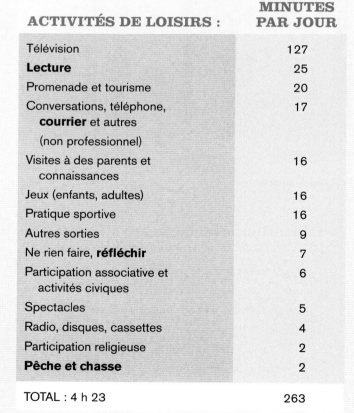

Temps consacré à des activités de loisirs

| ACTIVITÉS DE LOISIRS : | MINUTES PAR JOUR |
|---|---|
| Télévision | 127 |
| **Lecture** | 25 |
| Promenade et tourisme | 20 |
| Conversations, téléphone, **courrier** et autres (non professionnel) | 17 |
| Visites à des parents et connaissances | 16 |
| Jeux (enfants, adultes) | 16 |
| Pratique sportive | 16 |
| Autres sorties | 9 |
| Ne rien faire, **réfléchir** | 7 |
| Participation associative et activités civiques | 6 |
| Spectacles | 5 |
| Radio, disques, cassettes | 4 |
| Participation religieuse | 2 |
| **Pêche et chasse** | 2 |
| TOTAL : 4 h 23 | 263 |

---

**met à part les repas** *sets aside meals*   **de loin** *by far*   **à chacun à titre exclusif** *to each one exclusively*
**on peut** *one can*   **voire** *even*   **ne... que** *only*   **lecture** *reading*   **courrier** *mail*   **réfléchir** *to think, to reflect*
**pêche et chasse** *fishing and hunting*

**Actives** ou non, les femmes disposent **en moyenne** de moins de temps libre que les hommes: 4h12 par jour contre 4h52 (activités de loisir et de sociabilité). Dans le domaine des médias, les femmes inactives constituent **la cible privilégiée** des radios, mais elles regardent moins la télévision et sont moins souvent **lectrices des quotidiens nationaux** que les hommes. Elles lisent **en revanche davantage de** livres et de magazines et constituent la clientèle majoritaire du théâtre.

visit http://horizons.heinle.com

Temps quotidien consacré aux loisirs (en heures et en minutes)

| | Actifs | | Femmes au foyer* | 60 ans et plus | |
| | Hommes | Femmes | | Hommes | Femmes |
|---|---|---|---|---|---|
| Sociabilité | 47 | 43 | 57 | 58 | 1 h 00 |
| Télévision | 1 h 45 | 1 h 22 | 2 h 08 | 3 h 01 | 2 h 51 |
| Lecture | 16 | 17 | 19 | 51 | 41 |
| Promenade | 18 | 14 | 18 | 44 | 25 |
| Sport | 10 | 5 | 6 | 10 | 2 |
| Semi-loisirs** | 45 | 20 | 38 | 1 h 51 | 48 |

*Moins de 60 ans.

**Les semi-loisirs (jardinage, bricolage, **entretien** des voitures, **soins aux** animaux, **travaux d'aiguille, confection de conserves**, gâteaux, confitures) ont été considérés comme faisant partie du temps libre et non du temps domestique.

## À discuter

1. Comparez les passe-temps préférés des Français avec les passe-temps préférés dans votre région. Sont-ils les mêmes? Quelles sont les différences? Pourquoi est-ce qu'il y a des différences, à votre avis? Est-ce qu'il y a peut-être des différences de valeurs *(values)*, d'intérêts, de géographie ou de climat qui influencent les préférences des gens?

2. Est-ce qu'il y a une grande différence entre les loisirs préférés des hommes et des femmes en France? Entre les personnes actives et les retraités *(retired people)*? Quelles différences y a-t-il dans votre région?

---

**Actives** *Working*   **en moyenne** *on average*   **la cible privilégiée** *the favored target*   **lectrices des quotidiens nationaux** *readers of national daily newspapers*   **en revanche** *on the other hand*   **davantage de** *more*   **femmes au foyer** *homemakers*   **entretien** *maintenance*   **soins aux** *care for*   **travaux d'aiguille** *needlework*   **confection de conserves, gâteaux, confitures** *making preserves, cakes, jelly*

# Résumé de grammaire

— Tu prends ce sac?
— Oui, je **le** prends.
— *Are you taking this purse?*
— *Yes, I'm taking it.*

— Tu aimes cette ceinture aussi?
— Oui, je **l'**aime bien.
— *Do you like this belt too?*
— *Yes, I like it.*

— Tu achètes tes vêtements ici?
— Oui, je **les** achète souvent ici.
— *Do you buy your clothes here?*
— *Yes, I often buy them here.*

Je **les** achète.
Je ne **les** achète pas.
Je vais **les** acheter.
Je ne vais pas **les** acheter.

A-t-il acheté les chaussures?
Oui, il **les** a achet**ées**.
Non, il ne **les** a pas achet**ées**.

Je ne **fais** rien ce week-end.
Qu'est-ce que tu **fais?**
On **fait** quelque chose ensemble?
**Faisons** quelque chose avec mes amis.
Que **faites**-vous généralement?
Mes amis **font** beaucoup de sport.

— Quel temps fait-il?
— Il fait beau (mauvais, froid, chaud, frais, du soleil, du vent).

Ils font la cuisine et nous faisons la vaisselle.
*They cook and we do the dishes.*

— On fait du bateau?
— Je préfère faire du vélo.
— *Shall we go boating?*
— *I prefer to go bike riding.*

Je ne fais jamais **d'**exercice.
Mon colocataire ne fait jamais **le** ménage.

Rien **n'**est en solde?
Tu **n'**achètes **rien**?
Je **n'**ai besoin de **rien**.
Je préfère **ne rien** acheter.

## Direct object pronouns

The direct object pronouns are **le, la, l'**, and **les.** Use **le** *(him, it)* to replace masculine singular nouns and **la** *(her, it)* to replace feminine singular nouns. **Les** *(Them)* replaces all plural nouns. **Le** and **la** become **l'** when the following word begins with a vowel or silent **h.**

| | BEFORE A CONSONANT | BEFORE A VOWEL OR SILENT H |
|---|---|---|
| *him, it (masculine)* | le | l' |
| *her, it (feminine)* | la | l' |
| *them* | les | les |

These pronouns are generally placed *immediately* before the verb. They go before the infinitive if there is one. If not, they go before the conjugated verb. In the negative, the pronoun remains *immediately* before the conjugated verb or the infinitive.

In the **passé composé,** direct object pronouns are placed just before the auxiliary verb **avoir** and the past participle agrees with them for gender and plurality by adding **-e, -s,** or **-es.**

## *Faire*

The verb **faire** *(to do, to make)* is irregular.

| FAIRE *(to do)* | |
|---|---|
| je **fais** | nous **faisons** |
| tu **fais** | vous **faites** |
| il/elle/on **fait** | ils/elles **font** |

**Faire** is also used in many weather expressions, as well as the following idiomatic expressions.

| | |
|---|---|
| **faire de l'exercice** | **faire des courses** |
| **faire du bateau** | **faire du jardinage** |
| **faire du camping** | **faire du shopping** |
| **faire du jogging** | **faire la cuisine** |
| **faire du ski (nautique)** | **faire la lessive** |
| **faire du sport (du tennis... )** | **faire la vaisselle** |
| **faire du vélo** | **faire le ménage** |
| **faire une promenade** | |
| **faire un voyage** | |

The **un, une, des, du, de la,** and **de l'** in the expressions with **faire** become **de (d')** when the verb is negated. The definite article (**le, la, l', les**) does not change.

## *Ne... rien*

**Ne... rien** means *nothing* or *not anything*. This expression can be the subject or object of the verb, or the object of a preposition.

When negating an infinitive, place both parts of the negative expression before it.

## *Passé composé*

To say what happened in the past, put the verb in the **passé composé.** The **passé composé** is composed of an auxiliary verb and a past participle. It may be translated in a variety of ways. For most verbs the auxiliary verb is **avoir,** but for a few verbs it is **être.** All **-er** verbs have past participles with **-é** (**parler: j'ai parlé**) and most **-ir** verbs with **-i** (**dormir: j'ai dormi**).

J'ai mangé. = *I ate. / I have eaten. / I did eat.*

Ils n'ont pas beaucoup dormi. = *They didn't sleep much. They haven't slept much.*

|  PARLER → PARLÉ  |  |
|---|---|
| j' **ai parlé** | nous **avons parlé** |
| tu **as parlé** | vous **avez parlé** |
| il/elle/on **a parlé** | ils/elles **ont parlé** |

These verbs conjugated with **avoir** have irregular past participles.

| avoir: | j'ai eu | mettre: | j'ai mis | être: | j'ai été |
|---|---|---|---|---|---|
| il y a: | il y a eu | prendre: | j'ai pris | faire: | j'ai fait |
| boire: | j'ai bu | apprendre: | j'ai appris | écrire: | j'ai écrit |
| lire: | j'ai lu | comprendre: | j'ai compris | | |
| pleuvoir: | il a plu | | | | |
| voir: | j'ai vu | | | | |

— Qu'est-ce que tu **as fait** hier soir?
— J'**ai vu** un film avec des amis et après on **a pris** un verre au café.

A few verbs have **être** as their auxiliary. With these verbs, the past participle agrees with the subject for gender and plurality.

|  ALLER → ALLÉ  |  |
|---|---|
| je **suis allé(e)** | nous **sommes allé(e)s** |
| tu **es allé(e)** | vous **êtes allé(e)(s)** |
| il **est allé** | ils **sont allés** |
| elle **est allée** | elles **sont allées** |
| on **est allé(e)(s)** | |

Here are some verbs that have **être** as their auxiliary verb.

| aller: | je suis allé(e) | monter: | je suis monté(e) |
|---|---|---|---|
| arriver: | je suis arrivé(e) | descendre: | je suis descendu(e) |
| rester: | je suis resté(e) | venir: | je suis venu(e) |
| entrer: | je suis entré(e) | revenir: | je suis revenu(e) |
| sortir: | je suis sorti(e) | devenir: | je suis devenu(e) |
| partir: | je suis parti(e) | naître: | je suis né(e) |
| rentrer: | je suis rentré(e) | mourir: | il/elle est mort(e) |
| retourner: | je suis retourné(e) | | |

— Est-ce que ta mère et ta tante **sont allées** à Paris avec toi?
— Oui, elles ont fait le voyage avec moi mais je **suis restée** plus longtemps. Elles **sont rentrées** une semaine avant moi.

Place **ne... pas, ne... rien,** or **ne... jamais** around the auxiliary verb. Use **ne... pas encore** to say *not yet* and **déjà** to say *already* or *ever*. **Déjà** and adverbs indicating how often (**toujours, souvent...** ) and how well (**bien, mal...** ) are usually placed between the auxiliary verb and the past participle.

The following adverbs indicate when something happened in the past. They may be placed at the beginning or end of the sentence.

| hier (matin, après-midi, soir) | récemment |
|---|---|
| le week-end (le mois) dernier | pendant deux heures (longtemps) |
| la semaine (l'année) dernière | il y a quelques secondes (cinq |
| la dernière fois | minutes, cinq ans... ) |

— Tu as **déjà** visité Nice?
— Non, je **n'**ai **pas encore** été à Nice.
— Qu'est-ce que ton mari et toi avez fait l'année dernière pour les vacances?
— On **n'**a **rien** fait.

— Tu as été en vacances pendant combien de temps?
— Pendant quinze jours.
— Tu es rentré il y a combien de temps?
— Je suis rentré mardi dernier.

**Vocabulaire**

## Deciding what to wear and buying clothes

**NOMS MASCULINS**

| | |
|---|---|
| un anorak | a ski jacket |
| un bikini | a bikini |
| un centre | a center |
| un chapeau | a hat |
| un chemisier | a blouse |
| un costume | a suit (for a man) |
| un homme d'affaires | a businessman |
| un imperméable | a raincoat |
| un jean | jeans |
| un maillot de bain | a swimsuit |
| un manteau | an overcoat |
| un pantalon | pants |
| un parapluie | an umbrella |
| un polo | a knit shirt |
| un portefeuille | a wallet |
| un pull | a pullover sweater |
| un sac | a purse, a sack |
| un short | shorts |
| un survêtement | a jogging suit |
| un tee-shirt | a T-shirt |
| un vendeur | a salesclerk |

**NOMS FÉMININS**

| | |
|---|---|
| des baskets | tennis shoes |
| des bottes | boots |
| une cabine d'essayage | a fitting room |
| une casquette | a cap |
| une ceinture | a belt |
| des chaussettes | socks |
| des chaussures | shoes |
| une chemise | a shirt |
| une cravate | a tie |
| une femme d'affaires | a businesswoman |
| la haute couture | designer fashion |
| une jupe | a skirt |
| des lunettes (de soleil) | (sun)glasses |
| la mode | fashion |
| une montre | a watch |
| une robe | a dress |
| des sandales | sandals |
| une vendeuse | a salesclerk |

**EXPRESSIONS VERBALES**

| | |
|---|---|
| coûter | to cost |
| entrer (dans) | to enter, to go in |
| essayer | to try, to try on |
| Il/Elle me plaît. | I like it. |
| mettre (je mets, vous mettez) | to put, to put on |

**DIVERS**

| | |
|---|---|
| Bien sûr! | Of course! |
| en solde | on sale |
| Je peux vous aider? | May I help you? |
| le (l') / la (l') | him, it/her, it |
| les | them |
| mondial(e) (mpl mondiaux) | world (adj.) |
| par ici | this way |
| parfois | sometimes |
| Quelle taille faites-vous? | What size do you wear? |
| Je fais du... | I wear size . . . |
| sans doute | without doubt |
| travaillant | working |
| voyons | let's see |

## Discussing the weather and what to do

**NOMS MASCULINS**

| | |
|---|---|
| l'automne (en automne) | autumn (in autumn) |
| l'été (en été) | summer (in summer) |
| l'hiver (en hiver) | winter (in winter) |
| un jardin | a garden |
| le printemps (au printemps) | spring (in spring) |
| le temps | the weather, time |

**NOMS FÉMININS**

| | |
|---|---|
| des distractions | entertainment |
| la neige | snow |
| la pluie | rain |
| une saison | a season |

**EXPRESSIONS VERBALES**

| | |
|---|---|
| aller à la montagne | to go to the mountains |
| dépendre (de) | to depend (on) |
| faire de l'exercice | to exercise |
| faire des courses | to run errands |
| faire du bateau | to go boating |
| faire du camping | to go camping |
| faire du jardinage | to garden |
| faire du jogging | to go jogging |
| faire du shopping | to go shopping |
| faire du ski (nautique) | to (water)ski |
| faire du sport (du tennis, du hockey... ) | to play sports (tennis, hockey . . . ) |
| faire du vélo | to go bike-riding |
| faire la cuisine | to cook |
| faire la lessive | to do laundry |
| faire la vaisselle | to do the dishes |
| faire le ménage | to do housework |
| faire une promenade | to take a walk |
| faire un voyage | to take a trip |
| neiger | to snow |
| pleuvoir | to rain |

**DIVERS**

| | |
|---|---|
| ne... rien | nothing |
| pendant | during, for |
| Quel temps fait-il? | What's the weather like? |
| Il fait beau/chaud/frais/ froid/mauvais/du soleil/ du vent. | It's nice/hot/cool/ cold/bad/sunny/ windy. |
| Il pleut. | It is raining., It rains. |
| Il neige. | It is snowing., It snows. |
| Quel temps va-t-il faire? | What's the weather going to be like? |
| Il va faire... | It's going to be . . . |
| Il va pleuvoir/neiger. | It's going to rain / to snow. |
| si | if |

# COMPÉTENCE 3

## Saying what you did

**NOMS MASCULINS**

| | |
|---|---|
| un an | *a year* |
| le journal | *the newspaper* |
| le petit déjeuner | *breakfast* |

**NOMS FÉMININS**

| | |
|---|---|
| une heure | *an hour* |
| une minute | *a minute* |
| une seconde | *a second* (in time) |

**EXPRESSIONS ADVERBIALES**

| | |
|---|---|
| l'année dernière | *last year* |
| déjà | *already* |
| la dernière fois | *the last time* |
| hier (matin, après-midi) | *yesterday (morning, afternoon)* |
| hier soir | *last night, yesterday evening* |
| Il y a combien de temps? | *How long ago?* |
| il y a quelques secondes | *a few seconds ago* |
| longtemps | *a long time* |
| lundi (mardi... ) dernier | *last Monday (Tuesday . . . )* |
| le mois dernier | *last month* |
| ne... pas encore | *not yet* |
| Pendant combien de temps? | *For how long?* |
| pendant deux heures | *for two hours* |
| récemment | *recently* |
| la semaine dernière | *last week* |
| le week-end dernier | *last weekend* |

**DIVERS**

| | |
|---|---|
| dernier (dernière) | *last* |
| prendre son petit déjeuner | *to have one's breakfast* |
| quelques | *some, a few* |

# COMPÉTENCE 4

## Telling where you went

**NOMS MASCULINS**

| | |
|---|---|
| un camping | *a campground* |
| un club | *a club* |
| un hôtel | *a hotel* |
| des parents | *relatives* |

**NOMS FÉMININS**

| | |
|---|---|
| la chance | *luck* |
| une nuit | *a night* |
| une voiture de location | *a rental car* |

**EXPRESSIONS VERBALES**

| | |
|---|---|
| descendre (de / dans / à) | *to descend, to come down, to get off/out (of), to stay (at)* |
| monter (dans) | *to go up, to get on/in* |
| mourir (mort[e]) | *to die (dead)* |
| naître (né[e]) | *to be born (born)* |
| partir en week-end | *to go away for the weekend* |
| retourner | *to return, to go back* |

**DIVERS**

| | |
|---|---|
| Quelle chance! | *What luck!* |

# SYNTHÈSE VIDÉO

## Épisode: Prélude

### Avant la vidéo

In this episode of the video you will meet our heroine, Élodie, who is staying at her Tante Mathilde's house in Paris while she studies at the conservatory. You will also meet several of their friends and acquaintances and find out about their likes and dislikes.

What are your own likes and dislikes? What do you think you would like and dislike if you lived in Paris? List your thoughts and compare your list to those of your classmates.

### Après la vidéo

1. Which character from the video does each sentence describe?

- **a.** Élodie
- **b.** Julien (l'étudiant au conservatoire)
- **c.** Claire-Anse (la voisine)
- **d.** M. Leroy (le fleuriste)
- **e.** Youssef (le vendeur de journaux)
- **f.** M. Benoît (le boulanger)
- **g.** Lucas (le garçon)
- **h.** Mme Dutilleul (la concierge)
- **i.** Olivier (le voisin)
- **j.** Tante Mathilde
- **k.** Camus (le chat)

1. _____ adore le jazz et aime jouer au foot.

2. _____ adore voyager!

3. _____ étudie la musique et aime toutes sortes de bruits.

4. _____ adore les antiquités et son scooter.

5. _____ aime regarder par la fenêtre et manger dans un bol en cristal.

6. _____ aime la pluie et déteste les fleurs artificielles.

7. _____ n'aime pas les chiens dans les cafés.

8. _____ n'aime pas grand-chose, surtout pas les gens qui font trop de bruit et les courants d'air.

9. _____ aime la monnaie exacte et un bon couscous.

10. _____ est citoyen du monde et aime les arts martiaux et les vieilles cartes postales.

11. _____ aime dormir tard, passer du temps au parc et écouter du hip hop.

## Épisode: L'éducation et le métier idéal

### Avant la vidéo

In this episode, Élodie's efforts to complete an assignment for class are interrupted by Olivier. They take a break at a nearby café where they complain about the difficulties of being a student and talk with their friends about what they'd like to do in life.

Do you have a lot of work to do outside of class? Where do you go when you want to take a break? Are you happy with your career choice? If you could be anything in the world, what would you be?

### Après la vidéo

1. What are some of the complaints the students make about student life?

2. What are some of Claire-Anse's complaints about working life? What does she do? Does she like her job?

3. List five of the professions mentioned in the video.

Do you have the same complaints about school and working life? Do any of the professions mentioned interest you?

## Épisode: Les sondages

### Avant la vidéo

In this episode, Olivier dreams of winning the lottery, but ends up accepting a job doing surveys. It's not an easy job, but luckily Élodie is there to help.

Do you buy lottery tickets? When?

Are you willing to participate in surveys? Why or why not?

### Après la vidéo

1. How does Youssef analyze people?

2. According to the narrator, what could Olivier do with a million euros? What would Olivier himself like about winning?

3. Poor Olivier is paid per interview conducted, but no one wants to participate in his survey. Who does Élodie end up interviewing in the **jardin du Luxembourg?** How does he answer the question: **Que pensez-vous de la qualité de l'air à Paris?**

If you won the lottery, what would you do with the money?

In your opinion, why do some people not like to answer survey questions?

# Épisode: Une visite en famille

## Avant la vidéo

In this episode, Élodie and Claire-Anse spend the weekend at Élodie's parents' house.

Do you like to stay with a friend's parents? Why or why not? At whose house do you like to spend time? What is this person's house or apartment like?

## Après la vidéo

1. Claire-Anse et Élodie voyagent en train. Est-ce qu'elles achètent des billets... de première ou de deuxième classe? aller-retour ou un aller simple? fumeur ou non-fumeur?

2. Claire-Anse et Élodie parlent de leurs familles. Combien de frères et sœurs est-ce qu'Élodie a? Et Claire-Anse?

3. Quand elles arrivent chez les parents d'Élodie, sa mère montre la maison à Claire-Anse. Quelles pièces la mère d'Élodie montre-t-elle?

4. Qu'est ce qu'il y a sur les murs de la chambre d'Élodie? Pourquoi?

5. Qu'est-ce qui intéresse Claire-Anse dans la chambre d'amis? Qu'est-ce que le père d'Élodie et Claire-Anse ont en commun?

What did you think of Élodie's parents' house? Did anything about it surprise you?

# Épisode: L'amitié et l'amour possible

## Avant la vidéo

Dans cet épisode, Élodie et ses amis sont au café quand Julien, un étudiant du conservatoire, arrive. Il invite Élodie à sortir d'une façon plutôt unique. Après, on voit Élodie en train de se préparer pour sortir avec lui.

Et vous? Qu'est-ce que vous aimez mettre pour sortir avec quelqu'un pour la première fois?

## Après la vidéo

1. Les amis sont au café. Qu'est-ce que chacun commande?
   Élodie:     Olivier:     Claire-Anse:     Lucas:

2. Claire-Anse n'est pas contente. Est-ce à cause de... ?
   a. sa vie personnelle
   b. sa vie familiale
   c. sa situation professionnelle

3. Lucas est amoureux d'Élodie. Qu'est-ce qu'il fait pour essayer de la rendre jalouse?

4. Julien arrive au café et Élodie devient si nerveuse qu'elle renverse son vin. Qu'est-ce que chacun de ses amis recommande pour enlever la tache?
   Claire-Anse:     Olivier:     Lucas:

5. Élodie se prépare pour son rendez-vous avec Julien. Qu'est-ce qu'elle décide finalement de mettre? Pourquoi ne met-elle pas son ensemble beige? sa petite robe noire?

Est-ce que les actions et les réactions de Lucas et d'Élodie vous rappellent vos expériences personnelles ou celles de vos amis?

## Épisode: L'opéra

### Avant la vidéo

Dans cet épisode, Élodie, Claire-Anse et Lucas attendent Olivier devant l'Opéra Bastille, mais il n'arrive pas. Le problème c'est que lui, il est allé à l'Opéra Garnier. Mais tout est bien qui finit bien. Les quatre amis réussissent à se retrouver après l'opéra. Ils se promènent sur une des plus anciennes places de Paris, la place des Vosges, et ils découvrent un magasin unique.

Est-ce que vous vous êtes déjà trompé(e) d'endroit pour un rendez-vous avec quelqu'un? Qu'est-ce que vous avez fait? Quelle a été la réaction de la personne avec qui vous aviez rendez-vous?

### Après la vidéo

1. Élodie et ses amis attendent l'arrivée d'Olivier pour entrer dans l'opéra.
   a. Où est-ce qu'ils l'attendent?
   b. À quelle heure est-ce qu'Olivier devait arriver?
   c. Qu'est-ce qu'ils décident de faire de son billet quand il n'arrive pas?

2. Élodie, Claire-Anse et Lucas assistent à l'opéra sans Olivier.
   a. Quel opéra voient-ils, *Carmen* ou *La Bohème?*
   b. Qui aime beaucoup l'opéra? Qu'est-ce qu'ils/elles apprécient surtout?

3. Olivier n'aime pas l'architecture futuriste de l'Opéra Bastille. Il dit que l'Opéra Bastille ressemble à: *(deux choses)*
   _____ une prison
   _____ une gare routière
   _____ une boucherie

4. En se promenant sur la place des Vosges, les quatre amis associent cette place avec: *(deux choses)*
   _____ le mariage d'Henri IV
   _____ le mariage de Louis XIII
   _____ la vie de Victor Hugo
   _____ la vie de Charles Baudelaire

5. Quelle sorte de magasin est-ce qu'Élodie et ses amis découvrent? Ce magasin ressemble à une autre sorte de magasin parce que les ancêtres du propriétaire étaient:
   _____ des musiciens
   _____ des bouchers
   _____ des fermiers

L'Opéra Garnier, réalisé par l'architecte Garnier, est un exemple du style orné Napoléon III, tandis que l'Opéra Bastille est d'un style simpliste et moderne. Lequel préférez-vous? Pourquoi?

**EN EUROPE,** le français est une langue officielle dans quatre pays et une principauté. **Lesquels** voudriez-vous visiter?

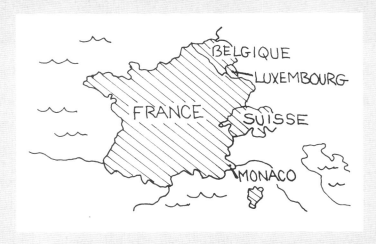

**Le duché** de Luxembourg est un des plus petits états d'Europe. **À la tête du gouvernement** se trouvent le Grand-Duc et le Premier ministre. Il y a trois langues **courantes** au Luxembourg: le luxembourgeois, le français et l'allemand. Le français est souvent employé dans l'administration, dans **les écoles** secondaires et dans **le monde** des affaires. Le Luxembourg **attire** l'attention internationale par sa place financière dans l'Europe moderne et **grâce à** une forte immigration (36%), le Luxembourg est devenu un microcosme de l'Europe.

**Le Luxembourg**

| | | | |
|---|---|---|---|
| **Bienvenue** *Welcome* | **Lesquels** *Which ones* | **Le duché** *The duchy* | **À la tête du gouvernement** *At the head of the government* |
| **courantes** *common* | **les écoles** *schools* | **le monde** *the world* | **attire** *attracts* **grâce à** *thanks to* |

Lausanne, Suisse

Genève, Suisse

La Suisse, ou Confédération Helvétique, est une république fédérale composée de 23 cantons **liés** par la Constitution de 1848. **Toutefois,** une grande partie du **pouvoir** politique **demeure au niveau du** canton. La Suisse **garde depuis** 1515 la neutralité dans tous les conflits internationaux. Ce pays a quatre langues officielles: l'allemand, le français, l'italien et le romanche.

**liés** *linked*　**Toutefois** *However*　**pouvoir** *power*　**demeure au niveau de** *remains at the level of*　**garde depuis** *has kept since*

La Belgique

La Belgique est une monarchie fondée sur une démocratie parlementaire. **Les Flamands** (58% de la population) parlent **néerlandais.** Les Wallons (32% de la population) parlent français. Pour le reste, neuf pour cent sont bilingues et un pour cent parle allemand. Cette division culturelle et linguistique a longtemps été une source de conflits. Pour dissiper cet antagonisme, un effort de décentralisation a donné plus de pouvoir aux trois régions qui forment ce pays: la Région flamande, la Région wallonne et la Région de Bruxelles (la capitale).

Monaco, **dont** la langue officielle est le français, est **une principauté** depuis plus de 300 ans. **Bien qu'elle soit devenue** un protectorat de la France en 1861, le prince y a gardé le pouvoir absolu jusqu'à l'établissement de la Constitution de 1911. Aujourd'hui une monarchie constitutionnelle, cette principauté est célèbre dans le monde entier pour le tourisme, le luxe, **les courses** de Formule 1 et ses casinos.

Monaco

Monaco

---

**Les Flamands** *The Flemish*  **néerlandais** *Dutch*  **dont** *whose, of which*  **une principauté** *a principality*
**Bien qu'elle soit devenue** *Although it became*  **les courses** *races*

Strasbourg, France

Avant d'être une république, la France a été une monarchie et un empire. Aujourd'hui, la France est un régime parlementaire qui a à sa tête le Président de la République et son Premier ministre. La France est divisée en 96 départements et 4 départements **d'outre-mer**: la Guadeloupe, la Martinique, la Guyane et la Réunion.

La France a aussi plusieurs territoires. La Polynésie française, Wallis-et-Futuna, Mayotte et Saint-Pierre-et-Miquelon sont des collectivités d'outre-mer. La Nouvelle-Calédonie est aujourd'hui considérée un pays d'outre-mer. La France possède aussi les Terres australes et antarctiques françaises.

La Corse, France

Un village en France

Aix-en-Provence, France

**d'outre-mer** *overseas*

To find a list of American businesses with offices in francophone countries, check the geographical index of the *Directory of Corporate Affiliations*, found in many libraries.

**For information about jobs in the travel industry, check with:**

The American Society of Travel Agents
1101 King Street, Suite 200
Alexandria, VA 22314
(703) 739-2782
www.astanet.com

**Association of Flight Attendants**

1275 K Street, NW, 5th floor
Washington, DC 20005
(202) 712-9799
www.afanet.org

**To do volunteer work in a francophone country, contact:**

United Nations Volunteers
www.unv.org

Peace Corps
(800) 424-8580
www.peacecorps.gov

SCI International Voluntary Service
www.sci-ivs.org

Operation Crossroads Africa
P. O. Box 5570
New York, NY 10027
(212) 289-1949
e-mail: oca@igc.org

WorldTeach
c/o Center for International Development
Harvard University
79 John F. Kennedy Street
Cambridge MA 02138
(800) 4-TEACH-0
(617) 495-5527
www.worldteach.org

**For information on working for the U.S. State Department, go to:**

www.state.gov/employment/

# French for Jobs in Business or for Government or International Organizations

Are you interested in business? Your knowledge of French can be useful whether you are working for a company here at home or abroad. You can help American businesses expand and provide services to markets in Canada, Europe, and Africa. Or you can work for an international company with offices in Europe, Africa, or Canada. Over 750 American companies (ExxonMobil, IBM, *Newsweek* magazine, Microsoft, and Hyatt Hotels, to name a few) do business in France, not to mention those with offices in other francophone countries around the globe. Or perhaps you would like to work for one of the companies from francophone countries with offices in the United States (Michelin, Dannon, Bic, etc.). If you wish to work in international business, consider specializing not only in French, but also in international finance, banking, business, economics, communications, journalism, or in a scientific or technical field. You can get experience and possibly an opportunity for permanent employment by doing an internship. Some interns are accepted on a volunteer basis, whereas others are paid a stipend. Check directly with the company for which you wish to work for more information about internships.

Another field of employment in which your language skills can be very useful is the travel industry. Working in the travel industry can be exciting, and your language skills can help you find employment as a travel agent, flight attendant, reservation and customer service agent, or tour manager. As a bilingual employee, you will have a better chance of getting hired, and you may be offered the best positions, routes, and pay.

Are you interested in working for a govermental or international organization? The United Nations offices in New York and Geneva hire French-speaking international lawyers, public information officers, demographers, secretaries, tour guides, translators, and interpreters. The United Nations also hires people with backgrounds in social work, language, education, health, technology, and economics to work in developing countries with organizations such as the United Nations Children's Fund, the World Health Organization, and the United Nations Development Program. One way to gain valuable experience with the United Nations that may eventually lead to a permanent job is to volunteer. For more information, visit www.unv.org.

**Les Nations unies à Genève**

Knowing French can also help you obtain a job in the Foreign Service, with the United States federal government, either in Washington or in offices in over 140 different countries. In fact, persons entering the Foreign Service with no foreign language skills are put on probation until competency in a second language is demonstrated. To enter the Foreign Service, you must take a written and oral exam that generally covers current events, history, geography, international relations, art, literature, culture, economics, and verbal expression. For more information about working for the United States State Department, visit www.state.gov/employment/.

The State Department is not the only part of the government that hires people because they are fluent in foreign languages. Nearly all governmental departments and agencies, from the Library of Congress to the Environmental Protection Agency, need people who know French.

## Catherine Kraus

*Où est-ce que vous travaillez et qu'est-ce que vous faites?*

Je suis **rédactrice adjointe** dans **une maison d'édition** américaine qui publie des livres universitaires.

*Comment est-ce que vous avez appris à parler français?*

Je l'ai étudié **au collège**, **au lycée** et à l'université. À l'université de Wisconsin-Madison, je me suis spécialisée en français et en anglais. J'ai aussi fait une année d'études à l'université d'Aix-en-Provence, en France.

*Quand avez-vous besoin d'**utiliser** le français dans votre travail?*

J'utilise le français tous les jours. Je travaille avec une rédactrice sur **des manuels** de français. Quelquefois je cherche des articles intéressants dans des journaux et des magazines français pour les utiliser dans nos manuels. **Je dois** aussi lire et écrire des lettres et **des factures** en français.

*Quels aspects de votre travail sont pour vous les plus satisfaisants?*

J'aime **surtout** les moments où je suis en contact avec la langue et la culture. Par exemple, quand je dois lire des textes ou éditer une vidéo. C'est dans ces moments-là que j'ai l'impression de **créer** quelque chose **qui servira**.

*Selon vous, quels sont les avantages de **savoir** parler une deuxième langue?*

**La connaissance** d'une deuxième langue non **seulement** ouvre **l'esprit** mais aussi donne la possibilité de comprendre une autre culture et **une façon de vivre** différente. **Par ailleurs,** j'aime voyager et le français **me permet de me sentir à l'aise** quand je visite la France.

*Quelles recommandations pouvez-vous faire à quelqu'un qui **souhaite** trouver un poste **dans lequel il peut** utiliser ses connaissances linguistiques?*

Vous ne savez jamais où vos connaissances de langues étrangères **vont vous mener! Vous pouvez** travailler pour le gouvernement, dans votre pays ou **à l'étranger.** Beaucoup de **sociétés** ont **des liens** internationaux et elles recherchent des employés bilingues. **J'ai voulu** mettre en pratique mon diplôme d'anglais en travaillant pour une maison d'édition. À ma grande surprise, cette entreprise m'a engagée pour mes connaissances des langues étrangères!

---

**rédactrice adjointe** *assistant editor*   **une maison d'édition** *a publishing company*   **au collège** *in middle school*   **au lycée** *in high school*   **utiliser** *to use*
**des manuels** *textbooks*   **Je dois** *I have to*   **des factures** *bills*   **surtout** *especially*   **créer** *to create*   **qui servira** *useful*   **savoir** *to know how to*   **La connaissance** *The knowledge*
**seulement** *only*   **l'esprit** *the mind*   **une façon de vivre** *a way of life*   **Par ailleurs** *Furthermore*   **me permet de me sentir à l'aise** *allows me to feel at ease*   **souhaite** *wishes*
**dans lequel il peut** *in which he can*   **vont vous mener** *will lead you*   **Vous pouvez** *You can*   **à l'étranger** *abroad*   **sociétés** *companies*   **des liens** *ties*   **J'ai voulu** *I wanted*

## Notre-Dame
### HENRI ROUSSEAU (1844–1910)

1909
The Phillips Collection

Ce tableau de **Notre-Dame de Paris** a été exécuté par le peintre *(painter)* Henri Rousseau dit le Douanier *(known as the Customs Agent)* pendant la dernière année de sa vie *(life)*. De nombreux artistes, parmi lesquels *(including)* Robert Delaunay et Paul Signac, ont également choisi de peindre *(also chose to paint)* Notre-Dame vue du quai Henri IV sur l'île Saint-Louis.

## Le Baiser
### CONSTANTIN BRANCUSI (1876–1957)

Circa 1911
Paris, Musée National d'Art Moderne
Giraudon/Art Resource
© 1998 Artists Rights Society (ARS),
New York/ADAGP, Paris

D'origine roumaine, Constantin Brancusi a fait *(studied)* les beaux-arts à Paris et s'est installé *(settled)* à Paris où il a vécu jusqu'à *(lived until)* sa mort. **Le Baiser** *(The Kiss)* fait partie d'une série de sculptures qui portent le même nom. Une des sculptures du **Baiser** a été érigée au cimetière Montparnasse à Paris.

# À Paris

**PARIS**
**SUPERFICIE:** 105 kilomètres carrés
**NOMBRE D'HABITANTS:** 2 145 000 (avec la région parisienne: plus de 11 000 000) (les Parisiens)
**DÉPARTEMENT:** Paris
**PROVINCE:** Île-de-France
**INDUSTRIES PRINCIPALES:** activités tertiaires *(service industries)*, tourisme, finance, haute-couture, industries mécaniques, technologie, transports
**LIEUX D'INTÉRÊT ET MUSÉES:** la tour Eiffel, l'arc de Triomphe, la cathédrale Notre-Dame, le centre Georges Pompidou, la basilique du Sacré-Cœur, l'Opéra, la Défense, le musée du Louvre, le musée d'Orsay, le musée de l'Homme

CHAPITRE **6**

# Les sorties

 Video activities are on pages 416–419.

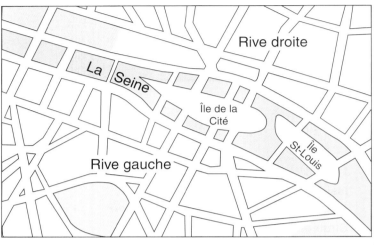

Paris, la capitale de la France, est une des plus belles villes **du monde.** La Seine sépare la ville en deux parties, la rive gauche et **la rive** droite. Les deux îles situées **au milieu de** la Seine sont l'île de la Cité et l'île St-Louis. C'est sur l'île de la Cité que la ville de Paris est née il y a plus de 2 000 ans.

La cathédrale Notre-Dame se trouve **au cœur de** Paris, sur l'île de la Cité.

Le Louvre, l'un des plus grands musées d'art du monde, fait presque un kilomètre de longueur.

---

**du monde** *in the world*    **la rive** *the bank (of a river)*    **au milieu de** *in the middle of*    **au cœur de** *in the heart of*

La célèbre avenue des Champs-Élysées **s'étend** de la place de la Concorde à l'arc de Triomphe.

Pour avoir une vue panoramique de la ville, on peut monter à la tour Eiffel.

Le Quartier latin est un des quartiers les plus sympathiques de Paris.

Si vous aimez **la vie** de bohème, visitez le quartier de Montmartre.

**s'étend** *extends*   **la vie** *life*

# Inviting someone to go out

## Les invitations

Éric Pérez **veut** inviter sa petite amie Michèle à sortir. Et vous, si **vous voulez** inviter **quelqu'un, vous pouvez dire...**

| À UN(E) AMI(E) | À UNE AUTRE PERSONNE OU À UN GROUPE DE PERSONNES |
|---|---|
| **Tu veux... ?** | Vous voulez... ? |
| Tu voudrais... ? | Vous voudriez... ? |
| Je t'invite à... | Je voudrais vous inviter à... |

Si **quelqu'un vous invite,** vous pouvez répondre...

| POUR DIRE OUI | POUR DIRE NON | POUR SUGGÉRER UNE AUTRE ACTIVITÉ |
|---|---|---|
| Oui, je veux bien... | Je regrette mais... | Je préfère... |
| Quelle bonne idée! | je ne suis pas libre. | J'aime mieux... |
| Avec plaisir! | **je ne peux** vraiment **pas.** | Allons plutôt à... |
| | **je dois** travailler. | |

Les Français **utilisent** l'heure officielle pour tous **les horaires** (le train, l'avion, le cinéma, le théâtre, la télé, **les heures d'ouverture**). Pour lire l'heure officielle, on utilise uniquement des chiffres. Aux USA, **on appelle** cette **façon** de lire l'heure *military time.*

**LA FEMME À VENIR**
d'après **CHRISTIAN BOBIN**　■ 18h30
"Coquine, déterminée, Bénédicte Charpentier provoque chez nous beaucoup d'émotion" - Pariscope

**LAURENT TERZIEFF**
**FLORILÈGE**　■ 20h

**LA TOUCHE ÉTOILE** de GILLES DYREK
"Une hilarante démonstration" - Pariscope　■ 21h30

**À LA RECHERCHE DU TEMPS PERDU**
de **MARCEL PROUST**　■ 18h30
"Extrait de tonalités cristallines pour une symphonie romanesque" - La Terrasse

**LUC ANTONI**
dans **ŒIL POUR ŒIL**　■ 20h
"Ce spectacle est exceptionnel" - Le Figaro

**LE PLAISIR** d'après CRÉBILLON Fils
"Sensuel" - Télérama. "Un bonheur" - Libération　■ 21h30
"Raffiné" - L'Express. "Coquin" - Pariscope

**LUCERNAIRE**
**01 45 44 57 34**
**www.lucernaire.fr**

| L'HEURE OFFICIELLE | | L'HEURE FAMILIÈRE |
|---|---|---|
| 0h05 | zéro heure cinq | minuit cinq |
| 1h15 | une heure quinze | une heure et quart (du matin) |
| 12h20 | douze heures vingt | midi vingt |
| 13h30 | treize heures trente | une heure et demie (de l'après-midi) |
| 15h40 | quinze heures quarante | quatre heures moins vingt |
| 21h45 | vingt et une heures quarante-cinq | dix heures moins le quart (du soir) |

**il veut (vouloir** *to want)* **vous voulez (vouloir** *to want)* **quelqu'un** *someone* **vous pouvez (pouvoir** *can, may, to be able)* **dire** *to say* **Tu veux (vouloir** *to want)* **quelqu'un vous invite** *someone invites you* **je ne peux pas (pouvoir** *can, may, to be able)* **je dois (devoir** *must, to have to)* **utiliser** *to use, to utilize* **un horaire** *a schedule* **les heures d'ouverture** *opening times* **appeler** *to call* **une façon** *a way*

CD 2-2

Éric téléphone à sa petite amie Michèle.

MICHÈLE:  Allô?
ÉRIC:  Salut, Michèle. C'est moi, Éric. Ça va?
MICHÈLE:  Oui, très bien. Et toi?
ÉRIC:  Moi, ça va. Écoute, tu es libre ce soir? Tu voudrais sortir?
MICHÈLE:  Oui, je veux bien. Qu'est-ce que tu as envie de faire?
ÉRIC:  **Je pensais** aller voir la nouvelle comédie qu'on **passe** au cinéma Gaumont.
MICHÈLE:  Tu sais, moi, je n'aime pas **tellement** les comédies. Je préfère les films d'**amour.** Allons plutôt voir le nouveau film d'amour au cinéma Rex.
ÉRIC:  Bon, je veux bien. À quelle heure?
MICHÈLE:  Il y a **une séance** à vingt heures quarante-cinq.
ÉRIC:  Alors, je passe chez toi vers huit heures?
MICHÈLE:  D'accord. Alors, au revoir.
ÉRIC:  À tout à l'heure, Michèle.

**A. Invitations.** Utilisez une variété d'expressions pour inviter un(e) partenaire. Il/Elle va accepter ou refuser chacune de vos invitations ou proposer une autre activité.

INVITEZ UN(E) AMI(E) À...

1. aller danser samedi soir
2. dîner au restaurant ce soir
3. aller voir une exposition demain
4. aller prendre un verre aujourd'hui après les cours

INVITEZ UN GROUPE D'AMIS À...

5. aller voir un film d'amour demain
6. préparer les cours ensemble ce soir
7. faire du vélo au parc ce week-end
8. aller au match de football américain / de basket ce week-end

**B. À quelle heure?** Regardez la liste des séances du film *RRRrrrr!!!* à la page 231. Exprimez l'heure de chaque séance de deux façons.

Exemple  10h55
**La première séance est à dix heures cinquante-cinq; c'est-à-dire (*that is to say*) à onze heures moins cinq.**

**C. Conversation.** Avec un(e) partenaire, relisez à haute voix la conversation entre Michèle et Éric en haut de la page. Ensuite, changez la conversation pour faire des projets pour aller au cinéma avec un(e) ami(e). Parlez de:

- quel(s) genre(s) de film vous aimez ou n'aimez pas. (Servez-vous des expressions données dans la liste de *Vocabulaire supplémentaire.*)
- quel film vous voudriez voir.
- où et à quelle heure on passe ce film.
- où et comment vous allez vous retrouver (*you are going to meet up*).

**VOCABULAIRE SUPPLÉMENTAIRE**

**LES FILMS**
**un dessin animé** *a cartoon*
**un drame**
**un film d'aventures**
**un film d'épouvante** *a horror film*
**un film de science-fiction**
**un film policier**

**POUR SE RETROUVER**
**Je passe chez toi / chez vous.** *I'll come by your place.*
**Passe / Passez chez moi.** *Come by my place.*
**Rendez-vous à...** *Let's meet at . . .*

---

**Je pensais** *I was thinking*  **passer (un film)** *to show (a movie)*  **tellement** *so much*  **l'amour** *(m) love*  **une séance** *a showing*

**1.** What does **vouloir** mean? What are three meanings of **pouvoir?** What are the meanings of **devoir?** What are the conjugations of these three verbs?

**2.** The **nous** and **vous** forms have the same vowel in the stem and the infinitive. What vowels do the other forms have?

**3.** What auxiliary verb do you use to form the **passé composé** of these three verbs? What are their past participles?

# Issuing and accepting invitations

*Les verbes* ***vouloir****,* ***pouvoir*** *et* ***devoir***

The verbs **vouloir** *(to want)* and **pouvoir** *(can, may, to be able)* are useful when inviting someone to do something. They have similar conjugations.

| VOULOIR *(to want)* | |
| --- | --- |
| je **veux** | nous **voulons** |
| tu **veux** | vous **voulez** |
| il/elle/on **veut** | ils/elles **veulent** |
| PASSÉ COMPOSÉ: **j'ai voulu** | |

| POUVOIR *(can, may, to be able)* | |
| --- | --- |
| je **peux** | nous **pouvons** |
| tu **peux** | vous **pouvez** |
| il/elle/on **peut** | ils/elles **peuvent** |
| PASSÉ COMPOSÉ: **j'ai pu** | |

Je **veux** sortir mais je ne **peux** pas.　　　*I **want** to go out, but I **can't**.*

Use **devoir** followed by an infinitive to say what you *must* or *have to* do. **Devoir** also means *to owe.*

| DEVOIR *(must, to have to, to owe)* | |
| --- | --- |
| je **dois** | nous **devons** |
| tu **dois** | vous **devez** |
| il/elle/on **doit** | ils/elles **doivent** |
| PASSÉ COMPOSÉ: **j'ai dû** | |

Je **dois** travailler demain.　　　*I **have to** work tomorrow.*
Je **dois** 100 dollars à mon frère.　　　*I **owe** my brother 100 dollars.*

In the **passé composé, devoir** can mean that someone *had to* do something or *must have* done something. Context will clarify the meaning.

Michèle n'est pas chez elle. Elle **a dû** partir.
*Michèle isn't home. She **had to** leave. / She **must have** left.*

Ils **ont dû** aller en ville.
*They **had to** go downtown. / They **must have** gone downtown.*

Il n'a pas pu sortir parce qu'il **a dû** travailler.
*He wasn't able to go out because he **had to** work.*

**A. Activités.** Demandez à votre partenaire ce que chacune de ces personnes veut faire aux moments indiqués. Si votre partenaire n'est pas sûr(e), il/elle doit proposer quelque chose.

　　Exemple　　toi (aujourd'hui après les cours?)
　　　　　　　　— **Qu'est-ce que tu veux faire aujourd'hui après les cours?**
　　　　　　　　— **Je veux rentrer à la maison.**

**1.** toi (ce soir? demain soir? ce week-end?)
**2.** tes amis et toi (vendredi soir? samedi après-midi? dimanche matin?)
**3.** ton meilleur ami / ta meilleure amie (demain soir? ce week-end? pendant les prochaines vacances *[vacation]?*)
**4.** les autres étudiants (après les cours aujourd'hui? au prochain cours de français? ce week-end?)

**B. En cours.** Dites si ces personnes peuvent faire chacune des choses indiquées en cours de français.

> **Exemple**    Je... (manger)
> **Je ne peux pas manger en cours.**

1. Je... (parler aux autres étudiants, boire un café, dormir)
2. Nous... (toujours parler anglais, fumer, réussir aux examens *[to pass the tests]* sans étudier)
3. Le prof... (quitter la classe maintenant, toujours comprendre les étudiants, parler au téléphone)
4. Les étudiants... (dormir, souvent partir en avance *[early]*, répondre à leur portable *[cell phone]*)

**C. Qu'est-ce qu'on doit faire?** Les étudiants veulent bien réussir au cours de français *(to do well in French class)*. Pour chaque paire proposée, indiquez ce que chacun doit et ne doit pas faire.

> **Exemple**    Le prof (être patient / être impatient)
> **Le prof doit être patient. Il ne doit pas être impatient.**

1. Le prof (insulter les étudiants / aider les étudiants)
   (donner de bons examens / donner des examens trop difficiles)
   (toujours parler anglais en classe / souvent parler français en classe)
2. Les étudiants (dormir en cours / écouter le prof)
   (faire les devoirs / sortir tous les soirs)
   (bien préparer l'examen / copier les réponses des autres)
3. Moi, je (bien préparer mes cours / toujours sortir avec des amis)
   (dormir en cours / écouter en cours)
   (souvent écouter le CD de français / regarder la télé tout le temps)

**D. On veut...** Aujourd'hui, les Pérez ne peuvent pas faire ce qu'ils veulent. Jouez le rôle d'Alice et expliquez ce que chacun veut et doit faire.

> **Exemple**    **Moi, je veux dormir, mais je dois promener le chien *(walk the dog).***

Moi...

**1.** Éric...

**2.** Éric et Cathy...

**3.** Vincent...

**4.** Nos amis...

**5.** Michel...

**E. Encore des explications.** Plus tard, Alice dit que chacun n'a pas pu faire ce qu'il voulait *(wanted)*. Qu'est-ce qu'elle dit? Utilisez le passé composé.

> **Exemple**    **Moi, je n'ai pas pu dormir.**

Maintenant, elle explique ce qu'ils ont dû faire. Qu'est-ce qu'elle dit?

> **Exemple**    **Moi, j'ai dû promener le chien.**

## Stratégies et Compréhension auditive

*Noting the important information*

When making plans, we often jot down important information for later reference. If a friend invited you to do something, what sort of information would you want to remember? Look at the following invitation and think about what information is given.

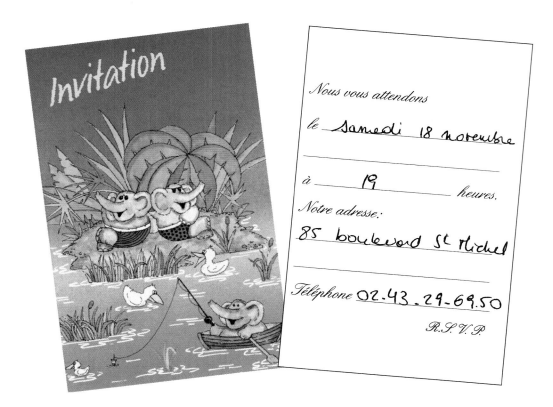

*Nous vous attendons*

*le* Samedi 18 novembre

*à* 19 *heures.*

*Notre adresse:*

85 boulevard St Michel

*Téléphone* 02.43.29.69.50

*R.S.V.P.*

CD 2-3

**A. Prenez des notes.** Trois amis invitent Éric à faire quelque chose. Écoutez chaque invitation et prenez des notes en français. Qu'est-ce qu'ils vont faire? Où? Quel jour? À quelle heure?

**B. À vous.** Éric demande à Michèle de l'accompagner. Utilisez vos notes de l'exercice précédent pour jouer les rôles d'Éric et de Michèle avec un(e) partenaire.

> Exemple
> — **Je vais jouer au tennis avec Marc demain à... Est-ce que tu voudrais jouer avec nous?**
> — **Oui, je veux bien!**

CD 2-4

## On va au cinéma?

Vincent demande à Alice si elle voudrait aller au cinéma. Lisez les questions de l'exercice suivant. Ensuite, écoutez la conversation et notez les détails importants sur une feuille de papier.

**A. Quel film?** Répondez aux questions suivantes d'après la conversation entre Alice et son mari.

1. Comment est-ce qu'Alice trouve les films de science-fiction?
2. Quel genre *(type)* de film est-ce qu'ils décident d'aller voir?
3. À quelle séance est-ce qu'ils vont aller?

**B. Vos notes.** Utilisez vos notes pour recréer *(to recreate)* la conversation entre Alice et Vincent avec un(e) camarade de classe.

**C. Tu veux sortir?** Invitez un(e) camarade de classe à aller voir un film avec vous. Choisissez une séance et décidez à quelle heure vous allez passer chez votre ami(e).

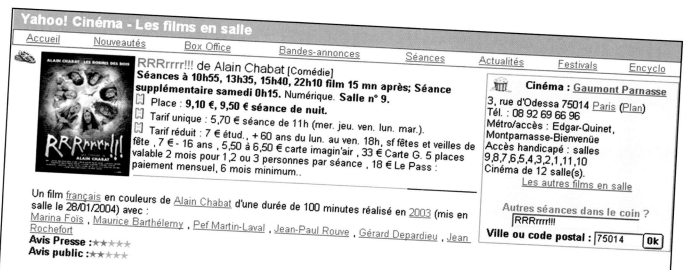

**Yahoo! Cinéma - Les films en salle**

| Accueil | Nouveautés | Box Office | Bandes-annonces | Séances | Actualités | Festivals | Encyclo |

**RRRrrrr!!! de Alain Chabat [Comédie]**
Séances à 10h55, 13h35, 15h40, 22h10 film 15 mn après; Séance supplémentaire samedi 0h15. Numérique. Salle n° 9.
Place : 9,10 €, 9,50 € séance de nuit.
Tarif unique : 5,70 € séance de 11h (mer. jeu. ven. lun. mar.).
Tarif réduit : 7 € étud., + 60 ans du lun. au ven. 18h, sf fêtes et veilles de fête , 7 € - 16 ans , 5,50 à 6,50 € carte imagin'air , 33 € Carte G. 5 places valable 2 mois pour 1,2 ou 3 personnes par séance , 18 € Le Pass : paiement mensuel, 6 mois minimum..

**Cinéma :** Gaumont Parnasse
3, rue d'Odessa 75014 Paris (Plan)
Tél. : 08 92 69 66 96
Métro/accès : Edgar-Quinet, Montparnasse-Bienvenüe
Accès handicapé : salles 9,8,7,6,5,4,3,2,1,11,10
Cinéma de 12 salle(s).
Les autres films en salle

Autres séances dans le coin ?
[RRRrrrr!!!]
**Ville ou code postal :** [75014] [Ok]

Un film français en couleurs de Alain Chabat d'une durée de 100 minutes réalisé en 2003 (mis en salle le 28/01/2004) avec : Marina Foïs , Maurice Barthélemy , Pef Martin-Laval , Jean-Paul Rouve , Gérard Depardieu , Jean Rochefort
**Avis Presse :** ★★★★★
**Avis public :** ★★★★★

**Résumé :**
[Comédie] Il y a 37.000 ans, deux tribus voisines vivaient en paix, sauf que, pas prêteuse, la tribu des cheveux propres gardait pour elle le secret de la formule du shampoing. Le chef de la tribu des cheveux sales décida d'envoyer un espion pour voler la recette. Mais un événement bien plus grave allait bouleverser la vie des cheveux propres: pour la première fois dans l'histoire de l'humanité, un crime venait d'être commis.
**Film tous publics.**

# Talking about how you spend and used to spend your time

>Note
*culturelle*

Il y a une grande différence entre un ami et un copain. Un copain, c'est quelqu'un qu'on aime bien et avec qui on sort de temps en temps. Le mot ami est plus souvent réservé pour parler d'une amitié *(friendship)* plus profonde. Un vrai ami, c'est presque comme de la famille. Y a-t-il des expressions comparables en anglais?

## Aujourd'hui et dans le passé

Michèle compare sa **vie** d'aujourd'hui avec sa vie quand elle était au **lycée**.

Aujourd'hui...

Quand **j'étais** au lycée...

J'ai 21 ans.
Je suis étudiante à l'université.
J'habite avec ma famille.
**J'ai cours** du lundi au vendredi.

J'aime l'université.
En général, je déjeune au **restau-u.**
Le week-end, je suis souvent
    **fatiguée** et **je dors** beaucoup.
Le vendredi soir, **je sors** souvent avec
    **des copains.** On va au cinéma, en
    boîte ou à une fête.
Chaque samedi, je joue au
    tennis avec des amis et je **fais**
    aussi souvent **du roller.**

**J'avais 15 ans.**
J'étais **lycéenne.**
**J'habitais** avec ma famille.
**J'avais** cours du lundi au vendredi et
    le samedi matin aussi.
Je n'aimais pas beaucoup **l'école** *(f).*
Je rentrais souvent à la maison pour déjeuner.
Le week-end, j'étais toujours fatiguée
    et je dormais beaucoup.
Le vendredi soir, je passais du temps avec ma
    famille ou je sortais avec des copains. On
    allait au cinéma, au café ou à une boum.
Le samedi, je faisais du sport avec des amis:
    on jouait au foot, on faisait du roller... et on
    jouait au tennis.

CD 2-5

Michèle demande à Éric **ce qu'il** faisait quand il était au lycée.

MICHÈLE: Qu'est-ce que tu aimais faire quand tu étais au lycée?
ÉRIC: J'aimais passer le temps avec des copains. Le vendredi soir, on allait aux matchs de football américain ou de basket au lycée.
MICHÈLE: Et le samedi?
ÉRIC: Le samedi matin, je travaillais. Le samedi après-midi, on faisait du skate-board. Le samedi soir, je sortais avec ma petite amie. On allait au cinéma.
MICHÈLE: Et qu'est-ce que tu faisais le dimanche?
ÉRIC: Le dimanche, je ne faisais rien de spécial. Je restais à la maison. Je regardais la télé ou je louais une vidéo.

---

**dans le passé** *in the past*    **la vie** *life*    **le lycée** *high school*    **j'étais** *I was*    **J'avais 15 ans.** *I was fifteen.*    **un(e) lycéen(ne)** *a high school student*    **J'habitais** *I lived, I used to live*    **J'ai cours (avoir cours** *to have class)*    **J'avais** *I had, I used to have*    **l'école** *(f) school*    **le restau-u** *the university cafeteria*    **fatigué(e)** *tired*    **je dors (dormir** *to sleep)*    **je sors (sortir** *to go out)*    **un copain (une copine)** *a friend, a pal*    **faire du roller** *to go in-line skating*    **ce que** *what*

**A. Maintenant ou dans le passé?** Est-ce que Michèle parle de sa vie maintenant ou de quand elle avait 15 ans?

1. J'étais lycéenne.
2. J'ai cours du lundi au vendredi.
3. Je n'aimais pas beaucoup l'école.
4. D'habitude, je déjeunais à la maison.
5. Je sors beaucoup le week-end.
6. J'aime sortir avec des copains.
7. Mes copains et moi, on aimait aller au café.
8. On faisait souvent du sport ensemble.

Quand j'avais 10 ans, j'aimais jouer avec mon chien.

**B. Et vous?** Dites si vous faites ces choses maintenant et si vous faisiez ces choses quand vous aviez 10 ans.

**Exemples**  Maintenant, j'habite avec ma famille.
**Maintenant, j'habite avec ma famille.**
**Maintenant, je n'habite pas avec ma famille.**

Quand j'avais 10 ans, j'habitais avec ma famille.
**Quand j'avais 10 ans, j'habitais avec ma famille.**
**Quand j'avais 10 ans, je n'habitais pas avec ma famille.**

1. Maintenant, je suis souvent fatigué(e).
   Quand j'avais 10 ans, j'étais souvent fatigué(e).
2. Maintenant, je dors bien.
   Quand j'avais 10 ans, je dormais bien.
3. Maintenant, je sors souvent le vendredi soir.
   Quand j'avais 10 ans, je sortais souvent le vendredi soir.
4. Maintenant, mes copains et moi, on fait souvent du sport ensemble.
   Quand j'avais 10 ans, on faisait souvent du sport ensemble.
5. Maintenant, je travaille.
   Quand j'avais 10 ans, je travaillais.

**C. Conversation.** Avec un(e) partenaire, relisez à haute voix la conversation entre Michèle et Éric en bas de la page précédente. Ensuite, changez la conversation pour parler de ce que vous faisiez *(what you used to do)* quand vous étiez au lycée. Si vous voulez utiliser des verbes que vous n'avez pas encore appris dans cette forme du passé, demandez à votre professeur comment les conjuguer.

**1.** Which form of the present tense do you use to create the stem for all verbs in the imperfect, except for **être**? What is the stem for **être**?

**2.** You use the **passé composé** to talk about a specific occurrence in the past. When do you use the imperfect?

**3.** Which imperfect endings are pronounced alike? What single letter distinguishes the **nous** and **vous** forms of the imperfect from the present?

**NOTE DE GRAMMAIRE**

Note that verbs like **étudier** retain the **i** of the stem before the **imparfait** endings.

j'étudiais        nous étudiions
vous étudiiez     ils étudiaient

# Saying how things used to be

## *L'imparfait*

You know to use the **passé composé** to talk about an action that took place on a specific occasion in the past. To tell what things used to be like in general, what someone used to do, or what happened over and over in the past, use the **imparfait** *(imperfect)*. The **imparfait** can be translated in a variety of ways in English.

> *I was working mornings.*
> *I used to work mornings.*      Je travaillais le matin.
> *I worked mornings.*

All verbs except **être** form this tense by dropping the **-ons** from the present tense **nous** form and adding the endings you see below. The stem for **être** is **ét-**.

|  | PARLER (nous parl~~ons~~ → parl-) | FAIRE (nous fais~~ons~~ → fais-) | PRENDRE (nous pren~~ons~~ → pren-) | ÊTRE (ét-) |
|---|---|---|---|---|
| je | parl**ais** | fais**ais** | pren**ais** | ét**ais** |
| tu | parl**ais** | fais**ais** | pren**ais** | ét**ais** |
| il/elle/on | parl**ait** | fais**ait** | pren**ait** | ét**ait** |
| nous | parl**ions** | fais**ions** | pren**ions** | ét**ions** |
| vous | parl**iez** | fais**iez** | pren**iez** | ét**iez** |
| ils/elles | parl**aient** | fais**aient** | pren**aient** | ét**aient** |

Verbs with spelling changes in the present tense **nous** form, like **manger** and **commencer,** retain the spelling changes in the **imparfait** only before endings beginning with an **a.**

| MANGER | COMMENCER |
|---|---|
| je mang**e**ais | je commen**ç**ais |
| tu mang**e**ais | tu commen**ç**ais |
| il/elle/on mang**e**ait | il/elle/on commen**ç**ait |
| nous mangions | nous commencions |
| vous mangiez | vous commenciez |
| ils/elles mang**e**aient | ils/elles commen**ç**aient |

Also learn these expressions in the imperfect.

| c'est → c'était | il y a → il y avait | il pleut → il pleuvait | il neige → il neigeait |
|---|---|---|---|

CD 2-6

# Prononciation

## *Les terminaisons de l'imparfait*

The **-ais, -ait,** and **-aient** endings of the imperfect are all pronounced alike. The **nous** and **vous** endings of the imperfect, **-ions** and **-iez,** are distinguished from the present only by the vowel **i** in the ending.

| Qu'est-ce que vous faisiez? | *What did you use to do?* |
| Ils travaillaient pour IBM. | *They worked for IBM.* |
| Nous allions à la plage. | *We used to go to the beach.* |

**A. Chez nous.** Que faisait votre famille quand vous aviez dix ans?

> **Exemple**   mes parents... (travailler le week-end)
> **Mes parents travaillaient le week-end.**
> **Mes parents ne travaillaient pas le week-end.**
> **Ma mère travaillait le week-end mais mon père ne travaillait pas.**

1. mes parents... (avoir beaucoup d'amis, être patients, prendre l'autobus pour aller au travail *[to work]*, quitter la maison tôt, rentrer tard, jouer aux cartes *[cards]*)
2. mon père / ma mère... (travailler beaucoup, faire souvent du sport, aimer lire, être à la maison le week-end, faire le ménage, jouer au golf)
3. moi, je... (aller à l'école, arriver à l'école avant neuf heures, aimer les maths, apprendre beaucoup de choses, avoir beaucoup de copains, nager bien)
4. nous... (voyager souvent, aller souvent voir mes grands-parents, aller à la plage le week-end, manger dans des fast-foods, avoir un chien, habiter à... )

**B. La jeunesse.** Interviewez un(e) camarade de classe pour savoir ce qu'il/elle faisait quand il/elle était au lycée.

> **Exemple**   — **Tu fumais quand tu étais au lycée?**
> — **Non, je ne fumais pas.**

fumer     aller toujours en cours     apprendre facilement

travailler          avoir beaucoup de copains

faire souvent du sport

pouvoir sortir tard     aller souvent en boîte     danser bien

aimer dormir tard          ???

Maintenant, avec votre partenaire, préparez six questions pour votre professeur. Demandez ce qu'il/elle faisait quand il/elle était à l'université.

**C. Entretien.** Interviewez votre partenaire.

1. Est-ce que tu habitais ici quand tu étais au lycée? Avec qui habitais-tu? Est-ce que tes grands-parents habitaient près de chez vous?
2. Passais-tu beaucoup de temps avec ta famille? Voyagiez-vous souvent ensemble? Alliez-vous à la plage en été?
3. Aimais-tu ton lycée? Quels étaient tes cours préférés? Faisais-tu du sport?
4. Est-ce que tes cours étaient faciles ou difficiles? Est-ce que tes profs étaient intéressants ou ennuyeux? Avais-tu beaucoup de devoirs?
5. Avais-tu beaucoup de copains? Qu'est-ce que tu faisais avec tes copains le week-end? Aimais-tu sortir le week-end? À quelle heure devais-tu rentrer chez toi le samedi soir? Comment s'appelait ton meilleur ami ou ta meilleure amie? Qu'est-ce que vous aimiez faire ensemble? Pouviez-vous rentrer chez vous après minuit?

**D. Ma jeunesse.** Préparez une conversation avec un(e) partenaire dans laquelle vous parlez de quand vous étiez au lycée. Expliquez...

- à quelle heure vos cours commençaient
- où vous déjeuniez à midi
- avec qui vous passiez beaucoup de temps
- ce que vous faisiez après les cours et le week-end

## Talking about activities
*Les verbes* **sortir, partir** *et* **dormir**

The verbs **sortir, partir,** and **dormir** have similar patterns of conjugation.

| SORTIR (to go out) | PARTIR (to leave) | DORMIR (to sleep) |
|---|---|---|
| je **sors** | je **pars** | je **dors** |
| tu **sors** | tu **pars** | tu **dors** |
| il/elle/on **sort** | il/elle/on **part** | il/elle/on **dort** |
| nous **sortons** | nous **partons** | nous **dormons** |
| vous **sortez** | vous **partez** | vous **dormez** |
| ils/elles **sortent** | ils/elles **partent** | ils/elles **dorment** |
| PASSÉ COMPOSÉ | PASSÉ COMPOSÉ | PASSÉ COMPOSÉ |
| **je suis sorti(e)** | **je suis parti(e)** | **j'ai dormi** |
| IMPARFAIT | IMPARFAIT | IMPARFAIT |
| **je sortais** | **je partais** | **je dormais** |

**Sortir** can mean *to go out,* in the sense of going out with friends.

Je suis sortie avec mes amis hier soir.

**Sortir** can also mean *to go out of,* in the sense of going out of a place. It is the opposite of **entrer.** Use **de** to say *of.*

Je suis sorti **de** l'appartement vers neuf heures.

**Partir** means *to leave* in the sense of *to go away.* It is the opposite of **arriver.** Some common expressions with **partir** are: **partir en week-end, partir en vacances, partir en voyage.** To name the place you are leaving, use **partir de.** To say where you are leaving *for,* use **partir pour.**

Il part en vacances aujourd'hui. Il est parti **de** son bureau à trois heures et il est parti **pour** l'aéroport vers cinq heures.

**Quitter** means *to leave* a person or a place and is *always* followed by a direct object. In the **passé composé,** it is conjugated with **avoir.**

Il **a quitté** sa famille pour aller travailler dans une autre ville. Il **est parti** hier.

CD 2-7

## Prononciation
*Les verbes* **sortir, partir** *et* **dormir**

You can distinguish aurally between the **il/elle** and **ils/elles** forms of verbs like **sortir, partir,** and **dormir.** Compare these sentences.

| ALICE | ALICE ET SA FILLE |
|---|---|
| Elle dort bien. | Elles dorment bien. |
| Elle sort ce soir. | Elles sortent ce soir. |
| Elle part demain. | Elles partent demain. |

When a word ends with a pronounced consonant sound in French, it must be released. Note that when you pronounce the boldfaced consonants in the following English phrases, your tongue or lips do not have to move back and release them.

What par**t**?          What sor**t**?          In the dor**m**.

Compare how the boldfaced consonants in the following plural verb forms are released.

Ils par**t**ent.          Ils sor**t**ent.          Ils dor**m**ent.

**A. Le week-end.** Dites si ces personnes font souvent les choses indiquées.

> **Exemple** je (dormir jusqu'à midi)
> **Je dors souvent jusqu'à midi. / Je ne dors jamais jusqu'à midi.**

1. je (sortir avec des amis, partir de chez moi avant 9 heures du matin, dormir toute la journée le samedi)
2. mon meilleur ami / ma meilleure amie (partir en vacances, sortir le vendredi soir, dormir jusqu'à 11 heures le week-end)
3. mes amis (partir en week-end, sortir le dimanche soir, dormir en cours le lundi)
4. mes amis et moi, nous (sortir ensemble, dormir en cours, partir ensemble en vacances)

Maintenant dites si ces personnes faisaient souvent les choses indiquées quand vous étiez lycéen(ne).

> **Exemple** je (dormir jusqu'à midi)
> **Je dormais souvent jusqu'à midi.**
> **Je ne dormais jamais jusqu'à midi.**

**B. Vos habitudes.** Formez des phrases pour parler de ce que vous faites les jours du cours de français et quand vous sortez avec des amis. Demandez à votre partenaire s'il/si elle fait les mêmes choses.

> **Exemples** Les jours du cours de français...
> je / dormir jusqu'à... heures
> **— Les jours du cours de français, je dors jusqu'à 7 heures.**
> **Et toi? Est-ce que tu dors jusqu'à 7 heures aussi?**
> **— Oui, je dors jusqu'à 7 heures aussi. / Non, je dors jusqu'à 8 heures.**
>
> Quand je sors avec des amis...
> nous / sortir le plus souvent le... soir
> **— Quand je sors avec des amis, nous sortons le plus souvent le samedi soir. Et vous? Est-ce que vous sortez le plus souvent le samedi soir aussi?**
> **— Oui, nous sortons le plus souvent le samedi soir aussi.**
> **Non, nous sortons le plus souvent le vendredi soir.**

Les jours du cours de francais...

1. je / dormir jusqu'à... heures
2. je / quitter la maison à... heures
3. je / prendre... pour aller à l'université
4. je / sortir de mon dernier cours à... heures

Quand je sors avec des amis...

5. nous / sortir le plus souvent le... soir
6. nous / quitter la maison à... heures
7. je / dormir jusqu'à... le lendemain *(the next day)*

**C. Toujours des questions!** Parlez avec votre partenaire de la dernière fois qu'il/elle est sorti(e) avec des amis. Posez les questions indiquées.

> **Exemple** quel jour / sortir ensemble
> **— Quel jour est-ce que vous êtes sortis ensemble?**
> **— On est sortis ensemble samedi dernier.**

1. quand / sortir ensemble
2. où / aller ensemble
3. qu'est-ce que / faire
4. à quelle heure / quitter la maison
5. jusqu'à quelle heure / dormir le lendemain *(the next day)*

# Talking about the past

>Note
*culturelle*

Aujourd'hui en France un repas *(meal)* sur cinq est pris en dehors du *(outside of)* domicile. 20% de ces repas sont pris dans un restaurant de chaîne comme McDonald's ou Quick. Les restaurants ethniques (tex-mex, chinois, grecs, japonais…) sont aussi très populaires. Est-ce que c'est la même chose chez vous?

## Une sortie

Cathy parle de la dernière fois qu'elle a dîné avec des amis. Et vous? La dernière fois que vous êtes sorti(e) avec des ami(e)s, comment était la soirée? **Qu'est-ce qui s'est passé?**

Il pleuvait quand j'ai quitté l'appartement.

Il était sept heures et demie quand je suis arrivée au restaurant.

On n'avait pas très faim et on n'a pas mangé **tout de suite.**

**Le repas** était **délicieux** et j'ai beaucoup mangé.

Après le repas, nous étions fatigués et je suis partie.

Quand je suis rentrée chez moi, il était environ dix heures.

**Le lendemain,** c'était dimanche et je suis restée au lit jusqu'à dix heures.

---

**Qu'est-ce qui s'est passé?** *What happened?*   **tout de suite** *right away*   **Le repas** *The meal*   **délicieux (délicieuse)** *delicious*
**Le lendemain** *The next day*

Cathy et une amie parlent de leurs activités du week-end dernier.

MICHELINE: Je suis allée au restaurant avec des copines ce week-end.
CATHY: Vous êtes allées où?
MICHELINE: Au Bistro Romain.
CATHY: **Ça t'a plu?**
MICHELINE: Beaucoup. C'était délicieux. On a bien mangé et on a beaucoup parlé. C'était vraiment bien!
CATHY: Et qu'est-ce que tu as fait après?
MICHELINE: **Rien du tout.** J'étais fatiguée et je suis rentrée. Et toi, qu'est-ce que tu as fait ce week-end?
CATHY: Moi aussi, je suis sortie avec des copains. On est allés au cinéma.

## A. Au restaurant.
La dernière fois que vous êtes allé(e) au restaurant, qu'est-ce qui s'est passé? Changez les mots en italique pour parler de votre sortie.

1. Quand j'ai quitté *la maison*, il était *huit heures* et il *faisait froid*.
2. Quand je suis arrivé(e) au restaurant, il était *neuf heures*.
3. On *avait très faim* et on *a mangé tout de suite*.
4. Le repas était vraiment *médiocre* et j'ai *peu* mangé.
5. Après le repas, nous avions envie de *continuer la soirée* et nous *sommes allés en boîte*.
6. Quand je suis rentré(e), il était *onze heures* et j'*étais fatigué(e)*.
7. Le lendemain, c'était *dimanche* et je *suis resté(e) au lit*.

## B. La journée d'Alice.
Décrivez la journée d'Alice vendredi dernier.

**NOTE DE GRAMMAIRE**

You usually answer a question in the same tense in which it is asked.

1. Alice était seule quand elle a quitté l'appartement? Quelle heure était-il? Est-ce qu'elle a pris son parapluie avec elle? Est-ce qu'il pleuvait? Est-ce qu'il faisait froid? Quels vêtements est-ce qu'Alice portait?
2. Alice était seule au café? Elle a mangé quelque chose? A-t-elle bu quelque chose?
3. Quelle heure était-il quand elle est rentrée chez elle?

## C. Conversation.
Avec un(e) partenaire, relisez à haute voix la conversation entre Micheline et Cathy en haut de la page. Ensuite, changez la conversation pour parler de la dernière fois que vous avez mangé avec des copains.

---

**Ça t'a plu?** *Did you like it?*     **Rien du tout.** *Nothing at all.*

# Telling what was going on when something else happened

*L'imparfait et le passé composé*

As you have seen, the **imparfait** is used to tell how things used to be, what someone used to do, or what happened over and over in the past. You also use the **imparfait** to say what was going on when something else occurred. To say what happened, interrupting the first activity, use the **passé composé.**

| ACTIONS IN PROGRESS | INTERRUPTING ACTIONS |
|---|---|
| Le professeur parlait... | quand je suis entré(e) dans la salle de classe. |
| Il pleuvait ce matin... | quand j'ai quitté la maison. |
| J'étais très fatigué(e)... | quand je suis rentré(e) hier soir. |

**A. Quand ils sont rentrés...** Deux couples ont laissé leurs enfants avec une nouvelle baby-sitter le week-end dernier. Qui faisait les choses suivantes quand ils sont rentrés?

**Exemple** porter les vêtements de sa mère
**Annick portait les vêtements de sa mère quand ils sont rentrés.**

1. embrasser *(to kiss)* son petit ami
2. parler au téléphone
3. fumer
4. jouer dans l'escalier
5. jouer à des jeux vidéo
6. manger quelque chose sur la table

Maintenant, répondez aux questions suivantes d'après l'illustration.

1. Quelle heure était-il quand les parents sont rentrés?
2. Qui écrivait *(was writing)* sur le mur?
3. Que faisait le chien?
4. Combien d'enfants est-ce qu'il y avait dans la maison?
5. Qui était avec la baby-sitter?

**B. En cours.** Qu'est-ce qui se passait quand vous êtes entré(e) dans la salle de classe aujourd'hui?

> **Exemple**　　le professeur / être dans la salle de classe
> **Quand je suis entré(e) dans la salle de classe, le professeur était dans la salle de classe / le professeur n'était pas dans la salle de classe.**

Quand je suis entré(e) dans la salle de classe...

1. la porte / être fermée *(closed)*
2. certains *(a few)* étudiants / parler
3. certains étudiants / faire leurs devoirs
4. je / avoir faim
5. il / faire froid dans la salle de classe
6. je / être fatigué(e)
7. le prof / parler sur son portable *(cell phone)*

**C. Quelques photos.** Alice montre des photos de sa famille en France. Qu'est-ce qu'ils faisaient quand on a pris ces photos? Dites aussi quel temps il faisait.

> **Exemple**　　**Quand on a pris cette photo, nous faisions du bateau.**
> **Il faisait beau.**

Quand on a pris cette photo...

nous...

**1.** les enfants...

**2.** Vincent...

**3.** Éric...

**4.** Vincent et moi...

**5.** Éric et Vincent...

**D. Hier.** Demandez à votre partenaire ce qui se passait *(what was happening)* quand il/elle est rentré(e) hier.

1. Quand tu es rentré(e) hier, quelle heure était-il?
2. Quel temps faisait-il?
3. Est-ce que tu étais seul(e)?
4. Est-ce que tu étais fatigué(e)?
5. Est-ce que tu avais envie de dormir?
6. Qu'est-ce que tu avais envie de faire?
7. Est-ce que tu avais des devoirs à faire?

**1.** Do you generally use the **passé composé** or the **imparfait** to say what happened at a specific moment? to describe how things were or used to be?

**2.** What are the three main uses of the **passé composé?** What are four uses of the **imparfait?**

**3.** Which would you use to talk about how you were feeling? to describe a setting? to tell what happened on a specific occasion?

# Telling what happened and describing the circumstances

*Le passé composé et l'imparfait*

In French, the **passé composé** and **imparfait** convey different meanings. In English, the use of different past tenses also changes a message. Consider these sentences. Is the message the same in each?

*When her husband came home, they kissed.*
*When her husband came home, they were kissing.*

You know to use the **imparfait** to tell how things used to be or what was going on when something else occurred. Also use the **imparfait** to:

- set the scene or describe the background *(how things were)*

Il était minuit et il faisait noir.        *It was midnight and it was dark.*

- describe physical or mental states *(how someone felt)*

Elle était fatiguée et elle avait faim.      *She was tired and she was hungry.*

- say what was about to be done *(what was going to happen)*

Il allait partir à cinq heures.        *He was going to leave at five o'clock.*

You know to use the **passé composé** to talk about what happened or what someone did at a particular moment. Also use the **passé composé** to:

- relate the sequence of events *(what happened next)*

Le voleur est entré par la fenêtre        *The thief entered through the window*
    et il a pris mon sac.            *and he took my purse.*

- say that a change of physical or mental state occurred *(what changed)* (Watch for words like **tout d'un coup** *[all at once]*, **tout à coup** *[all of a sudden]*, **soudain** *[suddenly]*, **une fois** *[once]*, and **un jour** *[one day]*.)

Tout à coup, elle a eu peur.      *All of a sudden, she got frightened.*

| USE THE *IMPARFAIT* TO SAY: | USE THE *PASSÉ COMPOSÉ* TO SAY: |
|---|---|
| **1. HOW THINGS USED TO BE OR WHAT USED TO HAPPEN**<br>• continuous actions or states<br>• repeated or habitual actions of an unspecified duration | **1. WHAT HAPPENED AT A PRECISE MOMENT OR FOR A SPECIFIC DURATION**<br>• completed actions<br>• actions within a specific duration |
| **2. WHAT WAS GOING ON**<br>• scene or setting<br>• interrupted actions in progress | **2. WHAT HAPPENED NEXT**<br>• sequence of events<br>• actions interrupting something in progress |
| **3. WHAT THINGS WERE LIKE OR HOW SOMEONE FELT**<br>• physical or mental states | **3. WHAT CHANGED**<br>• changes in states |
| **4. WHAT WAS GOING TO HAPPEN**<br>• **aller** + infinitive in the past | |

# Prononciation

*Le passé composé et l'imparfait*

Since the use of the **passé composé** or the **imparfait** imparts a different message, it is important that you differentiate what you hear and that you pronounce each tense distinctly. Listen to these pairs of sentences. Where do you hear a difference?

| | | | |
|---|---|---|---|
| Je travaillais. | Elle mangeait. | Tu parlais. | Il allait. |
| J'ai travaillé. | Elle a mangé. | Tu as parlé. | Il est allé. |

**A. Hier.** Est-ce que vous avez fait ces choses hier? Utilisez le passé composé.

> **Exemple** quitter la maison avant huit heures du matin
> **Oui, hier j'ai quitté la maison avant huit heures du matin.**

1. prendre l'autobus pour aller en cours
2. aller en cours
3. déjeuner avec des copains (des copines)
4. rester à la maison l'après-midi
5. dîner seul(e)
6. faire la lessive
7. sortir avec un(e) ami(e)
8. rentrer tard

**B. À dix ans.** Est-ce que vous faisiez ces choses quand vous aviez dix ans? Utilisez l'imparfait.

> **Exemple** parler souvent au téléphone
> **Oui, quand j'avais dix ans, je parlais souvent au téléphone.**

1. aimer l'école
2. passer beaucoup de temps à regarder la télé
3. faire du sport chaque week-end
4. jouer avec des copains (des copines) après l'école
5. prendre le car scolaire *(school bus)* pour aller à l'école
6. avoir un chat ou un chien
7. être sage
8. être timide

**Passiez-vous beaucoup de temps en famille?**

**C. Quand?** Alice parle de ce qu'elle a fait hier et aussi des choses qu'elle faisait quand elle était petite. Écoutez ce qu'elle dit et, sur une feuille de papier, écrivez le numéro de chaque phrase dans la colonne appropriée.

> **Exemple 1** Je jouais du piano.

> **Exemple 2** J'ai mangé un sandwich.

| HIER | QUAND J'ÉTAIS PETITE |
|---|---|
| EXEMPLE 2 | EXEMPLE 1 |

**D. On était en train de...** Expliquez ce qui s'est passé. Suivez l'exemple.

Exemple

Vincent (jouer au golf) / quand il (commencer à pleuvoir)
**Vincent jouait au golf quand il a commencé à pleuvoir.**

**1.** Cathy (préparer ses cours) / quand un ami (téléphoner)

**2.** Alice (lire un livre) / quand une amie (arriver)

**3.** Michèle (embrasser *[to kiss]* un copain) / Éric (arriver)

**4.** Quand le chien (entrer) / le chat (dormir)

**5.** Alice (faire la cuisine) / quand le chat (voir le chien)

**6.** Quand Vincent (rentrer) / Alice (nettoyer *[to clean]* la cuisine)

**E. La journée d'Alice.** Alice parle de sa journée. Décidez si chaque phrase décrit la scène / la situation ou raconte le déroulement des faits *(sequence of events)*. Récrivez les phrases dans chaque colonne.

Il est sept heures. Il pleut. Je quitte la maison. Il y a beaucoup de voitures sur la route. J'arrive au bureau en retard. Mon patron *(boss)* n'est pas content. Je travaille beaucoup. Je ne déjeune pas. Je rentre à cinq heures. Je suis fatiguée. Il n'y a rien à manger. Nous allons au restaurant. Nous rentrons. Je prends un bain. Il est 11 heures. Je vais au lit.

Exemple

| LA SCÈNE / LA SITUATION | LE DÉROULEMENT DES FAITS |
|---|---|
| **Il est sept heures.** | **Je quitte la maison.** |

Maintènant, récrivez le paragraphe en mettant les verbes racontant le déroulement des faits **au passé composé** et les verbes décrivant la scène ou la situation **à l'imparfait.**

**F. Qu'est-ce qu'ils voulaient faire?** Qu'est-ce que les Pérez et leurs amis ont fait hier? Qu'est-ce qu'ils voulaient faire?

> **Exemple**   **Moi, j'ai fait du jogging mais je voulais dormir.**

Moi...

**1.** Le chien et moi, nous...

**2.** Éric et Cathy...

**3.** Vincent...

**4.** Nos amis...

**5.** Michel...

**G. Pourquoi?** Expliquez pourquoi Cathy a fait ou n'a pas fait ces choses, comme dans l'exemple.

> **Exemple**   ne pas travailler / être malade *(sick)*
> **Cathy n'a pas travaillé parce qu'elle était malade.**

**1.** faire du shopping / vouloir acheter une nouvelle robe
**2.** ne pas aller en cours / être malade
**3.** ne pas faire les devoirs / être trop fatiguée
**4.** ne pas sortir avec ses amis / devoir préparer un examen
**5.** mettre un pull / avoir froid

**H. Entretien.** Interviewez votre partenaire au sujet de la dernière fois qu'il/elle est allé(e) au restaurant avec des amis.

La dernière fois que tu es allé(e) au restaurant avec des amis...

**1.** Quel temps faisait-il? Qu'est-ce que tu as mis pour sortir? Un jean? Une robe?
**2.** Quelle heure était-il quand tu es arrivé(e) au restaurant?
**3.** Avais-tu très faim? As-tu mangé tout de suite?
**4.** Comment était le repas?
**5.** Qu'est-ce que tu as fait après le repas?
**6.** Quelle heure était-il quand tu es rentré(e)? Étais-tu fatigué(e)? Est-ce que tu es allé(e) tout de suite au lit? As-tu bien dormi?
**7.** Le lendemain, jusqu'à quelle heure es-tu resté(e) au lit?

**I. Une sortie.** Préparez une conversation avec un(e) camarade de classe dans laquelle vous parlez d'une sortie avec des ami(e)s. Dites ce que vous vouliez faire et pourquoi, où vous êtes allé(e)s, le jour et l'heure. Ajoutez aussi d'autres détails pour faire une bonne description.

# Narrating in the past

>Note
*culturelle*

Le cinéma est né en France et la France joue un rôle très important dans l'histoire du cinéma. Georges Méliès a été le premier à utiliser des effets spéciaux. Les réalisateurs de la Nouvelle Vague *(directors of the New Wave)* comme Jean-Luc Godard et François Truffaut ont été les représentants les plus célèbres de l'esprit *(spirit)* innovateur des cinéastes *(filmmakers)* français. Quels films français connaissez-vous? Comment est-ce que ces films diffèrent des films faits à Hollywood?

## Les contes

Éric et Michèle sont allés voir le film classique ***La Belle et la Bête*** de Jean Cocteau. **Connaissez-vous** ce film? Connaissez-vous **le conte de fée sur lequel** il est basé?

**Il était une fois** un vieux **marchand** qui avait trois filles. Sa plus jeune fille, Belle, était très jolie, **douce** et **gracieuse.**

Un jour, la Bête a emprisonné le marchand. Belle **a promis** à la Bête de venir prendre la place de son père.

La Bête était horrible! Il était grand et laid et il avait l'air **féroce. Au début,** Belle avait très peur de **lui.** Mais elle était toujours gentille et patiente avec lui.

Petit à petit les choses ont changé. Belle et la Bête ont commencé à **se parler.** La Bête a beaucoup changé et Belle a appris à apprécier le monstre. Finalement, Belle **est tombée amoureuse de** lui! Et la Bête a aussi appris à aimer.

**À suivre...**

### NOTE DE GRAMMAIRE
**Tomber** takes **être** as its auxiliary verb in the passé composé (Elle est tombée... ).

CD 2-10

Cathy parle à son frère de ses activités du week-end dernier.

CATHY:   Tu es sorti ce week-end?
ÉRIC:   Oui, je suis allé au cinéclub avec Michèle.
CATHY:   Quel film est-ce que vous avez vu?
ÉRIC:   Nous avons vu *La Belle et la Bête* de Cocteau.
CATHY:   C'est un classique! Ça t'a plu?
ÉRIC:   Oui, ça m'a beaucoup plu. C'était très intéressant. Les acteurs **ont bien joué. Les effets spéciaux** étaient excellents et il n'y avait pas **trop de** violence.

---

**un conte** *a story*   ***La Belle et la Bête*** *Beauty and the Beast*   **Connaissez-vous... ?** *Do you know . . . ?*
**un conte de fée** *a fairy tale*   **lequel (laquelle)** *which*   **Il était une fois...** *Once upon a time there was . . .*
**un marchand** *a merchant, a shopkeeper*   **doux (douce)** *sweet, soft, gentle*   **gracieux (gracieuse)** *gracious*
**elle a promis** (**promettre** *to promise* [past participle **promis**])   **féroce** *ferocious*   **Au début** *At the beginning*   **lui** *him*
**se parler** *to talk to each other*   **tomber amoureux (amoureuse) de** *to fall in love with*   **À suivre** *To be continued*
**bien jouer** *to act well (in movies and theater)*   **Les effets spéciaux** *The special effects*   **trop de** *too much*

**A. Qu'est-ce qui s'est passé?** Relisez l'histoire *(the story)* de *La Belle et la Bête* à la page précédente. Sur une feuille de papier, faites une liste de *la séquence du déroulement des faits* (sequence of events) et *des changements* qui ont eu lieu *(took place)* dans l'histoire. Ne mettez pas sur votre liste les phrases qui décrivent les personnages, la scène ou les circonstances.

**B. C'est qui?** Décidez lequel des personnages les adjectifs suivants décrivent. Formez ensuite une phrase, comme dans l'exemple. N'oubliez pas d'utiliser l'imparfait pour faire une description!

**LE PÈRE DE BELLE          BELLE          LA BÊTE**

> **Exemple**     douce
> **Belle était douce.**

**1.** jolie                    **3.** toujours gentille       **5.** gracieuse
**2.** grande et laide          **4.** vieux

Maintenant, formez des phrases pour dire qui a fait les choses suivantes. N'oubliez pas d'utiliser le passé composé pour raconter la séquence d'événements *(sequence of events)* d'un récit!

**LE PÈRE DE BELLE          BELLE          LA BÊTE**

> **Exemple**     promettre de venir prendre la place de son père
> **Belle a promis de venir prendre la place de son père.**

**1.** emprisonner le marchand
**2.** prendre la place de son père
**3.** commencer à parler avec la Bête
**4.** beaucoup changer
**5.** apprendre à apprécier la Bête
**6.** tomber amoureuse de la Bête
**7.** apprendre à aimer

**C. Entretien.** Interviewez votre partenaire.

**1.** Quel film est-ce que tu as vu récemment? Est-ce que tu as vu ce film au cinéma ou à la télé? Est-ce que tu as aimé le film? Est-ce que tu recommandes ce film?
**2.** Qui a joué dans ce film? Est-ce que les acteurs ont bien joué? Est-ce qu'il y avait beaucoup de violence? Il y avait beaucoup d'effets spéciaux?
**3.** Qu'est-ce que tu as fait après le film?

**D. Conversation.** Avec un(e) partenaire, relisez à haute voix la conversation entre Cathy et Éric en bas de la page précédente. Ensuite, changez la conversation pour parler d'un film que vous avez vu récemment.

# Narrating what happened

*Le passé composé et l'imparfait (reprise)*

When recounting a story in the past, you use both the **passé composé** and the **imparfait**. Use the **imparfait** to set the scene and describe or give background information about the characters and the setting. Use the **passé composé** to narrate the sequence of events that advance the story. For example, if you were telling the old French tale **Cendrillon** *(Cinderella)*, you might begin . . .

> Il **était** une fois une belle jeune fille qui **s'appelait** Cendrillon. Son père **était** mort et elle **habitait** avec sa belle-mère et ses deux demi-sœurs. Sa belle-mère **était** cruelle et ses demi-sœurs **étaient** laides, bêtes et très gâtées *(spoiled)*. C'**était** Cendrillon qui **faisait** tout le travail mais elle **était** toujours belle et gracieuse. Un jour, le prince **a décidé** de donner un bal au palais et un messager **est allé** chez Cendrillon avec une invitation.

There are only two events that occur advancing the story in the preceding paragraph: the prince decided to give a ball and the messenger went to Cinderella's house. These two verbs are in the **passé composé.** All the rest of the paragraph is background information, setting the scene, so the verbs are in the **imparfait.**

When deciding whether to put a verb in the **passé composé** or the **imparfait**, learn to ask yourself whether you are talking about background information or something that was already in progress **(imparfait),** or the next thing that happened in the story **(passé composé).**

**A. Il était une fois...** Récrivez l'histoire de *La Belle et la Bête* au passé en mettant les verbes entre parenthèses à l'imparfait ou au passé composé.

> **Exemple**    Il y avait un marchand très riche qui **avait** (avoir) trois filles.

Il y avait un marchand très riche qui ___1___ (avoir) trois filles. Ils ___2___ (habiter) tous ensemble dans une belle maison en ville. Mais un jour, le marchand ___3___ (perdre *[to lose]*, *past participle* **perdu**) toute sa fortune et ses filles et lui ___4___ (devoir) aller habiter dans une petite maison à la campagne.

Ses deux filles aînées ___5___ (être) très malheureuses *(unhappy)*. Elles ___6___ (parler) constamment des choses qu'elles ___7___ (vouloir). Belle ___8___ (être) la plus jeune de ses filles. Elle ___9___ (être) très jolie et aussi très douce. Elle ___10___ (accepter) sa nouvelle vie et elle ___11___ (être) heureuse *(happy)*.

Un jour, le marchand ___12___ (partir) pour la ville voisine *(neighboring)*. Il ___13___ (neiger) et il ___14___ (faire) très froid et en route, il ne ___15___ (pouvoir) rien voir dans la forêt. Le marchand ___16___ (penser) qu'il ___17___ (aller) mourir quand, soudain, il ___18___ (trouver) un château. La porte du château ___19___ (être) ouverte et il ___20___ (décider) d'entrer. Il ___21___ (remarquer *[to notice]*) une grande table couverte de plats délicieux. Il ___22___ (manger), puis il ___23___ (faire) une sieste *(nap)*.

Après sa sieste, il ___24___ (sortir) dans le jardin où il ___25___ (trouver) une jolie rose qu'il ___26___ (vouloir) rapporter *(to bring back)* à Belle. À ce moment-là, un monstre horrible ___27___ (arriver) et ___28___ (commencer) à crier *(to shout)* qu'il ___29___ (vouloir) que Belle vienne habiter chez lui. Sinon *(Otherwise)*, la Bête ___30___ (aller) tuer *(to kill)* le marchand.

Quand le marchand ____31____ (rentrer), il ____32____ (raconter [to recount]) ses aventures à ses filles et Belle ____33____ (décider) d'aller habiter chez la Bête. Quand elle ____34____ (arriver) au château, elle ____35____ (trouver) tout ce dont (that) elle ____36____ (avoir) besoin. Chaque jour, elle ____37____ (avoir) tout ce qu'elle ____38____ (vouloir). Mais les cinq premiers jours, elle ____39____ (ne pas voir) la Bête.

Un jour, elle le (l') ____40____ (voir) pour la première fois pendant (while) qu'elle ____41____ (faire) une promenade dans le jardin. Elle le (l') ____42____ (trouver) horrible et elle ____43____ (crier). Belle ____44____ (avoir) peur et elle ____45____ (ne pas pouvoir) regarder la Bête dans les yeux, mais elle ____46____ (aller) faire une promenade avec lui. La conversation ____47____ (être) agréable. Quand la Bête ____48____ (demander) à Belle de faire une promenade deux jours plus tard, elle ____49____ (accepter).

Après ce jour-là, ils ____50____ (faire) une promenade chaque après-midi. Ils ____51____ (parler) de tout. Au début, Belle ____52____ (avoir) très peur de la Bête mais, finalement, Belle ____53____ (apprendre) à avoir confiance en lui. Après un certain temps, Belle ____54____ (commencer) à aimer le monstre et un jour elle l'____55____ (embrasser [to kiss]). Tout à coup, le visage (face) de la Bête ____56____ (changer) et il ____57____ (devenir) un beau et jeune prince.

### B. Le Petit Chaperon rouge. Racontez l'histoire du *Petit Chaperon rouge* *(Little Red Riding Hood)* en mettant les verbes entre parenthèses au passé composé ou à l'imparfait.

Une petite fille ____1____ (habiter) avec sa mère dans une grande forêt. Elle ____2____ (ne pas avoir) de père mais sa grand-mère ____3____ (habiter) dans une petite maison de l'autre côté de la forêt. On appelait cette petite fille le Petit Chaperon rouge parce qu'elle ____4____ (porter) toujours un chaperon rouge. Un jour, sa mère ____5____ (demander) au Petit Chaperon rouge d'apporter (to take) des choses à manger à sa grand-mère. La petite fille ____6____ (partir) tout de suite et elle ____7____ (traverser [to cross]) la forêt quand un grand loup (wolf) ____8____ (sortir) de derrière un arbre. Il ____9____ (avoir) très faim et il ____10____ (vouloir) savoir (to know) où le Petit Chaperon rouge ____11____ (aller) avec toutes ces choses à manger. Le Petit Chaperon rouge ____12____ (expliquer [to explain]) qu'elle les ____13____ (apporter) chez sa grand-mère. Le loup ____14____ (partir) dans la forêt et la petite fille ____15____ (continuer) son chemin (way). Mais le loup ____16____ (prendre) un chemin plus court pour aller chez la grand-mère et il ____17____ (arriver) le premier. Comme la porte ____18____ (ne pas être) fermée, il ____19____ (entrer) dans la maison. Il ____20____ (manger) la grand-mère toute entière (whole) et ____21____ (prendre) sa place. Quelques minutes plus tard, le Petit Chaperon rouge ____22____ (entrer) dans la chambre de sa grand-mère. Il y ____23____ (avoir) très peu de lumière (light) et le Petit Chaperon rouge ____24____ (ne pas pouvoir) voir très bien. La petite fille ____25____ (commencer) à parler à sa grand-mère:

— Quels gros yeux tu as, grand-mère!
— C'est pour mieux te voir, ma petite chérie!
— Quelles grandes oreilles tu as, grand-mère!
— C'est pour mieux t'entendre, ma petite chérie!
— Quelles grandes dents tu as, grand-mère!
— C'est pour mieux te manger, ma petite chérie!

À ce moment-là, le loup ____26____ (sauter [to jump]) du lit, il ____27____ (manger) le Petit Chaperon rouge tout entier et il ____28____ (sortir) de la maison. Par hasard (By chance), un chasseur (hunter) ____29____ (passer) devant la maison à ce moment-là. Il ____30____ (voir) le loup et il le (l') ____31____ (tuer [to kill]). Quand il a ouvert le ventre (belly) du loup, la petite fille et sa grand-mère ____32____ (sortir) vivantes (alive) parce que le loup les avait mangées toutes entières.

## Reprise

*Issuing invitations and talking about the past*

Dans le **Chapitre 6**, vous avez appris à faire des invitations et à raconter *(to tell)* ce qui s'est passé dans le passé. Maintenant vous allez réviser ce que vous avez appris.

**A. Invitations.** Invitez un(e) camarade de classe à faire les choses suivantes. Il/Elle va accepter une de vos invitations, refuser une de vos invitations et suggérer une autre activité pour la troisième. Utilisez une variété d'expressions.

> **Exemple**  aller au cinéma demain
> — **Tu voudrais aller au cinéma demain?**
> — **Oui, je voudrais bien.**

1. aller prendre un verre après les cours
2. aller danser samedi soir
3. aller voir une exposition au musée dimanche après-midi

Maintenant, refaites les trois invitations pour inviter toute la classe.

> **Exemple**  aller au cinéma demain
> **Vous voudriez aller au cinéma demain?**

**B. Non, merci.** Un ami téléphone à Éric pour l'inviter à sortir, mais Éric préfère ne rien faire et il refuse. L'ami insiste. Éric est très imaginatif dans ses excuses. Jouez les deux rôles avec un(e) partenaire.

**C. On ne peut pas toujours faire ce qu'on veut!** Éric explique ce que les Pérez ont envie de faire et ce qu'ils ont besoin de faire. Refaites ses phrases en utilisant **vouloir, pouvoir** et **devoir** comme dans l'exemple.

> **Exemple**  Maman a envie de dormir, mais elle a besoin de travailler.
> **Maman veut dormir, mais elle ne peut pas parce qu'elle doit travailler.**

1. Papa a envie de jouer au golf, mais il a besoin de faire des courses.
2. Michel a envie de faire du vélo, mais il a besoin de faire ses devoirs.
3. Michèle et moi, nous avons envie de sortir ce soir, mais nous avons besoin de préparer les cours.
4. Nos amis ont envie de sortir aussi, mais ils ont besoin de travailler.
5. Moi, j'ai envie de faire du vélo, mais j'ai besoin de faire la lessive.

**D. En cours.** Dites si les personnes suivantes font les choses indiquées.

> **Exemple**  Moi, je (dormir en cours)
> **Moi, je ne dors pas en cours.**

1. Moi, je (partir de la maison avant 8 heures pour aller en cours, dormir en cours, sortir avec des camarades de classe le samedi soir)
2. Les meilleurs étudiants (partir de la maison tôt pour arriver en cours à l'heure, sortir tous les soirs, dormir dans le laboratoire de langues, faire toujours les devoirs)
3. Les autres étudiants et moi, nous (dormir en cours, faire attention *[to pay attention]* en cours, sortir du cours en avance *[early]*, sortir ensemble après les cours)
4. Quand il y a un examen, le professeur (sortir de la salle de classe, dormir pendant l'examen, sortir au café avec nous après le cours)

**E. Entretien.** Les questions suivantes sont au présent. Mettez-les au passé composé ou à l'imparfait pour demander à un(e) camarade de classe ce qu'il/elle a fait le dernier jour que vous étiez en cours de français.

> **Exemple**   À quelle heure est-ce que tu quittes la maison?
> — **À quelle heure est-ce que tu as quitté la maison hier (jeudi... )?**
> — **J'ai quitté la maison à huit heures.**

1. Qu'est-ce que tu mets pour sortir? Un jean? Une robe?
2. Quel temps fait-il quand tu quittes la maison?
3. Est-ce que tu veux rester à la maison?
4. Est-ce que tu prends ta voiture ou l'autobus ou est-ce que tu vas en cours à pied?
5. À quelle heure est-ce que le cours de français commence?
6. Est-ce que tu as faim quand tu sors du cours?
7. Est-ce que tu peux faire ce que tu veux après les cours?
8. Quelle heure est-il quand tu rentres?
9. Qui prépare le dîner? Est-ce que c'est bon?
10. Qu'est-ce que tu veux faire après le dîner?
11. Est-ce que tu as besoin de faire quelque chose?
12. Qu'est-ce que tu fais?

Maintenant, écrivez un paragraphe décrivant votre journée le jour du dernier cours de français.

**F. Une aventure!** Regardez l'illustration et racontez *(tell)* ce qui s'est passé chez les Fédor le week-end dernier. Utilisez **le voleur** pour *the thief*, **voler** pour *to steal* et **entrer par la fenêtre** pour *to come in through the window.* Avant de commencer, réfléchissez *(think)* aux questions suivantes.

- What night was it?
- What time was it?
- What was the weather like?
- How many people were in the Fédors' living room?
- Why were they there?
- What was each person doing?
- What was in the bedroom?
- What happened?
- What happened next?

le voleur

Les Dupont    Les Fédor          Simon   Pascale

## Lecture: *Un peu d'histoire*

Les domaines spécialisés (le cinéma, les affaires, la musique, les mathématiques) utilisent un vocabulaire spécialisé. Vous allez lire un article du magazine *Jeune et Jolie* dans lequel on parle de **la découverte** des techniques de projection cinématographique et des débuts difficiles du cinéma. Avant de lire l'article, faites une liste (en anglais) de mots qui **se rapportent à ce sujet.** Cette liste **vous aidera à** deviner **le sens** des mots que vous ne connaissez pas.

**Devinez!** Devinez le sens des mots en italique dans les contextes du cinéma et de la science.

### LE CINÉMA

1. J'aime louer des vidéos, mais pour voir des films d'aventures, je préfère aller au cinéma parce que *l'écran* est plus grand.
2. Je préfère aller au cinéma l'après-midi parce que *l'entrée* est moins chère.
3. Quand le projecteur ne fonctionne pas bien, les *spectateurs* ne peuvent pas voir le film et ils ne sont pas contents.

### LA SCIENCE

1. Pierre et Marie Curie *ont découvert* le radium. Cela a été une découverte importante.
2. Une *expérience* scientifique mal *réglée* peut avoir de graves conséquences.

**Un peu d'histoire**

En 1895, les frères Lumière, Louis et Alphonse, font une découverte sur la projection d'images. Très vite, cette découverte devient une curiosité scientifique... Ainsi, le cinéma est né à Paris **lors d'**une projection officielle le 28 décembre 1895, dans un sous-sol du Grand-Café, **à deux pas de** l'Opéra de Paris, 14, boulevard des Capucines. L'écran faisait un mètre **de haut** et l'entrée coûtait un franc: **il y eut** 35 spectateurs. Le cinéma quitte alors le cercle académique pour des salles toutes simples, des cafés ou **des chapiteaux.** Malheureusement l'histoire commence mal! En 1897, plus de 150 personnes **meurent carbonisées** lors d'une séance, un projecteur mal réglé au Bazar de la Charité **prend feu... La classe aisée** est choquée et se réfugie vers le music-hall.

---

**une découverte** *a discovery*    **se rapportent à ce sujet** *are related to this subject*    **vous aidera à** *will help you to* **le sens** *the meaning*    **lors de** *at the time of*    **à deux pas de** *a short distance from*    **de haut** *high*    **il y eut** *there were* **des chapiteaux** *(m) tents*    **meurent carbonisées** *are burned to death*    **prend feu** *catches fire* **La classe aisée** *The upper class*

# Compréhension

## A. Vrai ou faux?

1. Le cinéma est né avec une découverte des frères Lumière.
2. Il y a une première projection officielle en 1895 au sous-sol du Grand-Café à Paris.
3. Le cinéma est immédiatement populaire et on commence tout de suite à construire *(to build)* des salles de cinéma.
4. En 1897, un accident choque les spectateurs et ils décident d'abandonner le cinéma pour retourner au music-hall.

## B. Un peu d'histoire.
Complétez les phrases avec un mot de la liste. Après, changez l'ordre des initiales de chacun de ces mots pour trouver un nom qu'on associe à l'histoire du cinéma. (Il est nécessaire de changer certains accents aussi!)

| entrée | Lumière | écran | images | mètre | réglé | un franc |
|--------|---------|-------|--------|-------|-------|----------|

En 1895, les frères _____ font une découverte sur la projection d' _____ et voilà que le cinéma est né. La première projection officielle est le 28 décembre 1895 au sous-sol d'un café à Paris. L' _____ coûte _____ et l' _____ n'est pas grand: il mesure un _____ de haut. Pendant un certain temps, les Parisiens ont la possibilité de voir ces «projections» dans les cafés ou dans d'autres salles simples. En 1897, un projecteur mal _____ prend feu et 150 spectateurs meurent carbonisés. L'histoire du cinéma ne commence pas bien!

MOT TROUVÉ: ❑ ❑ ❑ ❑ ❑ ❑

# Composition

## A. Organisez-vous.
Vous allez décrire un film que vous avez vu. D'abord, faites une liste de dix phrases à l'imparfait dans lesquelles vous décrivez les personnages *(characters)* (personnalité, apparence physique, etc.), le cadre *(setting)*. Ensuite, utilisez le passé composé pour décrire dix choses qui se sont passées *(happened)* dans le film.

### IMPARFAIT: DESCRIPTION DES PERSONNAGES, DU CADRE ET DE LA SITUATION

**Exemple**
Une jeune Américaine et son petit ami faisaient un voyage en France.
Elle était grande et très belle...

### PASSÉ COMPOSÉ: CE QUI S'EST PASSÉ

**Exemple**
Un jour, la jeune fille a rencontré un Français. Ils sont sortis ensemble.

## B. Rédaction: Un film.
Utilisez les phrases écrites dans **A. Organisez-vous** pour écrire un résumé du film.

## C. C'est quel film?
Lisez votre composition à la classe. Les autres étudiants doivent deviner de quel film vous parlez.

If you have access to SYSTÈME-D software, you will find the following phrases, vocabulary, grammar, and dictionary aids there.

**Phrases:** Describing people; Sequencing events; Linking ideas
**Vocabulary:** Personality; Hair colors
**Grammar:** Imperfect; Compound past tense; Verbs with auxiliary **être**

## Le cinéma français

Le cinéma est né en France avec **la découverte,** en 1895, de la projection d'images par les frères Lumière. Plus de cent ans après, la France reste **toujours** un des principaux producteurs de films **au monde.** Le cinéma français **demeure** le premier en Europe pour le nombre d'**entrées au cinéma** par habitant. La production cinématographique française continue d'être la plus dynamique en Europe avec la production de 212 films français en 2003 et la coproduction de 29 films étrangers.

La popularité du cinéma français n'est pas limité à l'Europe. Récemment, les films français **ont connu** un succès **inégalé** aux États-Unis et **les recettes** des films français y ont doublé depuis trois ans. Quelques films français qui ont eu du succès chez les Américains sont: *Le Fabuleux Destin d'Amélie Poulain, Le Pacte des loups, Le Placard, Le Peuple Migrateur, Les Triplettes de Belleville, L'Auberge espagnole, Décalage horaire, Swimming Pool* (tourné en anglais) et **bien d'autres.** Tous ces films sont **disponibles** en vidéo ou en DVD avec **des sous-titres** en anglais.

**Depuis que** *Le Fabuleux Destin d'Amélie Poulain,* interprétée par Audrey Tautou, a enchanté les Américains, le cinéma français connaît un succès inégalé aux États-Unis.

---

**la découverte** *the discovery*   **toujours** *still*   **au monde** *in the world*   **demeure** *remains*   **entrées au cinéma** *cinema attendance*   **ont connu** *have known*   **inégalé** *unequaled*   **les recettes** *the receipts*   **bien d'autres** *many others* **disponibles** *available*   **des sous-titres** *subtitles*   **Depuis que** *Since*

Les Césars et les Palmes d'Or (comme les Oscars aux USA) sont distribués chaque année dans les catégories de meilleur(e): film, acteur, actrice, second rôle masculin, second rôle féminin, **jeune espoir masculin,** jeune espoir féminin, première **œuvre,** scénario, dialogue ou adaptation, **réalisateur,** décor, musique, photo, **son,** costumes, **montage,** film étranger et **court métrage.** Chaque année, le célèbre festival de Cannes **attire** des artistes et **des cinéastes** du monde entier.

## À discuter

1. Les films américains sont très appréciés en France. Des 50 films les plus populaires en France entre 1945 et 2001, 24 sont des films américains et les films américains représentent presque 50% des entrées au cinéma en France. Certains Français trouvent qu'il y a trop d'influence américaine dans les salles de cinéma en France et que la culture française en est menacée *(is threatened by this)*. Est-ce que ce sentiment est justifié? Quel est le rôle du gouvernement dans la préservation de la culture? Est-ce qu'il doit y avoir une censure? des quotas? des subventions *(subsidies)*?

2. Tandis que *(While)* les Français trouvent que le cinéma français est supérieur dans la réflexion, le rire et l'émotion, ils trouvent que le cinéma américain réussit mieux dans l'action et le suspens. Est-ce que l'industrie cinématographique d'un pays est un reflet de *(a reflection of)* sa culture? Si oui, quelles comparaisons culturelles peut-on faire entre les Français et les Américains?

3. Le dynamisme dans la production des films français se trouve en partie dans le système de financement du cinéma. Le cinéma français est financé par des taxes sur les places de cinéma *(ticket sales)*, les revenus des chaînes de télévision et des éditeurs vidéo. Ces taxes retournent à l'industrie du cinéma sous forme de soutiens financiers *(financial support)* à l'écriture *(writing)*, à la production, à la distribution et à l'exportation. Que pensez-vous de ce système?

visit http://horizons.heinle.com

---

**jeune espoir masculin** *best new actor*   **œuvre** *work*   **réalisateur** *director*   **son** *sound*   **montage** *editing*
**court métrage** *short film*   **attire** *attracts*   **des cinéastes** *filmmakers*

# Résumé de grammaire

## The verbs *vouloir, pouvoir,* and *devoir*

Here are the conjugations of **vouloir** *(to want)*, **pouvoir** *(can, may, to be able)*, and **devoir** *(must, to have to, to owe)*.

| VOULOIR | POUVOIR | DEVOIR |
|---|---|---|
| je **veux** | je **peux** | je **dois** |
| tu **veux** | tu **peux** | tu **dois** |
| il/elle/on **veut** | il/elle/on **peut** | il/elle/on **doit** |
| nous **voulons** | nous **pouvons** | nous **devons** |
| vous **voulez** | vous **pouvez** | vous **devez** |
| ils/elles **veulent** | ils/elles **peuvent** | ils/elles **doivent** |
| PASSÉ COMPOSÉ | PASSÉ COMPOSÉ | PASSÉ COMPOSÉ |
| **j'ai voulu** | **j'ai pu** | **j'ai dû** |
| IMPARFAIT | IMPARFAIT | IMPARFAIT |
| **je voulais** | **je pouvais** | **je devais** |

Je veux sortir ce soir mais je ne peux pas. Je dois travailler.

Nous voulions partir en vacances, mais n'avons pas pu. Nous avons dû travailler.

Elle n'est pas chez elle. Elle **a dû** quitter la maison très tôt.
*She isn't home. She must have left / had to leave the house very early.*

In the **passé composé, devoir** can mean that someone *had to* do something or *must have* done something. Context will clarify the meaning.

## The verbs *sortir, partir,* and *dormir*

Here are the conjugations of **sortir** *(to go out)*, **partir** *(to leave)*, and **dormir** *(to sleep)*.

| SORTIR | PARTIR | DORMIR |
|---|---|---|
| je **sors** | je **pars** | je **dors** |
| tu **sors** | tu **pars** | tu **dors** |
| il/elle/on **sort** | il/elle/on **part** | il/elle/on **dort** |
| nous **sortons** | nous **partons** | nous **dormons** |
| vous **sortez** | vous **partez** | vous **dormez** |
| ils/elles **sortent** | ils/elles **partent** | ils/elles **dorment** |
| PASSÉ COMPOSÉ | PASSÉ COMPOSÉ | PASSÉ COMPOSÉ |
| **je suis sorti(e)** | **je suis parti(e)** | **j'ai dormi** |
| IMPARFAIT | IMPARFAIT | IMPARFAIT |
| **je sortais** | **je partais** | **je dormais** |

Je dors jusqu'à sept heures et je pars pour l'université à huit heures.

Ce matin j'ai dormi jusqu'à sept heures et demie et je suis partie pour l'université en retard *(late).*
Avant, je sortais souvent avec des amis mais nous ne sommes pas sortis le week-end dernier.

Je **sors** souvent avec ma sœur le samedi. Nous **sortons** de la maison vers neuf heures.
Il **quitte** Paris pour aller travailler à Nice. Il **part** demain.

Je sors **de** la maison à neuf heures.
Je pars **pour** Nice demain.
Je pars **de** chez moi à huit heures.

**Sortir** means *to go out* both in the sense of going out with friends and going out of a place. Use **partir** to say *to leave* in the sense of *to go away.* **Quitter** means *to leave* a person or a place and *must* be followed by a direct object.

Use these prepositions with these verbs:

*to go out of* = **sortir de**
*to leave for* = **partir pour**
*to leave (from)* = **partir de**

## L'imparfait and le passé composé

All verbs except **être** form the imparfait by dropping the **-ons** from the present tense **nous** form and adding these endings. The stem for **être** is **ét-**.

| | PARLER (nous parlons → parl-) | FAIRE (nous faisons → fais-) | PRENDRE (nous prenons → pren-) | ÊTRE (ét-) |
|---|---|---|---|---|
| je | parl**ais** | fais**ais** | pren**ais** | ét**ais** |
| tu | parl**ais** | fais**ais** | pren**ais** | ét**ais** |
| il/elle/on | parl**ait** | fais**ait** | pren**ait** | ét**ait** |
| nous | parl**ions** | fais**ions** | pren**ions** | ét**ions** |
| vous | parl**iez** | fais**iez** | pren**iez** | ét**iez** |
| ils/elles | parl**aient** | fais**aient** | pren**aient** | ét**aient** |

Quand j'avais 12 ans, j'allais au lycée. Je passais beaucoup de temps avec mes copains. On aimait faire du roller.

Verbs with spelling changes in the present tense **nous** form, like **manger** and **commencer,** retain the spelling changes in the **imparfait** only before endings beginning with an **a.**

Note these expressions in the **imparfait:**

| | | |
|---|---|---|
| il y a → il y avait | il pleut → il pleuvait | il neige → il neigeait |

Nous mangions bien, mais il mang**e**ait assez mal.
Vous commenciez vos cours à midi, mais moi, je commen**ç**ais mes cours à 11 heures.

Il y avait du vent, il pleuvait et il faisait froid, mais il ne neigeait pas.

When talking about the past, you will use both the **passé composé** and the **imparfait.** Note their uses:

**USE THE *IMPARFAIT* TO SAY:**

**1. HOW THINGS USED TO BE OR WHAT USED TO HAPPEN**
* continuous actions or states
* repeated or habitual actions of an unspecified duration

**2. WHAT WAS GOING ON**
* scene or setting
* interrupted actions in progress

**3. WHAT THINGS WERE LIKE OR HOW SOMEONE FELT**
* physical or mental states

**4. WHAT WAS GOING TO HAPPEN**
* **aller** + infinitive in the past

**USE THE *PASSÉ COMPOSÉ* TO SAY:**

**1. WHAT HAPPENED AT A PRECISE MOMENT OR FOR A SPECIFIC DURATION**
* completed actions
* actions within a specific duration

**2. WHAT HAPPENED NEXT**
* sequence of events
* actions interrupting something in progress

**3. WHAT CHANGED**
* changes in states

Cendrillon **pleurait** *(was crying)* quand sa marraine *(fairy godmother)* **est arrivée.** La marraine **a aidé** Cendrillon et Cendrillon **est allée** au bal du prince. Le prince **est tombé** immédiatement amoureux de Cendrillon. Ils **ont dansé** et ils **ont beaucoup parlé.** À minuit, Cendrillon **est partie** sans dire au prince qui elle **était,** mais elle **a laissé** tomber *(dropped)* une de ses chaussures.

# Vocabulaire

## COMPÉTENCE 1

### Inviting someone to go out

**NOMS MASCULINS**

| | |
|---|---|
| l'amour | love |
| un film d'amour | a romantic movie, a love story |
| un groupe | a group |
| un horaire | a schedule |

**NOMS FÉMININS**

| | |
|---|---|
| une comédie | a comedy |
| une façon | a way |
| l'heure officielle | official time |
| l'heure d'ouverture | opening time |
| une idée | an idea |
| une invitation | an invitation |
| une personne | a person |
| une séance | a showing |

**EXPRESSIONS VERBALES**

| | |
|---|---|
| appeler | to call |
| devoir | must, to have to, to owe |
| dire | to say, to tell |
| passer chez… | to stop by . . . 's house |
| passer un film | to show a movie |
| pouvoir | can, may, to be able |
| regretter | to regret, to be sorry |
| répondre (à) | to answer, to respond (to) |
| suggérer | to suggest |
| téléphoner (à) | to phone |
| utiliser | to use, to utilize |
| vouloir | to want |

**DIVERS**

| | |
|---|---|
| allô | hello (on the telephone) |
| avec plaisir | gladly, with pleasure |
| Je pensais | I was thinking |
| Je t'invite… | I'm inviting you . . . |
| Je voudrais vous inviter… | I'd like to invite you . . . |
| Quelle bonne idée! | What a good idea! |
| quelqu'un | someone, somebody |
| tellement | so much, so |
| uniquement | uniquely, only |
| Vous voudriez… ? | Would you like . . . ? |

## COMPÉTENCE 2

### Talking about how you spend and used to spend your time

**NOMS MASCULINS**

| | |
|---|---|
| un copain | a friend, a pal |
| un lycée | a high school |
| un lycéen | a high school student |
| un restau-u | a university cafeteria |

**NOMS FÉMININS**

| | |
|---|---|
| une copine | a friend, a pal |
| une école | a school |
| une lycéenne | a high school student |
| les vacances | vacation |
| la vie | life |

**EXPRESSIONS VERBALES**

| | |
|---|---|
| avoir cours | to have class |
| comparer | to compare |
| dormir | to sleep |
| faire du roller | to go in-line skating |
| faire du skateboard | to skateboard |
| partir (de / pour) | to leave (from / for), to go away (from / to) |
| partir en vacances | to leave on vacation |
| partir en voyage | to leave on a trip |
| partir en week-end | to go away for the weekend |
| quitter | to leave |
| sortir (de) | to go out (of) |

**DIVERS**

| | |
|---|---|
| ce que | what |
| dans le passé | in the past |
| fatigué(e) | tired |
| rien de spécial | nothing special |

## Talking about the past

**NOMS MASCULINS**

| | |
|---|---|
| un bistro | *a pub, a restaurant* |
| le lendemain | *the next day* |
| un repas | *a meal* |
| un voleur | *a thief* |

**NOMS FÉMININS**

| | |
|---|---|
| une fois | *once, one time* |
| une sortie | *an outing* |

**EXPRESSIONS ADVERBIALES**

| | |
|---|---|
| un jour | *one day* |
| soudain | *suddenly* |
| tout à coup | *all of a sudden* |
| tout de suite | *right away* |
| tout d'un coup | *all at once* |

**DIVERS**

| | |
|---|---|
| Ça t'a plu? | *Did you like it?* |
| délicieux (délicieuse) | *delicious* |
| Il faisait noir. | *It was dark.* |
| par la fenêtre | *through the window* |
| Qu'est-ce qui s'est passé? | *What happened?* |
| rien du tout | *nothing at all* |

## Narrating in the past

**NOMS MASCULINS**

| | |
|---|---|
| un acteur | *an actor* |
| un conte | *a story* |
| un conte de fée | *a fairy tale* |
| les effets spéciaux | *special effects* |
| un marchand | *a merchant, a shopkeeper* |
| un monstre | *a monster* |

**NOMS FÉMININS**

| | |
|---|---|
| une actrice | *an actress* |
| une bête | *a beast* |
| une marchande | *a merchant, a shopkeeper* |
| la violence | *violence* |

**EXPRESSIONS VERBALES**

| | |
|---|---|
| apprécier | *to appreciate* |
| à suivre | *to be continued* |
| changer | *to change* |
| Connaissez-vous… ? | *Do you know . . . ?* |
| emprisonner | *to imprison* |
| jouer | *to act* (in movies and theater) |
| se parler | *to talk to each other* |
| prendre la place de | *to take the place of* |
| promettre | *to promise* |
| tomber amoureux (amoureuse) de | *to fall in love with* |

**ADJECTIFS**

| | |
|---|---|
| amoureux (amoureuse) (de) | *in love (with)* |
| basé(e) (sur) | *based (on)* |
| classique | *classic* |
| doux (douce) | *sweet, soft, gentle* |
| excellent | *excellent* |
| féroce | *ferocious* |
| gracieux (gracieuse) | *gracious* |
| horrible | *horrible* |
| patient(e) | *patient* |

**DIVERS**

| | |
|---|---|
| au début (de) | *at the beginning (of)* |
| finalement | *finally* |
| Il était une fois… | *Once upon a time there was . . .* |
| ça m'a plu | *I liked it* |
| lequel (laquelle) | *which, which one* |
| lui | *him* |
| petit à petit | *little by little* |
| trop de | *too much* |

## Port de Rouen
### CAMILLE PISSARRO
### (1830–1903)

1896
Paris, musée d'Orsay

Pissarro est né à Saint Thomas, une île des Antilles. En 1841, ses parents l'envoient en pension *(boarding school)* à Paris, et là, il découvre le monde des arts. Il visite la ville de Rouen pour la première fois en 1883. L'activité fluviale de cette ville normande va servir de cadre à plusieurs de ses tableaux les plus connus.

## En Normandie

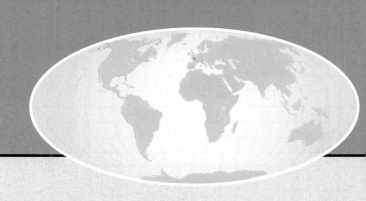

**LA NORMANDIE**
**SUPERFICIE:** 30 627 kilomètres carrés
**NOMBRE D'HABITANTS:** 3 242 000 habitants (les Normands)
**INDUSTRIES PRINCIPALES:** agriculture (céréalière et fruitière), élevage *(livestock)*, tourisme, pêche *(fishing)*, construction automobile et navale, industrie électrique et électronique

# La vie quotidienne

# La France et sa diversité

Existe-t-il une identité française? **une seule** culture française? un caractère français? Nous avons tous notre **propre** idée de ce que représente la France, mais en réalité la France n'a pas une seule identité, ou une seule culture. La France est un pays riche en diversité, où chaque région cherche à maintenir son héritage culturel: ses traditions, sa cuisine, sa musique, ses danses et **même parfois** sa langue.

Des Bretons dans leurs costumes traditionnels

En Bretagne, par exemple, il y a des Bretons qui parlent et écrivent **non seulement** le français mais aussi le breton—la seule langue d'origine celtique parlée **en dehors des** îles britanniques.

En Corse, de nombreuses personnes parlent corse et au Pays basque, le long de **la frontière** espagnole, **on entend** parler basque. Dans toute la région du sud, on entend parfois des vestiges d'anciennes langues dérivées du latin, **dont** le provençal, l'occitan et le catalan sont les exemples les plus **connus.**

Un accordéoniste au Pays basque

---

une seule *a single*    propre *own*    même parfois *even at times*    non seulement *not only*    en dehors de *outside of*
la frontière *the border*    on entend *one hears*    dont *of which*    connus *well-known*

Et **pourtant, malgré** cette diversité, les Français **se sentent** bien français! Une histoire qui date de plus de 2 000 ans, **un patrimoine** riche en architecture et en culture et une tradition **à la fois laïque** et catholique donnent à la France et aux Français leur unité, le sens d'être «français».

Récemment, l'immigration de gens venus surtout d'Asie, d'Afrique **occidentale** et d'Afrique du Nord **a beau-coup marqué** la France. Ces nouveaux immigrés cherchent aussi à maintenir leurs langues et leurs traditions. Comment peut-on préserver l'identité de la culture française **tout en** respectant les divers groupes ethniques qui habitent dans le pays? Est-il possible de combiner l'unité et la diversité? Voilà les questions auxquelles la France **essaie de** trouver une réponse.

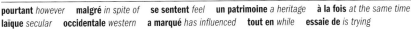

**pourtant** *however*   **malgré** *in spite of*   **se sentent** *feel*   **un patrimoine** *a heritage*   **à la fois** *at the same time*
**laïque** *secular*   **occidentale** *western*   **a marqué** *has influenced*   **tout en** *while*   **essaie de** *is trying*

# Describing your daily routine

### >Note *culturelle*

En France, on utilise souvent l'expression «métro, boulot, dodo» *("subway, work, bedtime")* pour exprimer la monotonie de la vie quotidienne. Y-a-t-il une expression en anglais pour exprimer *(to express)* cette même idée?

**NOTE DE VOCABULAIRE**

When saying that people are doing something to a part of their body, you generally use the definite article **(le, la, l', les)** in French, rather than a possessive adjective as in English.

Je me lave **les** mains.     *I'm washing **my** hands.*

## La vie de tous les jours

Voilà **la routine quotidienne** de Rose Richard, une jeune Américaine qui va bientôt visiter la France. Et vous? Quelle est votre routine quotidienne?

D'habitude le matin...

Je **fais ma toilette.**

Je me réveille vers six heures.

Je me lève tout de suite.

Je me lave **la figure** et **les mains** *(f)*.

Je prends un bain ou **une douche.**

Je me brosse les cheveux.

Je me brosse les dents.

Je me maquille.

Je m'habille.

Le soir...

Quelquefois **je me repose.**

**D'autres fois,** je m'amuse avec des amis.

Quand je suis seule, **je m'ennuie.**

Je me déshabille.

Je me couche et **je m'endors** facilement.

---

la routine quotidienne *daily routine*     faire sa toilette *to wash up*     la figure *the face*     les mains *(f) the hands*
une douche *a shower*     je me repose *I rest*     D'autres fois *Other times*     je m'ennuie *(s'ennuyer to be bored, to get bored)*
je m'endors *(s'endormir to fall asleep)*

Rosalie Toulouse Richard, d'origine française, habite à Atlanta **depuis** son mariage avec un Américain. **Veuve** maintenant, elle retourne en France avec sa **petite-fille** Rose qui ne **connaît** pas du tout la France. **Comme** elles partagent une chambre **pendant** leur **séjour,** elles parlent de leurs routines le matin.

ROSALIE:  Tu te lèves vers quelle heure d'habitude?

ROSE:  Entre six heures et six heures et demie. Je fais **vite** ma toilette, je m'habille et puis je me maquille. Je suis **prête** en une demi-heure.

ROSALIE:  C'est parfait. Moi, je prends quelquefois une douche le matin mais je préfère prendre mon bain le soir. Je peux très bien **attendre** jusqu'à sept heures pour faire ma toilette.

ROSE:  Et moi, je ne quitte jamais la maison avant huit heures et demie. Alors si tu veux, on peut prendre le petit déjeuner ensemble tous les matins.

---

**A. Ma routine.** Complétez les phrases avec une expression de la liste.

> **Exemple**  Je me réveille avant six heures.
> **Je me réveille rarement avant six heures.**

| | |
|---|---|
| toujours | tous les jours |
| souvent | le lundi, le mardi... |
| quelquefois | le matin, l'après-midi, le soir |
| de temps en temps | une (deux... ) fois par jour (semaine... ) |
| rarement | |
| ne... jamais | |

**NOTE DE GRAMMAIRE**

Place the **ne** in **ne... jamais** before the word **me** in these sentences, and **jamais** after the verb. Remember that **toujours, souvent,** and **rarement** go right after the verb, but the other adverbial phrases listed go at the end of the sentence.

1. Je me réveille après neuf heures.
2. Je me lève tout de suite.
3. Je prends une douche ou un bain.
4. Je me lave les mains.
5. Je me lave les cheveux.
6. Je me brosse les dents.
7. Je m'habille vite.
8. Je m'ennuie.
9. Je me repose.
10. Je m'amuse bien.
11. Je me couche tard.
12. Je m'endors sur le canapé.

**B. Conversation.** Avec un(e) partenaire, relisez la conversation entre Rose et sa grand-mère en haut de la page. Ensuite, imaginez que vous allez partager une maison avec votre partenaire et changez la conversation pour parler de votre routine le matin.

---

depuis *since*  Veuve (veuf) *Widow (widower)*  une petite-fille (un petit-fils) *a granddaughter (a grandson)*
elle connaît (connaître *to know*)  Comme *Since, As*  pendant *during*  un séjour *a stay*  vite *quickly, fast*  prêt(e) *ready*
attendre *to wait (for)*

**1.** What is the difference in usage between the reflexive verb **se laver** and the non-reflexive verb **laver?**

**2.** What are the different reflexive pronouns that are used with each subject pronoun when you conjugate a reflexive verb like **se laver?**

**3.** Where do you place **ne... pas** when negating reflexive verbs?

**4.** In which forms do verbs like **se lever, s'appeler,** and **s'ennuyer** have spelling changes? What are the changes? Which forms do not have spelling changes?

# Describing your daily routine

*Les verbes réfléchis au présent*

A verb can be used to say that you are doing something to or for yourself or that you are doing something to or for another person or thing. For example, one can dress oneself or one can dress one's children. When someone performs the action of a verb on or for himself/herself, a reflexive verb is generally used in French. Compare the differences depicted here.

**REFLEXIVE**

Je m'habille.

**NON-REFLEXIVE**

J'habille les enfants.

Je me lave les mains.

Je lave la voiture.

The infinitive of reflexive verbs is preceded by the reflexive pronoun **se.** When you conjugate these verbs, change the reflexive pronoun according to the subject. In the negative, place **ne** directly before the reflexive pronoun and **pas** after the conjugated verb.

| SE LAVER *(to wash [oneself])* | | NE PAS SE LAVER | |
|---|---|---|---|
| je me lave | nous nous lavons | je ne me lave pas | nous ne nous lavons pas |
| tu te laves | vous vous lavez | tu ne te laves pas | vous ne vous lavez pas |
| il/elle/on se lave | ils/elles se lavent | il/elle/on ne se lave pas | ils/elles ne se lavent pas |

Note that **me, te,** and **se** change to **m', t',** and **s'** before a vowel sound: **je m'habille, tu t'habilles, elle s'habille, ils s'habillent.**

Here are some reflexive verbs you can use to talk about your daily life:

| | |
|---|---|
| s'amuser | *to have fun* |
| s'appeler | *to be named* |
| se brosser (les cheveux, les dents) | *to brush (one's hair, one's teeth)* |
| se coucher / se recoucher | *to go to bed / to go back to bed* |
| s'endormir | *to fall asleep* |
| s'ennuyer | *to be bored, to get bored* |
| s'habiller / se déshabiller | *to get dressed / to get undressed* |
| se laver (les mains, la figure) | *to wash (one's hands, one's face)* |
| se lever | *to get up* |
| se maquiller | *to put on make-up* |
| se raser | *to shave* |
| se reposer | *to rest* |
| se réveiller | *to wake up* |

The verb **s'endormir** is conjugated like **dormir**.

| S'ENDORMIR *(to fall asleep)* | |
|---|---|
| je m'endors | nous nous endormons |
| tu t'endors | vous vous endormez |
| il/elle/on s'endort | ils/elles s'endorment |

Note the spelling change in **s'ennuyer** and other verbs ending in **-yer,** such as **essayer** and **payer.** The **y** changes to **i** in all forms except those of **nous** and **vous.**

| S'ENNUYER *(to be bored, to get bored)* | |
|---|---|
| je m'ennuie | nous nous ennuyons |
| tu t'ennuies | vous vous ennuyez |
| il/elle/on s'ennuie | ils/elles s'ennuient |

There is an accent spelling change in the conjugation of **se lever**. Its conjugation is similar to that of **acheter**. **S'appeler** changes its spelling by doubling the final consonant of the stem in all present tense forms except those of **nous** and **vous**.

| S'APPELER *(to be named)* | |
|---|---|
| je m'appelle | nous nous appelons |
| tu t'appelles | vous vous appelez |
| il/elle/on s'appelle | ils/elles s'appellent |

| SE LEVER *(to get up)* | |
|---|---|
| je me lève | nous nous levons |
| tu te lèves | vous vous levez |
| il/elle/on se lève | ils/elles se lèvent |

## A. Équivalents. Trouvez le verbe réfléchi correspondant à chaque définition.

1. aller au lit
2. sortir du lit
3. mettre des vêtements
4. faire quelque chose d'amusant
5. faire quelque chose d'ennuyeux
6. ne rien faire
7. commencer à dormir

a. s'endormir
b. s'ennuyer
c. se reposer
d. se lever
e. s'amuser
f. se coucher
g. s'habiller

## B. D'abord... Indiquez l'ordre logique des activités données.

**Exemple**     prendre un bain / se lever
         **D'abord, on se lève et puis on prend un bain.**

1. se réveiller / se lever
2. se raser / se lever
3. se laver la figure / se maquiller
4. s'habiller / prendre un bain ou une douche
5. se brosser les dents / manger
6. quitter la maison / s'habiller
7. se reposer / rentrer à la maison après les cours
8. s'amuser / retrouver des amis
9. se déshabiller / se coucher
10. s'endormir / se coucher

**C. Un samedi typique.** Voilà la routine de Rose le samedi matin. Qu'est-ce qu'elle fait?

Le samedi matin...

Exemple

... vers neuf heures.
**Elle se réveille vers neuf heures.**

**1.** ... tout de suite.　　**2.** ... la figure et les mains.　　**3.** ... les dents.

**4.** ... les cheveux.　　**5.** ... en jean.

La samedi soir...

**6.** ... avec des amis.　　**7.** ... vers deux heures du matin et... facilement.

**D. Et vous?** Regardez les illustrations de *C. Un samedi typique.* Est-ce que vous faites ces mêmes choses le samedi? Le samedi matin...

Exemple

... vers neuf heures
**Je me réveille vers neuf heures.**
**Je ne me réveille pas vers neuf heures.**

**E. Le week-end.** Demandez à votre partenaire s'il/si elle fait les choses suivantes le week-end.

> **Exemple**     se réveiller tôt ou tard le samedi matin
> — **Est-ce que tu te réveilles tôt ou tard le samedi matin?**
> — **En général, je me réveille tôt.**

1. se lever tôt ou tard le samedi matin
2. prendre un bain ou une douche
3. s'amuser ou s'ennuyer le week-end
4. se coucher tôt ou tard le samedi soir
5. s'endormir facilement

**F. Questions.** Avec un(e) partenaire, préparez cinq questions à poser au professeur au sujet de sa routine quotidienne. Utilisez des verbes réfléchis.

> **Exemple**     **Est-ce que vous vous couchez tôt ou tard d'habitude?**
> **À quelle heure est-ce que vous vous couchez d'habitude?**

**G. Un week-end entre amis.** Demandez à votre partenaire ce qu'il/elle fait avec ses amis quand ils passent un week-end ensemble dans une autre ville.

> **Exemple**     se réveiller tôt ou tard
> — **Est-ce que vous vous réveillez tôt ou tard?**
> — **Nous nous réveillons tard. / On se réveille tard.**

1. se réveiller avant ou après dix heures
2. se lever tôt ou tard
3. se reposer plus souvent le matin, l'après-midi ou le soir
4. s'amuser plus souvent le matin, l'après-midi ou le soir
5. s'ennuyer quelquefois
6. se coucher tôt ou tard

**H. Vous faites du baby-sitting.** Vous faites du baby-sitting pour les deux enfants d'un(e) ami(e). Demandez ces renseignements à votre ami(e). Votre partenaire va jouer le rôle de votre ami(e) et imaginer ses réponses.

*Find out . . .*

> **Exemple**     *what time they wake up*
> — **À quelle heure est-ce qu'ils se réveillent?**
> — **Ils se réveillent vers huit heures.**

1. *if they get up right away*
2. *if they take a bath or a shower in the morning or the evening*
3. *if they rest in the afternoon*
4. *what time they go to bed*
5. *if they fall asleep easily*

## Stratégies et Lecture

*Using word families and watching out for **faux amis***

Recognizing words that belong to the same word family can make reading easier. Can you supply the missing meanings below?

| **la vie** | **vivre** | **l'arrêt** | **s'arrêter** |
|---|---|---|---|
| *life* | *to live* | *stop* | *???* |

| **se marier** | **le mariage** | **espérer** | **l'espoir** |
|---|---|---|---|
| *to marry* | *marriage* | *to hope* | *???* |

Using cognates and word families can help you understand new texts more easily. However, beware of **faux amis,** words that look like cognates but have different meanings. For example, you already know that **rester** does not mean *to rest*, but *to stay*. Use cognates, but if a word does not seem right in the context, look it up.

**A. Familles de mots.** Voilà quelques mots que vous allez voir dans l'histoire à la page 271. Servez-vous du sens des mots donnés pour déterminer le sens des autres mots.

| **rêver** | **un rêve** |
|---|---|
| *to dream* | *a dream* |
| **se souvenir de** | **des souvenirs** |
| *to remember* | *???* |
| **saluer** | **une salutation** |
| *to greet* | *???* |
| **dire** | **dit(e)** |
| *to say, to tell* | *said, told* |
| **connaître** | **connu(e)** |
| *to know* | *???* |
| **reconnaître** | **reconnu(e)** |
| *to recognize* | *???* |
| **une rose** | **un rosier** |
| *a rose* | *???* |

**B. Faux amis.** Donnez le sens des faux amis en caractères gras selon le contexte.

M. Dupont est dans un fauteuil au jardin quand une jolie jeune fille qui passe **attire** son attention. Il la **salue** et lui dit: «Bonjour, mademoiselle.» Cette fille ressemble à quelqu'un qu'il connaissait dans le passé et il commence à rêver. Il a de beaux **souvenirs** du temps où il était jeune. Il aimait une jeune fille et il **garde** toujours l'espoir de la revoir un jour.

CD 2-12

## Il n'est jamais trop tard!

*Rosalie Toulouse Richard, qui habite à Atlanta depuis 1945, retourne à Rouen avec sa petite-fille Rose. Son vieil ami, André Dupont, ne sait pas encore que Rosalie est à Rouen.*

Andr é Dupont a toujours aimé passer des heures à travailler dans son jardin. Il a une passion pour les roses et depuis des années, il plante des rosiers de toutes les variétés et de toutes les couleurs!

Ses rosiers font l'admiration de tous les gens du quartier et beaucoup d'entre eux passent devant chez lui pour regarder son beau jardin. Aujourd'hui, trois jeunes filles s'arrêtent devant son jardin et lui disent bonjour. Il reconnaît deux d'entre elles, ce sont les petites-filles de son ami Jean Toulouse, mais c'est la troisième qui attire son attention. Il ne l'a jamais vue, et pourtant il a l'impression de la connaître! Elle ressemble à quelqu'un... quelqu'un qu'il a connu il y a très longtemps.

Les souvenirs lui reviennent, comme si c'était hier. C'était en 1945, il avait dix-huit ans et il était amoureux fou d'une jolie jeune fille de son âge. Elle s'appelait Rosalie... ! Il voulait lui dire combien il l'aimait, mais il n'en avait pas le courage. Il était trop timide. Un beau jour, il s'est décidé à tout lui dire. Il a choisi des fleurs de son jardin pour en faire un bouquet, il a pris son vélo et il est allé chez Rosalie. Mais en arrivant, il a trouvé Rosalie en compagnie d'un soldat américain et elle regardait ce jeune soldat d'un regard de femme amoureuse. André, lui, est rentré chez lui sans jamais parler à Rosalie.

Quelques mois après, Rosalie s'est mariée avec le jeune Américain et ils sont partis vivre aux États-Unis. De temps en temps, André avait des nouvelles car le frère de Rosalie et lui étaient de bons amis. Il savait qu'elle habitait à Atlanta, qu'elle avait eu trois enfants, et il y a trois ans, il a appris que son mari était mort. Il gardait toujours l'espoir de la revoir, mais les années passaient et elle ne revenait toujours pas.

— Vos rosiers sont magnifiques, monsieur!

C'est Rosalie qui parle! En un instant, André Dupont revient au présent et ouvre les yeux. C'est la jeune fille qui parle... celle qu'il ne connaît pas.

— Rosalie???

— Moi, monsieur? Non, je m'appelle Rose. Rosalie, c'est ma grand-mère.

— Ta grand-mère?

— Oui. Vous connaissez ma grand-mère?

— Rosalie Toulouse? Oui, je la connais, mais...

— Eh bien, venez la voir, elle est chez son frère Jean! Je suis sûre qu'elle sera contente de revoir un ami d'ici! Allez, venez donc avec nous!

Quoi? C'est trop beau! Est-ce qu'il rêve? Rosalie, ici à Rouen! Comme la vie est à la fois belle et bizarre! Va-t-elle le reconnaître? A-t-il le courage de lui dire qu'il l'aime toujours, après toutes ces années? André Dupont choisit les plus belles roses de son jardin et en fait un magnifique bouquet. Il va enfin pouvoir les offrir à la femme pour qui il a planté tous ces rosiers au cours des années.

**Qui parle?** Qui parle: André, Rosalie ou Rose?

1. J'adore les fleurs et j'aime faire du jardinage.
2. J'ai eu trois enfants, et mon mari est mort il y a trois ans.
3. Je suis passée devant une maison où il y avait des roses splendides.
4. Un monsieur m'a parlé. Il connaît ma grand-mère mais il ne l'a pas vue depuis longtemps.
5. J'ai invité ce monsieur à venir nous voir.
6. En 1945, je me suis mariée avec un Américain et je suis allée vivre aux États-Unis.
7. J'étais amoureux de Rosalie mais je n'ai jamais eu le courage de le lui dire.
8. Je garde toujours l'espoir de dire à Rosalie que je l'aime.

# Talking about relationships

**NOTE DE GRAMMAIRE**

**Se souvenir de** is conjugated like **venir.**

| | |
|---|---|
| je | me souviens |
| tu | te souviens |
| il/elle/on | se souvient |
| nous | nous souvenons |
| vous | vous souvenez |
| ils/elles | se souviennent |

## La vie sentimentale

À l'invitation de Rose, André va chez les Toulouse et André et Rosalie **se rencontrent** pour la première fois depuis des années. Voilà **ce qui se passe.**

André et Rosalie se regardent.

Ils s'embrassent.

Ils se parlent pendant des heures et ils **se souviennent de** leur **jeunesse** ensemble. C'est **le coup de foudre!**

Ils se quittent vers sept heures.

Pendant les semaines qui **suivent,** André et Rosalie passent beaucoup de temps ensemble. C'est **le grand amour!**

Ils se retrouvent en ville chaque après-midi.

Quelquefois ils se disputent.

Mais **la plupart du temps ils s'entendent** bien.

**Enfin,** André et Rosalie **prennent une décision.** Ils vont se marier et vont **s'installer** à Rouen. Ils vont être très **heureux.**

CD 2-13

Un soir, Rosalie parle à sa petite-fille Rose de sa relation avec André.

ROSE: Alors, **mamie,** tu as passé une bonne journée?
ROSALIE: Oui. André et moi, nous sommes allés visiter le Mont-Saint-Michel.
ROSE: Alors, vous vous entendez bien?
ROSALIE: Très bien. Nous nous retrouvons tous les jours, nous passons des heures ensemble et nous nous parlons de tout. Nous ne nous disputons presque jamais.
ROSE: **Formidable!** Moi, je **rêve d'une telle** relation.
ROSALIE: Et ton petit ami et toi, ça va?
ROSE: Pas très bien. Nous nous disputons souvent et nous ne nous entendons pas très bien.
ROSALIE: **C'est dommage!**

---

**se rencontrer** *to meet each other (by chance), to run into each other*   **ce qui** *what*   **se passer** *to happen*
**se souvenir de** *to remember*   **la jeunesse** *youth*   **le coup de foudre** *love at first sight*   **suivent** (**suivre** *to follow*)
**le grand amour** *true love*   **la plupart du temps** *most of the time*   **s'entendre** *to get along*   **Enfin** *Finally*
**prendre une décision** *to make a decision*   **s'installer (à / dans)** *to settle (in), to move (into)*   **heureux (heureuse)** *happy*
**mamie** *grandma*   **Formidable!** *Great!*   **rêver (de)** *to dream (of)*   **un(e) tel(le)** *such a*   **C'est dommage!** *That's too bad!*

**A. Test.** Faites ce test pour savoir si vous êtes romantique.

# Êtes-vous romantique?

## I. Indiquez vos opinions sur ces sujets.

**1** Pensez-vous que le grand amour...
  **a.** arrive une fois dans la vie?
  **b.** n'existe pas?
  **c.** est sans importance?

**2** Pensez-vous qu'un couple peut s'aimer pour toujours?
  **a.** Certainement.
  **b.** Je ne sais pas, on peut essayer.
  **c.** Probablement pas: la vie est trop longue.

**3** Au restaurant, **vous voyez** des amoureux qui se regardent dans les yeux pendant tout le dîner. Vous trouvez ça...
  **a.** un peu bête mais charmant.
  **b.** ridicule.
  **c.** adorable.

## II. Comment êtes-vous en couple?

**1** Vous vous rencontrez **par hasard** et c'est le coup de foudre. Que pensez-vous?
  **a.** C'est juste un désir sexuel.
  **b.** C'est peut-être l'amour.
  **c.** **Attention!**

**2** Vous vous disputez. Quelle est la meilleure manière de vous réconcilier?
  **a.** Nous devons nous embrasser.
  **b.** Nous devons essayer de parler calmement du problème.
  **c.** Nous devons nous quitter pendant un certain temps.

**3** Vous vous adorez. Vous voulez...
  **a.** essayer de vous voir tous les jours.
  **b.** vous téléphoner tous les jours et vous voir trois ou quatre fois par semaine.
  **c.** vous retrouver le week-end, si vous n'avez pas d'autres projets.

**SCORE:**    **Partie I.** 1. a–2 points 2. a–2 points, b–1 point 3. c–2 points, a–1 point
    **Partie II.** 1. b–2 points, a–1 point 2. a–2 points, b–1 point 3. a–2 points, b–1 point

◆ Si vous avez 10–12 points, vous êtes une personne très (peut-être même un peu trop?) romantique. Attention! **Ne perdez pas votre temps** à attendre un amour parfait. Essayez d'être un peu plus réaliste, quand même.
◆ Si vous avez 6–9 points, vous êtes romantique, mais vous n'exagérez pas. Vous êtes prêt(e) à aimer quand le bon moment arrivera, mais vous ne perdez pas votre temps à chercher l'amour idéal partout.
◆ Si vous avez 0–5 points, vous êtes réaliste, cynique même! Ne voulez-vous pas mettre un peu plus de poésie dans votre vie?

**B. Meilleurs amis.** Parlez de votre meilleur(e) ami(e) et vous.

1. Nous nous parlons *tous les jours / une fois par semaine / ???.*
2. Nous nous retrouvons *tous les jours / une fois par semaine / rarement / ???.*
3. Nous nous entendons *toujours bien / bien la plupart du temps / ???.*
4. Nous nous disputons *tout le temps / quelquefois / rarement / ???.*

**C. Conversation.** Avec un(e) partenaire, relisez la conversation entre Rosalie et Rose en bas de la page précédente. Ensuite, changez la conversation pour parler de votre relation avec votre mari, votre femme, votre petit(e) ami(e), votre meilleur(e) ami(e) ou votre camarade de chambre.

Le Mont-Saint-Michel

---

**vous voyez** *you see*    **par hasard** *by chance*    **Attention!** *Watch out!*    **Ne perdez pas votre temps** *Don't waste your time*

**1.** When do you use a reciprocal verb?

**2.** What verbs can be made into reciprocal verbs? How would you say *to look at each other* or *to listen to each other*?

**3.** When a reflexive or reciprocal verb is used in the infinitive, does the reflexive pronoun change with the subject? How would you say *I am going to get up at 6:00? I am not going to get up at 6:00?*

**NOTE DE GRAMMAIRE**

Note that although the verbs **se fiancer** and **se marier** are reflexive, **divorcer** is not.

## Saying what people do for each other

*Les verbes réciproques au présent et les verbes réfléchis et réciproques au futur immédiat*

You have seen that reflexive verbs are used when someone is doing something to or for himself/herself. You use similar verbs to describe reciprocal actions; that is, to indicate that people are doing something to or for each other. Here are some reflexive and reciprocal verbs commonly used to describe relationships.

| | |
|---|---|
| s'aimer | *to like each other, to love each other* |
| se détester | *to hate each other* |
| se disputer | *to argue* |
| s'embrasser | *to kiss each other, to embrace each other* |
| s'entendre (bien / mal) | *to get along (well / badly) with each other* |
| se fiancer | *to get engaged* |
| se marier (avec) | *to get married (to)* |
| se quitter | *to leave each other* |
| se réconcilier | *to make up* |
| se regarder | *to look at each other* |
| se rencontrer | *to meet* (for the first time), *to run into each other* (by chance) |
| se retrouver | *to meet* (by design) |
| se téléphoner | *to telephone each other* |

The verb **s'entendre** *(to get along)* is a regular **-re** verb. You will learn how to conjugate other **-re** verbs in the next section on page 278. The forms of **s'entendre** are:

| **S'ENTENDRE** *(to get along)* | |
|---|---|
| je m'entends | nous nous entendons |
| tu t'entends | vous vous entendez |
| il/elle/on s'entend | ils/elles s'entendent |

Notice that most verbs indicating actions done to other people can be used reciprocally.

| | |
|---|---|
| téléphoner à quelqu'un *(to phone someone)* | Je téléphone **à Liz.** |
| se téléphoner *(to phone each other)* | Nous **nous** téléphonons. |
| regarder quelqu'un *(to look at someone)* | Je regarde **Jim.** |
| se regarder *(to look at each other)* | Nous **nous** regardons. |

Form the immediate future of reflexive and reciprocal verbs with the verb **aller,** as always, to say what someone is going to do.

| **SE LEVER** *(to get up)* | |
|---|---|
| je vais me lever | nous allons nous lever |
| tu vas te lever | vous allez vous lever |
| il/elle/on va se lever | ils/elles vont se lever |

When you use a reflexive or reciprocal verb in the infinitive, the reflexive pronoun varies with the subject. In the negative, put **ne... pas** around the conjugated verb.

**Je** ne vais pas **me** lever tôt.    **Nous** aimons **nous** retrouver au café.
**Tu** préfères **te** coucher tard.    **Vous** allez **vous** marier?

**A. Une histoire d'amour.** Isabelle, la cousine de Rose, rencontre Luc et ils tombent amoureux. Qu'est-ce qui se passe?

se téléphoner se regarder se marier s'embrasser
s'installer dans une maison se quitter se fiancer
se réconcilier se parler se disputer se retrouver au parc

Exemple  **Ils se téléphonent.**

1. 2.  3.

4.  5.  6.

7.  8.  9.

**B. Questions.** Rose veut en savoir plus *(to know more)* sur Isabelle et Luc. Avec un(e) partenaire, imaginez ses questions et les réponses qu'Isabelle lui donne.

Exemple se disputer
— **Est-ce que vous vous disputez souvent?**
— **Non, nous ne nous disputons pas souvent.**

1. se téléphoner
2. se retrouver
3. s'embrasser
4. s'entendre
5. s'aimer

tous les jours bien
souvent mal
quelquefois beaucoup
la plupart du temps ne… jamais

**C. Isabelle et Luc.** Tout va très bien entre Isabelle et Luc. Ils se parlent et ils se retrouvent en ville tous les jours. Est-ce qu'ils vont faire les choses suivantes demain?

> **Exemple**  se disputer
> **Non, ils ne vont pas se disputer.**

1. se téléphoner
2. se retrouver en ville
3. se parler de tout
4. bien s'entendre
5. s'ennuyer ensemble
6. s'embrasser

**D. Et demain chez Rose.** Dites ce que Rose va faire demain d'après les illustrations.

**Exemple**  ... vers neuf heures.
**Elle va se réveiller vers neuf heures.**

**1.** ... tout de suite.

**2.** ... la figure et les mains.

**3.** ... les dents.

**4.** ... les cheveux.

**5.** ... en jean.

**6.** ... vers deux heures du matin.

**E. Et toi?** Regardez chaque illustration de *D. Et demain chez Rose.* Demandez à un(e) partenaire s'il/si elle va faire la même chose demain.

**Exemple**  ... vers neuf heures.
— **Est-ce que tu vas te réveiller vers neuf heures?**
— **Oui, je vais me réveiller vers neuf heures.**
**Non, je ne vais pas me réveiller vers neuf heures.**

**F. Ce week-end.** Est-ce que ces personnes vont peut-être faire ces choses ce week-end?

>    Exemple    Moi, je... (se lever tôt)
>    **Moi, je vais me lever tôt. / Je ne vais pas me lever tôt.**

1.  Moi, je... (se réveiller tôt, se réveiller tard, se lever tout de suite, rester au lit quelques minutes, s'habiller vite, quitter la maison tôt, travailler, s'amuser samedi soir, rentrer tard samedi soir)
2.  Mon meilleur ami / Ma meilleure amie... (se lever tôt, prendre son petit déjeuner avec moi, se reposer dimanche soir)
3.  Mes amis et moi, nous... (se retrouver en ville, sortir ensemble, s'amuser ensemble, s'ennuyer ensemble)

**G. Partons en week-end.** Vous allez faire du camping avec un groupe d'amis ce week-end. Travaillez avec un petit groupe d'étudiants et faites des projets.

>    Exemple    **On va se réveiller tôt.**

se lever tôt / tard                         faire un feu *(fire)*
faire des randonnées *(to go hiking)*       **???**
se coucher tôt / tard                       dormir sous une tente
            faire du canoë *(to go canoeing)*
se laver dans la rivière *(river)*                  nager
aller à la pêche *(to fish)*          s'amuser
        se brosser les dents avec l'eau de la rivière

**H. Entretien.** Interviewez votre partenaire.

1.  Est-ce que tu te réveilles facilement ou avec difficulté? Tu te lèves tôt ou tard pendant la semaine en général? Tu te lèves tout de suite? À quelle heure est-ce que tu vas te lever demain?
2.  Après les cours, est-ce que tu préfères te reposer ou t'amuser avec des amis? Est-ce que tu vas te reposer ce soir après les cours? Et demain soir?
3.  Est-ce que tu te couches tôt ou tard pendant la semaine d'habitude? À quelle heure vas-tu te coucher ce soir? Vas-tu te lever tôt ce week-end? À quelle heure vas-tu te lever? Est-ce que tu préfères te lever tôt ou tard?

**1.** What ending do you add for each subject pronoun after dropping the -**re** from the infinitive of these verbs? What is the conjugation of **perdre**?

**2.** Which of these -**re** verbs are conjugated with **être** in the **passé composé?**

# Talking about activities

*Les verbes en -re*

Many verbs that end in -**re,** like **s'entendre,** follow a regular pattern of conjugation. Study the verb **attendre** *(to wait for)* to learn this pattern.

| ATTENDRE *(to wait for)* | |
|---|---|
| j'attend**s** | nous attend**ons** |
| tu attend**s** | vous attend**ez** |
| il/elle/on attend | ils/elles attend**ent** |

PASSÉ COMPOSÉ: **j'ai attendu**
IMPARFAIT: **j'attendais**

Notice that you do not use **pour** after **attendre** to say *for* whom or what you are waiting.

J'attends des amis. *I'm waiting for friends.*

The following are some common -**re** verbs.

| | |
|---|---|
| descendre | *to go down, to get off, to stay* (at a hotel) |
| entendre | *to hear* |
| s'entendre (bien / mal) avec | *to get along (well / badly) with* |
| perdre | *to lose, to waste* |
| perdre du temps | *to waste time* |
| se perdre | *to get lost* |
| rendre quelque chose | *to return something to someone,* |
| à quelqu'un | *to turn in something to someone* |
| rendre visite à quelqu'un | *to visit someone* |
| répondre (à) | *to answer, to respond* |
| vendre / revendre | *to sell / to sell back, to resell* |

**NOTE DE VOCABULAIRE**
Use **rendre visite à** or **aller voir** to say that you visit a person, and only use **visiter** to say that you visit a place.

In the **passé composé, descendre** and the reflexive verbs are conjugated with **être** as the auxiliary verb. The other verbs in this list are all conjugated with **avoir.**

J'ai rendu visite à une amie à Paris.    Je suis descendu(e) à l'hôtel Floride Étoile.

**A. Votre vie.** Est-ce que ces personnes font les choses suivantes?

> **Exemple**    Moi, je... (attendre l'autobus pour aller en cours)
> **Moi, je n'attends pas l'autobus pour aller en cours.**

1. Moi, je... (attendre l'autobus pour aller en cours, rendre souvent visite à mes parents, attendre la fin du semestre / trimestre avec impatience, revendre mes livres à la fin du semestre / trimestre)
2. En cours de français, nous... (rendre nos devoirs au professeur tous les jours, répondre aux questions du prof, attendre quelquefois le professeur, perdre du temps *[to waste time]*)
3. Mes amis (descendre souvent en ville le week-end, s'entendre bien, se rendre souvent visite)
4. Mon meilleur ami / Ma meilleure amie... (perdre quelquefois patience avec moi, s'entendre bien avec mes autres amis, perdre souvent ses choses, se perdre facilement)

**B. La routine de Rose.** Rose décrit *(describes)* sa routine quotidienne quand elle est chez elle. Complétez ses phrases comme indiqué.

Le matin, je (j') __1__ l'autobus devant mon appartement. Quelquefois, le bus
<sub>wait for</sub>
arrive en retard *(late)* et je __2__ patience. Je n'aime pas __3__! Quand le bus
<sub>lose</sub> <sub>to wait</sub>
arrive, je monte dedans *(inside)* et je __4__ à l'université. Je n'aime pas __5__
<sub>get off</sub> <sub>to waste</sub>
mon temps, alors je fais mes devoirs dans l'autobus. Quand je suis en cours, je

__6__ toujours bien aux questions du prof. Quand il __7__ mes réponses, il est
<sub>answer</sub> <sub>hears</sub>
toujours content! Il y a d'autres étudiants qui ne __8__ pas très bien mais le prof
<sub>answer</sub>
ne __9__ jamais patience avec nous. Nous ne __10__ pas notre temps en cours —
<sub>loses</sub> <sub>waste</sub>
nous travaillons bien! Après les cours, je vais souvent à mon magasin préféré où

on __11__ des livres et des CD. Quelquefois, je __12__ à mon ami Trentin. Nous
<sub>sell</sub> <sub>visit</sub>
__13__ bien.
<sub>get along</sub>

Rose avait plus ou moins la même routine quand elle avait 15 ans. Servez-vous des verbes donnés pour dire quatre choses que Rose faisait quand elle avait 15 ans. Utilisez l'imparfait.

> **Exemple**   attendre
> **Le matin, elle attendait l'autobus.**

1. perdre
2. répondre
3. rendre visite à
4. s'entendre bien

**C. Et toi?** Choisissez le verbe logique et complétez les questions. Ensuite, posez les questions à votre partenaire. Utilisez le présent ou le passé composé comme indiqué.

## AU PRÉSENT

1. Est-ce que tu _____ souvent visite à tes parents? (rendre, entendre)
2. Ta famille et toi, est-ce que vous _____ bien la plupart du temps? (perdre, s'entendre)
3. Est-ce que tu _____ souvent patience avec tes parents? Est-ce qu'ils _____ souvent patience avec toi? (perdre, répondre)
4. Est-ce que tu _____ tes prochaines vacances avec impatience? (attendre, entendre)
5. Est-ce que tu _____ facilement quand tu es dans une autre ville? (se perdre, vendre)
6. Quand tu voyages avec des amis, est-ce que vous _____ dans un hôtel de luxe? (vendre, descendre)

## AU PASSÉ COMPOSÉ

7. Est-ce que tu _____ visite à tes parents récemment? (revendre, rendre)
8. La dernière fois que tu as vu tes parents, est-ce qu'ils _____ patience avec toi? (perdre, vendre)
9. La dernière fois que vous êtes partis en week-end ensemble, est-ce que vous _____ à un hôtel? (descendre, entendre)

# Talking about what you did and used to do

## Les activités d'hier

Rose parle de ce qu'elle a fait hier.

**Le réveil a sonné** et je me suis réveillée.

Je me suis levée.

J'ai pris un bain.

**NOTE DE GRAMMAIRE**

**Se promener** is a spelling change verb like **acheter**: **je me promène, nous nous promenons.**

Je me suis brossé les dents.

Je me suis peignée.

Je me suis habillée.

J'ai passé le reste de la journée avec ma cousine et son nouvel ami.

Nous nous sommes promenés.

**Nous nous sommes arrêtés** au restaurant pour manger.

Nous nous sommes bien amusés.

Nous nous sommes quittés vers 10 heures et je me suis couchée vers 11 heures.

**Le réveil** *The alarm clock* **sonner** *to ring* **s'arrêter** *to stop*

Rose parle à sa cousine, Isabelle, qui **raconte** comment elle a rencontré son ami, Luc.

CD 2-14

ROSE:       Alors, Luc et toi, vous vous êtes rencontrés où?

ISABELLE:   J'étais au parc et Luc était à côté de moi. On s'est vus et on s'est parlé un peu. Quelques jours plus tard, il était dans une librairie où j'achetais un livre et **on s'est reconnus.** Il m'a demandé si je voulais aller prendre un verre et j'ai accepté son invitation. On a passé le reste de la journée ensemble.

ROSE:       Vous vous êtes bien entendus, **donc?**

ISABELLE:   **Parfaitement** bien. On s'est très bien amusés et on s'est retrouvés le lendemain pour aller au cinéma. **Depuis cela,** on s'est téléphoné ou on s'est vus presque tous les jours.

---

**A. Récemment.** Quand avez-vous fait ces choses?

| | | |
|---|---|---|
| **ce matin** | **hier matin** | **il y a deux semaines** |
| **cet après-midi** | **hier soir** | **(un mois, longtemps... )** |
| **???** | **lundi dernier** | **???** |

1. Le réveil a sonné et je me suis levé(e) tout de suite...
2. J'ai pris un bain ou une douche...
3. Je me suis brossé les cheveux ou je me suis peigné(e)...
4. Mes amis et moi, nous nous sommes bien amusés ensemble...
5. Nous nous sommes promenés en ville...
6. Je me suis arrêté(e) dans un fast-food pour manger...
7. Je me suis couché(e) après minuit...

**B. Ils se sont retrouvés.** Décrivez la première fois que Rosalie et André se sont revus après toutes ces années en mettant ces phrases dans l'ordre logique.

**1.**    **2.**    **3.**    **4.**

_____ Ils se sont embrassés.

___1___ André et Rosalie se sont vus.

_____ Ils se sont quittés.

_____ Ils se sont reconnus.

_____ Ils se sont parlé pendant plusieurs heures et ils se sont souvenus du passé.

**C. Conversation.** Avec un(e) partenaire, relisez la conversation entre Rose et sa cousine en haut de la page. Ensuite, parlez avec votre partenaire de comment vous avez rencontré votre meilleur(e) ami(e) ou votre petit(e) ami(e).

---

**raconter** *to tell*   **on s'est reconnus** (**passé composé** of **se reconnaître** *to recognize each other*)   **donc** *then, thus, so*
**Parfaitement** *Perfectly*   **Depuis cela** *since then* (**cela** *that*)

**1.** Do you use **être** or **avoir** as the auxiliary verb with reflexive and reciprocal verbs in the **passé composé**?

**2.** Where are reflexive pronouns placed with respect to the auxiliary verb? How do you conjugate **s'amuser** in the **passé composé**?

**3.** Where do you place **ne... pas** in the negative? How do you say *I didn't wake up early*?

**4.** When does the past participle agree with the reflexive pronoun and subject? When does it not agree? What are three verbs that you know that do not have agreement?

**NOTES DE GRAMMAIRE**

**1.** When **on** means *we*, its verb may either be left in the masculine singular form **(on s'est levé)** or it may agree **(on s'est levé[e][s])**. Either form is considered correct.
**2.** Note the past participles of these verbs:
**Je me suis souvenu(e).**
**Je me suis endormi(e).**
**Je me suis ennuyé(e).**
**Nous nous sommes entendu(e)s.**

# Saying what people did

*Les verbes réfléchis et réciproques au passé composé*

All reflexive and reciprocal verbs have **être** as the auxiliary verb in the **passé composé.** Always place the reflexive pronoun directly before the auxiliary verb. In the negative, place **ne** just before the reflexive pronoun and **pas** or **jamais** after **être.**

| SE LEVER | NE PAS SE LEVER |
|---|---|
| je me suis levé(e) | je ne me suis pas levé(e) |
| tu t'es levé(e) | tu ne t'es pas levé(e) |
| il s'est levé | il ne s'est pas levé |
| elle s'est levée | elle ne s'est pas levée |
| on s'est levé(e)(s) | on ne s'est pas levé(e)(s) |
| nous nous sommes levé(e)s | nous ne nous sommes pas levé(e)s |
| vous vous êtes levé(e)(s) | vous ne vous êtes pas levé(e)(s) |
| ils se sont levés | ils ne se sont pas levés |
| elles se sont levées | elles ne se sont pas levées |

In the **passé composé,** the past participle agrees in gender and number with the reflexive pronoun (and the subject) when it is the direct object of the verb.

Rosalie **s**'est lev**é**e tôt.          André et Rosalie **se** sont mari**é**s.

In this chapter, make the past participle agree except in these cases:

- There is no agreement when a reflexive verb is followed by a noun that is the direct object of the verb. Past participles of verbs like **se laver, se maquiller,** or **se brosser** do not agree with the subject when they are followed by the name of a part of the body.

Rose et Rosalie se sont lav**ées.**     BUT     Rose et Rosalie se sont lavé **les mains.**
Rose s'est maquill**ée.**                          Rose s'est maquillé **les yeux.**

- With the verbs **se parler, se téléphoner,** and **s'écrire,** there is no agreement because the reflexive pronoun is an *indirect* object, not a *direct* object.

Ils se sont parlé.     Nous nous sommes téléphoné.     Ils se sont écrit.

**A. Hier chez Henri et Patricia.** Patricia, la cousine de Rose, parle de ce qu'elle a fait hier. Qu'est-ce qu'elle dit?

Exemple     **Je me suis réveillée à six heures.**

Exemple    Je...          1. Je...          2. Je...

**3.** Je...  **4.** Je...  **5.** Henri et moi, nous...

**B. Hier.** Regardez les illustrations de *A. Hier chez Henri et Patricia* et expliquez ce que Patricia a fait.

**Exemple**  **Patricia s'est réveillée à six heures.**

**C. Et toi?** Demandez à votre partenaire s'il/si elle a fait les choses suivantes hier.

**Exemple**    se lever tôt
   — **Est-ce que tu t'es levé(e) tôt hier?**
   — **Oui, je me suis levé(e) tôt hier.**
   **Non, je ne me suis pas levé(e) tôt hier.**

**1.** se réveiller tôt
**2.** se lever tout de suite
**3.** prendre un café au lit
**4.** prendre un bain ou une douche
**5.** se laver les cheveux

**6.** passer la soirée à la maison
**7.** s'ennuyer
**8.** s'amuser
**9.** se coucher tard
**10.** s'endormir facilement

**D. Je veux tout savoir.** Utilisez les verbes suivants pour poser des questions à votre partenaire sur ses interactions avec son (sa) meilleur(e) ami(e) cette semaine.

**Exemple**    se téléphoner
   — **Est-ce que vous vous êtes téléphoné cette semaine?**
   — **Oui, on s'est téléphoné hier.**
   **Non, on ne s'est pas téléphoné hier.**

se retrouver en ville   ???   se promener au parc
se voir beaucoup   se parler   se disputer
s'ennuyer   s'amuser

**E. Entretien.** Posez ces questions à votre partenaire.

**1.** À quelle heure est-ce que tu t'es couché(e) hier soir? Est-ce que tu as bien dormi? Jusqu'à quelle heure est-ce que tu as dormi ce matin? Est-ce que tu t'es levé(e) facilement?

**2.** À quelle heure est-ce que tu dois te réveiller les jours du cours de français? À quelle heure est-ce que tu aimes te lever? À quelle heure est-ce que tu t'es levé(e) ce matin?

**3.** Avec qui est-ce que tu es sorti(e) récemment? Où est-ce que vous vous êtes retrouvé(e)s? Où est-ce que vous êtes allé(e)s ensemble? Qu'est-ce que vous avez fait? Est-ce que vous vous êtes bien amusé(e)s?

**1.** How do you form the **imparfait** of all verbs except **être?** What is the **imparfait** of **je m'amuse?** of **je ne m'amuse pas?**

**2.** Do you use the **imparfait** or the **passé composé** to say what happened on a specific occasion? to say how things used to be?

# Saying what people did and used to do

*Les verbes réfléchis et réciproques à l'imparfait et reprise de l'usage du passé composé et de l'imparfait*

Just as with all other verbs (except **être**), the **imparfait** of reflexive verbs is formed by dropping the **-ons** from the present tense **nous** form and adding the endings **-ais, -ais, -ait, -ions, -iez, -aient.**

| **SE LEVER** | **NE PAS SE LEVER** |
| --- | --- |
| je me levais | je ne me levais pas |
| tu te levais | tu ne te levais pas |
| il/elle/on se levait | il/elle/on ne se levait pas |
| nous nous levions | nous ne nous levions pas |
| vous vous leviez | vous ne vous leviez pas |
| ils/elles se levaient | ils/elles ne se levaient pas |

When talking about your life in the past, remember to use the **imparfait** to tell *what things were like in general* or *what was going on when something else happened* and the **passé composé** to tell *what happened on specific occasions* or to recount *a sequence of events.* Before doing the exercises in this section, review the specific uses of the **passé composé** and the **imparfait** on page 242.

Ce matin, **je me suis levé(e)** à six heures.
Quand j'étais au lycée, **je me levais** à sept heures.

**A. À seize ans.** Parlez de votre routine quotidienne à l'âge de 16 ans.

    **Exemple**    se réveiller souvent tôt
        **À l'âge de seize ans, je me réveillais souvent tôt.**
        **Je ne me réveillais pas souvent tôt.**

1. se réveiller souvent avant six heures
2. se lever facilement
3. prendre un bain / une douche le matin
4. se laver les cheveux tous les jours
5. prendre toujours le petit déjeuner
6. aller toujours en cours
7. s'ennuyer souvent en cours

**B. Et hier?** Utilisez les verbes de l'exercice précédent pour parler de ce que vous avez fait hier.

    **Exemple**    se réveiller tôt
        **Hier, je me suis réveillé(e) tôt.**
        **Je ne me suis pas réveillé(e) tôt.**

**C. Et alors?** Rosalie parle de ce qui s'est passé hier. Complétez ses phrases logiquement en mettant les verbes donnés au passé composé ou à l'imparfait.

> **Exemple**    Hier matin, je (j') _____ (être) fatiguée et alors,
> je _____ (rester) au lit.
> Hier matin, j'**étais** fatiguée et alors, je **suis restée** au lit.

1. Je (J') _____ (vouloir) préparer le petit déjeuner et alors, je _____ (se laver) les mains.
2. Vers midi, André et moi, nous _____ (avoir) faim et alors, nous _____ (se préparer) des sandwichs.
3. Nous _____ (boire) deux bouteilles d'eau minérale aussi parce que nous _____ (avoir) très soif.
4. Après, André _____ (se coucher) parce qu'il _____ (être) fatigué.
5. Il _____ (se lever) vers trois heures parce qu'il n' _____ (être) plus fatigué.
6. Il _____ (faire) très beau. Alors, nous _____ (se promener).
7. Quand nous _____ (rentrer), Rose et ses copains _____ (être) à la maison.
8. Nous _____ (se quitter) assez tôt parce que nous _____ (vouloir) nous reposer.

**D. Le mariage d'André et de Rosalie.** André et Rosalie se sont enfin mariés. Décrivez le jour de leur mariage en mettant les verbes donnés au passé composé ou à l'imparfait.

Le jour de son mariage, Rosalie ___1___ (se lever) tôt. André ___2___ (arriver) vers neuf heures mais tout de suite après, il ___3___ (se souvenir) d'une course qu'il ___4___ (devoir) faire et il ___5___ (repartir).

Il ___6___ (être) trois heures quand André ___7___ (revenir). La cérémonie ___8___ (commencer) à quatre heures. Tous les invités *(guests)* ___9___ (être) dans le jardin. Il ___10___ (faire) beau et Rosalie et André ___11___ (être) contents. Rosalie ___12___ (porter) une jolie robe beige et André ___13___ (porter) un costume noir. Rosalie ___14___ (être) très jolie! Après la cérémonie, les amis ___15___ (rester) et ils ___16___ (manger) du gâteau *(cake)*. Ils ___17___ (s'amuser) bien quand tout d'un coup il ___18___ (commencer) à pleuvoir et alors, ils ___19___ (devoir) rentrer dans la maison.

André ___20___ (partir) et il ___21___ (revenir) avec assez de chaises pour tout le monde *(everyone)*. Vers huit heures les invités ___22___ (partir). André et Rosalie ___23___ (se regarder) et ils ___24___ (commencer) à sourire *(to smile)*. Ils ___25___ (être) fatigués mais très, très heureux.

**E. Entretien.** Interviewez votre partenaire.

1. Est-ce que tu t'entendais bien avec tes parents quand tu avais quinze ans? Qu'est ce que vous faisiez en famille? Est-ce que vous vous disputiez quelquefois? Est-ce que vous vous êtes disputés récemment?
2. À quelle heure est-ce que tu t'es réveillé(e) ce matin? Est-ce que tu t'es levé(e) tout de suite? Qu'est-ce que tu as fait ensuite? À quelle heure est-ce que tu te levais quand tu étais au lycée? Est-ce que tu te levais facilement?
3. Avec qui est-ce que tu es sorti(e) récemment? Où est-ce que vous êtes allé(e)s ensemble? Qu'est-ce que vous avez fait? Est-ce que vous vous êtes bien amusé(e)s? Avec qui aimais-tu sortir quand tu étais au lycée? Qu'est-ce que vous aimiez faire pour vous amuser?

# Describing traits and characteristics

>Note
*culturelle*

En France, un peu plus de 5 personnes sur mille se marient chaque année. Aux États-Unis, c'est 9 personnes sur mille. 39% des mariages en France se terminent en divorce comparé à 50% aux États-Unis. Les Français ont 31 ans et les Françaises 29 ans en moyenne *(on average)* quand ils se marient pour la première fois. À votre avis, pourquoi est-ce qu'il y a plus de mariages et de divorces aux États-Unis qu'en France? À quel âge est-ce qu'on se marie en moyenne dans votre région?

## Le caractère

### Rencontres en ligne: Test de compatibilité

**Rangez** chaque groupe de réponses de 1 (la réponse qui **exprime** le mieux vos sentiments) à 4 (la réponse qui exprime le moins bien vos sentiments).

Je préfère partager la vie avec quelqu'un qui **s'intéresse**...

1 2 3 4    aux arts
1 2 3 4    au sport
1 2 3 4    à la politique
1 2 3 4    à la nature

Je préfère quelqu'un qui cultive...

1 2 3 4    sa spiritualité
1 2 3 4    son **corps**
1 2 3 4    son **esprit**
1 2 3 4    sa vie professionnelle

Un trait que je cherche chez un(e) parte-naire, c'est...

1 2 3 4    un bon sens de l'humour
1 2 3 4    la passion
1 2 3 4    la beauté
1 2 3 4    **la compréhension**

Un trait que je ne **supporte** pas chez une autre personne, c'est...

1 2 3 4    l'indécision *(f)*
1 2 3 4    l'inflexibilité *(f)*
1 2 3 4    **l'insensibilité** *(f)*
1 2 3 4    la vanité

**Ce que** je supporte le moins dans une relation, c'est...

1 2 3 4    la jalousie
1 2 3 4    l'indifférence *(f)*
1 2 3 4    l'infidélité *(f)*
1 2 3 4    la violence

Chez un(e) partenaire, ce qui a le moins d'importance pour moi, c'est...

1 2 3 4    son argent
1 2 3 4    sa profession
1 2 3 4    sa religion
1 2 3 4    son **aspect physique**

**ranger** *to arrange, to order*   **exprimer** *to express*   **s'intéresser à** *to be interested in*   **le corps** *the body*
**l'esprit** *(m) the mind, the spirit*   **la compréhension** *understanding*   **supporter** *to bear, to tolerate, to put up with*
**l'insensibilité** *insensitivity*   **Ce que** *What*   **l'aspect physique** *(m) physical appearance*

Rose parle à sa cousine, Isabelle, de son petit ami, Luc.

CD 2-15

ROSE: Alors, tu as trouvé **le bonheur** avec ton nouvel ami, Luc? Il est comment?

ISABELLE: Il a un bon sens de l'humour et il est sympa. Son seul trait que je n'aime pas, c'est qu'il est un peu **jaloux** si je ne passe pas tout mon temps avec lui.

ROSE: Vous vous intéressez aux mêmes choses?

ISABELLE: Oui et non. On aime plus ou moins la même musique et les mêmes films et il s'intéresse à la politique comme moi, mais il est très **conservateur** et moi, tu sais, je suis plutôt libérale.

---

**A. Et vous?** Changez les mots en italique pour décrire votre propre situation ou pour exprimer votre opinion.

1. J'ai beaucoup d'amis qui s'intéressent *au sport.*
2. Je ne m'intéresse pas du tout *à la politique.*
3. Je ne supporte pas quelqu'un qui *parle tout le temps des autres.*
4. La plupart de mes amis sont *libéraux.*
5. Dans une relation, je supporte *l'infidélité* moins bien que *la jalousie.*
6. Pour moi, la beauté est *plus* importan*te* que le sens de l'humour.
7. Je pense que *la religion* d'une personne est plus importante que *sa profession.*

**B. Entretien.** Interviewez votre partenaire.

1. Est-ce que tu t'intéresses au sport? aux arts? au cinéma? à la politique? à la philosophie? Est-ce que tu t'ennuies si quelqu'un parle de ces choses?
2. Est-ce que tu passes plus de temps à cultiver ton corps, ton esprit, ta spiritualité ou ta vie professionnelle? Qu'est-ce que tu fais pour le (la) cultiver?
3. Où est-ce que tu as rencontré ton (ta) meilleur(e) ami(e)? Est-ce qu'il/elle a un bon sens de l'humour? Quels sont ses meilleurs traits? A-t-il/elle des traits que tu n'aimes pas? Est-ce qu'il/elle fait des choses quelquefois que tu ne supportes pas? Est-ce que vous vous disputez de temps en temps?

**C. Test de compatibilité.** Travaillez avec un(e) partenaire pour préparer deux questions supplémentaires pour le test de compatibilité.

> Exemple  **Quelle activité aimez-vous le moins faire avec une autre personne?**
>
> 1 2 3 4   faire la cuisine
> 1 2 3 4   faire de l'exercice
> 1 2 3 4   faire du shopping
> 1 2 3 4   voyager

**D. Conversation.** Avec un(e) partenaire, relisez la conversation entre Rose et Isabelle en haut de la page. Ensuite, changez la conversation pour parler d'un(e) ami(e), de votre petit(e) ami(e) ou de votre mari ou femme. Si vous préférez, vous pouvez commencer la conversation en disant: **Alors, tu passes beaucoup de temps avec...** (au lieu de dire: **Alors, tu as trouvé le bonheur avec...** ).

---

**le bonheur** *happiness*   **jaloux (jalouse)** *jealous*   **conservateur (conservatrice)** *conservative*

**1.** Which relative pronoun functions as the subject of a verb? Which one functions as the direct object of a verb? Which one replaces the preposition **de** and its object?

**2.** Can **qui, que,** and **dont** all be used for both people and things?

**3.** Where are relative clauses placed with respect to the noun they describe?

**NOTE DE GRAMMAIRE**

Remember that past participles agree with preceding direct objects and therefore agree with the noun that **que** represents: **Je sors avec une femme que j'ai rencontrée pendant mes vacances.**

# Specifying which one

## Les pronoms relatifs *qui, que* et *dont*

Sometimes you need to use a whole phrase to clarify which person or object you are talking about. The phrase that describes the noun is the relative clause. The word that begins the phrase, referring back to the noun described, is a relative pronoun.

Je sors avec une femme
{
**qui** est beaucoup plus âgée que moi.
**que** j'ai rencontrée pendant mes vacances.
**dont** je suis amoureux.
}

*I'm going out with a woman*
{
*who is a lot older than I am.*
*that I met during my vacation.*
*with whom I'm in love.*
}

The relative pronouns **qui, que,** and **dont** are all used for both people and things. The choice depends on how the pronoun functions in the relative clause.

- Use **qui** for both people or things when they are the *subject* of the relative clause. Since **qui** is the subject, it is followed by a verb and it can mean *that, which,* or *who.*

Note how relative pronouns are used to combine two sentences talking about the same thing. The relative clause is placed immediately after the noun it describes.

> **Mon ami** vient avec nous ce soir. **Mon ami** travaille avec moi.
> Mon ami **qui** travaille avec moi vient avec nous ce soir.

> Tu vas mettre **la robe? Cette robe** est sur ton lit.
> Tu vas mettre la robe **qui** est sur ton lit?

- Use **que (qu')** for people or things when they are the *direct object* in the relative clause. **Que (qu')** can mean *that, which,* or *whom,* or it may be omitted in English.

> **Mon ami** vient avec nous ce soir. J'ai invité **cet ami.**
> Mon ami **que** j'ai invité vient avec nous ce soir.

> Tu dois mettre **cette robe.** Tu **l'**as achetée hier.
> Tu dois mettre la robe **que** tu as achetée hier.

Note that the pronoun **que** changes to **qu'** before a vowel sound, but **qui** does not change.

- Use **dont** to replace the preposition **de** + *a person or thing* in relative clauses with verbs such as the following. It can mean *whom, of (about, with) whom, whose, that,* or *of (about, with) which.*

| | |
|---|---|
| avoir besoin de | faire la connaissance de |
| avoir envie de | parler de |
| avoir peur de | rêver de |
| être amoureux (amoureuse) de | se souvenir de |
| être jaloux (jalouse) de | tomber amoureux (amoureuse) de |

> **Mon ami** est un homme très sympa. Tu vas tomber amoureuse **de cet homme.**
> Mon ami est un homme très sympa **dont** tu vas tomber amoureuse.

> **Cette robe** est sale. Tu parles **de cette robe.**
> La robe **dont** tu parles est sale.

**A. Préférences.** Posez des questions à votre partenaire comme dans l'exemple. Utilisez le pronom **qui** et conjuguez le verbe.

> **Exemple**     les personnes (avoir un bon sens de l'humour, avoir beaucoup d'argent)
> — **Est-ce que tu préfères les personnes qui ont un bon sens de l'humour ou les personnes qui ont beaucoup d'argent?**
> — **Je préfère les personnes qui ont un bon sens de l'humour.**

1. les amis (sortir tout le temps, rester à la maison)
2. les films (avoir beaucoup d'action, avoir peu de violence)
3. les voitures (être grandes et confortables, être plus économiques)
4. les amis (parler de leurs problèmes, ne pas parler de leurs problèmes)
5. les personnes (cultiver leur corps, cultiver leur esprit)

**B. Encore des préférences.** Posez des questions à votre partenaire comme dans l'exemple. Utilisez le pronom relatif **que (qu')**.

> **Exemple**     les personnes (tu rencontres au musée, tu rencontres en boîte)
> — **Est-ce que tu préfères les personnes que tu rencontres au musée ou les personnes que tu rencontres en boîte?**
> — **Je préfère les personnes que je rencontre en boîte.**

1. les personnes (on rencontre au club de gym, on rencontre à la bibliothèque)
2. les activités (on fait seul, on fait en groupe)
3. la musique (on fait maintenant, on faisait il y a vingt ans)
4. les voyages (tu fais avec ta famille, tu fais avec tes amis)
5. les vêtements (tu portes aujourd'hui, tu as mis hier)

**C. Test psychologique.** Imaginez qu'un psychologue vous demande de nommer les choses suivantes. Quelle est votre réponse?

Nommez…

1. une chose dont vous avez envie en ce moment.
2. une chose dont vous avez peur dans la vie.
3. une chose dont vous avez besoin dans une relation.
4. une chose dont vous rêvez.
5. un événement *(event)* passé dont vous vous souvenez bien.
6. un trait d'une autre personne dont vous êtes jaloux (jalouse).
7. une personne dont vous voudriez faire la connaissance et une chose dont vous voudriez parler avec cette personne.

**D. Qui est-ce?** Sur une feuille de papier, écrivez le nom d'une des personnes suivantes: **votre petit(e) ami(e), meilleur(e) ami(e), mari, femme, père, mère, frère** ou **sœur.** Votre partenaire va utiliser un élément de chaque colonne pour poser cinq questions et ensuite il/elle va deviner la personne sur votre feuille de papier.

| | | |
|---|---|---|
| | | est marié? |
| | | tu te souviens depuis toujours? |
| | | tu embrasses souvent? |
| | qui | est plus âgé ou plus jeune que toi? |
| C'est quelqu'un | que | tu as rencontré à l'école ou à l'université? |
| | dont | tu es tombé(e) amoureux (amoureuse)? |
| | | habite chez toi? |
| | | a les mêmes parents (enfants, amis) que toi? |
| | | sort quelquefois en boîte avec toi? |

## Reprise

*Talking about daily life and relationships*

Dans le **Chapitre 7,** vous avez appris à parler de votre routine quotidienne et des relations personnelles. Maintenant vous allez réviser ce que vous avez appris.

**A. En cours de français.** D'abord, dites si ces personnes font les choses indiquées en cours de français. Ensuite, dites si ces mêmes personnes ont fait ces choses la dernière fois que vous étiez en cours.

1. les étudiants / répondre bien aux questions du professeur
2. le professeur / perdre patience avec les étudiants
3. les étudiants / s'entendre bien
4. nous / perdre du temps en cours
5. je / rendre visite au professeur dans son bureau avant le cours
6. je / rendre les devoirs au professeur

**B. En cours.** Qu'est-ce qui se passe les jours du cours de français? Formez des questions et posez-les à votre partenaire.

> **Exemple**  tu / s'amuser en cours
> — **Est-ce que tu t'amuses en cours?**
> — **Oui, je m'amuse en cours.**
> **Non, je ne m'amuse pas en cours.**

Les jours du cours de français...

1. tu / se lever tôt
2. tu / s'ennuyer en cours
3. tu / s'endormir en cours
4. les autres étudiants et toi, vous / s'amuser bien en cours
5. vous / se disputer
6. vous / se retrouver après les cours
7. les autres étudiants / s'intéresser au cours
8. ils / s'entendre bien
9. le prof / s'amuser en cours
10. le prof / s'endormir en cours

**C. Et au dernier cours?** Demandez à votre partenaire si chacun a fait les choses indiquées dans **B. En cours** au dernier cours de français.

Au dernier cours de français...

> **Exemple**  tu / s'amuser en cours
> — **Est-ce que tu t'es amusé(e) en cours?**
> — **Oui, je me suis amusé(e) en cours.**
> **Non, je ne me suis pas amusé(e) en cours.**

**D. Samedi prochain.** Dites si chacun va faire les choses indiquées samedi prochain.

> **Exemple**  je / se réveiller avant six heures
> **Je vais me réveiller avant six heures.**
> **Je ne vais pas me réveiller avant six heures.**

1. je / se lever tôt
2. je / se laver les cheveux
3. mes amis et moi, nous / sortir ensemble
4. nous / s'amuser
5. je / se coucher tôt

**E. Entretien.** D'abord, complétez les questions avec le pronom relatif convenable. Ensuite, interviewez votre partenaire.

1. As-tu plus d'amis _____ tu as rencontrés à l'université ou au lycée? Quand tu sors avec tes amis, quels sont les sujets de conversation _____ vous parlez le plus souvent? Est-ce que tu t'intéresses à des choses _____ tes amis trouvent ennuyeuses ou est-ce que vous vous intéressez aux mêmes choses? As-tu des amis _____ se disputent souvent? Pourquoi?

2. Est-ce que tu as beaucoup d'amis _____ sont mariés? Es-tu marié(e)? Est-ce que tu t'es marié(e) avec la première personne _____ tu es tombé(e) amoureux (amoureuse)? Est-ce que le mariage est quelque chose _____ tu trouves important ou _____ n'est pas important pour toi? Pourquoi?

3. Qu'est-ce qu'on doit faire pour avoir une relation _____ dure *(lasts)?* Y a-t-il des choses _____ tu as peur dans une relation? Est-ce que tu préfères être avec quelqu'un _____ est jaloux ou indifférent?

**F. L'histoire de Rosalie.** Racontez l'histoire de Rosalie en mettant les verbes donnés à l'imparfait ou au passé composé.

Une jeune fille qui ___1___ (s'appeler) Rosalie ___2___ (habiter) à la campagne près de Rouen. Quand elle ___3___ (avoir) 18 ans, Rosalie ___4___ (finir) ses études et elle ___5___ (devenir) professeur de musique.

En 1944, un jeune soldat américain ___6___ (venir) en France et un jour ce jeune homme et Rosalie ___7___ (se rencontrer). Ils ___8___ (se voir) et ils ___9___ (se parler). Ils ___10___ (passer) des heures ensemble. À partir de ce jour-là *(From that day on),* Rosalie et son jeune soldat ___11___ (se retrouver) tous les jours. Le soldat ___12___ (venir) chez Rosalie ou ils ___13___ (se retrouver) en ville. Finalement, ils ___14___ (se marier) et ils ___15___ (aller) s'installer à Atlanta. Leur vie ensemble ___16___ (être) très heureuse.

Après la mort de son mari, Rosalie ___17___ (revenir) en France avec sa petite-fille, Rose. Un jour, Rose ___18___ (se promener) avec ses cousines quand elle ___19___ (commencer) à parler avec un monsieur. Ce monsieur, André Dupont, ___20___ (être) l'ancien ami de Rosalie. Il ___21___ (se souvenir) très bien de Rosalie parce qu'il ___22___ (être) amoureux d'elle quand il ___23___ (avoir) 18 ans.

Rosalie ___24___ (être) chez son frère Jean quand elle ___25___ (revoir) André. Ils ___26___ (se voir) et ils ___27___ (tomber) amoureux.

# LECTURE ET COMPOSITION

## Lecture: *Tous les matins, je me lève*

Comment est-ce que vous passez votre matinée? Vous allez lire des interviews du magazine *Vogue Hommes* faites il y a quelques années avec Nicolas Sarkozy, ministre de l'Intérieur français, et Alain de Pouzhilac, President-directeur général du groupe de communication Havas. Avant de lire les interviews, faites cet exercice.

**Familles de mots.** Devinez le sens des mots en caractères gras.

| |
|---|
| s'endormir |
| se réveiller |
| rêver |
| la banque |

Je me réveille tôt mais j'aime **me rendormir** quelques minutes.
L'heure du **réveil** chez nous est entre sept et huit heures.
Quand je suis d'humeur **rêveuse**, j'aime prendre un bain chaud.
Mon ami est **banquier**. Il travaille dans une banque en ville.

---

### NICOLAS SARKOZY

*Prêt en trente-cinq minutes.*

**Heure du réveil?**
Entre 6h30 et 6h45. J'adore me lever tôt parce que j'ai l'impression de gagner du temps dans la journée.

**Nombre d'heures de sommeil?**
Sept heures.

**Quelle est la première chose que vous faites en vous levant?**
Je vais dans ma salle de bains.

**La radio?**
J'adore écouter la radio et **zapper;** je passe d'Europe 1 à RTL ou France Inter.

**Le petit déjeuner?**
Jamais de petit déjeuner à la maison. Je suis un adepte des petits déjeuners d'affaires dans les grands hôtels, mon préféré est le George V, ou dans les restaurants. J'aime **traîner** le matin dans les grands hôtels parisiens. Et puis un petit déjeuner, c'est mieux qu'un déjeuner, parce qu'en une heure on a généralement terminé.

J'ai beaucoup d'appétit. **J'avale** une omelette au fromage et je bois du thé.

**Vêtements?**
**Je choisis** mes vêtements **en fonction de** mes activités du jour. On ne s'habille pas de la même manière pour une cérémonie ou pour présider un match de football.

---

### ALAIN DE POUZHILAC

*Prêt en une heure et demie.*

**Heure du réveil?**
6h45, et je passe trois quarts d'heure dans ma salle de bains. Je suis **une** véritable «**cocotte**». Deux fois par semaine, je me lève à 5h pour prendre l'avion.

**Nombre d'heures de sommeil?**
Entre six et sept heures par nuit. **Malheureusement,** je me réveille, **je réfléchis, j'angoisse,** je rêve et **je finis par** me rendormir.

**Le petit déjeuner?**
Tous les matins, j'ai un petit déjeuner d'affaires avec mes collaborateurs ou des clients. Je ne mange pas, je prends juste un café. Nous nous retrouvons souvent à l'hôtel Bristol. J'adore **cet endroit** parce que je peux m'y rendre à pied; le salon et le jardin sont très agréables.

**Bain ou douche?**
Si j'ai l'humeur dynamique, je prends une douche; si j'ai l'humeur plutôt rêveuse, c'est un bain assez chaud.

**Vêtements?**
Jacques Séguéla a l'habitude de dire à mon sujet que je m'habille comme «un banquier de province». Mais, en vérité, je choisis mes vêtements selon mon instinct du matin, la couleur du temps et mon humeur.

**Le moment préféré?**
Celui où je me réveille, où **je découvre** que je suis en vie, avec **des tas de** projets à **réaliser.** Je n'aime pas la solitude. J'adore m'amuser et **rire.**

---

**zapper** to channel surf, to switch back and forth   **traîner** to hang around   **J'avale** I gobble (down)   **Je choisis** I choose   **en fonction de** depending on   **une cocotte** a primper
**Malheureusement** Unfortunately   **je réfléchis** I think   **j'angoisse** I worry   **je finis par** I end up   **cet endroit** that place   **je découvre** I discover   **des tas de** lots of
**réaliser** to carry out   **rire** to laugh

## Compréhension

**Trois interviews.** Indiquez ce qui est vrai pour les trois personnes indiquées.

|  | NICOLAS SARKOZY | ALAIN DE POUZHILAC | VOUS |
|---|---|---|---|
| • *Profession* | _____ | _____ | _____ |
| • *Prêt(e) en… minutes* | _____ | _____ | _____ |
| • *Heure du réveil* | _____ | _____ | _____ |
| • *Nombre d'heures de sommeil* | _____ | _____ | _____ |
| • *Première activité du matin* | _____ | _____ | _____ |
| • *Petit déjeuner* | _____ | _____ | _____ |
| • *Toilette (bain? douche?)* | XXX | _____ | _____ |
| • *Vêtements* | _____ | _____ | _____ |

## Composition

**A. Organisez-vous.** Vous allez écrire une petite annonce *(ad)*. D'abord, organisez-vous en écrivant un bref profil de vous-même. Servez-vous du profil de Marie-Laure Augry, journaliste à la télévision française, comme modèle.

---

**NOM:** *AUGRY*

**PRÉNOM:** *MARIE-LAURE*

**ÂGE:** *40 ANS*

**PROFESSION:** *JOURNALISTE*

**ANIMAL FAVORI:** *MON CHAT ARMAND*

**DÉTENTE:** *LE LIT ET L'HERBE VERTE*

**MUSIQUE:** *LE ROCK-AND-ROLL*

**LIVRE DE CHEVET:** *«UNE CHAÎNE SUR LES BRAS»*
*(HERVÉ BOURGES)*

**SPORTS:** *TENNIS, RUGBY, CYCLISME*

**VACANCES:** *À FONDETTES (EN TOURAINE)*

**LOISIRS:** *LE TENNIS ET LA CHAISE LONGUE*

**AIME:** *LA BONNE CUISINE*

**DÉTESTE:** *L'INTOLÉRANCE*

---

**B. Rédaction: Une annonce.** Vous allez mettre une petite annonce dans le journal. Lisez ces annonces de *Rouen Poche* et utilisez votre autoportrait de l'exercice précédent pour écrire une annonce.

**RENCONTRES**

**ÉVASION CLUB**

RENCONTRES SÉLECTIONNÉES
HOMMES—FEMMES—COUPLES
CONTACTS IMMÉDIATS DE
QUALITÉ. TÉL. 02.35.73.52.18
Discrétion assurée

419
Homme, la trentaine, seul, recherche femme, sympa, câline, pour passer moments agréables. Écrire au journal qui transmettra.

420
Dame, souhaite rencontrer monsieur, 60 à 65 ans pour sorties et voyages. Écrire au journal qui transmettra.

422
Homme, 36 ans, sensible au charme et à l'humour, recherche femme sportive, jolie et dotée d'un heureux caractère. Écrire au journal qui transmettra.

423
Robert, 27 ans, ambitieux et sentimental, souhaite rencontrer blonde, 25 à 30 ans pour sorties + si affinités. Écrire au journal qui transmettra.

455
Cadre, 45 ans, grand, mince, souhaite rencontrer femme distinguée, vive, sensuelle, peu attachée aux valeurs matérielles, pour partager loisirs, et vivre une relation tendre et sincère. Écrire au journal qui transmettra.

456
Si vous désirez partir avec moi en Espagne du 25 août au 30 septembre, prenez dès maintenant contact avec moi. Écrire au journal qui transmettra.

If you have access to SYSTÈME-D software, you will find the following phrases, vocabulary, grammar, and dictionary aids there.

**Phrases:** Writing a news item; Describing people; Writing a letter; Introducing; Asking for information

**Vocabulary:** Trades, occupation; Professions; Animals; Leisure; Sports; People; Personality

**C. Une lettre.** Échangez votre petite annonce avec un(e) camarade de classe. Imaginez que vous êtes un homme / une femme qui répond à son annonce. Écrivez-lui une lettre dans laquelle vous vous présentez et vous lui posez des questions.

## L'amour et le couple

**Voici** les résultats de **sondages** sur les opinions des Français sur le couple et les relations entre les hommes et les femmes. Quelles sont vos opinions?

### Les Français et les Françaises parlent de l'amour.

➠ Êtes-vous amoureux en ce moment?

| Oui | Non | Sans réponse |
|-----|-----|--------------|
| 70% | 29% | 1% |

➠ Pour vous, l'amour, est-ce quelque chose de très important, assez important, peu important ou pas important du tout?

| Très | Assez | Peu | Pas du tout | Sans opinion |
|------|-------|-----|-------------|--------------|
| 68% | 27% | 3% | 1% | 1% |

➠ Pour être heureux en amour, estimez-vous que la sexualité est très importante, assez importante, peu importante ou pas importante du tout?

| Très | Assez | Peu | Pas du tout | Sans opinion |
|------|-------|-----|-------------|--------------|
| 35% | 55% | 7% | 1% | 2% |

➠ Parlez-vous de votre vie amoureuse avec vos amis?

| Souvent | Rarement | Jamais | Sans réponse |
|---------|----------|--------|--------------|
| 21 | 38 | 40 | 1 |

### Les femmes parlent de la vie en couple et des hommes.

Pour vous, un couple, c'est **avant tout...**

| | |
|---|---|
| **Vieillir** ensemble | 53%* |
| Partager ses idées, ses **valeurs** | 49% |
| Avoir des enfants | 32% |
| **Vivre** un grand amour | 23% |
| **Se soutenir** matériellement | 14% |

Avoir un homme dans votre vie, aujourd'hui, **diriez-vous** que...

| | |
|---|---|
| C'est indispensable à votre bonheur | 59% |
| **Vous pourriez vous en passer** | 36% |
| Sans opinion | 5% |

Avoir des enfants, diriez-vous que...

| | |
|---|---|
| C'est indispensable à votre bonheur | 88% |
| Vous pourriez vous en passer | 9% |
| Sans opinion | 3% |

*La totalité des % est supérieure à 100, les personnes interrogées **ayant pu** donner trois réponses.

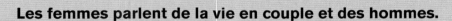

**sondages** *polls*　**avant tout** *above all*　**Vieillir** *To grow old*　**valeurs** *values*　**Vivre** *To live*　**Se soutenir** *To support each other*
**diriez-vous** *would you say*　**Vous pourriez vous en passer** *You could do without*　**ayant pu** *having been able*

## Les hommes parlent des femmes.

Quelles sont les principales qualités que vous recherchez chez une femme?

| | |
|---|---|
| **La tendresse** | 48% |
| L'intelligence | 45% |
| La fidélité | 45% |
| L'humour | 39% |
| La beauté | 24% |
| **Qu'elle tienne bien sa maison** | 22% |
| La sensualité | 21% |
| L'indépendance | 14% |

**Qu'est-ce qui pourrait vous faire peur** chez une femme?

| | |
|---|---|
| **Le fait qu'elle ait eu** beaucoup d'hommes dans sa vie | 25% |
| Sa très grande beauté | 21% |
| Son milieu social | 17% |
| **Son audace**, le fait qu'elle prenne l'initiative | 14% |
| Son indépendance | 13% |
| Son désir d'avoir un enfant | 10% |
| Son désir de se marier | 10% |
| Son intelligence et sa culture supérieure à la vôtre | 10% |
| Son appétit sexuel | 6% |
| Le fait qu'elle ait une situation professionnelle supérieure à la vôtre | 4% |

## À discuter

**A. Vrai ou faux?** D'abord, complétez les phrases suivantes avec le pronom relatif convenable: **qui, que** ou **dont.** Ensuite, dites si les phrases sont vraies ou fausses.

1. Il y a beaucoup plus de Français _____ trouvent que l'amour est très important que de Français _____ sont amoureux.
2. La vie amoureuse est quelque chose _____ la majorité des Français parlent ouvertement *(openly)* avec leurs amis.
3. Une bonne relation sexuelle est quelque chose _____ la majorité des Français trouvent important pour être heureux en amour.
4. Pour beaucoup de Françaises, un couple, c'est surtout deux personnes _____ restent ensemble jusqu'à la fin *(end)* de la vie.
5. Il y a plus de femmes _____ veulent absolument avoir des enfants dans leur vie que de femmes _____ veulent absolument avoir un homme.
6. Le trait _____ les Français recherchent le plus chez les femmes, c'est la sensualité.
7. La chose _____ les Français ont le plus peur chez les femmes, c'est le désir de se marier.
8. Il y a beaucoup plus d'hommes _____ préfèrent les femmes indépendantes que d'hommes _____ ont peur des femmes indépendantes.

## B. Comparaisons. Discutez les questions suivantes.

1. Qu'est-ce que vous trouvez surprenant *(surprising)* dans les réponses aux sondages des Français? Qu'est-ce qui ne vous surprend pas? Pourquoi?
2. Posez les questions du sondage aux étudiants de votre classe. Quelles différences y a-t-il dans les réponses? Pouvez-vous expliquer ces différences?
3. Dans un sondage sur ce sujet fait dans votre pays, quelles autres questions est-ce qu'on poserait *(would one ask)?* Voyez-vous des attitudes différentes sur ce sujet?

---

**La tendresse** *Tenderness* **Qu'elle tienne bien sa maison** *That she keeps house well* **Qu'est-ce qui pourrait vous faire peur?**
*What could frighten you?* **Le fait qu'elle ait eu** *The fact that she has had* **Son audace** *Her boldness*

# Résumé de grammaire

## Reflexive verbs

Reflexive verbs are used to say that people do something to or for themselves. In French, the reflexive pronoun corresponding to the subject is placed before the verb.

Je **me** réveille à six heures et puis, je réveille mes enfants à sept heures.
*I wake up (**myself**) at six o'clock, and then I wake up my children at seven.*

| SE COUCHER *(to go to bed)* | |
|---|---|
| je **me** couche | nous **nous** couchons |
| tu **te** couches | vous **vous** couchez |
| il/elle/on **se** couche | ils/elles **se** couchent |

Mon fils de trois ans s'habille tout seul.
*My three-year-old son dresses all by himself.*

The reflexive pronouns **me, te,** and **se** become **m', t',** and **s'** before vowel sounds. Also note the spelling changes with **s'ennuyer, s'appeler** and **se lever.** All verbs ending with **-yer,** such as **essayer** and **payer,** follow the same pattern as **s'ennuyer. Se promener** is also conjugated like **se lever.**

— Comment vous appelez-vous?
— Je m'appelle Catherine Faure.

— À quelle heure est-ce que vous vous levez?
— Je me lève très tôt.

| S'ENNUYER *(to be / get bored)* | S'APPELER *(to be named)* | SE LEVER *(to get up)* |
|---|---|---|
| je m'ennuie | je m'appelle | je me lève |
| tu t'ennuies | tu t'appelles | tu te lèves |
| il/elle/on s'ennuie | il/elle/on s'appelle | il/elle/on se lève |
| nous nous ennuyons | nous nous appelons | nous nous levons |
| vous vous ennuyez | vous vous appelez | vous vous levez |
| ils/elles s'ennuient | ils/elles s'appellent | ils/elles se lèvent |

— Tu **ne** t'ennuies **pas** dans ce cours?
— Non, je m'intéresse beaucoup au français.

With negated reflexive verbs, place **ne** before the reflexive pronoun and **pas** after the verb.

Mon père **s'**achète une nouvelle voiture chaque année.
*My father buys **himself** a new car each year.*

Verbs that are reflexive in English, such as *to amuse **oneself*** or *to buy **oneself*** something will generally also be reflexive in French. Many other verbs are reflexive in French that are not in English. Consult the end-of-chapter vocabulary list to find all 28 reflexive verbs learned in this chapter.

Je me brosse **les** dents trois fois par jour.
*I brush **my** teeth three times a day.*

Verbs indicating that people are doing something to their own body are generally reflexive in French. After such verbs, in French, you use the definite article (**le, la, l', les**) with a following body part, rather than the possessive adjective *(my, your, his . . .).*

## Reciprocal verbs

Reciprocal verbs indicate that two or more people do something to or for one another. Reciprocal verbs look like reflexive verbs. Most verbs naming something one person might do to another can be made reciprocal by adding a reciprocal pronoun.

Vous **vous** retrouvez après les cours?
*Do you meet **each other** after class?*

Mes voisins ne **se** parlent pas.
*My neighbors don't talk **to one another.***

| aimer | *to love* | s'aimer | *to love each other* |
|---|---|---|---|
| détester | *to hate* | se détester | *to hate each other* |
| regarder | *to look at* | se regarder | *to look at each other* |

— **Vous** voulez **vous** marier?
— Oui, et **nous** allons **nous** installer dans un petit appartement.

When reflexive / reciprocal verbs are used in the infinitive, the reflexive / reciprocal pronoun changes to match the subject of the conjugated verb.

## Past tenses of reflexive and reciprocal verbs

All reflexive / reciprocal verbs are conjugated with **être** in the **passé composé.** The past participle agrees in gender and number with the reflexive / reciprocal pronoun (and the subject) when it is the direct object of the verb.

| S'AMUSER | |
|---|---|
| je me suis amusé(e) | nous nous sommes amusé(e)s |
| tu t'es amusé(e) | vous vous êtes amusé(e)(s) |
| il s'est amusé | ils se sont amusés |
| elle s'est amusée | elles se sont amusées |
| on s'est amusé(e)(s) | |

— Tous tes amis se sont retrouvé**s** chez toi?
— Oui, et on s'est bien amusé**s** jusqu'à très tard. Mon amie Rose s'est endorm**ie** sur le canapé.

With negated verbs place **ne** before the reflexive / reciprocal pronoun and **pas** after **être.**

Past participles do not agree with reflexive / reciprocal pronouns that are indirect objects. For this reason, there is no agreement with **se parler, se téléphoner, s'écrire,** or when a reflexive verb is followed directly by a noun that is the direct object of the verb, such as a part of the body.

As with all verbs except **être,** form the imperfect of reflexive verbs by dropping the **-ons** from the **nous** form of the verb and adding the imperfect endings: **-ais, -ais, -ait, -ions, -iez, -aient.**

— Vous ne vous êtes pas vus hier?
— Non, mais nous nous sommes téléphoné trois fois.

Ma petite sœur s'est maquill**ée.**
Ma petite sœur s'est maquillé **les yeux.**

— Tu te levais plus tôt l'année dernière?
— Oui, je me levais à six heures.

## Regular *-re* verbs

The following verbs are conjugated like **répondre: descendre, entendre, s'entendre (bien / mal) (avec), perdre, se perdre, rendre visite à quelqu'un, rendre quelque chose à quelqu'un, vendre, revendre.** They all take **avoir** in the **passé composé** except **descendre** and the reflexive verbs.

| RÉPONDRE (to answer) | |
|---|---|
| je répond**s** | nous répond**ons** |
| tu répond**s** | vous répond**ez** |
| il/elle/on répond | ils/elles répond**ent** |

PASSÉ COMPOSÉ: **j'ai répondu**
IMPARFAIT: **je répondais**

— Tu ne rends jamais visite à ton ex-petite amie?
— Non, on a perdu contact. On ne s'entend pas très bien. Si je téléphone chez elle, elle ne répond pas au téléphone.

## Relative pronouns

A relative clause is a phrase that describes a noun. The word that begins the phrase, referring back to the noun described is a relative pronoun. The relative pronouns **qui, que,** and **dont** are all used for both people and things. The choice of relative pronoun depends on the pronoun's function in the relative clause. **Qui** replaces the subject of the relative clause, **que** replaces the direct object, and **dont** replaces the preposition **de** and its object.

Place relative clauses directly after the noun they describe. When **que** is the object of a verb in the **passé composé,** the past participle agrees in number and gender with the noun it represents.

La femme **qui** habite à côté est française. (= La femme est française. **Cette femme** habite à côté.)
La femme **que** j'ai invit**ée** est française. (= La femme est française. J'ai invité **cette femme.**)
La femme **dont** je parle souvent est française. (= La femme est française. Je parle souvent **de cette femme.**)

# Vocabulaire

## COMPÉTENCE 1

### Describing your daily routine

**NOMS MASCULINS**

| | |
|---|---|
| le mariage | marriage |
| un petit-fils | a grandson |
| un séjour | a stay |
| un veuf | a widower |

**NOMS FÉMININS**

| | |
|---|---|
| une demi-heure | a half hour |
| la figure | the face |
| la main | the hand |
| une petite-fille | a granddaughter |
| une routine | a routine |
| une veuve | a widow |

**EXPRESSIONS VERBALES**

| | |
|---|---|
| s'amuser | to have fun |
| s'appeler | to be named |
| attendre | to wait (for) |
| se brosser (les cheveux / les dents) | to brush (one's hair / one's teeth) |
| connaître | to be familiar with, to be acquainted with, to know |
| se coucher / se recoucher | to go to bed / to go back to bed |
| s'endormir | to fall asleep |
| s'ennuyer | to be bored, to get bored |
| faire sa toilette | to wash up |
| s'habiller / se déshabiller | to get dressed / to get undressed |
| se laver (la figure / les mains) | to wash (one's face / one's hands) |
| se lever | to get up |
| se maquiller | to put on makeup |
| prendre un bain / une douche | to take a bath / a shower |
| se raser | to shave |
| se reposer | to rest |
| se réveiller | to wake up |

**DIVERS**

| | |
|---|---|
| comme | since, as |
| d'autres fois | other times |
| depuis | since, for |
| d'origine... | of . . . origin |
| facilement | easily |
| parfait(e) | perfect |
| pendant | during |
| quotidien(ne) | daily |
| vite | quick(ly), fast |

## COMPÉTENCE 2

### Talking about relationships

**NOMS MASCULINS**

| | |
|---|---|
| le coup de foudre | love at first sight |
| le grand amour | true love |

**NOMS FÉMININS**

| | |
|---|---|
| la jeunesse | youth |
| une relation | a relationship |

**EXPRESSIONS VERBALES**

| | |
|---|---|
| s'aimer | to like each other, to love each other |
| descendre | to go down, to get off, to stay (at a hotel) |
| se détester | to hate each other |
| se disputer | to argue |
| s'embrasser | to kiss each other, to embrace each other |
| entendre | to hear |
| s'entendre (bien / mal) (avec) | to get along (well / badly) (with) |
| se fiancer | to get engaged |
| s'installer (dans / à) | to move (into), to settle (in) |
| se marier (avec) | to get married (to) |
| se parler | to talk to each other |
| se passer | to happen |
| perdre | to lose |
| perdre du temps | to waste time |
| se perdre | to get lost |
| prendre une décision | to make a decision |
| se quitter | to leave each other |
| se réconcilier | to make up with each other |
| se regarder | to look at each other |
| se rencontrer | to meet each other (by chance, for the first time), to run into each other |
| rendre quelque chose à quelqu'un | to return something to someone |
| rendre visite à quelqu'un | to visit someone |
| répondre (à) | to answer |
| se retrouver | to meet each other (by design) |
| revendre | to sell back |
| rêver (de) | to dream (of, about) |
| se souvenir de | to remember |
| suivre | to follow |
| se téléphoner | to phone each other |
| vendre | to sell |

**DIVERS**

| | |
|---|---|
| ce qui | what |
| C'est dommage! | That's too bad! |
| enfin | finally |
| formidable | great |
| heureux (heureuse) | happy |
| la plupart du temps | most of the time |
| mamie | grandma |
| sentimental(e) (mpl sentimentaux) | sentimental, emotional |
| un(e) tel(le) | such a |

# COMPÉTENCE 3

## Talking about what you did and used to do

### NOMS MASCULINS

| | |
|---|---|
| le reste (de) | *the rest (of)* |
| un réveil | *an alarm clock* |

### EXPRESSIONS VERBALES

| | |
|---|---|
| accepter | *to accept* |
| s'arrêter | *to stop* |
| se peigner | *to comb one's hair* |
| se promener | *to go walking* |
| raconter | *to tell* |
| se reconnaître | *to recognize each other* |
| sonner | *to ring* |
| se voir | *to see each other* |

### DIVERS

| | |
|---|---|
| cela | *that* |
| donc | *then, so, thus, therefore* |
| parfaitement | *perfectly* |

# COMPÉTENCE 4

## Describing traits and characteristics

### NOMS MASCULINS

| | |
|---|---|
| l'aspect physique | *physical appearance* |
| le bonheur | *happiness* |
| le corps | *the body* |
| l'esprit | *the mind, the spirit* |
| un groupe | *a group* |
| un partenaire | *a partner* |
| le sens de l'humour | *the sense of humor* |
| un sentiment | *a feeling* |
| un test | *a test* |
| un trait | *a trait* |

### NOMS FÉMININS

| | |
|---|---|
| la beauté | *beauty* |
| la compatibilité | *compatibility* |
| la compréhension | *understanding* |
| l'importance | *importance* |
| l'indécision | *indecision* |
| l'indifférence | *indifference* |
| l'infidélité | *infidelity* |
| l'inflexibilité | *inflexibility* |
| l'insensibilité | *insensitivity* |
| la jalousie | *jealousy* |
| la nature | *nature* |
| une partenaire | *a partner* |
| la passion | *passion* |
| la politique | *politics* |
| la profession | *the profession* |
| la religion | *the religion* |
| une rencontre | *an encounter* |
| la spiritualité | *spirituality* |
| la vanité | *vanity* |

### VERBES

| | |
|---|---|
| cultiver | *to cultivate* |
| exprimer | *to express* |
| s'intéresser à | *to be interested in* |
| ranger | *to arrange, to order* |
| supporter | *to bear, to tolerate, to put up with* |

### DIVERS

| | |
|---|---|
| ce que | *what* |
| chez (une personne) | *with, in (a person)* |
| conservateur (conservatrice) | *conservative* |
| dont | *whom, of (about, with) whom, whose, that, of (about, with) which* |
| en ligne | *online* |
| jaloux (jalouse) | *jealous* |
| libéral(e) (*mpl* libéraux) | *liberal* |
| professionnel(le) | *professional* |
| que | *that, which, whom* |
| qui | *that, which, who* |

## Les affiches à Trouville
### RAOUL DUFY
### (1877–1953)

1906
Paris, Musée National d'Art Moderne
© 1998 Artists Rights Society (ARS), New York/ADAGP, Paris

Né au Havre, Dufy a souvent choisi *(chose)* des scènes de la côte normande *(Normandy coast)*, comme sujet de ses tableaux: les vues de la mer, les régates et les villes touristiques de Trouville, Deauville et Honfleur.

## La tapisserie de Bayeux

11ᵉ siècle *(century)*
Bayeux, Musée de la Tapisserie
Erich Lessing/Art Resource

La tapisserie de Bayeux, appelée aussi «la tapisserie de la reine Mathilde», est une œuvre *(work)* unique. Mesurant plus de 70 mètres de long, cette broderie raconte en images l'histoire de la conquête de l'Angleterre par Guillaume le Conquérant *(William the Conqueror)*, duc de Normandie.

## En Normandie

**ROUEN**
**NOMBRE D'HABITANTS:** 105 100 habitants (avec ses agglomérations *[metropolitan region]*: 527 000) (les Rouennais)
**DÉPARTEMENT:** Seine-Maritime
**RÉGION:** Haute-Normandie
**INDUSTRIES PRINCIPALES:** import-export, raffineries de pétrole, métallurgie, construction, mécanique, industries chimiques, alimentaires *(food)* et textiles

# La bonne cuisine

 Video activities are on pages 416–419.

Comment imaginez-vous la Normandie? Imaginez-vous...

des villes **au bord de la mer telles que** Deauville?

d'anciennes villes historiques?

des bateaux **de pêche?**

---

**au bord de la mer** *at the seaside*   **telles que** *such as*   **de pêche** *fishing*

**des falaises** isolées?

des pâturages (avec **des moutons** ou des vaches)?

**des fermes normandes?**

La Normandie, **c'est tout cela! Et même plus!**

## Qu'en savez-vous?

Que savez-vous de *(What do you know about)* l'histoire de la Normandie? Trouvez la date qui correspond à chacun de ces événements historiques.

    **a.** 1066      **b.** le 6 juin 1944      **c.** 820-911      **d.** 1453

1. le Jour J, jour du débarquement en Normandie des forces alliées (américaines, anglaises, canadiennes et françaises) commandées par le général Eisenhower
2. la conquête de la région par les Vikings (Le nom de Normandie veut dire «*Land of the Northmen*».)
3. la guerre de Cent Ans entre la France et l'Angleterre (que la France a gagnée grâce surtout aux batailles *[thanks especially to the battles]* gagnées par Jeanne d'Arc)
4. la conquête de l'Angleterre *(England)* par Guillaume le Conquérant, duc de Normandie

La tapisserie de Bayeux raconte en images la conquête de l'Angleterre par Guillaume le Conquérant, duc de Normandie.

---

**des falaises** *cliffs*   **des moutons** *sheep*   **des vaches** *cows*   **des fermes normandes** *Norman farms*
**c'est tout cela! Et même plus!** *It's all that and even more!*

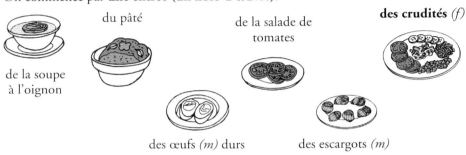

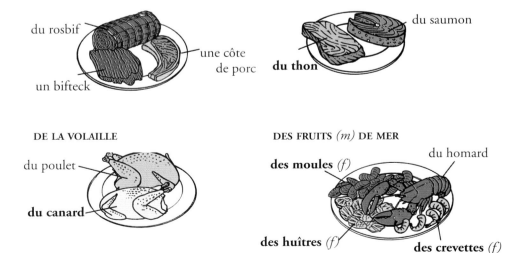

# Ordering at a restaurant

## Au restaurant

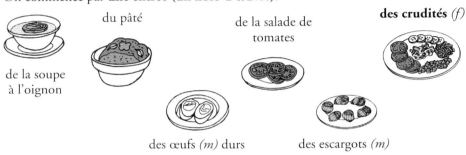

Aimez-vous la cuisine française? **Savez-vous** préparer des plats typiquement français? En famille, entre amis ou au restaurant, les Français aiment bien les grands repas traditionnels.

On commence par **une entrée (un hors-d'œuvre):**

du pâté

de la salade de tomates

**des crudités** *(f)*

de la soupe à l'oignon

des œufs *(m)* durs

des escargots *(m)*

Sur la table, il y a aussi...

du pain

du sel et du poivre

de l'eau

Ensuite, on **sert** le plat principal:

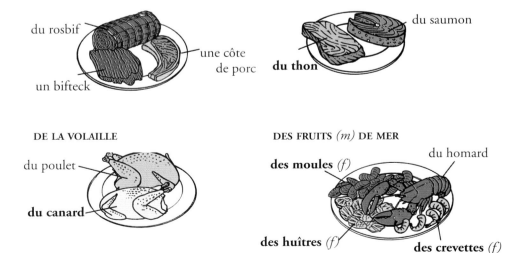

**DE LA VIANDE**

du rosbif

un bifteck

une côte de porc

**DU POISSON**

du saumon

**du thon**

**DE LA VOLAILLE**

du poulet

**du canard**

**DES FRUITS** *(m)* **DE MER**

**des moules** *(f)*

du homard

**des huîtres** *(f)*

**des crevettes** *(f)*

> Note
*culturelle*

Les Français passent en moyenne environ deux heures à table aux repas, mais le temps consacré à la préparation d'un repas a beaucoup diminué avec l'augmentation du nombre de femmes qui travaillent et de l'équipement culinaire comme, par exemple, le four à micro-ondes. De plus, les Français se servent de plus en plus des produits prépréparés. Est-ce que la même chose est vraie dans votre région?

**NOTE DE GRAMMAIRE**

The article you see in front of many of the nouns on this page is called the partitive. It expresses the idea of *some* or *any*. Why are there four different forms of this article?

**du pâté** *some pâté*
**de la soupe** *some soup*
**de l'eau** *some water*
**des œufs** *some eggs*

You will learn how to use the partitive article in the next section.

The verb **servir** *(to serve)* is irregular: **je sers, tu sers, il/elle/on sert, nous servons, vous servez, ils/elles servent;** PASSÉ COMPOSÉ: **j'ai servi;** IMPARFAIT: **je servais.**

---

**Savez-vous... ?** *Do you know (how to) . . . ?* **une entrée** *a first course* **un hors-d'œuvre** *an appetizer*
**des crudités** *(f) raw vegetables* **sert** *(servir to serve)* **de la viande** *meat* **du poisson** *fish* **du thon** *tuna*
**de la volaille** *poultry* **du canard** *duck* **des fruits** *(m)* **de mer** *shellfish* **des moules** *(f) mussels* **des huîtres** *(f) oysters*
**des crevettes** *(f) shrimp*

Le plat principal **comprend** aussi **du riz** et des légumes *(m):*

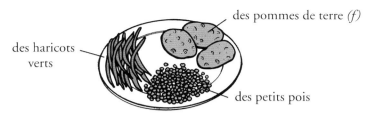

des haricots verts

des pommes de terre *(f)*

des petits pois

On sert généralement la salade verte après le plat principal. On sert le fromage après la salade.

une salade

du fromage

On finit le repas avec des fruits—ou un dessert.

des fruits *(m)*

de la tarte aux pommes

de la glace à la vanille

du gâteau au chocolat

Pour finir, on sert le café.

du café

Prenez-vous **du sucre**, du lait ou de la crème dans votre café?

CD 2-16

# Prononciation

*Le **h** aspiré*

In French, **h** is never pronounced and there is usually liaison and elision before it.

J'aime les ͡z huîtres.        Il y a beaucoup **d'**huile *(oil)* dans la salade.

Before a few words beginning with **h,** there is no liaison or elision, even though the **h** is silent. These words are said to begin with **h aspiré**. In vocabulary lists, they are indicated by an asterisk (*). The following words have **h aspiré: le homard, les haricots, les hors-d'œuvre.** English words that begin with *h* often have an **h aspiré** when used in French: **les hot-dogs, les hamburgers.**

---

**comprend (comprendre** *to include)*    **du riz** *rice*    **du sucre** *sugar*

**VOCABULAIRE SUPPLÉMENTAIRE**

**bleu(e)** *very rare*
**saignant(e)** *rare*
**à point** *medium rare*
**cuit(e)** *medium*
**bien cuit(e)** *well-done*
**végétarien(ne)** *vegetarian*
**végétalien(ne)** *vegan*
**D'AUTRES PLATS** *(dishes):*
  **de l'agneau** *(m) lamb*
  **du bifteck haché** *ground meat*
  **des coquilles St-Jacques** *(f) scallops*
  **de la dinde** *turkey*
  **du rôti de porc** *pork roast*
  **de la sole** *sole*
  **de la truite** *trout*
  **du veau** *veal*
**POUR METTRE LA TABLE** *(to set the table):*
  **une assiette** *a plate*
  **un bol** *a bowl*
  **un couteau** *a knife*
  **une cuillère (cuiller)** *a spoon*
  **une fourchette** *a fork*
  **une nappe** *a tablecloth*
  **une serviette** *a napkin*
  **une tasse** *a cup*
  **un verre** *a glass*

Pour une liste de fruits et de légumes, voir la page 315.

André a invité Rosalie au restaurant Maraîchers. Regardez le menu de ce restaurant aux pages 308–309.

| | |
|---|---|
| LE SERVEUR: | Bonsoir, monsieur. Bonsoir, madame. Aimeriez-vous **un apéritif** avant de commander? |
| ANDRÉ: | Rosalie? |
| ROSALIE: | Non, merci, pas ce soir. |
| ANDRÉ: | Pour moi non plus. |
| LE SERVEUR: | Et pour dîner? Est-ce que vous avez décidé? |
| ANDRÉ: | Nous allons prendre le menu à 22 euros. |
| LE SERVEUR: | Très bien, monsieur. Et qu'est-ce que vous désirez **comme** entrée? |
| ANDRÉ: | Pour madame, le saumon fumé. Et pour moi, les huîtres. |
| LE SERVEUR: | Et comme plat principal? |
| ROSALIE: | Pour moi, **la raie,** s'il vous plaît. |
| ANDRÉ: | Et pour moi, **le pavé de saumon.** |
| LE SERVEUR: | Bien, monsieur. Et comme boisson? |
| ANDRÉ: | Une carafe de vin blanc et **une bouteille d'**eau minérale. |
| LE SERVEUR: | Évian ou Perrier? |
| ROSALIE: | Évian, s'il vous plaît. |
| LE SERVEUR: | Très bien, madame. |

**A. Préférences.** Demandez à votre partenaire ce qu'il/ce qu'elle aime mieux. Pour répondre *neither . . . nor . . .*, dites **ne... ni... ni...** comme dans l'exemple.

**Exemple**     la viande ou le poisson
     — Est-ce que tu aimes mieux la viande ou le poisson?
     — J'aime mieux la viande. / J'aime les deux. /
     **Je n'aime ni la viande ni le poisson.**

1. la viande rouge ou la volaille
2. les légumes ou la viande
3. la volaille ou le poisson
4. le poisson ou les fruits de mer
5. les crudités ou la salade verte
6. les pommes de terre ou le riz
7. les haricots verts ou les petits pois
8. les escargots ou les œufs durs
9. le gâteau, la glace ou la tarte
10. les crevettes ou le homard

**B. Catégories logiques.** Quel mot ne va pas logiquement avec les autres? Pourquoi?

**Exemple**     le thé, le jus de fruit, le sel, le lait, l'eau
     **Le sel, parce que ce n'est pas une boisson.**

1. le pain, les petits pois, les pommes de terre, les haricots verts
2. le gâteau au chocolat, le poivre, la tarte aux pommes, la glace
3. la salade de tomates, le pâté, la soupe à l'oignon, le rosbif
4. le déjeuner, le dîner, le petit déjeuner, le sel
5. le homard, le rosbif, les crevettes, les huîtres, les moules
6. les pommes de terre, les petits pois, les haricots verts, le gâteau

---

**un serveur (une serveuse)** *a server*     **un apéritif** *a before-dinner drink*     **comme** *for, as a*     **la raie** *skate, rayfish*
**le pavé de saumon** *salmon steak*     **une bouteille de** *a bottle of*

**C. Aujourd'hui on sert...** Voilà ce qu'on sert aujourd'hui. Regardez la liste et indiquez ce qu'il y a par catégorie.

| | | |
|---|---|---|
| de l'eau minérale | du vin | du saumon |
| du thon | des crevettes | des huîtres |
| des petits pois | des pommes de terre | du gâteau |
| de la tarte aux pommes | des côtes de porc | du bifteck |
| du pâté | des œufs durs | du poulet |
| du canard | | |

**Exemple** viande
**Comme viande, il y a des côtes de porc et...**

1. entrée
2. volaille
3. viande
4. poisson

5. dessert
6. légume
7. boisson
8. fruits de mer

**D. Vos préférences.** Regardez la liste de catégories dans *C. Aujourd'hui on sert...* et indiquez vos préférences pour chaque catégorie.

**Exemple** **Comme viande, je préfère les côtes de porc.**
**Je n'aime pas la viande.**

**E. Un dîner.** Voici ce que Rosalie a mangé hier soir. Qu'est-ce qu'elle a mangé? Dans quel ordre? Et vous? Qu'est-ce que vous avez mangé hier soir? Dans quel ordre?

**F. Conversation.** Avec deux camarades de classe, relisez à haute voix la conversation à la page précédente. Ensuite, imaginez que vous dînez au restaurant Maraîchers avec un(e) ami(e). Commandez un repas complet. Le (La) troisième camarade de classe va jouer le rôle du serveur (de la serveuse).

# BISTROT D'ADRIAN

**37** **37**

## RESTAURANT

# MARAICHERS

**Servis
Jusqu'à 23 H.**

## Le Bistrot - 15 €.

**Service 15% Compris**

*Adrian vous propose son petit Menu Bistrot
composé uniquement de produits frais de saison*

### Première Assiette

9 Huîtres "Fines de Claires n°3" Sur lit de glace
Assiette de Coquillages farcis à l'ail
Cocotte de moules marinières
Salade aux lardons, Oeuf poché
Terrine de canard maison, au poivre vert
Plateau de fruits de mer "l'écailler" + 10 €

### Deuxième Assiette

Brochette de poissons, beurre blanc
Moules de pays, frites
Sardines grillées aux herbes
Langue de boeuf, sauce piquante
Poêlée de Rognon de boeuf, flambée au cognac
Bavette Poêlée à la fondue d'oignons

### Troisième Assiette

Crème Caramel
Fraises au vin ou fraises au sucre
Feuillantine aux pommes
Glace et sorbet artisanaux
Île flottante
Coupe normande

**Arrivage Journalier
de Poissons, d'Huîtres et de Fruits de Mer**

## Les Maraîchers - 22 €.

**Service 15% Compris**

*Les plus beaux produits du Terroir sélectionnés
et cuisinés dans la grande tradition des Maraîchers*

### Première Assiette

12 Huîtres "Fines de Claires n°3" Sur Lit de glace
Saumon fumé par nos soins, Toasts chauds
Poêlon de 12 Escargots de Bourgogne à l'ail
Beignets de langoustines, Sauce tartare
Salade de cervelle d'agneau poêlée
Plateau de fruits de mer "l'écailler" + 10 €

### Deuxième Assiette

Aile de Raie capucine
Daurade entière au lard fumé
Pavé de Saumon Rôti, beurre de moules
Filet de Canard à la Rouennaise
Andouillette à la ficelle "du Père Tafournel"
Faux-filet grillé ou Sauce Poivre

### Troisième Assiette

Salade de Saison, ou plateau de fromages

### Quatrième Assiette

Tarte tatin chaude, crème fraîche
Bavarois ananas coco
Symphonie aux trois chocolats
Feuillantine aux fraises ou fraises Melba
Glace et Sorbet artisanaux
Crème Brûlée

*depuis 1912*

## La Carte

*Service 15% Compris*

### Nos Huîtres et Fruits de Mer (Arrivage Journalier)

12 Huîtres "Fines de claires" Sur lit de glace n° "3" 14€" n° "2" 16€"

12 Huîtres "Spéciales St Vaast" Sur lit de glace n° "3" 15€" n° "2" 17€"

Plateau de fruits de mer "L'écailler" 18€ "Le marayeur" 30€ "Le Royal" 60€ 1 ou 2 personnes avec 1 Homard frais

### Fraîcheur du Marché & Préparations Maison

Soupe de poissons maison, sa rouille et ses croûtons, 6€    Assiette de coquillages farcis 6€

Moules à la crème 7€ – Salade aux lardons, œuf poché 6€    Terrine de canard maison au poivre 6€

Salade de cervelle d'agneau poêlée 8€    Beignets de langoustines, Sauce Tartare 10€

Saumon fumé par nos soins Toasts chauds 10€    Poêlon de 12 Escargots de Bourgogne à l'ail 10€

### Poissons Frais d'Arrivage

_ Brochette de poissons frais, beurre Blanc 7,50€   Moules de pays Frites 7,50€

_ Sardines grillées aux herbes 7,50€   Pavé de Saumon Rôti, Beurre de Moules 10,50€

_ Aile de Raie capucine 10,50€   Daurade entière au lard fumé 10,50€

_ Sole Meunière ou Sole Normande 19€

### Traditionnels & Spécialités

Langue de Bœuf, sauce piquante 7,50€   Tête de veau ravigote 7,50€  Bavette poêlée à la fondue d'oignons 7,50€  Poêlée de Rognon de bœuf Flambée au cognac 7,50€  Faux-Filet Grillé ou Sauce Poivre 10,50€ Filet de canard à la Rouennaise 10,50€  Andouillette à la ficelle 10,50€

Cœur de Filet au Poivre Flambé au calvados 15€  Chateaubriand Grillé Beurre Persillé 14,50€

### Desserts

Plateau de Fromages 5,50€

Île flottante au caramel 4€    Crème au Caramel 4€    Baiser de vierge 5€    Glace et Sorbet artisanaux 5€   Fraises au vin ou sucrées 5€   After eight 5€    Coupe normande 5€   Feuillantine aux Pommes 5,50€ Tarte Tatin crème fraîche 5,50€  Crème Brûlée 5,50€  Bavarois ananas coco 5,50€  Feuillantine aux fraises 6€   Fraises Melba 6€    Symphonie aux trois chocolats 6,50€

**1.** How do you express the idea of *some* in French? What are the forms of the partitive and when do you use each? Can you drop the word for *some* or *any* in French, as you can in English?

**2.** In what two circumstances do you use **de** instead of the partitive?

# Talking about what you eat

*Le partitif*

To express the idea of *some* or *any*, use the partitive article (**du, de la, de l', des**).

| MASCULINE SINGULAR BEGINNING WITH A CONSONANT SOUND | FEMININE SINGULAR BEGINNING WITH A CONSONANT SOUND | SINGULAR NOUNS BEGINNING WITH A VOWEL SOUND | ALL PLURAL NOUNS |
|---|---|---|---|
| du pain | de la glace | de l'eau | des fruits |

The words *some* or *any* may be left out in English, but the partitive article must be used in French.

The partitive article becomes **de (d'):**

- after negated verbs (except after the verb **être**).

  Je voudrais **du café.**     *I'd like **(some) coffee.***
  Tu **ne** veux **pas de café?**     *Don't you want **(any) coffee?***

- after expressions of quantity like **beaucoup, combien,** and **trop.**

  J'ai acheté **trop de café.**     *I bought **too much coffee.***

**A. Qu'est-ce qu'on sert?** Demandez à votre partenaire ce qu'on sert pour chaque plat en France.

> **Exemple**    Comme entrée...
>         du riz, de la soupe, du gâteau, de la glace?
>         — **Comme entrée, est-ce qu'on sert du riz, de la soupe, du gâteau ou de la glace?**
>         — **On sert de la soupe.**

Comme entrée...
1. du café, des œufs durs, des petits pois ou de la tarte?
2. de la salade verte, de la salade de tomates ou du rosbif?

Comme plat principal...
1. du pâté, du saumon, des fruits ou de la salade verte?
2. du fromage, du gâteau, des crevettes ou des œufs durs?

Comme légume...
1. des petits pois, des huîtres, des moules ou du rosbif?
2. du fromage, des pommes, de la volaille ou des pommes de terre?

Après le plat principal...
1. de la salade verte, du poulet, des escargots ou de la soupe?
2. de la viande, des œufs durs, des fruits de mer ou du fromage?

**B. Qu'est-ce que vous prenez?** Dites si vous prenez souvent les choses suivantes avec vos repas.

> **Exemple** vin
> **Je prends souvent (rarement) du vin avec mes repas.**
> **Je ne prends jamais de vin avec mes repas.**

**1.** pain     **3.** eau minérale     **5.** crevettes     **7.** volaille
**2.** œufs     **4.** viande rouge     **6.** poisson     **8.** soupe

**C. Comparaisons.** Indiquez si les Français prennent souvent ces choses comme entrée, comme plat principal, comme boisson, comme dessert ou comme légume. Ensuite, dites si vous faites souvent la même chose.

> **Exemple** pâté    **Les Français prennent souvent du pâté comme entrée.**
> **Moi aussi, je prends souvent du pâté comme entrée.**
> **Moi, je ne prends pas souvent de pâté comme entrée.**

**1.** salade de tomates     **3.** petits pois     **5.** canard     **7.** gâteau
**2.** eau minérale     **4.** saumon     **6.** tarte     **8.** vin

**D. Sur la table.** Rose est invitée à une fête où il y a beaucoup à manger et à boire. Voici la table de la salle à manger et la table de la cuisine. Faites des comparaisons entre les deux.

> **Exemple**    **Il y a des chips dans la cuisine et dans la salle à manger.**
> **Il y a de l'eau minérale dans la salle à manger mais il n'y a pas d'eau minérale dans la cuisine.**

la salle à manger            la cuisine

**E. Entretien.** Interviewez votre partenaire.

**1.** Qu'est-ce que tu manges souvent le soir? Qu'est-ce que tu aimes boire le soir? Qu'est-ce que tu as mangé hier soir?
**2.** Que préfères-tu manger à midi? (Une salade, un sandwich ou un hamburger?)
**3.** Est-ce que tu aimes manger dans les fast-foods? Est-ce que tu manges souvent dans un fast-food? Est-ce que tu préfères boire de l'eau ou du coca avec tes repas?

**F. Préparatifs.** Vous allez inviter des amis chez vous pour un grand repas traditionnel à la française. Avec un(e) partenaire, faites des projets pour ce dîner.

Parlez de:

- quand et où vous allez faire ce dîner et qui vous allez inviter.
- ce que vous allez servir. (Imaginez que vous n'aimez pas les mêmes choses et proposez au moins trois choses comme entrée, comme plat principal, comme dessert et comme boisson.)

## Stratégies et Compréhension auditive

*Planning and predicting*

Since no two cultures are identical, you may sometimes find yourself lacking the cultural knowledge to understand what you hear in French. For example, if the waiter asks **Évian ou Perrier?** you will not be able to answer unless you recognize that these are brand names of French mineral waters. In such situations, try to infer what is being asked from the context. Also, when possible, prepare and predict from previous experiences what might be asked or said. For example, before ordering mineral water, glance at the menu to see what kinds are sold.

CD 2-18

**A. Pendant le repas.** Vous êtes au restaurant. Est-ce qu'on vous dit les choses que vous entendez **avant le repas** ou **à la fin du repas?**

**B. Questions.** Faites une liste de trois questions qu'un(e) client(e) pose souvent au serveur ou à la serveuse dans un restaurant.

## Au restaurant

CD 2-19

Deux touristes se trouvent dans un restaurant français. Écoutez leur conversation. Qu'est-ce qu'ils commandent? Nommez au moins quatre choses.

**A. Que demandent-ils?** Écoutez encore une fois la conversation au restaurant et écrivez deux questions que les clients posent à la serveuse.

**B. Qu'allez-vous choisir?** Avec un(e) partenaire, jouez une scène au restaurant entre un serveur (une serveuse) et un(e) client(e). Commandez une entrée, un plat principal, un légume, un dessert et une boisson.

# Buying food

> Note
> *culturelle*

Dans le passé, les Français faisaient leurs courses presque tous les jours chez les petits commerçants. Aujourd'hui, les Français font 66% de leurs achats alimentaires *(food purchases)* dans les grandes surfaces. Et vous? Combien de fois par semaine faites-vous les courses? Où préférez-vous les faire? Faites-vous les courses chez les petits commerçants de temps en temps?

**VOCABULAIRE SUPPLÉMENTAIRE**

**la crémerie** *the dairy store*
**la fromagerie** *the cheese shop*
**la pâtisserie** *the pastry shop*
**le marchand de fruits et légumes** *the fruit and vegetable market*

## Les courses

De plus en plus de Français **font leurs courses** dans les supermarchés et **les grandes surfaces** où on vend de tout. Mais beaucoup préfèrent aller chez les petits **commerçants** du quartier où le service est plus personnalisé.

À la boulangerie, on peut acheter du pain et **des pâtisseries** *(f)*:

| une baguette | un pain au chocolat | **un pain complet** | une tarte **aux cerises** | une tartelette **aux fraises** |

À la boucherie, on achète de la viande:

du poulet          du bœuf          du porc

À la charcuterie, on achète **de la charcuterie** et **des plats préparés:**

du saucisson     du jambon     des saucisses *(f)*     des plats préparés

On achète du poisson et des fruits de mer à la poissonnerie.

Et on va à l'épicerie pour acheter des fruits, des légumes, **des conserves** *(f)* et des produits **surgelés.**

---

**faire les courses** *to go grocery shopping*   **une grande surface** *a superstore*   **un(e) commerçant(e)** *a shopkeeper*
**une pâtisserie** *a pastry*   **un pain complet** *a loaf of whole-grain bread*   **une cerise** *a cherry*   **une fraise** *a strawberry*
**de la charcuterie** *deli meats, cold cuts*   **un plat préparé** *a ready-to-serve dish*   **des conserves** *(f) canned goods*
**surgelé(e)** *frozen*

Beaucoup de Français **disent** que pour avoir un bon **choix** de légumes et de fruits vraiment **frais, il faut** aller au marché.

**VOCABULAIRE SUPPLÉMENTAIRE**

**LÉGUMES**
**des asperges** (f) asparagus
**une aubergine** an eggplant
**des brocolis** (m)
**du céleri**
**des champignons** (m) mushrooms
**du chou** cabbage
**du chou-fleur** cauliflower
**des choux de Bruxelles** (m) Brussels sprouts
**un concombre** a cucumber
**une courgette** a zucchini
**des épinards** (m) spinach
**du maïs** corn

**FRUITS**
**des abricots** (m) apricots
**un ananas** a pineapple
**un citron vert** a lime
**des framboises** (f) raspberries
**un kiwi**
**une mandarine** a tangerine
**une mangue** a mango
**un melon**
**des myrtilles** (f) blueberries
**une nectarine**
**un pamplemousse** a grapefruit
**une pastèque** a watermelon
**une prune** a plum
**un pruneau** a prune
**des raisins secs** (m) raisins

Au marché, on peut acheter:

des oranges *(f)*      des poires *(f)*      des bananes *(f)*      des pêches *(f)*

du raisin      **des laitues** *(f)*      des oignons *(m)*      des carottes *(f)*

---

**disent** (**dire** *to say, to tell*)   **un choix** *a choice*   **frais (fraîche)** *fresh*   **il faut** *it is necessary, one needs, one must*
**une laitue** *a head of lettuce*

CD 2-20

Rosalie fait ses courses au marché.

| | |
|---|---|
| ROSALIE: | Bonjour, monsieur. |
| LE MARCHAND: | Bonjour, madame. **Qu'est-ce qu'il vous faut aujourd'hui?** |
| ROSALIE: | Euh... voyons... un kilo de pommes de terre et **une livre** de tomates. Vous avez des haricots verts? |
| LE MARCHAND: | Non, madame, pas aujourd'hui. Mais j'ai des petits pois. Regardez comme ils sont beaux. |
| ROSALIE: | Non, merci, pas de petits pois aujourd'hui. |
| LE MARCHAND: | Alors, qu'est-ce que je peux vous proposer d'autre? |
| ROSALIE: | Donnez-moi aussi 500 grammes de fraises. |
| LE MARCHAND: | Et voilà, 500 grammes. Et avec ça? |
| ROSALIE: | C'est tout, merci. Ça fait combien? |
| LE MARCHAND: | Voilà... Alors, un kilo de pommes de terre —1,20 €, une livre de tomates —1,36 € et 500 grammes de fraises —1,50 €. Ça fait 4,06 €. |
| ROSALIE: | Voici 5 euros. |
| LE MARCHAND: | Et voici votre monnaie. Merci, madame, et à bientôt! |
| ROSALIE: | Merci. Au revoir, monsieur. |

## A. Devinettes. Qu'est-ce que c'est?

**Exemple**    C'est un fruit rond, orange et plein de vitamine C.
**C'est une orange.**

1. C'est le légume préféré de Bugs Bunny.
2. C'est un fruit long et jaune que les chimpanzés adorent.
3. Beaucoup de gens pensent que c'est un légume, mais en réalité, c'est un fruit. Ce fruit est rond et rouge. On le sert souvent en salade.
4. C'est un fruit qui peut être jaune, rouge ou vert. On peut le manger cru *(raw)*, mais on peut aussi faire des gâteaux, des tartes, du jus ou du cidre avec.
5. C'est le légume vert qui est l'ingrédient principal d'une salade.
6. On utilise ce fruit pour faire du vin.
7. Ce sont de petits légumes ronds et verts.
8. Ce sont de petits fruits rouges qu'on utilise souvent pour faire une tarte.

## B. Que peut-on acheter... ?

Que peut-on acheter dans une boulangerie?

| | | | |
|---|---|---|---|
| du pain | du bœuf | du raisin | des oignons |
| des légumes | une tarte | des tartelettes | une baguette |
| des cerises | un pain complet | du jambon | des produits surgelés |

Que peut-on acheter dans une poissonnerie?

| | | | |
|---|---|---|---|
| des carottes | des œufs | des moules | des crevettes |
| des haricots | du poisson | de la volaille | de la viande |
| du café | de la glace | du gâteau | des fruits de mer |

Que peut-on acheter dans une boucherie?

| | | | |
|---|---|---|---|
| du poulet | du thon | du bœuf | du homard |
| des laitues | du rosbif | du saucisson | du pâté |
| du porc | des crevettes | du riz | du sel |

---

**Qu'est-ce qu'il vous faut aujourd'hui?** *What do you need today?*    **une livre** *half a kilo (≈a pound)*

Que peut-on acheter dans une charcuterie?

| du jambon | un pain complet | des conserves | du vin |
|---|---|---|---|
| des légumes | du saucisson | du poivre | du sucre |
| des tartes | des saucisses | des plats préparés | des conserves |

### C. Quel magasin? Dans quels magasins est-ce qu'on vend ces produits? (Utilisez l'article partitif!)

| à la charcuterie | au marché |
|---|---|
| à la boulangerie | à la boucherie |
| à l'épicerie | à la poissonnerie |

**Exemple**     le rosbif
**On vend du rosbif à la boucherie.**

1. la viande
2. le pain
3. les plats préparés
4. le porc
5. les crevettes

6. les tartes
7. les produits surgelés
8. le saucisson
9. les conserves
10. le homard

À la charcuterie

### D. Qu'est-ce qu'on vend? Nommez au moins quatre choses qu'on vend dans les endroits mentionnés dans l'exercice précédent.

**Exemple**     à la charcuterie
**À la charcuterie, on vend du jambon...**

### E. Entretien. Interviewez votre partenaire.

1. Aimes-tu faire les courses? Combien de fois par semaine est-ce que tu fais les courses? Où est-ce que tu fais tes courses d'habitude? Est-ce que tu achètes quelquefois des choses chez les petits commerçants?
2. En France, où est-ce qu'on achète du pain? des plats préparés? des fruits et des légumes frais? Qu'est-ce qu'on vend à l'épicerie? à la boulangerie? à la poissonnerie?
3. Aimes-tu les fruits? les légumes? Préfères-tu les fruits ou les légumes? Quels légumes préfères-tu? Quels légumes est-ce que tu n'aimes pas? Quels fruits préfères-tu? Quels fruits est-ce que tu n'aimes pas?

### F. Conversation. Avec un(e) partenaire, relisez à haute voix la conversation à la page précédente. Ensuite, imaginez que vous êtes à la boulangerie. Achetez ce que vous voudriez. (Déterminez un prix logique en euros pour chaque chose.)

**Pour vérifier**

What word follows quantity expressions before nouns? Do you use **de** or **des** after a quantity expression followed by a plural noun?

# Saying how much

*Les expressions de quantité*

When ordering in a restaurant or shopping for food, you need to specify how much you want.

| | | | |
|---|---|---|---|
| un verre de | *a glass of* | une boîte de | *a box of, a can of* |
| un litre de | *a liter of* | un pot de | *a jar of* |
| une carafe de | *a carafe of* | un paquet de | *a bag of, a sack of* |
| une bouteille de | *a bottle of* | une douzaine de | *a dozen* |
| | | | |
| une tranche de | *a slice of* | 300 grammes de | *300 grams of* |
| un morceau de | *a piece of* | un kilo de | *a kilo of* |
| | | un kilo et demi de | *a kilo and a half of* |
| | | une livre de | *a half a kilo (≈ a pound of)* |

When specifying a quantity with expressions like those above, always use **de (d')** in front of a noun instead of **du, de la, de l',** or **des.** This is also true for imprecise quantities such as:

| | |
|---|---|
| combien de | *how much, how many* |
| (un) peu de | *(a) little* |
| assez de | *enough* |
| beaucoup de | *a lot of* |
| trop de | *too much, too many* |
| beaucoup trop de | *much too much, much too many* |

J'ai acheté une bouteille **de** vin rouge, 500 grammes **de** viande, un litre **de** lait et beaucoup **de** légumes!

**A. C'est assez?** Est-ce que la quantité indiquée est suffisante?

**Exemple**  Vous prenez le petit déjeuner seul(e) le matin et il y a un verre de lait dans le réfrigérateur.
**Il y a trop de lait. / Il y a assez de lait. / Il y a trop peu de lait.**

| beaucoup trop | trop | assez | trop peu |
|---|---|---|---|

1. Vous êtes quatre au restaurant et il y a une demi-bouteille d'eau.
2. Vous allez préparer une salade de tomates pour deux personnes. Vous avez un kilo de tomates.
3. Vous allez faire une omelette pour deux personnes et vous avez un seul œuf.
4. C'est le matin et il y a un verre de lait dans le réfrigérateur chez vous.
5. Vous dînez seul(e) au restaurant et il y a trois carafes d'eau.
6. Vous voulez préparer des carottes pour six personnes et vous avez deux carottes.

**B. Je voudrais...** Précisez quelque chose de logique pour chacune des quantités proposées.

Je voudrais...

1. une bouteille de
2. un paquet de
3. une boîte de
4. une livre de
5. deux kilos de
6. un morceau de
7. un litre de
8. dix tranches de

| | | |
|---|---|---|
| thon | cerises | jambon |
| vin | tomates | fromage |
| jus de fruit | rosbif | lait |
| sel | sucre | riz |

**C. Donnez-moi...** Demandez les quantités indiquées des provisions suivantes.

**Exemple**  **Une bouteille de vin, s'il vous plaît.**

**D. Au marché.** Imaginez que vous préparez un dîner pour quatre amis. Décidez ce que vous voulez servir et achetez les provisions au marché. Un(e) camarade de classe va jouer le rôle du/de la marchand(e).

Pour vérifier

1. Which article do you use to say *a* in French? Which articles do you use to express the idea of *some* or *any?*

2. Which article do you use to say *the?* to talk about likes, dislikes, and preferences? to make statements about entire categories?

3. Which articles change to **de?** When do they make this change? Which articles never change?

# Talking about foods

## *L'usage des articles*

Each article you use with a noun conveys a different meaning. **Un** and **une** mean *a,* whereas **du, de la, de l',** and **des** mean *some* or *any.*

Vous voulez **une** tarte?
*Do you want **a** pie?*
(This refers to a whole pie.)

Vous voulez **de la** tarte?
*Do you want **(some)** pie?*
(This refers to a portion or serving.)

The indefinite article (**un, une, des**) and the partitive (**du, de la, de l'**) change to **de** (**d'**) after expressions of quantity, such as **trop, beaucoup, un kilo, une bouteille...,** and after most negated verbs.

Il ne veut pas **de** dessert parce qu'il a mangé trop **de** chocolats.

Remember to use the definite article (**le, la, l', les**) to say *the,* to express likes, dislikes, and preferences, to make statements about entire categories, or to order from a menu. The definite article does *not* change to **de** after a negative or an expression of quantity.

| | |
|---|---|
| **Le** poisson qu'on achète ici est très bon. | *The fish you buy here is very good.* |
| Je n'aime pas beaucoup **le** poisson. | *I don't like fish very much.* |
| **Le** poisson n'a pas beaucoup de calories. | *Fish doesn't have a lot of calories.* |
| Je vais prendre **le** saumon fumé. | *I'll have the smoked salmon.* |

When using **beaucoup, trop,** or **assez** with **aimer** to say how much you do or don't like something, continue to use the definite article **le, la, l',** or **les.**

J'aime **beaucoup le** thé.    J'aime **assez le** café.    Je n'aime pas **trop le** coca.

| | AFFIRMATIVE | NEGATIVE |
|---|---|---|
| **PARTITIVE ARTICLE** *to say* some *or* any | Je voudrais **du** café. | Je ne veux pas **de** café. |
| **INDEFINITE ARTICLE** *to say* a; *to indicate a whole or several* | Je voudrais **un** café. | Je ne veux pas **de** café. |
| ***DE* WITH AN EXPRESSION OF QUANTITY** | Je voudrais un kilo **de** café. | Je n'ai pas acheté beaucoup **de** café. |
| **DEFINITE ARTICLE** *to say* the; *to express likes; to make general statements about categories* | J'aime beaucoup **le** café. | Je n'aime pas **le** café. |

**A. Manges-tu bien?** Demandez à votre partenaire s'il/si elle mange souvent les choses suivantes.

Exemple    fruits    — **Manges-tu souvent des fruits?**
                      — **Je mange rarement des fruits.**
                         **Je ne mange jamais de fruits.**

1. escargots
2. tarte
3. légumes
4. viande rouge

5. poulet
6. crudités
7. glace
8. pâté

Maintenant, demandez à votre partenaire s'il/si elle aime ces mêmes choses.

Exemple    fruits    — **Aimes-tu les fruits?**
                     — **J'aime assez les fruits. / Je n'aime pas les fruits.**

### B. Vos préférences. Dites si vous achetez souvent les choses suivantes et expliquez pourquoi.

Exemple    pâté    **J'achète souvent du pâté parce que j'aime le pâté.**
                   **Je n'achète jamais de pâté parce que je n'aime pas le pâté.**

1. fromage
2. bananes
3. viande rouge
4. huîtres

5. raisin
6. eau minérale
7. jus
8. café

### C. Vos goûts. Complétez les phrases suivantes avec le nom d'un aliment (food) ou d'une boisson logique. Utilisez les articles convenables.

1. Moi, j'adore...
2. J'aime bien...
3. Comme viande, je mange souvent...
4. Chez moi, il n'y a jamais...
5. Pour le déjeuner, je prends souvent...
6. La dernière fois que je suis allé(e) au restaurant, j'ai mangé...

### D. Chez Rosalie. Rosalie parle du dîner qu'elle va préparer pour André ce soir. Complétez ce qu'elle dit avec l'article convenable: **un, une, du, de la, de l', des, le, la, l', les** ou **de.**

Ce soir, je vais servir ___1___ soupe de légumes, ___2___ poulet, ___3___ riz et ___4___ petits pois. Et comme dessert, je pense préparer ___5___ tarte aux cerises. Moi, je préfère ___6___ gâteau, mais André aime beaucoup ___7___ tarte! Cet après-midi, je dois aller acheter ___8___ sucre, 500 grammes ___9___ cerises et beaucoup ___10___ légumes. Il y a un marché tout près où ___11___ légumes sont toujours très frais! Je ne mets pas ___12___ oignons dans la soupe parce qu'André n'aime pas ___13___ oignons. C'est dommage parce que ___14___ oignons sont bons pour la santé (health).

### E. Entretien. Interviewez votre partenaire.

1. Quels fruits de mer aimes-tu? Quelles viandes? Quelles boissons?
2. Manges-tu plus souvent des fruits ou des légumes? Quel fruit préfères-tu? Quels fruits est-ce que tu n'aimes pas? Quel légume préfères-tu? Quels légumes est-ce que tu n'aimes pas? Est-ce que tu préfères acheter des légumes surgelés, frais ou en conserve?
3. Tu aimes les desserts? Est-ce que tu préfères le gâteau ou la tarte? la glace au chocolat ou la glace à la vanille? Est-ce que tu manges souvent un dessert quand tu vas au restaurant? Quel dessert prends-tu le plus souvent?
4. À la maison, qu'est-ce que tu manges la plupart du temps? Qu'est-ce que tu ne manges jamais? Pourquoi?

# Talking about meals

Seulement 10% des Français ne prennent pas de petit déjeuner. Parmi ceux qui mangent le matin, la plus grande majorité (70%) mangent à la française (pain ou croissant et boisson). 13% aiment prendre un petit déjeuner à l'américaine et 15% prennent seulement une boisson.

En France, les repas se font de moins en moins à une heure fixe et les familles mangent moins souvent ensemble. Les Français mangent de plus en plus sans se mettre à table: au travail, dans la rue, en voiture ou dans les transports publics, au parc. En effet, à midi, 32% des Français mangent sans se mettre à table. Est-ce que la situation est la même chez vous?

## Les repas

En France, le petit déjeuner est généralement un repas **léger.** On prend:

du café au lait     du thé     **des tartines** *(f)* ou des croissants *(m)*

du chocolat     du beurre     de la confiture

De plus en plus de Français, **surtout** les jeunes, prennent aussi des céréales le matin.

Les Américains et les Canadiens prennent souvent un petit déjeuner plus **copieux.** Ils prennent:

des œufs au bacon     des céréales *(f)*     du pain grillé     des fruits

À midi, certains Français prennent un déjeuner complet. D'autres prennent un repas rapide. Dans les cafés, les fast-foods et les self-services, on peut manger:

    une soupe
    une omelette
    **un steak-frites**
    une salade
    un hamburger
    une pizza
    un sandwich

Les gens qui prennent un repas rapide à midi mangent souvent un repas plus complet le soir. **Ceux** qui mangent un repas plus copieux à midi mangent **seulement** de la soupe, des légumes, de la charcuterie, une salade, du fromage ou une omelette comme dîner.

---

**léger (légère)** *light*    **une tartine** *bread with butter and jelly*    **surtout** *especially*    **copieux (copieuse)** *copious, large*
**un steak-frites** *steak and fries*    **Ceux (Celles)** *Those*    **seulement** *only*

CD 2-21

Rose prépare le petit déjeuner avec sa cousine Lucie.

LUCIE: Tu as faim? Je peux te faire des œufs au bacon si tu veux—un vrai petit déjeuner à l'américaine.

ROSE: Merci, c'est gentil, mais je mange très peu le matin. **Pourtant je prendrais volontiers** des céréales et du thé si tu **en** as.

LUCIE: Ah, je regrette... il **n'**y a **plus** de thé. Mais il y a du café. Tu en veux?

ROSE: Oui, je veux bien. Et toi? Qu'est-ce que tu vas prendre?

LUCIE: Le matin, **je bois** toujours du chocolat chaud et quelquefois je prends des tartines.

ROSE: Oh, regarde! **Il n'y a presque plus** de pain.

LUCIE: Mais **si!** Il y a **encore** une baguette, **là.**

---

## A. Vrai ou faux? Corrigez les phrases fausses.

1. En France, on prend plus souvent des œufs le soir ou à midi que le matin.
2. Les Français prennent un repas copieux le matin.
3. Les Américains et les Canadiens préfèrent prendre un petit déjeuner plus léger que les Français.
4. Beaucoup de Français prennent seulement du pain et du café le matin.
5. Certains, surtout les jeunes, aiment prendre des céréales.
6. Rose a l'habitude de beaucoup manger au petit déjeuner.
7. Ce matin, Rose va boire du thé.
8. Il n'y a plus de café chez Lucie.
9. Il y a encore une baguette chez Lucie.

## B. Chez nous. Aux États-Unis et au Canada, à quel repas mange-t-on le plus souvent ces choses: **au petit déjeuner, au déjeuner** ou **au dîner?**

**Exemple**    une omelette
**On mange une omelette au petit déjeuner.**

1. des croissants
2. des céréales
3. du poisson
4. du gâteau
5. un hamburger et des frites
6. du saumon
7. des œufs au bacon
8. des légumes
9. de la soupe
10. du pain grillé avec de la confiture et du beurre

**VOCABULAIRE SUPPLÉMENTAIRE**

**des gaufres** (f) waffles
**des muffins anglais**
**des pancakes**
**des petites saucisses** breakfast sausages
**du sirop d'érable** maple syrup
**du yaourt**
**des flocons d'avoine** oatmeal
**une barre de céréales**
**du pain perdu** French toast

## C. Conversation. Avec un(e) partenaire, relisez à haute voix la conversation entre Lucie et Rose en haut de la page. Ensuite, imaginez que vous passez des vacances avec un(e) ami(e) français(e). Parlez de ce que vous mangez d'habitude le matin.

---

**Pourtant** However    **je prendrais volontiers** I would gladly have    **en** some, any    **ne... plus** no more, no longer
**je bois** (**boire** to drink)    **Il n'y a presque plus** There is almost no more    **si** yes (in response to a question / statement in the negative)    **encore** still, again, more    **là** there

**1.** In what three instances do you use the pronoun **en?** How is **en** usually translated in English? Can you omit **en** in French as you often can its equivalent in English?

**2.** How do you say *to drink* in French? What is the conjugation of this verb? How do you say *I drank some coffee this morning? I used to drink a lot of coffee?*

# Saying what you eat and drink

*Le pronom **en** et le verbe **boire***

Use the pronoun **en** to replace a noun preceded by a partitive article, an expression of quantity, **un, une, des,** or a number. In English, **en** is usually translated as *some, any, of it,* or *of them.* Although the equivalent expression may be omitted in English, **en** is always used in French.

| | |
|---|---|
| — Tu veux un croissant? | — *Do you want a croissant?* |
| — Oui, j'**en** veux un. | — *Yes, I want one (of them).* |

**En** is placed *immediately* before the verb. It goes before the infinitive if there is one. If not, it goes before the conjugated verb. In the **passé composé,** it is placed before the auxiliary verb.

— Tu prends du gâteau?
— Oui, je vais **en** prendre. / Oui, j'**en** prends. / Non, merci, j'**en** ai déjà pris.

Use **en** to replace:

- a noun preceded by **de, du, de la, de l',** or **des.**

| | |
|---|---|
| — Tu veux **du café?** | — *Do you want **some coffee?*** |
| — Non merci, je n'**en** veux pas. | — *No thanks, I don't want **any.*** |

- a noun preceded by an expression of quantity. (In this case, repeat the expression of quantity in the sentence containing **en,** unless it's negative.)

| | |
|---|---|
| — Vous voulez un kilo **de cerises?** | — *Do you want a kilo **of cherries?*** |
| — Oui, j'**en** veux un kilo. | — *Yes, I want a kilo **(of them).*** |
| Non, je n'**en** veux pas. | *No, I don't want **any.*** |

- a noun preceded by **un, une,** or a number. (In this case, include **un, une,** or a number in the sentence containing **en,** unless it's negative.)

| | |
|---|---|
| — Tu as mangé une **tartelette?** | — *You ate a **tart?*** |
| — Oui, j'**en** ai mangé une. | — *Yes, I ate one **(of them).*** |
| J'**en** ai mangé deux! | *I ate two **(of them)!*** |
| Non, je n'**en** ai pas mangé. | *No, I didn't eat **any.*** |

Here is the conjugation of **boire** *(to drink).*

| **BOIRE (to drink)** | |
|---|---|
| je bois | nous buvons |
| tu bois | vous buvez |
| il/elle/on boit | ils/elles boivent |
| PASSÉ COMPOSÉ: j'ai bu | |
| IMPARFAIT: je buvais | |

Vous avez bu du vin hier soir?        Elle buvait du lait quand elle était petite.

**A. À table.** Un(e) ami(e) vous propose les choses suivantes au petit déjeuner. Comment répondez-vous? Utilisez le pronom **en** dans vos réponses.

**Exemple**     du café     — **Tu veux du café?**
                           — **Non merci, je n'en veux pas. / Oui, j'en veux bien.**

**1.** du café          **3.** des œufs          **5.** des tartines
**2.** du thé           **4.** de l'eau          **6.** des céréales

**B. Combien?** Voilà la liste de Rosalie pour les courses. Combien est-ce qu'il faut acheter de chaque chose? Utilisez des quantités logiques et le pronom **en** dans vos réponses.

un paquet de sucre
6 pommes
un kilo de bœuf
2 litres de lait
une douzaine d'œufs
une bouteille de vin rouge
500 grammes de cerises
300 grammes de pâté
une boîte de céréales

**Exemple**  du sucre
**Il faut en acheter un paquet.**

1. des pommes
2. du bœuf
3. du lait
4. des œufs
5. du vin rouge
6. des cerises
7. du pâté
8. des céréales

**C. Et vous?** Faites-vous attention à votre santé *(health)*? Répondez à ces questions. Employez le pronom **en**.

**Exemple**  Vous mangez des œufs?
**Oui, j'en mange trop / beaucoup / assez / peu. /**
**Oui, mais je n'en mange pas assez. / Non, je n'en mange pas.**

| trop | beaucoup | assez | (un) peu |
|---|---|---|---|
| ne... pas assez | | ne... pas | |

1. Vous buvez de l'eau?
2. Vous mangez des desserts?
3. Vous faites de l'exercice?
4. Vous mangez des fruits?
5. Vous mangez du poisson?
6. Vous fumez des cigarettes?
7. Vous mangez des légumes?
8. Vous mangez de la viande?

**D. Boissons.** Complétez les phrases logiquement en utilisant le verbe **boire**.

**Exemple**  Le matin, je **bois du lait.**

1. Au petit déjeuner, les Français...
2. Au petit déjeuner, les Américains / Canadiens...
3. Le matin, je...
4. Quand j'étais jeune, le matin, je...
5. Ce matin, je (j')...
6. Avec un hamburger, on...
7. Dans cette région, quand il fait chaud, nous...
8. Quand j'ai très soif, je...
9. *(À un[e] camarade de classe)* À une fête, qu'est-ce que tu... ?
10. *(Au professeur)* Est-ce que vous... beaucoup de café?

**E. Entretien.** Interviewez votre partenaire. Répondez à chaque question en utilisant le pronom **en**.

1. Manges-tu souvent des légumes? Est-ce que tu en as déjà mangé aujourd'hui? Manges-tu souvent de la viande rouge? En manges-tu tous les jours? Est-ce que tu vas en manger demain?
2. Fais-tu souvent de l'exercice? Combien de fois par semaine est-ce que tu en fais?
3. Est-ce que tu bois du café? En bois-tu trop? Quand est-ce que tu en bois? Et tes amis, est-ce qu'ils en boivent souvent?

**1.** How do you find the stem of a regular **-ir** verb? What are the endings? What is the conjugation of **grandir?** of **grossir?**

**2.** What auxiliary do you use in the **passé composé** with the verbs listed here? How do you form the past participle? How do you say *I finished?* What is the conjugation of **-ir** verbs in the imperfect?

**3.** How do you pronounce an initial **s?** a single **s** between vowels? How do you pronounce double **ss?** How can you hear the difference between the singular and plural forms of **-ir** verbs in the present tense?

## Talking about choices

*Les verbes en -ir*

To conjugate regular **-ir** verbs in the present tense, drop the **-ir** and add the following endings:

| CHOISIR *(to choose)* | |
|---|---|
| je chois**is** | nous chois**issons** |
| tu chois**is** | vous chois**issez** |
| il/elle/on chois**it** | ils/elles chois**issent** |
| PASSÉ COMPOSÉ: j'ai choisi | |
| IMPARFAIT: je choisissais | |

All **-ir** verbs presented here form the **passé composé** with **avoir**.

Many verbs that describe a change in physical appearance *(to get older, to turn red . . . )* end in **-ir**. Notice that some are based on the related adjective: (**vieille** → **vieillir**, **rouge** → **rougir**).

Here are some common **-ir** verbs.

| | |
|---|---|
| choisir (de faire) | *to choose (to do)* |
| finir (de faire) | *to finish (doing)* |
| grandir | *to grow (up), to grow taller* |
| grossir | *to get fatter* |
| maigrir | *to get thinner, to slim down* |
| obéir (à quelqu'un / à quelque chose) | *to obey (somebody / something)* |
| réfléchir (à) | *to think (about)* |
| réussir (à) | *to succeed (at), to pass* [a test] |
| rougir | *to blush, to turn red* |
| vieillir | *to age* |

CD 2-22

## Prononciation

*La lettre **s** et les verbes en -ir*

It can be difficult to remember whether to use one **s** or two when spelling forms of verbs such as **choisir** or **réussir**. Keep in mind that a single **s** between vowels is pronounced like a **z**, and double **ss** is pronounced like an **s**. Initial **s** is always pronounced like an **s**.

ils choisissent    nous réussissons    je choisissais    je grossissais

poison / poisson    un désert / un dessert    vous choisissez / vous réussissez

In the present tense, an **s** sound in the ending of **-ir** verbs indicates that you are talking about more than one person.

il rougit / ils rougissent    elle finit / elles finissent    il choisit / ils choisissent

**A. C'est-à-dire...** Trouvez une expression équivalente. Utilisez un verbe en **-ir**.

**Exemple**    Il devient rouge.
                **Il rougit.**

1. Il devient plus gros.
2. Il a l'air plus âgé.
3. Il pense à quelque chose.
4. Il devient plus mince.
5. L'enfant devient plus grand.
6. Il fait un choix.
7. Il termine quelque chose.
8. Il a un bon résultat à son examen.

**B. Il faut bien choisir.** Rosalie dit ce que chacun choisit de manger. Qu'est-ce qu'elle dit? Variez vos réponses.

> **Exemple**    Rose veut maigrir. Elle **choisit de la salade.**

| | | |
|---|---|---|
| des légumes | de la salade | des fruits |
| de la viande rouge | du poisson | des œufs |
| des desserts | de la glace | ??? |

1. André veut grossir. Il...
2. Moi, je veux rester en bonne santé *(healthy)*. Je...
3. André et Henri veulent de la vitamine C dans leur régime *(diet)*. Ils...
4. Rose et moi, nous voulons maigrir. Nous...
5. Et toi, Patricia, tu veux être plus forte *(stronger)*? Tu... ?
6. Et vous, les enfants, vous voulez grandir vite? Vous... ?

**C. En cours de français.** Comment est votre cours de français? Dites si les personnes suivantes font les choses indiquées généralement.

> **Exemple**    Le professeur... (choisir des questions faciles pour l'examen)
> **Généralement, le professeur choisit des questions faciles pour l'examen. / Généralement, le professeur ne choisit pas des questions faciles pour l'examen.**

1. Le professeur... (réussir à comprendre les questions des étudiants, finir le cours à l'heure, rougir facilement)
2. Les étudiants... (finir les devoirs, obéir au prof, réussir à bien parler français)
3. Moi, je... (finir les devoirs, réussir à comprendre la leçon, réfléchir avant des répondre)

**D. Et au dernier cours?** Dites si les personnes nommées ont fait les choses indiquées dans *C. En cours de français* au dernier cours.

> **Exemple**    Le professeur (choisir des questions faciles pour l'examen)
> **Au dernier cours, le professeur a choisi des questions faciles pour l'examen. / Au dernier cours, le professeur n'a pas choisi des questions faciles pour l'examen.**

**E. Au lycée.** Demandez à votre partenaire s'il/si elle faisait les choses suivantes quand il/elle était au lycée.

> **Exemple**    réfléchir toujours avant de répondre
> — **Quand tu étais au lycée, est-ce que tu réfléchissais toujours avant de répondre?**
> — **Oui, je réfléchissais toujours avant de répondre.**
>   **Non, je ne réfléchissais pas toujours avant de répondre.**

1. réussir à tous tes cours
2. obéir toujours à tes parents
3. finir toujours tes devoirs
4. réfléchir souvent à l'avenir *(the future)*

# Choosing a healthy lifestyle

## La bonne santé

**Note culturelle**

Les Français font de plus en plus d'effort pour rester en bonne santé. 66% des Français pratiquent un sport régulièrement au moins une fois par semaine. Ils aiment autant *(as much)* les sports individuels (randonnées, gymnastique, natation *[swimming]*, vélo, tennis, roller, ski, judo...) que les sports d'équipe *(team)* (football, basketball, rugby, handball...). Ils mangent moins de graisses et de viande et plus de légumes. 42% des foyers *(households)* achètent quelquefois des produits bios. Qu'est-ce qu'on fait pour rester en bonne santé dans votre région?

**NOTES DE GRAMMAIRE**

**Se sentir** *(to feel)* is conjugated like **sortir (je me sens, tu te sens, il/elle/on se sent, nous nous sentons, vous vous sentez, ils/elles se sentent)**.

Note that **prendre** and **faire** are followed by an indefinite or partitive article **(prendre des vitamines, faire de l'aérobic)**, whereas **éviter** and **contrôler** are often followed by the definite article **(éviter le tabac, contrôler le stress)**.

**Faites-vous attention à** votre santé? **À votre avis,** qu'est-ce qu'il faut faire pour rester en bonne santé?

Pour rester en bonne santé, est-ce qu'**on devrait...**

    manger des plats **sains** et légers?
    manger plus de produits **bios**?
    manger moins de **matières grasses** *(f)*?
    manger plus de protéines et de produits **laitiers**?
    manger moins de **féculents** *(m)*?
    manger plus **lentement**?
    prendre des vitamines?
    **éviter** l'alcool et le tabac?
    contrôler le stress? (faire du yoga ou de la méditation, parler entre ami[e]s...)

Pour être en forme et pour devenir plus **fort,** est-ce qu'on devrait...

    **marcher** et **faire des randonnées** *(f)*?
    faire de l'aérobic?
    **faire de la muscu(lation)?**

CD 2-23

Patricia demande **des conseils** à Rosalie.

PATRICIA: **Je me sens** toujours fatiguée ces jours-ci. J'ai besoin d'**améliorer** ma santé. Toi, tu as l'air toujours en forme. **Pourrais-tu** me donner des conseils?

ROSALIE: Tu dors assez la nuit?

PATRICIA: Je me couche assez tôt mais je dors très mal. Je me réveille **plusieurs** fois pendant la nuit. Si je pouvais dormir mieux, **je serais** contente.

ROSALIE: Tu devrais boire moins de café pendant la journée. **Tu ferais mieux de** bien manger aussi et de faire de l'exercice régulièrement.

PATRICIA: J'aime bien marcher. Si j'avais plus de temps libre, **j'aimerais** bien faire du sport tous les jours.

ROSALIE: Si tu marchais tous les jours et que tu mangeais mieux, **tu te sentirais sans doute** mieux. Et **n'oublie pas** de boire moins de café et plus d'eau!

---

**la santé** *health*    **faire attention (à)** *to pay attention (to), to watch out (for)*    **À votre avis** *In your opinion*
**on devrait** *one should*    **sain(e)** *healthy*    **bios (biologiques)** *organic*    **les matières grasses** *(f) fats*
**laitier (laitière)** *dairy*    **les féculents** *(m) carbohydrates*    **lentement** *slowly*    **éviter** *to avoid*    **fort(e)** *strong*
**marcher** *to walk*    **faire des randonnées** *(f) to go hiking*    **faire de la muscu(lation)** *to do weight training, to do bodybuilding*
**des conseils** *(m) advice*    **Je me sens (se sentir** *to feel)*    **améliorer** *to improve*    **Pourrais-tu...?** *Could you...?*
**plusieurs** *several*    **je serais** *I would be*    **Tu ferais mieux de** *You would do better to*    **j'aimerais** *I would like*
**tu te sentirais** *you would feel*    **sans doute** *probably*    **n'oublie pas** *don't forget* **(oublier** *to forget)*

**A. Des conseils.** C'est **un bon conseil** ou **un mauvais conseil** pour rester en bonne santé?

1. Il faut faire de l'exercice plusieurs fois par semaine.
2. On devrait manger moins de féculents et plus de protéines.
3. Il est important de faire de l'aérobic.
4. On devrait éviter les matières grasses.
5. Les plats sains et légers sont bons pour la santé.
6. On peut devenir plus fort si on fait de la muscu.
7. On devrait manger plus vite pour éviter de trop manger.
8. On devrait manger des produits bios.
9. On ferait mieux de rester très stressé, ça donne de l'énergie.
10. Si vous voulez améliorer votre santé, n'oubliez pas de boire assez d'eau.

**B. Il faut...** Complétez ces phrases. Dites au moins deux choses pour chaque phrase.

on devrait...
faire...          éviter...          obéir...
prendre...        contrôler...       manger...

1. Pour améliorer sa santé...
2. Pour contrôler le stress...
3. Pour devenir plus fort...
4. Pour se sentir moins fatigué...

**C. Entretien.** Interviewez votre partenaire.

1. Est-ce que tu te sens bien en général? Est-ce que tu te sens souvent fatigué(e)? Comment est-ce que tu te sens aujourd'hui?
2. Fais-tu attention à ta santé? Que fais-tu pour ta santé?
3. Manges-tu bien? Manges-tu beaucoup de fruits et de légumes? beaucoup de plats sains et légers? beaucoup de produits laitiers? Est-ce que tu prends des vitamines?
4. Dors-tu assez? Combien d'heures dors-tu par nuit?
5. Est-ce que tu évites l'alcool ou est-ce que tu en bois? Est-ce que tu fumes?
6. Es-tu stressé(e)? Que fais-tu pour contrôler le stress?
7. Aimes-tu faire de l'exercice? Fais-tu de l'aérobic? de la muscu? des randonnées? Aimes-tu marcher? Combien de fois par semaine fais-tu de l'exercice?

**D. Conversation.** Avec un(e) partenaire, relisez à haute voix la conversation entre Rosalie et Patricia à la page précédente. Ensuite, imaginez que vous voudriez faire plus attention à votre santé. Demandez des conseils à votre partenaire.

**1.** What other verb tense has the same endings as the conditional? What is the stem for the conditional of most verbs? Which 12 verbs have irregular stems in the conditional? What is the stem of each? Do they use the regular conditional endings? How do you say *there would be? it would rain? it would be necessary?*

**2.** How do you express *could* and *should* in French?

**3.** When do you use the conditional?

# Saying what you would do

*Le conditionnel*

To say what one *would, could,* or *should* do, use the conditional form of the verb.

> *would* + verb in English = verb in the conditional in French

*I would like* to improve my health.　　　**Je voudrais** améliorer ma santé.

The conditional of most verbs is formed by adding the same endings as the **imparfait** to the infinitive of the verb. If an infinitive ends in **-e,** the **e** is dropped.

| PARLER | FINIR | PERDRE |
|---|---|---|
| je parlerais | je finirais | je perdrais |
| tu parlerais | tu finirais | tu perdrais |
| il/elle/on parlerait | il/elle/on finirait | il/elle/on perdrait |
| nous parlerions | nous finirions | nous perdrions |
| vous parleriez | vous finiriez | vous perdriez |
| ils/elles parleraient | ils/elles finiraient | ils/elles perdraient |

Most irregular verbs follow this same pattern.

dormir → je dormirais...　　　prendre → je prendrais...　　　boire → je boirais...

Verbs like **se lever, payer,** and **appeler** have spelling changes in the conditional stem in *all* the forms **(je me lèverais, je paierais, j'appellerais).** Those like **préférer** do not **(je préférerais).**

The following verbs have irregular stems in the conditional. The endings are regular.

| -r- | | -vr- / -dr- | | -rr- | |
|---|---|---|---|---|---|
| aller | ir- | devoir | devr- | voir | verr- |
| avoir | aur- | vouloir | voudr- | pouvoir | pourr- |
| être | ser- | venir | viendr- | mourir | mourr- |
| faire | fer- | devenir | deviendr- | | |
| | | revenir | reviendr- | | |

Si j'avais le temps, **j'irais** plus souvent au club de gym. **Voudriez-vous** venir aussi?
*If I had time,* **I would go** to the gym more often. **Would you like** to come too?

You need to learn these forms too.

| | | |
|---|---|---|
| il y a | il y aurait | *there would be* |
| il pleut | il pleuvrait | *it would rain* |
| il faut | il faudrait | *it would be necessary* |

To say *should,* use the conditional of **devoir** plus an infinitive.

> *should* + verb in English = **devoir** in the conditional + infinitive

*I should* eat better.　　　**Je devrais** manger mieux.

To say *could,* use the conditional of **pouvoir** plus an infinitive.

> *could* + verb in English = **pouvoir** in the conditional + infinitive

*Could you* give me some advice?　　　**Pourrais**-tu me donner des conseils?

As you have seen, the conditional is used to say what one *would, could,* or *should* do.

Use the conditional:

- to make polite requests or offers.

  Pourrais-tu me passer le sel?    *Could you pass me the salt?*
  Voudriez-vous du café?    *Would you like some coffee?*

- to say what someone would do if circumstances were different (to make hypothetical or contrary-to-fact statements).

  Si je savais faire la cuisine, je mangerais mieux.
  *If I knew how to cook, I would eat better.*

In statements such as the one above, the **si** clause is in the imperfect and the result clause is in the conditional. Note that either clause can come first.

---

**si** + imperfect → result in conditional

---

Si nous **avions** plus de temps libre, nous **ferions plus d'exercice.**
*If we **had** more free time, we **would exercise more.***

Nous **ferions plus d'exercice** si nous **avions** plus de temps libre.
*We **would exercise more** if we **had** more free time.*

CD 2-24

# Prononciation

*La consonne **r** et le conditionnel*

---

The conditional stems of all verbs in French end in **-r.** To pronounce a French **r,** arch the back of the tongue firmly in the back of the mouth, as if to pronounce a *g,* and pronounce a strong English *h* sound.

| je pourrais | tu trouverais | nous serions | il reviendrait | ils devraient |
|---|---|---|---|---|

**A. Réactions.** Quelle serait votre réaction dans les circonstances suivantes?

Je serais... / Je ne serais pas...

heureux (heureuse)    furieux (furieuse)    horrifié(e)

étonné(e) *(astonished)*    surpris(e)    triste *(sad)*

indifférent(e)    fatigué(e)    ???

1. Si mon meilleur ami (ma meilleure amie) commençait un cours de muscu...
2. Si je ne pouvais plus manger de viande...
3. Si on découvrait *(discovered)* que le chocolat était très bon pour la santé...
4. Si je devais faire de l'exercice tous les jours...
5. Si mon meilleur ami (ma meilleure amie) devenait végétarien(ne)...
6. S'il était interdit partout de fumer...
7. Si le médecin *(doctor)* me disait *(told me)* d'éviter le sucre...

**B. Scrupules.** Que feriez-vous dans ces circonstances?

1. Si vous voyiez *(saw)* la fiancée de votre frère embrasser un autre garçon, est-ce que vous...
   **a.** le diriez *(would tell)* à votre frère?
   **b.** ne feriez rien?
   **c.** demanderiez 50 dollars à sa fiancée pour garder le silence?

2. Si vous voyiez une copie de l'examen de fin de semestre / trimestre sur le bureau du prof deux jours avant l'examen, est-ce que vous...
   **a.** la prendriez?
   **b.** ne feriez rien?
   **c.** liriez l'examen tout de suite?

3. Si vous trouviez un chien dans la rue, est-ce que vous...
   **a.** téléphoneriez à la Société protectrice des animaux?
   **b.** prendriez le chien et chercheriez son maître *(owner)*?
   **c.** ne feriez rien?

4. Si vous ne veniez pas en cours le jour d'un examen important parce que vous n'étiez pas préparé(e), est-ce que vous...
   **a.** expliqueriez *(explain)* la situation au professeur?
   **b.** diriez au professeur que vous étiez malade?
   **c.** choisiriez d'avoir un zéro à l'examen?

5. Si vous voyiez quelqu'un qui attaquait votre professeur de français, est-ce que vous...
   **a.** téléphoneriez à la police?
   **b.** resteriez là pour aider votre professeur?
   **c.** resteriez là pour aider l'agresseur?

**C. Une interview.** Vous avez une interview avec Barbara Walters et elle vous pose les questions suivantes. Comment lui répondez-vous?

1. Si vous étiez une autre personne, qui voudriez-vous être?
2. Si vous habitiez dans une autre ville, où voudriez-vous habiter?
3. Si vous étiez un animal, quel animal seriez-vous: un chien, un chat, un poisson, un rat ou un oiseau *(a bird)*?
4. Si vous étiez une saison, quelle saison seriez-vous: l'hiver, l'été... ?
5. Si on écrivait *(wrote)* votre biographie, comment s'appellerait le livre?
6. Si votre vie était un morceau de musique, est-ce que ce serait de la musique populaire, de la musique classique, du rock, du blues... ?
7. Si votre vie était un film, est-ce que ce serait un drame, une comédie, un film d'épouvante *(horror)* ou un film d'aventures?

**D. Temps libre.** Feriez-vous les choses suivantes si vous aviez plus de temps libre?

**Exemple**   préparer plus souvent des plats sains et légers
   **Oui, je préparerais plus souvent des plats sains et légers.**
   **Non, je ne préparerais pas plus souvent des plats sains et légers.**

1. dormir plus
2. être moins stressé(e)
3. pouvoir me reposer plus
4. apprendre une autre langue
5. aller plus souvent au parc
6. faire plus d'exercice
7. voir plus souvent mes amis
8. rendre plus souvent visite à ma famille

**E. Situations.** Qu'est-ce que ces gens feraient dans les situations suivantes?

> **Exemple**     Si nous n'avions pas cours aujourd'hui, mes amis et moi... (aller au parc)
> **Si nous n'avions pas cours aujourd'hui, nous irions au parc.**
> **Si nous n'avions pas cours aujourd'hui, nous n'irions pas au parc.**

1. Si nous n'avions pas cours aujourd'hui, mes amis et moi... (manger au restaurant, faire de l'aérobic, aller prendre un verre, se reposer)
2. Si Rose voulait améliorer sa santé, elle... (fumer beaucoup, devoir faire plus d'exercice, prendre des vitamines, boire assez d'eau)
3. Si les étudiants voulaient mieux réussir au cours, ils... (faire tous les devoirs, aller à tous les cours, dormir en cours, écouter des CD en français)
4. Si mes parents allaient en vacances en France, ils... (être contents, manger dans des restaurants français, boire du vin français, marcher beaucoup)

**F. Décisions.** Qu'est-ce que ces gens feraient dans les circonstances données?

> **Exemple**     Si je pouvais quitter la classe maintenant, je **rentrerais chez moi.**

1. Si je pouvais faire ce que je voulais en ce moment, je...
2. Si j'avais des vacances la semaine prochaine, je...
3. Si mon meilleur ami (ma meilleure amie) pouvait faire ce qu'il/elle voulait en ce moment, il/si elle...
4. S'il/si elle gagnait à la loterie, il/elle...
5. Si nous pouvions sortir ensemble ce soir, nous...
6. Si nous avions envie de faire de l'exercice, nous...
7. Si mes parents gagnaient à la loterie, ils...
8. S'ils pouvaient partir en vacances maintenant, ils...
9. Si le professeur nous disait *(told us)* qu'il n'y aurait plus d'examens dans ce cours, nous...

**G. Par politesse.** Mettez ces phrases au conditionnel pour être plus poli(e) *(polite).*

> **Exemple**     Veux-tu rester en forme?
> **Voudrais-tu rester en forme?**

1. Tu veux faire de l'exercice?
2. Quand as-tu le temps d'aller au club de gym avec moi?
3. Peux-tu passer chez moi vers dix heures?
4. Ton amie veut venir aussi?
5. Qu'est-ce que vous voulez faire après?
6. On peut aller au restaurant végétarien?
7. Est-ce que vous voulez manger leur nouvelle salade?

## Reprise
*Talking about food and health*

Dans le *Chapitre 8,* vous avez appris à commander dans un restaurant, à acheter des provisions au marché, à parler des repas français et à dire ce que vous feriez pour améliorer votre santé. Maintenant vous allez réviser ce que vous avez appris.

**A. Chez les petits commerçants.** Dites au moins quatre choses qu'on peut acheter dans les endroits suivants.

> **Exemple**   dans un supermarché
> **On peut acheter de l'eau minérale...**

1. dans une boulangerie
2. dans une charcuterie
3. dans une épicerie
4. dans une boucherie
5. au marché
6. dans une poissonnerie

**B. Les courses.** Rose va préparer un grand dîner ce soir. Voilà la liste de ce qu'elle va acheter. Dites où elle va aller pour acheter chaque chose.

> **Exemple**   *a jar of jelly*
> **Elle va acheter un pot de confiture à l'épicerie.**

a jar of jelly
a kilo of potatoes
a bag of sugar
6 slices of ham
some ice cream
an apple
a chicken

**C. Des gens en bonne santé.** Ces personnes font très attention à leur santé. Répondez à chaque question de façon logique pour dire ce qu'elles font ou vont faire. Employez le pronom **en.**

> **Exemple**   Rose mange beaucoup **de desserts sucrés?**
> **Non, elle n'en mange pas beaucoup.**

1. Son meilleur ami mange **de la viande rouge** tous les soirs?
2. Ses petits-enfants mangent **des fruits** le matin?
3. Rosalie boit beaucoup **de vin** tous les jours?
4. Les enfants de Patricia boivent trop **de coca?**
5. Patricia et Henri vont faire **de l'exercice** ce matin?
6. André va boire moins **de café?**
7. Il va prendre **un dessert** ce soir?

**D. Qu'est-ce qu'on prend?** Indiquez ce qu'on mange et ce qu'on boit dans chacune de ces circonstances. Ensuite, dites ce que vous prenez dans les mêmes circonstances. Nommez autant de choses que possible.

> **Exemple**   En France, au petit déjeuner, on **mange des tartines ou des croissants et on boit...**
> Moi, au petit déjeuner,...

1. En France, au petit déjeuner, on...
   Moi, au petit déjeuner, je...
2. En France, pour un déjeuner dans un fast-food, on...
   Moi, pour un déjeuner dans un fast-food, je...

**3.** En France, pour un repas traditionnel, comme entrée, on...
Comme plat principal, on...
Comme légume, on...
Comme dessert, on...
Et comme boisson, on...
Moi, comme entrée, je...
Comme plat principal, je...
Comme légume, je...
Comme dessert, je...
Et comme boisson, je...

**4.** En France, pour un dîner léger, on...
Moi, pour un dîner léger, je...

**E. À table!** Complétez avec la forme correcte de l'article convenable.

Ce qu'on mange varie d'une culture à l'autre. Aux États-Unis, par exemple, on prend ____1____ petit déjeuner copieux. On mange souvent ____2____ œufs au bacon et ____3____ pain grillé. On boit ____4____ jus, ____5____ lait ou ____6____ café. En France, ____7____ petit déjeuner est un repas léger. On boit ____8____ café au lait, ____9____ thé ou ____10____ chocolat et on mange ____11____ tartines.

À midi, en France, on peut manger un repas complet ou un repas rapide. Si on mange dans un café on peut prendre ____12____ omelette, ____13____ salade ou ____14____ sandwich avec ____15____ vin ou ____16____ eau minérale. ____17____ vin français est très bon, mais ____18____ eau minérale est populaire aussi. On peut toujours finir un repas avec une tasse *(cup)* ____19____ café — peut-être avec un peu ____20____ sucre ou un peu ____21____ lait.

**F. Qu'est-ce qu'ils font?** Dites si ces personnes font ou ne font pas les choses indiquées. Suivez l'exemple et soyez logique.

> **Exemple**   Je ne veux pas grossir. Alors, je (finir) tous mes repas avec un dessert.
> **Je ne veux pas grossir. Alors, je ne finis pas tous mes repas avec un dessert.**

**1.** Tu fais attention à ta santé. Alors, tu (choisir) des plats sains et tu (boire) beaucoup d'eau.
**2.** Mes amis (maigrir) parce qu'ils marchent tous les jours.
**3.** Nous n'aimons pas les boisson alcoolisées. Alors, nous (boire) beaucoup de bière.
**4.** Comme nous voulons éviter le sucre, nous (finir) tous nos repas avec un dessert.
**5.** Mes amis veulent rester en bonne forme. Alors, ils (boire) peu de bière.
**6.** Si on veut rester en forme, on (boire) du jus de fruit et on (choisir) des plats sains.
**7.** Tes amis et toi, vous voulez rester en forme? Alors, vous (choisir) de bien manger et vous (boire) trop de café.

**G. Si...** Si ces personnes avaient plus de temps libre, est-ce qu'elles feraient les choses indiquées?

> **Exemple**   Moi, je (voyager plus)
> **Je voyagerais plus. / Je ne voyagerais pas plus.**

**1.** Mon meilleur ami (Ma meilleure amie) (faire de la muscu, travailler plus)
**2.** Mes parents (faire plus attention à leur santé, partir souvent en voyage)
**3.** Moi, je (dormir plus, réussir mieux à mes cours)
**4.** Mes amis (réfléchir plus à leur santé, boire moins de boissons alcoolisées)
**5.** Mes amis et moi (se reposer, sortir plus souvent, être moins stressés)

# LECTURE ET COMPOSITION

## Lecture: *Déjeuner du matin*

Jacques Prévert (1900–1977), l'un des poètes les plus célèbres du vingtième **siècle,** aimait parler de la vie de tous les jours dans sa poésie. Avant de lire le poème qui suit, faites cet exercice.

**En contexte.** Devinez le sens des mots en caractères gras.

Il a pris son paquet de cigarettes qui était sur la table. Il a pris une cigarette et il l'**a allumée. La fumée** grise a rempli la pièce. Il a posé sa cigarette dans **le cendrier.** Il a laissé quelques **cendres** dans **le cendrier.** Il **a reposé** le paquet de cigarettes sur la table.

### Déjeuner du matin
#### Jacques Prévert

Il a mis le café
Dans **la tasse**
Il a mis le lait
Dans la tasse de café
Il a mis le sucre
Dans le café au lait
Avec la petite **cuiller**
Il a tourné
Il a bu le café au lait
Et il a reposé la tasse
Sans me parler
Il a allumé
Une cigarette
Il a fait **des ronds**
Avec la fumée
Il a mis les cendres

Dans le cendrier
Sans me parler
Sans me regarder
Il s'est levé
Il a mis
Son chapeau sur **sa tête**
Il a mis
Son manteau de pluie
Parce qu'il pleuvait
Et il est parti
Sous la pluie
Sans **une parole**
Sans me regarder
Et moi j'ai pris
Ma tête dans mes mains
Et **j'ai pleuré.**

## Compréhension

### Qu'est-ce qui s'est passé? Qu'est-ce qui s'est passé dans le poème?

1. Faites une liste des choses qu'il a faites.
2. Nommez deux choses qu'il n'a pas faites.
3. Quelle a été la réaction de l'autre personne?

---

**siècle** *century*   **la tasse** *the cup*   **cuiller** *spoon*   **des ronds** *smoke rings*   **sa tête** *his head*   **une parole** *a word*
**j'ai pleuré** *I cried*

# Composition

## A. Organisez-vous.
Vous allez imaginer ce qui s'est passé entre les personnages du poème. D'abord, organisez-vous en répondant aux questions suivantes.

1. Qui sont ces personnages? Sont-ils amis? parents? Sont-ils mariés, fiancés, divorcés... ?
2. Comment sont-ils? Faites un portrait physique (grand, petit, gros, jeune... ) et psychologique (intelligent, bête, sympathique, égoïste... ) des personnages.
3. Pourquoi est-ce qu'ils ne se parlent pas? Qu'est-ce qui s'est passé?

If you have access to SYSTÈME-D software, you will find the following phrases, vocabulary, grammar, and dictionary aids there.

**Phrases:** Describing people; Expressing an opinion; Linking ideas; Persuading
**Vocabulary:** Personality; Hair colors; Family members
**Grammar:** Imperfect; Compound past tense

## B. Rédaction: Leur vie ensemble.
Imaginez le passé des personnages du poème. Écrivez une rédaction qui explique leur passé ensemble.

## C. Un scénario.
Comparez votre rédaction à celle d'un(e) camarade de classe et choisissez une explication de la situation dans le poème. Préparez une scène dans laquelle chacun des personnages explique à un troisième son point de vue sur ce qui s'est passé. Présentez la scène à la classe.

## À table!

**Ce** qui est considéré «normal» ou «**poli**» diffère souvent d'une culture à l'autre. Chaque société a ses **propres coutumes** à table, ses plats préférés, et même sa propre **façon** de manger. En France, par exemple, on **garde** toujours les deux mains sur la table. **Après avoir coupé** la viande, on garde sa **fourchette** dans la main gauche. On ne boit jamais de lait avec les repas comme le font certains Américains. De nombreux restaurants et cafés acceptent que leurs clients viennent en compagnie de leur chien, du moment qu'il **se comporte** correctement.

Regardez ces photos. Qu'est-ce que vous **remarquez?**

**poli** *polite*   **propres coutumes** *own customs*   **façon** *way, manner*   **on garde** *one keeps*
**Après avoir coupé** *After cutting*   **fourchette** *fork*   **se comporte** *behaves*   **remarquez** *notice*

Lisez ces phrases concernant les coutumes et les bonnes manières. Lesquelles sont vraies dans votre région? Et en France?

| | CHEZ NOUS | EN FRANCE |
|---|---|---|
| 1. Avant de manger, on dit souvent «bon appétit»! | ☐ | ☐ |
| 2. On boit quelquefois du lait aux repas. | ☐ | ☐ |
| 3. On mange souvent des œufs le matin. | ☐ | ☐ |
| 4. On mange plus souvent des œufs le soir ou à midi. | ☐ | ☐ |
| 5. On mange assez souvent dans des fast-foods. | ☐ | ☐ |
| 6. La présentation est presque aussi importante que le goût *(taste)* d'un plat. | ☐ | ☐ |
| 7. Le pain est presque indispensable à tous les repas. | ☐ | ☐ |
| 8. Le pain se mange généralement sans beurre, sauf le matin. | ☐ | ☐ |
| 9. On fait assez souvent les courses chez les petits commerçants. | ☐ | ☐ |
| 10. On mange beaucoup de choses avec les mains. | ☐ | ☐ |
| 11. Quand on mange, on garde toujours les deux mains sur la table. | ☐ | ☐ |
| 12. On met le pain directement sur la table, pas sur l'assiette *(plate)*. | ☐ | ☐ |
| 13. Au restaurant, on peut commander à la carte ou on peut choisir un menu à prix fixe. | ☐ | ☐ |
| 14. La carte est toujours affichée *(posted)* à l'extérieur d'un restaurant. | ☐ | ☐ |

> *Pour la France - Vrai: 1, 4, 5, 6, 7, 8, 9, 11, 12, 13, 14*

## À discuter

1. Quelles différences est-ce qu'il y a entre ce qu'on fait chez vous et ce qu'on fait en France? Quelles similarités?
2. Les opinions des Français ne sont pas toujours reflétées *(reflected)* dans leur vie de tous les jours. Comment pouvez-vous expliquer ce contraste entre ce que les Français pensent et ce qu'ils font?

| Opinions | Actions |
|---|---|
| Selon *(According to)* les Français: | En France: |
| Les repas, c'est surtout un moment pour se retrouver en famille ou entre amis. | Les repas se font de moins en moins à heures fixes et à la maison et les familles mangent de moins en moins souvent ensemble. |
| On devrait continuer à préparer des repas traditionnels à la maison quand c'est possible. | De plus en plus les grands repas traditionnels se limitent aux fêtes. |
| Les plats déjà préparés, c'est juste pour quand on est pressé *(in a hurry)*. | On passe de moins en moins de temps à préparer les repas en se servant *(using)* de produits pré-préparés (salades composées, légumes mélangés *[mixed]*... ), du surgelé et du four à micro-onde *(microwave)*. |
| Le service et la qualité sont meilleurs chez les petits commerçants que dans les grandes surfaces. | On fait de plus en plus souvent les courses dans les grandes surfaces. |

**visit http://horizons.heinle.com**

# Résumé de grammaire

## The partitive and review of using the articles

Je vais acheter **de l'**eau, **du** pain, **de la** crème et **des** légumes.
*I'm going to buy (some) water, (some) bread, (some) cream and (some) vegetables.*

— Je vais prendre **un** sandwich et **des** frites.
— Je **ne** prends **pas de** frites parce qu'elles ont **trop de** calories.

— Tu **n'**aimes **pas les** frites?
— Mais si, j'aime **beaucoup les** frites, mais **le** riz est meilleur pour **la** santé.
— Mais **les** frites qu'ils servent ici sont délicieuses.

Use the partitive to convey the idea of *some* or *any*. Use the partitive in French even when *some* or *any* can be omitted in English. Use **de l'** before all singular nouns beginning with a vowel sound, **du** before masculine singular nouns beginning with a consonant, **de la** before feminine singular nouns beginning with a consonant, and **des** before all plural nouns.

**Un** and **une** mean *a* and **du, de la, de l',** and **des** express the idea of *some* or *any*. All of these forms change to **de (d')** after most negated verbs and after expressions of quantity. (See page 318 for a list of quantity expressions.)

Use the definite article (**le, la, l', les**) to say *the,* to express likes, dislikes, and preferences, or to make statements about entire categories. The definite article does *not* change to **de** after a negative or an expression of quantity.

## The verb *boire* and regular *-ir* verbs

The verb **boire** *(to drink)* is irregular.

Le matin, je **bois** du thé mais mon mari **boit** du café. À midi, nous **buvons** de l'eau.

Qu'est-ce que tu **as bu** ce matin?
Qu'est-ce qu' tu **buvais** quand tu étais petit?

| BOIRE *(to drink)* | |
|---|---|
| je **bois** | nous **buvons** |
| tu **bois** | vous **buvez** |
| il/elle/on **boit** | ils/elles **boivent** |
| PASSÉ COMPOSÉ: **j'ai bu** | |
| IMPARFAIT: **je buvais** | |

The stem for the present tense of regular **-ir** verbs is obtained by dropping the **-ir**. Add the following endings for the present tense.

Les étudiants **réussissent** bien au cours. Tu **réussis** à tes cours?

**J'ai fini** mes devoirs.
Je ne **réfléchissais** pas beaucoup à mon avenir *(future)* quand j'étais jeune.

| RÉUSSIR *(to succeed)* | |
|---|---|
| je réuss**is** | nous réuss**issons** |
| tu réuss**is** | vous réuss**issez** |
| il/elle/on réuss**it** | ils/elles réuss**issent** |
| PASSÉ COMPOSÉ: **j'ai réussi** | |
| IMPARFAIT: **je réussissais** | |

— Tu veux **de l'**eau?
— Oui, j'**en** veux bien.
  Non merci, je n'**en** veux pas.

See page 326 for a list of common **-ir** verbs. All **-ir** verbs presented in this chapter form the **passé composé** with **avoir**.

— Tu prends un **sandwich?**
— Oui, j'**en** prends **un**.
  Non, j'**en** prends **deux**.
  Non, je n'**en** prends pas.

## The pronoun *en*

— Tu as acheté un kilo **de carottes?**
— Oui, j'**en** ai acheté **un kilo**.
  Non, j'**en** ai acheté **une livre**.
  Non, je n'**en** ai pas acheté.

**En** replaces a noun preceded by a partitive article, an expression of quantity, **un, une,** or a number. When replacing a noun preceded by **un, une,** a number, or an expression of quantity, repeat the **un, une,** number, or expression of quantity in the sentence containing **en,** unless it's negative. In English, **en** is usually translated by *some, any, of it,* or *of them.* Although the equivalent expression may be omitted in English, **en** is always used in French.

**En** is placed *immediately* before the verb. It goes before the infinitive if there is one. If not, it goes before the conjugated verb. In the **passé composé,** place it before the auxiliary verb.

Je vais **en** prendre.
J'**en** prends.
J'**en** ai pris.

## The conditional *(Le conditionnel)*

Use the conditional to say what someone *would, could,* or *should* do. To form the conditional of most verbs, add the same endings as the **imparfait** to the infinitive of the verb. If an infinitive ends in **-e,** drop the **e** before adding the endings.

| PARLER | FINIR | PERDRE |
|---|---|---|
| je parlerais | je finirais | je perdrais |
| tu parlerais | tu finirais | tu perdrais |
| il/elle/on parlerait | il/elle/on finirait | il/elle/on perdrait |
| nous parlerions | nous finirions | nous perdrions |
| vous parleriez | vous finiriez | vous perdriez |
| ils/elles parleraient | ils/elles finiraient | ils/elles perdraient |

Si j'avais plus de temps, **je préparerais** mieux mes cours. **Je finirais** tous mes devoirs et **le prof perdrait** moins souvent patience avec moi.

Most irregular verbs follow this same pattern.

dormir → je dormirais, tu dormirais...
prendre → je prendrais, tu prendrais...
boire → je boirais, tu boirais...

Verbs like **se lever, payer,** and **appeler** have spelling changes in the conditional stem in *all* the forms **(je me lèverais, je paierais, j'appellerais).** Those like **préférer** do not **(je préférerais).**

Si tu voulais être en bonne forme, **tu dormirais** plus, **tu prendrais** des vitamines et **tu boirais** assez d'eau.

Si nous étions en vacances, **nous nous lèverions** plus tard. **Mon ami préférerait** se lever vers neuf heures.

The following verbs have irregular stems in the conditional. The endings are regular.

aller → j'irais, tu irais...
avoir → j'aurais, tu aurais...
être → je serais, tu serais...
faire → je ferais, tu ferais...
devoir → je devrais, tu devrais...
vouloir → je voudrais, tu voudrais...
venir → je viendrais, tu viendrais...
devenir → je deviendrais, tu deviendrais...
revenir → je reviendrais, tu reviendrais...
voir → je verrais, tu verrais...
pouvoir → je pourrais, tu pourrais...
mourir → je mourrais, tu mourrais...

Si j'avais plus de temps libre, **je ferais** beaucoup de choses. **J'irais** plus souvent au parc, **je verrais** plus souvent mes amis et **je serais** content!

Also learn the following:

il y a → il y aurait          il pleut → il pleuvrait          il faut → il faudrait

Si tu visitais la Normandie au printemps, **il y aurait** du vent et **il pleuvrait. Il te faudrait** un parapluie!

To say *should,* use the conditional of **devoir** plus an infinitive. To say *could,* use the conditional of **pouvoir** plus an infinitive.

Use the conditional:
* to make polite requests or offers.
* to say what someone would do if circumstances were different.

— **Pourrais-tu** me donner des conseils pour rester en bonne santé?
— **Tu devrais** bien manger et faire de l'exercice.

**Voudrais-tu** y aller avec moi?

S'il savait faire la cuisine, **il mangerait** mieux.

# Vocabulaire

## Ordering at a restaurant

### NOMS MASCULINS

| | |
|---|---|
| un apéritif | a before-dinner drink |
| un dessert | a dessert |
| un fruit | a fruit |
| des fruits de mer | shellfish, crustaceans |
| *un hors-d'œuvre | an hors d'œuvre, an appetizer |
| du lait | milk |
| des légumes | vegetables |
| un menu à prix fixe | a set-price menu |
| du pain | bread |
| un pavé de | a thick slice of |
| le plat (principal) | the (main) dish |
| du poisson (fumé) | (smoked) fish |
| du poivre | pepper |
| un repas | a meal |
| du riz | rice |
| du sel | salt |
| un serveur | a server, a waiter |
| du sucre | sugar |

### NOMS FÉMININS

| | |
|---|---|
| une bouteille (de) | a bottle (of) |
| une carafe (de) | a carafe (of) |
| la carte | the menu |
| de la crème | cream |
| une entrée | a first course |
| de la raie | rayfish, skate |
| une salade | a salad |
| une serveuse | a server, a waitress |
| de la viande | meat |
| de la volaille | poultry |

### DIVERS

| | |
|---|---|
| Aimeriez-vous… ? | Would you like . . . ? |
| comme | for, as (a) |
| comprendre | to include |
| décider | to decide |
| du, de la, de l', des | some, any |
| finir | to finish |
| fumé(e) | smoked |
| Savez-vous… ? | Do you know (how to) . . . ? |
| servir | to serve |
| traditionnel(le) | traditional |
| typiquement | typically |

*Pour les noms des différentes sortes d'entrées, voir la page 304.*

*Pour les noms des différentes sortes de viandes, de volailles, de poissons et de fruits de mer, voir la page 304.*

*Pour les noms des différentes sortes de légumes et de fruits, voir les pages 305 et 315.*

*Pour voir les différentes possibilités pour finir un repas, voir la page 305.*

## Buying food

### NOMS MASCULINS

| | |
|---|---|
| du bœuf | beef |
| un choix | a choice |
| un commerçant | a shopkeeper |
| un marché | a market |
| un oignon | an onion |
| un pain au chocolat | a chocolate-filled croissant |
| un pain complet | a loaf of whole-grain bread |
| un plat préparé | a ready-to-serve dish |
| du porc | pork |
| un produit | a product |
| du raisin | grapes |
| du saucisson | salami |
| le service personnalisé | personal service |
| un supermarché | a supermarket |

### NOMS FÉMININS

| | |
|---|---|
| une baguette | a loaf of bread |
| une banane | a banana |
| la boucherie | the butcher's shop |
| la boulangerie | the bakery |
| une carotte | a carrot |
| une cerise | a cherry |
| la charcuterie | the deli |
| de la charcuterie | deli meats, cold cuts |
| une commerçante | a shopkeeper |
| des conserves | canned goods |
| l'épicerie | the grocery store |
| une fraise | a strawberry |
| une grande surface | a superstore |
| une laitue | lettuce |
| une orange | an orange |
| une pâtisserie | a pastry |
| une pêche | a peach |
| une poire | a pear |
| la poissonnerie | the fish market |
| des saucisses | sausages |
| une tartelette (aux fraises / aux cerises) | a (strawberry / cherry) tart |

### DIVERS

| | |
|---|---|
| C'est tout. | That's all. |
| de plus en plus | more and more |
| faire les courses | to go grocery-shopping |
| frais (fraîche) | fresh |
| il faut | it is necessary, one needs, one must |
| Qu'est-ce que je peux vous proposer d'autre? | What else can I get you? |
| Qu'est-ce qu'il vous faut? | What do you need? |
| surgelé(e) | frozen |

*Pour les expressions de quantité, voir la page 318.*

## COMPÉTENCE 3

### Talking about meals

**NOMS MASCULINS**

| | |
|---|---|
| du bacon | bacon |
| du beurre | butter |
| du chocolat | chocolate |
| un croissant | a croissant |
| le déjeuner | lunch |
| le dîner | dinner |
| *un hamburger | a hamburger |
| du pain grillé | toast |
| un self-service | a self-service restaurant |
| un steak-frites | steak and fries |

**NOMS FÉMININS**

| | |
|---|---|
| des céréales | cereal |
| de la confiture | jelly |
| une omelette | an omelet |
| une pizza | a pizza |
| une tartine | bread with butter and jelly |

**EXPRESSIONS VERBALES**

| | |
|---|---|
| boire | to drink |
| choisir (de faire) | to choose (to do) |
| finir (de faire) | to finish (doing) |
| grandir | to grow, to grow up, to get taller |
| grossir | to get fatter |
| maigrir | to get thinner, to slim down |
| obéir (à) | to obey |
| réfléchir (à) | to think (about) |
| réussir (à) | to succeed (at, in), to pass [a test] |
| rougir | to blush, to turn red |
| vieillir | to age |

**DIVERS**

| | |
|---|---|
| à l'américaine | American-style |
| ceux (celles) | those |
| complet (complète) | complete |
| copieux (copieuse) | copious, large |
| en | some, any, of it, of them |
| encore | still, again, more |
| grillé(e) | toasted, grilled |
| je prendrais | I would have, I would take |
| là | there |
| léger (légère) | light |
| ne... plus | no more, no longer |
| pourtant | however |
| rapide | rapid, fast, quick |
| seulement | only |
| si | yes (in response to a question or statement in the negative) |
| surtout | especially |
| volontiers | gladly |
| vrai(e) | true |

## COMPÉTENCE 4

### Choosing a healthy lifestyle

**NOMS MASCULINS**

| | |
|---|---|
| l'alcool | alcohol |
| des conseils | advice |
| des féculents | carbohydrates |
| des produits bios | organic products |
| des produits laitiers | milk products |
| le stress | stress |
| le tabac | tobacco |

**NOMS FÉMININS**

| | |
|---|---|
| des matières grasses | fats |
| des protéines | protein |
| la santé | health |
| des vitamines | vitamins |

**EXPRESSIONS VERBALES**

| | |
|---|---|
| améliorer | to improve |
| contrôler | to control |
| éviter | to avoid |
| faire attention (à) | to pay attention (to), to watch out (for) |
| faire de l'aérobic | to do aerobics |
| faire de la méditation | to meditate |
| faire de la muscu(lation) | to do weight training, to do bodybuilding |
| faire des randonnées | to go hiking |
| faire du yoga | to do yoga |
| faire mieux (de) | to do better (to) |
| marcher | to walk |
| oublier | to forget |
| se sentir | to feel |

**DIVERS**

| | |
|---|---|
| à votre avis | in your opinion |
| content(e) | content, happy |
| en forme | in shape |
| fort(e) | strong |
| lentement | slowly |
| moins de (+ noun) | less (+ noun) |
| plus de (+ noun) | more (+ noun) |
| plusieurs | several |
| régulièrement | regularly |
| sain(e) | healthy |
| sans doute | probably |

## Man in Orange Hat
### JOSEPH-JEAN LAURENT
### (1893–1976)

1970
Milwaukee Art Museum
Gift of Richard and Erna Flagg

Joseph-Jean Laurent, tailleur *(tailor)* de Port-au-Prince, Haïti, a commencé à peindre *(to paint)* à l'âge de soixante-huit ans. Ce tableau d'une figure vaudou *(voodoo)* appelée Legba reflète les couleurs vives *(bright)* des Antilles.

# Aux Antilles

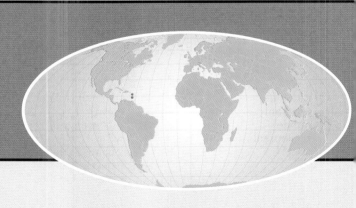

**LA GUADELOUPE**
**SUPERFICIE:** 1 780 kilomètres carrés
**NOMBRE D'HABITANTS:** 445 000 (les Guadeloupéens)
**CHEF-LIEU *(ADMINISTRATIVE CENTER)*:** Basse-Terre
**INDUSTRIES PRINCIPALES:** agriculture, tourisme, pêche, exploitation minière, industries manufacturières

**LA MARTINIQUE**
**SUPERFICIE:** 1 128 kilomètres carrés
**NOMBRE D'HABITANTS:** 393 000 (les Martiniquais)
**CHEF-LIEU:** Fort-de-France
**INDUSTRIES PRINCIPALES:** agriculture, tourisme, pêche, exploitation minière, industries manufacturières, pétrole

CHAPITRE **9**

# En vacances

 Video activities are on pages 416–419.

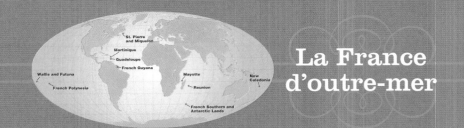

# La France d'outre-mer

Quand on pense à la France on imagine l'Hexagone, la France métropolitaine en Europe. Mais la République française **comprend** aussi quatre départements **d'outre-mer** (les DOM), la Guadeloupe, la Martinique, la Guyane et la Réunion, qui **font partie de** la France depuis 1946 tout comme Hawaii fait partie des États-Unis. Leurs habitants sont **citoyens** français avec les mêmes **droits** qu'un Parisien ou tout autre citoyen du pays. Regardez **la carte du monde au début du livre** pour trouver chacun de ces départements.

Fort-de-France, **chef-lieu** de la Martinique

La Guadeloupe

Colonisées par la France en 1635, la Guadeloupe et la Martinique se trouvent dans la mer des Caraïbes. La majorité des habitants sont descendants d'**esclaves** africains **emmenés** dans ces îles pour travailler dans les plantations. La France a aboli l'esclavage en 1848.

Colonisée en 1605, la Guyane se trouve en Amérique du Sud. Au 19ᵉ siècle, la France a envoyé ses prisonniers politiques aux **bagnes** de la région, comme la célèbre **île du Diable,** bagne fermé en 1945.

L'île du Diable

---

**comprend** *includes*    **d'outre-mer** *overseas*    **font partie de** *are part of*    **citoyens** *citizens*    **droits** *rights*
**la carte du monde au début du livre** *the world map at the beginning of the book*    **chef-lieu** *administrative center*
**esclaves** *slaves*    **emmenés** *brought*    **bagnes** *penal colonies*    **île du Diable** *Devil's Island*

Les Français se sont établis à l'île de la Réunion en 1642. Située dans l'océan Indien à 640 kilomètres de Madagascar, c'est le département d'outre-mer le plus peuplé. Les Réunionnais constituent une société multi-ethnique: les Africains, les Européens, les Indiens, les Chinois et les **Malgaches.**

Plages à la Réunion

Saint-Denis, chef-lieu de la Réunion

La France a aussi **plusieurs** territoires, **pareils** aux territoires américains de Puerto Rico et Guam. Appelés «territoires d'outre-mer» (TOM) jusqu'en 2003, la Polynésie française, Wallis-et-Futuna, Mayotte et Saint-Pierre-et-Miquelon s'appellent aujourd'hui «collectivités d'outre-mer». Depuis 2004, l'ancien TOM de la Nouvelle-Calédonie est considéré «pays d'outre-mer **au sein de** la République». La France possède aussi les Terres **australes** et antarctiques françaises. Trouvez chacune de ces régions sur la carte du monde au début du livre.

Saint-Pierre-et-Miquelon

La Polynésie française

---

**Malgaches** *(from Madagascar)*   **plusieurs** *several*   **pareils** *similar*   **au sein de** *within*   **australes** *southern*

# Talking about vacation

## Les vacances

Luc, un jeune Parisien, va passer ses vacances en Guadeloupe. Et vous? Où aimez-vous passer vos vacances?

dans un pays étranger ou exotique • sur une île tropicale ou **à la mer** • dans une grande ville • à la montagne

Qu'est-ce qu'on peut faire dans chaque **endroit?**

admirer **les paysages** *(m)* • visiter des sites *(m)* historiques et touristiques • profiter des activités culturelles

**bronzer** ou **courir** le long des plages • **goûter** la cuisine locale **assis** sur la terrasse d'un restaurant • **faire des randonnées** *(f)*

CD 2-25

Luc parle à son ami Alain de ses prochaines vacances en Guadeloupe.

LUC: Je vais bientôt partir en vacances.
ALAIN: Et tu vas où?
LUC: Je vais aller en Guadeloupe.
ALAIN: La Guadeloupe? Quelle chance! Tu pars quand?
LUC: Je vais partir le 20 juillet et je **compte** passer trois semaines **là-bas.**
ALAIN: Génial! J'espère que **ça te plaira!**

---

**à la mer** *at the coast, by the sea*   **un endroit** *a place*   **les paysages** *(m) scenery, landscapes*   **bronzer** *to tan*   **courir** *to run*
**goûter** *to taste*   **assis(e)** *seated*   **faire des randonnées** *(f) to go for hikes*   **compter** *to plan on, to count on*
**là-bas** *over there*   **ça te plaira** *you'll like it*

**A. Où?** Où fait-on les choses suivantes?

Exemple  **On nage à la mer.**

dans un pays étranger
à la mer    à la montagne
dans une grande ville
sur une île tropicale

1.     2.     3.

4.     5.     6.

**B. Voyages.** Imaginez qu'un(e) ami(e) a passé ses vacances dans les endroits suivants. Préparez une conversation dans laquelle vous parlez de l'endroit où il/elle est allé(e) et de ce qu'il/elle a fait, comme dans l'exemple.

Exemple    en Espagne
— **Alors, tu as passé tes vacances dans un pays étranger?**
— **Oui, je suis allé(e) en Espagne.**
— **Qu'est-ce que tu as fait en Espagne?**
— **J'ai visité des sites historiques et touristiques.**

1. à Palm Beach    4. en Guadeloupe
2. à Paris    5. à New York
3. au Colorado    6. en France

**C. Entretien.** Interviewez votre partenaire.

1. Est-ce que tu voyages beaucoup? Comment est-ce que tu préfères voyager? en avion? en train? en voiture? Aimes-tu voyager seul(e) parfois?
2. Où est-ce que tu aimerais passer tes prochaines vacances? Qu'est-ce qu'on peut faire dans cette région?
3. Où est-ce que tu as passé tes meilleures vacances? Pourquoi as-tu trouvé ces vacances agréables? Qu'est-ce que tu as fait?

**D. Conversation.** Avec un(e) partenaire, relisez la conversation entre Luc et Alain à la page précédente. Ensuite, imaginez que vous allez faire le voyage de vos rêves *(dreams)* et changez la conversation pour dire où vous allez, avec qui, quand et combien de temps vous comptez rester.

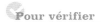
**1.** What other verb form has the same stem as the future?

**2.** All but two of the future tense endings look like the present tense forms of the verb **avoir.** Which two are they?

**NOTE DE GRAMMAIRE**

The future/conditional stem always ends with **-r**. Do you remember these irregular ones?

| | |
|---|---|
| aller | ir- |
| avoir | aur- |
| être | ser- |
| faire | fer- |
| devoir | devr- |
| vouloir | voudr- |
| venir | viendr- |
| revenir | reviendr- |
| devenir | deviendr- |
| voir | verr- |
| pouvoir | pourr- |
| mourir | mourr- |

Note these forms in the future:

| | |
|---|---|
| il y a | il y aura |
| il faut | il faudra |
| il pleut | il pleuvra |

Verbs like **se lever, payer,** and **appeler** have spelling changes in all forms of the future (**il se lèvera, il paiera, il appellera**). Those like **préférer** do not (**il préférera**).

# Talking about how things will be
## *Le futur*

You have learned to use **aller** + *infinitive* to say what someone *is going to do.* You can also use the future tense forms of the verb to say what someone *will do.* The future of most verbs is formed by adding the boldfaced endings listed below to the same stem you used for the conditional in *Chapitre 8.* The future tense endings look like the present tense forms of the verb **avoir,** except for the **nous** and **vous** forms.

| PARLER | ÊTRE | VENIR |
|---|---|---|
| je parler**ai** | je ser**ai** | je viendr**ai** |
| tu parler**as** | tu ser**as** | tu viendr**as** |
| il/elle/on parler**a** | il/elle/on ser**a** | il/elle/on viendr**a** |
| nous parler**ons** | nous ser**ons** | nous viendr**ons** |
| vous parler**ez** | vous ser**ez** | vous viendr**ez** |
| ils/elles parler**ont** | ils/elles ser**ont** | ils/elles viendr**ont** |

Although the future is generally used in French as it is in English, one difference is its use in clauses with **quand** referring to the future. English has the present in such clauses.

> Quand j'**arriverai** en Guadeloupe, je prendrai un taxi pour aller à l'hôtel.
> *When I **arrive** in Guadeloupe, I'll take a taxi to go to the hotel.*

Just as in English, you also use the future tense to indicate what will happen if another event occurs first. Unlike with **quand,** you use the present tense in the clause with **si.**

> Si je peux visiter la Martinique, je **serai** vraiment content!
> *If I can visit Martinique, I **will be** really happy!*

**A. Des prédictions.** Comment sera la vie des personnes suivantes dans cinq ans? Est-ce que ces gens feront les choses indiquées?

Dans cinq ans...

**Exemple**     je (être riche)
**Je serai riche. / Je ne serai pas riche.**

1. Moi, je... (avoir mon diplôme, travailler pour une grande société *[company]* comme IBM, voyager beaucoup, étudier à l'université, parler français, comprendre mieux la vie, habiter ici, être marié[e], avoir des enfants, être content[e], trouver un bon travail)
2. La personne de mes rêves et moi, nous (se marier, avoir des enfants, acheter une maison, faire beaucoup de voyages ensemble)
3. Mon meilleur ami (Ma meilleure amie)... (passer les vacances avec moi chaque année, habiter avec moi, être comme maintenant, travailler en France, sortir avec moi tous les week-ends, avoir un diplôme universitaire)

Maintenant, dites si vous espérez que les personnes suivantes feront ou ne feront pas les choses indiquées dans les cinq années à venir.

**Exemple**     mon meilleur ami (se marier, habiter très loin d'ici)
**J'espère que mon meilleur ami se mariera.**
**J'espère qu'il n'habitera pas très loin d'ici.**

4. *[au prof de français]* vous (pouvoir prendre des vacances, aller bientôt en France, avoir beaucoup d'étudiants intelligents, devoir enseigner *[to teach]* toujours à 7h00 du matin)

5. *[à l'étudiant(e) à côté de vous]* tu (avoir une vie intéressante, finir tes études, trouver un bon travail, devoir trop travailler, apprendre à bien parler le français)

**B. Un voyage.** Décrivez un voyage réel ou imaginaire que vous ferez pendant les prochaines vacances d'hiver, de printemps ou d'été. Dans votre description, répondez aux questions suivantes.

1. Où irez-vous?
2. Quand est-ce que vous partirez et quand est-ce que vous reviendrez?
3. Comment est-ce que vous voyagerez? en avion? en train? en bateau?
4. Descendrez-vous dans des hôtels de luxe, dans des hôtels économiques ou ferez-vous du camping?
5. Qu'est-ce que vous ferez pendant le voyage? Qu'est-ce que vous verrez d'intéressant? Quels sites touristiques est-ce que vous visiterez?
6. Qui fera le voyage avec vous et qu'est-ce que chacun devra apporter *(bring)*?
7. Combien est-ce que le voyage coûtera?

**C. Quand.** Créez des phrases logiques en utilisant un élément de chaque groupe ou d'autres verbes de votre choix. Écrivez au moins deux phrases pour chaque sujet.

**Exemple**    **Je me reposerai quand je finirai mes études.**
           **Je serai content(e) quand j'aurai mon diplôme.**

1. Je...
2. Dans ma famille, nous...
3. Mon/Ma meilleur(e) ami(e)…
4. Beaucoup d'étudiants...

| | | | | |
|---|---|---|---|---|
| être content(e)(s) | ??? | | avoir son diplôme | aller à la plage |
| parler français | être ensemble | | voyager en France | gagner à la loterie |
| faire un voyage | se reposer | quand | prendre des vacances | finir ses études |
| s'amuser | bronzer | | rentrer à la maison | ??? |
| faire du ski | étudier | ??? | avoir plus de temps | sortir ce week-end |
| être plus (moins) stressé(e)(s) | | | pouvoir dormir plus | ??? |

**D. Entretien.** Demandez à votre partenaire d'imaginer sa vie dans dix ans.

1. Est-ce que tu habiteras encore *(still)* ici? Sinon *(If not)*, où habiteras-tu?
2. Est-ce que tu seras marié(e)? Combien d'enfants auras-tu?
3. Auras-tu des cheveux gris? Feras-tu de l'exercice tous les jours? Seras-tu plus stressé(e) ou moins stressé(e) que maintenant?
4. Seras-tu encore étudiant(e)? Où travailleras-tu? Est-ce que ta vie sera plus facile ou plus difficile que maintenant? Pourquoi?
5. Comment passeras-tu ton temps? Qu'est-ce que tu feras pour t'amuser? Est-ce que tu voyageras beaucoup?

## Stratégies et Lecture

*Recognizing compound tenses*

---

You have learned to use the **passé composé** to say what someone has done. In the **passé composé,** one uses the present tense of the auxiliary verbs **avoir** and **être** with the past participle of the verb.

J'**ai** commencé.  
*I've begun. / I began.*

Je **suis** rentré(e)  
*I've returned. / I returned.*

While reading, you will see other compound tenses that look like the **passé composé,** but with the auxiliary verb **avoir** or **être** in the imperfect, the future, or the conditional. When you see the auxiliary verb in the imperfect followed by a past participle, translate it as *had* plus a past participle. This tense is called the pluperfect (**le plus-que-parfait**) and it indicates that an action preceded another action in the past.

J'**avais** déjà commencé.  
*I had already begun.*

Je n'**étais** pas encore rentré(e).  
*I hadn't returned yet.*

The future perfect tense is used to say what *will have happened* before another action in the future, and the auxiliary verb is in the future tense.

J'**aurai** déjà commencé.  
*I will have already begun.*

Je ne **serai** pas encore rentré(e).  
*I will not have returned yet.*

The conditional perfect is used to say what *would have happened* under certain conditions, and the auxiliary verb is in the conditional.

J'**aurais** déjà commencé.  
*I would have already begun.*

Je ne **serais** pas encore rentré(e).  
*I would not have returned yet.*

---

**A. Et vous?** Traduisez les phrases suivantes en anglais.

1. Avant de partir en vacances, j'avais réservé une chambre d'hôtel.
2. Je suis allé(e) à Miami. J'y étais déjà allé(e) deux fois avant.
3. Si j'avais eu assez d'argent, j'aurais passé mes vacances en Europe.
4. J'aurais aimé avoir une semaine de plus de vacances.
5. Mes vacances auraient été plus agréables s'il n'avait pas plu tout le temps.
6. Quand je suis rentré du voyage, j'avais dépensé (**dépenser** *to spend*) plus de mille dollars.
7. Quand j'aurai fini mes études, je ferai un long voyage.
8. Je visiterai la Guadeloupe quand j'aurai fini mes quatre semestres de français.

**B. Le temps des verbes.** Dans le texte qui suit, trouvez tous les verbes au plus-que-parfait, au futur antérieur et au conditionnel passé. Donnez le sens de chaque verbe.

# Quelle aventure!

CD 2-26 Luc, un jeune Parisien qui passe ses vacances en Guadeloupe, raconte ses aventures dans un mail à son ami Alain.

```
Salut Alain:
    Je passe des vacances formidables ici en Guadeloupe! Je
t'aurais écrit plus tôt si je n'avais pas été si occupé. Il y
a beaucoup de choses intéressantes à faire ici! Les gens sont
très sympas et tout le reste est parfaitement à mon goût… la
cuisine, le paysage, le climat, les femmes! En fait, j'ai
rencontré une jeune Guadeloupéenne très sympa. Elle s'appelle
Micheline et nous passons beaucoup de temps ensemble depuis
notre rencontre assez comique au parc naturel. J'étais allé
au parc pour faire l'escalade de la Soufrière, un énorme
volcan en repos… mais comme j'allais bientôt voir, pas si en
«en repos» que ça! En montant vers le volcan, j'avais remar-
qué qu'il y avait un peu de vapeur qui sortait du cratère,
mais je n'avais pas fait trop attention. Quand j'étais
presque au sommet du volcan, je m'étais assis par terre pour
me reposer un peu et c'est là que la comédie a commencé. Là
où j'étais assis, la terre était toute chaude, mais vraiment
chaude, et je voyais des jets de vapeur qui sortaient
du sommet! J'ai pensé que le volcan allait exploser!
    J'ai commencé à crier aux autres touristes: «Atten-
tion! Attention! Le volcan entre en éruption, il va
exploser! Sauvez-vous!» Heureusement, Micheline était
parmi le groupe et elle nous a expliqué calmement:
«Mais non, mais non… calmez-vous! C'est tout à fait
normal. Le volcan est en repos, il n'y a pas de dan-
ger!» Si elle n'avait pas été avec nous, on aurait
tous commencé à courir paniqués.
    J'aurais dû lire plus sur la Soufrière dans le guide
touristique avant d'y aller! Sur le moment, j'ai eu
l'impression d'être complètement ridicule! Mais cette
impression n'a pas duré. On s'est présentés et on a
commencé à parler et elle était super sympa. Nous
avons continué l'escalade du volcan ensemble. Arrivés
au sommet, nous avons trouvé une vue impressionnante…
la lave…, les fissures…, l'odeur… C'était un paysage
presque irréel. Pendant un instant, j'ai eu l'impres-
sion d'être sur une autre planète!
    Mais, tout est bien qui finit bien. Si je n'avais pas fait
cette bêtise, Micheline et moi n'aurions jamais commencé à
parler et je n'aurais pas fait la connaissance de cette
femme extraordinaire. Depuis, nous sortons ensemble presque
tous les soirs et j'ai décidé de rester en Guadeloupe un peu
plus longtemps que prévu. Je ne sais pas encore quand je
rentrerai à Paris, mais je t'enverrai un mail quand j'aurai
décidé. Entre temps, voici quelques photos.
        À bientôt,
        Luc
```

**Compréhension.** Répondez aux questions suivantes d'après la lecture.

1. Quel site touristique est-ce que Luc visitait quand il a rencontré Micheline?
2. Est-ce qu'il avait lu une description du volcan avant d'y aller?
3. Qu'est-ce que Luc avait vu quand il a commencé à crier que le volcan allait exploser?
4. Qu'est-ce que tous les touristes auraient fait si Micheline n'avait pas été là pour les calmer?
5. Combien de temps est-ce que Luc a décidé de rester en Guadeloupe?

# Buying your ticket

## À l'agence de voyages

Pour faire un voyage **à l'étranger**, il vous faut...

un passeport
des chèques *(m)* de voyage
un billet d'avion avec un itinéraire
une carte de crédit
une carte bancaire

Il faut aussi **savoir...**

le numéro de votre **vol**
l'heure de départ
l'heure d'arrivée
**la porte d'embarquement**
**la porte d'arrivée**

Aimez-vous préparer vos voyages à l'avance? Il faut lire des guides touristiques pour mieux **connaître...**

la région, l'histoire, la géographie et les sites touristiques

les gens et leur culture

les hôtels, les restaurants et le système de **transports** *(m)* **en commun, tels que** le métro ou le train

CD 2-27

Avant son voyage, Luc va acheter son billet à l'agence de voyages.

LUC: Bonjour, monsieur. Je voudrais acheter un billet Paris–Pointe-à-Pitre.
L'AGENT DE VOYAGES: Très bien, monsieur. Vous voulez un billet aller-retour ou un aller simple?
LUC: Un billet aller-retour.
L'AGENT DE VOYAGES: À quelle date est-ce que vous voulez partir?
LUC: Le 20 juillet.
L'AGENT DE VOYAGES: Quand est-ce que vous voudriez rentrer?
LUC: Le 12 août.
L'AGENT DE VOYAGES: Vous voulez un billet de première classe ou de classe touriste?
LUC: De classe touriste.
L'AGENT DE VOYAGES: Très bien. Il y a un vol le 20 juillet, départ Paris-Orly à 15h15, arrivée à Pointe-à-Pitre à 17h30. Pour le retour, il y a un vol qui part de Pointe-à-Pitre le 12 août à 20h15 et qui arrive à Paris-Orly à 10h15 le 13 août. **Ça vous convient?**
LUC: Oui, c'est parfait. Combien coûte le billet?
L'AGENT DE VOYAGES: C'est 759 euros.
LUC: Bon. Alors, faites ma réservation. Voilà ma carte de crédit.

**à l'étranger** abroad    **savoir** to know    **un vol** a flight    **la porte d'embarquement** the departure gate
**la porte d'arrivée** the arrival gate    **connaître** to know, to be familiar with, to be acquainted with
**les transports** *(m)* **en commun** public transportation    **tel(le) que** such as    **Ça vous convient?** Is that good for you?

**A. Le voyage de Luc.** Lisez l'itinéraire de Luc et répondez à ces questions.

1. Est-ce que Luc a acheté un billet aller-retour ou un aller simple?
2. Est-ce que Luc voyagera en première classe ou en classe touriste?
3. Quelle est la date de son départ? de son retour? De quel aéroport partira-t-il?
4. Il devra arriver à l'aéroport combien d'heures avant le départ?
5. À quelle heure est son départ de Paris? À quelle heure est son arrivée à Pointe-à-Pitre?
6. Est-ce qu'un repas sera servi en route?
7. Quelle est la date de son retour à Paris? C'est quel jour de la semaine?

---

### ITINÉRAIRE

À l'intention de: Moreau/Luc

**ALLER:** Mardi 20 juillet:
| | |
|---|---|
| Départ de Paris-Orly | 15h15 |
| Air France-Vol 624 | Classe touriste |
| Arrivée à Pointe-à-Pitre | 17h30 |

• Un repas et une collation seront servis en vol.

**RETOUR:** Jeudi 12 août:
| | |
|---|---|
| Départ de Pointe-à-Pitre | 20h15 |
| Air France-Vol 625 | Classe touriste |
| Arrivée à Paris-Orly | 10h15 |

• Un repas et une collation seront servis en vol.

Prix du billet aller-retour: 759€.

Prévoyez d'arriver à l'aéroport deux heures avant l'heure de départ et n'oubliez pas de reconfirmer votre retour 72 heures avant le départ.

*BON VOYAGE!*

---

**B. Et vous?** Choisissez la phrase qui vous décrit le mieux quand vous voyagez.

1. **a.** Je préfère voyager en première classe.
   **b.** Je préfère voyager en classe touriste.
   **c.** Ça dépend de qui va payer.

2. **a.** J'arrive à l'aéroport bien en avance.
   **b.** J'arrive à l'aéroport au dernier moment.
   **c.** Je manque *(miss)* quelquefois mon vol.

3. **a.** Si je dois attendre l'avion, je préfère lire.
   **b.** Si je dois attendre l'avion, je préfère manger.
   **c.** Si je dois attendre l'avion, je préfère faire les petits magasins de l'aéroport.

4. **a.** Si on perd mes bagages, je reste calme.
   **b.** Je suis furieux (furieuse) si on les perd.
   **c.** On n'a jamais perdu mes bagages.

5. **a.** Dans une grande ville comme Paris, j'utilise les moyens de transport en commun.
   **b.** Je prends toujours un taxi ou je loue une voiture.
   **c.** Je ne sors pas de l'hôtel.

**C. Conversation.** Avec un(e) partenaire, relisez la conversation entre Luc et l'agent de voyages à la page précédente. Ensuite, imaginez que vous êtes dans une agence de voyages d'une ville francophone et que vous achetez un billet pour rentrer chez vous. Votre partenaire jouera le rôle de l'agent de voyages.

**1.** What is the conjugation of **savoir?** of **connaître?**

**2.** Which verb meaning *to know* do you use to say that you are familiar with people and places? Which verb do you use to say you know information or facts? a language?

**3.** How do you say that you know how to do something?

**NOTE DE GRAMMAIRE**

Use **savoir** to translate the verb *to know* if it is followed by a question word, *if* (**si**), or the conjunction *that* (**que**), since one is talking about knowing information.

Sais-tu **où** tu vas aller?
Je ne sais pas **si** je vais avoir des vacances.
Savez-vous **que** la France a quatre départements d'outre-mer?

# Saying what people know

*Les verbes **savoir** et **connaître** et reprise des pronoms compléments d'objet direct **le, la, l'** et **les***

Both **savoir** and **connaître** mean *to know*.

| **SAVOIR** (to know [how]) | |
|---|---|
| je **sais** | nous **savons** |
| tu **sais** | vous **savez** |
| il/elle/on **sait** | ils/elles **savent** |

PASSÉ COMPOSÉ: j'**ai su**
IMPARFAIT: je **savais**
FUTUR: je **saurai**
CONDITIONNEL: je **saurais**

| **CONNAÎTRE** (to know, to be familiar with, to be acquainted with) | |
|---|---|
| je **connais** | nous **connaissons** |
| tu **connais** | vous **connaissez** |
| il/elle/on **connaît** | ils/elles **connaissent** |

PASSÉ COMPOSÉ: j'**ai connu**
IMPARFAIT: je **connaissais**
FUTUR: je **connaîtrai**
CONDITIONNEL: je **connaîtrais**

Use **savoir** to say you *know* . . .

FACTS OR INFORMATION:

Est-ce que tu **sais** ma réponse?
Nous ne **savons** pas où ils sont.

A LANGUAGE:

Je **sais** le français.
Je ne **sais** pas l'allemand.

HOW TO DO SOMETHING:

Je **sais** nager.
Je ne **sais** pas danser.

Use **connaître** to say you *know (of)* or *are familiar* or *acquainted with* . . .

PEOPLE:

Vous **connaissez** mon amie Micheline?
Je la **connais** bien.

PLACES:

Est-ce que tu **connais** bien la Guadeloupe?
Qui **connaît** le quartier?

THINGS:

Je ne **connais** pas bien l'histoire des Antilles.
Tu **connais** ce film?

Remember that if you wish to replace the object of a verb such as **connaître** or **savoir** with a pronoun, you use the direct object pronoun **le** *(him, it)*, **la** *(her, it)*, **l'** *(him, her, it)*, or **les** *(them)*. Also remember that object pronouns go before an infinitive in a sentence if there is one, otherwise they go before the conjugated verb.

— Tu sais **ma réponse**?
— Non, je ne **la** sais pas.

— Est-ce que tu connais bien **le quartier**?
— Non, je ne **le** connais pas bien.

**A. Quel pays?** Luc vous parle des gens qu'il connaît et des pays où ils habitent. Quels pays est-ce que ces personnes connaissent bien?

Exemple    J'habite à Paris.
                    Je **connais bien la France.**

la France    l'Allemagne    ???    l'Espagne
les États-Unis    le Sénégal    le Canada

1. Mon amie Sophie habite à Berlin. Elle...
2. Mes cousins habitent à Barcelone. Ils...
3. Mes parents et moi habitons à Paris. Nous...
4. Mon frère habite à Dakar. Il...
5. Et vous, vous habitez à *[votre ville]*. Alors, vous... ?

Maintenant, Luc dit quelle langue chaque personne sait parler. Qu'est-ce qu'il dit?

**Exemple**     J'habite à Paris.
                    Je **sais parler français.**

**B. Tu connais... ?** Demandez à un(e) camarade de classe s'il/si elle connaît bien différents endroits de votre ville. Donnez un nom précis. Utilisez le pronom **le, la, l'** ou **les** dans la réponse.

**Exemple**     la rue...
                    — **Est-ce que tu connais la rue Canyon?**
                    — **Oui, je la connais. / Non, je ne la connais pas.**

1. le magasin...
2. la librairie...
3. le parc...
4. le restaurant...
5. le centre commercial...
6. la rue...
7. les appartements...
8. le cinéma...

**C. Qui sait faire ça?** Dites qui sait faire les choses suivantes dans votre famille. Dites **Tout le monde sait** pour dire *Everyone knows how . . . to* and **Personne ne sait...** pour dire *No one knows how to . . .*

**Exemple**     nager
                    **Tout le monde sait nager dans ma famille.**
                    **Moi, je sais nager mais les autres ne savent pas nager.**
                    **Personne ne sait nager dans ma famille.**

1. bien faire la cuisine
2. faire du ski
3. bien danser
4. jouer au tennis
5. bien chanter
6. parler français

Maintenant demandez aux personnes de votre classe si elles savent faire ces choses.

**Exemple**     nager
                    — **Marc, tu sais nager? / Monsieur Grant, vous savez nager?**
                    — **Non, je ne sais pas nager.**

**D. Les voyages et la géographie.** Complétez chaque question avec la forme correcte de **connaître** ou de **savoir** et posez-la à votre partenaire.

1. _____-tu une bonne agence de voyages? Est-ce que tu _____ combien coûte un billet d'ici à Paris? _____-tu combien de temps prend un vol d'ici à Paris? Est-ce que tu _____ le taux de change *(exchange rate)* de l'euro?
2. Combien de langues est-ce que tu _____ parler? Est-ce que tu _____ l'allemand? _____-tu un peu l'Europe? _____ -tu quelle ville est la capitale de la Belgique?
3. _____-tu la Guadeloupe? Est-ce que tu _____ quelle ville est le chef-lieu *(administrative center)* de la Guadeloupe? _____ -tu bien l'histoire et la géographie des Antilles? _____ -tu en quelle année Christophe Colomb est arrivé en Guadeloupe?

**1.** What four pronouns are used for both direct and indirect objects? Where are they usually placed in a sentence with an infinitive? Where are they placed otherwise?

**2.** When is an unaccented **e** silent? When must you pronounce it?

# Indicating who does what to whom

*Les pronoms* **me, te, nous** *et* **vous**

The following pronouns are used as direct or indirect objects to say *me, to me, you, to you, us,* or *to us.* **Me** and **te** become **m'** and **t'** before vowel sounds.

| | | |
|---|---|---|
| *me, to me* | **me (m')** | Tu ne **m'**attends pas? |
| *you, to you* (familiar) | **te (t')** | Nous **t'**avons attendu(e) une heure. |
| *us, to us* | **nous** | Tu peux venir **nous** chercher? |
| *you, to you* (plural / formal) | **vous** | Je **vous** téléphonerai plus tard. |

Remember that object pronouns go before an infinitive in a sentence if there is one, otherwise they go before the conjugated verb. In the **passé composé,** they go before the auxiliary verb.

Je vais **te** voir demain.     Il ne **nous** connaît pas bien.     Je **vous** ai vu(e)(s).

The expression **il faut** followed by an infinitive generally means *it is necessary* or *one must.*

Il faut arriver une heure
  à l'avance.

*It is necessary to arrive one hour in advance.*
*One must arrive one hour in advance.*

Use **il faut** with indirect object pronouns such as **me, te, nous,** and **vous** to say that someone needs something.

Qu'est-ce qu'il vous faut?     *What do you need?*
Il me faut un passeport.     *I need a passport.*

CD 2-28

# Prononciation

*Le* **e** *caduc*

Unaccented **e** is usually not pronounced if you can drop it without bringing three pronounced consonants together.

Tu m¢ parles?
Je n¢ veux pas d¢ vin.
Vous n¢ voulez pas m¢ donner cinq dollars?

Pronounce an unaccented **e** if dropping it would bring three pronounced consonants together.

Le professeur m<u>e</u> parle.     Luc t<u>e</u> cherche.     Karim l<u>e</u> veut.

**A. Ça se prononce?**   Vous parlez à votre meilleur(e) ami(e). Lisez la phrase que vous diriez le plus probablement à votre ami(e). Ne prononcez pas les **e** en italique.

1. **a.** Tu m*e* parles trop.         **b.** Tu n*e* me parles pas trop.
2. **a.** Je vais t*e* donner 100 dollars.     **b.** Je n*e* vais pas t*e* donner 100 dollars.
3. **a.** Tu peux m*e* téléphoner d*e*main.     **b.** Tu n*e* peux pas m*e* téléphoner d*e*main.
4. **a.** Tu m*e* rends souvent visite.     **b.** Tu n*e* me rends pas souvent visite.
5. **a.** Tu vas v*e*nir me voir sam*e*di.     **b.** Tu n*e* vas pas v*e*nir me voir sam*e*di.

**B. Qu'est-ce qu'il vous faut?** Dites la même chose en utilisant **il faut** avec le pronom complément d'objet indirect **me, te, nous** ou **vous**.

> Exemple     J'ai besoin d'un passeport.
> **Il me faut un passeport.**

1. Tu as besoin d'une carte de crédit.
2. Nous avons besoin d'un guide.
3. Vous avez besoin d'un billet.
4. J'ai besoin d'un nouveau bikini.
5. Tu as besoin d'une pièce d'identité *(identification)*.
6. Vous avez besoin d'une réservation.

Maintenant, dites pourquoi il vous faut chacune de ces choses.

> Exemple     **Il me faut un passeport pour faire un voyage à l'étranger.**

changer un chèque de voyage     avoir une chambre d'hôtel
faire un voyage à l'étranger     payer le voyage
monter dans l'avion     préparer un itinéraire     aller à la plage

**C. Je te promets!** Un jeune homme dit à sa fiancée qu'il fait et qu'il va faire tout ce qu'elle veut. Elle lui pose les questions suivantes. Comment répond-il?

> Exemple     Tu m'aimes vraiment beaucoup?
> **Oui, je t'aime vraiment beaucoup.**

1. Tu m'adores?
2. Tu me trouves laide?
3. Tu me comprends?
4. Tu m'écoutes quand je te parle?
5. Tu veux me voir tous les jours?
6. Tu vas venir me voir demain?
7. Tu vas me donner ta photo?
8. Tu vas m'aider avec mon travail?
9. Tu vas m'abandonner?
10. Tu vas m'aimer pour toujours?

**D. Meilleurs amis.** Demandez à votre partenaire si son meilleur ami (sa meilleure amie) fait les choses suivantes.

> Exemple     téléphoner souvent
> **— Il/Elle te téléphone souvent?**
> **— Non, il/elle ne me téléphone pas souvent.**

parler tous les jours     rendre toujours visite le week-end
retrouver souvent en ville     embêter *(to annoy)* quelquefois
écouter toujours     donner de l'argent     comprendre bien
demander beaucoup de services *(favors)*

**E. Professeurs et étudiants.** Dites au professeur trois choses que les autres étudiants et vous faites pour lui et trois choses que le professeur fait pour vous. Faites deux listes sur une feuille de papier.

> Exemple     **Nous vous écoutons...**     **Vous nous donnez trop de devoirs...**

**F. Entretien.** Interviewez votre partenaire.

1. Est-ce que tes amis t'invitent souvent à partir en voyage avec eux *(them)*?
2. As-tu des amis qui te téléphonent d'un autre pays de temps en temps?
3. De tous les endroits où tu as passé tes vacances, quelle ville est-ce que tu me recommandes de visiter? Pourquoi ?

# Preparing for a trip

>Note
*culturelle*

Comme en France métropolitaine, l'euro est la monnaie d'usage utilisée dans les départements d'outre-mer français (la Guadeloupe, la Martinique, la Réunion et la Guyane), à Mayotte, à Saint-Pierre-et-Miquelon et aux Terres australes et antarctiques françaises. En Polynésie française, à Wallis-et-Futuna et en Nouvelle-Calédonie la monnaie est le franc CFP (Comptoir français du Pacifique). Quelle est la monnaie des territoires américains tels que Puerto Rico et Guam?

**NOTE DE GRAMMAIRE**

**Obtenir** is conjugated like **venir (j'obtiens, tu obtiens, il/elle obtient, nous obtenons, vous obtenez, ils/elles obtiennent).** The past participle is **obtenu** and the **passé composé** is formed with **avoir (j'ai obtenu... ).** The root of the future and conditional is **obtiendr.**

## Les préparatifs

Avant de faire un voyage à l'étranger, il faut faire beaucoup de **préparatifs** *(m)*. Avant le départ, il faut...

s'informer sur des sites Web pour **obtenir** des renseignements.

lire des guides touristiques.

téléphoner à l'hôtel pour réserver une chambre.

dire à votre famille où vous allez.

demander à **vos voisins** de donner à manger à votre chien.

**faire vos valises.**

À votre arrivée, vous devez...

montrer votre passeport.

passer la douane.

changer de l'argent ou des chèques de voyage.

---

**des préparatifs** *(m)* preparations   **obtenir** *to obtain*   **un(e) voisin(e)** *a neighbor*   **faire ses valises** *(f) to pack one's bags*

CD 2-29

Alain, l'ami de Luc, parle à sa femme de son mail de Luc.

CATHERINE: Qu'est-ce que **tu lis?**

ALAIN: C'est un mail que **j'ai reçu** de mon ami Luc. Il m'écrit de la Guade-loupe où il passe ses vacances.

CATHERINE: Et **ça lui plaît,** la Guadeloupe?

ALAIN: Ça lui plaît beaucoup! Il dit qu'il a décidé d'y rester un peu plus longtemps que **prévu.**

CATHERINE: La Guadeloupe doit être jolie. J'aimerais bien voir les plages et les paysages tropicaux.

ALAIN: Luc dit qu'il aime beaucoup le paysage, la cuisine et le climat. Il me parle aussi d'une «femme extraordinaire» qu'il a rencontrée là-bas et qui s'appelle Micheline.

### A. Avant le départ ou après l'arrivée? Quand on voyage, fait-on les choses suivantes **avant le départ** ou **après l'arrivée?**

> **Exemple** acheter un billet d'avion
> **avant le départ**

1. passer la douane
2. écrire pour obtenir des renseignements
3. s'informer sur des sites Web
4. acheter des chèques de voyage
5. changer des chèques de voyage
6. réserver une chambre
7. montrer son passeport
8. lire des guides touristiques
9. demander à un ami de donner à manger à son chien
10. faire des préparatifs

### B. Mon dernier voyage? Dites si vous avez fait chaque chose de l'activité précédente avant ou pendant vos dernières vacances.

> **Exemple** acheter un billet d'avion
> **Je n'ai pas acheté de billet d'avion.**

### C. Que fait-on? Faites une liste de ce qu'on fait dans chacun des endroits suivants.

1. à l'agence de voyages
2. à l'aéroport
3. à la banque
4. à l'hôtel
5. sur des sites Web

### D. Conversations. Avec un(e) partenaire, relisez la conversation entre Alain et Catherine en haut de la page. Ensuite, imaginez que vous recevez un mail d'un(e) ami(e) qui visite une autre région francophone. Parlez avec votre partenaire de vos impressions de cette région et dites pourquoi vous voudriez ou ne voudriez pas y aller.

---

**tu lis** (**lire** *to read*)   **j'ai reçu** (**recevoir** *to receive*)   **Ça lui plaît?** (**plaire** *to please*) *Does he like it?*
**prévu(e)** *planned, foreseen*

**1.** What are the conjugations of **dire, lire,** and **écrire?** What is unusual about the **vous** form of **dire?** What are the future and conditional stems of these verbs?

**2.** Which two of these verbs have similar past participles? What are they? What is the past participle of **lire?**

# Contacting people

*Les verbes **dire**, **lire** et **écrire***

You have already seen the verbs **dire** *(to say, to tell)*, **lire** *(to read)*, and **écrire** *(to write)*. Here are their full conjugations. The verb **décrire** *(to describe)* is conjugated like **écrire.**

| DIRE *(to say, to tell)* | |
|---|---|
| je **dis** | nous **disons** |
| tu **dis** | vous **dites** |
| il/elle/on **dit** | ils/elles **disent** |

PASSÉ COMPOSÉ: j'**ai dit**
IMPARFAIT: je **disais**
FUTUR: je **dirai**
CONDITIONNEL: je **dirais**

| LIRE *(to read)* | |
|---|---|
| je **lis** | nous **lisons** |
| tu **lis** | vous **lisez** |
| il/elle/on **lit** | ils/elles **lisent** |

PASSÉ COMPOSÉ: j'**ai lu**
IMPARFAIT: je **lisais**
FUTUR: je **lirai**
CONDITIONNEL: je **lirais**

| ÉCRIRE *(to write)* | |
|---|---|
| j' **écris** | nous **écrivons** |
| tu **écris** | vous **écrivez** |
| il/elle/on **écrit** | ils/elles **écrivent** |

PASSÉ COMPOSÉ: j'**ai écrit**
IMPARFAIT: j'**écrivais**
FUTUR: j'**écrirai**
CONDITIONNEL: j'**écrirais**

Here are some things you might want to read or write.

| | |
|---|---|
| **un article** *an article* | **une lettre** *a letter* |
| **une carte postale** *a postcard* | **un magazine** *a magazine* |
| **un mail** *an e-mail* | **un poème** *a poem* |
| **une histoire** *a story* | **une rédaction** *a composition* |
| **un journal** (*pl* **des journaux**) *a newspaper* | **un roman** *a novel* |

**A. En cours de français.** Est-ce que ces personnes font souvent les choses indiquées en cours de français?

> souvent     quelquefois     rarement     ne… jamais

> **Exemple**    je / écrire des poèmes
> **Je n'écris jamais de poèmes en cours de français.**

1. le professeur / écrire au tableau
2. les étudiants / écrire au tableau
3. je / écrire quelque chose dans mon cahier
4. nous / écrire une rédaction
5. les autres étudiants et moi / s'écrire des mails après le cours
6. je / lire le journal
7. le professeur / (nous) lire des poèmes en français
8. nous / lire des phrases à haute voix (*aloud*)
9. les étudiants / lire des romans en français

Maintenant, dites si ces personnes feront probablement ces choses en cours la semaine prochaine.

> **Exemple**    **Je n'écrirai pas de poèmes en cours de français la semaine prochaine.**

**B. Qu'est-ce qu'on dit?** Vous dites à un ami quand on utilise les expressions suivantes. Complétez les phrases avec la forme correcte du verbe **dire** et l'expression logique.

> Exemple     Vos amis vont partir en voyage. Vous **dites «Bon voyage».**

> **Vous pouvez répéter, s'il vous plaît?     Bon voyage!**
> **Je veux bien.     À tout à l'heure!     À demain!     Salut!**

**1.** Nous n'avons pas compris le professeur. Nous...
**2.** Tes camarades de classe et toi allez voir le prof demain. Vous...
**3.** Tu vas voir tes camarades de classe plus tard, à la bibliothèque. Tu...
**4.** J'accepte une invitation au cinéma avec des amis. Je...
**5.** Mes amis retrouvent d'autres amis au cinéma. Ils...

**C. En vacances.** Vous faites le voyage de vos rêves avec un(e) bon(ne) ami(e). Avec un(e) partenaire, faites des phrases logiques en utilisant un élément de chaque colonne. Faites au moins deux phrases pour chaque sujet de la colonne de gauche. Le groupe qui écrit le plus grand nombre de phrases logiques gagne!

> Exemple     **Je dis la date de notre départ à l'agent de voyages.**

| | | | |
|---|---|---|---|
| Je...<br>Nous...<br>L'agent de voyages (nous)...<br>Nos amis (nous)... | écrire<br>lire<br>dire | des cartes postales<br>des mails<br>des sites Web<br>des guides touristiques<br>«au revoir»<br>«bon voyage»<br>à l'hôtel<br>les prix des billets<br>le numéro de notre vol<br>le nom de notre hôtel<br>notre destination<br>la date de notre départ | quand nous achetons le billet<br>avant de partir<br>à notre départ<br>pendant le voyage<br>pour faire une réservation<br>pour obtenir des renseignements<br>à des amis<br>à nos familles<br>à l'agent de voyages |

**D. Entretien.** Interviewez votre partenaire.

**1.** Est-ce que tu écris plus de lettres ou plus de mails? À qui? Est-ce que tu as écrit un mail ce matin? À qui? Est-ce que des personnes que tu ne connais pas t'écrivent des mails quelquefois? Est-ce que tu écris quelquefois des mails à des personnes que tu ne connais pas?
**2.** Lis-tu le journal tous les jours? Est-ce que tu l'as lu ce matin? Quel magazine lis-tu le plus souvent? Est-ce que tu l'as lu ce mois-ci?
**3.** Lis-tu beaucoup de romans? Lis-tu plus de romans d'aventures ou d'amour? Quel est le dernier roman que tu as lu? Quand est-ce que tu l'as lu?

**E. Préparatifs.** Vous partez en vacances avec un(e) ami(e) qui veut savoir si vous avez tout préparé. Préparez une conversation où vous dites si vous avez fait les choses suivantes.

- écrire pour réserver une chambre
- acheter les billets
- acheter des chèques de voyage
- lire des guides touristiques
- dire à un(e) ami(e) où vous allez
- faire vos valises
- demander à un(e) ami(e) de donner à manger à vos animaux

**1.** What types of verbs are frequently followed by indirect objects?

**2.** Where do you place the object pronoun when there is an infinitive in the sentence? Where does it go otherwise?

**3.** Where do you place the object pronoun in the **passé composé?**

# Avoiding repetition

*Les pronoms compléments d'objet indirect*

You already know how to use **le, la, l',** and **les** to replace the direct object of the verb.

    — Tu fais **ta valise** maintenant?    — Tu as acheté **ton billet?**
    — Oui, je **la** fais.    — Oui, je **l'ai** acheté.

Use the indirect pronouns **lui** *(him, to him, her, to her)* and **leur** *(them, to them)* to replace a noun that is the indirect object of the verb. Generally, indirect objects can only be people or animals, not things. In French, you can recognize a noun that is an indirect object because it is preceded by the preposition **à** (**à la, à l', au, aux**).

Verbs indicating communication or exchanges between people, such as **parler à, téléphoner à, dire à, écrire à, demander à, rendre visite à,** and **donner à** are often followed by indirect objects.

    — Tu écris **à ta mère?**    — Tu vas rendre visite **à tes parents?**
    — Oui, je **lui** écris un mail.    — Oui, je vais **leur** rendre visite ce week-end.

Remember that the pronouns **me, te, nous,** and **vous** function as both direct and indirect objects.

| DIRECT OBJECT PRONOUNS | | INDIRECT OBJECT PRONOUNS | |
|---|---|---|---|
| me (m') | nous | me (m') | nous |
| te (t') | vous | te (t') | vous |
| le, la (l') | les | lui | leur |

All object pronouns are generally placed immediately before the verb. They go before the infinitive if there is one. If not, they go before the conjugated verb. In the **passé composé,** they go before the auxiliary verb.

    — Luc écrit **à son ami?**    — *Is Luc writing **to his friend?***
    — Oui, il **lui** écrit.    — *Yes, he is writing **(to) him.***

    — Il va téléphoner **à Micheline?**    — *Is he going to call **Micheline?***
    — Oui, il va **lui** téléphoner.    — *Yes, he's going to call **her.***

    — Il a parlé **à ses parents?**    — *Has he talked **to his parents?***
    — Non, il ne **leur** a pas parlé.    — *No, he hasn't talked **to them.***

Notice the placement of object pronouns in negated sentences.

Je ne veux pas **lui** écrire.
Je ne **lui** écris jamais.
Je ne **lui** ai pas écrit.

When you use object pronouns in the **passé composé,** the past participle agrees with direct object pronouns, but not with indirect objects.

Luc a invité Micheline.    Luc a téléphoné à Micheline.
Luc **l'a** invité**e.**    Luc **lui** a téléphoné.

**A. Une excursion.** Quand un groupe de touristes fait une excursion guidée, est-ce qu'un bon guide fait les choses suivantes pour les touristes généralement? Utilisez le pronom **leur,** comme dans l'exemple.

    **Exemple**    parler de ses problèmes personnels
                 **Non, il ne leur parle pas de ses problèmes personnels.**

1. dire son nom
2. expliquer *(to explain)* l'itinéraire
3. parler de choses ennuyeuses
4. parler de l'histoire de la région
5. décrire la culture
6. montrer les sites historiques
7. répondre poliment *(politely)*
8. demander un pourboire *(tip)*
9. parler dans une langue qu'ils ne comprennent pas

Maintenant, dites si les touristes sympas font les choses suivantes au guide. Utilisez le pronom **lui.**

> **Exemple**    demander son nom
> **Oui, ils lui demandent son nom.**

1. téléphoner à minuit
2. obéir
3. poser des questions
4. parler
5. donner un pourboire *(tip)*
6. dire «merci»

### B. Habitudes de voyage?  Est-ce que vous faites généralement les choses suivantes quand vous partez en vacances? Répondez en utilisant **lui** ou **leur.**

> **Exemple**    Vous dites à vos parents où vous allez?
> **Oui, je leur dis où je vais. / Non, je ne leur dis pas où je vais.**

1. Vous téléphonez à vos amis pendant le voyage?
2. Vous demandez de l'argent à vos parents?
3. Vous écrivez des cartes postales à vos amis?
4. Vous rapportez *(bring back)* un souvenir à votre meilleur(e) ami(e)?
5. Vous parlez du voyage à vos parents?
6. Vous écrivez des mails à votre meilleur(e) ami(e)?
7. Vous montrez des photos du voyage à votre mère?
8. Vous décrivez le voyage à vos amis?
9. Vous demandez à votre meilleur(e) ami(e) de vous accompagner?
10. Vous demandez à vos voisins de donner à manger à votre chien ou chat?

### C. Et votre dernier voyage?  Posez les questions de l'exercice *B. Habitudes de voyage* à un(e) partenaire au passé composé pour décrire la dernière fois qu'il/elle est parti(e) en vacances. Votre partenaire doit répondre en utilisant **lui** ou **leur.**

> **Exemple**    Tu as dit à tes parents où tu allais?
> **Oui, je leur ai dit où j'allais.**
> **Non, je ne leur ai pas dit où j'allais.**

### D. À l'agence de voyages.  Vous êtes dans une agence de voyages. Travaillez avec un(e) partenaire pour compléter les phrases suivantes de façon logique. Écrivez plusieurs choses pour chaque situation. Le groupe avec le plus de phrases logiques gagne.

> **Exemple**    L'agent de voyages me demande **quand je veux partir.**
> Il me demande **si je veux un billet aller-retour.**

1. L'agent de voyages me demande...
2. Je lui demande...
3. L'agent de voyages me dit...
4. Je lui dis...
5. L'agent de voyages me donne…
6. Je lui donne…

# Deciding where to go on a trip

> Note
*culturelle*

De tous les pays du monde, la France est le pays le plus visité par les étrangers chaque année, et plus de 8 Français sur 10 passent leurs vacances dans leur propre pays aussi. Les Français qui partent à l'étranger préfèrent l'Espagne, l'Italie, la Grèce et le Portugal. Quelles sont les destinations étrangères les plus populaires des gens que vous connaissez? Pourquoi?

**VOCABULAIRE SUPPLÉMENTAIRE**

| | |
|---|---|
| **EN AFRIQUE** | l'Afrique du Sud |
| | la Tunisie |
| **EN ASIE** | la Corée |
| | l'Inde |
| | l'Indonésie |
| | l'Iran |
| | l'Irak |
| | la Turquie |
| **EN EUROPE** | le Danemark |
| | la Grèce |
| | la Norvège |
| | la Pologne |
| | le Portugal |
| | la République tchèque |
| | la Suède *(Sweden)* |

## Un voyage

Luc visite la Guadeloupe. Et vous? Quels continents et pays aimeriez-vous visiter?

Moi, j'aimerais visiter...

l'Afrique: **le Maroc,** l'Algérie, l'Égypte, le Sénégal, la Côte d'Ivoire

L'oasis Kerzaz, Algérie

l'Asie et **le Moyen-Orient:** la Chine, Israël, le Japon, le Viêt Nam

l'Amérique du Nord ou l'Amérique centrale: **les Antilles,** le Canada, les États-Unis, le Mexique

La Guadeloupe

l'Amérique du Sud: l'Argentine, le Brésil, le Pérou, la Colombie, le Chili

l'Océanie: l'Australie, la Nouvelle-Calédonie, la Polynésie française

l'Europe: l'Allemagne, la Belgique, l'Espagne, la France, **la Grande-Bretagne,** l'Italie, la Russie, la Suisse

L'Arcade du Cinquantenaire, Bruxelles

**le Maroc** *Morocco*    **le Moyen-Orient** *the Middle East*    **les Antilles** *the West Indies*    **la Grande-Bretagne** *Great Britain*

CD 2-30

Luc et Micheline parlent des voyages qu'ils ont faits.

MICHELINE: Pourquoi es-tu venu tout seul en Guadeloupe? Tu aimes voyager?
LUC: Oui, j'adore!
MICHELINE: Quels pays étrangers as-tu visités?
LUC: J'ai visité les États-Unis, la Chine et le Canada. Et toi? Tu aimes voyager à l'étranger?
MICHELINE: Je n'ai jamais quitté la Guadeloupe, mais j'aimerais bien visiter l'Afrique un jour.
LUC: Où aimerais-tu aller en Afrique?
MICHELINE: Moi, j'aimerais surtout visiter le Sénégal et la Côte d'Ivoire.

## A. Quel continent? Où se trouvent ces pays?

> Exemple   la Chine
>           **La Chine se trouve en Asie.**

1. les États-Unis
2. l'Algérie
3. le Japon
4. l'Australie
5. l'Allemagne
6. le Sénégal
7. le Viêt Nam
8. le Maroc

> **en Afrique      en Asie**
> **en Amérique du Nord**
> **en Amérique du Sud**
> **en Océanie      en Europe**

## B. Quels pays? Dites quels pays vous aimeriez visiter dans la région indiquée.

> Exemple   en Europe
>           **En Europe, j'aimerais visiter la France, l'Espagne...**

1. en Asie et au Moyen-Orient
2. en Amérique du Nord et du Sud
3. en Océanie
4. en Afrique
5. en Europe

**Marrakech, Maroc**

## C. Associations. Travaillez avec un(e) partenaire pour trouver l'endroit de chaque groupe qui ne va pas avec les autres. Expliquez pourquoi.

> Exemple   l'Allemagne, les États-Unis, la France, la Suisse
>           **les États-Unis: Tous les autres sont en Europe.**

1. le Canada, l'Argentine, l'Espagne, le Pérou, le Mexique
2. l'Australie, la Polynésie française, la Grande-Bretagne, le Sénégal
3. la France, les États-Unis, l'Australie, la Grande-Bretagne
4. le Sénégal, l'Égypte, le Brésil, l'Algérie, le Maroc
5. la France, la Belgique, le Sénégal, la Suisse, le Mexique

## D. Conversation. Avec un(e) partenaire, relisez la conversation entre Micheline et Luc en haut de la page. Ensuite, changez la conversation pour parler des régions et pays que vous avez visités et de ceux que vous aimeriez visiter.

**1.** With which one of the following do you generally not use a definite article when it is the subject or direct object of a verb: cities, states, provinces, countries, or continents? Would you use **le, la, l'**, or **les** before the following place names: _____ **Italie**, _____ **Antilles**, _____ **Ohio**, _____ **Japon?**

**2.** Which countries, states or provinces are generally feminine? masculine?

**3.** How do you say *to* or *in* with a city? with a feminine country? with a masculine country beginning with a vowel sound? with a masculine country beginning with a consonant? with plural countries?

**NOTE DE GRAMMAIRE**

The following places are exceptions to the rule that countries and states ending in **-e** are feminine: **le Mexique, le Delaware, le Maine, le New Hampshire, le Nouveau-Mexique, le Rhode Island, le Tennessee.**

# Saying where you are going

*Les expressions géographiques*

When a place name is used as the subject or object of a verb, you generally need to use the definite article with continents, countries, states, and provinces, but not with cities. Most continents, countries, states, and provinces ending in **-e** are feminine, whereas most others are masculine. **Le Mexique** is an exception.

J'adore **l'Europe. La** France est très belle. Nous allons visiter Londres, Paris et Nice. J'aimerais aussi voir **les** États-Unis: **la** Californie, **le** Texas et **la** Floride.

To say *to* or *in* with a geographical location, the preposition you use varies.

|  |  | *to / in* |
|---|---|---|
| **à** | with cities | **à** Paris |
| **en** | with all feminine countries, states, provinces, or continents, and masculine ones beginning with a vowel | **en** France **en** Ontario |
| **au** | with masculine countries, states, or provinces beginning with a consonant | **au** Canada |
| **aux** | with plural countries and regions | **aux** États-Unis |

## A. C'est quelle ville? Quelle est la capitale de ces régions francophones?

**Exemple**    Quelle est la capitale de la France?
**Paris est la capitale de la France.**

Quelle est la capitale ou le chef-lieu *(administrative center)* ... ?

du Sénégal? du Maroc? du Québec? de la Belgique? d'Haïti? de Tahiti? de la Louisiane? de la Guyane? de la Guadeloupe? de la Martinique?

Dakar   Paris   Rabat
Basse-Terre   Baton Rouge
Papeete   Cayenne   Bruxelles
Port-au-Prince   Québec
Fort-de-France

## B. C'est connu! D'abord, mettez la forme convenable de l'article défini devant le nom de chaque pays. Ensuite, demandez à votre partenaire quel pays est connu *(known)* pour les choses indiquées.

| | | |
|---|---|---|
| _____ Grande-Bretagne | _____ Égypte | _____ Suisse |
| _____ Colombie | _____ États-Unis | _____ France |
| _____ Mexique | _____ Italie | _____ Brésil |

**Exemple**    — **Quel pays est connu pour le café?**
                 — **La Colombie.**

Quel pays est connu pour... ?

1. le fromage et le vin
2. le carnaval
3. le chocolat
4. le thé
5. les spaghetti
6. les pyramides
7. la musique rock
8. le sphinx

**C. Leçon de géographie.** Votre ami(e) n'est pas très fort(e) en géographie et il/elle vous pose des questions. Répondez-lui. D'abord, donnez la préposition convenable pour dire *to / in* avec chaque pays. Ensuite, jouez les deux rôles avec votre partenaire.

> **Exemple** Londres (_____ Grande-Bretagne, _____ Canada)
> — **Londres se trouve en Grande-Bretagne ou au Canada?**
> — **Londres se trouve en Grande-Bretagne.**

1. Tokyo (_____ Chine, _____ Japon)
2. Mexico (_____ Mexique, _____ Pérou)
3. Moscou (_____ Italie, _____ Russie)
4. Berlin (_____ Espagne, _____ Allemagne)
5. Hanoi (_____ Viêt Nam, _____ Brésil)
6. Alger (_____ Algérie, _____ Maroc)
7. Le Caire (_____ Maroc, _____ Égypte)
8. Dakar (_____ Sénégal, _____ Côte d'Ivoire)
9. La Nouvelle-Orléans (_____ États-Unis, _____ France)
10. Abidjan (_____ Côte d'Ivoire, _____ Sénégal)

**D. C'est où?** Devinez où dans le monde francophone se trouvent ces sites touristiques. Donnez le nom de la ville et du pays.

1.

la Grand-Place

2.

le Château Frontenac

3.

Chambord

**E. Entretien.** Interviewez votre partenaire.

1. Dans quels pays étrangers as-tu voyagé? Quels pays voudrais-tu visiter? Pourquoi?
2. Dans quelles villes as-tu habité? Quelles grandes villes aux États-Unis as-tu visitées? Est-ce que tu voudrais habiter dans ces villes? Pourquoi (pas)?
3. Qu'est-ce qu'on peut faire en vacances à Washington, D.C.? à New York? au Colorado? en Floride? De ces quatre endroits, où est-ce que tu aimerais le mieux passer tes vacances? Pourquoi?

## Reprise

*Making travel plans and preparing for a trip*

Dans le ***Chapitre 9,*** vous avez appris à parler des vacances. Maintenant vous allez réviser ce que vous avez appris.

**A. Qu'est-ce qu'on fait?** Après son voyage en Guadeloupe, Luc décide d'aller visiter l'Afrique francophone avec Micheline. Dites ce qu'ils pourraient faire dans les endroits *(places)* suivants.

> **Exemple**  dans une grande ville
> > **Dans une grande ville ils pourraient profiter des activités culturelles...**
>
> Qu'est-ce qu'ils pourraient faire dans une grande ville? à la mer? à la montagne?

**B. Destinations.** Donnez l'article défini qui correspond aux pays suivants.

| | | | |
|---|---|---|---|
| _____ | Égypte | _____ | Maroc |
| _____ | États-Unis | _____ | Algérie |
| _____ | Sénégal | _____ | Côte d'Ivoire |
| _____ | Japon | _____ | Brésil |

Luc et Micheline visiteront tous les pays africains de la liste précédente. Quels pays visiteront-ils?

> Ils visiteront...

Maintenant, complétez les phrases suivantes avec le nom du pays logique. N'oubliez pas d'utiliser la préposition correcte: **en, au** ou **aux.**

> D'abord, Luc et Micheline iront au Caire...
> Après l'Égypte, ils prendront l'avion pour Alger...
> D'Algérie, ils prendront l'autocar pour aller à Fès...
> De Fès, il iront à Abidjan…
> Finalement, avant de rentrer chez Luc à Paris, ils passeront quelques jours à Dakar...

**C. En Égypte.** Micheline parle avec une amie de son itinéraire pour le voyage en Égypte avec Luc. D'abord, mettez le verbe de chaque phrase au futur. Ensuite, mettez les phrases dans l'ordre logique.

> _____ On arrive au Caire après plus de 14 heures en avion.
>
> _____ Quelqu'un de l'hôtel vient nous chercher à l'aéroport à notre arrivée. L'hôtel coûte très cher et Luc paie tout.
>
> _____ Le premier soir, nous restons à l'hôtel et nous nous reposons. Le lendemain, un guide nous montre les pyramides et nous visitons le sphinx aussi.
>
> _____ D'abord, notre avion part de Guadeloupe à 3 heures de l'après-midi.
>
> _____ Nous sommes en première classe dans l'avion.
>
> _____ Après notre séjour au Caire, nous allons à Alexandrie où nous passons trois jours.
>
> _____ L'après-midi de notre arrivée, nous prenons un guide privé pour visiter Le Caire.

**D. Un bon guide.** Quand Luc et Micheline visitent les pyramides avec un groupe de touristes, ils ont un bon guide qui est très bien informé. Complétez les phrases suivantes avec la forme convenable du verbe **savoir** ou **connaître**.

**1.** Le guide _____ parler arabe et plusieurs langues européennes.
**2.** Après cinq minutes, il _____ le nom de tous les touristes qui font l'excursion.
**3.** Il _____ très bien la culture égyptienne.
**4.** Il _____ très bien les pyramides aussi.
**5.** Il _____ répondre à toutes nos questions.

**E. Qu'est-ce qu'ils ont fait?** Qu'est-ce que le guide a fait avec les touristes pendant leur visite aux pyramides? Récrivez le paragraphe suivant en remplaçant les compléments d'objets indirects en italique par le pronom **lui** ou **leur** pour éviter la répétition.

Un très bon guide a accompagné Luc et Micheline et les autres touristes pendant l'excursion. Il a montré tous les sites historiques *aux touristes* et il a expliqué *(explained)* l'histoire de chacun *aux touristes*. Il a dit *aux touristes* qu'ils pouvaient prendre des photos mais il a demandé *aux touristes* de ne rien toucher. Le groupe a trouvé le guide très intéressant et tout le monde *(everyone)* a posé beaucoup de questions *au guide*. À la fin de l'excursion, ils ont donné un bon pourboire *(tip) au guide*.

**F. Correspondance.** Luc correspond par mail avec Micheline après leur retour à Paris et en Guadeloupe. Dans le paragraphe suivant, il parle à son ami, Alain, de ses relations avec elle. Complétez le paragraphe suivant avec la forme correcte des verbes entre parenthèses.

Micheline et moi _____ (s'écrire) des mails. Je lui _____ (écrire) tous les jours mais récemment elle m' _____ (écrire) moins. Normalement, nous _____ (se dire) tout, mais maintenant, quand je _____ (lire) ses mails, je suis certain qu'il y a quelque chose qu'elle ne me _____ (dire) pas. Je lui _____ (dire) que je l'aime mais elle ne me _____ (dire) jamais qu'elle m'aime.

Maintenant, Alain lui pose des questions sur ses relations avec Micheline. Complétez ses questions avec la forme correcte du verbe indiqué. Ensuite, imaginez les réponses de Luc d'après le paragraphe précédent.

**1.** Est-ce que Micheline t'_____ (écrire) tous les jours?
**2.** Est-ce que tu lui _____ (écrire) aussi?
**3.** Est-ce qu'elle te _____ (dire) qu'elle t'aime?

**G. Des reproches.** Luc commence à faire des reproches à Micheline. Il pense qu'elle va l'oublier. Qu'est-ce qu'il dit? Utilisez le pronom **me**.

> **Exemple**  ne pas aimer
> **Tu ne m'aimes pas.**

**1.** ne pas demander mon opinion
**2.** ne pas écrire tous les jours
**3.** ne jamais téléphoner
**4.** ne pas parler de tes projets
**5.** parler très peu de tes amis en Guadeloupe
**6.** quitter pour un autre

Pour rassurer Luc, Micheline dit qu'elle va ou ne va pas faire chacune de ces choses. Qu'est-ce qu'elle dit?

> **Exemple**  **Je vais t'aimer!**

## Lecture: *Berceuse*

Vous allez lire le conte **Berceuse** *(Lullaby)* par l'Haïtienne Jan Dominique. Née à Port-au-Prince en 1953, Jan Dominique a passé une grande partie de sa vie au Québec. Dans ce conte elle change la phrase typique du commencement d'un conte pour enfants **Il était une fois** *(Once upon a time there was. . .)* et la met au futur **Il sera une fois...** *(Once upon a time there will be . . .)* pour parler des espoirs *(hopes)* d'une mère pour l'avenir *(the future)* de son fils.

### *Berceuse*

Il sera une fois **la Terre.** (À quoi bon, me dit-elle, nous n'y serons plus, toi et moi.) Peu importe, il faut. Il sera une fois la Terre. Et sur la Terre, les animaux, les arbres, **les fleurs,** les vraies maisons et les humains. Et dans la Terre, les plantes qui auront **germé** pour nourrir les hommes et **les bêtes.** Et tout **autour,** il y aura des rivières, **des champs à perte de vue,** des océans au loin. (Qu'en sais-tu, dit-elle.) J'ai oublié l'ordre, mais je sais qu'il sera une fois tout cela et bien plus encore. Je sais que tout sera **pareil** et différent. Je sais qu'il faut que je lui dise. Il faut lui raconter que cette époque n'est pas la fin **car** plus loin, **au-delà** du regard, il ne peut y avoir **pire,** que nous essayons de **lutter** pour lui. Je dois lui faire comprendre qu'un jour les choses changeront. Plus de misères et d'injustices, plus de crimes à la face de la vie, plus d'**opprimés** ni d'oppresseurs, plus de **guerres,** plus de carnages, nous n'en voulons plus. (Plus de Terre, dit-elle.) **Tais-toi!** Tu dois, comme moi, y **croire.** Pour lui. Je vois déjà ses yeux quand je lui raconterai qu'il ne sera plus jamais seul. Je vois déjà son **sourire** quand il entendra ma **voix** lui chanter les villes **pleines de rires** et de fleurs, les campagnes vertes, les animaux dans **les bois.** (Il ne connaît rien de tout cela, dit-elle.) Il apprendra. Je lui apprendrai comment il sera une fois la Terre, je lui ferai des dessins qu'**il accrochera** aux murs bas de sa chambre, pour ne pas oublier. **Je collerai** des paysages sur **les grilles** des fenêtres. À droite, une rivière, des arbres bruns, **un âne** et un petit garçon **étendu dans l'herbe;** à gauche, un lac **gelé, des pins** couverts de neige, un chien **à la fourrure épaisse** et une petite fille au manteau rouge **glissant dans un traîneau.** Il connaîtra les deux Terres que maintenant plus rien ne distingue. Il oubliera les eaux **boueuses, la poussière,** le soleil moribond, la fumée qu'**aucune brise ne chasse.** Il oubliera les murs, les grilles, les portes barricadées. (Pour une autre prison, dit-elle.) Non, pour d'autres horizons. Je veux tout cela pour lui. Pour nous, c'est peut-être trop tard, je ne sais pas. Mais lui, je ne le laisserai pas connaître la peur **en grandissant.** (Il la connaît déjà, dit-elle.) Il oubliera. Il **ne** se souviendra **que** des histoires racontées la nuit pour qu'il s'endorme.

---

**la Terre** *Earth*   **les fleurs** *flowers*   **germé** *sprouted*   **les bêtes** *beasts*   **autour** *around*
**des champs à perte de vue** *fields as far as you can see*   **pareil** *the same*   **car** *because*   **au-delà** *beyond*   **pire** *worse*
**lutter** *to struggle*   **opprimés** *oppressed*   **guerres** *wars*   **Tais-toi!** *Be quiet!*   **croire** *to believe*   **sourire** *smile*
**voix** *voice*   **pleines de rires** *full of laughter*   **les bois** *the woods*   **il accrochera** *he will hang*   **Je collerai** *I will stick*
**les grilles** *the bars*   **un âne** *a donkey*   **étendu dans l'herbe** *stretched out on the grass*   **gelé** *frozen*
**des pins** *pine trees*   **à la fourrure épaisse** *with thick fur*   **glissant dans un traîneau** *gliding on a sled*   **boueuses** *muddy*
**la poussière** *dust*   **aucune brise ne chasse** *no breeze makes go away*   **en grandissant** *while growing up*   **ne... que** *only*

Il oubliera **le son aigu** de ma voix pour couvrir le bruit des machines qui jamais ne s'arrêtent, il oubliera **l'oreiller** sur **la tête** pour trouver le sommeil. Il ne se souviendra que des histoires répétées la nuit pour **éloigner** l'angoisse. (**Tu échoueras,** dit-elle.) Je forcerai sa mémoire. Nuit après nuit, je lui écrirai tout, je lui raconterai tout. (Il ne t'entendra pas, dit-elle.) Je l'obligerai. Ouvre les yeux. Je sais que tu n'arrives pas à t'endormir. Je vais te raconter une histoire. Il sera une fois la Terre... Non, dit l'enfant aux yeux **tristes,** je n'aime pas le commencement de ton histoire. Dis-moi, comment veux-tu que je l'invente? Tu le sais, dit mon fils de sa voix fatiguée, commence par le commencement. Commence en racontant il est une fois la Terre. Pour ne jamais oublier.

## Compréhension

Répondez aux questions suivantes d'après la lecture.

1. À votre avis, qui fait les commentaires mis entre parenthèses dans la lecture?
2. Dans la liste des choses qu'il y aura sur la Terre imaginée par la mère, elle parle de **vraies maisons.** Pourquoi emploie-t-elle le mot **vraies?**
3. Comment imaginez-vous le monde actuel de la mère? Elle dit que son fils connaîtra les deux Terres que plus rien ne distingue. À votre avis, quelles sont ces deux Terres?
4. Comment commence l'histoire de la mère? Normalement, quelle phrase commence les histoires pour les enfants? Quel commencement est-ce que le fils préfère? Pourquoi, à votre avis?

## Composition

**A. Organisez-vous.** Votre classe de français va faire un voyage d'une semaine dans un pays francophone et vous êtes chargé(e) de préparer l'itinéraire. Avant de commencer, recherchez sur Internet des itinéraires de vacances ou des excursions dans la région que vous allez visiter pour trouver des idées sur les points d'intérêt de la région et d'autres renseignements importants pour les voyageurs.

**B. Rédaction: un itinéraire.** Écrivez une description détaillée du voyage que fera la classe ensemble. Dans la description, donnez les renseignements suivants.

- quand vous partirez et quand vous reviendrez
- comment vous voyagerez et le prix par personne
- où vous descendrez et où vous prendrez les repas
- ce que vous ferez chaque jour de la semaine

**C. À l'agence de voyages.** Comparez votre itinéraire et celui d'un(e) partenaire. Ensuite, préparez la conversation suivante.

Un agent de voyages décrit les deux itinéraires à un client qui fait des projets de vacances. Le client lui pose des questions sur chaque voyage et choisit l'un des deux.

---

**le son aigu** *the shrill sound*   **l'oreiller** *the pillow*   **la tête** *head*   **éloigner** *to remove*   **Tu échoueras** *You will fail*   **tristes** *sad*

## La Francophonie

**Depuis** les années soixante, on parle souvent de la Francophonie pour décrire l'ensemble des pays où on parle français. Le français et l'anglais sont les seules langues parlées comme langue maternelle sur tous les continents.

Pour beaucoup de gens, le terme «Francophonie» représente beaucoup plus qu'une définition des régions où le français s'emploie. C'est plutôt un esprit d'unité entre les personnes qui le parlent.

Voici des citations de deux pères fondateurs du concept de la Francophonie, l'ex-président et écrivain sénégalais, Léopold Sédar Senghor, et l'ex-président tunisien, Habib Bourguiba.

Léopold Sédar Senghor

«La Francophonie, c'est cet humanisme intégral qui **se tisse autour de** la Terre: cette symbiose des énergies dormantes de tous les continents, de toutes les races qui se réveillent à leur **chaleur** complémentaire.»

> *Léopold Sédar Senghor, dans une interview avec la revue* Esprit *en 1962*

«La langue est **un lien** remarquable de **parenté** qui **dépasse** en force le lien de l'idéologie [...]. La langue française constitue **l'appoint** à notre patrimoine culturel, enrichit notre pensée, exprime notre action, contribue à forger notre destin intellectuel et à faire de nous des hommes **à part entière**.»

> *Habib Bourguiba, devant l'Assemblée nationale du Niger, en décembre 1965*

Plus récemment, pour certains, la Francophonie **sert de contrepoids** à la globalisation de l'anglais.

Habib Bourguiba, ancien président de la Tunisie

«La Francophonie nous permet de nous organiser, nous Arabes, Africains et autres identités menacées par **le rouleau compresseur** des industries culturelles américaines **car**, seuls, nous ne serions pas assez forts pour nous défendre... »

> *Youssef Chahine, cinéaste égyptien, membre du Haut-Conseil de la Francophonie*

«La Francophonie a **vocation** à appeler toutes les autres langues du monde à se rassembler pour faire en sorte que la diversité culturelle, qui résulte de la diversité linguistique, que cette diversité **soit sauvegardée**. **Au-delà du** français, au-delà de la Francophonie, il nous faut être les militants du multiculturalisme dans le monde pour **lutter contre l'étouffement**, par une langue unique, des diverses cultures qui font la richesse et la dignité de l'humanité.»

> *Jacques Chirac, président de la République française, 1997*

---

**se tisse autour de** *is woven around*   **chaleur** *warmth*   **un lien** *a link*   **parenté** *relationship*   **dépasse** *goes beyond*
**l'appoint** *the exact contribution needed*   **à part entière** *complete*   **sert de contrepoids** *serves as a counterbalance*
**le rouleau compresseur** *the steamroller*   **car** *because*   **vocation** *calling*   **soit sauvegardée** *be preserved*
**Au-delà de** *Beyond*   **lutter conter l'étouffement** *to struggle against suffocation*

«La Francophonie sera subversive et imaginative ou ne sera pas!»

«La Francophonie est née d'un désir **ressenti hors de** France.»

*Boutros Boutros-Ghali, Secrétaire général (égyptien) des Nations unies, 1995*

## À discuter

1. Est-ce qu'on entend parler de «l'Anglophonie» de la même façon qu'on parle de «la Francophonie»? À votre avis, pourquoi (pas)?

2. Quel rôle est-ce qu'une langue joue dans la culture d'un peuple? Est-il important de protéger la diversité culturelle? Et la diversité linguistique? Quels sont les avantages et les inconvénients de la diversité linguistique? Et de l'uniformité linguistique?

3. À votre avis, est-il juste ou exagéré de parler du «rouleau compresseur des industries culturelles américaines»? Pourquoi?

4. Étant donné qu'on parle français sur les cinq continents en grande partie à cause de la colonisation par la France, comment peut-on expliquer le sentiment chez beaucoup d'Africains et d'Arabes que la Francophonie protège la diversité culturelle?

---

**ressenti hors de** *felt outside of*

# Résumé de grammaire

## The future tense (Le futur)

Use the future tense to say what someone *will do.* Form it by adding the boldfaced endings below to the same stem that you used for the conditional. For most verbs, it is the infinitive, but drop the final **e** of infinitives ending with **-re.**

**Je prendrai** des vacances en été.

**Tu resteras** ici?

**J'irai** en Europe.

**Tu partiras** tout seul?

**Mes parents voyageront** avec moi.

| VISITER | CONNAÎTRE | FINIR |
|---|---|---|
| je visiter**ai** | je connaîtr**ai** | je finir**ai** |
| tu visiter**as** | tu connaîtr**as** | tu finir**as** |
| il/elle/on visiter**a** | il/elle/on connaîtr**a** | il/elle/on finir**a** |
| nous visiter**ons** | nous connaîtr**ons** | nous finir**ons** |
| vous visiter**ez** | vous connaîtr**ez** | vous finir**ez** |
| ils/elles visiter**ont** | ils/elles connaîtr**ont** | ils/elles finir**ont** |

The following verbs have irregular stems.

| -r- | -vr- / -dr- | -rr- |
|---|---|---|
| aller: ir- | devoir: devr- | voir: verr- |
| avoir: aur- | vouloir: voudr- | pouvoir: pourr- |
| être: ser- | venir: viendr- | mourir: mourr- |
| faire: fer- | devenir: deviendr- | |
| savoir: saur- | revenir: reviendr- | |

Combien de temps **serez-vous** en Europe?

**On reviendra** après trois semaines.

As in English, use the future tense in *if / then* sentences to say what will happen if something else occurs, but use the present tense in the clause with **si.** Unlike English, use the future in French in clauses with **quand** referring to the future. English has the present in such clauses.

**S'il peut,** mon frère **ira** en vacances avec nous.

**Il décidera** quand **on saura** la date exacte de notre départ.

## The verbs savoir and connaître

**Savoir** and **connaître** both mean *to know.*

| SAVOIR | CONNAÎTRE |
|---|---|
| je sais | je connais |
| tu sais | tu connais |
| il/elle/on sait | il/elle/on connaît |
| nous savons | nous connaissons |
| vous savez | vous connaissez |
| ils/elles savent | ils/elles connaissent |

Quelles langues **sais-tu?**

**Je sais** parler français mais **mes parents savent** l'allemand.

**Savez-vous** si vous allez visiter l'Allemagne?

On ira à Berlin, où **mes parents connaissent** beaucoup de gens.

**Je ne connais pas** du tout l'Europe. Est-ce que **tu connais** bien l'histoire de la région?

Use **savoir** to say that someone knows facts, information, or languages. If the verb *to know* is followed by a question word, *if* (**si**), or the conjunction *that* (**que**), use **savoir,** since one is talking about knowing information. **Savoir** is also used with an infinitive to state what one knows how to do.

Use **connaître** to say that someone knows a person, place or thing, in the sense that they are familiar with it.

## The verbs *dire, lire,* and *écrire*

The verbs **dire, lire,** and **écrire** are irregular in the present tense and the **passé composé** (j'ai dit, j'ai lu, j'ai écrit). As with other verbs, use the stem for **nous** in the present tense to form the imperfect (**je disais, je lisais, j'écrivais**). Obtain the future / conditional stem by dropping the final **e** of the infinitive (**je dirai, je lirai, j'écrirai**).

| DIRE | LIRE | ÉCRIRE |
|---|---|---|
| je dis | je lis | j' écris |
| tu dis | tu lis | tu écris |
| il/elle/on dit | il/elle/on lit | il/elle/on écrit |
| nous disons | nous lisons | nous écrivons |
| vous dites | vous lisez | vous écrivez |
| ils/elles disent | ils/elles lisent | ils/elles écrivent |

Est-ce que **tu lis** ton mail quand tu voyages?

**J'écris** à mes amis et je leur montre des photos de mon voyage.

**Mes parents disent** que la Méditerranée est très jolie.

## Indirect object pronouns

Generally, indirect objects are people or animals, not things, and they follow the preposition **à.** They often are used with verbs indicating communication or exchanges (**parler à, téléphoner à, dire à, écrire à, demander à, rendre visite à, donner à**).

Indirect object pronouns replace indirect object nouns. Compare them to the direct object pronouns.

| DIRECT OBJECT PRONOUNS | | | INDIRECT OBJECT PRONOUNS | | |
|---|---|---|---|---|---|
| **me** *me* | **nous** *us* | | **me** *(to) me* | **nous** *(to) us* | |
| **te** *you* | **vous** *you* | | **te** *(to) you* | **vous** *(to) you* | |
| **le (l')** *him, it* | **les** *them* | | **lui** *(to) him* | **leur** *(to) them* | |
| **la (l')** *her, it* | | | **lui** *(to) her* | | |

Est-ce que tu **m'**écriras si je **te** donne mon adresse mail?

Mon frère habite à Paris. Je vais **te** donner son numéro de téléphone et tu pourras **lui** téléphoner quand tu seras en France.

Indirect object pronouns have the same placement rules as direct object and reflexive pronouns. They go before the infinitive if there is one. If not, they go before the conjugated verb. In the **passé composé,** they go before the auxiliary verb. The past participle agrees with direct object pronouns, but not with indirect objects.

Les amis de mes parents **nous** ont demandé de **leur** rendre visite. Mes parents ne **les** ont pas vus depuis vingt ans, la dernière fois qu'ils **leur** ont rendu visite.

## Geographical expressions

Use the definite article with names of continents, countries, states, and provinces used as the subject or object of a verb, but not with cities. Most continents, countries, states, and provinces ending in **e** are feminine, whereas most others are masculine.

To say *to* or *in* with a geographical location, use...

Pendant notre voyage, on ira **à** Berlin **en** Allemagne, **à** Copenhague **au** Danemark, **à** Amsterdam **aux** Pays-Bas et **à** Paris et **à** Nice **en** France.

| à | with cities |
|---|---|
| **en** | with all feminine countries, states, provinces, or continents, and masculine ones beginning with a vowel |
| **au** | with masculine countries, states, or provinces beginning with a consonant |
| **aux** | with plural countries and regions |

**Vocabulaire**

## Talking about vacation

### NOMS MASCULINS

| | |
|---|---|
| un endroit | a place |
| un Parisien | a Parisian |
| le paysage | the landscape, scenery |
| un site | a site, a spot |

### NOMS FÉMININS

| | |
|---|---|
| une île | an island |
| la mer | the sea |
| une Parisienne | a Parisian |
| une terrasse | a terrace |

### EXPRESSIONS VERBALES

| | |
|---|---|
| admirer | to admire |
| bronzer | to tan |
| compter | to count on, to plan on |
| courir | to run |
| goûter | to taste |
| profiter de | to take advantage of |

### ADJECTIFS

| | |
|---|---|
| assis(e) | seated |
| exotique | exotic |
| historique | historic |
| local(e) (mpl locaux) | local |
| touristique | touristic |
| tropical(e) (mpl tropicaux) | tropical |

### DIVERS

| | |
|---|---|
| Ça te plaira. | You'll like it. |
| là-bas | over there |
| le long de | along |

## Buying your ticket

### NOMS MASCULINS

| | |
|---|---|
| un agent de voyages | a travel agent |
| un aller simple | a one-way ticket |
| un billet aller-retour | a round-trip ticket |
| un chèque de voyage | a travelers' check |
| un départ | a departure |
| les gens | the people |
| un guide | a guidebook; a guide |
| un itinéraire | an itinerary |
| un passeport | a passport |
| le retour | the return |
| le système de transports en commun | the public transportation system |
| un vol | a flight |

### NOMS FÉMININS

| | |
|---|---|
| une agence de voyages | a travel agency |
| une arrivée | an arrival |
| une carte bancaire | a bank card |
| une carte de crédit | a credit card |
| la classe touriste | tourist class, coach |
| la culture | the culture |
| la géographie | the geography |
| la porte d'arrivée | the arrival gate |
| la porte d'embarquement | the departure gate |
| la première classe | first class |

### EXPRESSIONS VERBALES

| | |
|---|---|
| connaître | to know, to be familiar with, to be acquainted with |
| faire une réservation | to make a reservation |
| savoir | to know |

### DIVERS

| | |
|---|---|
| à l'avance | in advance |
| à l'étranger | abroad |
| Ça te/vous convient? | Does that work for you? |
| il me (te/nous/vous) faut | I (you/we/you) need |
| me | (to) me |
| nous | (to) us |
| te | (to) you |
| tel(le) que | such as |
| vous | (to) you |

# COMPÉTENCE 3

## Preparing for a trip

### NOMS MASCULINS

| | |
|---|---|
| un article | an article |
| le climat | the climate |
| un magazine | a magazine |
| un poème | a poem |
| des préparatifs | preparations |
| un roman | a novel |
| un site Web | a website |
| un voisin | a neighbor |

### NOMS FÉMININS

| | |
|---|---|
| une carte postale | a postcard |
| la douane | customs |
| une histoire | a story |
| une lettre | a letter |
| une rédaction | a composition |
| une valise | a suitcase |
| une voisine | a neighbor |

### EXPRESSIONS VERBALES

| | |
|---|---|
| changer | to change, to exchange |
| décrire | to describe |
| dire | to say, to tell |
| donner à manger à | to feed |
| écrire | to write |
| faire ses valises | to pack your bags |
| s'informer | to find out information |
| lire | to read |
| obtenir | to obtain |
| passer | to pass (through) |
| recevoir | to receive |
| réserver | to reserve |

### DIVERS

| | |
|---|---|
| Ça lui plaît? | Does he/she like it? |
| extraordinaire | extraordinary, great |
| leur | to them |
| lui | (to) him, (to) her |
| prévu(e) | planned, foreseen |

# COMPÉTENCE 4

## Deciding where to go on a trip

### NOMS MASCULINS

| | |
|---|---|
| le Brésil | Brazil |
| le Canada | Canada |
| le Chili | Chile |
| un continent | a continent |
| les États-Unis | the United States |
| Israël | Israel |
| le Japon | Japan |
| le Maroc | Morocco |
| le Mexique | Mexico |
| le Moyen-Orient | the Middle East |
| le Pérou | Peru |
| le Sénégal | Senegal |
| le Viêt Nam | Vietnam |

### NOMS FÉMININS

| | |
|---|---|
| l'Afrique | Africa |
| l'Algérie | Algeria |
| l'Allemagne | Germany |
| l'Amérique centrale | Central America |
| l'Amérique du Nord | North America |
| l'Amérique du Sud | South America |
| les Antilles | the West Indies |
| l'Argentine | Argentina |
| l'Asie | Asia |
| l'Australie | Australia |
| la Belgique | Belgium |
| la Chine | China |
| la Colombie | Colombia |
| la Côte d'Ivoire | Ivory Coast |
| l'Égypte | Egypt |
| l'Espagne | Spain |
| l'Europe | Europe |
| la France | France |
| la Grande-Bretagne | Great Britain |
| l'Italie | Italy |
| la Nouvelle-Calédonie | New Caledonia |
| l'Océanie | Oceania |
| la Polynésie française | French Polynesia |
| la Russie | Russia |
| la Suisse | Switzerland |

### DIVERS

| | |
|---|---|
| adorer | to adore, to love |

## Coumbite
**GÉRARD VALCIN**
**(1923–1988)**

Private Collection. Manu Sassoonian / Art Resource, NY

L'agriculture est une des industries principales des Antilles. Sur ce tableau, un homme joue du tambour *(drum)* pour établir *(to establish)* le rythme du travail pour les travailleurs.

## Une maison antillaise

Robert Fried Photography

Les maisons en Martinique et en Guadeloupe sont souvent peintes avec des couleurs vives qui reflètent les couleurs naturelles tropicales des Antilles.

## Aux Antilles

**LA GUADELOUPE**
**SUPERFICIE:** 1 780 kilomètres carrés
**NOMBRE D'HABITANTS:** 445 000 (les Guadeloupéens)
**CHEF-LIEU *(ADMINISTRATIVE CENTER):*** Basse-Terre
**INDUSTRIES PRINCIPALES:** agriculture, tourisme, pêche, exploitation minière, industries manufacturières

**LA MARTINIQUE**
**SUPERFICIE:** 1 128 kilomètres carrés
**NOMBRE D'HABITANTS:** 393 000 (les Martiniquais)
**CHEF-LIEU:** Fort-de-France
**INDUSTRIES PRINCIPALES:** agriculture, tourisme, pêche, exploitation minière, industries manufacturières, pétrole

**COMPÉTENCE**

 Video activities are on pages 416–419.

# Les Antilles

Les Antilles françaises **comprennent** la Martinique et la Guadeloupe et son **archipel** (Marie-Galante, les Saintes, Saint-Martin, Saint-Barthélemy, la Désirade et Petite-Terre). La Guadeloupe et la Martinique sont **à la fois** départements d'outre-mer et régions de France. Cette situation donne à leurs **citoyens** tous les **droits** et les responsabilités des citoyens français. Ces îles offrent donc aux visiteurs **un monde** caraïbe **à la française.**

Depuis le temps de ses premiers habitants, on appelle la Martinique «l'île aux **fleurs»,** et la beauté de ses paysages et **la chaleur** de son peuple sont **renommées.**

La montagne Pelée

Une forêt tropicale

Fort-de-France, **le chef-lieu,** est une ville pleine d'activité. Saint-Pierre, l'**ancien** chef-lieu de la Martinique, a été **détruit** par une éruption de la montagne Pelée en 1902. **Au milieu de** la ville **vivante** d'aujourd'hui, on peut voir des ruines de l'ancienne ville.

Saint-Pierre

---

**comprennent** *include*    **archipel** *archipelago*    **à la fois** *at the same time*    **citoyens** *citizens*    **droits** *rights*    **un monde** *a world*
**à la française** *French-style*    **fleurs** *flowers*    **la chaleur** *the warmth*    **renommées** *renowned*
**le chef-lieu** *the administrative center*    **ancien** *former*    **détruit** *destroyed*    **Au milieu de** *In the midst of*    **vivante** *living*

Grande-Terre

La Guadeloupe est composée de deux îles, Grande-Terre et Basse-Terre. Grande-Terre est plutôt **plate** et **sèche** et **recouverte de champs** de canne à sucre. Pointe-à-Pitre, la plus grande ville de la Guadeloupe, se trouve sur Grande-Terre.

Pointe-à-Pitre

L'île de Basse-Terre

Basse-Terre est **couverte de** montagnes volcaniques et de forêts tropicales. La Soufrière, un volcan actif, domine la partie sud de l'île et une grande partie de l'île est protégée par le parc national de la Guadeloupe. Basse-Terre, le chef-lieu de la Guadeloupe, se trouve sur l'île de Basse-Terre.

Basse-Terre

La mer des Caraïbes

Mais ce sont surtout les vastes plages et l'eau calme, claire et transparente de la mer des Caraïbes qui **attirent** aux Antilles des visiteurs de tous les pays **du monde.**

---

**plate** *flat*  **sèche** *dry*  **recouverte de champs** *covered with fields*  **couverte de** *covered with*  **attirent** *attract*
**du monde** *of the world*

# Deciding where to stay

## Le logement

Quand vous êtes en vacances, est-ce que vous aimez mieux descendre dans... ?

un hôtel (de luxe)  **une auberge de jeunesse**  un chalet de ski  **une station estivale**

Préférez-vous avoir une chambre... ?

à deux lits ou avec un grand lit  avec ou sans salle de bains et W.-C.  avec douche

Comment préférez-vous **régler la note?**

**en espèces** *(f)*  en chèques de voyage  par carte de crédit

CD 2-31

Luc a quitté la Guadeloupe pour aller passer quelques jours en Martinique. Il arrive à la réception d'un hôtel.

| | |
|---|---|
| LUC: | Bonjour, monsieur. |
| L'HÔTELIER: | Bonjour, monsieur. |
| LUC: | Avez-vous une chambre pour ce soir? |
| L'HÔTELIER: | Eh bien... nous avons une chambre avec salle de bains et W.-C. privés. |
| LUC: | C'est combien la nuit? |
| L'HÔTELIER: | 108 euros, monsieur. |
| LUC: | Vous avez quelque chose de moins cher? |
| L'HÔTELIER: | Voyons... nous avons une chambre avec douche et **lavabo** à 88 euros, si vous préférez. |

---

**une auberge de jeunesse** *a youth hostel*  **une station estivale** *a summer resort*  **régler la note** *to pay the bill*
**en espèces** *(f) in cash*  **un lavabo** *a sink*

| | |
|---|---|
| Luc: | Je préfère une chambre calme. |
| L'hôtelier: | Alors, **il vaut mieux** prendre la chambre avec douche. C'est **côté cour** et il y a moins de **bruit.** |
| Luc: | Bon, d'accord. Le petit déjeuner est **compris?** |
| L'hôtelier: | Non, monsieur. Il y a un supplément de 6 euros. Il est servi entre sept heures et neuf heures dans la salle à manger. |
| Luc: | Eh bien, je vais prendre la chambre avec douche. Vous préférez que je vous paie maintenant? |
| L'hôtelier: | Non, monsieur. Vous pouvez régler la note à votre départ. Voici **la clé.** C'est la chambre 210. C'est au bout du couloir. |
| Luc: | Y a-t-il un restaurant dans le quartier? |
| L'hôtelier: | Je vous recommande le Tropical. |
| Luc: | Est-ce qu'il faut réserver? |
| L'hôtelier: | Oui, il vaut mieux. |
| Luc: | Merci, monsieur. |
| L'hôtelier: | **Bon séjour.** |

## A. Préférences. Indiquez vos préférences.

1. Quand je pars en vacances, je préfère *visiter un autre pays / rester dans mon propre* (my own) *pays.*
2. J'aime mieux *visiter une grande ville / aller à la montagne / aller à la mer / ???.*
3. Comme activités en vacances, j'aime *nager / goûter la cuisine locale / ???.*
4. Je préfère descendre dans *un hôtel pas cher / un hôtel de luxe / une auberge de jeunesse / une station estivale / ???. (Ça dépend de qui va payer!)*
5. À mon avis, *il vaut mieux réserver une chambre d'hôtel à l'avance / on peut toujours trouver un hôtel à son arrivée.*
6. Je préfère une chambre *avec douche / avec salle de bains. (Je préfère la chambre la moins chère.)*
7. Quand je descends dans un hôtel, je préfère prendre mon petit déjeuner *dans ma chambre / dans le restaurant de l'hôtel / dans un autre restaurant / dans un fast-food / ???. (Je ne prends pas de petit déjeuner.)*
8. Je préfère régler la note *en espèces / en chèques de voyage / par carte de crédit.*

## B. Réponses. Votre meilleur(e) ami(e) et vous allez passer six jours dans un petit hôtel en Martinique. Répondez aux questions de l'hôtelier selon vos besoins et vos goûts.

1. Vous voulez une chambre pour une seule personne?
2. C'est pour combien de nuits?
3. Vous voulez une chambre à deux lits ou avec un grand lit?
4. Vous préférez une chambre avec ou sans salle de bains?
5. Nous avons une chambre à 75 euros. Vous préférez régler la note maintenant ou à votre départ?
6. Il y a un supplément de 6 euros pour le petit déjeuner. Vous allez prendre le petit déjeuner à l'hôtel?
7. Comment voulez-vous payer?
8. C'est à quel nom?

## C. Conversation. Avec un(e) partenaire, relisez à haute voix la conversation entre Luc et l'hôtelier. Ensuite, imaginez que vous allez visiter la Martinique ensemble. Parlez de quelle sorte de chambres vous voulez et comment vous allez payer.

---

**il vaut mieux** *it's better*   **côté cour** *on the courtyard side*   **un bruit** *a noise*   **compris(e)** *included*   **la clé** *the key*
**Bon séjour.** *Enjoy your stay.*

**NOTES DE GRAMMAIRE**

**1.** Note that the expressions that have **être (Il est important / essentiel / bon...)** require the preposition **de** before an infinitive. Remember that **de** elides before a vowel sound.
**2.** **C'est bien...** is less formal than **Il est bon...** and is more likely to be used when talking with a friend. You will also hear **C'est important / essentiel / bon...** in less formal conversation.
**3.** Remember to place both parts of a negative expression before the infinitive when negating an infinitive: **Il est important de ne pas perdre la clé.**

# Giving general advice

*Les expressions impersonnelles et l'infinitif*

The following expressions can be used to give advice and state opinions. When talking in general, follow them with an infinitive.

Notice that although **il faut** means *it is necessary*, **il ne faut pas** means *one should not* or *one must not*. Use **il n'est pas nécessaire** to say *it's not necessary.*

| | |
|---|---|
| Il faut | Il faut payer un supplément pour le petit déjeuner. |
| Il ne faut pas | Il ne faut pas faire trop de bruit. |
| Il vaut mieux | Il vaut mieux réserver à l'avance. |
| Il est nécessaire (de) | Il est nécessaire de réserver. |
| Il n'est pas nécessaire (de) | Il n'est pas nécessaire de téléphoner à l'avance. |
| Il est essentiel (de) | Il est essentiel de régler la note. |
| Il est important (de) | Il est important de ne pas perdre la clé. |
| Il est bon (de) | Il est bon de choisir une chambre calme. |
| Il est mauvais (de) | Il est mauvais de faire trop de bruit. |
| C'est bien (de)... | C'est bien de profiter de la piscine. |

**A. Qu'est-ce qu'il faut faire?** Qu'est-ce qu'il faut faire dans les situations suivantes quand on voyage?

> **Exemple**    Si on est fatigué?    **Il faut rentrer à l'hôtel.**

> rentrer à l'hôtel    téléphoner à l'ambassade *(embassy)*
> acheter un plan *(map)* de la ville    aller à la banque
> aller au restaurant    se coucher    téléphoner à des amis
> changer d'hôtel    acheter un guide touristique

**1.** Si on perd son passeport?
**2.** Si on veut visiter la ville?
**3.** Si on a faim?
**4.** Si l'hôtel est trop bruyant *(noisy)?*
**5.** Si on cherche une liste de bons restaurants et de sites touristiques?
**6.** Si on a sommeil?
**7.** Si on se sent un peu seul *(lonely)?*
**8.** Si on a besoin de changer de l'argent?

**B. Pour réussir.** Un nouvel étudiant veut réussir à l'université. Dites-lui **s'il vaut mieux** ou **s'il ne faut pas** faire ces choses.

> **Exemples**    On copie les réponses des autres étudiants?
> **Non, il ne faut pas copier les réponses des autres étudiants.**
>
> On fait tous les devoirs?
> **Oui, il vaut mieux faire tous les devoirs.**

**1.** On arrive en classe à l'heure?
**2.** On va en boîte tous les soirs?
**3.** On prépare les examens bien à l'avance?
**4.** On dort en classe?
**5.** On écoute le professeur?
**6.** On fait attention en cours?
**7.** On lit le journal en classe?
**8.** On prend des notes en cours?

**C. Qu'est-ce qu'il faut faire?** Un ami fait les préparatifs pour un voyage que vous allez faire ensemble. Utilisez un élément de chaque colonne pour lui expliquer ce qu'il faut faire.

Exemple **Il vaut mieux réserver une chambre à l'avance.**

Il faut
Il vaut mieux
Il est bon de
Il n'est pas bon de
Il est important de
Il n'est pas important de
Il ne faut pas

réserver une chambre à l'avance
obtenir les passeports bien à l'avance
oublier les billets
savoir le numéro et l'heure de départ du vol
tout payer par carte de crédit
choisir une chambre côté rue
choisir une chambre côté cour
faire beaucoup de bruit dans l'hôtel

**D. Chez vous.** Un groupe de Martiniquais va venir visiter votre région. Donnez-leur des conseils.

Exemple Il est essentiel d'aller **au City Arts Museum.**

1. Il vaut mieux venir au mois de (d')...
2. Il ne faut pas venir au mois de (d')...
3. Il est important d'apporter *(to bring)*...
4. Il est essentiel de ne pas oublier...
5. Il est bon de descendre à l'hôtel...
6. Il est bon de goûter la cuisine locale au restaurant...
7. Il n'est pas bon de manger au restaurant...
8. Il est essentiel de voir...

Que faut-il faire pour préparer un voyage en Martinique?

## Stratégies et Compréhension auditive

*Anticipating a response*

When you cannot understand everything you hear, use what you can understand, as well as non-verbal cues such as circumstances, tone of voice, and written materials such as ads or signs to anticipate what someone will say. Read the two hotel ads at the bottom of this page and on the next page and list five things you learned about each hotel from its ad.

**CD 2-32**

**A. Quel hôtel?** On parle de l'hôtel de l'Anse Bleue ou de l'hôtel Bakoua.

**CD 2-33**

**B. Le ton de la voix.** Écoutez le début de ces conversations dans un hôtel. Pour chacune, écoutez le ton de la voix *(tone of voice)* pour deviner la suite *(what follows)*, **a** ou **b.**

1. **a.** C'est bien. Nous allons prendre la chambre.
   **b.** Est-ce que vous avez quelque chose de moins cher?
2. **a.** Nous préférons une chambre avec salle de bains.
   **b.** Bon, c'est bien. Je vais prendre cette chambre.
3. **a.** Voici votre clé, monsieur. Vous avez la chambre numéro 385.
   **b.** Je regrette, mais nous n'avons pas de réservation à votre nom.

**CD 2-34**

## À la réception

Deux touristes arrivent dans un hôtel. Écoutez cette conversation pour déterminer le prix de leur chambre.

**À l'hôtel.** Écoutez la conversation une seconde fois et répondez à ces questions.

1. Pourquoi est-ce que les touristes ne veulent pas la première chambre?
2. Combien coûte le petit déjeuner? Où est-ce qu'il est servi?
3. Quel est le numéro de leur chambre?

# *Bienvenue dans l'univers enchanté du Bakoua*

Charme suranné des splendeurs coloniales...
Ici le temps semble s'être arrêté. A la Pointe
du Bout, face à l'une
des plus belles baies
du monde : une oasis
de confort et de
volupté pour votre
plus grand plaisir.

- Un hôtel Sofitel
  Coralia 4 étoiles du
  Groupe Accor.
- 132 chambres grand confort climatisées
  avec terrasse ou balcon.

  - 6 suites de luxe
    de style colonial.
  - 2 restaurants proposant
    une cuisine raffinée
    créole et internationale.
  - 2 bars face à la piscine
    ou sur la plage.

### INFORMATIONS - RESERVATIONS

Tel : 0596 66 02 02 • Fax : 0596 66 00 41
SOFITEL BAKOUA CORALIA
LA POINTE DU BOUT
97229 LES TROIS ILETS

Hotel Sofitel
CORALIA

L'esprit
ACCOR

# Going to the doctor

> Note
*culturelle*

Voici quelques statistiques intéressantes sur les pratiques de santé des Français: Les Français consultent leur médecin en moyenne sept fois par an et dépensent à peu près *(spend more or less)* 10% de leur PIB *(GNP)* pour les soins médicaux *(medical care)*. 75% de leurs dépenses médicales sont remboursées par la Sécurité sociale. La majorité des Français traitent quelquefois leurs maladies eux-mêmes *(themselves)* et achètent des médicaments en vente libre *(over the counter)*. Est-ce que la situation est semblable dans votre pays?

## Chez le médecin

Luc tombe **malade** pendant son séjour en Martinique. Savez-vous communiquer avec le médecin si vous tombez malade **au cours d'**un voyage?

— Où est-ce que vous **avez mal?**
— J'ai mal à la tête et au ventre.
— Quels autres symptômes avez-vous?

— Je tousse.

— J'éternue.

— J'ai une indigestion et j'ai envie de vomir.

LE CORPS

la tête — l'oreille (f)
l'œil (m) (pl les yeux) — la bouche
le nez — **la gorge**
les dents (f)
la main
le dos — le bras
les doigts (m) — le ventre
la jambe
le pied (m) — les doigts de pied

Avez-vous **la grippe? un rhume?** un virus? des allergies?
Êtes-vous **enceinte?**

 Luc va chez le médecin.

CD 2-35

| | |
|---|---|
| LE MÉDECIN: | Bonjour, monsieur. **Qu'est-ce qui ne va pas** aujourd'hui? |
| LUC: | Je ne sais pas exactement. Je me sens mal. Je tousse, j'**ai des frissons** et j'ai mal un peu partout. |
| LE MÉDECIN: | Vous avez mal à la gorge? |
| LUC: | Oui, très. |
| LE MÉDECIN: | Eh bien, vous avez tout simplement la grippe. |
| LUC: | Qu'est-ce que je dois faire? |
| LE MÉDECIN: | Je vais vous donner **une ordonnance.** Il faut que vous preniez ces médicaments trois fois par jour. Il est important que vous finissiez tous ces médicaments. N'oubliez pas de boire beaucoup de liquides, mais il ne faut pas que vous buviez d'alcool et il est essentiel que vous restiez au lit. |

---

**le médecin** the doctor   **malade** sick   **au cours de** in the course of, during, while on   **avoir mal (à)...** one's . . . hurts
**la gorge** the throat   **la grippe** the flu   **un rhume** a cold   **enceinte** pregnant   **Qu'est-ce qui ne va pas?** What's wrong?
**avoir des frissons** to have the shivers   **une ordonnance** a prescription

**A. J'ai mal partout!** Un hypocondriaque va voir son médecin. Selon lui *(according to him)*, il a mal partout, de la tête jusqu'aux pieds. De quoi se plaint-il? *(What does he complain about?)*

> **Exemple**   **Mon Dieu, docteur! J'ai mal à la tête, j'ai mal aux yeux, j'ai mal au nez...**

**B. Descriptions.** Décrivez le corps des personnes ou des animaux suivants.

> **Exemple**   un vampire   **Il a les yeux rouges et des dents pointues *(pointy).***

**1.** un cyclope     **2.** un serpent     **3.** un éléphant     **4.** un extra-terrestre

**C. Qu'est-ce qui ne va pas?** Quels symptômes ont-ils?

> **Exemple**   **Il a mal aux yeux.**

Exemple                    1.                    2.

3.                    4.                    5.

**D. Des symptômes.** Nommez autant de symptômes que possible pour chacune de ces conditions.

> **Exemple**   Quand on a la grippe, **on a mal partout. On a des frissons et...**

**1.** Quand on a un rhume...
**2.** Quand on a des allergies...
**3.** Quand on un virus intestinal...
**4.** Quand on est enceinte...

**E. Entretien.** Interviewez votre partenaire.

**1.** La dernière fois que tu as été malade, est-ce que tu avais mal à la tête? à la gorge? Est-ce que tu avais des frissons? Est-ce que tu es allé(e) chez le médecin? Qu'est-ce que tu avais? *(What was wrong?)* Est-ce que tu as pris des médicaments?
**2.** Est-ce que tu as des allergies? Quels symptômes as-tu? Pendant quels mois as-tu ces symptômes? Est-ce que tu prends des médicaments? Est-ce que tu vas chez le médecin pour une ordonnance ou est-ce que tu achètes des médicaments sans ordonnance?

**F. Conversation.** Avec un(e) partenaire, relisez à haute voix la conversation entre Luc et le médecin. Ensuite, imaginez que vous êtes malade et créez une conversation entre le médecin et vous.

**VOCABULAIRE SUPPLÉMENTAIRE**

**un antibiotique** *an antibiotic*
**un antihistaminique** *an antihistamine*
**une aspirine** *an aspirin*
**le cou** *the neck*
**l'épaule** *(f) the shoulder*
**le genou** *the knee*
**des pastilles** *(f)* **contre la toux** *cough drops*
**la poitrine** *the chest*
**du sirop** *cough syrup*
**avoir de la fièvre** *to have a fever*
**avoir le nez bouché** *to have a stuffy nose*
**avoir le nez qui coule** *to have a runny nose*
**se brûler / se casser / se couper la main** *to burn / break / cut your hand*
**se fouler la cheville** *to sprain your ankle*
**faire une piqûre** *to give a shot*
**prendre sa température** *to take your temperature*

**1.** When do you use the subjunctive?

**2.** What do you use as the subjunctive stem for all verb forms except **nous** and **vous?** What endings do you use?

**3.** For most verbs, the **nous** and **vous** forms of the subjunctive look just like what other verb tense?

### NOTE DE GRAMMAIRE

The **de** in expressions like **il est important de** is replaced by **que** in these structures. Remember that verbs ending in **–ier**, like **étudier** and **oublier**, will have two **i**'s in the **nous** and **vous** forms of the subjunctive, just as they did in the **imparfait: nous oubliions, vous étudiiez.**

# Giving advice to someone in particular

*Les expressions impersonnelles et les verbes réguliers au subjonctif*

You know you can use impersonal expressions like **il faut** and **il est important de** followed by an infinitive to give general advice or state opinions. When talking to or about a particular person, you can use these same expressions followed by **que** and a second clause with a conjugated verb.

Il est important **de bien manger.**
*It's important **to eat well.***

Il est important **que tu manges mieux.**
*It's important **that you eat better.***

When giving advice to a particular person, the verb in the second clause is in a form called the subjunctive. You have used verbs in the indicative mode to say what happens. The subjunctive is another verb mode. The subjunctive is generally used in the second clause of a sentence, when the first clause expresses a feeling, attitude, or opinion about what should or might be done, rather than simply stating what is happening. The present subjunctive may imply either present or future actions.

| | |
|---|---|
| Il faut que | Il faut que tu restes au lit. |
| Il ne faut pas que | Il ne faut pas que tu sortes du lit. |
| Il vaut mieux que | Il vaut mieux que tu ne travailles pas. |
| Il est nécessaire que | Il est nécessaire que tu prennes ces médicaments. |
| Il n'est pas nécessaire que | Il n'est pas nécessaire que tu prennes de l'aspirine. |
| Il est essentiel que | Il est essentiel que tu finisses tous tes médicaments. |
| Il est important que | Il est important que tu te reposes. |
| Il est bon que | Il est bon que tu te sentes mieux. |
| Il est mauvais que | Il est mauvais que tu boives de l'alcool. |
| C'est bien que | C'est bien que tu ne fumes plus. |

For most verbs, the subjunctive is formed as follows:

* For **nous** and **vous,** the subjunctive looks like the imperfect.
* For the other forms, find the stem of the subjunctive by dropping the **-ent** ending of the **ils/elles** form of the present indicative and use the endings: **-e, -es, -e, -ent.**

| | **PARLER** | **FINIR** | **RENDRE** |
|---|---|---|---|
| que je | parl**e** | finiss**e** | rend**e** |
| que tu | parl**es** | finiss**es** | rend**es** |
| qu'il/qu'elle/qu'on | parl**e** | finiss**e** | rend**e** |
| que nous | parl**ions** | finiss**ions** | rend**ions** |
| que vous | parl**iez** | finiss**iez** | rend**iez** |
| qu'ils/qu'elles | parl**ent** | finiss**ent** | rend**ent** |

Most irregular verbs follow the same rule.

| | | |
|---|---|---|
| connaître | que je connaiss**e** | que nous connaiss**ions** |
| dire | que je dis**e** | que nous dis**ions** |
| dormir | que je dorm**e** | que nous dorm**ions** |
| écrire | que j'écriv**e** | que nous écriv**ions** |
| lire | que je lis**e** | que nous lis**ions** |
| partir | que je part**e** | que nous part**ions** |
| sortir | que je sort**e** | que nous sort**ions** |

These verbs follow the same rule, but have two different stems.

| | | |
|---|---|---|
| acheter | que j'achèt**e** | que nous achet**ions** |
| boire | que je boiv**e** | que nous buv**ions** |
| devoir | que je doiv**e** | que nous dev**ions** |
| payer | que je pai**e** | que nous pay**ions** |
| prendre | que je prenn**e** | que nous pren**ions** |
| venir | que je vienn**e** | que nous ven**ions** |

**A. Conseils.** Selon les circonstances indiquées, dites **s'il faut** ou **s'il ne faut pas** que ces personnes fassent ces choses.

**Exemple**  Je suis fatigué(e). Alors... je (se reposer, sortir)
**Il faut que je me repose. Il ne faut pas que je sorte.**

1. J'ai la grippe. Alors... je (se reposer, rendre visite à ma famille, acheter des médicaments, prendre de l'aspirine, boire beaucoup d'eau)
2. *(à votre professeur)* Vous avez la grippe aussi? Alors... vous (boire beaucoup de liquides, venir en cours, sortir, finir tous vos médicaments, fumer)
3. *(à un[e] camarade de classe)* Il y a un examen de français bientôt. Alors... tu (écrire tous les exercices dans le cahier, le dire au professeur si tu ne comprends pas, connaître bien les conjugaisons, sortir tous les soirs)
4. Les autres étudiants et moi voulons réussir au cours de français. Alors... nous (partir avant la fin du cours, écouter bien en cours, perdre notre temps en cours, prendre des notes, dormir en cours)
5. Mon meilleur ami veut réussir à ses examens. Alors... il (finir tous ses devoirs, obéir à ses professeurs, attendre ses professeurs s'ils arrivent en retard, regarder les examens des autres)
6. Mes amies s'ennuient. Alors... elles (trouver de nouveaux passe-temps, s'amuser plus, rester toujours à la maison, partir en voyage, sortir plus, apprendre quelque chose de nouveau, venir me voir)

**B. Encore des conseils.** Complétez ces phrases logiquement.

1. Vous êtes enceinte? Alors, il faut que vous... Il ne faut pas que vous...
2. Votre ami a la grippe? Il vaut mieux qu'il... Il est important qu'il...
3. Vos enfants ont un virus intestinal? Il est essentiel qu'ils... Il ne faut pas qu'ils...
4. Vous voulez rester en forme? Il est bon que vous... Il est mauvais que vous...

**1.** What are the seven verbs that are irregular in the subjunctive?

**2.** Which four of these verbs have a different stem for the **nous** and **vous** forms?

**3.** What are the conjugations of these seven verbs in the subjunctive?

**4.** What is the subjunctive of **il y a?** of **il pleut?**

# Giving advice

*Les verbes irréguliers au subjonctif*

The following seven verbs are irregular in the subjunctive. Note that **être, avoir, aller,** and **vouloir** have a different stem for the **nous** and **vous** forms. All except **être** and **avoir** have the regular subjunctive endings.

|  | **ÊTRE** | **AVOIR** | **ALLER** | **VOULOIR** |
|---|---|---|---|---|
|  | *soi- / soy-* | *aie- / ay-* | *aill- / all-* | *veuill- / voul-* |
| que je | sois | aie | aille | veuille |
| que tu | sois | aies | ailles | veuilles |
| qu'il/qu'elle/qu'on | soit | ait | aille | veuille |
| que nous | soyons | ayons | allions | voulions |
| que vous | soyez | ayez | alliez | vouliez |
| qu'ils/qu'elles | soient | aient | aillent | veuillent |

|  | **FAIRE** | **POUVOIR** | **SAVOIR** |
|---|---|---|---|
|  | *fass-* | *puiss-* | *sach-* |
| que je | fasse | puisse | sache |
| que tu | fasses | puisses | saches |
| qu'il/qu'elle/qu'on | fasse | puisse | sache |
| que nous | fassions | puissions | sachions |
| que vous | fassiez | puissiez | sachiez |
| qu'ils/qu'elles | fassent | puissent | sachent |

The subjunctive of **il y a** is **qu'il y ait** and the subjunctive of **il pleut** is **qu'il pleuve.**

**A. Réactions.** Une amie vous parle des habitudes de sa famille. Réagissez *(React)* à ce qu'elle dit avec **c'est bien que...** ou **ce n'est pas bien que...**

> Exemple    Je ne fume plus.
> **C'est bien que tu ne fumes plus.**

1. Je veux améliorer ma santé.
2. Je vais souvent au club de gym.
3. Mes enfants font très attention à leur santé.
4. Mon mari n'est pas en forme.
5. Il a souvent mal.
6. Le médecin ne sait pas pourquoi.
7. Mon mari ne veut pas arrêter de fumer.
8. Nous sommes stressés.
9. Nous avons beaucoup de problèmes.
10. Nous ne pouvons pas bien dormir la nuit.
11. Nous ne savons pas contrôler le stress.
12. Nous voulons apprendre à faire du yoga.
13. Nous faisons des promenades ensemble.
14. Nous allons au club de gym ensemble aussi.

**B. La grossesse.** Une femme enceinte parle avec son médecin. Lui dit-il de faire ou de ne pas faire les choses indiquées à droite.

> **Exemples** **Il faut que vous mangiez bien.**
> **Il ne faut pas que vous fumiez.**

manger bien
se reposer assez
avoir beaucoup de stress
fumer
faire attention à votre santé
être très agitée
boire de l'alcool
savoir contrôler le stress
grossir beaucoup
prendre des vitamines

**C. Conseils.** Vous êtes conseiller (conseillère). Expliquez à des parents s'il faut ou s'il ne faut pas que leurs enfants fassent ces choses.

> **Exemple** dormir assez
> **Il faut qu'ils dorment assez.**

1. faire de l'exercice
2. aller toujours en cours
3. manger toujours dans un fast-food
4. avoir des responsabilités à la maison
5. savoir que vous les aimez
6. pouvoir faire tout ce qu'ils veulent
7. vouloir réussir à l'école
8. être toujours sages

**D. Préparatifs.** Une amie va bientôt partir en vacances. Dites-lui ce qu'il faut qu'elle fasse pour préparer son voyage, selon les illustrations.

s'informer sur des sites Web
changer de l'argent
faire ta valise
passer la douane
dire à tes parents où tu vas
lire des guides
téléphoner à l'hôtel pour
    réserver une chambre

> **Exemple**  **Il faut que tu t'informes sur des sites Web.**

1.
2.
3.
4.
5.
6.

**E. L'ange et le diable.** Vous vous trouvez dans les situations suivantes. Imaginez ce que l'ange *(angel)* et le diable *(devil)* vous disent de faire. Utilisez **Il faut que... / il ne faut pas que...**

> **Exemple** Mes amis m'ont invité à sortir ce soir, mais j'ai un examen de français demain.
> LE DIABLE: **Il faut que tu sortes!**
> L'ANGE: **Il ne faut pas que tu sortes! Il faut que tu prépares ton examen!**

1. Je devrais aller en cours, mais je suis fatigué(e) et je voudrais rentrer.
2. J'aime fumer, mais le médecin m'a dit d'arrêter de fumer.
3. J'ai envie d'aller au cinéma, mais j'ai des devoirs à faire.
4. J'ai acheté un cadeau *(gift)* pour une amie, mais maintenant je voudrais le garder *(to keep it)*.
5. Ma mère veut que je l'aide à la maison samedi, mais je voudrais sortir.
6. Ma sœur veut qu'on sorte ensemble ce soir, mais je préfère sortir avec mon meilleur ami.

# Running errands on a trip

**NOTES DE GRAMMAIRE**

1. **Envoyer** is a **-yer** spelling change verb, like **s'ennuyer** (j'envoie, tu envoies, il/elle/on envoie, nous envoyons, vous envoyez, ils/elles envoient). The stem for the future and conditional is **enverr-**.
2. Remember that nouns ending in **-eau**, like **cadeau**, form their plurals in **-x** (**des cadeaux**).

**NOTE DE VOCABULAIRE**

The post office is referred to as **le bureau de poste, la Poste**, or **les PTT**.

## Des courses en voyage

Des touristes en Martinique ont beaucoup de choses à faire aujourd'hui. Où vont-ils aller?

Il faut qu'il/qu'elle aille...

au **distributeur de billets** pour **retirer de l'argent**

à la banque pour changer des chèques de voyage

à la pharmacie pour acheter de l'aspirine *(f)*

chez le marchand de **cadeaux** pour acheter un cadeau pour un ami

au kiosque pour acheter le journal et une carte téléphonique

au bureau de poste pour **envoyer** des cartes postales et acheter **des timbres** *(m)*

CD 2-36

Luc quitte la Martinique pour retourner en Guadeloupe. Il parle au téléphone avec Micheline.

MICHELINE: Je suis contente que tu reviennes bientôt de Martinique. Quand penses-tu arriver en Guadeloupe?
LUC: Je prends l'avion vendredi matin.
MICHELINE: Voudrais-tu que j'**aille te chercher** à l'aéroport?
LUC: Non, non, je ne veux pas que tu perdes ton temps à l'aéroport si l'avion arrive **en retard. J'aimerais autant** prendre **la navette.**
MICHELINE: Mais non, j'insiste! L'avion arrive à quelle heure?
LUC: À 10 heures.
MICHELINE: Alors, je viendrai te chercher devant la porte principale de l'aéroport vers dix heures et quart. Et si tu n'as pas d'autres projets, nous pouvons passer la journée à Pointe-à-Pitre.
LUC: Bonne idée! J'aimerais faire un tour de la ville.
MICHELINE: Parfait. À demain, alors.
LUC: Oui, au revoir, à demain.

**un distributeur de billets** *an ATM machine*   **retirer** *to withdraw*   **l'argent** *(m) money*   **un cadeau** *a gift*   **envoyer** *to send*
**un timbre** *a stamp*   **aller / venir chercher** *to go / come pick up*   **en retard** *late*   **J'aimerais autant** *I would just as soon*
**la navette** *the shuttle*

**A. Où faut-il aller?** Dites où il faut que les personnes suivantes aillent.

> **Exemple**     Notre vol va partir dans deux heures.
> **Il faut que nous allions à l'aéroport.**

à la banque     à un restaurant     au distributeur de billets
à la pharmacie     au bureau de poste     à la réception de l'hôtel
chez le marchand de cadeaux     au kiosque     à l'aéroport

1. Vous voulez changer des chèques de voyages.
2. Tu as perdu la clé de ta chambre.
3. Tes amis ont besoin d'acheter une carte téléphonique.
4. J'ai besoin de retirer de l'argent.
5. Nous voulons envoyer des cartes postales.
6. Luc veut acheter de l'aspirine.
7. Micheline a besoin d'acheter des timbres.
8. Luc veut acheter un cadeau pour Micheline.

**B. Une journée chargée.** Pourquoi est-ce que Luc est probablement allé aux endroits indiqués?

> **Exemple**     Luc est allé au marché pour **acheter des fruits.**

1. Luc est allé au bureau de poste pour...
2. Il est allé à la pharmacie pour...
3. Il a cherché un distributeur de billets pour...
4. Il est allé à la banque pour...
5. Il est allé au restaurant pour...
6. Il est allé au kiosque pour...
7. Il est allé à l'agence de voyages pour...
8. Il est allé chez le marchand de cadeaux pour...

**C. Conversation.** Avec un(e) partenaire, relisez à haute voix la conversation entre Luc et Micheline à la page précédente. Ensuite, imaginez qu'un(e) ami(e) va venir vous rendre visite. Votre partenaire va jouer le rôle de votre ami(e). Créez une conversation dans laquelle vous parlez de quel jour votre ami(e) va arriver, où vous allez vous retrouver et ce que vous allez faire ensemble au cours de son séjour.

**1.** What are eight expressions that indicate feelings that trigger the subjunctive? What expressions do you know that indicate desires, doubts, fears, opinions, and requests that trigger the subjunctive?

**2.** Do you use the subjunctive after the verb **espérer** *(to hope)*?

**3.** Does the present subjunctive always indicate present time?

**NOTES DE GRAMMAIRE**

**1.** Although most verbs that express desires trigger the subjunctive, **espérer** *(to hope)* does not. J'espère que tu **es** heureuse ici.

**2.** Traditionally, **ne** was always used in a clause following the expression **avoir peur que**. This **ne explétif** does not change the meaning of the clause and is now optional. J'ai peur qu'il **n'**arrive en retard. = J'ai peur qu'il arrive en retard. = *I'm afraid he'll arrive late.*

# Expressing wishes and emotions

*Les expressions d'émotion et de volonté et le subjonctif*

The indicative mood is used to talk about reality. The subjunctive mood conveys subjectivity: feelings, desires, opinions, requests, doubts, and fears.

You know that you use the subjunctive to give advice and state opinions to someone in particular after impersonal expressions like **il faut que** and **il vaut mieux que**.

You also use the subjunctive in a second clause beginning with **que** when:

- the verb in the first clause "triggers" the subjunctive in the second clause by expressing feelings, desires, doubts, fears, opinions, or requests.
- the subject of the first clause is not the same as the subject of the second clause.

Verbal expressions such as those that follow will "trigger" the subjunctive in the second clause.

| FEELINGS | DESIRES |
|---|---|
| être content(e) que *to be glad that* | vouloir que *to want that* |
| être heureux (heureuse) que *to be happy that* | préférer que *to prefer that* |
| être furieux (furieuse) que *to be furious that* | aimer mieux que *to prefer that* |
| être surpris(e) que *to be surprised that* | |
| être étonné(e) que *to be astonished that* | **DOUBTS AND FEARS** |
| être triste que *to be sad that* | douter que *to doubt that* |
| être désolé(e) que *to be sorry that* | avoir peur que *to be afraid that* |
| regretter que *to regret that* | |

| OPINIONS | REQUESTS / DEMANDS |
|---|---|
| c'est dommage que *it's too bad that* | insister que *to insist that* |
| il est bon / mauvais, etc., que *it's good / bad, etc., that* | |

Je suis désolé que votre chambre n'ait pas de vue sur la mer.
Je préfère que la chambre soit au premier étage.
J'ai peur que le quartier de l'hôtel ne soit pas calme.
C'est dommage que votre lit ne soit pas confortable.
J'insiste que nous changions d'hôtel.

Remember that the present subjunctive expresses either the present or the future.

| Je doute qu'elle soit ici. | *I doubt she **is** / **will be** here.* |
| Je doute qu'il arrive demain. | *I doubt he **will arrive** tomorrow.* |

**A. Quel hôtel?** Vous allez faire un voyage. Quelle sorte d'hôtel préférez-vous? Donnez votre réaction comme indiqué.

**Exemple**    l'hôtel / être près des sites touristiques
              **Je préfère que l'hôtel soit près des sites touristiques.**

1. l'hôtel / avoir une piscine
2. le réceptionniste / parler anglais
3. l'hôtel / accepter les cartes de crédit
4. la chambre / être grande
5. la chambre / avoir une salle de bains privée
6. on / (ne pas) pouvoir fumer dans la chambre
7. l'hôtel / (ne pas) être cher
8. on / pouvoir acheter de beaux cadeaux dans la boutique

**Je veux absolument que...**
**Je préfère que...**
**Il n'est pas important que...**

**B. Réactions.** Vous êtes parti(e) en voyage organisé en Martinique et vous partagez votre chambre d'hôtel avec un(e) autre touriste. Donnez votre réaction à ce qu'il/elle vous dit.

**Exemple**  Je parle français couramment *(fluently).*
**Je suis content(e) que vous parliez français couramment.**

Je (ne) suis (pas) content(e) que...     Je suis furieux (furieuse) que...
Je suis triste que...     Je suis désolé(e) que...
Je regrette que...

1. Notre hôtel est tout près de la mer.
2. Il y a deux grands lits.
3. Les lits sont très confortables.
4. Je fume dans la chambre.
5. Je ne dors pas bien la nuit.
6. Je tousse toute la nuit.
7. L'hôtel n'accepte pas les cartes de crédit.
8. Il n'y a pas de distributeur de billets à l'hôtel.
9. Je n'ai pas assez d'argent pour payer ma part de la chambre.

**C. Tu m'accompagnes?**  Une amie de Micheline est en vacances avec sa famille. Qu'est-ce qu'elle veut que ces personnes fassent avec elle?

**Exemple**     **Elle veut que son fils joue au tennis avec elle.**

son fils

**1.** sa fille

**2.** son fils

**3.** son mari

**4.** ses enfants

**5.** son amie

**D. Réactions.**  Votre partenaire et vous pensez peut-être partir en voyage ensemble. Posez ces questions à votre partenaire pour parler de ses habitudes quand il/elle est en vacances. Réagissez chaque fois à sa réponse.

**Exemple**     — **Tu passes beaucoup de temps à l'hôtel?**
— **Non, je ne passe pas beaucoup de temps à l'hôtel.**
— **Je suis content(e) que tu ne passes pas beaucoup de temps à l'hôtel.**

1. Tu préfères aller à la plage ou à la montagne?
2. Tu descends dans un hôtel de luxe ou dans un hôtel moins cher?
3. Tu sors souvent le soir ou tu restes à l'hôtel?
4. Tu fumes?
5. Tu dînes dans un restaurant ou dans ta chambre?

**1.** Do you use the infinitive or the subjunctive when people have feelings about what *others* should or might do? When they have feelings about what *they themselves* should or might do?

**2.** When do you use the infinitive after impersonal expressions such as **il faut?** When do you use the subjunctive?

## Saying who you want to do something

*Le subjonctif ou l'infinitif?*

You know to use the subjunctive in a second clause when the first clause expresses feelings, desires, doubts and fears, requests, or opinions about what someone else does, might do, or should do. In this case, the subjunctive is used only when there are different subjects in the main and dependent clauses. When there is no change of subject, you normally use the infinitive.

| FEELINGS ABOUT SOMEONE ELSE | FEELINGS ABOUT ONESELF |
|---|---|
| Je veux que tu le fasses. *I want you to do it.* | Je veux le faire. *I want to do it.* |
| Nous préférons qu'il soit à l'heure. *We prefer that he be on time.* | Nous préférons être à l'heure. *We prefer to be on time.* |

Use **de** before an infinitive after the verb **regretter** and when the expression includes the verb **être.**

Je regrette **de** partir demain.     Elle est contente **de** venir.

Remember to use an infinitive after expressions such as **il faut** or **il est important de** to talk about people in general, rather than someone specific.

| TALKING ABOUT SOMEONE SPECIFIC | TALKING ABOUT PEOPLE IN GENERAL |
|---|---|
| Il faut que nous le fassions. *We have to do it.* | Il faut le faire. *It has to be done.* |
| Il est important qu'il y aille. *It's important for him to go there.* | Il est important **d'**y aller. *It's important to go there.* |

**A. De bons conseils.** Dites s'il faut ou s'il ne faut pas faire ces choses quand on voyage à l'étranger.

Exemple     prendre la photo d'un tableau avec un flash dans un musée
**Il ne faut pas prendre la photo d'un tableau avec un flash dans un musée.**

1. arriver à l'aéroport bien à l'avance
2. oublier son passeport
3. montrer son passeport à la douane
4. passer par la sécurité
5. fumer dans l'avion
6. faire beaucoup de bruit à l'hôtel

Maintenant, imaginez que vous donnez ces mêmes conseils à un groupe de jeunes qui partent en voyage.

**Exemple**    prendre la photo d'un tableau avec un flash dans un musée
**Il ne faut pas que vous preniez la photo d'un tableau avec un flash dans un musée.**

**B. Des courses.** Micheline et sa sœur se préparent pour aller voir leur oncle qui habite dans une autre ville. Micheline préfère faire ce qu'on peut faire à la maison et elle veut que sa sœur aille faire les courses. Que dit-elle à sa sœur de faire?

**Exemple**    faire le ménage / faire des courses
**Je voudrais que tu fasses des courses. Moi, je préfère faire le ménage.**

1. aller retirer de l'argent du distributeur de billets / faire les valises
2. acheter une carte téléphonique au kiosque / téléphoner à l'oncle Jean
3. écrire une lettre à l'oncle Jean / envoyer ces lettres
4. téléphoner à l'hôtel / aller à la pharmacie
5. acheter de la nourriture pour chien *(dog food)* / donner à manger au chien
6. écrire des mails pour obtenir des renseignements sur la région / acheter des chèques de voyage à la banque

**C. Préférences.** Choisissez les mots entre parenthèses qui décrivent le mieux vos préférences quand vous voyagez. Conjuguez le verbe au subjonctif ou utilisez l'infinitif comme il convient.

1. Pour un long voyage, je préfère... (prendre l'avion, prendre le train, prendre ma voiture, ???)
2. Je préfère que mon vol... (être le matin, être l'après-midi, être le soir)
3. Pendant le vol, j'aime... (lire, voir le film, écouter de la musique, dormir, parler avec d'autres passagers, ???)
4. Je n'aime pas que les autres passagers près de moi... (parler tout le temps, avoir un petit bébé, se lever tout le temps, ???)
5. Je préfère que l'hôtel... (être agréable et de luxe, être grand mais pas trop cher)
6. Je préfère que ma chambre d'hôtel... (avoir un grand lit, avoir un petit lit)
7. Généralement, j'aime... (dîner dans ma chambre d'hôtel, manger au restaurant de l'hôtel, sortir dîner dans un autre restaurant)
8. À l'hôtel, je préfère... (payer en chèques de voyage, payer par carte de crédit, payer en espèces)

**D. Entretien.** Interviewez votre partenaire sur un voyage qu'il/elle voudrait faire.

1. Où est-ce que tu voudrais faire un voyage? Quand est-ce que tu voudrais le faire? Est-ce que tu veux que ta famille ou que tes amis voyagent avec toi?
2. Est-ce que tu préfères que ton hôtel soit de luxe ou pas cher? Est-il important qu'il y ait une piscine? Aimes-tu nager dans la piscine d'un hôtel?
3. As-tu peur de prendre l'avion? Aimes-tu parler avec les personnes à côté de toi dans l'avion ou préfères-tu dormir?

# Giving directions

## Les indications

Luc et Micheline visitent Pointe-à-Pitre. Ils sont à l'office de tourisme. Voilà un plan du centre-ville. Qu'est-ce qu'il y a dans le quartier?

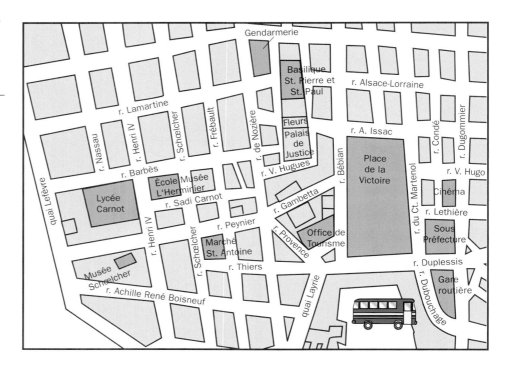

L'employé à l'office de tourisme va **expliquer** à Luc et à Micheline comment arriver au musée Schœlcher. Voilà quelques expressions **utiles** pour **indiquer le chemin.**

| | |
|---|---|
| Prenez la rue… | **Traversez la place…** |
| Continuez **tout droit jusqu'à…** | C'est dans la rue… |
| Tournez à droite. | sur le boulevard… |
| Tournez à gauche. | sur l'avenue… |
| Descendez la rue… | sur la place… |
| Montez la rue… | C'est **au coin de** la rue. |

---

**expliquer** *to explain*    **utile** *useful*    **indiquer le chemin** *to give directions, to show the way*
**tout droit jusqu'à…** *straight ahead until / as far as . . .*    **traverser** *to cross, to go across*    **la place** *the square*
**au coin de** *on the corner of*

CD 2-37

Micheline demande à l'office de tourisme comment aller au musée Schœlcher.

MICHELINE: S'il vous plaît, monsieur, pourriez-vous m'expliquer comment aller au musée Schœlcher?

L'EMPLOYÉ: Bien sûr, mademoiselle, il n'y a rien de plus simple. C'est tout près. Montez la rue Provence jusqu'à la rue Peynier. Tournez à gauche...

MICHELINE: À gauche dans la rue Peynier?

L'EMPLOYÉ: Oui, c'est ça. Continuez tout droit et le musée Schœlcher est sur votre gauche, juste après la rue Henri IV.

MICHELINE: Je vous remercie, monsieur.

L'EMPLOYÉ: Je vous en prie, mademoiselle.

**A. Où allez-vous?** Imaginez que vous êtes à l'office de tourisme avec Luc et Micheline. D'abord, complétez les explications suivantes en traduisant les mots entre parenthèses. Ensuite regardez le plan à la page précédente et dites où vous arrivez.

1. _____ *(Go up)* la rue Provence _____ *(as far as)* la rue Peynier. _____ *(Turn left)*. _____ *(Continue straight ahead)* et il est sur votre gauche, juste après la rue Henri IV.

2. _____ *(Cross)* la place de la Victoire et entrez dans la rue Lethière. _____ *(Continue straight ahead)* jusqu'à la rue Condé et _____ *(turn left)*. Il est sur votre _____ *(right)* entre la rue Victor Hugo et la rue Lethière.

3. _____ *(Go up)* la rue Bébian _____ *(as far as)* la rue Alsace-Lorraine. _____ *(Turn left)*. Elle est juste devant vous.

4. _____ *(Go up)* la rue Provence, _____ *(turn left)* dans la rue Peynier. _____ *(Continue straight ahead)* et il est sur votre gauche, entre la rue Frébault et la rue Schœlcher.

**B. Conversation.** D'abord, avec un(e) partenaire, relisez à haute voix la conversation entre Micheline et l'employé de l'office de tourisme. Ensuite, votre partenaire va vous demander comment aller chez vous en partant de *(leaving from)* l'université. Expliquez-lui comment y aller. Il/Elle va créer un plan selon vos indications.

**1.** How do you form the imperative of most verbs? Which verbs drop the final **s** in the **tu** form of the imperative? Which two verbs are irregular and what are their forms?

**2.** Where do you place **y, en,** and object and reflexive pronouns in affirmative commands? What happens to **me** and **te** in an affirmative command? Where do you place **y, en,** and object and reflexive pronouns in negative commands?

**3.** When do you reattach the **s** to a **tu** form command?

## Telling how to go somewhere

*Reprise de l'impératif et les pronoms avec l'impératif*

You use the **impératif** (command) form of the verb to give directions. As you have seen, the imperative is the **tu, vous,** or **nous** form of the verb without the subject pronoun.

| | |
|---|---|
| Descends cette rue! | *Go down this street!* |
| Traversez la place! | *Cross the square!* |
| Allons à la banque! | *Let's go to the bank!* |

Remember to drop the final **s** of **er** verbs and of **aller,** but not of other verbs, in **tu** form commands.

|  | | | | |
|---|---|---|---|---|
| | Tourne à gauche! | *Turn left!* | Va en ville! | *Go to town!* |
| BUT: | Prend**s** la navette! | *Take the shuttle!* | Fai**s** ta valise! | *Pack your bag!* |

Review the irregular command forms of **être** and **avoir.**

| | | | |
|---|---|---|---|
| Sois calme! | *Be calm!* | Aie de la patience! | *Have patience!* |
| Soyons gentils! | *Let's be nice!* | Ayons confiance! | *Let's have confidence!* |
| Soyez à l'heure! | *Be on time!* | Ayez pitié! | *Have pity!* |

In negative commands, reflexive pronouns, direct and indirect object pronouns, **y,** and **en** are placed before the verb.

| | |
|---|---|
| Ne te perds pas! | *Don't get lost!* |
| Ne les prends pas! | *Don't take them!* |
| N'y va pas! | *Don't go there!* |

In affirmative commands, pronouns are attached to the end of the verb with a hyphen.

| | |
|---|---|
| Cherche-le à l'aéroport. | *Pick him up at the airport.* |
| Dis-lui que nous arriverons bientôt. | *Tell her that we will arrive soon.* |

When **me** and **te** are attached to the end of the verb, they become **moi** and **toi.**

| | | | |
|---|---|---|---|
| Attendez-moi! | *Wait for me!* | Lève-toi! | *Get up!* |

When **y** or **en** follows a **tu** form command, the final **s** is reattached to the end of the verb.

| | | | |
|---|---|---|---|
| Va**s**-y! | *Go ahead!* | Mange**s**-y! | *Eat there!* |
| Achète**s**-en! | *Buy some!* | Mange**s**-en! | *Eat some!* |

**A. Le chemin.** Consultez le plan à la page 402 et expliquez comment aller...

- de l'office de tourisme à la gendarmerie *(police station)*
- de la gendarmerie au musée Schœlcher
- du musée Schœlcher à la sous-préfecture *(administrative building)*

**B. Un drôle de touriste.** Votre nouvel ami, un extra-terrestre, descend dans un hôtel. Dites-lui ce qu'il faut et ce qu'il ne faut pas faire.

> **Exemple** Je m'habille avant de prendre une douche?
> **Non, ne t'habille pas avant de prendre une douche.**
> **Habille-toi après.**

1. Je me couche par terre?
2. Je m'habille dans le jardin?
3. Je me brosse les mains?
4. Je me lave à la réception?
5. Je me lève à minuit?
6. Je me couche à midi?
7. Je me déshabille dans le couloir?
8. Je me brosse les dents avec l'eau de la piscine?

**C. Luc est amoureux.** Luc est tombé amoureux de Micheline et il ne veut pas qu'elle l'oublie quand il sera de retour en France. Vous êtes son ami(e). Répondez à ses questions. Dites-lui de faire ou de ne pas faire chaque chose.

> **Exemple** — Est-ce que je devrais lui écrire des mails de la France?
> **— Oui, écris-lui des mails.**
> **Non, ne lui écris pas de mails. Téléphone-lui.**

1. Est-ce que je devrais l'inviter à venir me voir l'été prochain?
2. Je devrais lui téléphoner deux fois par jour?
3. Est-ce que je devrais lui dire que je suis amoureux d'elle?
4. Est-ce que je devrais lui donner des fleurs *(flowers)*?
5. Est-ce que je devrais l'oublier?
6. Je ferais mieux de la quitter pour toujours?
7. Est-ce que je devrais l'embrasser avant de partir?

**D. Micheline aussi!** Micheline aussi est amoureuse de Luc. Est-ce qu'elle lui dirait de faire les choses indiquées dans *C. Luc est amoureux?*

> **Exemple** **Écris-moi des mails. / Ne m'écris pas de mails. Téléphone-moi.**

**E. Conseils.** Un touriste pose des questions. Répondez à ses questions. Utilisez l'impératif et le pronom convenable.

> **Exemple** — Quand est-ce que je devrais confirmer mon vol?
> **— Confirmez-le 72 heures avant votre départ.**

1. Quand est-ce que je devrais régler la note de la chambre?
2. Comment est-ce que je peux régler la note?
3. Où est-ce que je peux prendre le petit déjeuner?
4. Où est-ce que je peux changer mes chèques de voyage?
5. Où est-ce que je peux acheter des timbres?
6. Où est-ce que je peux acheter un plan de la ville?
7. Comment est-ce que je peux aller à l'aéroport?
8. Où est-ce que je peux acheter de l'aspirine?

## Reprise

*Being on a trip*

Dans le ***Chapitre 10,*** vous avez appris à obtenir une chambre d'hôtel, à demander et à suivre des indications, à parler avec un médecin si vous êtes malade, à faire des recommandations, à exprimer vos désirs et à donner votre réaction à ce qui se passe. Maintenant vous allez réviser ce que vous avez appris.

### A. À l'étranger. Dites ce qu'il vaut mieux faire si on part à l'étranger.

**Exemple**  apporter *(to bring)* beaucoup de choses ou apporter une seule valise?
**Il vaut mieux apporter une seule valise.**

1. chercher un hôtel à l'arrivée ou réserver une chambre à l'avance?
2. faire les valises à l'avance ou faire les valises au dernier moment?
3. arriver à l'aéroport juste avant le départ ou être à l'aéroport au moins deux heures avant le départ?
4. se souvenir de prendre les passeports ou oublier les passeports à la maison?
5. envoyer des cartes postales pendant le voyage ou envoyer les cartes postales après le retour?

Deux de vos amis partent à l'étranger pour la première fois. Dites-leur ce qu'il faut qu'ils fassent.

**Exemple**  **Il vaut mieux que vous apportiez une seule valise.**

### B. Des préparatifs. Vous faites les préparatifs pour un voyage avec un(e) ami(e). Dites à votre ami(e) ce que vous préférez faire et ce que vous préférez qu'il/elle fasse.

**Exemple**  aller à la banque pour acheter des chèques de voyage / aller à l'agence de voyages pour acheter les billets
**Je préfère aller à l'agence de voyages pour acheter les billets et je préfère que tu ailles à la banque pour acheter des chèques de voyage.**

1. choisir l'hôtel / choisir le vol
2. faire les réservations d'hôtel / louer une voiture
3. lire le guide touristique / chercher des renseignements sur le Web
4. être assis(e) *(seated)* côté hublot *(window)* / être assis(e) côté couloir *(aisle)*
5. dormir dans le lit / dormir sur le canapé
6. acheter des timbres au bureau de poste / changer des chèques de voyage
7. payer le voyage / ne rien payer

### C. En voyage. Votre ami(e) vous demande les choses suivantes pendant votre voyage. Répondez en utilisant l'impératif avec un pronom complément d'objet direct.

**Exemple**  Je mets le réveil *(set the alarm)* pour six heures ou pour huit heures?
**Ne le mets pas pour six heures. Mets-le pour huit heures.**

1. J'apporte *(I bring)* mon passeport avec moi ou je le laisse à l'hôtel?
2. Je paie l'hôtel avec ma carte de crédit ou avec ta carte de crédit?
3. Je fais le lit ou je le laisse pour la femme de chambre *(maid)?*
4. Je prends la clé avec moi ou je la laisse à la réception?
5. J'appelle le taxi une heure ou deux heures avant le vol?
6. J'écris ces cartes postales avant de partir ou je les écris dans l'avion?

**D. Une réservation perdue.** Vous êtes dans les situations suivantes pendant votre voyage. Décrivez vos réactions.

**Exemple**   Votre avion est en retard.
**Je suis furieux (furieuse) que mon avion soit en retard.**

**Je suis content(e) que...**   **Je ne suis pas content(e) que...**
**Je regrette que...**   **Je suis furieux (furieuse) que...**
**Il est bon que...**   **C'est dommage que...**
**Il n'est pas important...**

1. On ne peut pas trouver votre réservation d'hôtel.
2. Il n'y a pas de chambres disponibles *(available)*.
3. Il n'y a pas de télé dans la chambre d'hôtel.
4. L'hôtel a un grand restaurant.
5. Les repas à l'hôtel sont excellents.
6. Votre ami(e) veut passer toute la journée dans la chambre d'hôtel.
7. Il fait très mauvais et il pleut tous les jours.
8. Il n'y a pas assez d'eau chaude le matin.

**E. On cherche un hôtel.**   On a perdu votre réservation d'hôtel, alors vous cherchez un autre hôtel. Avec un(e) partenaire, préparez une conversation avec le (la) réceptionniste dans laquelle vous discutez les choses suivantes.

- say that you are looking for a room and for how many nights
- explain what sort of room you are looking for, including the number of beds and the sort of bathroom you need
- discuss the price, including breakfast, and ask where and at what time breakfast is served **(est servi)**

**F. Pourriez-vous m'indiquer le chemin?**   Regardez le plan de Pointe-à-Pitre à la page 402. Vous êtes à la Gare routière dans la rue Dubouchage. (Cherchez le petit autobus.) Vous désirez aller au marché Saint-Antoine. Votre partenaire va vous dire comment y aller. Ensuite, changez de rôles. Cette fois, votre partenaire voudrait aller de la Gare routière au lycée Carnot.

**G. Chez le médecin.**   Vous tombez malade pendant votre voyage. Avec un(e) partenaire, préparez la conversation suivante avec un médecin.

- The doctor greets you and asks what is wrong.
- You say that you are coughing, sneezing, and you have a sore throat and a headache.
- The doctor says you have the flu and gives you a prescription for medicine. He/She says that it is important that you take it every morning and gives you other advice on what to do.

## Lecture: *Je vais camper...*

Selon cet **extrait** d'un article de *France-Antilles Magazine*, le camping devient de plus en plus populaire chez les Martiniquais. Et vous? Aimez-vous faire du camping?

Avant de lire l'article, lisez les paires de phrases qui suivent avec un(e) partenaire. Dites quelle phrase de chaque paire exprime le mieux votre opinion et expliquez pourquoi.

1. **a.** J'aime faire du camping parce que c'est différent de la routine quotidienne.
   **b.** Je n'aime pas faire du camping parce que je n'aime pas changer de routine.

2. **a.** J'aime faire du camping parce que c'est moins cher que les vacances dans un hôtel.
   **b.** Je préfère payer plus pour avoir les commodités *(comforts)* d'un hôtel.

3. **a.** J'aime la vie en communauté quand on fait du camping.
   **b.** Je n'aime pas tout partager avec d'autres gens pendant plusieurs jours.

---

### *Je vais camper...*

Le camping est un mode de **villégiature** de plus en plus **prisé** par les Martiniquais, **que ce soit** par goût, ou pour faire des économies...

Synonyme de liberté et d'indépendance, le camping est aussi **une façon de vivre** différente qui **séduit** de plus en plus de personnes, désireuses de «**couper**» avec la routine quotidienne. Recherche de **dépaysement** total jusque dans les gestes de tous les jours, **souci** de passer des vacances agréables sans faire trop de **dépenses**, envie de partager des moments de **détente** et de **convivialité** en groupe, que ce soit en famille ou entre amis, désir de changer ses **codes de fonctionnement** habituels pour vraiment «**décompresser**», sont **autant** de raisons qui **poussent** les gens, **inconditionnels** ou **débutants**, à choisir ce style de vie, généralement **au bord de la mer.**

Faire du camping suppose que l'on aime la vie en communauté, et que l'on en connaît les «codes» de bonne **conduite.** Il en est de même en matière de respect de l'environnement. Le bon campeur aime, par définition, la nature, puisque, en principe, c'est pour **se rapprocher d'**elle qu'il a opté pour ce style de villégiature...

Où camper en Martinique? Sur le territoire de la commune de Sainte-Anne, les lieux de camping autorisés sont le Cap Chevalier et la Plage des Salines; vous pouvez **également** camper à la Pointe Marin. Sur le territoire de la commune du Vauclin, les lieux autorisés sont la plage de la Pointe Faula et la plage du Macabou. Il existe également des terrains de camping privés à l'Anse-à-l'Ane, aux Trois-Îlets.

---

**extrait** *excerpt*   **villégiature** *vacation*   **prisé** *appreciated*   **que ce soit** *whether it be*   **une façon de vivre** *a way of life*   **séduit** *seduces*   **couper** *to cut off*   **dépaysement** *change of scene*   **souci** *care, a desire to*   **dépenses** *expenses*   **détente** *relaxation*   **convivialité** *sharing a good time*   **codes de fonctionnement** *way of doing things*   **décompresser** *to let off steam*   **autant** *as many*   **poussent** *push*   **inconditionnels** *devotees*   **débutants** *beginners*   **au bord de la mer** *by the sea*   **conduite** *conduct*   **se rapprocher de** *to get closer to*   **également** *equally, likewise, as well*

## Compréhension

### A. Avez-vous compris? Répondez selon l'article.

1. Donnez trois raisons pour lesquelles certaines personnes aiment le camping.
2. Qu'est-ce que le bon campeur aime par définition?
3. Où peut-on faire du camping en Martinique?

### B. Allons faire du camping. Préparez une conversation avec un(e) camarade de classe dans laquelle vous essayez de persuader un(e) ami(e) d'aller faire du camping. Votre ami(e) hésite à accepter et vous utilisez les arguments pour faire du camping donnés dans l'article *Je vais camper...* pour le/la persuader.

## Composition

### A. Organisez-vous. Vous organisez une visite dans votre ville pour un groupe de touristes venant de France et vous êtes chargé(e) d'écrire un bulletin aux participants. Avant d'écrire votre bulletin, répondez d'abord aux questions suivantes.

1. Quelles sont les dates de la visite?
2. Dans quel hôtel est-ce que les touristes vont loger *(to lodge)*?
3. Où allez-vous vous réunir *(to meet)*?
4. Quels moyens de transport leur recommandez-vous?
5. Quelles sont les indications pour aller de l'aéroport à l'hôtel?
6. Quels restaurants leur recommandez-vous?
7. Quelles autres recommandations ou conseils avez-vous pour les visiteurs?

### B. Rédaction: Un bulletin. En utilisant ce que vous avez préparé dans l'exercice précédent, écrivez un bulletin donnant tous les renseignements nécessaires aux visiteurs qui viendront dans votre ville pour la visite.

### C. Un coup de téléphone. Comparez votre bulletin et celui d'un(e) partenaire. Ensuite, choisissez l'un des deux et préparez la conversation suivante.

Un(e) des touristes a perdu les renseignements que vous lui avez envoyés et il/elle téléphone pour s'informer.

If you have access to SYSTÈME-D software, you will find the following phrases, vocabulary, grammar, and dictionary aids there.

**Phrases:** Writing a news item; Giving directions: Advising
**Vocabulary:** Calendar; Telling time; City; Means of transportation; Traveling; Direction and distance; Restaurant; Meals

## La négritude

**Au** cours **des années trente,** des **écrivains** francophones noirs ont commencé à utiliser le terme «négritude» pour décrire la culture noire, **l'opposant** à la culture imposée par les colonisateurs européens. En 1934, Aimé Césaire, poète martiniquais, Léopold Sédar Senghor, poète sénégalais, et Léon Damas, poète de Guyane française, ont fondé le journal *L'Étudiant Noir* et sont devenus **les porte-paroles de** la négritude. Ce mouvement, **avant tout** littéraire, représente aussi une attitude culturelle, sociale et politique et l'affirmation d'une identité et d'une culture noires.

Vous allez lire un poème qui parle de la vie à Haïti, un pays indépendant à quelques centaines de kilomètres de la Floride. Ce pays, qui a des plages très **attirantes,** est un des plus **pauvres** pays du monde. Avant de lire le poème **qui suit,** faites une liste de tout ce que vous savez sur Haïti. Regardez aussi cette photo et la photo à la page suivante et écrivez les mots **qui vous viennent à l'esprit.**

---

**des années trente** *of the thirties*    **écrivains** *writers*    **l'opposant** *contrasting it*    **les porte-paroles de** *the spokespersons for*
**avant tout** *above all*    **attirantes** *attractive*    **pauvres** *poor*    **qui suit** *that follows*    **qui vous viennent à l'esprit** *that come to mind*

## À qui

*Tiré d'Haïti blues Echopoèmes*

*J. F. Ménard*

**À qui**
**Devine**
Qui devine
**Au bord de mer**
L'hôtel de touristes **plein**
À qui
Dis
Qui dira
La compagnie sur le port
Les cargos
L'avion **particulier**
Sur l'avenue
**Les devantures** le journal
À qui
Le compte en banque
Secret
Devine
Qui devine
**Quelques-uns**
Tous les autres grand goût
**Pieds nus** sur les asphaltes
Et sur la route **crevassée**
Les **lourdes** limousines
**Dans les hauts** les villas piscine
L'autre côté de la ravine
Qui
Sait lire compter **mentir**
Et qui ne pourra plus **courber l'échine**
**Davantage**
**Lambi!**

## À discuter

Étudie-t-on la littérature caraïbe, la littérature africaine et la littérature afro-américaine à l'école dans votre région? Devrait-on les étudier plus? Est-ce qu'il y a des mouvements pour protéger et promouvoir *(to promote)* les cultures des divers groupes ethniques dans votre pays?

**À qui?** *Whose is it?*    **Devine** *Guess*    **Au bord de mer** *By the sea*    **plein** *full*    **particulier** *private*
**Les devantures** *The shop windows*    **Quelques-uns** *A few*    **Pieds nus** *Barefoot*    **crevassée** *cracked*    **lourdes** *heavy*
**Dans les hauts** *Up in the hills*    **mentir** *to lie*    **courber l'échine** *to bend their backs*    **Davantage** *Any further*
**Lambi!** *a type of shell commonly sold to tourists*

# Résumé de grammaire

## Impersonal expressions and the infinitive

Use an infinitive after the following expressions to state general advice and opinions. Notice that **il faut** means *it is necessary*, **il ne faut pas** means *one should / must not*, and **il n'est pas nécessaire** means *it's not necessary*.

Pour préparer un voyage à l'étranger, **il faut obtenir** (*to obtain*) des passeports. **Il vaut mieux réserver** une chambre à l'avance. **Il ne faut pas attendre** au dernier moment.

Il faut... / Il ne faut pas...
Il est nécessaire de... / Il n'est pas nécessaire de...
Il vaut mieux...
Il est essentiel / important / bon / mauvais de...
C'est bien de...

## The subjunctive (*Le subjonctif*)

The indicative mood expresses reality. The subjunctive mood conveys subjectivity; that is, feelings, desires, doubts and fears, opinions, and requests about what happens or might happen. The present subjunctive may imply either present or future actions.

The subjunctive is used in a second clause preceded by **que:**

S'il est malade, il faut **qu'il téléphone** au médecin.

J'ai peur **qu'il soit** très malade. Je suis content **qu'il aille** chez le médecin.

- to give advice for someone in particular after impersonal expressions like those listed above. (In expressions like **il est bon de, que** replaces **de.**)
- when the verb in the first clause "triggers" the subjunctive in the second clause by expressing feelings, desires, doubts and fears, opinions, or requests, provided that the subject of the first clause is not the same as the subject of the second clause. (See page 398 for a list of such "trigger" verbs.)

For most verbs, form the subjunctive as follows.

- For **nous** and **vous,** the subjunctive looks like the imperfect.
- For the other forms, drop the **-ent** ending of the **ils/elles** form of the present indicative and add the endings: **-e, -es, -e, -ent.**

Le médecin veut **qu'il reste au lit** et **qu'il finisse** tous ses médicaments. Il vaut mieux **qu'il ne rende pas** visite à ses amis.

|  | PARLER | FINIR | RENDRE |
|---|---|---|---|
| que je | parle | finisse | rende |
| que tu | parles | finisses | rendes |
| qu'il/qu'elle/qu'on | parle | finisse | rende |
| que nous | parlions | finissions | rendions |
| que vous | parliez | finissiez | rendiez |
| qu'ils/qu'elles | parlent | finissent | rendent |

Most irregular verbs follow the same pattern.

Il ne veut pas **que je dise** à ses parents qu'il est malade. Il faut **qu'il dorme** beaucoup. Il ne faut pas **qu'il sorte** ce soir.

| connaître | que je connaiss**e** | que nous connaiss**ions** |
|---|---|---|
| dire | que je dis**e** | que nous dis**ions** |
| dormir | que je dorm**e** | que nous dorm**ions** |
| écrire | que j'écriv**e** | que nous écriv**ions** |
| lire | que je lis**e** | que nous lis**ions** |
| partir | que je part**e** | que nous part**ions** |
| sortir | que je sort**e** | que nous sort**ions** |

These verbs follow the same pattern, but have two different stems.

| acheter | que j'achè**te** | que nous achet**ions** |
| boire | que je boiv**e** | que nous buv**ions** |
| devoir | que je doiv**e** | que nous dev**ions** |
| payer | que je pai**e** | que nous pay**ions** |
| prendre | que je prenn**e** | que nous pren**ions** |
| venir | que je vienn**e** | que nous ven**ions** |

Il faut **que nous achetions** ces médicaments à la pharmacie.
Il veut **que tu viennes** le voir.

Only seven verbs are irregular in the subjunctive: **avoir, être, aller, faire, vouloir, savoir,** and **pouvoir.** Memorize their conjugations from the charts on page 394. The subjunctive of **il y a** is **qu'il y ait** and the subjunctive of **il pleut** is **qu'il pleuve.**

Je regrette **qu'il soit** malade mais je suis content **qu'il aille** voir le médecin.

## The subjunctive or the infinitive?

The subjunctive is used when there are different subjects in the main and dependent clauses. When there is no change of subject, you normally use the infinitive. Use **de** before an infinitive after the verb **regretter** and when the expression includes the verb **être.** Also remember to use an infinitive after expressions such as **il faut** or **il est important de** to talk about what should be done as a general rule, rather than what specific people should do.

Je ne veux pas **changer** mes chèques de voyage. Je préfère **que tu changes** tes chèques de voyage.

## Commands and using pronouns with commands

The imperative (command form) is the **tu, nous,** or **vous** form of the verb without the subject pronoun. Remember to drop the final **s** of -er verbs and of **aller,** but not of other verbs, in **tu** form commands.

**Prends** la rue Provence, **va** jusqu'à la rue Thiers et **tourne** à gauche.
**Prenons** la rue Provence.
**Prenez** la rue Provence.

**Être** and **avoir** have irregular command forms: **sois, soyons, soyez** and **aie, ayons, ayez.**

**Sois** à l'heure. **Aie** de la patience.

In negative commands, reflexive and object pronouns, **y,** and **en** are placed before the verb.

**Ne lui achète pas** de cadeau dans la boutique de l'aéroport.

In affirmative commands, pronouns are attached to the end of the verb with a hyphen. In an affirmative command, **me** and **te** become **moi** and **toi.** When **y** or **en** follows a **tu** form command, the final **s** is reattached to the end of the verb.

**Achète-lui** un cadeau au marché.
**Réveille-toi** tôt et **vas-y** le matin.

# Vocabulaire

## COMPÉTENCE 1

### Deciding where to stay

**NOMS MASCULINS**

| | |
|---|---|
| un bruit | a noise |
| un chalet de ski | a ski lodge |
| un hôtelier | a hotel manager |
| un lavabo | a washbasin, a sink |
| le logement | lodging |
| un supplément | an extra charge, a supplement |

**NOMS FÉMININS**

| | |
|---|---|
| une auberge de jeunesse | a youth hostel |
| une clé | a key |
| une hôtelière | a hotel manager |
| la réception | the front desk |
| une station estivale | a summer resort |

**EXPRESSIONS VERBALES**

| | |
|---|---|
| C'est bien de... | It's good to . . . |
| Il est bon de... | It's good to . . . |
| Il est essentiel de... | It's essential to . . . |
| Il est important de... | It's important to . . . |
| Il est mauvais de... | It's bad to . . . |
| Il est nécessaire de... | It's necessary to . . . |
| Il n'est pas nécessaire de... | It's not necessary to . . . |
| Il faut... | One must . . . , It's necessary to . . . |
| Il ne faut pas... | One shouldn't . . . , One must not . . . |
| Il vaut mieux... | It's better to . . . |

**ADJECTIFS**

| | |
|---|---|
| calme | calm |
| compris(e) | included |
| privé(e) | private |
| servi(e) | served |

**DIVERS**

| | |
|---|---|
| bon séjour | enjoy your stay |
| côté cour | on the courtyard side |
| de luxe | deluxe |
| en espèces | in cash |
| régler la note | to pay the bill |

## COMPÉTENCE 2

### Going to the doctor

**NOMS MASCULINS**

| | |
|---|---|
| les frissons | the shivers |
| un liquide | a liquid |
| un médecin | a doctor |
| un médicament | a medecine, a medication |
| un rhume | a cold |
| un symptôme | a symptom |
| un virus | a virus |

**NOMS FÉMININS**

| | |
|---|---|
| une allergie | an allergy |
| la grippe | the flu |
| une indigestion | indigestion |
| une ordonnance | a prescription |

**LES PARTIES DU CORPS**

| | |
|---|---|
| la bouche | the mouth |
| le bras | the arm |
| le corps | the body |
| les dents (f) | the teeth |
| les doigts (m) | the fingers |
| les doigts de pied | the toes |
| le dos | the back |
| la gorge | the throat |
| la jambe | the leg |
| la main | the hand |
| le nez | the nose |
| l'œil (m) (pl les yeux) | the eye |
| l'oreille (f) | the ear |
| le pied | the foot |
| la tête | the head |
| le ventre | the stomach |

**EXPRESSIONS VERBALES**

| | |
|---|---|
| avoir des frissons | to have the shivers |
| avoir mal à... | one's . . . hurt(s) |
| communiquer | to communicate |
| éternuer | to sneeze |
| tomber malade | to get sick |
| tousser | to cough |
| vomir | to vomit, to throw up |

**DIVERS**

| | |
|---|---|
| au cours de | in the course of, during, while on |
| enceinte | pregnant |
| exactement | exactly |
| Qu'est-ce qui ne va pas? | What's wrong? |
| tout simplement | quite simply |

# COMPÉTENCE 3

## Running errands on a trip

**NOMS MASCULINS**

| | |
|---|---|
| un aéroport | an airport |
| un bureau de poste | a post office |
| un cadeau | a present |
| un distributeur de billets | an ATM machine |
| un kiosque | a kiosk |
| un marchand de cadeaux | a gift shop |
| un timbre | a stamp |

**NOMS FÉMININS**

| | |
|---|---|
| de l'aspirine | aspirin |
| une banque | a bank |
| une carte téléphonique | a telephone card |
| une navette | a shuttle |
| une pharmacie | a pharmacy |

**EXPRESSIONS VERBALES**

| | |
|---|---|
| aller / venir chercher quelqu'un | to go / come pick someone up |
| c'est dommage que... | it's too bad that . . . |
| douter que... | to doubt that . . . |
| envoyer | to send |
| être content(e) que... | to be happy that . . . |
| être désolé(e) que... | to be sorry that . . . |
| être étonné(e) que... | to be astonished that . . . |
| être furieux (furieuse) que... | to be furious that . . . |
| être heureux (heureuse) que... | to be happy that . . . |
| être surpris(e) que... | to be surprised that . . . |
| être triste que... | to be sad that . . . |
| insister que... | to insist that . . . |
| j'aimerais autant | I would just as soon |
| regretter que... | to regret that . . . |
| retirer de l'argent | to withdraw money |

**DIVERS**

| | |
|---|---|
| en retard | late |
| principal(e) (mpl principaux) | principal, main |

# COMPÉTENCE 4

## Giving directions

**NOMS MASCULINS**

| | |
|---|---|
| un employé | an employee |
| l'office de tourisme | the Tourist Office |
| un plan | a map |

**NOMS FÉMININS**

| | |
|---|---|
| une employée | an employee |
| une expression | an expression |
| les indications | directions |
| une place | a (town) square, a plaza |

**EXPRESSIONS VERBALES**

| | |
|---|---|
| continuer (tout droit) | to continue (straight ahead) |
| descendre la rue... | to go down . . . Street |
| expliquer | to explain |
| indiquer le chemin | to give directions, to show the way |
| monter la rue... | to go up . . . Street |
| prendre la rue... | to take . . . Street |
| remercier | to thank |
| tourner (à droite / à gauche) | to turn (right / left) |
| traverser | to cross, to go across |

**EXPRESSIONS PRÉPOSITIONNELLES**

| | |
|---|---|
| au coin de | on the corner of |
| dans la rue... | on . . . Street |
| jusqu'à | until, up to, as far as |
| sur l'avenue / le boulevard / la place... | on . . . Avenue / Boulevard / Square |

**DIVERS**

| | |
|---|---|
| juste | just |
| tout droit | straight (ahead) |
| utile | useful |

## Épisode: La vie quotidienne

### Avant la vidéo

Dans cet épisode, c'est vendredi. Élodie fait ses courses et elle fait des projets pour le week-end. Ses amis lui font des suggestions. Finalement, on entend que ce sont souvent les petites choses ordinaires qui procurent du bonheur aux gens.

Et vous? Qu'est-ce que vous aimez faire quand vous avez du temps libre? Quelles sont les petites choses ordinaires qui vous rendent heureux (heureuse)?

### Après la vidéo

1. Pourquoi est-ce que la journée d'Élodie commence mal? Qu'est-ce qu'elle a oublié d'acheter hier?

2. Élodie veut trouver quelque chose de passionnant à faire ce week-end. Quelles activités est-ce que ses amis lui suggèrent?
   Claire-Anse:              Olivier:

3. Olivier a fait des sondages sur les goûts des Français. Selon lui, quelles sont les activités les plus populaires... ?
   chez les plus de trente ans:
   chez les jeunes de moins de trente ans:
   chez les enfants:

4. Quelles sont les petites choses qui procurent du bonheur à... ?
   M. Benoît:
   le fleuriste:
   Youssef:

Comment trouvez-vous les activités qui sont populaires parmi les Français?

Que pensez-vous des goûts de M. Benoît, du fleuriste et de Youssef?

## Épisode: Marché aux puces

### Avant la vidéo

Dans cet épisode, Élodie et Olivier décident de faire une surprise à Claire-Anse. Ils veulent lui acheter un cadeau d'anniversaire très spécial. Il vont au célèbre **marché aux puces de Saint-Ouen** à Paris.

Êtes-vous déjà allé(e) à un marché aux puces? Qu'est-ce que vous avez acheté? Avez-vous payé le prix demandé ou avez-vous essayé d'avoir un meilleur prix?

### Après la vidéo

1. De qui est-ce qu'Élodie reçoit une carte postale? Quelles sont deux choses dont cette personne parle?

2. Où est-ce qu'Élodie devait aller avec Claire-Anse? Pourquoi est-ce qu'Élodie ne dit pas à Claire-Anse qu'elle va aller au marché aux puces avec Olivier?

3. Comment est-ce qu'Élodie et Olivier vont au marché aux puces? En arrivant, qu'est-ce qu'ils regardent en premier? Pourquoi?

4. Qu'est-ce qu'ils achètent pour Claire-Anse? Quel prix demande le marchand? Combien d'argent est-ce qu'ils lui offrent?

Aimez-vous faire des surprises à vos amis de temps en temps? Qu'est-ce que vous faites?

## Épisode: La fête d'un anniversaire

### Avant la vidéo

Dans cet épisode, Élodie et Olivier font faire une chasse au trésor dans tout Paris à Claire-Anse. Finalement, Claire-Anse retrouve Élodie et Olivier pour une fête d'anniversaire surprise qu'ils lui ont préparée.

Avez-vous déjà participé à une chasse au trésor? Si vous faisiez une chasse au trésor à Paris, par quels endroits pensez-vous que vous passeriez? Faites une liste.

### Après la vidéo

1. Élodie envoie Claire-Anse à travers tout Paris. Dans quel ordre est-ce qu'elle passe par ces endroits?

   _____ **1.** Le Lapin Agile      _____ **3.** le Passe-Muraille

   _____ **2.** le parc de la Turlure      _____ **4.** Drôle d'Endroit

2. Quel endroit de la question **1** correspond à chacune de ces descriptions?
   **a.** une statue créée par Jean Marais
   **b.** un café à Paris
   **c.** un cabaret de Montmartre, fréquenté autrefois par des artistes et des écrivains célèbres
   **d.** un espace vert avec une vue sur le Sacré-Cœur

Est-ce que Claire-Anse est passée par des endroits qui sont sur votre liste pour l'activité *Avant la vidéo?*

## Épisode: La pharmacie

### Avant la vidéo

Dans cet épisode, Élodie a mal à la tête. Comme sa tante Mathilde préfère la médecine homéopathique, il n'y a pas d'aspirine chez elle et Élodie doit aller à la pharmacie. En rentrant, elle trouve une carte postale de sa tante.

Et vous? Si vous ne vous sentez pas bien, qui consultez-vous: un médecin, un pharmacien ou des amis? Qu'est-ce que vous faites quand vous avez mal à la tête?

### Après la vidéo

1. Pourquoi est-ce qu'Élodie a mal à la tête? Qu'est-ce que sa mère lui préparait quand elle était petite et qu'elle ne se sentait pas bien? Qu'est-ce que Claire-Anse lui dit de faire?

2. Le pharmacien pose des questions à Élodie pour savoir ce qu'elle a. Quels sont cinq symptômes qu'il mentionne? Qu'est-ce qu'il finit par lui donner?

3. Qu'est-ce que Youssef suggère pour guérir le mal de tête d'Élodie?

4. Quand Élodie rentre, elle trouve une carte postale de sa tante Mathilde. D'où écrit-elle? Quelles sont deux choses qu'elle a admirées dans ce pays?

Et vous, envoyez-vous des cartes postales quand vous êtes en vacances? À qui? Qu'est-ce que vous leur écrivez généralement?

## Épisode: Le retour de tante Mathilde

### Avant la vidéo

Dans cet épisode, Élodie prépare une fête pour célébrer le retour de voyage de sa tante Mathilde.

Et vous? Voyagez-vous souvent? Pourquoi ou pourquoi pas? Quels sont les pays ou les régions que vous avez déjà visités? Lesquels voudriez-vous explorer?

Quand vous rentrez de vos vacances, rapportez-vous des souvenirs et des cadeaux? Pour qui? Qu'est-ce que vous leur rapportez?

### Après la vidéo

1. Selon le mail de tante Mathilde, quand est-ce qu'elle va rentrer?

2. Nommez trois des cadeaux qu'elles a rapportés de son voyage.

3. De quels trois pays est-ce que tante Mathilde parle?

4. Quelle langue étrangère avait-elle étudiée avant de partir?

5. Qu'est-ce qui arrive au dîner qu'Élodie a préparé? Quelle est la solution?

Êtes-vous d'accord avec tante Mathilde quand elle dit: «On ne connaît bien une culture que lorsqu'on connaît sa langue.»

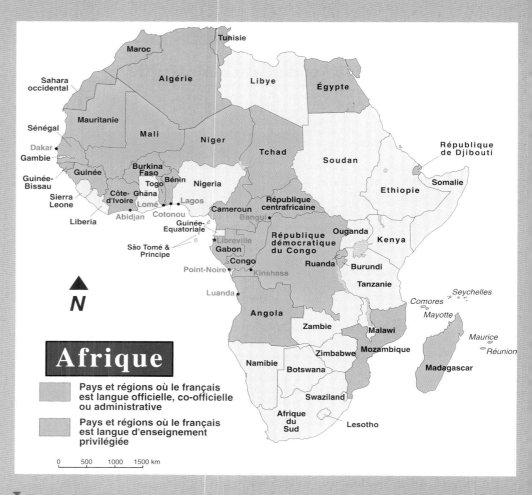

**Afrique**

Pays et régions où le français est langue officielle, co-officielle ou administrative

Pays et régions où le français est langue d'enseignement privilégiée

0    500    1000    1500 km

**LE FRANÇAIS** est une langue importante dans 22 pays d'Afrique, et plus de 200 millions d'habitants de ce continent parlent français. La colonisation de l'Afrique par la France est en grande partie à l'origine de la francophonie en Afrique.

Allons visiter quelques pays francophones africains!

La Côte d'Ivoire est un pays fascinant par sa diversité géographique et culturelle.

Dans ce seul pays, vous pouvez voir des régions géographiques très variées. Le long de **la côte,** il y a des plages et **des falaises.** Au centre, il y a la jungle et des forêts tropicales. Dans le nord, il y a la savane.

Il y a plus de 60 **tribus** différentes en Côte d'Ivoire, **chacune** avec ses **propres** traditions.

---

**la côte** *the coast*   **des falaises** *cliffs*   **tribus** *tribes*   **chacune** *each one*   **propres** *own*

Avec plus de 500 tribus différentes, la République Démocratique du Congo, **anciennement** le Zaïre, est un pays de diversité et de contradictions.

Kinshasa, la capitale, est une grande ville moderne.

**Pourtant,** 70% de la population du pays habite dans des régions rurales où les traditions remontent à plus de mille ans.

anciennement *formerly*   **Pourtant** *However*

Le Maroc, appelé aussi «le pays du soleil couchant» (*al-Maghrib al-aqsa*), est l'état le plus occidental de l'Afrique du Nord.

Par sa situation entre la Méditerranée, l'Atlantique et le Sahara, le Maroc **appartient à la fois** au monde méditerranéen, occidental et berbère. Composé de montagnes, de déserts, de plages, de **côtes escarpées** et de forêts, et **doté de** villes fascinantes (la capitale, Rabat, Casablanca et Marrakech) et de sites archéologiques (Fès, Salé), le Maroc est un des plus beaux pays du monde.

Encore plus **attirante** que la beauté de ses paysages, la culture marocaine est très riche **car** elle reflète l'histoire et les traditions du peuple marocain, **tant d'**origine arabe que berbère et saharienne.

---

**appartient à la fois** *belongs at the same time*    **côtes escarpées** *rocky coasts*    **doté de** *endowed with*    **attirante** *attractive*
**car** *because*    **tant de** *as much*

## French for Study and Temporary Work Abroad

**H**ow would you like to spend some time in a French-speaking country? There are many opportunities to spend a semester or a year studying abroad or to obtain a temporary position working in a francophone country.

Study abroad offers you experiences that will enrich your life forever, but you may have questions about how to organize and finance such studies. The cost of studying abroad varies, depending on the program, its location, and your length of stay. Many American universities organize study abroad programs in France, Quebec, and other francophone countries. Financial aid programs can often be used for study abroad if your university agrees to transfer credit, and there are also fellowships available. Check with the financial aid officer or international studies office at your campus.

Once you have chosen a study abroad program, check with your university to see

L'université Laval, Québec

if the courses will count toward your degree. If you enroll in a program sponsored by an American university, transfer credit is easier to determine, because that school will issue a transcript. If a foreign institution will be issuing the transcript, your registrar's office may need additional information.

Opportunities for temporary work abroad are also varied. Would you enjoy living with a family and helping with the children, teaching English to students, working on an archaeological restoration, or working on a farm in a French-speaking country? There is a variety of temporary jobs available that may pay a small stipend, or perhaps only room and board, and allow you to practice your French and observe the culture.

One of the most popular ways for college-age students to spend time in France is to work with a family as an **au pair.** As an **au pair,** you live with a family and, in exchange for room, board, and a small allowance, help around the house, especially with the children. Lengths of stay generally range from a few months to a year.

Perhaps you would prefer to teach English to French speakers in an elementary, middle, or high school in France. If so, you can apply to a program supported by the French government to become an English **assistant(e).** As an **assistant(e),** you would either assist an experienced English teacher or teach English to groups of French students. You would be paid a small salary, but would be responsible for most of your own expenses. Most **assistant(e)** positions are for one school year.

Interested in history or archaeology? You might enjoy working on an archaeological site or restoring old buildings. In exchange for working on a site, you receive free room and board. The Council on International Education Exchange can arrange work at an archaeological site in France or in other francophone countries. The CIEE also arranges short jobs abroad in nature conservation or working with children and the elderly, where room and board are provided during your stay.

---

Check out these sources to get more information on study programs or temporary work in a francophone country.

English Assistants in France (Cultural Services of the French Embassy in the United States)
www.info-france-usa.org/visitingfrance/teach.asp

Alliances Abroad
1221 South Mopac Expressway, Suite 250
Austin, Texas 78746
(512) 457-8062
(888)-6-ABROAD
www.alliancesabroad.com

Inter-Exchange
161 Sixth Avenue
New York, NY 10013
(212) 924-0446
www.interexchange.org

Council on International Education Exchange CIEE
7 Custom House Street, 3rd Floor
Portland, ME 04101
(800)-40-Study
(207) 553-7600
www.CIEE.org

Traditionally, a popular late summer job among young foreigners was grape-picking. Today, with mechanization and a rising number of immigrant laborers, farmers hire fewer and fewer inexperienced college students. However, if you are already in France visiting, and you want to practice your French for a few more weeks while learning about the wine industry, you might consider trying it. Students interested in agriculture can also find work on a variety of organic and dairy farms year-round. These jobs are usually not paid, but you receive room and board.

## Anthony Muñoz

*Quand vous étiez en France, où est-ce que vous travailliez et qu'est-ce que vous faisiez?*

J'étais assistant dans une école primaire à Compiègne où **j'enseignais** l'anglais aux enfants.

*Comment est-ce que vous avez appris à parler français?*

J'ai étudié le français pendant un an dans une université au Texas.

*Comment s'organisait votre journée typique d'assistant?*

Je me réveillais vers huit heures, je mangeais quelque chose et puis, je partais à l'école. Je donnais des cours le matin jusqu'à midi. Comme les enfants ne comprenaient pas l'anglais, je devais tout le temps parler français. À midi, je rentrais chez moi pour déjeuner et pour me reposer. Je recommençais mes cours à une heure et quart et je les finissais vers quatre heures.

*Quels aspects de votre travail trouviez-vous difficiles? **Lesquels** étaient les plus satisfaisants?*

J'ai trouvé que c'était très difficile d'enseigner aux enfants. Mais j'ai trouvé la vie quotidienne en France très sympa. Oh là là, **qu'est-ce que la France me manque!**

*Qu'est-ce que ces expériences vous ont appris?*

Quand on voyage dans un autre pays, il est très **utile** de connaître d'autres langues si on veut communiquer avec les habitants et comprendre leur culture. **Tout le monde** ne parle pas anglais!

*Quelles recommandations pouvez-vous faire à un(e) étudiant(e) qui voudrait travailler à l'étranger?*

J'ai trouvé le programme *English Assistants in France* (www.info-france-usa.org/visitingfrance/teach.asp) excellent. On peut passer de six à neuf mois en France. C'est **une façon** excellente d'apprendre le français et de connaître la France.

---

**j'enseignais** *I taught*   **Lesquels** *Which ones*   **qu'est-ce que la France me manque** *how I miss France*   **utile** *useful*
**Tout le monde** *Everyone*   **une façon** *a way*

### Return of the Hunters
**PIETER BRUEGEL (DIT L'ANCIEN) (1525–1569)**

1565
Kunsthistorisches Museum,
Gemäldegalerie,
Vienna Erich Lessing/
Art Resource, NY

Bruegel habitait et travaillait à Anvers *(Antwerp),* en Belgique. Cette scène montrant la stérilité de l'hiver est typique de ses œuvres *(works),* qui représentaient l'activité humaine sur fond *(background)* d'un paysage panoramique.

## En Europe: En Belgique

**LA BELGIQUE (LE ROYAUME DE BELGIQUE)**
**SUPERFICIE:** 30 513 kilomètres carrés
**NOMBRE D'HABITANTS:** 10 402 000 (les Belges)
**CAPITALE:** Bruxelles
**LANGUES OFFICIELLES:** le flamand *(Flemish)* (58%), le français (32%), l'allemand (1%). Neuf pour cent de la population est bilingue.
**INDUSTRIES PRINCIPALES:** industries métallurgiques, textiles et chimiques; verrerie *(glassworks);* agriculture; communications; commerce

# Un drôle de mystère

Quelqu'un a été assassiné et c'est à vous, le détective, de trouver le criminel. En même temps, vous allez faire une révision de ce que vous avez appris dans *Horizons*. Si vous avez des difficultés en faisant un exercice, référez-vous aux pages indiquées en marge *(in the margin)*.

**Les personnages**

**Un mystère dans les Ardennes**

**Épilogue**

 Video activities are on pages 416–419.

# La Belgique

Bruxelles, la capitale belge, est une ville bilingue. Dans la Région **flamande,** dans **le nord** du pays, on parle un dialecte **néerlandais,** le flamand. Dans la Région **wallonne,** dans **le sud,** on parle français. Dans **l'est,** un pour cent de la population parle allemand, la troisième langue officielle en Belgique.

La Grand-Place, Bruxelles, Belgique

Anvers est la plus grande ville de la Région flamande.

La Belgique est une monarchie parlementaire. L'opposition linguistique entre les Flamands et les Wallons est reflétée dans une opposition politique. Comme la majorité des Belges, le Premier ministre est généralement flamand. Pour certains Belges, **le roi ne** joue **aucun** rôle important dans le gouvernement, mais pour d'autres, sa présence assure le respect des **droits** de la minorité wallonne.

Liège est la plus grande ville wallonne.

---

**flamande** *Flemish*   **le nord** *the north*   **néerlandais** *Dutch*   **wallonne** *Walloon (French-speaking Belgian)*   **le sud** *the south*
**l'est** *the east*   **le roi** *the king*   **ne... aucun(e)** *not any, no*   **droits** *(m) rights*

**Siège de l'OTAN** (Organisation du traité de l'Atlantique Nord), la Belgique a été **un champ de bataille** pendant les deux **guerres mondiales.** Au cours de la Première Guerre mondiale, les Allemands ont occupé le pays pendant quatre ans et près d'un million de Belges se sont réfugiés en France, en Grande-Bretagne et aux **Pays-Bas.** L'histoire s'est répétée pendant la Seconde Guerre mondiale. Occupée **à partir de 1940,** la Belgique a été libérée par les Alliés en décembre 1944, **lors de la** célèbre **bataille des Ardennes** qui **a eu lieu** près de la ville de Bastogne. **Les villageois** de la région racontent que, dans une neige **qui leur arrivait jusqu'aux genoux,** les troupes américaines ont demandé aux **citoyens** belges de leur donner leurs **draps** pour servir de camouflage. Après la guerre, ces villages **ont reçu des paquets de** draps de la part du gouvernement américain. Cette coopération entre l'Amérique et la Belgique au cours de la guerre a continué jusqu'à **nos jours.**

Le musée militaire à Novion-Porcien, Ardennes

## À deviner

1. Quelles sont les trois langues officielles de la Belgique?
2. Quel pourcentage de la population belge parle chacune de ces langues?
3. Bruxelles, une ville bilingue, est la capitale du pays. Quelle est la plus grande ville francophone en Belgique après Bruxelles?
4. Quels sont les pays européens dont le français est la (ou une des) langue(s) officielle(s)?

---

**Siège de l'OTAN** *Seat of NATO*   **un champ de bataille** *a battlefield*   **guerres mondiales** *world wars*   **les Pays-Bas** *the Netherlands*   **à partir de 1940** *starting in 1940*   **lors de** *at the time of*   **la bataille des Ardennes** *the Battle of the Bulge*   **a eu lieu** *took place*   **Les villageois** *The villagers*   **qui leur arrivait jusqu'aux genoux** *that came up to their knees*   **citoyens** *citizens*   **draps** *bedsheets*   **ont reçu des paquets de** *received packages of*   **nos jours** *current time*

Dans ce chapitre, vous allez **résoudre** l'énigme d'un crime. C'est **un meurtre** qui **a lieu** dans un vieux château de la forêt des Ardennes, dans **le sud** de la Belgique. En résolvant le mystère, vous allez aussi réviser ce que vous avez appris dans ce livre. D'abord, faisons la connaissance des personnages de l'histoire.

Regardez les personnages suivants. Comment sont-ils?

François Fédor, millionnaire excentrique

Laurent Lavare, **le comptable** de François Fédor

Valérie Veutoux, l'ex-femme de François Fédor

Bernard Boncorps, le neveu de François Fédor

Nathalie Lanana, la petite amie de Bernard Boncorps

le/la domestique

le détective

Il y a encore un dernier petit détail. Le/La domestique sera joué(e) par votre professeur. Et le détective, qui est-ce? Oui, vous avez **deviné** juste (comme un bon détective); c'est vous!

---

**résoudre** *to resolve*   **un meurtre** *a murder*   **a lieu** *takes place*   **le sud** *the south*   **le comptable** *the accountant*
**deviné** *guessed*

**A. Descriptions.** Choisissez quatre adjectifs pour décrire chacun des personnages.

• Pour réviser l'accord des adjectifs, voir les pages 34, 40 et 48.

riche ??? malhonnête *(dishonest)* beau ???
âgé ??? snob bête paresseux laid blond
suspect méchant sympathique irresponsable
??? (mal)heureux désagréable sexy froid
hostile grand petit intelligent ???
sportif matérialiste frivole sérieux intéressant

**B. Explications.** Avec un(e) partenaire, devinez qui va être la victime et qui va commettre le crime. Imaginez une explication. Utilisez un dictionnaire si nécessaire.

• Pour réviser le futur immédiat, voir la page 156.

**C. Stratégies.** Vous avez appris plusieurs stratégies pour lire plus facilement en français. Avant de lire *Un mystère dans les Ardennes*, révisez les stratégies suivantes.

**a.** Utilisez les mots apparentés et le contexte pour donner le sens de ces phrases.

   **1.** L'aptitude de François Fédor à faire fortune était sans égal. Et on pouvait dire la même chose de son aptitude à se faire des ennemis.
   **2.** Dans le village, où il n'allait jamais, on l'appelait le vieux Midas parce qu'on disait que tout ce qu'il touchait se transformait en or.

**b.** Utilisez les mots entre parenthèses pour deviner le sens des mots en italique.

   **1.** (jeune) On disait que François Fédor avait fait fortune en Afrique pendant sa *jeunesse*.
   **2.** (attendre) Cette *attente* avait duré presque deux jours.

**c.** Vous avez appris à reconnaître la signification des temps composés. Comparez ces phrases.

| | | | |
|---|---|---|---|
| Je l'**ai** fait. | *I **have** done it.* | Il **est** parti. | *He **has** left.* |
| Je l'**avais** fait. | *I **had** done it.* | Il **était** parti. | *He **had** left.* |
| Je l'**aurai** fait. | *I **will have** done it.* | Il **sera** parti. | *He **will have** left.* |
| Je l'**aurais** fait. | *I **would have** done it.* | Il **serait** parti. | *He **would have** left.* |

Donnez les sens des expressions en italique dans les phrases suivantes.

**1.** François Fédor *avait toujours fait* ce qu'il voulait mais il *avait toujours négligé* (négliger *to neglect*) les membres de sa famille.
**2.** Ils acceptaient son argent chaque mois sans poser de questions et ils *n'auraient jamais pensé* que François Fédor puisse choisir un acte de charité plus méritoire *(deserving)*.
**3.** Si M. Lavare, le comptable, *n'avait pas été* là, on *n'aurait pas dit* quatre mots durant tout le dîner.

Maintenant, utilisez ces stratégies pour lire le dossier *(file)* sur ce cas aux pages suivantes.

CD 2-38 Certains l'admiraient, d'autres le détestaient. Il avait toujours fait ce qu'il voulait et **personne ne discutait** ce qu'il faisait. François Fédor habitait dans un vieux château **au fond de** la forêt des Ardennes. Dans le village, où il n'allait jamais, on l'appelait le vieux Midas parce qu'on disait que tout ce qu'il touchait se transformait en or. Personne ne savait exactement d'où venait sa fortune, mais on disait qu'il avait fait fortune en Afrique pendant sa jeunesse.

Son aptitude à faire fortune était sans égal. Et on pouvait dire la même chose de son aptitude à se faire des ennemis. François Fédor avait toujours négligé les membres de sa famille et il n'avait jamais pris le temps de se faire des amis. Quand je dis qu'il avait négligé les membres de sa famille, je ne veux pas donner l'impression qu'il ne partageait pas sa richesse avec **eux;** au contraire, ils ne **manquaient de** rien. Comme dans **un trou** noir, chaque mois, François Fédor **versait** une petite fortune sur **les comptes en banque** de son neveu Bernard Boncorps et de son ex-femme Valérie Veutoux. Il payait cet argent depuis vingt ans sans avoir **le moindre** contact avec l'un ou l'autre. En fait, il n'avait jamais rencontré son neveu, qui **vivait** une vie de play-boy à Monaco **grâce à** son vieil oncle. Et eux non plus, ils n'avaient jamais essayé de venir le voir. Ils acceptaient son argent chaque mois sans poser de questions et ils n'auraient jamais pensé que François Fédor puisse choisir un jour un acte de charité plus **méritoire.**

C'était donc avec grande surprise que son neveu et son ex-femme avaient reçu un coup de téléphone de Laurent Lavare, le comptable de François Fédor, quelques semaines **auparavant.** Ils étaient **priés de se rendre** chez le vieux Midas le dernier jour du mois **courant** avant midi. Chacun se demandait ce que le vieux Fédor pouvait bien vouloir après tout ce temps. Mais M. Lavare avait refusé de leur donner plus de détails. Quand ils étaient arrivés au grand château sombre, Valérie Veutoux, Bernard Boncorps et sa petite amie Nathalie Lanana s'étaient sentis un peu **mal à l'aise.** Après avoir passé deux journées entières dans le château sans voir leur hôte, les invités avaient senti leur **malaise** se transformer en panique. Mais que pouvaient-ils faire sinon accepter **les caprices** de leur **bienfaiteur** et chercher une manière de passer le temps? Quand Bernard n'était pas avec Nathalie, il jouait au billard pendant qu'elle nageait dans la piscine. Valérie Veutoux restait toute la journée dans sa chambre. Cette attente avait duré presque deux jours quand le/la domestique les avait enfin informés qu'ils verraient M. Fédor au dîner à huit heures, dans la salle à manger.

Accompagné de son comptable, François Fédor les attendait, assis à table, quand ils étaient descendus. Sans dire un mot, le vieil hôte leur avait indiqué d'un geste de la main où chacun devait **s'asseoir,** à l'autre bout de la table. Le/La domestique avait servi un excellent dîner mais les invités, qui n'avaient pas l'habitude d'apprécier ce

---

**personne ne discutait** *no one questioned*   **au fond de** *deep in*   **eux** *them*   **manquaient de** *lacked*   **un trou** *a hole*
**versait** *poured, deposited*   **les comptes en banque** *the bank accounts*   **le moindre** *the least*   **vivait** *lived*
**grâce à** *thanks to*   **méritoire** *deserving*   **auparavant** *beforehand*   **priés de se rendre** *requested to appear*
**courant** *current*   **mal à l'aise** *ill at ease*   **malaise** *uneasiness*   **les caprices** *the whims*   **bienfaiteur** *benefactor*
**s'asseoir** *to sit*

qu'on leur donnait, **n'**avaient fait **aucun** compliment. Ils étaient trop curieux de connaître la raison de cette réunion soudaine et **inattendue.** Si M. Lavare, le comptable, n'avait pas été là, on n'aurait pas dit quatre mots durant tout le dîner.

Le repas fini, François Fédor s'était retiré à la bibliothèque et il avait demandé au/à la domestique de faire entrer son neveu et son ex-femme l'un après l'autre pour boire un cognac avec lui… Il avait quelque chose d'important à leur dire. Ils avaient eu avec M. Fédor une conférence d'une demi-heure chacun, puis le/la domestique les avait raccompagnés à leur chambre et leur avait **souhaité** une bonne nuit. Devinaient-ils la scène qui les attendrait le lendemain matin en sortant de leur chambre? Savaient-ils qu'un détective voudrait leur parler et qu'ils seraient **soupçonnés** d'un meurtre? Au moins une personne présente cette nuit-là le savait. Mais qui était-ce?

Quand ils s'étaient levés, ils avaient appris que tôt le matin, le/la domestique avait téléphoné à la police pour dire que François Fédor avait été victime d'un meurtre au cours de la nuit. Qui avait **commis** ce crime? Quel était **le mobile** du meurtre? Pourquoi est-ce que François Fédor leur avait demandé de venir? Qu'est-ce qu'il leur avait dit dans la bibliothèque? Qu'est-ce que M. Lavare savait? Et le/la domestique? Qu'est-ce qui s'était passé ce soir-là?

C'est à vous de résoudre le mystère. Qu'est-ce que le célèbre inspecteur Maigret aurait fait à votre place? Vous allez sans doute vouloir poser beaucoup de questions et prendre des notes.

**D. Détails.** Lisez le texte *Un mystère dans les Ardennes* et répondez aux questions suivantes.

1. Où est-ce que François Fédor habitait?
2. D'où venait sa fortune?
3. Avait-il beaucoup d'amis?
4. Qui profitait aussi de son argent?
5. Qui a téléphoné à Bernard Boncorps et à Valérie Veutoux pour les inviter au château?
6. Combien de temps ont-ils dû attendre avant de voir François Fédor?
7. À votre avis *(opinion)*, qu'est-ce que François Fédor a dit à Bernard Boncorps et à Valérie Veutoux dans la bibliothèque?

Un château de la forêt des Ardennes

---

**ne... aucun** *no, not any*    **inattendue** *unexpected*    **souhaité** *wished*    **soupçonnés** *suspected*    **commis** *committed*
**le mobile** *the motive*

• Pour réviser l'imparfait, voir la page 234.

• Pour réviser comment dire l'heure, voir la page 12.

**E. Vous êtes le détective.** Pour commencer votre enquête *(investigation)*, CD 2-39 écoutez la déclaration de chacun des personnages qui a passé la nuit au château. En les écoutant, notez les réponses aux questions qui suivent sur une autre feuille de papier.

Bernard Boncorps    Valérie Veutoux    Laurent Lavare    le/la domestique

**1.** Qu'est-ce que chaque personne a fait après le dîner?
**2.** À quelle heure est-ce que chacun s'est couché?
**3.** Qu'est-ce que chacun a entendu dans le couloir pendant la nuit?

Écoutez une fois de plus les déclarations de Valérie Veutoux, de Laurent Lavare et de Bernard Boncorps et notez qui faisait chaque chose à l'heure indiquée.

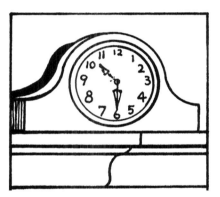

**Exemple**    être déjà au lit
**À dix heures et demie, Valérie Veutoux était déjà au lit.**

**1.** avoir mal à la tête
travailler sur
   l'ordinateur
être au village

**2.** prendre un verre au
   café
lire
parler au téléphone

**3.** jouer aux cartes
dormir

**F. Il a disparu.** Le corps de François Fédor a disparu *(disappeared)*. Vous devez bien examiner le lieu *(place)* du crime. Observez bien tous les indices *(clues)*. Voici la chambre de François Fédor avant le dîner et le lendemain du crime. Quelles différences y a-t-il?

• Pour réviser les prépositions, voir la page 116.

• Pour réviser les meubles, voir les pages 112 et 118.

avant le dîner

le lendemain du crime

Regardez encore une fois les deux dessins. Demandez au/à la domestique si chaque chose qui se trouve dans la chambre le lendemain du crime et qui n'était pas là la nuit précédente appartenait *(belonged)* à François Fédor. Dites à qui pourraient appartenir les choses qui n'étaient pas à lui.

• Pour réviser comment exprimer la possession, voir les pages 120 et 122.

> **Exemple** — **Est-ce que c'était son ordinateur?**
> — **Non, ce n'était pas l'ordinateur de M. Fédor.**
> — **Alors, c'est peut-être l'ordinateur de M. Lavare.**

• Pour réviser les prépositions, voir la page 116.

 CD 2-40

### G. Dans quelle chambre?
Tout le monde *(Everyone)* a dormi le long du même couloir hier soir. Écoutez le/la domestique pour déterminer qui a dormi dans chaque chambre.

**Exemple**  **Mme Veutoux était au bout du couloir, en face de la salle de bains.**

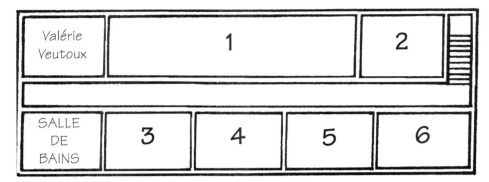

• Pour réviser les pronoms compléments d'objet direct et indirect, voir les pages 180, 358 et 364.

 CD 2-41

### H. Relations.
Utilisez le pronom **le** ou le pronom **lui** avec les verbes suivants à l'imparfait pour interroger le/la domestique sur ses relations avec M. Fédor. Écoutez ses réponses.

**Exemple**  connaître M. Fédor depuis longtemps
 — **Est-ce que vous le connaissiez depuis longtemps?**
 — **Je le connaissais depuis 15 ans.**

**1.** aimer bien M. Fédor
**2.** parler à M. Fédor de sa famille
**3.** emprunter quelquefois de l'argent à M. Fédor
**4.** réveiller M. Fédor à la même heure tous les jours
**5.** trouver M. Fédor sévère

CD 2-42

Maintenant demandez au/à la domestique si M. Fédor faisait les choses suivantes. Écoutez ses réponses.

**Exemple**  vous irriter quelquefois
 — **Est-ce que M. Fédor vous irritait quelquefois?**
 — **Oui, il m'irritait quelquefois. Ce n'était pas un homme facile.**

**1.** vous dire tout
**2.** vous payer bien
**3.** vous parler de sa vie privée

• Pour réviser le subjonctif, voir les pages 392-394, 398 et 400.

### I. Je ne veux pas que...
Dites aux suspects ce qu'ils doivent et ne doivent pas faire.

**Exemple**  **Je ne veux pas que vous partiez d'ici.**

Il faut que...
Il ne faut pas que...
Je veux que...
Je ne veux pas que...
Il vaut mieux que...

partir d'ici
dire tout ce que vous savez
être calmes
avoir peur
toucher aux affaires *(things)* de M. Fédor
faire une déposition
parler à la presse
m'obéir
être patients
???

**J. Savoir ou connaître?** Votre enquête *(investigation)* progresse. Dites si vous savez ou si vous connaissez les choses ou les personnes suivantes en utilisant le verbe **savoir** ou le verbe **connaître**.

• Pour réviser **savoir** et **connaître,** voir la page 356.

1. la date du crime
2. le/la domestique de M. Fédor
3. l'heure approximative du crime
4. le château de M. Fédor
5. tous les amis de M. Fédor
6. tous les détails de la vie de M. Fédor
7. des mobiles *(motives)* possibles
8. l'identité de l'assassin

**K. Il faut penser comme le/la criminel(le).** Pour attraper le/la criminel(le), il faut penser comme lui/elle. Si vous étiez le/la criminel(le), est-ce que vous feriez les choses suivantes? Utilisez le conditionnel.

• Pour réviser le conditionnel, voir les pages 330–331.

Si j'étais le/la criminel(le),...

**Exemple**    faire quelque chose d'inhabituel
**Si j'étais le/la criminel(le), je ne ferais rien d'inhabituel.**

1. être calme
2. parler beaucoup du crime
3. savoir tous les détails du crime
4. obéir à la police
5. s'intéresser beaucoup à l'enquête
6. dire la vérité *(truth)*
7. avoir envie de partir
8. devenir de plus en plus nerveux (nerveuse)
9. accuser quelqu'un d'autre
10. ???

**L. Une matinée typique.** Voici comment François Fédor passait ses matinées. Décrivez sa journée typique. Utilisez l'imparfait.

• Pour réviser les verbes réfléchis, voir les pages 266–267, 274 et 282.

• Pour réviser l'imparfait, voir la page 234.

• Pour réviser comment dire l'heure, voir la page 12.

1.

2.

3.

4.

5.

6.

• Pour réviser le passé composé et l'imparfait, voir les pages 240, 242 et 248.

**M. Accusations.** Dans le château Fédor, chacun des suspects vient vous expliquer pourquoi il/elle soupçonne *(suspects)* les autres. Complétez les paragraphes suivants en mettant les verbes entre parenthèses au passé composé ou à l'imparfait.

### BERNARD BONCORPS

Je crois que c'est Laurent Lavare, le comptable de mon oncle qui le (l') _____ (assassiner). Je (J') _____ (entendre) dire récemment qu'il _____ (avoir) des problèmes financiers. Certains disent qu'il _____ (emprunter *to borrow*) des millions d'euros à mon oncle sans le lui dire. En fait, un ami suisse qui travaille à la banque de mon oncle me (m') _____ (dire) qu'il y _____ (avoir) très peu d'argent sur son compte. Je pense que mon oncle _____ (apprendre) ce qui _____ (se passer) et je suis certain qu'il _____ (dire) à M. Lavare qu'il _____ (aller) le dénoncer à la police.

### VALÉRIE VEUTOUX

Il faut que vous sachiez que Bernard Boncorps _____ (être) furieux contre son oncle. François Fédor _____ (penser) que son neveu _____ (faire) des études de droit à l'université de Nice. En vérité, Bernard _____ (passer) tout son temps sur les plages et dans les casinos de Monaco. Quand son oncle _____ (comprendre) la situation, il _____ (se fâcher *to get angry*) et il _____ (dire) à son neveu qu'il _____ (vouloir) qu'il vienne finir ses études en Belgique, à l'université de Liège. Quand sa sœur, la mère de Bernard, _____ (mourir), elle lui _____ (demander) de se charger de l'éducation de son neveu. Bernard _____ (ne pas comprendre) pourquoi son oncle, qu'il n'avait jamais vu, _____ (s'intéresser) après tout ce temps à ce qu'il _____ (faire). Bernard _____ (ne pas vouloir) abandonner sa vie de play-boy sur la Côte d'Azur et il _____ (avoir) peur que sa petite amie, Nathalie Lanana, refuse de venir ici avec lui. Et puis, il faut ajouter aussi que Bernard _____ (avoir) des dettes énormes dans les casinos. Il _____ (ne pas pouvoir) payer ses dettes avec l'argent que son oncle lui _____ (donner) chaque mois. Bernard _____ (ne pas vouloir) attendre la mort naturelle de son oncle pour hériter de sa part de la fortune.

### LAURENT LAVARE

Je suis presque certain que Valérie Veutoux _____ (assassiner) François Fédor. Récemment, elle _____ (faire) la connaissance de Jean Jigaulaux, un jeune homme de 25 ans, et elle _____ (tomber) amoureuse de lui. Ils _____ (sortir) quelques mois ensemble, puis il lui _____ (demander) de l'épouser *(to marry)*. La vieille Veutoux _____ (ne pas comprendre) qu'il ne _____ (vouloir) que *(only)* son argent et le jeune Jigaulaux _____ (ne pas savoir) qu'elle ne recevrait plus un centime de François Fédor si elle _____ (se remarier). La vaniteuse Valérie Veutoux _____ (sans doute comprendre) qu'elle n'aurait jamais le joli Jigaulaux tant que *(as long as)* François Fédor _____ (être) en vie et elle _____ (se débarrasser *to get rid*) de lui.

• Pour réviser les pronoms compléments d'objet direct et indirect, **y** et **en,** voir les pages 150, 180, 324, 358 et 364.

Répondez aux questions suivantes au sujet des suspects. Utilisez un pronom dans chaque réponse pour remplacer les mots en italique.

Laurent Lavare

1. Qui a accusé *Laurent Lavare* du crime?
2. D'après son accusateur, est-ce que Laurent Lavare avait *des problèmes financiers?*
3. Disait-il *à François Fédor* qu'il lui empruntait de l'argent?
4. Combien empruntait-il *à François Fédor?*
5. D'après le banquier, ami de Bernard Boncorps, combien *d'argent* y avait-il sur le compte de son oncle?

Bernard Boncorps

1. Est-ce que Bernard Boncorps rendait souvent visite *à son oncle?*
2. Combien de fois est-ce que Bernard avait vu *son oncle?*
3. Est-ce que Bernard voulait aller *à Liège* pour finir ses études?
4. Combien de temps passait-il *sur les plages et dans les casinos?*
5. Est-ce qu'il avait *des dettes?*
6. Est-ce que Bernard avait assez *d'argent* pour payer *ses dettes?*

Valérie Veutoux

1. Qui pense que Valérie Veutoux a assassiné *François Fédor?*
2. Après combien de temps est-ce que Jean Jigaulaux a demandé *à Valérie Veutoux* de l'épouser?
3. Pourquoi est-ce que le jeune Jigaulaux aimait *la vieille Veutoux?*

**N. Qui est-ce?** Que savons-nous des suspects? Complétez les phrases suivantes avec **il est** ou **c'est.** Ensuite, dites si vous pensez que chaque phrase décrit plutôt Laurent Lavare ou Bernard Boncorps.

> • Pour réviser l'usage de **c'est** et **il/elle est,** voir les pages 34 et 48.

**Exemple**    **C'est** quelqu'un qui travaille beaucoup.
**C'est Laurent Lavare.**

1. _____ le neveu de François Fédor.
2. _____ comptable.
3. _____ suisse.
4. _____ jeune.
5. _____ un play-boy.
6. _____ peut-être l'assassin.

**O. Le dîner.** Complétez le paragraphe suivant avec l'article défini (**le, la, l', les**), l'article indéfini (**un, une, des**), le partitif (**du, de la, de l'**) ou **de.**

> • Pour réviser les produits alimentaires, voir les pages 88, 304–305, 314–315 et 322.
>
> • Pour réviser les articles, voir les pages 46, 52, 310 et 320.

_____ soir où M. Fédor est mort, M. Fédor et M. Lavare sont descendus vers sept heures et demie et ils ont pris _____ vin blanc avant de dîner. Pendant le repas, M. Fédor n'avait pas très faim; il a mangé _____ soupe et un peu _____ pain. Ensuite, il a pris _____ poulet et un peu _____ riz. Il n'a pas pris _____ légumes ni _____ tarte aux pommes. Il a pris un peu _____ fromage à la fin du repas. Normalement, il mangeait beaucoup. Il aimait bien _____ viande et _____ pommes de terre mais il ne prenait pas beaucoup _____ choses sucrées. Je pense qu'il n'avait pas _____ appétit ce soir-là, parce que ses problèmes le préoccupaient. Il n'a pas bu _____ vin rouge avec son repas, seulement _____ eau minérale et il a pris _____ café quand j'ai servi _____ dessert. Après _____ dîner, M. Fédor s'est retiré à _____ bibliothèque où il a bu un verre _____ cognac. Il est resté assis dans _____ fauteuil près de _____ porte pendant _____ heure après avoir parlé avec M. Boncorps et Mme Veutoux, puis il est monté se coucher.

Maintenant, dites si François Fédor a mangé ou a bu les choses suivantes le soir de son meurtre.

**Exemple**    **Il n'a pas mangé de pâté. Il a mangé de la soupe.**

• Pour réviser les pronoms relatifs, voir la page 288.

**P. Les gens du village.** Vous demandez aux gens du village ce qu'ils savaient au sujet de François Fédor. Faites des phrases en utilisant un élément de chaque colonne.

| | | |
|---|---|---|
| François Fédor était un homme... | qui...<br>que (qu')...<br>dont... | ne parlait pas beaucoup.<br>avait un passé mystérieux.<br>avait une personnalité un peu bizarre.<br>beaucoup de gens trouvaient difficile.<br>n'avait pas beaucoup d'amis.<br>je ne connaissais pas bien.<br>faisait toujours ce qu'il voulait.<br>tout le monde *(everyone)* avait un peu peur. |

• Pour réviser le passé composé et l'imparfait, voir les pages 240, 242 et 248.

**Q. Valérie se marie.** Vous avez demandé à des collègues d'observer les activités de chacun des suspects. Celui qui suit *(The one who is following)* Valérie Veutoux a rapporté ces photos prises le lendemain du crime. Vous lui demandez de vous raconter la journée de Valérie Veutoux mais ses notes sont en désordre. D'abord, remettez ses notes dans l'ordre; ensuite, racontez la journée de Valérie Veutoux en mettant les verbes au passé composé ou à l'imparfait.

**Exemple**    **Mme Veutoux est sortie de sa chambre à 8h20 du matin. Elle est descendue...**

- M. Jigaulaux *arrive* ici quelques heures après. Il *retrouve* Mme Veutoux dans la forêt à midi et ils *s'embrassent* passionnément.

- Comme M. Jigaulaux *est* fatigué, il *prend* une chambre à l'hôtel du village, où il *passe* l'après-midi.

- Mme Veutoux *sort* de sa chambre à 8h20 du matin. Elle *descend* au rez-de-chaussée et elle *téléphone* à M. Jigaulaux au Luxembourg. Ensuite, elle *téléphone* à une agence de voyages à Bruxelles.

- Ils *quittent* le restaurant à 20h50. À ce moment-là, un chien m'*attaque* dans les rosiers derrière lesquels je m'étais caché et je les *perds* de vue.

- À 17h00, M. Jigaulaux et Mme Veutoux *se retrouvent* devant l'hôtel, ils *montent* dans la voiture de M. Jigaulaux et *vont* dans le village voisin où ils *se marient* en secret à 18h20.

- Après la cérémonie, ils *dînent* au restaurant du village. À part le serveur, ils *sont* seuls dans le restaurant.

- Pendant le dîner, je les *observe* de l'extérieur. M. Jigaulaux ne *parle* pas beaucoup mais Mme Veutoux lui *explique* quelque chose.

**R. Réactions.** Valérie Veutoux est furieuse. Imaginez sa réaction quand vous lui dites les choses suivantes.

• Pour réviser le subjonctif, voir les pages 392-394, 398 et 400.

Il est bon que...          Il est nécessaire que...
Il est impossible que...   Il est important que...
Il est ridicule que...     Il est essentiel que...

**Exemple**    Vous ne pouvez pas partir pour quelques jours.
               **Il est ridicule que je ne puisse pas partir.**

1. Oui madame, vous êtes suspecte.
2. Nous ne savons pas où se trouve le corps de la victime.
3. M. Lavare dit que vous aviez des raisons d'assassiner M. Fédor.
4. Nous savons que vous avez retrouvé M. Jigaulaux dans la forêt.
5. Nous avons des photos de M. Jigaulaux avec vous.
6. Je veux lui parler demain.
7. Il pourra partir après l'interrogatoire.
8. Vous devez tout nous expliquer.

CD 2-43

**S. Deux billets pour Tahiti.** Pendant l'enquête, vous apprenez que François Fédor enregistrait *(recorded)* toutes les conversations téléphoniques chez lui. Vous découvrez que Valérie Veutoux a téléphoné à une agence de voyages à Bruxelles le lendemain du crime. Écoutez la conversation entre Valérie Veutoux et l'agent de voyages. Sur une autre feuille de papier, complétez les détails qui manquent sur l'itinéraire de Valérie ci-dessous.

• Pour réviser comment acheter un billet d'avion, voir la page 354.

> **ITINÉRAIRE**
>
> **À l'intention de:** _(Nom)_ et de _(Nom)_
>
> **ALLER**                     **Air France—Vol** _(Numéro)_
> _(Date)_
> **Départ de Bruxelles** _(Heure)_    **Boeing 747**
>                                **Première classe/Vol direct**
>
> _(Date)_
> **Arrivée à Tahiti**    _(Heure)_
>
>                                **Prix du billet:** _(Prix)_
>                                **Total des deux billets:** _(Prix)_
>
> **Prévoyez d'arriver à l'aéroport deux heures avant l'heure de départ.**
>
>                   **BON VOYAGE!**

On parle français à Tahiti.

• Pour réviser le futur, voir la page 350.

• Pour réviser l'impératif, voir les pages 152 et 404.

## T. Une conversation téléphonique.

Voici une transcription de la conversation téléphonique entre Valérie Veutoux et son amant *(lover),* Jean Jigaulaux, le lendemain du crime. La première partie a été effacée *(erased)* accidentellement. Complétez ce qui reste en mettant les verbes entre parenthèses au futur ou à l'impératif.

— ... Après cela, François ne _____ (faire) plus obstacle à notre bonheur *(happiness)*. Nous _____ (pouvoir) nous marier quand tu _____ (vouloir).

— Je _____ (venir) aujourd'hui et nous _____ (se marier) ce soir. Je vais partir tout de suite et j' _____ (arriver) un peu avant midi.

— À deux kilomètres d'ici, il y a une vieille école abandonnée. _____ (Tourner) à gauche juste après cette école et _____ (entrer) dans la forêt. Là, personne ne nous _____ (voir). Je t' _____ (attendre) à cet endroit à midi.

— On _____ (être) heureux ensemble.

— Après-demain, nous _____ (partir) pour Tahiti et nous _____ (commencer) notre nouvelle vie ensemble.

• Pour réviser les chiffres, voir les pages 10, 90 et 108.

• Pour réviser les dates, voir la page 158.

## U. Le compte en banque.

Quand vous comparez les relevés de compte *(bank statements)* de François Fédor, vous remarquez que quelqu'un avait retiré presque tout son argent ces derniers mois. Combien d'argent est-ce qu'il y avait aux dates suivantes de l'année dernière et de cette année?

**Exemple** 30/9  20 789 067 euros

**Le 30 septembre de l'année dernière, il y avait 20 789 067 euros sur son compte.**

1. 15/10      16 136 978 euros
2. 10/11      12 194 456 euros
3. 24/12       8 714 387 euros
4.  1/1       1 000 090 euros
5. 15/2          90 506 euros
6.  4/3          11 871 euros

• Pour réviser comment poser une question, voir les pages 42, 84 et 86.

## V. Une vidéo révélatrice.

Vous venez de découvrir qu'une caméra de sécurité cachée dans le couloir filmait chaque personne qui entrait dans la chambre de François Fédor. Entre 20h et 8h du matin, la caméra a enregistré une seule personne qui est entrée dans la chambre de la victime. La caméra s'est arrêtée à 8h30 le lendemain matin. Préparez cinq questions que vous voudriez poser à Valérie Veutoux.

pourquoi   ???   à quelle heure   combien de temps
comment   ???   que   quand   qui   où

**W. La dernière volonté de François.** Vous avez interrogé Valérie Veutoux et elle a répondu que François Fédor n'était pas fâché *(upset)* qu'elle ait un amant, mais, qu'au contraire, il l'avait encouragée à l'épouser *(to marry him)*. Elle vous raconte ce que François Fédor lui a dit. Est-ce qu'il voulait qu'elle fasse les choses suivantes ou est-ce qu'il voulait les faire lui-même *(himself)*?

• Pour réviser l'usage de l'infinitif ou du subjonctif, voir la page 400.

**Exemples**   se marier avec Jean Jigaulaux
**Il voulait que je me marie avec Jean Jigaulaux.**

nous offrir un cadeau de mariage
**Il voulait nous offrir un cadeau de mariage.**

1. tout savoir sur Jean Jigaulaux
2. dire à Jean Jigaulaux de venir ici
3. se marier tout de suite
4. nous offrir un voyage de noces *(honeymoon trip)*
5. téléphoner pour réserver le billet pour Tahiti le lendemain
6. partir pour Tahiti cette semaine
7. être heureuse
8. venir dans sa chambre après le dîner prendre l'argent pour payer le voyage

CD 2-44

**X. Que faisait le/la domestique?** Reformulez les questions suivantes avec l'inversion et posez-les au/à la domestique. Ensuite, écoutez ses réponses.

• Pour réviser l'inversion, voir la page 86.

1. À quelle heure est-ce que vous vous êtes levé(e) le lendemain du crime?
2. Qu'est-ce que vous avez fait après?
3. Est-ce que les autres invités dormaient encore dans le château?
4. Quand est-ce que vous avez découvert *(discover)* que François Fédor était mort?
5. Est-ce que vous avez été surpris(e)?
6. Pourquoi est-ce que vous n'avez pas crié *(scream)*?
7. Est-ce que vous avez réveillé quelqu'un pour vous aider?
8. Vous avez téléphoné à la police à 8h12. À quelle heure est-ce que vous êtes entré(e) dans la chambre?
9. Combien de portes est-ce qu'il y a pour entrer dans la chambre de la victime?
10. Pourquoi est-ce que vous ne dites pas la vérité *(truth)*?
11. Ne faites pas l'innocent(e)! Comment est-ce que vous saviez que François Fédor était mort sans entrer dans sa chambre?
12. Pourquoi est-ce que vous n'êtes pas sur la vidéo de sécurité?
13. Pourquoi est-ce que la vidéo s'arrête à 8h30?
14. Alors, est-ce que vous voulez dire que François Fédor n'est pas mort?

• Pour réviser le passé composé et l'imparfait, voir les pages 240, 242 et 248.

**Y. Une confession.** Le/La domestique confesse que François Fédor n'est pas mort. En lisant sa confession, mettez les verbes entre parenthèses au passé composé ou à l'imparfait.

Je ___1___ (ne pas vouloir) le faire mais c' ___2___ (être) la seule manière! C' ___3___ (être) la seule manière de sauver le château. M. Fédor m' ___4___ (expliquer) que M. Lavare ___5___ (venir) de l'informer qu'il avait tout perdu. Il avait tout investi dans une société qui avait fait faillite *(had gone bankrupt)*. Il ___6___ (devoir) vendre le château pour payer les créanciers. «Mais, non», je lui ___7___ (dire). Il ___8___ (savoir) que je (j') ___9___ (adorer) ce château et que je ferais tout pour ne pas le perdre. Je ___10___ (naître) pas loin d'ici. Quand je (j') ___11___ (être) jeune, je (j') ___12___ (rêver) d'habiter ici un jour et je (j') ___13___ (inventer) des histoires fantastiques qui ___14___ (avoir) lieu *(to take place)* ici. Mais toutes ces histoires-là ___15___ (finir) toujours bien. Puis, M. Fédor ___16___ (suggérer) qu'il y ___17___ (avoir) peut-être un moyen de garder le château et que, si on ___18___ (réussir), il me le donnerait. Le château serait à moi pour toujours. C'est alors qu'il me (m') ___19___ (révéler) son plan. Il prendrait une assurance vie de 10 000 000 d'euros et j'en serais le/la bénéficiaire.

M. Fédor ___20___ (ne jamais le dire), mais je (j') ___21___ (avoir) l'impression que c' ___22___ (être) M. Lavare qui avait inventé ce plan. Je sais que M. Lavare avait dit à M. Fédor que Mme Veutoux avait pris ce M. Jigaulaux comme amant. Cela ___23___ (rendre) M. Fédor furieux. Chaque fois que M. Fédor ___24___ (parler) de son ex-femme avec M. Lavare, l'un ___25___ (devenir) tout rouge et l'autre tout pâle. La vérité, c'est que c' ___26___ (être) elle qui avait quitté M. Fédor il y a 15 ans et pas le contraire, comme tout le monde le disait. Il ___27___ (ne jamais lui pardonner) et il ___28___ (toujours vouloir) contrôler sa vie. Il ___29___ (ne pas être) obligé de lui donner cet argent depuis le divorce, mais M. Lavare l'avait persuadé de continuer à lui en donner beaucoup. Il ___30___ (dire) à M. Fédor que si Mme Veutoux ___31___ (dépendre) de lui financièrement, il pourrait contrôler sa vie. M. Fédor me (m') ___32___ (dire) que M. Lavare inviterait M. Boncorps et Mme Veutoux à la maison. M. Fédor expliquerait à son neveu qu'il ___33___ (ne plus pouvoir) lui donner d'argent. Mais il dirait à Mme Veutoux qu'il ___34___ (vouloir) qu'elle soit heureuse et qu'il ___35___ (avoir) l'intention de lui offrir un voyage à Tahiti pour sa lune de miel *(honeymoon)* si elle ___36___ (se marier) tout de suite.

D'après le plan, tout le monde *(everyone)* penserait que Mme Veutoux avait assassiné M. Fédor et qu'elle était partie pour Tahiti. On la verrait sur la vidéo entrer dans sa chambre la nuit du meurtre et on penserait qu'elle l'avait assassiné pour pouvoir se marier avec son jeune amant. Mais en réalité, on assassinerait Mme Veutoux et on laisserait *(would leave)* son corps au fond de la forêt. M. Fédor s'habillerait comme elle et il partirait pour Tahiti à sa place. À l'aéroport de Bruxelles, on verrait Mme Veutoux partir pour Tahiti et personne ne saurait que c' ___37___ (être) elle la vraie victime. On accuserait Mme Veutoux de s'être échappée *(of having escaped)* après le meurtre de M. Fédor et on ne la reverrait plus. M. Fédor me laisserait le château et après quelques mois, je mettrais les 10 000 000 d'euros d'assurance sur un compte secret pour M. Fédor.

*À ce moment-là, pendant la confession, un policier ___38___ (entrer) et il ___39___ (annoncer) que des chasseurs* (hunters) *avaient trouvé le corps d'une femme morte dans la forêt et qu'ils avaient donné la description de Mme Veutoux.*

CD 2-45 Vous pensez probablement avoir compris le mystère du meurtre de François Fédor. Vous pensez que le/la domestique va être **arrêté(e)** et que le vieux Midas est parti vivre sur une île tropicale. Mais êtes-vous certain(e) d'avoir trouvé les vrais criminels? Ah! Les voilà **en croisière** quelque part dans l'océan Pacifique. Écoutons un peu leur conversation.

— Quel coup! Tu es **un** vrai **génie,** mon chéri. Qui aurait pensé que nous pourrions réussir! **Tout le monde** pense que je suis morte et que François est l'assassin. Après toutes ces années, nous allons enfin pouvoir vivre ensemble **sans nous préoccuper de** ce vieux tyran. **Je me souviens de** la première fois que je t'ai vu quand tu as commencé à travailler pour lui! Quel coup de foudre! Et le pauvre François! Il n'avait aucune idée que je l'ai quitté parce que nous étions amants.

— Je trouve toujours **incroyable** qu'il ait investi toute sa fortune dans cette société qui n'existait pas. Il avait tellement confiance en moi! Ha ha ha!

— Mais pourquoi pas? Le vrai vieux Midas, c'était toi. Tu avais multiplié dix fois sa fortune. Sans toi, cet imbécile aurait perdu tout son argent longtemps avant! Mais maintenant, toute cette fortune est à nous! S'il avait su que tous ces **créanciers** que tu payais n'étaient personne d'autre que moi, son ex-femme! Ha ha ha! Qu'est-ce que tu as fait de son corps?

— Il était vraiment surpris quand, **au lieu de l'amener à** l'aéroport de Bruxelles, nous sommes allés au fond des Ardennes! Quand je lui ai expliqué que toi et moi, nous étions amants depuis le début, j'ai pensé pendant un moment que je n'aurais pas besoin de l'assassiner. Le pauvre, **il a failli avoir** une attaque! Et il était très comique, habillé comme toi.

— Quel dommage que nous n'ayons pas de photos! J'aurais aimé voir ça! Ha ha ha! Mais qu'est-ce qu'on dira si on trouve son corps?

— On pensera sans doute que c'est le/la domestique qui l'a assassiné pour ces 10 000 000 d'euros d'assurance!

— Mais il y a un dernier détail que je ne comprends pas. Comment est-ce que tu as persuadé ton jeune associé de jouer le rôle de Jean Jigaulaux? Il a si bien joué! Pendant un moment, j'ai vraiment eu l'impression que j'allais me marier avec lui.

— Ce jeune homme était tellement ambitieux qu'il aurait fait **n'importe quoi** pour avoir ma clientèle. Je lui ai promis de lui laisser tous mes clients, mais il ne savait pas que je n'en avais qu'un seul, et que c'était François Fédor.

— Ça, c'est trop! Tu es cruel... vicieux! C'est pour ça que je t'aime! Ha ha ha!

Naturellement Valérie Veutoux et Laurent Lavare ont dû changer de noms. Si on vous les présente aujourd'hui, vous ferez la connaissance d'Anabelle Atout et de son mari Richard!

---

**arrêté(e)** *arrested*　**en croisière** *on a cruise*　**un génie** *a genius*　**Tout le monde** *Everyone*
**sans nous préoccuper de** *without worrying about*　**Je me souviens de** *I remember*　**incroyable** *unbelievable*
**créanciers** *creditors*　**au lieu de l'amener à** *instead of taking him to*　**il a failli avoir** *he almost had*　**n'importe quoi** *anything*

# Appendice A

## L'ALPHABET PHONÉTIQUE

### Voyelles

[a] madame      [i] qui      [œ] sœur

[e] thé      [o] eau      [u] vous

[ɛ] être      [ɔ] porte      [y] sur

[ə] que      [ø] peu

### Semivoyelles

[j] bien      [ɥ] puis      [w] oui

### Voyelles nasales

[ɑ̃] quand      [ɛ̃] vin      [ɔ̃] non

### Consonnes

[b] bleu      [l] lire      [s] sur

[d] dormir      [m] marron      [ʃ] chat

[f] faire      [n] nouveau      [t] triste

[g] gris      [ɲ] enseigner      [v] vers

[ʒ] jaune      [p] parler      [z] rose

[k] quand      [ʀ] rester

# Appendice B

## TABLEAU DES VERBES

### Verbes auxiliaires

| VERBE INFINITIF | PRÉSENT | PASSÉ COMPOSÉ | IMPARFAIT | FUTUR | CONDITIONNEL PRÉSENT | SUBJONCTIF PRÉSENT | IMPÉRATIF |
|---|---|---|---|---|---|---|---|
| | | INDICATIF | | | | | |
| **avoir** | ai | ai eu | avais | aurai | aurais | aie | |
| *to have* | as | as eu | avais | auras | aurais | aies | aie |
| | a | a eu | avait | aura | aurait | ait | |
| | avons | avons eu | avions | aurons | aurions | ayons | ayons |
| | avez | avez eu | aviez | aurez | auriez | ayez | ayez |
| | ont | ont eu | avaient | auront | auraient | aient | |
| **être** | suis | ai été | étais | serai | serais | sois | |
| *to be* | es | as été | étais | seras | serais | sois | sois |
| | est | a été | était | sera | serait | soit | |
| | sommes | avons été | étions | serons | serions | soyons | soyons |
| | êtes | avez été | étiez | serez | seriez | soyez | soyez |
| | sont | ont été | étaient | seront | seraient | soient | |

### Verbes réguliers

| VERBE INFINITIF | PRÉSENT | PASSÉ COMPOSÉ | IMPARFAIT | FUTUR | CONDITIONNEL PRÉSENT | SUBJONCTIF PRÉSENT | IMPÉRATIF |
|---|---|---|---|---|---|---|---|
| | | INDICATIF | | | | | |
| **-er** verbs | | | | | | | |
| **parler** | parle | ai parlé | parlais | parlerai | parlerais | parle | |
| *to talk,* | parles | as parlé | parlais | parleras | parlerais | parles | parle |
| *to speak* | parle | a parlé | parlait | parlera | parlerait | parle | |
| | parlons | avons parlé | parlions | parlerons | parlerions | parlions | parlons |
| | parlez | avez parlé | parliez | parlerez | parleriez | parliez | parlez |
| | parlent | ont parlé | parlaient | parleront | parleraient | parlent | |
| **-ir** verbs | | | | | | | |
| **finir** | finis | ai fini | finissais | finirai | finirais | finisse | |
| *to finish* | finis | as fini | finissais | finiras | finirais | finisses | finis |
| | finit | a fini | finissait | finira | finirait | finisse | |
| | finissons | avons fini | finissions | finirons | finirions | finissions | finissons |
| | finissez | avez fini | finissiez | finirez | finiriez | finissiez | finissez |
| | finissent | ont fini | finissaient | finiront | finiraient | finissent | |
| **-re** verbs | | | | | | | |
| **vendre** | vends | ai vendu | vendais | vendrai | vendrais | vende | |
| *to sell* | vends | as vendu | vendais | vendras | vendrais | vendes | vends |
| | vend | a vendu | vendait | vendra | vendrait | vende | |
| | vendons | avons vendu | vendions | vendrons | vendrions | vendions | vendons |
| | vendez | avez vendu | vendiez | vendrez | vendriez | vendiez | vendez |
| | vendent | ont vendu | vendaient | vendront | vendraient | vendent | |

## Verbes réfléchis

| VERBE INFINITIF | INDICATIF PRÉSENT | PASSÉ COMPOSÉ | IMPARFAIT | FUTUR | CONDITIONNEL PRÉSENT | SUBJONCTIF PRÉSENT | IMPÉRATIF |
|---|---|---|---|---|---|---|---|
| **se laver** *to wash oneself* | me lave | me suis lavé(e) | me lavais | me laverai | me laverais | me lave | |
| | te laves | t'es lavé(e) | te lavais | te laveras | te laverais | te laves | lave-toi |
| | se lave | s'est lavé(e) | se lavait | se lavera | se laverait | se lave | |
| | nous lavons | nous sommes lavé(e)s | nous lavions | nous laverons | nous laverions | nous lavions | lavons-nous |
| | vous lavez | vous êtes lavé(e)(s) | vous laviez | vous laverez | vous laveriez | vous laviez | lavez-vous |
| | se lavent | se sont lavé(e)s | se lavaient | se laveront | se laveraient | se lavent | |

## Verbes à changements orthographiques

| VERBE INFINITIF | INDICATIF PRÉSENT | PASSÉ COMPOSÉ | IMPARFAIT | FUTUR | CONDITIONNEL PRÉSENT | SUBJONCTIF PRÉSENT | IMPÉRATIF |
|---|---|---|---|---|---|---|---|
| **préférer** *to prefer* | préfère | ai préféré | préférais | préférerai | préférerais | préfère | |
| | préfères | as préféré | préférais | préféreras | préférerais | préfères | préfère |
| | préfère | a préféré | préférait | préférera | préférerait | préfère | |
| | préférons | avons préféré | préférions | préférerons | préférerions | préférions | préférons |
| | préférez | avez préféré | préfériez | préférerez | préféreriez | préfériez | préférez |
| | préfèrent | ont préféré | préféraient | préféreront | préféreraient | préfèrent | |
| **acheter** *to buy* | achète | ai acheté | achetais | achèterai | achèterais | achète | |
| | achètes | as acheté | achetais | achèteras | achèterais | achètes | achète |
| | achète | a acheté | achetait | achètera | achèterait | achète | |
| | achetons | avons acheté | achetions | achèterons | achèterions | achetions | achetons |
| | achetez | avez acheté | achetiez | achèterez | achèteriez | achetiez | achetez |
| | achètent | ont acheté | achetaient | achèteront | achèteraient | achètent | |
| **appeler** *to call* | appelle | ai appelé | appelais | appellerai | appellerais | appelle | |
| | appelles | as appelé | appelais | appelleras | appellerais | appelles | appelle |
| | appelle | a appelé | appelait | appellera | appellerait | appelle | |
| | appelons | avons appelé | appelions | appellerons | appellerions | appelions | appelons |
| | appelez | avez appelé | appeliez | appellerez | appelleriez | appeliez | appelez |
| | appellent | ont appelé | appelaient | appelleront | appelleraient | appellent | |
| **essayer** *to try* | essaie | ai essayé | essayais | essaierai | essaierais | essaie | |
| | essaies | as essayé | essayais | essaieras | essaierais | essaies | essaie |
| | essaie | a essayé | essayait | essaiera | essaierait | essaie | |
| | essayons | avons essayé | essayions | essaierons | essaierions | essayions | essayons |
| | essayez | avez essayé | essayiez | essaierez | essaieriez | essayiez | essayez |
| | essaient | ont essayé | essayaient | essaieront | essaieraient | essaient | |
| **manger** *to eat* | mange | ai mangé | mangeais | mangerai | mangerais | mange | |
| | manges | as mangé | mangeais | mangeras | mangerais | manges | mange |
| | mange | a mangé | mangeait | mangera | mangerait | mange | |
| | mangeons | avons mangé | mangions | mangerons | mangerions | mangions | mangeons |
| | mangez | avez mangé | mangiez | mangerez | mangeriez | mangiez | mangez |
| | mangent | ont mangé | mangeaient | mangeront | mangeraient | mangent | |
| **commencer** *to begin* | commence | ai commencé | commençais | commencerai | commencerais | commence | |
| | commences | as commencé | commençais | commenceras | commencerais | commences | commence |
| | commence | a commencé | commençait | commencera | commencerait | commence | |
| | commençons | avons commencé | commencions | commencerons | commencerions | commencions | commençons |
| | commencez | avez commencé | commenciez | commencerez | commenceriez | commenciez | commencez |
| | commencent | ont commencé | commençaient | commenceront | commenceraient | commencent | |

# Verbes irréguliers

| VERBE INFINITIF | INDICATIF PRÉSENT | PASSÉ COMPOSÉ | IMPARFAIT | FUTUR | CONDITIONNEL PRÉSENT | SUBJONCTIF PRÉSENT | IMPÉRATIF |
|---|---|---|---|---|---|---|---|
| **aller** *to go* | vais | suis allé(e) | allais | irai | irais | aille | |
| | vas | es allé(e) | allais | iras | irais | ailles | va |
| | va | est allé(e) | allait | ira | irait | aille | |
| | allons | sommes allé(e)s | allions | irons | irions | allions | allons |
| | allez | êtes allé(e)(s) | alliez | irez | iriez | alliez | allez |
| | vont | sont allé(e)s | allaient | iront | iraient | aillent | |
| **s'asseoir** *to sit (down)* | m'assieds | me suis assis(e) | m'asseyais | m'assiérai | m'assiérais | m'asseye | |
| | t'assieds | t'es assis(e) | t'asseyais | t'assiéras | t'assiérais | t'asseyes | assieds-toi |
| | s'assied | s'est assis(e) | s'asseyait | s'assiéra | s'assiérait | s'asseye | |
| | nous asseyons | nous sommes assis(es) | nous asseyions | nous assiérons | nous assiérions | nous asseyions | asseyons-nous |
| | vous asseyez | vous êtes assis(es) | vous asseyiez | vous assiérez | vous assiériez | vous asseyiez | asseyez-vous |
| | s'asseyent | se sont assis(es) | s'asseyaient | s'assiéront | s'assiéraient | s'asseyent | |
| **battre** *to beat* | bats | ai battu | battais | battrai | battrais | batte | |
| | bats | as battu | battais | battras | battrais | battes | bats |
| | bat | a battu | battait | battra | battrait | batte | |
| | battons | avons battu | battions | battrons | battrions | battions | battons |
| | battez | avez battu | battiez | battrez | battriez | battiez | battez |
| | battent | ont battu | battaient | battront | battraient | battent | |
| **boire** *to drink* | bois | ai bu | buvais | boirai | boirais | boive | |
| | bois | as bu | buvais | boiras | boirais | boives | bois |
| | boit | a bu | buvait | boira | boirait | boive | |
| | buvons | avons bu | buvions | boirons | boirions | buvions | buvons |
| | buvez | avez bu | buviez | boirez | boiriez | buviez | buvez |
| | boivent | ont bu | buvaient | boiront | boiraient | boivent | |
| **conduire** *to drive* | conduis | ai conduit | conduisais | conduirai | conduirais | conduise | |
| | conduis | as conduit | conduisais | conduiras | conduirais | conduises | conduis |
| | conduit | a conduit | conduisait | conduira | conduirait | conduise | |
| | conduisons | avons conduit | conduisions | conduirons | conduirions | conduisions | conduisons |
| | conduisez | avez conduit | conduisiez | conduirez | conduiriez | conduisiez | conduisez |
| | conduisent | ont conduit | conduisaient | conduiront | conduiraient | conduisent | |
| **connaître** *to be acquainted with, to know* | connais | ai connu | connaissais | connaîtrai | connaîtrais | connaisse | |
| | connais | as connu | connaissais | connaîtras | connaîtrais | connaisses | connais |
| | connaît | a connu | connaissait | connaîtra | connaîtrait | connaisse | |
| | connaissons | avons connu | connaissions | connaîtrons | connaîtrions | connaissions | connaissons |
| | connaissez | avez connu | connaissiez | connaîtrez | connaîtriez | connaissiez | connaissez |
| | connaissent | ont connu | connaissaient | connaîtront | connaîtraient | connaissent | |
| **courir** *to run* | cours | ai couru | courais | courrai | courrais | coure | |
| | cours | as couru | courais | courras | courrais | coures | cours |
| | court | a couru | courait | courra | courrait | coure | |
| | courons | avons couru | courions | courrons | courrions | courions | courons |
| | courez | avez couru | couriez | courrez | courriez | couriez | courez |
| | courent | ont couru | couraient | courront | courraient | courent | |
| **croire** *to believe* | crois | ai cru | croyais | croirai | croirais | croie | |
| | crois | as cru | croyais | croiras | croirais | croies | crois |
| | croit | a cru | croyait | croira | croirait | croie | |
| | croyons | avons cru | croyions | croirons | croirions | croyions | croyons |
| | croyez | avez cru | croyiez | croirez | croiriez | croyiez | croyez |
| | croient | ont cru | croyaient | croiront | croiraient | croient | |

## Verbes irréguliers (suite)

| VERBE INFINITIF | INDICATIF PRÉSENT | PASSÉ COMPOSÉ | IMPARFAIT | FUTUR | CONDITIONNEL PRÉSENT | SUBJONCTIF PRÉSENT | IMPÉRATIF |
|---|---|---|---|---|---|---|---|
| **devoir** | dois | ai dû | devais | devrai | devrais | doive | |
| *must,* | dois | as dû | devais | devras | devrais | doives | |
| *to have to,* | doit | a dû | devait | devra | devrait | doive | |
| *to owe* | devons | avons dû | devions | devrons | devrions | devions | |
| | devez | avez dû | deviez | devrez | devriez | deviez | |
| | doivent | ont dû | devaient | devront | devraient | doivent | |
| **dire** | dis | ai dit | disais | dirai | dirais | dise | |
| *to say,* | dis | as dit | disais | diras | dirais | dises | dis |
| *to tell* | dit | a dit | disait | dira | dirait | dise | |
| | disons | avons dit | disions | dirons | dirions | disions | disons |
| | dites | avez dit | disiez | direz | diriez | disiez | dites |
| | disent | ont dit | disaient | diront | diraient | disent | |
| **dormir** | dors | ai dormi | dormais | dormirai | dormirais | dorme | |
| *to sleep* | dors | as dormi | dormais | dormiras | dormirais | dormes | dors |
| | dort | a dormi | dormait | dormira | dormirait | dorme | |
| | dormons | avons dormi | dormions | dormirons | dormirions | dormions | dormons |
| | dormez | avez dormi | dormiez | dormirez | dormiriez | dormiez | dormez |
| | dorment | ont dormi | dormaient | dormiront | dormiraient | dorment | |
| **écrire** | écris | ai écrit | écrivais | écrirai | écrirais | écrive | |
| *to write* | écris | as écrit | écrivais | écriras | écrirais | écrives | écris |
| | écrit | a écrit | écrivait | écrira | écrirait | écrive | |
| | écrivons | avons écrit | écrivions | écrirons | écririons | écrivions | écrivons |
| | écrivez | avez écrit | écriviez | écrirez | écririez | écriviez | écrivez |
| | écrivent | ont écrit | écrivaient | écriront | écriraient | écrivent | |
| **envoyer** | envoie | ai envoyé | envoyais | enverrai | enverrais | envoie | |
| *to send* | envoies | as envoyé | envoyais | enverras | enverrais | envoies | envoie |
| | envoie | a envoyé | envoyait | enverra | enverrait | envoie | |
| | envoyons | avons envoyé | envoyions | enverrons | enverrions | envoyions | envoyons |
| | envoyez | avez envoyé | envoyiez | enverrez | enverriez | envoyiez | envoyez |
| | envoient | ont envoyé | envoyaient | enverront | enverraient | envoient | |
| **faire** | fais | ai fait | faisais | ferai | ferais | fasse | |
| *to do,* | fais | as fait | faisais | feras | ferais | fasses | fais |
| *to make* | fait | a fait | faisait | fera | ferait | fasse | |
| | faisons | avons fait | faisions | ferons | ferions | fassions | faisons |
| | faites | avez fait | faisiez | ferez | feriez | fassiez | faites |
| | font | ont fait | faisaient | feront | feraient | fassent | |
| **falloir** | faut | a fallu | fallait | faudra | faudrait | faille | |
| *to be necessary* | | | | | | | |
| **lire** | lis | ai lu | lisais | lirai | lirais | lise | |
| *to read* | lis | as lu | lisais | liras | lirais | lises | lis |
| | lit | a lu | lisait | lira | lirait | lise | |
| | lisons | avons lu | lisions | lirons | lirions | lisions | lisons |
| | lisez | avez lu | lisiez | lirez | liriez | lisiez | lisez |
| | lisent | ont lu | lisaient | liront | liraient | lisent | |
| **mettre** | mets | ai mis | mettais | mettrai | mettrais | mette | |
| *to put,* | mets | as mis | mettais | mettras | mettrais | mettes | mets |
| *to place,* | met | a mis | mettait | mettra | mettrait | mette | |
| *to set* | mettons | avons mis | mettions | mettrons | mettrions | mettions | mettons |
| | mettez | avez mis | mettiez | mettrez | mettriez | mettiez | mettez |
| | mettent | ont mis | mettaient | mettront | mettraient | mettent | |

# Verbes irréguliers (suite)

| VERBE INFINITIF | INDICATIF PRÉSENT | PASSÉ COMPOSÉ | IMPARFAIT | FUTUR | CONDITIONNEL PRÉSENT | SUBJONCTIF PRÉSENT | IMPÉRATIF |
|---|---|---|---|---|---|---|---|
| **obtenir** *to obtain* | obtiens | ai obtenu | obtenais | obtiendrai | obtiendrais | obtienne | |
| | obtiens | as obtenu | obtenais | obtiendras | obtiendrais | obtiennes | obtiens |
| | obtient | a obtenu | obtenait | obtiendra | obtiendrait | obtienne | |
| | obtenons | avons obtenu | obtenions | obtiendrons | obtiendrions | obtenions | obtenons |
| | obtenez | avez obtenu | obteniez | obtiendrez | obtiendriez | obteniez | obtenez |
| | obtiennent | ont obtenu | obtenaient | obtiendront | obtiendraient | obtiennent | |
| **ouvrir** *to open* | ouvre | ai ouvert | ouvrais | ouvrirai | ouvrirais | ouvre | |
| | ouvres | as ouvert | ouvrais | ouvriras | ouvrirais | ouvres | ouvre |
| | ouvre | a ouvert | ouvrait | ouvrira | ouvrirait | ouvre | |
| | ouvrons | avons ouvert | ouvrions | ouvrirons | ouvririons | ouvrions | ouvrons |
| | ouvrez | avez ouvert | ouvriez | ouvrirez | ouvririez | ouvriez | ouvrez |
| | ouvrent | ont ouvert | ouvraient | ouvriront | ouvriraient | ouvrent | |
| **partir** *to leave* | pars | suis parti(e) | partais | partirai | partirais | parte | |
| | pars | es parti(e) | partais | partiras | partirais | partes | pars |
| | part | est parti(e) | partait | partira | partirait | parte | |
| | partons | sommes parti(e)s | partions | partirons | partirions | partions | partons |
| | partez | êtes parti(e)(s) | partiez | partirez | partiriez | partiez | partez |
| | partent | sont parti(e)s | partaient | partiront | partiraient | partent | |
| **pleuvoir** *to rain* | pleut | a plu | pleuvait | pleuvra | pleuvrait | pleuve | |
| **pouvoir** *to be able, can* | peux | ai pu | pouvais | pourrai | pourrais | puisse | |
| | peux | as pu | pouvais | pourras | pourrais | puisses | |
| | peut | a pu | pouvait | pourra | pourrait | puisse | |
| | pouvons | avons pu | pouvions | pourrons | pourrions | puissions | |
| | pouvez | avez pu | pouviez | pourrez | pourriez | puissiez | |
| | peuvent | ont pu | pouvaient | pourront | pourraient | puissent | |
| **prendre** *to take* | prends | ai pris | prenais | prendrai | prendrais | prenne | |
| | prends | as pris | prenais | prendras | prendrais | prennes | prends |
| | prend | a pris | prenait | prendra | prendrait | prenne | |
| | prenons | avons pris | prenions | prendrons | prendrions | prenions | prenons |
| | prenez | avez pris | preniez | prendrez | prendriez | preniez | prenez |
| | prennent | ont pris | prenaient | prendront | prendraient | prennent | |
| **recevoir** *to receive* | reçois | ai reçu | recevais | recevrai | recevrais | reçoive | |
| | reçois | as reçu | recevais | recevras | recevrais | reçoives | reçois |
| | reçoit | a reçu | recevait | recevra | recevrait | reçoive | |
| | recevons | avons reçu | recevions | recevrons | recevrions | recevions | recevons |
| | recevez | avez reçu | receviez | recevrez | recevriez | receviez | recevez |
| | reçoivent | ont reçu | recevaient | recevront | recevraient | reçoivent | |
| **rire** *to laugh* | ris | ai ri | riais | rirai | rirais | rie | |
| | ris | as ri | riais | riras | rirais | ries | ris |
| | rit | a ri | riait | rira | rirait rie | | |
| | rions | avons ri | riions | rirons | ririons | riions | rions |
| | riez | avez ri | riiez | rirez | ririez | riiez | riez |
| | rient | ont ri | riaient | riront | riraient | rient | |
| **savoir** *to know* | sais | ai su | savais | saurai | saurais | sache | |
| | sais | as su | savais | sauras | saurais | saches | sache |
| | sait | a su | savait | saura | saurait | sache | |
| | savons | avons su | savions | saurons | saurions | sachions | sachons |
| | savez | avez su | saviez | saurez | sauriez | sachiez | sachez |
| | savent | ont su | savaient | sauront | sauraient | sachent | |

## Verbes irréguliers (suite)

| VERBE INFINITIF | PRÉSENT | INDICATIF PASSÉ COMPOSÉ | IMPARFAIT | FUTUR | CONDITIONNEL PRÉSENT | SUBJONCTIF PRÉSENT | IMPÉRATIF |
|---|---|---|---|---|---|---|---|
| **sortir** *to go out* | sors | suis sorti(e) | sortais | sortirai | sortirais | sorte | |
| | sors | es sorti(e) | sortais | sortiras | sortirais | sortes | sors |
| | sort | est sorti(e) | sortait | sortira | sortirait | sorte | |
| | sortons | sommes sorti(e)s | sortions | sortirons | sortirions | sortions | sortons |
| | sortez | êtes sorti(e)(s) | sortiez | sortirez | sortiriez | sortiez | sortez |
| | sortent | sont sorti(e)s | sortaient | sortiront | sortiraient | sortent | |
| **suivre** *to follow* | suis | ai suivi | suivais | suivrai | suivrais | suive | |
| | suis | as suivi | suivais | suivras | suivrais | suives | suis |
| | suit | a suivi | suivait | suivra | suivrait | suive | |
| | suivons | avons suivi | suivions | suivrons | suivrions | suivions | suivons |
| | suivez | avez suivi | suiviez | suivrez | suivriez | suiviez | suivez |
| | suivent | ont suivi | suivaient | suivront | suivraient | suivent | |
| **venir** *to come* | viens | suis venu(e) | venais | viendrai | viendrais | vienne | |
| | viens | es venu(e) | venais | viendras | viendrais | viennes | viens |
| | vient | est venu(e) | venait | viendra | viendrait | vienne | |
| | venons | sommes venu(e)s | venions | viendrons | viendrions | venions | venons |
| | venez | êtes venu(e)(s) | veniez | viendrez | viendriez | veniez | venez |
| | viennent | sont venu(e)s | venaient | viendront | viendraient | viennent | |
| **vivre** *to live* | vis | ai vécu | vivais | vivrai | vivrais | vive | |
| | vis | as vécu | vivais | vivras | vivrais | vives | vis |
| | vit | a vécu | vivait | vivra | vivrait | vive | |
| | vivons | avons vécu | vivions | vivrons | vivrions | vivions | vivons |
| | vivez | avez vécu | viviez | vivrez | vivriez | viviez | vivez |
| | vivent | ont vécu | vivaient | vivront | vivraient | vivent | |
| **voir** *to see* | vois | ai vu | voyais | verrai | verrais | voie | |
| | vois | as vu | voyais | verras | verrais | voies | vois |
| | voit | a vu | voyait | verra | verrait | voie | |
| | voyons | avons vu | voyions | verrons | verrions | voyions | voyons |
| | voyez | avez vu | voyiez | verrez | verriez | voyiez | voyez |
| | voient | ont vu | voyaient | verront | verraient | voient | |
| **vouloir** *to want, to wish* | veux | ai voulu | voulais | voudrai | voudrais | veuille | |
| | veux | as voulu | voulais | voudras | voudrais | veuilles | veuille |
| | veut | a voulu | voulait | voudra | voudrait | veuille | |
| | voulons | avons voulu | voulions | voudrons | voudrions | voulions | veuillons |
| | voulez | avez voulu | vouliez | voudrez | voudriez | vouliez | veuillez |
| | veulent | ont voulu | voulaient | voudront | voudraient | veuillent | |

# Vocabulaire français–anglais

This list contains words appearing in *Horizons,* except for absolute cognates. The definitions of active vocabulary words are followed by the number of the chapter where they are first presented. A (P) refers to the *Chapitre préliminaire.* When several translations, separated by commas, are listed before a chapter number, they are all considered active. Since verbs are sometimes introduced lexically in the infinitive before the conjugation of the present indicative is presented, consult the *Index* to find out the chapter where a conjugation is introduced. An *(m)*, *(f)*, or *(pl)* following a noun indicates that it is masculine, feminine, or plural. *Inv* means that a word is invariable. An asterisk before a word beginning with an **h** indicates that the **h** is aspirate.

## A

**à** to, at, in (P); **À bientôt.** See you soon. (P); **à cause de** due to, because of; **À ce soir.** See you tonight/this evening. (2); **à côté (de)** next to (3); **À demain.** See you tomorrow. (P); **à la campagne** in the country (3); **à la française** French-style; **à la maison** at home (P); **à la page...** on page . . . (P); **à l'avance** in advance (9); **à l'étranger** abroad (9); **à l'heure** on time (4); **à peu près** about; **à pied** on foot (4); **À quelle heure?** At what time? (P); **à suivre** to be continued (6); **À tout à l'heure.** See you in a little while. (P); **au café** at the café (2); **au centre-ville** downtown (3); **au coin (de)** on the corner (of) (10); **au cours de** in the course of, during, while on (10); **au dessus de** above; **au premier étage** on the second floor (3); **Au revoir.** Good-bye. (P); **à votre avis** in your opinion (8); **café au lait** coffee with milk (2); **j'habite à** (+ city) I live in (+ city) (P)
**abandonner** to abandon, to leave
**abattre** to strike down
**abbaye** *(f)* abbey
**abolir** to abolish
**abonnement** *(m)* subscription
**abonner: s'abonner à** to subscribe to
**abord: d'abord** first (4)
**abrégé(e)** abbreviated
**abricot** *(m)* apricot
**abriter** to shelter
**absolu(e)** absolute
**absolument** absolutely
**académique** academic
**Acadie** *(f)* Acadia
**accent** *(m)* accent (P); **sans accent** without an accent (P)
**acceptation** *(f)* acceptance
**accepter** to accept (7)
**accès** *(m)* access
**accessoire** *(m)* accessory
**accidentellement** accidentally
**accompagner** to accompany
**accomplir** to accomplish
**accord** *(m)* agreement; **D'accord!** Okay! Agreed! (2); **se mettre d'accord** to come to an agreement
**accordéon** *(m)* accordion
**accorder: s'accorder** to grant each other
**accrocher** to hang
**accueil** *(m)* welcome, reception
**accueillant(e)** welcoming
**achat** *(m)* purchase
**acheter** to buy (4)

**acier** *(m)* steel
**acteur** *(m)* actor (6)
**actif (active)** active, working
**Action** *(f)* **de Grâce: jour** *(m)* **d'Action de Grâce** Thanksgiving Day
**activité** *(f)* activity (2)
**actrice** *(f)* actress (6)
**actuellement** currently
**adapter: s'adapter** to adapt
**addition** *(f)* check, bill
**adepte** *(mf)* one who believes in
**adhésion** *(f)* joining
**adjectif** *(m)* adjective (1)
**adjoint(e)** assistant
**admettre** to admit
**administratif(-ive): centre administratif** *(m)* administration building
**admirer** to admire (9)
**adopter** to adopt
**adorer** to love, to adore (9)
**adresse** *(f)* address (3); **adresse** *(f)* **mail** e-mail address (3)
**adresser** to address; **s'adresser à** to go and see, to speak to
**adulte** *(mf)* adult
**aérien(ne)** aerial
**aérobic** *(f)* aerobics (8)
**aéronautique** aeronautical, space
**aéroport** *(m)* airport (10)
**affaire** *(f)* thing, belonging, business; **avoir affaire à** to deal with; **femme d'affaires** businesswoman (5); **homme d'affaires** businessman (5)
**affichage: affichage public** *(m)* signage
**affiche** *(f)* poster (3)
**affiché(e)** posted
**affinité** *(f)* affinity
**africain(e)** African
**Afrique** *(f)* Africa (9); **Afrique du Sud** *(f)* South Africa
**âge** *(m)* age; **Quel âge a... ?** How old is . . . ? (4)
**âgé(e)** old (4)
**agence** *(f)* **de voyages** travel agency (9)
**agent** *(m)* agent; **agent** *(m)* **de police** policeman; **agent** *(m)* **de voyages** travel agent (9)
**aggraver** to worsen
**agir** to act, to take action
**agitation** *(f)* agitation
**agité(e)** agitated
**agneau** *(m)* lamb
**agréable** pleasant (1)
**agricole** agricultural
**agriculture** *(f)* agriculture

**aider** to help (5)
**aïe** ouch
**aigle** *(m)* eagle
**aigu(ë)** acute, shrill
**aiguille** *(f)* needle; **travaux** *(mpl)* **d'aiguille** needlework
**ail** *(m)* garlic
**aile** *(f)* wing
**ailleurs** elsewhere; **par ailleurs** furthermore
**aimable** kind, amiable
**aimer** to like (2), to love (7); **Aimeriez-vous... ?** Would you like. . . ? (8); **aimer mieux** to like better, to prefer (2); **Est-ce que tu aimes/ vous aimez... ?** Do you like. . . ? (1); **J'aime...** I like . . . (1); **J'aimerais...** I would like . . . ; **J'aimerais autant...** I would just as soon… (10); **s'aimer** to love each other (7)
**aîné(e)** oldest (child)
**ainsi** thus; **ainsi que** as well as
**air** *(m)* air, look, appearance; **avoir l'air** (+ *adjective*) to look / to seem (+ *adjective*) (4); **de plein air** outdoor (4)
**aise** *(f)* ease; **mal à l'aise** ill at ease
**aisé(e): classe aisée** *(f)* upper class
**ajouter** to add
**alcool** *(m)* alcohol (8)
**alcoolisé(e)** alcoholic
**alcoolisme** *(m)* alcoholism
**Algérie** *(f)* Algeria (9)
**algérien(ne)** Algerian
**aliment** *(m)* food
**alimentaire** food
**Allemagne** *(f)* Germany (9)
**allemand** *(m)* German (1)
**allemand(e)** German
**aller (à)** to go (to) (2); **aller à la chasse** to go hunting; **aller à la pêche** to go fishing; **aller à pied** to walk, to go on foot (4); **aller très bien à quelqu'un** to look very good on someone; **aller voir** to go see, to visit (a person) (4); **aller-retour** *(m)* round-trip ticket (9); **Allez au tableau.** Go to the board. (P); **billet aller simple** *(m)* one-way ticket (9); **Ça va.** It's going fine. (P); **Comment allez-vous?** How are you? (P); **Comment ça va?** How's it going? (P); **Comment vas-tu?** How are you? (informal); **je vais** I go, I am going (1); **On va... ?** Shall we go . . . ? (2); **Qu'est-ce qui ne va pas?** What's wrong? (10); **s'en aller** to go away; **tu vas/vous allez** you go, you are going (2)
**allergie** *(f)* allergy (10)
**allié(e)** allied

**allô** hello (on the telephone) (6)
**allumer** to light
**allumette** *(f)* match
**alors** so, then (1)
**alpinisme** *(m)* mountain climbing; **faire de l'alpinisme** to go mountain climbing
**amande** *(f)* almond
**amant(e)** *(mf)* lover
**ambassade** *(f)* embassy
**ambassadeur(-drice)** *(mf)* ambassador
**ambitieux(-ieuse)** ambitious
**améliorer** to improve (8)
**aménagé(e)** fitted out
**amener** to take, to bring
**américain(e)** American (P); **à l'américaine** American style (8)
**amérindien(ne)** Native American
**Amérique** *(f)* America (9); **Amérique centrale** *(f)* Central America (9); **Amérique** *(f)* **du Nord** North America (9); **Amérique** *(f)* **du Sud** South America (9)
**ami(e)** *(mf)* friend (P); **petit ami** *(m)* boyfriend (2); **petite amie** *(f)* girlfriend (2)
**amitié** *(f)* friendship
**amour** *(m)* love (6); **film** *(m)* **d'amour** romantic movie (6); **le grand amour** *(m)* true love (7)
**amoureux(-euse)** in love (6); **tomber amoureux(-euse) de** to fall in love with (6); **vie amoureuse** *(f)* love life
**amovible** detachable
**amphithéâtre** *(m)* lecture hall (1)
**amusant(e)** fun (1)
**amuser** to amuse; **On s'amuse bien.** One has a good time. (4); **s'amuser** to have fun (7)
**an** *(m)* year (5); **avoir... ans** to be . . . years old (4); **jour** *(m)* **de l'an** *(m)* New Year's Day
**ananas** *(m)* pineapple
**ancêtre** *(mf)* ancestor
**anchois** *(m)* anchovy
**ancien(ne)** former, old, ancient
**anciennement** formerly
**andouille** *(f)* sausage of chitterlings
**âne** *(m)* donkey
**ange** *(m)* angel
**angine** *(f)* tonsillitis
**anglais** *(m)* English (P)
**anglais(e)** English
**Angleterre** *(f)* England; **Nouvelle-Angleterre** *(f)* New England
**anglophone** English-speaking
**angoisse** *(f)* anguish
**angoisser** to agonize, to worry; **angoissé(e)** anguished
**animal** *(m)* *(pl animaux)* animal (3)
**animé(e)** animated; **dessin animé** *(m)* cartoon
**année** *(f)* year (4); **les années** *(fpl)* **trente** the thirties
**anniversaire** *(m)* birthday (4); **anniversaire** *(m)* **de mariage** wedding anniversary
**annonce** *(f)* advertisement, announcement
**annuaire** *(m)* telephone book
**annuel(le)** annual
**annuler** to annul, to cancel; **annulé(e)** canceled
**anorak** *(m)* ski jacket, anorak (5)
**Antarctique** *(m)* Antarctica
**anticiper** to anticipate
**antillais(e)** West Indian
**Antilles** *(fpl)* West Indies (9)
**anxiété** *(f)* anxiety
**août** *(m)* August (4)
**apercevoir** to see, to notice
**apéritif** *(m)* before-dinner drink (8)
**apparaître** to appear

**appareil** *(m)* apparatus, appliance; **appareil** *(m)* **téléphonique** telephone
**apparencé** *(f)* appearance
**apparenté(e)** related
**appartement** *(m)* apartment (3)
**appartenir (à)** to belong (to)
**appeler** to call; **Comment s'appelle... ?** What is . . . 's name? (4); **Comment t'appelles-tu?** What's your name? (informal); **Comment vous appelez-vous?** What's your name? (formal) (P); **Il/Elle s'appelle...** His/Her name is . . . (4); **Je m'appelle...** My name is . . . (P); **s'appeler** to be named, to be called (7); **Tu t'appelles comment?** What's your name? (informal) (P)
**appétit** *(m)* appetite
**applaudir** to applaud
**appoint** *(m)* exact amount needed
**apporter** to bring
**apprécier** to appreciate (6)
**apprendre** to learn (4); **Apprenez...** Learn. . . (P)
**approcher: s'approcher (de)** to approach
**approprié(e)** appropriate
**approuver** to approve
**approximatif(-ive)** approximate
**après** after, afterward (P); **d'après** according to
**après-demain** the day after tomorrow
**après-midi** *(m)* afternoon (P); **cet après-midi** this afternoon (4); **Il est une heure de l'après-midi.** It's one o'clock in the afternoon. (P); **l'après-midi** in the afternoon, afternoons (P)
**arabe** *(m)* Arabic
**arachide** *(f)* groundnut, peanut
**arbre** *(m)* tree (1)
**arc** *(m)* arch, bow; **tir** *(m)* **à l'arc** archery
**archange** *(m)* archangel
**archéologique** archeological
**archipel** *(m)* archipelago
**ardent(e)** ardent, fervent
**argent** *(m)* money, silver (2)
**Argentine** *(f)* Argentina (9)
**aristocratie** *(f)* aristocracy
**armée** *(f)* army
**arrêt** *(m)* stop; **arrêt** *(m)* **d'autobus** bus stop (3)
**arrêter** to stop; **s'arrêter** to stop (7)
**arrivée** *(f)* arrival (9); **porte** *(f)* **d'arrivée** arrival gate (9)
**arriver** to arrive (3), to happen
**arrondi(e)** rounded
**arrondissement** *(m)* district
**art** *(m)* art; **les beaux-arts** the fine arts (1)
**article** *(m)* article (9)
**artificiel(le)** artificial
**artisanat** *(m)* crafts
**artiste** *(mf)* artist, performer
**ascenseur** *(m)* elevator (3)
**Asie** *(f)* Asia (9)
**aspect physique** *(m)* physical appearance (7)
**asperge** *(f)* asparagus
**aspirant(e)** *(mf)* candidate
**aspirine** *(f)* aspirin (10)
**assassin** *(m)* murderer, assassin
**assassiner** to murder, to assassinate
**assaut** *(m)* assault, attack
**assemblage** *(m)* assembly, gathering
**assemblée** *(f)* assembly
**asseoir: Asseyez-vous.** Sit down.; **s'asseoir** to sit (down)
**assez** fairly, rather (P); **assez (de)** enough (1)
**assiette** *(f)* plate
**assis(e)** seated (9)
**assister à** to attend
**associatif(-ive)** in the community
**associer** to associate; **associé(e)** associated

**Assomption** *(f)* the Assumption
**assurance** *(f)* insurance
**assuré(e)** provided, assured
**astronomie** *(f)* astronomy
**astucieux(-euse)** astute
**atelier** *(m)* workshop
**Atlantique** *(m)* Atlantic
**attaché(e)** attached
**attaque** *(f)* attack; **attaque** *(f)* **d'apoplexie** stroke
**attendre** to wait (for) (7); **s'attendre à** to expect to
**attente** *(f)* waiting
**attention: faire attention (à)** to pay attention (to), to watch out (for) (8)
**attirant(e)** attractive
**attirer** to attract
**attraper** to catch
**attribuer** assign, allocate
**aube** *(f)* dawn
**auberge** *(f)* inn; **auberge** *(f)* **de jeunesse** youth hostel (10)
**aubergine** *(f)* eggplant
**aucun(e): ne... aucun(e)** no, none, not one
**audace** *(f)* boldness
**audacieux(-euse)** audacious, bold
**au-delà** beyond
**au-dessus** above
**auditif(-ive)** auditory
**aujourd'hui** today (P)
**aumenter** to augment, to raise
**auparavant** beforehand
**auquel (à laquelle, auxquels, auxquelles)** to which
**aussi** too, also (P); **aussi... que** as . . . as (1)
**aussitôt que** as soon as
**austral(e)** southern
**Australie** *(f)* Australia (9)
**autant (de)... (que)** as much . . . (as), as many . . . (as); **J'aimerais autant...** I would just as soon... (10)
**authenticité** *(f)* authenticity
**autobus** *(m)* bus (4); **arrêt** *(m)* **d'autobus** bus stop (3); **en autobus** by bus (4)
**autocar** *(m)* bus (4); **en autocar** by bus (4)
**automatique** automatic
**automne** *(m)* autumn, fall (5); **en automne** in autumn (5)
**autonomie** *(f)* autonomy
**autoportrait** *(m)* self-portrait (P)
**autorisé(e)** authorized
**autoritaire** authoritarian
**autour de** around
**autre** other (1); **quelquefois... d'autres fois** sometimes . . . other times (7); **Qu'est-ce que je peux vous proposer d'autre?** What else can I get you? (8)
**autrefois** formerly, in the past
**Autriche** *(f)* Austria
**auxiliaire** *(m)* auxiliary
**avaler** to swallow, to gulp
**avance** *(f)* **advance; à l'avance** in advance (9); **en avance** early
**avancer** to advance
**avant** before (P); **avant de partir** before leaving; **avant tout** above all
**avantage** *(m)* advantage
**avec** with (P); **Avec plaisir!** With pleasure! (6)
**avenir** *(m)* future
**aventure** *(f)* adventure ; **film** *(m)* **d'aventures** adventure movie
**avenue** *(f)* avenue (10)
**avion** *(m)* airplane (4); **en avion** by airplane (4)
**avis** *(m)* opinion; **à votre avis** in your opinion (8)
**avocat(e)** *(mf)* lawyer

**avoir** to have (3); **avoir... ans** to be . . . years old (4); **avoir besoin de** to need (4); **avoir chaud** to be hot (4); **avoir cours** to have class (6); **avoir de la fièvre** to have fever; **avoir du mal à...** to have difficulty . . . , to have a hard time. . .; **avoir envie de** to feel like, to desire (4); **avoir faim** to be hungry (4); **j'ai faim** I'm hungry (2); **avoir froid** to be cold (4); **avoir \*honte** to be ashamed; **avoir l'air** (+ *adjective*) to look / to seem (+ *adjective*) (4); **avoir le nez bouché** to have a stopped-up nose; **avoir le nez qui coule** to have a runny nose; **avoir les cheveux/les yeux...** to have . . . hair/eyes (4); **avoir lieu** to take place; **avoir l'intention de** to plan on, to intend to (4); **avoir mal (à)** one's . . . hurts, to ache (10); **avoir peur (de)** to be afraid (of), to fear (4); **avoir raison** to be right (4); **avoir soif** to be thirsty (4); **j'ai soif** I'm thirsty (2); **avoir sommeil** to be sleepy (4); **avoir tort** to be wrong (4); **il y a** there is, there are (1), ago (5); **Quel âge a... ?** How old is . . . ? (4)
**avouer** to admit
**avril** *(m)* April (4)
**ayant** having

## B

**baby-sitter** *(mf)* babysitter
**baccalauréat (bac)** *(m)* a comprehensive examination at the end of secondary school
**bachelier(-ière)** *(mf)* someone having passed the baccalauréat
**bacon** *(m)* bacon (8)
**bagages** *(mpl)* baggage (9)
**bagne** *(m)* penal colony
**bague** *(f)* ring
**baguette** *(f)* loaf of French bread (8)
**baie** *(f)* bay
**baigner: se baigner** to bathe, to go swimming
**bain** *(m)* bath (7); **bain** *(m)* **de soleil** sunbath (4); **maillot** *(m)* **de bain** swimsuit (5); **salle** *(f)* **de bains** bathroom (3)
**baiser** *(m)* kiss
**baisser** to lower
**bal** *(m)* dance
**bambou** *(m)* bamboo
**banane** *(f)* banana (8)
**bancaire: carte** *(f)* **bancaire** bank card (9)
**banlieue** *(f)* suburbs (3)
**banque** *(f)* bank (10)
**banquette** *(f)* bench, seat
**banquier** *(m)* banker
**bar** *(m)* bar (4)
**barbe** *(f)* beard (4)
**barrer** to cross out
**barricadé(e)** barricaded
**bas** *(m)* bottom
**bas(se)** low; **table basse** *(f)* coffee table
**base** *(f)* base; **de base** basic
**basé(e) sur** based on (6)
**base-ball** *(m)* baseball (2)
**basilique** *(f)* basilica
**basket** *(m)* basketball (1)
**baskets** *(fpl)* tennis shoes (5)
**basque** *(m)* Basque
**bataille** *(f)* battle
**bateau** *(m)* boat (4); **en bateau** by boat (4); **faire du bateau** to go boating (5)
**bâtiment** *(m)* building (1)
**batterie** *(f)* drums (2)
**battre** to beat; **se battre** to fight
**bavette** *(f)* undercut

**beau (bel, belle,** *pl* **beaux, belles)** beautiful, handsome (1); **beau-frère** *(m)* brother-in-law (4); **beau-père** *(m)* father-in-law (4); **beaux-arts** *(mpl)* fine arts (1); **beaux-parents** *(mpl)* stepparents, in-laws; **belle-mère** *(f)* mother-in-law (4); **belle-sœur** *(f)* sister-in-law (4); **Il fait beau.** The weather's nice. (5)
**beaucoup** a lot (P); **beaucoup de** a lot of (1)
**beauté** *(f)* beauty (7)
**bébé** *(m)* baby
**beige** beige (3)
**beignet** *(m)* fritter
**belge** Belgian
**Belgique** *(f)* Belgium (9)
**bénéficiaire** *(mf)* beneficiary
**bénéfique** beneficial
**bénévole** benefit, benevolent, voluntary
**bénir** to bless
**berbère** Berber
**berceuse** *(f)* lullaby
**besoin** *(m)* need; **avoir besoin de** to need (4)
**bête** *(f)* beast (6), animal
**bête** stupid, dumb (1)
**beurre** *(m)* butter (8)
**beurré(e)** buttered
**bibliothèque** *(f)* library (1), bookcase
**bien** well (P), very; **bien d'autres** many others; **bien que** although; **Bien sûr!** Of course! (5); **c'est bien de...** it's good to... (10); **Je voudrais bien.** Sure, I'd like to. (2)
**bien-être** *(m)* well-being
**bienfaiteur** *(m)*, **bienfaitrice** *(f)* benefactor
**biens** *(mpl)* goods
**bientôt** soon (P); **À bientôt.** See you soon. (P)
**bienvenu(e)** welcome
**bière** *(f)* beer (2)
**bifteck** *(m)* steak (8); **bifteck hâché** *(m)* ground meat
**bijoux** *(mpl)* jewelry
**bikini** *(m)* bikini (5)
**bilingue** bilingual
**billard** *(m)* billiards
**billet** *(m)* ticket (9), bill; **distributeur** *(m)* **de billets** ATM machine (10)
**biologie** *(f)* biology (1)
**bios: produits bios** *(mpl)* organic products (8)
**biscotte** *(f)* melba toast
**bise** *(f)* kiss
**bistro(t)** *(m)* restaurant, pub (6)
**bizarre** bizarre, strange
**blanc(he)** white (3); **vin blanc** *(m)* white wine (2)
**blanquette** *(f)* stew (usually veal)
**bleu(e)** blue (3); **bleu clair** light blue; **bleu foncé** dark blue; **bleu vif** bright blue
**blond(e)** blond (4)
**blouson** *(m)* windbreaker, jacket
**bœuf** *(m)* beef (8); **bœuf bourguignon** *(m)* beef burgandy
**bohème** bohemian
**boire** to drink (4)
**bois** *(m)* wood, woods
**boisson** *(f)* drink (2)
**boîte** *(f)* box, can (8); **boîte** *(f)* **de nuit** nightclub (1)
**bol** *(m)* bowl
**bombardement** *(m)* bombing
**bon(ne)** good (1); **Bonne année!** Happy New Year!; **Bon anniversaire!** Happy birthday!; **Bonne idée!** Good idea! (4); **Bonne journée!** Have a good day!; **Bon séjour!** Enjoy your stay! (10); **Bon week-end!** Have a good weekend!
**bonbon** *(m)* candy
**bonheur** *(m)* happiness (7)

**Bonjour!** Hello! Good morning! (P)
**bonne** *(f)* maid, nanny
**Bonsoir!** Good evening! (P)
**bord** *(m)* edge; **à bord** on board; **au bord de** at the edge of; **bord** *(m)* **de la mer** seaside
**bordé(e)** bordered
**bordure: en bordure de** along the edge of
**botte** *(f)* boot (5)
**bouche** *(f)* mouth (10)
**bouché(e)** stopped-up; **cidre bouché** *(m)* bottled cider
**boucherie** *(f)* butcher's shop (8)
**boucle** *(f)* **d'oreille** earring
**boudin** *(m)* blood sausage
**boue** *(f)* mud
**boueux(-euse)** muddy
**bouger** to move
**bouillabaisse** *(f)* fish soup
**bouillir** to boil
**boulangerie** *(f)* bakery (8)
**boule** *(f)* ball
**boulevard** *(m)* boulevard (10)
**boulot** *(m)* work (familiar)
**boum** *(f)* party (1), bash
**bourgeoisie: haute bourgeoisie** *(f)* upper-middle class
**bout** *(m)* end (3); **au bout (de)** at the end (of) (3)
**bouteille** *(f)* bottle (8)
**boutique** *(f)* shop
**bouton** *(m)* button, pimple
**branché(e)** up with things
**brancher: se brancher sur** to get into
**bras** *(m)* arm (10)
**brasier** *(m)* inferno
**bref(-ève)** brief
**Brésil** *(m)* Brazil (9)
**Bretagne** *(f)* Brittany
**breton** *(m)* Breton
**brevet** *(m)* certificate, diploma
**bricolage** *(m)* handiwork
**bricoler** to do handiwork (2)
**brioche** *(f)* brioche (a type of soft bread)
**brise** *(f)* breeze
**briser** to break
**britannique** British
**brochette** *(f)* skewer
**brocolis** *(mpl)* broccoli
**bronchite** *(f)* bronchitis
**bronzer** to tan (9)
**brosser** to brush; **se brosser** to brush (7)
**brouillard** *(m)* fog, mist, haze
**bruit** *(m)* noise (10)
**brûler** to burn; **se brûler la main** to burn your hand
**brun(e)** (with hair) brown, brunette, dark-haired (4)
**Bruxelles** Brussels
**bulletin** *(m)* report, bulletin
**bureau** *(m)* desk (3), office (1); **bureau** *(m)* **de poste** post office (10); **bureau** *(m)* **de tabac** tobacco shop
**bus** *(m)* bus (4)
**but** *(m)* goal

## C

**ça** that (P); **Ça fait combien?** How much is it? (2); **Ça fait... euros.** That's . . . euros. (2); **Ça me plaît!** I like it! (3); **Ça lui plaît?** Does he like it? (9); **Ça s'écrit comment?** How is that written? (P); **Ça te/vous dit?** How does that sound to you? (4); **Ça te/vous plaît!** You like it! (3); **Ça va.** It's going fine. (P); **C'est ça!** That's right!; **comme ci comme ça** so-so (2); **Comment ça va?** How's it going? (P); **Qu'est-**

**ce que ça veut dire?** What does that mean? (P)

**cabine** *(f)* **d'essayage** fitting room (5)

**cacao** *(m)* cocoa

**cacher** to hide; **se cacher** to hide oneself, to be hidden

**cadien(ne)** Cajun (4)

**cadeau** *(m)* gift (10); **marchand** *(m)* **de cadeaux** gift shop (10)

**cadre** *(m)* executive

**café** *(m)* café (1), coffee (2); **café** *(m)* **au lait** coffee with milk (2)

**cahier** *(m)* notebook (P)

**calcul** *(m)* calculation

**calculer** to calculate

**câlin(e)** cuddly

**calme** calm (4)

**calmement** calmly

**calmer: se calmer** to calm down

**calvaire** *(m)* Calvary

**camarade** *(mf)* pal; **camarade** *(mf)* **de chambre** roommate (P); **camarade** *(mf)* **de classe** classmate

**camerounais(e)** Cameroonian

**campagne** *(f)* country (3), campaign; **à la campagne** in the country (3)

**camping** *(m)* camping, campground (5); **faire du camping** to go camping (5)

**camper** to camp

**campeur** *(m)* camper

**campus** *(m)* campus (1)

**Canada** *(m)* Canada (9)

**canadien(ne)** Canadian (P)

**canapé** *(m)* couch (3), open-faced sandwich

**canard** *(m)* duck (8)

**candidat(e)** *(mf)* candidate, applicant

**canne à sucre** *(f)* sugar cane

**canton** *(m)* canton, district

**capacité** *(f)* capacity, ability

**capitale** *(f)* capital

**caprice** *(m)* whim

**car** *(m)* bus (4)

**car** because

**caractère** *(m)* character; **en caractères gras** boldfaced

**caractériser** to characterize

**caractéristique** *(f)* characteristic

**carafe** *(f)* carafe (a decanter) (8)

**caraïbe** Caribbean; **mer** *(f)* **des Caraïbes** Caribbean Sea

**carbonisé(e): mourir carbonisé(e)** to be burned to death

**cardiaque** cardiac, of the heart

**cargo** *(m)* cargo boat

**carie** *(f)* cavity

**carotte** *(f)* carrot (8)

**carré(e)** square; **Vieux Carré** French Quarter (4)

**carrière** *(f)* career

**carte** *(f)* menu (8), card, map; **carte** *(f)* **bancaire** bank card (9); **carte** *(f)* **de crédit** credit card (9); **carte** *(f)* **d'identité** identity card; **carte** *(f)* **postale** postcard (9); **carte** *(f)* **téléphonique** telephone card (10)

**cas** *(m)* case; **dans tous les cas** in any case

**case** *(f)* box

**casier: casier postal** *(m)* mailbox

**casquette** *(f)* cap (5)

**casse-cou** *(inv)* *(mf)* daredevil

**casse-pieds** *(inv)* *(mf)* nuisance

**casser** to break; **se casser la jambe** to break one's leg

**cassette** *(f)* cassette (3)

**catastrophe** *(f)* disaster

**catégorie** *(f)* category

**cathédrale** *(f)* cathedral

**catholique** *(mf)* Catholic (1)

**cauchemar** *(m)* nightmare

**cause** *(f)* cause; **à cause de** because of

**causer** to cause

**CD** *(m)* CD (P)

**ce (cet, cette)** this, that (3); **ce que** what, that which; **ce qui** what, that which (7); **ces** these, those (3); **ce semestre** this semester (P); **ce soir** tonight, this evening (2); **ce sont** they are, those are (1); **c'est** it's (P), he is, she is, that is, this is (1); **c'est-à-dire** in other words

**céder** to give up

**ceinture** *(f)* belt (5)

**cela** that (7)

**célèbre** famous (4)

**célébrer** to celebrate

**célébrité** *(f)* celebrity

**céleri** *(m)* celery

**célibataire** single, unmarried (1)

**celte** Celtic

**celtique** Celtic

**celui (celle)** the one

**cendre** *(f)* ash; **mercredi** *(m)* **des Cendres** Ash Wednesday

**cendrier** *(m)* ashtray

**censure** *(f)* censorship

**cent** *(m)* one hundred (2)

**centaine** *(f)* about one hundred

**centime** *(m)* centime (one hundredth part of a euro) (2)

**central(e)** *(mpl* **centraux)** central; **Amérique** *(f)* **centrale** Central America (9)

**centre** *(m)* center (5); **centre administratif** *(m)* administration building; **centre commercial** *(m)* shopping center, mall (4); **centre** *(m)* **d'étudiants** student center

**centre-ville** *(m)* downtown (3)

**cercle** *(m)* circle

**céréales** *(fpl)* cereal (8)

**céréalier(-ière)** cereal

**cérémonie** *(f)* ceremony

**cerise** *(f)* cherry (8)

**certain(e)** certain; **certains** some, certain people

**certainement** certainly

**certes** true, indeed, of course

**certificat** *(m)* certificate

**cervelle** *(f)* brain

**cesser** to cease

**ceux (celles)** those (ones) (8)

**chacun(e)** each one

**chagrin** *(m)* sorrow

**chaîne** *(f)* chain; **chaîne hi-fi** *(f)* stereo (2)

**chaise** *(f)* chair (3)

**chalet de ski** *(m)* a ski lodge (10)

**chaleur** *(f)* warmth

**chaleureux(-euse)** warm-hearted

**chambre** *(f)* bedroom (3); **camarade** *(mf)* **de chambre** roommate (P)

**champ** *(m)* field; **champ** *(m)* **de bataille** battlefield

**champignon** *(m)* mushroom

**chance** *(f)* luck

**changement** *(m)* change

**changer** to change (6); **changer de l'argent** to exchange money (9)

**chanson** *(f)* song

**chanter** to sing (2)

**chanteur(-euse)** *(mf)* singer

**chapeau** *(m)* hat (5)

**chapelle** *(f)* chapel

**chaperon:** *(m)* hood; **le Petit Chaperon rouge** Little Red Riding Hood

**chapiteau** *(m)* tent

**chapitre** *(m)* chapter

**chaque** each, every (3)

**charbon** *(m)* coal

**charcuterie** *(f)* delicatessen, deli meats, cold cuts (8)

**charger** to charge, to load; **chargé(e) (de)** busy, in charge (of); **se charger de** to take charge of

**charité** *(f)* charity

**charmant(e)** charming

**chasse** *(f)* hunt, hunting; **aller à la chasse** to go hunting

**chasser** to hunt, to make go away

**chasseur** *(m)* hunter

**chat** *(m)* cat (3)

**châtain** (light to medium) brown (hair) (4)

**château** *(m)* castle

**chaud(e)** hot (2); **avoir chaud** to be hot (4); **chocolat chaud** *(m)* hot chocolate (2); **Il fait chaud.** It's hot. (5)

**chauffant(e)** heating

**chauffé(e)** heated

**chauffeur** *(m)* driver

**chaume** *(m)* thatch

**chaussette** *(f)* sock (5)

**chausson** *(m)* **aux pommes** apple turnover

**chaussure** *(f)* shoe (5)

**chef** *(m)* head, boss, chief

**chef-d'œuvre** *(m)* masterpiece

**chemin** *(m)* road; **chemin** *(m)* **de fer** railroad; **indiquer le chemin** to give directions, to show the way (10)

**chemise** *(f)* shirt (5); **chemise** *(f)* **de nuit** nightgown

**chemisier** *(m)* blouse (5)

**chêne** *(m)* oak

**chèque** *(m)* check (9); **chèque** *(m)* **de voyage** traveler's check (9)

**cher(-ère)** expensive (3), dear

**chercher** to look for (3), to seek; **aller / venir chercher quelqu'un** to go / to come get someone (10)

**chercheur(-euse)** *(mf)* researcher

**chéri(e)** *(mf)* honey, darling

**cheval** *(m)* horse; **faire du cheval** to go horseback riding

**chevet: livre** *(m)* **de chevet** bedside book

**cheveux** *(mpl)* hair (4)

**cheville** *(f)* ankle; **se fouler la cheville** to sprain one's ankle

**chèvre** *(m)* goat cheese

**chez...** at / in / to / by . . . 's house/place (2); in (a person) (7)

**chien** *(m)* dog (3)

**chiffre** *(m)* number, numeral (P)

**Chili** *(m)* Chile (9)

**chimie** *(f)* chemistry (1)

**chimique** chemical

**Chine** *(f)* China (9)

**chinois** *(m)* Chinese

**chirurgie** *(f)* surgery

**choc** *(m)* shock, impact

**chocolat** *(m)* chocolate (2); **gâteau au chocolat** *(m)* chocolate cake (8); **pain au chocolat** *(m)* chocolate-filled croissant (8)

**choisir (de faire)** to choose (to do) (8)

**choix** *(m)* choice (8)

**choquer** to shock

**chose** *(f)* thing (3); **quelque chose** something (2)

**chou** *(m)* cabbage; **choux** *(mpl)* **de Bruxelles** Brussels sprouts

**chouette** neat, great

**chou-fleur** *(m)* cauliflower

**chrétien(ne)** Christian

**chrysanthème** *(m)* chrysanthemum

**ci: ce (cet, cette)... ci** this. . . (3); **ce mois-ci** this month (4); **ces... ci** these. . . (3); **ci-dessous**

below; **ci-dessus** above; **comme ci comme ça** so-so (2)

**ciao** bye (informal)

**cible** *(f)* target

**ciel** *(m)* sky

**cinéaste** *(mf)* filmmaker

**cinéclub** *(m)* cinema club (2)

**cinéma** *(m)* cinema, movie theater (1); **aller au cinéma** to go to the movies (2)

**cinématographique** film

**cinq** five (P)

**cinquante** fifty (2)

**cinquième** fifth (3)

**circonstance** *(f)* circumstance

**circuit** *(m)* circuit, course

**circulation** *(f)* traffic

**circuler** to circulate

**cité universitaire** *(f)* residence halls complex

**citoyen(ne)** *(mf)* citizen

**citoyenneté** *(f)* citizenship

**citron** *(m)* lemon (2); **citron vert** *(m)* lime; **thé** *(m)* **au citron** tea with lemon (2)

**civet** *(m)* stew

**civil(e)** civil

**civique** civic

**clair(e)** light, clear; **bleu clair** light blue

**clairement** clearly

**classe** *(f)* class (1); **classe aisée** *(f)* upper class; **classe** *(f)* **touriste** tourist class, coach (9); **première classe** *(f)* first class (9); **salle** *(f)* **de classe** classroom (1)

**classique** classical (1), classic (2)

**clavier** *(m)* keyboard

**clé** *(f)* key (10)

**client(e)** *(mf)* customer

**climat** *(m)* climate (9)

**climatisé(e)** air-conditioned

**clinique** *(f)* clinic

**cloche** *(f)* bell

**clos(e)** closed

**clôture** *(f)* closure, closing date

**club** *(m)* club; **club** *(m)* **de gym** gym, fitness club (1); **club** *(m)* **de sport** sports club

**coca** *(m)* cola (2)

**cocotier** *(m)* coconut tree

**cocotte** *(f)* casserole, primper

**code** *(m)* code; **code** *(m)* **de fonctionnement** responsibility; **code postal** *(m)* zip code (3)

**cœur** *(m)* heart; **au cœur de** in the heart of

**coiffure** *(f)* hair style

**coin** *(m)* corner (3); **au coin (de)** on the corner (of) (10); **café** *(m)* **du coin** neighborhood café; **dans le coin de** in the corner of (3)

**colère** *(f)* anger; **en colère** angry

**colis** *(m)* package

**collaborateur(-trice)** *(mf)* colleague

**collant** *(m)* pantyhose

**collation** *(f)* snack

**collectionner** to collect

**collectivité** *(f)* community

**collège** *(m)* secondary school

**collègue** *(mf)* colleague

**coller** to glue

**collier** *(m)* necklace

**colocataire** *(mf)* housemate, co-renter (P)

**Colombie** *(f)* Columbia (9)

**colonie** *(f)* colony

**colonisateur(-trice)** *(mf)* colonizer

**coloniser** to colonize

**colonne** *(f)* column

**combattre** to fight, to combat

**combien (de)** how much, how many (3); **Ça fait combien? / C'est combien?** How much is it? (2); **combien de** how many, how much (3);

**Combien font... et... / moins... ?** How much is . . . plus . . . / minus . . . ? (P); **Pendant combien de temps?** For how long? (5); **Vous êtes combien?** How many are there (of you)? (4)

**combinaison** *(f)* slip

**combiner** to combine

**comédie** *(f)* comedy (6); **comédie musicale** *(f)* musical

**comédien(ne)** *(mf)* actor

**comique** comical

**commander** to order (2), to command

**comme** like, as (1) , since (7), for (8); **comme ci comme ça** so-so (2); **comme tu vois** as you see (3)

**commencement** *(m)* beginning

**commencer (à)** to begin (to), to start (2); **Le cours de français commence...** The French class starts . . . (P)

**comment** how (P); **Ça s'écrit comment?** How do you write that? (P); Comment? What? (P); **Comment allez-vous?** How are you? (P); **Comment ça va?** How's it going? (P); **Comment dit-on... en français?** How do you say . . . in French? (P); **Comment est (sont)... ?** What is (are) . . . like? (1); **Comment s'appelle... ?** What is . . . 's name? (4); **Comment vas-tu?** How are you? (informal); **Comment vous appelez-vous?** What's your name? (formal) (P); **Tu t'appelles comment? / Comment t'appelles-tu?** What's your name? (informal)

**commerçant(e)** *(mf)* shopkeeper, merchant (8)

**commerce** *(m)* business (1)

**commercial: centre commercial** *(m)* shopping center, mall (4)

**commettre** to commit

**commode** *(f)* dresser, chest of drawers (3)

**commode** convenient (3)

**commodité** *(f)* convenience, comfort

**commun(e)** common

**communauté** *(f)* community

**commune** *(f)* parish

**communiquer** to communicate (10)

**compagnie** *(f)* company; **en compagnie de** accompanied by

**comparaison** *(f)* comparison

**comparer** to compare (6)

**compatibilité** *(f)* compatibility (7)

**compétence** *(f)* skill, competency

**complément d'objet direct / indirect** *(m)* direct / indirect object

**complémentaire** complementary

**complet(-ète)** complete (8); **en phrases complètes** *(f)* in complete sentences (P); **pain complet** *(m)* wholegrain bread (8)

**complètement** completely

**compléter** to complete

**complexe** complex, complicated

**compliqué(e)** complicated

**comporter: se comporter** to behave

**composer** to compose; **composé(e) de** composed of; **se composer de** to be made up of

**compote** *(f)* stewed fruit

**compotier** *(m)* fruit bowl

**compréhension** *(f)* understanding (7)

**comprenant** including

**comprendre** to understand (4), to include (8); **compris(e)** included (10); **Je comprends.** I understand. (P); **Vous comprenez?** Do you understand? (P)

**comptabilité** *(f)* accounting (1)

**comptable** *(mf)* accountant

**compte** *(m)* **en banque** bank account

**compter** to count (2), to plan (9); **Comptez de... à...** Count from . . . to . . . (P)

**concentrer: se concentrer sur** to concentrate on

**concerner** to concern

**concert** *(m)* concert (1); **de concert avec** along with

**concevoir** to conceive

**concombre** *(m)* cucumber

**concours** *(m)* competition, competitive entrance examination

**concurrent(e)** *(mf)* competitor

**conducteur(-trice)** *(mf)* driver

**conduire** to drive

**conduite** *(f)* conduct

**confection** *(f)* making

**confiance** *(f)* confidence; **avoir confiance** to have confidence (4)

**confidence** *(f)* secret

**confier à** to confide in, to entrust to

**confirmer** to confirm

**confit** *(m)* **de canard** conserve of duck

**confiture** *(f)* jam, jelly (8)

**conflit** *(m)* conflict

**confondre** to confuse; confondu(e) combined

**confort** *(m)* comfort

**confortable** comfortable (3)

**confus(e)** confused

**conjugal(e)** *(mpl* **conjuguaux)** married, conjugal

**conjuguer** to conjugate

**connaissance** *(f)* acquaintance, knowledge; **faire connaissance** to meet (1);

**connaître** to know, to get to know, to be familiar / acquainted with (4); **Connaissez-vous... ?** Do you know . . . ? (6); **faire connaître** to inform

**connu(e)** known

**conquérant(e)** *(mf)* conqueror

**conquête** *(f)* conquest

**consacrer** to devote; **consacré(e) à** devoted to

**conseil** *(m)* a piece of advice (8), council, committee

**conseiller(-ère)** *(mf)* counselor, adviser

**conséquence** *(f)* consequence; **en conséquence** as a consequence

**conséquent: par conséquent** consequently

**conservateur(-trice)** conservative (7)

**conserver** to keep

**conserves** *(fpl)* canned goods (8)

**considérer** to consider; **considéré(e)** considered; **se considérer** to consider oneself

**consommation** *(f)* consumption, drink

**consonne** *(f)* consonant

**constamment** constantly

**constituer** to make up

**construire** to construct, to build

**consulat** *(m)* consulate

**consulter** to consult

**conte** *(m)* story (6); **conte** *(m)* **de fée** fairy tale (6)

**contemporain(e)** contemporary

**contenir** to contain

**content(e)** happy, glad (8)

**conteur(-euse)** *(mf)* storyteller

**contexte** *(m)* context

**continent** *(m)* continent (9)

**continuer** to continue (10)

**contraire** *(m)* contrary; **au contraire** on the contrary

**contraste** *(m)* contrast

**contrat** *(m)* contract

**contre** against; **par contre** on the other hand

**contrepoids** *(m)* counterbalance

**contribuer** to contribute

**contrôle** *(m)* control

**contrôler** to control (8)

**convenable** appropriate, suitable

**convenir** to be suitable; **Ça vous convient?** Does that work for you? (9)

**convivialité** (f) friendliness

**convoité(e)** coveted

**cool: assez cool** pretty cool (P)

**copain** (m) (male) friend, pal (6)

**copieux(-euse)** copious, large (8)

**copine** (f) (female) friend, pal (6)

**coq au vin** (m) chicken in wine sauce

**coquillage** (m) shellfish

**coquilles St-Jacques** (fpl) scallops

**corporel(le)** of the body

**corps** (m) body (7); **Corps** (m) **de la Paix** Peace Corps

**correspondant(e)** corresponding

**correspondre (à)** to correspond (to)

**Corse** (f) Corsica

**corse** (m) Corsican (language)

**costume** (m) man's suit (5)

**côte** (f) coast; **côte** (f) **de porc** pork chop (8)

**côté** (m) side (3); **à côté (de)** next to (3); **côté cour** on the courtyard side (10); **de l'autre côté (de)** on the other side (of) (3)

**Côte d'Ivoire** (f) Ivory Coast (9)

**coton** (m) cotton

**cou** (m) neck

**couchant** setting

**coucher: se coucher** to go to bed (7); **chambre à coucher** (f) bedroom

**coulée** (f) flow

**couler** to run (liquids)

**couleur** (f) color (3); **De quelle couleur est/sont... ?** What color is/are . . . ? (3)

**coulis** (m) purée

**couloir** (m) hall, corridor (3)

**coup** (m) stroke, blow; **coup** (m) **de foudre** love at first sight (7); **coup** (m) **d'état** coup; **coup** (m) **de téléphone** telephone call; **tout d'un coup** all of a sudden (6)

**coupe** (f) dessert dish

**couper** to cut; **se couper le doigt** to cut one's finger

**cour** (f) court, courtyard; **côté cour** on the courtyard side (10)

**couramment** fluently

**courant(e)** present, current, common

**courber l'échine** to bend one's back

**courgette** (f) zucchini

**courir** to run (9)

**courrier** (m) mail; **courrier électronique** (m) email

**cours** (m) class (P), course; **au cours de** in the course of, during, while on (10); **avoir cours** to have class (6); **suivre un cours** to take a course

**course** (f) errand (5), race; **faire des courses** to run errands (5); **faire les courses** to go grocery shopping

**court** (m) **de tennis** tennis court

**court(e)** short (4); **court métrage** (m) short film

**cousin(e)** (mf) cousin (4)

**coûter** to cost (5)

**coutume** (f) custom

**couture** (f) sewing, dressmaking; ***haute couture** (f) designer fashion (5)

**couvert(e)** de covered by

**couverture** (f) blanket, cover (3)

**couvrir** to cover

**cravate** (f) tie (5)

**crayon** (m) pencil (P)

**créancier(-ière)** (mf) creditor

**créateur(-trice)** (mf) creator

**crèche** (f) (government-sponsored) day care

**crédit: carte** (f) **de crédit** credit card (9)

**créer** to create

**crème** (f) cream (8)

**créole** Creole

**crevette** (f) shrimp (8)

**crier** to shout

**criminel(le)** (mf) criminal

**crise** (f) crisis; **crise cardiaque** (f) heart attack

**critique** (f) criticism

**croc** (m) fang

**croire (à) (que)** to believe (in) (that) (10); **je crois** I think

**croissant** (m) croissant

**croque-madame** (m) toasted ham-and-cheese sandwich with an egg on top

**croque-monsieur** (m) toasted ham-and-cheese sandwich

**cru(e)** raw

**crudités** (fpl) raw vegetables (8)

**cuiller** (f) spoon

**cuillerée** (f) spoonful

**cuir** (m) leather

**cuire** to cook

**cuisine** (f) kitchen (3), cuisine, cooking (4); **faire la cuisine** to cook (5)

**cuisinière** (f) stove

**cuisson** (f) cooking

**cuivre** (m) copper

**cultiver** to cultivate (7)

**culture** (f) culture (9), cultivation

**culturel(le)** cultural (4)

**curieux(-euse)** curious, odd

**curiosité** (f) curiosity

**cyclisme** (m) cycling

**cycliste** (mf) cyclist

# D

**dactylographie** (f) typing

**dame** (f) lady; **messieurs-dames** gentlemen-ladies

**Danemark** (m) Denmark

**danger** (m) danger

**dangereux(-euse)** dangerous

**dans** in (P); **dans la rue...** on . . . street (10)

**danse** (f) dance

**danser** to dance (2)

**danseur(-euse)** (mf) dancer

**date** (f) date (4); **Quelle est la date aujourd'hui?** What is the date today? (4)

**dater de** to date from

**daurade** (f) sea bream

**davantage** more

**de** from, of (P), about (1); **de la, de l'** some (8); **de luxe** deluxe (10); **de rien** you're welcome (P); **parler de** to talk about

**débarquement** (m) landing

**débrouiller: se débrouiller** to get by

**début** (m) beginning (6)

**débutant(e)** (mf) beginner

**décembre** (m) December (4)

**décennie** (f) decade

**déchets** (mpl) trash, rubbish

**décidément** decidedly, for sure

**décider** to decide (8); **se décider** to make up one's mind

**décision** (f) decision (7); **prendre une décision** to make a decision (7)

**décompresser** to let off steam

**décorer** to decorate

**découper** to cut out

**découverte** (f) discovery

**découvrir** to discover

**décrire** to describe (9)

**décrocher** to unhook, to get, to land

**défaire: défaire ses valises** to unpack

**défendre** to defend, to forbid; **défendu(e)** forbidden; **se défendre** to defend oneself

**défi** (m) challenge

**défilé** (m) parade

**défini(e)** definite

**définir** to define

**degré** (m) degree

**dégustation** (f) sampling

**dehors** outside; **en dehors de** outside of

**déjà** already (5)

**déjeuner** (m) lunch; **petit déjeuner** (m) breakfast (5)

**déjeuner** to have lunch (2)

**délicieux(-euse)** delicious (6)

**délivrance** (f) issue, delivery

**déluge** (m) flood

**demain** tomorrow (P); **À demain!** See you tomorrow! (P)

**demande** (f) request

**demander** to ask (for) (2); **se demander** to wonder

**demeurer** to remain

**demi** (m) draft beer (2)

**demi(e)** half (P); **demi-heure** (f) half hour (7); **Il est deux heures et demie.** It's half past two. (P); **un kilo et demi** a kilo and a half (8)

**démocratie** (f) democracy

**démocratique** democratic

**dénoncer** to denounce, to turn in

**dent** (f) tooth (7)

**dentaire** dental

**départ** (m) departure (9)

**département** (m) department (a French administrative region)

**dépasser** to go beyond

**dépaysement** (m) change of scenery

**dépêcher: se dépêcher** to hurry

**dépendre (de)** to depend (on) (5); **Ça dépend.** That depends.

**dépense** (f) expense

**déplier** to unfold

**déposer** to deposit

**déprime** (f) depression

**déprimé(e)** depressed

**depuis** since, for (7), from; **depuis que** since

**député** (m) deputy

**dérivé(e)** derived

**dernier(-ère)** last (5)

**derrière** behind (3)

**des** some (1)

**dés** (mpl) dice

**dès** since, right after; **dès que** as soon as

**désagréable** unpleasant (1)

**descendre (de)** to go down, to get off (5); **descendre dans / à** to stay at (a hotel) (5)

**déshabiller** to undress; **se déshabiller** to get undressed (7)

**désir** (m) desire

**désirer** to desire; **Vous désirez?** What would you like?, May I help you? (2)

**désireux (désireuse)** desirous

**désolé(e)** sorry (10)

**désordre: en désordre** in disorder (3)

**désormais** henceforth, from now on

**dessert** (m) dessert (8)

**dessin** (m) drawing; **dessin animé** (m) cartoon

**dessinateur** (m) artist

**dessiner** to draw

**dessous: ci-dessous** below

**dessus: au dessus de** above

**destin** (m) destiny

**détaillé(e)** detailed

**détendre: se détendre** to relax

**détenir** to hold, to possess

**détente** (f) relaxation

**détenteur(-trice)** (mf) holder

**déterminer** to determine

**détester** to hate (7); **se détester** to hate each other (7)

**détruit(e)** destroyed

**dette** *(f)* debt

**deux** two (P); **deux-tiers** two-thirds

**deuxième** second (3)

**devant** in front of (3)

**devanture** *(f)* shop window

**développement** *(m)* development

**développer** to develop

**devenir** to become (4)

**deviner** to guess

**devinette** *(f)* riddle

**devise** *(f)* currency

**devoir** must, to have to, to owe (6); **il/elle doit** he/she must (3)

**devoirs** *(mpl)* homework (P)

**diabète** *(m)* diabetes

**diable** *(m)* devil

**diamant** *(m)* diamond

**diarrhée** *(f)* diarrhea

**dictature** *(f)* dictatorship

**dictée** *(f)* dictation

**dictionnaire** *(m)* dictionary

**dieu** *(m)* god

**différemment** differently

**différent(e)** different

**difficile** difficult (P)

**difficulté** *(f)* difficulty

**digérer** to digest

**dignité** *(f)* dignity

**digue** *(f)* causeway

**dimanche** *(m)* Sunday (P)

**diminuer** to diminish

**dinde** *(f)* turkey

**dîner** *(m)* dinner (8)

**dîner** to have dinner, to dine (2)

**diplôme** *(m)* diploma, degree

**diplômé(e)** *(mf)* graduate

**dire** to say, to tell (6); **Ça te/vous dit?** How does that sound to you? (4); **Comment dit-on... en français?** How do you say . . . in French? (P); **On dit que...** They say that . . . ; **Qu'est-ce que ça veut dire?** What does that mean? (P)

**direct(e)** direct

**directement** directly

**directeur(-trice)** *(mf)* director

**diriger** to direct, to conduct

**discothèque** *(f)* dance club

**discuter** to discuss

**disparaître** to disappear; **disparu(e)** having disappeared

**disponible** available

**disposer de** to have available

**disposition: à la disposition de** available to

**disputer** to dispute; **se disputer (avec)** to argue (with) (7)

**disque** *(m)* record; **disque compact** *(m)* compact disc

**dissiper** to dissipate

**distingué(e)** distinguished

**distinguer** to distinguish

**distraction** *(f)* entertainment (5)

**distribué(e)** distributed

**distributeur** *(m)* **de billets** ATM machine (10)

**divers(e)** diverse, different

**diversité** *(f)* diversity

**diviser** to divide; **se diviser (en)** to divide (into)

**divorcer** to divorce; **divorcé(e)** divorced (1)

**dix** ten (P); **dix-huit** eighteen (P); **dix-huitième** eighteenth (3); **dix-neuf** nineteen (P); **dix-sept** seventeen (P)

**dixième** tenth (3)

**doctorat** *(m)* doctorate

**documentaire** *(m)* documentary

**dodo** *(m)* bedtime (familiar)

**doigt** *(m)* finger (10); **doigt** *(m)* **de pied** toe (10)

**dollar** *(m)* dollar (3)

**dolmen** *(m)* dolmen (an ancient megalithic structure)

**domaine** *(m)* domain, field

**domestique** *(mf)* servant

**domestique** domestic, household; **tâche domestique** *(f)* household chore

**domicile** *(m)* place of residence

**dominer** to dominate

**dommage: C'est dommage!** It's a shame! It's a pity! (7)

**donc** so, therefore, thus, then (7)

**donner** to give (2); **donner à manger à** to feed (9); **donner lieu à** to give rise to; **Donnez-moi...** Give me . . . (P)

**dont** of which, among which, whose

**dormir** to sleep (2)

**dos** *(m)* back (10)

**dossier** *(m)* file

**doté(e)** endowed

**douane** *(f)* customs (9)

**douanier(-ière)** customs

**doublé(e)** doubled, dubbed

**douche** *(f)* shower (7)

**douleur** *(f)* pain, ache

**douloureux(-euse)** painful

**doute** *(m)* doubt; **sans doute** without doubt (5); probably (8)

**douter** to doubt (10)

**doux (douce)** sweet, soft, gentle (6)

**douzaine** *(f)* dozen (8)

**douze** twelve (P)

**dramatique** dramatic

**dramaturge** *(m)* playwright

**drame** *(m)* drama

**drap** *(m)* sheet

**dresser** to set up

**droit** *(m)* law (field of study), right (legal); **droits** *(mpl)* **de l'homme** human rights; **tout droit** straight (10)

**droite** *(f)* right (direction): **à droite (de)** to the right (of) (3)

**du (de la, de l', des)** some (8)

**dû (due, dus, dues) à** due to

**duc** *(m)* duke

**duché** *(m)* dukedom, duchy

**dur(e)** hard; **œuf dur** *(m)* hard-boiled egg (8)

**durant** during

**durée** *(f)* duration

**durer** to last

**DVD** *(m)* DVD (2), **lecteur DVD** *(m)* DVD player (3)

**dynamique** active (1)

## E

**eau** *(f)* water (2)

**écailler** to open (shellfish)

**échange** *(m)* exchange

**échanger** to exchange

**échapper** to escape; **s'échapper** to escape

**écharpe** *(f)* winter scarf

**échelle** *(f)* ladder

**échouer** to fail

**éclair** *(m)* éclair (a pastry)

**éclairage** *(m)* lighting

**éclaircie** *(f)* sunny spell

**éclairé(e)** lighted

**école** *(f)* school (6)

**écolo(giste)** *(mf)* environmentalist

**économie** *(f)* economy; **faire des économies** to save money

**économique** economic; **sciences économiques** *(fpl)* economics

**écossais(e)** plaid

**écossé(e)** shelled

**écoute: être à l'écoute de** to be listening to

**écouter** to listen (to) (2); **Écoutez...** Listen to . . . (P)

**écran** *(m)* screen

**écrevisse** *(f)* crawfish

**écrire** to write (2); **Ça s'écrit comment?** How do you write that? (P); **écrit(e)** written; **Écrivez...** Write . . . (P)

**écrivain** *(m)* writer

**éditer** to edit

**édition: maison** *(f)* **d'édition** publishing company

**éduquer** to educate

**effectuer** to carry out

**effet** *(m)* effect; **effets personnels** personal belongings (10); **effets spéciaux** special effects (6)

**efforcer: s'efforcer (de)** to endeavor

**égal(e)** *(mpl* **égaux***)* equal; **Ça m'est égal.** It's all the same to me.

**également** also, as well, equally, likewise

**égalité** *(f)* equality

**égard** *(m)* respect

**église** *(f)* church (4)

**égoïste** selfish

**Égypte** *(f)* Egypt (9)

**élection** *(f)* election

**électricité** *(f)* electricity

**électrique** electrical

**électronique** electronic; **courrier électronique** *(m)* e-mail

**élément** *(m)* element

**élevage** *(m)* raising livestock

**élève** *(mf)* pupil, student

**élevé(e)** high, elevated

**elle** she, it (1), her; **elles** they (1), them; **elle-même** herself

**éloigner** to remove, to make go away

**embarquement** *(m)* boarding; **porte** *(f)* **d'embarquement** departure gate (9)

**embêtant(e)** annoying (3)

**embrasser** to kiss (7); **s'embrasser** to kiss each other, to embrace each other (7)

**émincé(e)** thinly sliced

**emmener** to take

**emploi** *(m)* employment, use; **emploi** *(m)* **du temps** schedule (P)

**employé(e)** *(mf)* employee (10)

**employer** to use; **s'employer** to be used

**emporter** to carry away

**emprisonner** to imprison (6)

**emprunter (à)** to borrow (from)

**en** in (P); **de temps en temps** from time to time (4); **en avance** early; **en avion** by plane (4); **en désordre** in disorder (3); **en face (de)** across from, facing (3); **en ligne** online (7); **en même temps** at the same time; **en ordre** in order (3); **en plus** furthermore (8); **en retard** late (10); **en solde** on sale (5); **en tout temps** at all times; **en vacances** on vacation; **être en train de...** to be in the process of . . . ; **partir en week-end** to go away for the weekend (5); **payer en espèces** to pay cash (10)

**en** some, any, about it/them, of it/them (8); **Je vous/t'en prie.** You're welcome.; **s'en aller** to go away

**enceinte** pregnant (10)

**enchaîné(e)** chained up

**Enchanté(e).** Delighted to meet you.

**enchanter** to enchant

**encore** still (4), again, more (8); **ne... pas encore** not yet (5)
**encourager** to encourage
**endormir: s'endormir** to fall asleep (7)
**endroit** *(m)* place (9)
**énergie** *(f)* energy
**énergique** energetic
**énerver** to irritate
**enfance** *(f)* childhood
**enfant** *(mf)* child (4)
**enfanter** to give birth to
**enfer** *(m)* hell
**enfin** finally (7)
**enflé(e)** swollen
**engager** to hire
**ennemi(e)** *(mf)* enemy
**ennui** *(m)* trouble
**ennuyer** to bore; **s'ennuyer (de)** to get bored (with), to be bored (with) (7)
**ennuyeux(-euse)** boring (1)
**énorme** enormous
**enquête** *(f)* investigation, survey
**enregistrer** to record
**enrichir** to enrich
**enseignement** *(m)* teaching, education; **enseignement supérieur** higher education
**enseigner** to teach
**ensemble** *(m)* whole group
**ensemble** together (2)
**ensuite** next, then (4)
**entendre** to hear (7); **s'entendre bien/mal (avec)** to get along well/badly (with) (7)
**enthousiasme** *(m)* enthusiasm
**entier(-ère)** entire, whole; **à part entière** complete
**entouré(e) (de)** surrounded (by)
**entre** between (3), among
**entrée** *(f)* appetizer (8), entry ticket, entrance, entry; **entrée au cinéma** *(f)* cinema attendance
**entreprise** *(f)* firm, enterprise
**entrer (dans)** to enter, to go in (5)
**entretien** *(m)* conversation, interview, maintenance
**envahir** to invade
**enveloppe** *(f)* envelope
**envers** towards
**envie: avoir envie de** to feel like, to desire (4)
**environ** around, about (4)
**environnement** *(m)* environment
**environs** *(mpl)* surrounding area
**envoyer** to send (10)
**épais(se)** thick
**épaisseur** *(f)* thickness
**épanouir: s'épanouir** to flourish
**épaule** *(f)* shoulder
**épée** *(f)* sword
**épicerie** *(f)* grocer's shop (8)
**épicier(-ière)** *(mf)* grocer
**épinards** *(mpl)* spinach
**époque** *(f)* time period; **à cette époque-là** at that time, in those days
**épouser** to marry; **s'épouser** to get married
**épouvante: film** *(m)* **d'épouvante** horror movie (6)
**époux (épouse)** *(mf)* spouse
**épreuve** *(f)* test
**épuisé(e)** exhausted
**équilibré(e)** balanced
**équipe** *(f)* team
**équipé(e)** equipped
**équipée** *(f)* venture
**équipement** *(m)* equipment
**érotique** erotic
**escalade** *(f)* (rock) climbing

**escale** *(f)* stopover
**escalier** *(m)* stairs, staircase (3)
**escargot** *(m)* snail (8)
**escarpé(e)** steep
**esclavage** *(m)* slavery
**esclave** *(mf)* slave
**espace** *(m)* space
**Espagne** *(f)* Spain (9)
**espagnol** *(m)* Spanish (P)
**espagnol(e)** Spanish
**espèce** *(f)* species; **Espèce de... !** You . . . !; **payer en espèces** to pay cash (10)
**espérer** to hope (3)
**espiègle** mischievous
**espion(ne)** *(mf)* spy
**espionnage** *(m)* spying
**espoir** *(m)* hope; **meilleur jeune espoir** *(m)* best new actor
**esprit** *(m)* mind, spirit (7)
**essayage** *(m)* fitting; **cabine** *(f)* **d'essayage** fitting room (5)
**essayer** to try on (5); **essayer (de faire)** to try (to do)
**essentiel(le)** essential
**essoufflé(e)** to be out of breath
**est** *(m)* east
**est-ce que** (question marker) (1)
**estimer** to estimate, to reakon
**estival(e): station estivale** *(f)* a summer resort (10)
**et** and (P)
**établir** to establish; **s'établir** to establish oneself, to settle
**établissement** *(m)* establishment
**étage** *(m)* floor (3); **à l'étage** on the same floor, down the hall; **À quel étage?** On what floor? (3); **au premier étage** on the second floor (3)
**étagère** *(f)* shelf, bookcase (3)
**étain** *(m)* tin
**étape** *(f)* stopping place, step
**état** *(m)* state (3), condition
**États-Unis** *(mpl)* United States (3)
**été** *(m)* summer (5); **en été** in summer (5)
**étendre: s'étendre** to extend; **étendu(e)** stretched out
**éternuer** to sneeze (10)
**ethnique** ethnic
**étoile** *(f)* star
**étonner** to surprise, to amaze; **étonné(e)** surprised, amazed (10)
**étouffant(e)** stifling
**étouffement** *(m)* suffocation
**étranger(-ère)** foreign (1); **à l'étranger** abroad (9)
**être** to be (1); **c'est** it's (P), he is, she is this is, that is (1); **C'est quel jour aujourd'hui?** What day is today? (P); **Comment est/sont... ?** What is/are . . . like? (1); **être à** to belong to; **je suis** I'm (P); **le français est...** French is . . . (P); **Nous sommes six.** There are six of us. (4); **Quelle est la date aujourd'hui?** What is the date today? (4); **tu es/vous êtes** you are (P)
**être humain** *(m)* human being
**étroit(e)** tight
**étude: études** *(fpl)* studies (1), **salle** *(f)* **d'étude** study room
**étudiant(e)** *(mf)* student (P)
**étudier** to study (1)
**euro** *(m)* euro (2)
**Europe** *(f)* Europe (9)
**européen(ne)** European
**eux** them, they; **eux-mêmes** themselves
**évader: s'évader** to escape
**évasion** *(f)* escape
**événement** *(m)* event

**évidemment** of course, obviously
**éviter** to avoid (8)
**exact(e)** exact
**exactement** exactly (10)
**examen** *(m)* test, exam (P)
**excentrique** eccentric
**excessivement** excessively
**exclamer: s'exclamer** to exclaim, to cry out
**excuser** to excuse, to forgive; **Excusez-moi.** Excuse me. (P); **s'excuser** to apologize
**exécutif(-ive)** executive
**exemple** *(m)* example; **par exemple** for example (2)
**exercer** to exert
**exercice** *(m)* exercise (P); **faire de l'exercice** to exercise (5)
**exiger** to require
**exister** to exist
**exotique** exotic (9)
**expérience** *(f)* experience, experiment
**explication** *(f)* explanation
**expliquer** to explain (10)
**explorateur(-trice)** *(mf)* explorer
**exploser** to explode
**exposé(e)** exposed
**exposition** *(f)* exhibit (4)
**expresso** *(m)* espresso (2)
**expression** *(f)* expression (10)
**exprimer** to express
**expulser** to throw out
**extérieur** *(m)* outside, exterior
**extinction** *(f)* extinguishing
**extra** great, terrific (4); **extra-scolaire** extracurricular
**extrait** *(m)* excerpt
**extraordinaire** extraordinary (9)
**extraverti(e)** outgoing, extroverted (1)

**F**
**fac** *(f)* university, campus (2)
**face** *(f)* face; **en face (de)** across from, facing (3); **face à** across from, confronted with; **faire face à** to face
**facile** easy (P)
**facilement** easily (7)
**faciliter** to facilitate, to make easy
**façon** *(f)* way
**facture** *(f)* bill
**faculté (fac)** *(f)* university, campus (2)
**faillir: j'ai failli tomber** I almost fell
**faim** *(f)* hunger; **avoir faim** to be hungry (4); **j'ai faim** I'm hungry (2)
**faire** to do, to make (2); **Ça fait... euros.** That's . . . euros. (2); **Ça ne se fait pas!** That is not done!; **faire attention (à)** to pay attention (to), to watch out (for) (8); **faire connaissance** to meet (1); **faire connaître** to inform; **faire de l'aérobic** to do aerobics (8); **faire de l'alpinisme** to go mountain climbing; **faire de la marche à pied** to go walking; **faire de la musculation** to do weight training, to do bodybuilding (8); **faire de la musique** to play music (2); **faire de la planche à voile** to go windsurfing; **faire de la plongée sous-marine** to go scuba diving; **faire de la varappe** to go rock climbing; **faire de l'exercice** to exercise (5); **faire des courses** to run errands (5); **faire des économies** to save up (money); **faire des projets** to make plans (4); **faire du bateau** to go boating (5); **faire du camping** to go camping (5); **faire du cheval** to go horseback riding; **faire du jardinage** to garden (5); **faire du jogging** to jog (2); **faire du patin (à glace)** to go (ice-)skating; **faire du roller** to go

rollerblading (6); **faire du shopping** to go shopping (2); **faire du skateboard(ing)** to skateboard (6); **faire du ski (nautique)** to go (water-)skiing (5); **faire du sport** to play sports (2); **faire du tuba** to go snorkeling; **faire du vélo** to go bike-riding (5); **faire face à** to face; **faire la cuisine** to cook (5); **faire la fête** to party; **faire la lessive** to do laundry (5); **faire la vaisselle** to do the dishes (5); **faire le ménage** to do housework (5); **faire les courses** to go grocery shopping; **faire mal** to hurt; **faire noir** to be dark (6); **faire sa toilette** to wash up (7); **faire ses valises** to pack one's bags (9); **faire une promenade** to go for a walk (5); **faire une randonnée** to go for a hike (8); **faire une réservation** to make a reservation (9); **faire un tour** to take a tour, to go for a ride (4); **faire un voyage** to take a trip (5); **Faites les devoirs dans le cahier.** Do the homework in the workbook. (P); **Faites l'exercice A à la page 21.** Do exercise A on page 21. (P); **Il fait beau / chaud / du soleil / du vent / frais / froid / mauvais.** It's nice / hot / sunny / windy / cool / cold / bad. (5); **Il fait bon / du brouillard.** It's nice / foggy.; **Il va faire beau. . .** It's going to be nice. . . (5); **Je fais du 42.** I wear a 42. (5); **Je ne fais pas de musique / de sport.** I don't play music / sports. (2); **Quelle taille faites-vous?** What size do you need? (5); **Quel temps fait-il?** What's the weather like? (5); **Quel temps va-t-il faire?** What's the weather going to be like? (5); **Qu'est-ce que vous faites/tu fais?** What are you doing? What do you do? (2)
**faisan** *(m)* pheasant
**falaise** *(f)* cliff
**falloir: il faut. . .** it is necessary . . . , one must . . . , one needs . . . (8); **il me/te/nous/vous faut** I/you/we/you need (9); **il ne faut pas** one shouldn't, one must not . . . (10)
**fameux(-euse)** famous
**familial(e)** *(mpl* **familiaux)** family
**familiariser: se familiariser (avec)** to get to know
**familier(-ère)** familiar, informal
**familièrement** colloquially
**famille** *(f)* family (P)
**famine** *(f)* famine, starvation
**fantastique** fantastic; **film fantastique** *(m)* fantasy movie
**farci(e)** stuffed
**farine** *(f)* flour
**fascinant(e)** fascinating
**fasciner** to fascinate
**fast-food** *(m)* fast food restaurant (1)
**fatigant(e)** tiring
**fatigué(e)** tired (6)
**faut** See **falloir.**
**faute** *(f)* lack, mistake, fault
**fauteuil** *(m)* armchair (3)
**faux (fausse)** false
**favoriser** to favor, to further
**féculents** *(mpl)* carbohydrates
**fédéral(e)** *(mpl* **fédéraux)** federal
**fée** *(f)* fairy; **conte** *(m)* **de fée** fairy tale (6)
**femme** *(f)* woman (1), wife (2); **ex-femme** *(f)* ex-wife; **femme au foyer** homemaker; **femme** *(f)* **d'affaires** businesswoman (5)
**fenêtre** *(f)* window (3)
**fenouil** *(m)* fennel
**fer** *(m)* iron; **chemin** *(m)* **de fer** railroad
**férié(e): jour férié** *(m)* holiday
**ferme** *(f)* farm
**fermer** to close (2); **Fermez votre livre.** Close your book. (P)

**féroce** ferocious (6)
**festival** *(m)* festival (4)
**fête** *(f)* holiday, celebration (4), party (P); **faire la fête** to party; **fête des mères** *(f)* Mother's Day; **fête des pères** *(f)* Father's Day; **fête du travail** *(f)* Labor Day; **fête nationale** *(f)* national holiday
**fêter** to celebrate
**feu** *(m)* fire; **prendre feu** to catch fire
**feuille** *(f)* **de papier** sheet of paper (P)
**feuilleté(e)** flaky (pastry)
**février** *(m)* February (4)
**fiancé(e)** engaged (1)
**fiancer: se fiancer** to get engaged (7)
**ficelle** *(f)* string
**fiche** *(f)* form
**fidélité** *(f)* faithfulness
**fier(-ère)** proud
**fièvre** *(m)* fever; **avoir de la fièvre** to have fever; **fièvre jaune** *(f)* yellow fever
**figure** *(f)* face (7)
**filière** *(f)* career path
**fille** *(f)* girl; daughter (4); **fille unique** *(f)* only child
**film** *(m)* movie (1)
**filmer** to film
**fils** *(m)* son (4); **fils unique** *(m)* only child
**fin** *(f)* end
**fin(e)** fine
**finalement** finally (6)
**financier(-ère)** financial
**financièrement** financially
**finir (de faire)** to finish (doing) (8); **finir par faire** to end up doing; **Le cours de français finit. . .** The French class ends . . . (P)
**fixe** fixed (8)
**fixer** to set, to fix
**flamand** *(m)* Flemish (language)
**fleur** *(f)* flower
**fleuri(e)** with a floral pattern
**fleuriste** *(mf)* florist
**fleuve** *(m)* river
**flore** *(f)* flora
**foie** *(m)* liver
**fois** *(f)* time, occasion (5); **à la fois** at the same time; **d'autres fois** other times (7); **Il était une fois. . .** Once upon a time . . . (6)
**folk** *(m)* folk music
**folklore** *(m)* folklore (4)
**foncé(e)** dark; **bleu foncé** dark blue
**fonction** *(f)* function; **en fonction de** according to; **voiture** *(f)* **de fonction** company car
**fonctionner** to function, to work
**fond** *(m)* bottom, back, background; **dans le fond** really, basically
**fondateur : père fondateur** *(m)* founding father
**fonder** to found; **fondé(e )** founded
**fonderie** *(f)* foundry
**fondre** to melt
**fontaine** *(f)* fountain
**football** *(m)* soccer (1); **football américain** football (1)
**force** *(f)* force, strength
**forcément** necessarily, inevitably
**forcer** to force
**forestier(-ère): exploitation forestière** *(f)* forestry
**forêt** *(f)* forest
**forger** to forge, to mold
**formation** *(f)* education
**forme** *(f)* shape; **en forme** in shape (8)
**former** to form, to educate
**formidable** great (7)
**formulaire** *(m)* form
**formule** *(f)* formula, expression

**fort(e)** strong (8)
**fort** very
**fortifié(e)** fortified
**fou (folle)** crazy
**foudre: coup** *(m)* **de foudre** love at first sight (7)
**foulard** *(m)* dress scarf
**fouler: se fouler la cheville** to sprain your ankle
**four (à micro-ondes)** *(m)* (microwave) oven
**fourchette** *(f)* fork
**fournir** to furnish
**fourrure** *(f)* fur
**foyer** *(m)* home; **femme au foyer** homemaker; **foyer** *(m)* **des étudiants** student center
**fragile** fragile
**fragmenté(e)** fragmented
**frais (fraîche)** fresh (8); **Il fait frais.** It's cool. (5)
**fraise** *(f)* strawberry (8)
**framboise** *(f)* raspberry
**franc** *(m)* franc
**français** *(m)* French (P)
**français(e)** French (1); **à la française** French-style
**France** *(f)* France (1)
**franchir** to cross
**francophone** French-speaking
**francophonie** *(f)* French-speaking world
**frapper** to strike
**fraternité** *(f)* brotherhood
**frénésie** *(f)* frenzy
**fréquemment** frequently
**fréquenter** to frequent, to hang out at
**frère** *(m)* brother (1); **beau-frère** *(m)* brother-in-law (4); **demi-frère** *(m)* stepbrother, halfbrother
**frigo** *(m)* refrigerator
**frire** to fry
**frisbee: jouer au frisbee** to play frisbee (4)
**frisé(e)** curly
**frisée** *(f)* curly endive
**frisson** *(m)* shiver (10)
**frites** *(fpl)* French fries (2); **steak-frites** *(m)* steak and fries (8)
**frivole** frivolous
**froid(e)** cold (4); **avoir froid** to be cold (4); **Il fait froid.** It's cold. (5)
**fromage** *(m)* cheese (2)
**frontière** *(f)* border (10)
**fruit** *(m)* fruit (8); **fruits** *(mpl)* **de mer** shellfish (8); **jus** *(m)* **de fruit** fruit juice (2)
**fruitier(-ière)** fruit
**fuir** to flee, to run away
**fumé(e)** smoked (8)
**fumée** *(f)* smoke
**fumer** to smoke (3)
**fumeur(-euse)** *(mf)* smoker; **section (non-) fumeur** *(f)* (non-)smoking section
**funérailles** *(fpl)* funeral
**furieux(-euse)** furious (10)
**futon** *(m)* futon (3)
**futur** *(m)* future (tense)

**G**

**gagner** to win (2), to gain; **gagner de l'argent** to earn money, to make money
**gai(e)** gay, lively
**gaieté** *(f)* cheerfulness
**gant** *(m)* glove
**garage** *(m)* garage
**garantir** to guarantee
**garçon** *(m)* boy (4), waiter (2)
**garder** to keep
**gare** *(f)* train station
**garni(e)** served with vegetables
**garniture** *(f)* garnish
**gaspiller** to waste

**gâteau** *(m)* cake (8)

**gauche** *(f)* left; **à gauche (de)** to the left (of) (3)

**gaulois(e)** from Gaul (ancient name for the region of modern France)

**gaz: gaz naturel** *(m)* natural gas

**géant** *(m)* giant

**gelé(e)** frozen

**gêné(e)** embarrassed

**généalogie** *(f)* genealogy

**général(e)** *(mpl* **généraux)** general; **en général** in general (2)

**généralement** generally (7)

**génial(e)** *(mpl* **géniaux)** great (4)

**genou** *(m)* knee

**genre** *(m)* gender, kind, type, genre

**gens** *(mpl)* people (1)

**gentil(le)** nice (1)

**géographie** *(f)* geography (9)

**géographique** geographical

**géographiquement** geographically

**géologie** *(f)* geology

**germer** to sprout

**geste** *(m)* gesture

**gestion** *(f)* management

**gilet** *(m)* vest

**glace** *(f)* ice cream (8), ice; **glace à la vanille** vanilla ice cream (8)

**glacier** *(m)* ice cream shop

**glisser** to glide

**global(e)** *(mpl* **globaux)** global

**gloire** *(f)* glory

**goéland** *(m)* seagull

**golf** *(m)* golf (2)

**gommage** *(m)* rubbing out

**gorge** *(f)* throat (10); **soutien-gorge** *(m)* bra

**gorille** *(m)* gorilla

**gosse** *(mf)* kid

**goulu(e)** gluttonous

**gousse** *(f)* clove

**goût** *(m)* taste

**goûter** to taste (9)

**goutte** *(f)* drop

**gouvernement** *(m)* government

**gouverner** to govern

**grâce** *(f)* grace; **jour** *(m)* **d'Action de grâce** Thanksgiving

**grâce à** thanks to, because of

**gracieux(-euse)** gracious (6)

**grammaire** *(f)* grammar

**gramme** *(m)* gram (8)

**grand(e)** big, large, tall (1); **grande surface** *(f)* superstore (8); **le grand amour** *(m)* true love (7)

**grand-chose: ne... pas grand-chose** not much, not a lot

**Grande-Bretagne** *(f)* Great Britain (9)

**grandir** to grow up, to grow, to get taller (8)

**grand-mère** *(f)* grandmother (4)

**grand-père** *(m)* grandfather (4)

**grands-parents** *(mpl)* grandparents (4)

**gras(se)** *(f)* fatty; **en caractères gras** boldfaced; **matière grasse** *(f)* fat (8)

**gratuit(e)** free (of charge)

**gratuitement** without charge

**grave** serious, grave

**Grèce** *(f)* Greece

**grenade** *(f)* pomegranate

**grille** *(f)* bars

**grillé(e)** grilled (8); **pain grillé(e)** toast (8)

**grippe** *(f)* flu (10)

**gris(e)** gray (3)

**gros(se)** big, fat (1)

**grossir** to get fatter (8)

**groupe** *(m)* group (6); **en groupe** in a group

**grouper** to group

**gruyère** *(m)* Swiss cheese

**guérir** to cure, to heal

**guerre** *(f)* war

**guichet** *(m)* ticket window; **guichet automatique** *(m)* automatic teller machine

**guide** *(m)* guide, guidebook (9)

**guitare** *(f)* guitar (2)

**Guyane** *(f)* Guiana

**gym: club** *(m)* **de gym** gym, fitness club (1)

**gymnase** *(m)* gym

## H

**habiller** to dress; **s'habiller** to get dressed (7)

**habitant(e)** *(mf)* inhabitant

**habiter** to live (2); **j'habite à** (+ city) I live in (+ city) (P); **Vous habitez... ?** Do you live. . . ? (P)

**habitude** *(f)* habit; **d'habitude** usually (2)

**habitué(e) à** used to, accustomed to

**habituel(le)** customary, usual

**\*haché(e)** chopped (up)

**\*haine** *(f)* hatred

**Haïti** *(m)* Haiti

**\*hamburger** *(m)* hamburger (8)

**\*handicapé(e)** handicapped

**\*Hanoukka** *(f)* Hanukkah

**\*haricots verts** *(mpl)* green beans (8)

**harmonie** *(f)* harmony

**\*hasard: par hasard** by chance

**\*haut: dans les hauts** high above; **(tout) en haut** at the (very) top

**\*haut(e)** high; **haute couture** *(f)* high fashion (5); **haut talon** *(m)* high heel

**hébergement** *(m)* accommodation

**hébreu** *(m)* Hebrew

**\*hein?** huh?

**helvétique** Helvetic (Swiss)

**hépatite** *(f)* hepatitis

**herbe** *(f)* grass

**héritage** *(m)* inheritance, heritage

**hériter** to inherit

**hésiter** to hesitate

**heure** *(f)* hour (P); **à l'heure** on time (4); **À tout à l'heure.** See you in a little while. (P); **heure officielle** military time, 24-hour clock; **Il est... heure(s).** It's . . . o'clock. (P); **Quelle heure est-il?** What time is it? (P); **tout à l'heure** in a little while (P), a little while ago

**heureusement** luckily

**heureux(-euse)** happy (7)

**hier** yesterday (5)

**hi-fi: chaîne hi-fi** *(f)* stereo (2)

**histoire** *(f)* history (1); story (9)

**historique** historical (9)

**historiquement** historically

**hiver** *(m)* winter (5); **en hiver** in winter (5)

**\*hockey** *(m)* hockey (2)

**\*homard** *(m)* lobster (8)

**homme** *(m)* man (1); **homme** *(m)* **d'affaires** businessman (5)

**homogène** homogeneous

**honnête** honest

**honnêteté** *(f)* honesty

**honneur** *(f)* honor

**hôpital** *(m)* hospital

**horaire** *(m)* schedule

**horreur** *(f)* horror

**horrible** horrible (6)

**\*hors de** outside of; **\*hors-d'œuvre** *(m)* (inv) hors d'oeuvre, appetizer (8)

**hôte** *(m)* host

**hôtel** *(m)* hotel (5)

**hôtelier(-ère)** *(mf)* hotel manager (10)

**hôtesse** *(f)* hostess

**huile** *(f)* oil

**\*huit** eight (P); **huit jours** one week

**\*huitième** eighth (3)

**huître** *(f)* oyster (8)

**humain(e)** human; **sciences humaines** *(fpl)* social sciences (1)

**humanité** *(f)* humanity

**humer** to breathe in

**humeur** *(f)* mood; **de bonne humeur** in a good mood

**humour** *(m)* humor; **sens** *(m)* **de l'humour** sense of humor (7)

**hypermarché** *(m)* superstore

**hypertension** *(f)* high blood pressure

## I

**ici** here (P); **par ici** this way (5)

**idéaliste** idealistic (1)

**idée** *(f)* idea (4)

**identifier** to identify

**identité** *(f)* identity; **carte** / **pièce** *(f)* **d'identité** identity card

**igname** *(f)* yam

**il** he (1), it (P); **il faut...** it is necessary . . . , one must . . . (8); **il ne faut pas** one should not, one must not (10); **ils** they (1); **il y a** there is, there are (1), ago (5); **Qu'est-ce qu'il y a?** What's the matter?; **s'il vous plaît** please (P)

**île** *(f)* island (9)

**imaginaire** imaginary

**imaginer** to imagine

**immédiatement** immediately

**immeuble** *(m)* apartment building (3)

**immigré(e)** *(mf)* immigrant

**immobilier(-ère)** real estate

**imparfait** *(m)* imperfect

**impatient(e)** impatient (4)

**impératif** *(m)* imperative

**imperméable** *(m)* raincoat (5)

**impoli(e)** impolite

**importance** *(f)* importance (7)

**important(e)** important (5)

**importer** to be important; **n'importe où** (just) anywhere; **n'importe quel(le)** (just) any; **n'importe qui** (just) anyone; **n'importe quoi** (just) anything

**imposer** to impose, to lay down

**impressionnant(e)** impressive

**imprimé(e)** printed

**inaccessibilité** *(f)* inaccessibility

**inactif(-ive)** inactive, non-working

**inattendu(e)** unexpected

**inciter à** to make one feel

**inclure** to include; **inclus(e)** included

**inconditionnel(le)** *(mf)* devotee

**inconstitutionnel(le)** unconstitutional

**inconvénient** *(m)* disadvantage

**incroyable** incredible

**Inde** *(f)* India

**indécision** *(f)* indecision (7)

**indéfini** indefinite

**indépendant(e)** independent

**indicatif régional** *(m)* area code

**indications** *(fpl)* directions (10)

**indifférence** *(f)* indifference (7)

**indigène** native

**indigestion** *(f)* indigestion (10)

**indiquer** to show, to indicate (3); **indiqué(e)** indicated; **indiquer le chemin** to give directions, to show the way (10)

**indispensable** essential

**individu** *(m)* individual

**Indochine** *(f)* Indochina

**industrie** *(f)* industry
**inégalé(e)** unequaled
**inégalité** *(f)* inequality
**inférieur(e)** inferior, lower
**infidélité** *(f)* unfaithfulness (7)
**infinitif** *(m)* infinitive
**infirmier(-ère)** *(mf)* nurse
**influencer** to influence; **s'influencer** to influence each other
**informatique** *(f)* computer science (1)
**informer** to inform; **s'informer** to find out information (9)
**infusion** *(f)* herbal tea
**ingénieur** *(m)* engineer
**innover** to innovate
**inquiétant(e)** disturbing
**inscription** *(f)* registration
**inscrire** to register; **s'inscrire** to register (3)
**insecte** *(m)* insect
**insensibilité** *(f)* insensitivity (7)
**insister** to insist (10)
**instabilité** *(f)* instability
**installation** *(f)* arrangements
**installer: s'installer (à / dans)** to settle (in), to move (into) (7), to set up business
**instant** *(m)* instant; **Un instant!** Just a moment!
**institut** *(m)* institute
**instituteur(-trice)** *(mf)* elementary school teacher
**institution** *(f)* institution
**instrument** *(m)* instrument; **instrument** *(m)* **de musique** musical instrument
**insulter** to insult
**insupportable** unbearable, intolerable
**intellectuel(le)** intellectual (1)
**intelligent(e)** intelligent (1)
**intention: avoir l'intention de** to plan on, to intend to (4)
**interdire** to forbid; **interdit(e)** forbidden
**intéressant(e)** interesting (P)
**intéresser** to interest; **s'intéresser à** to be interested in (7)
**intérêt** *(m)* interest
**intérieur** *(m)* inside
**intermédiaire** intermediate
**interprète** *(mf)* interpreter
**interprété(e)** interpreted
**interrogatif(-ive)** interrogative, question
**interroger** to question
**interrompre** to interrupt
**intitulé(e)** titled, called
**introduire** to introduce
**introverti(e)** introverted
**investir** to invest
**invitation** *(f)* invitation (6)
**invité(e)** *(mf)* guest
**inviter (à)** to invite (to) (2)
**irresponsable** irresponsible
**irriter** to irritate
**isolé(e)** isolated
**Israël** *(m)* Israel (9)
**issu(e): être issu(e) de** to come from
**Italie** *(f)* Italy (9)
**italien(ne)** Italian
**italique: en italique** in italics
**itinéraire** *(m)* itinerary (9)
**ivoirien(ne)** from Côte d'Ivoire

## J
**jadis** formerly
**jalousie** *(f)* jealousy (7)
**jaloux(-ouse)** jealous (7)
**jamais: ne... jamais** never (2)
**jambe** *(f)* leg (10); **se casser la jambe** to break your leg

**jambon** *(m)* ham (2); **sandwich** *(m)* **au jambon** ham sandwich (2)
**janvier** *(m)* January (4)
**Japon** *(m)* Japan (9)
**japonais** *(m)* Japanese
**jardin** *(m)* garden (5), yard
**jardinage** *(m)* gardening; **faire du jardinage** to garden (5)
**jardiner** to garden
**jaune** yellow (3)
**jazz** *(m)* jazz (1)
**je (j')** I (P)
**jean** *(m)* jeans (5)
**jet** *(m)* stream
**jeu** *(m)* game; **jeu** *(m)* **de société** board game; **jeu** *(m)* **vidéo** video game (2)
**jeudi** *(m)* Thursday (P)
**jeune** young (1); **jeunes** *(pl)* young people
**jeunesse** *(f)* youth (7); **auberge** *(f)* **de jeunesse** youth hostel (10)
**jogging: faire du jogging** to jog (2)
**joie** *(f)* joy
**joindre: se joindre à** to join
**joli(e)** pretty (1)
**jouer** to act (in movies and theater) (6); **jouer à** to play (a sport or game) (2); **jouer de** to play (an instrument) (2)
**jour** *(m)* day (P); **C'est quel jour, aujourd'hui?** What day is today? (P); **huit jours** one week; **jour** *(m)* **de l'an** New Year's Day; **jour J** *(m)* D-day; **quinze jours** two weeks; **tous les jours** every day (2)
**journal** *(m)* newspaper (5), journal
**journaliste** *(mf)* journalist
**journée** *(f)* day (2), daytime; **Bonne journée!** Have a good day!; **journée continue** nine-to-five schedule; **toute la journée** the whole day (2)
**joyeux(-euse)** happy; **Joyeux Noël!** Merry Christmas!
**juif(-ive)** *(mf)* Jew
**juillet** *(m)* July (4)
**juin** *(m)* June (4)
**jumeau (jumelle)** twin (1)
**jupe** *(f)* skirt (5)
**jus (de fruit)** *(m)* (fruit) juice (2)
**jusqu'à** until, up to (2)
**jusque** until
**juste** just (10), fair; **juste là** right there
**justement** precisely, exactly; as a matter of fact (3)
**justifier** to justify

## K
**kilo** *(m)* kilo(gram) (2.2 pounds) (8)
**kilomètre** *(m)* kilometer (.6 miles)
**kiosque** *(m)* kiosk

## L
**la** the (1), her, it (5)
**là** there (8); **à ce moment-là** at that time; **ce... là** that. . . (3); **là-bas** over there (8)
**laboratoire: laboratoire** *(m)* **de langues / d'informatique** language / computer laboratory (1)
**lac** *(m)* lake
**laid(e)** ugly (1)
**laïque** lay, secular, civil
**laisser** to leave (behind) (3), to let; **laisser tomber** to drop
**lait** *(m)* milk (8); **café au lait** coffee with milk (2)
**laitier(-ère)** milk, dairy (8)
**laitue** *(f)* lettuce (8)
**lambi** a type of shell
**lampe** *(f)* lamp (3); **lampe** *(f)* **de poche** flashlight

**langouste** *(f)* spiny lobster
**langoustines** *(fpl)* scampi
**langue** *(f)* language (1); tongue
**lapin** *(m)* rabbit
**laqué(e)** lacquered, with a gloss finish
**lardon** *(m)* piece of bacon
**large** wide
**largement** widely
**laser: platine laser** *(f)* CD player (3)
**lavabo** *(m)* washbasin, sink (10)
**laver** to wash; **se laver** to wash (up) (7)
**lave-vaisselle** *(m)* dishwasher
**le** the (1), him, it (5); **le lundi** on Mondays (P); **le matin** in the morning, mornings (P); **le week-end** on the weekend, weekends (P)
**leçon** *(f)* lesson
**lecteur (lectrice)** *(mf)* reader; **lecteur DVD** *(m)* DVD player (3)
**lecture** *(f)* reading
**légende** *(f)* legend
**léger(-ère)** light (8)
**légume** *(m)* vegetable (8)
**lendemain** *(m)* the next day (6)
**lentement** slowly (8)
**lequel (laquelle, lesquels, lesquelles)** which, which one(s) (7)
**les** the (1); them (5);
**lessive** *(f)* laundry (5)
**lettre** *(f)* letter; **lettres** *(fpl)* study of literature
**leur** (to, for) them (9)
**leur** their (9)
**levant** *(m)* east, sunrise
**lever: se lever** to get up (7)
**lèvre** *(f)* lip
**liaison** *(f)* linking, link
**libéral(e)** *(mpl* **libéraux)** liberal (7)
**libérer: se libérer** to free oneself
**liberté** *(f)* freedom
**librairie** *(f)* bookstore (1)
**libre** free (2); **temps libre** *(m)* free time (4)
**licence** *(f)* three-year university degree
**licencié(e)** *(mf)* someone with the licence degree
**lien** *(m)* link
**lié(e)** linked
**lier** to connect, to link
**lieu** *(m)* place; **avoir lieu** to take place
**ligne** *(f)* figure; line; **en ligne** online (7)
**limande** *(f)* dab
**limité(e)** limited
**limiter** to limit, to border; **se limiter à** to limit oneself to
**linguistique** linguistic
**liquide** *(m)* liquid (10)
**lire** to read (2); **Lisez...** Read . . . (P)
**liste** *(f)* list
**lit** *(m)* bed (3); **rester au lit** to stay in bed (2)
**litre** *(m)* liter (approximately one quart) (8)
**littéraire** literary
**littérature** *(f)* literature (1)
**living** *(m)* living room
**livre** *(m)* book (P)
**livre** *(f)* pound, half-kilo (8)
**livrer: se livrer à** to participate in
**local(e)** *(mpl* **locaux)** local (9)
**locataire** *(mf)* renter
**location** *(f)* rental; **voiture** *(f)* **de location** rental car (5)
**logement** *(m)* lodging (3)
**loger** to lodge
**logique** logical
**logiquement** logically
**loi** *(f)* law
**loin (de)** far (from) (3); **au loin** in the distance; **de loin** by far

**loisir** (m) leisure activity
**Londres** London
**long: le long de** along (9); **au long de** along
**long(ue)** long (4)
**longtemps** a long time (5)
**longueur** (f) length
**lors de** at the time of
**lorsque** when
**loterie** (f) lottery
**loto** (m) lotto, bingo
**louer** to rent (4)
**Louisiane** (f) Louisiana
**loup** (m) wolf
**lourd(e)** heavy
**loyer** (m) rent (3)
**lui** him (6), (to, for) him (9); **lui-même** himself
**lundi** (m) Monday (P)
**lune** (f) moon; **lune** (f) **de miel** honeymoon
**lunettes** (fpl) glasses (4); **lunettes** (fpl) **de soleil** sunglasses (5)
**lutte** (f) struggle, fight
**lutter** to struggle, to fight
**luxe** (m) luxury; **de luxe** deluxe (10)
**luxembourgeois** (m) Luxemburgian (native language of Luxembourg)
**luxembourgeois(e)** from Luxembourg
**lycée** (m) French secondary school (6)
**lycéen(ne)** (mf) high school student (6)

## M

**macérer** to soak
**madame (Mme)** (f) madam (Mrs.) (P)
**mademoiselle (Mlle)** (f) miss (P)
**magasin** (m) store, shop (4)
**magazine** (m) magazine (9)
**magnétoscope** (m) video cassette recorder
**magnifique** magnificent
**mai** (m) May (4)
**maigre** skinny (8)
**maigrir** to get thinner, to slim down (8)
**mail** (m) e-mail (2)
**maillot** (m) **de bain** swimsuit (5)
**main** (f) hand (7)
**maintenant** now (P)
**maintenir** to maintain
**maire** (m) mayor
**mairie** (f) town hall
**mais** but (P)
**maïs** (m) corn
**maison** (f) house (1); **à la maison** (at) home (P); **maison** (f) **d'édition** publishing company
**maître** (m) master
**maîtrise** (f) master's degree
**majoré(e)** with a surcharge
**majoritaire** (adj) majority
**majorité** (f) majority
**mal** (m) bad, evil; **avoir mal à...** one's. . . hurts; **faire mal (à)** to hurt
**mal** badly (P); **mal à l'aise** ill at ease; **pas mal** not bad(ly) (P)
**malade** (mf) sick person
**malade** ill, sick (10)
**maladie** (f) illness; **maladie** (f) **des nerfs** nervous disorder
**malaise** (f) discomfort
**malgache** Madagascan
**malgré** in spite of
**malheureusement** unfortunately
**malheureux(-euse)** unhappy
**malhonnête** dishonest
**maman** (f) mama, mom
**mamie** (f) granny, grandma (7)
**Manche** (f) English Channel

**mandarine** (f) tangerine
**mandat** (m) money order
**manger** to eat (2); **donner à manger à** to feed (9); **salle** (f) **à manger** dining room (3)
**mangue** (f) mango
**manière** (f) manner, way
**manifestation** (f) demonstration; **manifestation sportive** (f) sports event
**manifester: se manifester** to be reflected
**manoir** (m) manor, country house
**manquer** to miss, to lack
**manteau** (m) overcoat (5)
**manuel** (m) textbook
**manufacturier(-ère)** manufacturing
**manuscrit** (m) manuscript
**maquillage** (m) make-up
**maquiller: se maquiller** to put on make-up (7)
**marais** (m) swamp
**marchand(e)** (mf) merchant, shopkeeper (6); **marchand** (m) **de cadeaux** gift shop (10)
**marche à pied** (f) walking; **faire de la marche à pied** to go walking
**marché** (m) market (8)
**marcher** to walk (8), to work
**mardi** (m) Tuesday (P); **Mardi gras** (m) Fat Tuesday
**maréchal** (m) marshall
**marée** (f) tide
**marge** (f) margin
**mari** (m) husband (2); **ex-mari** (m) ex-husband
**mariage** (m) marriage (7)
**marié(e)** married (1)
**marier: se marier (avec)** to get married (to) (7)
**marinier(-ère): moules marinières** (f) mussels cooked with onions and white wine
**marketing** (m) marketing (1)
**Maroc** (m) Morocco (9)
**marocain(e)** Moroccan
**marquer** to mark
**marron** (inv) brown (3)
**mars** (m) March (4)
**martiniquais(e)** from Martinique
**masse** (f) **d'eau** body of water
**massif** (m) group of mountains, clump
**match** (m) match, game (1)
**matelas** (m) mattress
**matérialiste** materialistic
**matériel(le)** material
**matériellement** materially
**maternel(le)** maternal; **école maternelle** (f) kindergarten
**mathématiques** (fpl) mathematics (1)
**maths** (fpl) math (1)
**matière** (f) matter; **matières grasses** fat (8)
**matin** (m) morning (P); **À huit heures du matin.** At eight o'clock in the morning. (P); **le matin mornings,** in the morning (P)
**matinée** (f) morning (2)
**matrimonial(e)** (mpl **matrimoniaux**) marriage
**mauvais(e)** bad (1); **Il fait mauvais.** The weather's bad. (5)
**me** (to, for) me (9), myself (7); **Ça me plaît!** I like it! (3); **il me faut...** I need. . . (9)
**méchant(e)** mean (1)
**mécontent(e)** displeased
**médaille** (f) medal
**médecin** (m) doctor, physician (10)
**médicament** (m) medication, medicine, drugs (10)
**médiocre** mediocre (6)
**Méditerranée: (mer) Méditerranée** (f) Mediterranean (Sea)
**méditerranéen(ne)** Mediterranean
**méfiance** (f) mistrust

**meilleur(e)** best (1), better
**mélange** (m) mixture
**membre** (m) member
**même** same (1), even; **moi-même** myself; **quand même** all the same
**mémoire** (f) memory
**menacer** to threaten
**ménage** (m) housework (5), household
**ménager(-ère)** household
**mener** to lead
**menhir** (m) menhir (an ancient megalithic structure)
**menthe** (f) mint
**mentionner** to mention
**mentir** to lie
**menu** (m) menu (8)
**mépris** (m) scorn
**mer** (f) sea (9); **bord** (m) **de la mer** seaside; **fruits** (mpl) **de mer** shellfish (8)
**merci (bien)** thank you, thanks (P)
**mercredi** (m) Wednesday (P)
**mère** (f) mother (4)
**méritoire** deserving
**merveille** (f) marvel, wonder
**merveilleux(-euse)** marvelous
**messager(-ère)** (mf) messenger
**messieurs (MM.)** gentlemen, sirs
**mesurer** to measure
**métier** (m) occupation
**métrage: court métrage** (m) short film
**mètre** (m) meter
**métrique** metric
**métro** (m) subway (4); **en métro** by subway (4)
**metteur** (m) **en scène** director
**mettre** to put (on), to place (5); **mettre à part** to set aside; **mettre en scène** to present; **mettre en valeur** to emphasize; **mettre la table** to set the table; **se mettre d'accord** to come to an agreement
**meublé(e)** furnished
**meubles** (mpl) furniture, furnishings (3)
**meurtre** (m) murder
**meurtrier** (m) murderer
**meurtrière** (f) murderess
**Mexico** Mexico City
**Mexique** (m) Mexico (9)
**mi-** mid-, half-; **cheveux mi-longs** (mpl) shoulder-length hair (4)
**micro-ondes** (m) microwave oven
**midi** (m) noon (P)
**mie: pain** (m) **de mie** soft sandwich bread
**mieux (que)** better (than) (2); **aimer mieux** to prefer (2); **il vaut mieux** it's better (10); **le mieux** the best
**milieu** (m) middle, milieu, environment; **au milieu (de)** in the middle (of)
**militaire** military
**mille** one thousand (3)
**mille-feuille** (f) mille-feuille (a layered pastry)
**millénaire** (m) millennium
**million: un million (de)** (m) one million (3)
**millionnaire** (mf) millionaire
**mince** thin (1)
**minéral(e)** (mpl **minéraux**): **eau minérale** (f) mineral water (8)
**minier(-ère): exploitation minière** (f) mining
**ministère** (m) ministry, department
**ministre** (m) minister, secretary
**minoritaire** minority
**minorité** (f) minority
**minuit** (m) midnight (P)
**minute** (f) minute (5)
**miroir** (m) mirror

**mise** *(f)* putting; **mise** *(f)* **en bouteille** bottling;
  **mise** *(f)* **en place** establishment; **mise** *(f)* **en relief** highlighting, accentuating
**misère** *(f)* misery
**mobile** *(m)* motive
**mobilier** *(m)* furnishings
**mode** *(f)* fashion (5), *(m)* type
**modèle** *(m)* model
**moderne** modern (1)
**moi** me (P); **chez moi** at my house (2); **Donnez-moi...** Give me . . . (P); **Excusez-moi.** Excuse me. (P); **moi-même** myself
**moindre: le moindre** the least
**moins** minus (P); **au moins** at least; **de moins en moins** fewer and fewer, less and less; **Il est trois heures moins le quart.** It's a quarter to three. (P); **le moins** the least; **moins de** fewer, less (8); **moins... que** less . . . than (1)
**mois** *(m)* month (3); **ce mois-ci** this month (4); **par mois** per month (3)
**moitié** *(f)* half
**moment** *(m)* moment; **à ce moment-là** at that time; **au dernier moment** at the last minute
**mon (ma, mes)** my (3); **ma famille** my family (P); **mes amis** my friends (1)
**monarchie** *(f)* monarchy
**monde** *(m)* world, crowd; **faire le tour du monde** to take a trip around the world; **Tiers Monde** *(m)* Third World; **tout le monde** everybody, everyone
**mondial(e)** *(mpl* **mondiaux)** world(-wide) (5)
**monétaire** monetary
**monnaie** *(f)* change (2), currency
**monoparental(e)** *(mpl* **monoparentaux)** singleparent
**monotonie** *(f)* monotony
**monsieur (M.)** *(m)* mister (Mr.), sir (P), man
**monstre** *(m)* monster (6)
**mont** *(m)* mount
**montagne** *(f)* mountain (5); **aller à la montagne** to go to the mountains (5)
**montagneux(-euse)** mountainous
**monter (dans)** to go up; to get on/in (5), to set up, to climb
**montre** *(f)* watch (5)
**montrer** to show (3)
**morceau** *(m)* piece (8)
**moribond(e)** moribund, dying
**mort** *(f)* death
**mort(e)** dead (4)
**mosaïque** *(f)* mosaic
**mosquée** *(f)* mosque
**mot** *(m)* word (P)
**moule** *(f)* mussel (8)
**moulin** *(m)* mill
**mourant(e)** dying
**mourir** to die (5)
**moustache** *(f)* mustache (4)
**moutarde** *(f)* mustard
**mouton** *(m)* sheep
**mouvement** *(m)* movement
**moyen** *(m)* means; **moyen** *(m)* **de transport** means of transportation (4)
**moyen(ne)** medium; **de taille moyenne** medium-sized (4); **Moyen-Orient** *(m)* Middle East (9)
**moyenne** *(f)* average; **en moyenne** on average
**MST** *(f)* STD
**muet(te)** silent
**multiplier** to multiply
**mur** *(m)* wall (3)
**musculation: faire de la musculation** to do weight training, to do bodybuilding (8)
**musée** *(m)* museum (4)
**musical(e)** *(mpl* **musicaux): comédie musicale**

*(f)* musical
**musicien(ne)** *(mf)* musician
**musicien(ne)** musical
**musique** *(f)* music (1); **musique zydeco** zydeco music (4)
**musulman(e)** Muslim
**myrtille** *(f)* blueberry
**mystère** *(m)* mystery

## N

**nager** to swim (2)
**naissance** *(f)* birth
**naître** to be born (5); **être né(e)** to be born (5)
**natal(e)** native
**nationalité** *(f)* nationality (3)
**nature** *(f)* nature (7); **grandeur nature** *(f)* life-sized; **nature morte** *(f)* still life; **omelette nature** *(f)* plain omelet
**naturel(le)** natural
**naturellement** naturally
**nausée** *(f)* nausea
**nautique: ski nautique** *(m)* water-skiing (5)
**navette** *(f)* shuttle (10)
**ne: je ne travaille pas** I don't work (P); **ne... aucun(e)** none, not one; **ne... jamais** never (2); **ne... ni... ni...** neither . . . nor; **ne... nulle part** nowhere; **ne... pas (du tout)** not (at all) (1); **ne... pas encore** not yet (5); **ne... personne** nobody, no one; **ne... plus** no more, no longer (8); **ne... que** only; **ne... rien** nothing (5); **ne... rien que** nothing but; **n'est-ce pas?** right? (1); **n'importe où (just) anywhere
**né(e): être né(e)** to be born (5)
**nécessaire** necessary (10)
**nécessiteux** *(mpl)* needy
**néerlandais(e)** Dutch
**néfaste** harmful
**négliger** to neglect
**négocier** to negociate
**nègre** negro
**négritude** *(f)* negritude
**neige** *(f)* snow (5)
**neiger** to snow (5)
**nerf** *(m)* nerve; **maladie** *(f)* **des nerfs** nervous disorder; **nerfs à vif** nerves on edge
**nerveux(-euse)** nervous
**n'est-ce pas?** right? (1)
**Net: surfer le Net** to surf the Net (2)
**neuf** nine (P)
**neuf (neuve)** brand-new
**neutralité** *(f)* neutrality
**neutre** neutral
**neuvième** ninth (3)
**neveu** *(m)* *(pl* **neveux)** nephew (4)
**nez** *(m)* nose (10); **avoir le nez bouché** to have a stopped-up nose
**ni: ne... ni... ni...** neither . . . nor
**niçois(e)** from Nice
**nièce** *(f)* niece (4)
**niveau** *(m)* level
**Noël** *(m)* Christmas
**noir(e)** black (3); **Il faisait noir.** It was dark. (6)
**nom** *(m)* name (3); **au nom de** in the name of
**nombre** *(m)* number
**nombreux(-euse)** numerous
**nommé(e)** named
**nommer** to name
**non** no (P); **non?** right? (1); **non plus** neither (3)
**non-pratiquant(e)** *(mf)* non-churchgoer
**nord** *(m)* north; **Amérique** *(f)* **du Nord** North America (9)
**normal(e)** *(mpl* **normaux)** normal
**normalement** normally
**Norvège** *(f)* Norway

**note** *(f)* grade, note; **régler la note** to pay the bill (10)
**noter** to note, to notice
**notre** *(pl* **nos)** our (3)
**nourrir** to feed, to nourish
**nourriture** *(f)* food, nourishment
**nous** we (1); (to, for) us (9), ourselves (7); **avec nous** with us (2); **Nous sommes six.** There are six of us. (4)
**nouveau (nouvel, nouvelle)** new (1); **de nouveau** again, anew; **Nouvelle-Angleterre** *(f)* New England; **Nouvelle-Calédonie** *(f)* New Caledonia (9); **La Nouvelle-Orléans** *(f)* New Orleans (4)
**novembre** *(m)* November (4)
**noyau** *(m)* pit
**nu(e)** naked; **pieds nus** barefoot
**nuage** *(m)* cloud
**nuageux(-euse)** cloudy
**nucléaire** nuclear
**nuisible** harmful
**nuit** *(f)* night (5); **boîte** *(f)* **de nuit** nightclub (1)
**nul(le) (en)** no good (at), really bad (at); **ne... nulle part** nowhere
**numéro** *(m)* number (3), issue
**numéroté(e)** numbered

## O

**obéir (à)** to obey (8)
**objectif** *(m)* objective
**objet** *(m)* object
**obligatoire** obligatory, required
**obligeance** *(f)* kindness
**obliger** to force, to make; **obligé(e)** obliged, forced
**observer** to observe
**obtenir** to get, to obtain
**occasion: d'occasion** second-hand
**occidental(e)** *(mpl* **occidentaux)** western
**occitan** *(m)* Occitan
**occupé(e)** busy
**occuper** to occupy; **s'occuper de** to take care of
**océan** *(m)* ocean
**Océanie** *(f)* Oceania (9)
**octobre** *(m)* October (4)
**œil** *(pl* **yeux)** *(m)* eye (10); **avoir les yeux...** to have . . . eyes (4)
**œuf** *(m)* egg (8); **œuf dur** *(m)* hard-boiled egg (8)
**œuvre** *(f)* work
**office** *(m)* **de tourisme** tourist office (10)
**officiel(le)** official
**officiellement** officially
**offrir** to offer; **offrant** offering
**oignon** *(m)* onion (8); **soupe** *(f)* **à l'oignon** onion soupe (8)
**oiseau** *(m)* bird
**ombre** *(f)* shadow, shade
**omelette** *(f)* omelet (8)
**on** one, they, we, people, you (4); **Comment dit-on... en français?** How do you say . . . in French? (P); **On... ?** Shall we . . . ?, How about. . . ? (4); **On dit que...** They say that . . . (4); **On va... ?** Shall we go. . . ? (2)
**oncle** *(m)* uncle (4)
**onze** eleven (P)
**opposer** to oppose; **s'opposer** to confront each other
**oppresseur** *(m)* oppressor
**opprimé(e)** oppressed
**opter** to opt
**optimiste** optimistic (1)
**or** *(m)* gold
**orage** *(m)* storm
**orange** *(f)* orange (8); **jus** *(m)* **d'orange** orange juice (2)

orange *(inv)* orange (3)

**Orangina** *(m)* Orangina (an orange drink) (2)

**oratoire** *(m)* oratory, small chapel

**orchestre** *(m)* orchestra, band (4)

**ordinateur** *(m)* computer (2)

**ordonnance** *(f)* prescription (10)

**ordre** *(m)* order; **en ordre** in order (3)

**oreille** *(f)* ear (10)

**oreiller** *(m)* pillow

**oreillons** *(mpl)* mumps

**organisation** *(f)* organization

**organiser** to organize; **s'organiser** to get organized

**organisme** *(m)* organism, body

**originaire de** coming from

**origine** *(f)* origin; **d'origine...** of... origin (7)

**orner** to decorate

**orthographique** spelling

**os** *(m)* bone

**ou** or (P)

**où** where (1); **d'où** from where (1); **n'importe où** (just) anywhere

**oublier** to forget (8)

**ouest** *(m)* west

**oui** yes (P)

**outre-mer** overseas

**ouvert(e)** open

**ouverture** *(f)* opening

**ouvrir** to open; **Ouvrez...** Open... (P)

## P

**pacifique** pacific, peaceful

**page** *(f)* page (P)

**paiement** *(m)* payment

**pain** *(m)* bread (8); **pain au chocolat** *(m)* croissant with chocolate filling (8); **pain complet** *(m)* wholegrain bread (8); **pain grillé** *(m)* toast (8)

**pair: jeune fille au pair** au pair, nanny

**paisible** peaceful, calm

**paix** *(f)* peace; **Corps** *(m)* **de la Paix** Peace Corps

**palais** *(m)* palace

**pâle** pale

**palme** *(f)* palm leaf

**paludisme** *(m)* paludism, malaria

**pamplemousse** *(m)* grapefruit

**panique** *(f)* panic

**panoramique** panoramic

**pantalon** *(m)* pants (5)

**papa** *(m)* dad, papa

**papier** *(m)* paper; **feuille** *(f)* **de papier** sheet of paper (P)

**pâque juive** *(f)* Passover

**Pâques** *(fpl)* Easter

**paquet** *(m)* package, bag (8)

**par** per (3), by; **par ailleurs** furthermore; **par conséquent** consequently; **par contre** on the other hand; **par exemple** for example (2); **par \*hasard** by chance; **par ici** this way (5); **par la fenêtre** through the window (6); **par mois** per month (3); **par terre** on the ground / floor (3)

**paradis** *(m)* paradise, heaven

**paraître** to appear

**parapluie** *(m)* umbrella (5)

**parc** *(m)* park (1); **parc naturel** natural park, nature reserve

**parce que** because (P)

**parcourir** to skim, to glance through

**Pardon.** Excuse me. (P)

**pardonner** to forgive, to pardon

**pareil(le) (à)** similar (to)

**parent** *(m)* parent (4), relative (5)

**parenté** *(f)* relationship

**parenthèses** *(fpl)* parentheses

**paresseux(-euse)** lazy (1)

**parfait(e)** perfect (7)

**parfaitement** perfectly (7)

**parfois** sometimes

**parfum** *(m)* perfume

**Parisien(ne)** *(mf)* Parisian (9)

**parking** *(m)* parking lot (1), parking garage

**parlementaire** parlementary

**parler** to talk, to speak (2); **je parle** I speak (P); **se parler** to talk to each other (7); **Vous parlez... ?** Do you speak... ? (P)

**parmi** among

**paroisse** *(f)* parish

**parole** *(f)* word, lyric

**part: à part...** besides... ; **à part entière** complete; **mettre à part** to set aside; **ne... nulle part** nowhere; **quelque part** somewhere

**partager** to share (3), to divide up; **partagé(e)** shared, divided (3)

**partenaire** *(mf)* partner (7)

**parti (politique)** *(m)* (political) party

**participer (à)** to participate (in)

**particulier(-ère)** particular, private; **en particulier** especially

**partie** part *(f)*; **en grande partie** mostly, in large part; **en partie** partially; **faire partie de** to be a part of

**partir (de... pour)** to leave (from... for), to go away (4); **à partir de** starting from

**partout** everywhere (3)

**pas** not (P); **je ne comprends pas** I don't understand (P); **ne... pas (du tout)** not (at all) (1); **ne... pas encore** not yet (5); **Pas de problème!** No problem! (3); **pas plus** no more (4)

**passant(e)** *(mf)* passerby

**passé** *(m)* past (6)

**passeport** *(m)* passport (9)

**passer** to spend, to pass (2); **passer chez** to go by...'s house (2); **passer le temps / la matinée** to spend one's time / the morning (2); **passer un film** to show a movie (6); **Qu'est-ce qui s'est passé?** What happened? (7); **s'en passer** to do without; **se passer** to happen (7)

**passe-temps** *(m)* pastime (2)

**passion** *(f)* passion (7)

**pastèque** *(f)* watermelon

**pâte** *(f)* paste, dough

**pâté** *(m)* pâté, meat spread (8)

**patience** *(f)* patience; **avoir de la patience** to have patience (4)

**patient(e)** *(mf)* patient

**patient(e)** patient (6)

**patin** *(m)* skate; **patin** *(m)* **à glace** ice-skate, iceskating; **patin** *(m)* **à roulettes** roller skate, roller skating

**pâtisserie** *(f)* pastry shop, pastry

**patrie** *(f)* homeland

**patrimoine** *(m)* patrimony, heritage

**patron(ne)** *(mf)* owner, boss

**pâturage** *(m)* pasture

**pauvre** poor

**pavé** *(m)* thick slice (8)

**pavé(e)** paved

**payant(e)** not free

**payer** to pay (2)

**pays** *(m)* country (3)

**paysage** *(m)* landscape (9)

**Pays-Bas** *(mpl)* Netherlands

**peau** *(f)* skin

**pêche** *(f)* peach (8), fishing; **aller à la pêche** to go fishing

**peigner: se peigner** to comb one's hair (7)

**peintre** *(m)* painter

**peinture** *(f)* painting

**pèlerin** *(m)* pilgrim

**pendant** during, for (7); **pendant que** while

**pensée** *(f)* thought

**penser** to think (2); **penser à** think about; **je pense que** I think that (P)

**pension** *(f)* room and board

**perçu(e)** perceived

**perdre** to lose, to waste (time) (7); **perdu(e)** lost; **se perdre** to get lost (7)

**père** *(m)* father (4); **le père Noël** Santa Claus

**perfectionnement** *(m)* perfecting

**perfectionner** to perfect

**période** *(f)* period

**permettre (de)** to permit, to allow; **permis(e)** permitted, allowed

**Pérou** *(m)* Peru (9)

**perpétuel(le)** perpetual

**personnage** *(m)* character

**personnalisé(e)** personalized (8)

**personnalité** *(f)* personality (1)

**personne** *(f)* person (6); **ne... personne** nobody, no one

**personnel(le)** personal; **effets personnels** *(mpl)* personal belongings (3)

**persuader** to persuade

**perte: à perte de vue** as far as you can see

**pessimiste** pessimistic (1)

**petit(e)** small, little, short (1); **petit ami** *(m)* boyfriend (2); **petit à petit** little by little (6); **petit déjeuner** *(m)* breakfast (5); **petite amie** *(f)* girlfriend (2); **petite annonce** *(f)* classified ad; **petits pois** *(mpl)* peas (8)

**petite-fille** *(f)* granddaughter (7)

**petit-fils** *(m)* grandson (7)

**petits-enfants** *(mpl)* grandchildren (7)

**pétrole** *(m)* oil

**pétrolier(-ière): industries pétrolières** *(f)* oil industry

**peu** little (P); **à peu près** approximately, about

**peuple** *(m)* people

**peur** *(f)* fear; **avoir peur (de)** to be afraid (of), to fear (4); **faire peur à** to frighten

**peut-être** perhaps, maybe (3)

**pharmacie** *(f)* pharmacy (10)

**pharmacien(ne)** *(mf)* pharmacist

**philosophe** *(mf)* philosopher

**philosophie** *(f)* philosophy (1)

**photo** *(f)* photo

**phrase** *(f)* sentence (P)

**physiologique** physiological

**physique** *(f)* physics (1)

**physique** physical; **aspect physique** *(m)* physical appearance (7)

**piano** *(m)* piano (2)

**pièce** *(f)* room (3); **pièce** *(f)* **de théâtre** play (4); **pièce** *(f)* **d'identité** identity card

**pied** *(m)* foot (10); **aller à pied** to walk, to go on foot (4); **doigt** *(m)* **de pied** toe (10); **pieds nus** barefoot

**pin** *(m)* pine

**pique-nique** *(m)* picnic

**pire** worse

**piscine** *(f)* swimming pool (4)

**piste** *(f)* trail, lead

**pitié** *(f)* pity

**pizza** *(f)* pizza (8)

**placard** *(m)* closet (3)

**place** *(f)* square, place, plaza (10); **à sa place** in its place (3)

**plage** *(f)* beach (4)

**plaine** *(f)* plain

**plaire** to please (9); **Ça me plaît!** I like it! (3); **Ça**

**te plaît!** You like it! (3); **Ça t'a plu?** Did you like it? (6); **Ça te plaira!** You'll like it! (9); **s'il vous plaît** please (P)

**plaisant(e)** pleasant

**plaisir** (m) pleasure; **Avec plaisir!** It would be a pleasure! (6); **faire plaisir à** to please

**plan** (m) map, level; **plan** (m) **d'eau** stretch of water

**planche** (f) **à voile** windsurfing; **faire de la planche à voile** to windsurf

**plante** (f) plant (3)

**planter** to plant

**plastique** (m) plastic; **sac** (m) **en plastique** plastic bag

**plat** (m) dish (8); **plat préparé** (m) ready-to-serve dish (8)

**plat(e)** flat; **œuf au plat** (m) fried egg

**plateau** (m) tray

**platine** (m) platinum; **platine laser** (f) CD player (3)

**plein(e)** full; **de plein air** outdoor (4); **plein de** full of, a lot of

**pleur** (m) sobbing

**pleurer** to cry

**pleuvoir** to rain (5)

**plongée sous-marine** (f) scuba diving

**plonger** to dive, to plunge

**pluie** (f) rain (5)

**plupart: la plupart** (f) the most part; **la plupart de** (f) the majority of (7); **la plupart du temps** most of the time (7)

**plus** plus; **À plus tard!** See you later! (2); **de plus** in addition; **de plus en plus** more and more (8); **en plus** besides, furthermore (8); **ne... plus** no more, no longer (8); **non plus** neither (3); **pas plus** no more (4); **plus de** more (8); **plus... que** more . . . than (1); **plus tard** later (4)

**plusieurs** several (8)

**plutôt** rather (1); instead (4); **plutôt que** rather than

**pneumonie** (f) pneumonia

**poche** (f) pocket; **lampe** (f) **de poche** flashlight

**poêle** (f) frying pan

**poêlée (de)** (f) frying pan full (of)

**poème** (m) poem (9)

**poésie** (f) poetry

**poète** (m) poet

**poids** (m) weight

**poing** (m) fist

**point** (m) point; **au point de** to be about to; **point** (m) **de vue** viewpoint

**poire** (f) pear (8)

**poireau** (m) leek

**pois: petits pois** (mpl) peas (8)

**poisson** (m) fish (8); **poissons** (mpl) **d'avril** April Fool's Day

**poissonnerie** (f) fish shop (8)

**poitrine** (f) chest

**poivre** (m) pepper (8)

**poivron** (m) (bell) pepper

**poli(e)** polite

**police** (f) police, policy

**policier(-ère)** detective, police

**politesse** (f) politeness

**politique** (f) politics (7), policy

**politique** political; **homme politique** (m) politician

**polo** (m) knit shirt (5)

**Pologne** (f) Poland

**Polynésie française** (f) French Polynesia (9)

**pomme** (f) apple (8); **pomme** (f) **de terre** potato (8)

**pommier** (m) apple tree

**populaire** popular, pop (1)

**porc** (m) pork (8); **côte** (f) **de porc** pork chop (8)

**porte** (f) door (3); **porte** (f) **d'arrivée** arrival gate (9); **porte** (f) **d'embarquement** departure gate (9)

**portefeuille** (m) wallet (5)

**porte-parole de** (m, inv) spokesperson for

**porter** to wear, to carry (4)

**portugais** (m) Portuguese

**poser** to place; **poser une question** to ask a question (3)

**posséder** to possess, to own

**possibilité** (f) possibility (4)

**postal(e)** (mpl **postaux**): **carte postale** (f) postcard (9); **code postal** (m) zip code (3)

**poste** (f) post office; **bureau** (m) **de poste** post office (10)

**poste** (m) position

**pot** (m) jar (8)

**poubelle** (f) trash can

**poudre** (f) powder

**poulet** (m) chicken (8)

**poumon** (m) lung

**pour** for (P), in order to (1); **pour cent** percent; **pour que** so that

**pourcentage** (m) percentage

**pourquoi** why (2)

**poursuite** (f) pursuit, chase

**poursuivre** to pursue

**pourtant** however (8)

**pousser** to push

**poussière** (f) dust

**pouvoir** (m) power

**pouvoir** to be able, can, may (6); **Je peux vous aider?** Can I help you? (5); **on peut** one can (4)

**pratique** (f) practice

**pratique** practical

**pratiquement** practically

**pratiquer** to practice, to play (a sport), to do

**préavis** (m) (previous) notice

**précédent(e)** preceding

**prêcher** to preach

**précipitamment** hurriedly

**préciser** to specify

**préféré(e)** favorite (3)

**préférence** (f) preference; **de préférence** preferably

**préférer** to prefer (2); **je préfère** I prefer (1)

**premier(-ère)** first (1); **Premier ministre** Prime Minister

**prendre** to take (4); **prendre contact** to get in touch; **prendre du poids** to put on weight; **prendre feu** to catch fire; **prendre possession de** to take possession of; **prendre son petit déjeuner** to have one's breakfast (5); **prendre un bain** to take a bath (7); **prendre un bain de soleil** to sunbathe (4); **prendre une décision** to make a decision (7); **prendre une douche** to take a shower (7); **prendre un verre** to have a drink (2); **Prenez une feuille de papier et un crayon ou un stylo.** Take out a piece of paper and a pencil or a pen. (P)

**prénom** (m) first name (3)

**préoccuper** to worry; **se préoccuper (de)** to worry (about)

**préparatifs** (mpl) preparations (9)

**préparatoire** preparatory

**préparer** to prepare (2); **plat préparé** ready-to-serve dish (8); **préparer les cours** to prepare for class, to study (2); **Préparez l'examen.** Prepare / Study for the exam. (P)

**près (de)** near (1), nearly; **à peu près** approximately, about

**présentation** (f) introduction

**présenter** to introduce, to present; **Je vous/te présente...** I would like to introduce . . . to you.; **se présenter** to arise, to introduce oneself

**préservatif** (m) condom

**préserver** to preserve

**présider (à)** to preside

**presque** almost, nearly (2)

**presse** (f) press

**pressé(e)** hurried

**pression** (f) pressure

**prestigieux(-euse)** prestigious

**prêt(e)** ready (4)

**prétendre** to claim

**prêter** to loan, to lend (9)

**preuve** (f) proof

**prévisions météo** (fpl) weather forecast

**prévu(e)** planned, foreseen (9)

**prier** to beg, to request, to pray; **Je vous en prie.** You're welcome.

**prière** (f) prayer

**primaire: école primaire** (f) elementary school

**primeur** (m) produce

**principal(e)** (mpl **principaux**) main (8); **à titre principal** mainly

**principauté** (f) principality

**principe** (m) principle

**printemps** (m) spring (5); **au printemps** in spring (5)

**prise** (f) electrical outlet; **prise en charge** (f) taking up

**prisé(e)** sought after

**privé(e)** private (10)

**privilégié(e)** privileged, favored

**prix** (m) price; **à prix fixe** with a set price (8)

**probablement** probably

**problème** (m) problem; **pas de problème** no problem (3)

**prochain(e)** next (4); **le prochain cours** the next class (P)

**proche (de)** near (to)

**production** (f) **cinématographique** cinematic production

**produire** to produce

**produit** (m) product (8); **produits bios** (mpl) organic products (8)

**professeur** (m) professor (P)

**profession** (f) profession (7)

**professionnel(le)** professional (7)

**profil** (m) profile

**profiter de** to take advantage of (9)

**profond(e)** deep

**programme** (m) program

**programmeur(-euse)** (mf) computer programmer

**progrès** (m) progress

**projecteur** (m) projector

**projet** (m) plan (4); **faire des projets** to make plans (4)

**promenade** (f) walk (5); **faire une promenade** to take a walk (5)

**promener: se promener** to go walking (7)

**promettre (de)** to promise (6)

**promouvoir** to promote

**promulguer (des lois)** to create laws

**pronom** (m) pronoun

**prononcer** to pronounce

**prononciation** (f) pronunciation

**proposer** to offer, to suggest, to propose; **Qu'est-ce que je peux vous proposer d'autre?** What else can I get you? (8); **se proposer de** to intend

**propre** clean (3), own

**propriétaire** (mf) owner

**propriété** (f) property

**prospérité** *(f)* prosperity
**protectorat** *(m)* protectorate
**protéger** to protect; **protégé(e) par** protected by
**protéines** *(fpl)* protein (8)
**protestant(e)** *(mf)* Protestant
**provençal** *(m)* Provençal
**provenir de** to come from
**province** *(f)* province (3)
**provisions** *(fpl)* supplies, groceries
**proximité: à proximité de** in the vicinity of
**prune** *(f)* plum
**pruneau** *(m)* prune
**psychologie** *(f)* psychology (1)
**psychologique** psychological
**public(-que)** public; **santé publique** *(f)* public health
**publicité** *(f)* advertising, advertisement
**publier** to publish
**puis** then (4)
**puisque** since
**puissant(e)** powerful
**pull** *(m)* pullover sweater (5)
**punir** to punish
**purée** *(f)* mashed potatoes
**pureté** *(f)* purity
**pyjama** *(m)* pajamas

## Q

**quai** *(m)* quay, wharf
**qualité** *(f)* quality
**quand** when (2); **quand même** all the same
**quantité** *(f)* quantity
**quarante** forty (2)
**quart** *(m)* quarter; **Il est deux heures et quart.** It's a quarter past two. (P)
**quartier** *(m)* neighborhood (1)
**quatorze** fourteen (P)
**quatre** four (P)
**quatre-vingt-dix** ninety (2)
**quatre-vingts** eighty (2)
**quatrième** fourth (3)
**que** that (P), than, as (1), what (2), which, whom (7); **ce que** what, that which; **ne... que** only; **ne... rien que** nothing but; **que ce soit** whether it be; **qu'est-ce que** what (1); **Qu'est-ce que ça veut dire?** What does that mean? (P)
**quel(le)** which, what (3); **À quelle heure?** At what time? (P); **C'est quel jour aujourd'hui?** What day is today? (P); **n'importe quel(le)...** (just) any . . . ; **Quel âge a... ?** How old is . . . ? (4)
**quelconque** any
**quelque** some; **quelque chose** something (2); **quelque part** somewhere; **quelques** a few, several (5); **quelqu'un** someone, somebody (6); **quelques-uns** a few
**quelquefois** sometimes (2)
**quelques-un(e)s** *(mf)* a few
**question** *(f)* question (P)
**qui** who (2), that, which, who (7); **ce qui** what (7); **Qu'est-ce qui s'est passé?** What happened? (6); **Qu'est-ce qui ne va pas?** What's wrong? (10)
**quinze** fifteen (P); **quinze jours** two weeks
**quinzième** fifteenth
**quitter** to leave (4); **se quitter** to leave each other (7)
**quoi** what; **n'importe quoi** (just) anything
**quoique** although
**quotidien(ne)** daily (7)

## R

**raccompagner** to (re)accompany
**raccrocher** to hang up

**racisme** *(m)* racism
**raconter** to tell, to recount (7)
**radio** *(f)* radio (2), X-ray
**rafale** *(f)* blast, gust
**raffinerie** *(f)* refinery
**raie** *(f)* skate (fish), rayfish (8)
**raisin** *(m)* grape(s) (8); **raisins secs** *(mpl)* raisins
**raison** *(f)* reason; **avoir raison** to be right (4)
**raisonnable** reasonable
**ralenti** *(m)* slow motion
**ralentir** to slow down
**ramadan** *(m)* Ramadan
**randonnée** *(f)* hike (8); **faire une randonnée** to go for a hike (8)
**rangé(e)** straightened up, arranged, put away (3)
**ranger** to arrange, to order (7)
**rapide** rapid (8)
**rappeler** to remind
**rapport** *(m)* relationship, report
**rapporter** to bring back; **se rapporter à** to be related to
**rapprochement** *(m)* drawing together
**rapprocher: se rapprocher de** to get closer to
**rarement** rarely (2)
**raser: se raser** to shave (7)
**rasoir** *(m)* razor
**rassembler: se rassembler** to gather
**rassis(e)** stale
**rassurant(e)** reassuring
**rater** to miss
**ratifier** to ratify
**ravigote** *(f)* vinaigrette
**rayé(e)** striped
**réagir (à)** to react (to)
**réalisateur** *(m)* producer
**réalisation** *(f)* carrying out
**réaliser** to accomplish
**réaliste** realistic (1)
**réalité** *(f)* reality
**réapparaître** to reappear
**récemment** recently (5)
**réception** *(f)* front desk (10), receiving
**recette** *(f)* recipe, receipt
**recevoir** to receive (9)
**recherche** *(f)* research
**rechercher** to seek; **recherché(e)** sought
**réciproque** reciprocal
**recommander** to recommend; **recommandé(e)** recommended
**récompenser** to recompense
**réconcilier: se réconcilier** to make up with each other (7)
**reconfirmer** to reconfirm
**reconnaître** to recognize; **se reconnaître** to recognize each other (7)
**reconstruire** to reconstruct
**recopier** to copy
**recoucher: se recoucher** to go back to bed (7)
**recouvert(e)** covered
**recréer** to recreate
**récrire** to rewrite
**rédacteur(-trice)** *(mf)* **en chef** editor-in-chief
**rédaction** *(f)* composition (9)
**redéfinir** to redefine
**réduire** to reduce
**réel(le)** real
**référer: se référer à** to refer to
**refermer** to close back up
**réfléchi(e)** reflexive
**réfléchir (à)** to think (about), to reflect (on) (8)
**reflet** *(m)* reflection
**refléter** to reflect
**réflexion** *(f)* reflection, thought
**réfrigérateur** *(m)* refrigerator

**réfugier: se réfugier** to take refuge
**regagner** to regain
**regard** *(m)* look
**regarder** to look at, to watch (2); **se regarder** to look at each other (7)
**régime** *(m)* diet; regime; **être au régime** to be on a diet
**région** *(f)* region (4)
**régional(e)** *(mpl* **régionaux)** regional (4)
**régir** to govern
**règle** *(f)* rule
**règlement** *(m)* payment
**réglementé(e)** regulated
**régler** to adjust; **régler la note** to pay the bill (10)
**regretter** to regret (6)
**regrouper** to regroup
**régulier(-ière)** regular
**régulièrement** regularly (8)
**rein** *(m)* kidney; **reins** *(mpl)* lower back
**reine** *(f)* queen
**rejeter** to reject
**rejoindre** to join
**relais** *(m)* inn
**relation** *(f)* relationship (7)
**relativement** relatively
**relier** to connect
**religieuse** *(f)* cream puff
**religieux(-euse)** religious
**religion** *(f)* religion (7)
**relire** to reread
**remarquable** remarkable
**remarquer** to notice
**remède** *(m)* remedy, cure
**remercier (de)** to thank (for) (10)
**remettre** to put back; **remettre en cause** to call into question
**remonter** to go back (up)
**remplacer** to replace
**remporter** to win
**rencontre** *(f)* meeting, encounter (7)
**rencontrer** to meet, to run into (7); **se rencontrer** to run into each other (7)
**rendez-vous** *(m)* date, appointment; **Rendez-vous à...** Let's meet at . . .
**rendormir: se rendormir** to fall back asleep
**rendre (quelque chose à quelqu'un)** to return, to give something back to someone (7); **rendre (+ *adjective*)** to make (+ *adjective*); **rendre visite à** to visit (someone) (7); **se rendre (à / chez)** to go (to)
**renommée** *(f)* fame
**renommé(e)** renowned
**rénové(e)** renovated
**renseignement** *(m)* a piece of information (3)
**renseigner** to inform
**rentrée** *(f)* return
**rentrer** to return, to come / go back (home) (2)
**repartir** to start again, to leave again
**repas** *(m)* meal (6)
**répéter** to repeat (2); **Répétez, s'il vous plaît.** Repeat, please. (P); **se répéter** to be repeated
**répondre (à)** to answer (6); **Répondez à la question.** Answer the question. (P)
**réponse** *(f)* answer (P)
**reposant(e)** restful
**reposer** to set down; **se reposer** to rest (7)
**représentant(e)** *(mf)* representative
**représenter** to represent
**reproche** *(m)* reproach
**république** *(f)* republic
**requis(e)** required
**réseau** *(m)* network
**réservation** *(f)* reservation (9); **faire une réservation** to make a reservation (9)

**réserve: sous réserve de** subject to
**réserver** to reserve (9)
**résidence** *(f)* dormitory, residence hall (1); **résidence secondaire** *(f)* second home
**résoudre** to solve
**respecter** to respect
**respirer** to breathe
**responsabilité** *(f)* responsiblity
**ressemblance** *(f)* similarity
**ressembler à** to look like, to resemble
**ressentir** to feel
**ressortir: faire ressortir** to make stand out
**restaurant** *(m)* restaurant (1); **dîner au restaurant** to dine out (2); **restau-u** *(m)* university cafeteria (6)
**reste** *(m)* rest (7); **le reste (de)** the rest (of) (7)
**rester** to stay (2); **rester au lit** to stay in bed (2)
**résultat** *(m)* result
**résumé** *(m)* summary
**retard** *(m)* delay; **en retard** late (10)
**retirer** to take out, to withdraw (10)
**retour** *(m)* return (9); **(billet) aller-retour** *(m)* round-trip ticket (9)
**retourner** to return (5); **se retourner** to turn around
**retravailler** to rework
**rétrécir** to shrink
**retrouver** to meet (4), to find (again); **se retrouver** to meet (each other), to find each other again (7)
**réunion** *(f)* meeting
**réunir: se réunir** to meet
**réussir (à)** to succeed (in) (8)
**revanche: en revanche** on the other hand
**rêve** *(m)* dream
**réveil** *(m)* alarm clock (7), awakening
**réveiller** to wake up; **se réveiller** to wake up (7)
**réveillon** *(m)* **du jour de l'an** New Year's Eve
**révélateur(-trice)** revealing
**révéler** to reveal; **se révéler** to turn out to be
**revendre** to resell, to sell back (7)
**revenir** to come back (4)
**revenu** *(m)* income; **Revenu National Brut (R.N.B)** *(m)* gross national product (GNP)
**rêver (de)** to dream (about) (7)
**rêveur(-euse)** dreamy
**réviser** to review
**révision** *(f)* review
**revoir** to see again; **Au revoir.** Good-bye. (P)
**révolte** *(f)* revolt
**revue** *(f)* magazine
**rez-de-chaussée** *(m)* ground floor (3)
**rhum** *(m)* rum
**rhume** *(m)* cold (10)
**riche** rich (2)
**richesse** *(f)* wealth
**ride** *(f)* wrinkle
**rideau** *(m)* curtain (3)
**ridicule** ridiculous
**rien: de rien** you're welcome (P); **ne... rien** nothing (5); **ne... rien que** nothing but; **rien de spécial** nothing special (6); **rien du tout** nothing at all (6)
**rigoureux(-euse)** rigorous, harsh
**rillettes** *(fpl)* potted pork or goose
**rire** *(m)* laugh, laughter,
**rire** to laugh
**rive** *(f)* bank
**rivière** *(f)* river
**riz** *(m)* rice (8)
**robe** *(f)* dress (5)
**rocher** *(m)* rock, boulder
**rocheux(-euse)** rocky
**rock** *(m)* rock music (1)
**roi** *(m)* king

**rôle** *(m)* role
**roller: faire du roller** to go rollerblading (6)
**romain(e)** Roman
**roman** *(m)* novel (9)
**romanche** *(m)* Romansh
**romancier** *(m)* novelist
**romantique** romantic
**rond** *(m)* circle
**rosbif** *(m)* roast beef (8)
**rose** pink (3)
**rosier** *(m)* rosebush
**rôti(e)** roasted; **rôti** *(m)* **de porc** pork roast
**roue** *(f)* wheel
**rouge** red (3); **vin rouge** *(m)* red wine (2)
**rougeole** *(f)* measles
**rougir** to turn red, to blush (8)
**roulette: patin** *(m)* **à roulettes** roller skate
**route** *(f)* route, way
**routine** *(f)* routine (7)
**roux (rousse)** red (hair) (4)
**royaume** *(m)* kingdom; **Royaume-Uni** *(m)* United Kingdom
**rue** *(f)* street (3); **dans la rue...** on . . . street (10)
**ruine** *(f)* ruin
**ruminer** to ponder
**rupture** *(f)* breaking up
**rural(e)** *(mpl* **ruraux)** rural
**russe** *(m)* Russian
**Russie** *(f)* Russia (9)

## S

**sable** *(m)* sand
**sac** *(m)* purse (5)
**sage** good, well-behaved (4)
**saharien(ne)** Saharan
**sain(e)** healthy (8)
**Saint-Valentin** *(f)* Valentine's Day
**saison** *(f)* season (5)
**salade** *(f)* salad (8); **salade** *(f)* **de tomates** tomato salad (8)
**salaire** *(m)* salary
**sale** dirty (3)
**salé(e)** salted
**salle** *(f)* room; **salle** *(f)* **à manger** dining room (3); **salle** *(f)* **de bains** bathroom (3); **salle** *(f)* **de classe** classroom (1)
**salon** *(m)* living room (3)
**saluer** to greet
**Salut!** Hi! (P), Bye!
**salutation** *(f)* greeting
**samedi** *(m)* Saturday (P)
**sandale** *(f)* sandal (5)
**sandwich** *(m)* sandwich (2)
**sang** *(m)* blood
**sanglier** *(m)* wild boar
**sanitaires** *(mpl)* bathroom
**sans** without (P)
**santé** *(f)* health (8); **santé publique** *(f)* public health
**satisfaisant(e)** satisfying
**satisfait(e)** satisfied
**sauce** *(f)* sauce, gravy, dip
**saucière** *(f)* sauceboat
**saucisse** *(f)* sausage (8)
**saucisson** *(m)* salami (8)
**sauf** except (2)
**saumon** *(m)* salmon (8)
**sauvage** wild
**sauvegardé(e)** preserved
**sauver** to save; **sauvé(e)** saved
**savane** *(f)* savanna
**savoir** to know (how) (9); **Je ne sais pas.** I don't know. (P); **Savez-vous... ?** Do you know (how to). . . ? (8)

**savon** *(m)* soap
**scénario** *(m)* screenplay
**scène** *(f)* stage, scene, skit
**sceptique** skeptical
**science** *(f)* science (1); **film** *(m)* **de science-fiction** science fiction movie; **sciences économiques** *(fpl)* economics; **sciences humaines** *(fpl)* social sciences (1); **sciences politiques** *(fpl)* political science, government (1)
**scientifique** scientific
**scolaire** school; **extra-scolaire** extracurricular
**sculpteur** *(m)* sculptor
**se** herself, himself, itself, oneself, themselves (7); **Il/Elle se trouve...** It is located. . . (3)
**séance** *(f)* showing (6)
**sec (sèche)** dry
**second(e)** second
**secondaire** secondary
**seconde** *(f)* second (5)
**secrétaire** *(mf)* secretary
**secteur** *(m)* sector, area
**section (non-)fumeur** *(f)* (non-)smoking section
**sécurité** *(f)* security, safety
**séduire** to seduce
**séduisant(e)** seductive
**sein** *(m)* breast; **au sein de** within
**seize** sixteen (P)
**seizième** sixteenth
**séjour** *(m)* stay (7)
**séjourner** to stay
**sel** *(m)* salt (8)
**self-service** *(m)* self-service restaurant (8)
**selon** according to
**semaine** *(f)* week (P); **en semaine** weekdays
**semblable** similar
**sembler** to seem
**semestre** *(m)* semester (P)
**Sénégal** *(m)* Senegal (9)
**sénégalais(e)** Senegalese
**sens** *(m)* meaning, sense; **sens** *(m)* **de l'humour** sense of humor (7)
**sensible** sensitive
**sensuel(le)** sensual
**sensualité** *(f)* sensuality
**sentiment** *(m)* feeling (7)
**sentimental(e)** *(mpl* **sentimentaux)** sentimental, emotional (7)
**sentir: se sentir** to feel (8)
**séparé(e)** separated
**sept** seven (P)
**septembre** *(m)* September (4)
**septième** seventh (3)
**série** *(f)* series, category
**sérieusement** seriously
**sérieux(-euse)** serious
**serveur** *(m)* waiter (8)
**serveuse** *(f)* waitress (8)
**service** *(m)* service (8)
**serviette** *(f)* towel
**servir** to serve (4); **servi(e)** served (10); **se servir de** to use
**seul(e)** alone (P), only (1), single, lonely
**seulement** only (8)
**sévère** strict
**sexualité** *(f)* sexuality
**sexuel(le)** sexual
**sexy** *(inv)* sexy (2)
**shopping: faire du shopping** to go shopping (2)
**short** *(m)* shorts (5)
**si** if (5), yes (8); **s'il vous plaît** please (P)
**SIDA** *(m)* AIDS
**siècle** *(m)* century
**siège** *(m)* seat
**sieste** *(f)* nap
**sigle** *(m)* set of initials

**signaler** to draw attention to
**signifier** to mean, to signify
**similaire (à)** similar (to)
**similarité** *(f)* similarity
**simple** simple; **billet aller** simple *(m)* one-way ticket (9)
**simplement** simply (10)
**singe** *(m)* monkey
**sinon** if not, otherwise
**sinusite** *(f)* sinusitis
**site** *(m)* site (9)
**situer: se situer** to be situated; **situé(e)** situated
**six** six (P)
**sixième** sixth (3)
**skateboard(ing): faire du skateboard(ing)** to skateboard (6)
**ski (nautique)** *(m)* (water-)skiing (5); **chalet de ski** *(m)* a ski lodge (10); **faire du ski (nautique)** to go (water-)skiing (5)
**skier** to ski
**slip** *(m)* briefs, panties
**sociabilité** *(f)* socializing
**social(e)** *(mpl* **sociaux)** social
**société** *(f)* company, society; **jeu** *(m)* **de société** board game
**sociologie** *(f)* sociology
**sœur** *(f)* sister (1); **belle-sœur** *(f)* sister-in-law (4); **demi-sœur** *(f)* stepsister, half-sister
**soi** oneself
**soif: avoir soif** to be thirsty (4); **j'ai soif** I'm thirsty (2)
**soin** *(m)* care
**soir** *(m)* evening (P); **à huit heures du soir** at eight in the evening (P); **ce soir** tonight, this evening (2); **le soir** evenings, in the evening (P)
**soirée** *(f)* evening (4)
**soixante** sixty (2)
**soixante-dix** seventy (2)
**soja** *(m)* soya
**sol** *(m)* ground
**soldat** *(m)* soldier
**solde: en solde** on sale (5)
**sole** *(f)* sole (fish)
**soleil** *(m)* sun; **Il fait du soleil.** It's sunny. (5); **lunettes** *(fpl)* **de soleil** sunglasses (5); **prendre un bain de soleil** to sunbathe (4)
**solitaire** lonely
**solitude** *(f)* loneliness
**sombre** dark, gloomy
**somme** *(f)* sum
**sommeil** *(m)* sleep; **avoir sommeil** to be sleepy (4)
**son** *(m)* sound
**son (sa, ses)** her, his, its (3)
**sondage** *(m)* poll
**sonner** to ring (7)
**sorcière** *(f)* witch
**sorte** *(f)* kind, sort; **en sorte que** so that
**sortie** *(f)* outing (6), exit
**sortir (de)** to go out (2); to leave (6); to take out
**souci** *(m)* care
**soudain** suddenly (6)
**soudain(e)** sudden
**soudainement** suddenly
**souffrance** *(f)* suffering
**souffrir** to suffer
**souhait** *(m)* wish
**souhaiter** to wish
**soumettre: se soumettre à** to submit to
**soupçonner** to suspect
**soupe** *(f)* soup (8); **soupe** *(f)* **à l'oignon** onion soup (8)
**souper** to have supper

**sourire** *(m)* smile
**sous** under (3); **sous réserve de** subject to
**sous-estimer** to underestimate
**sous-marin(e)** underwater; **plongée sous-marine** *(f)* scuba diving
**sous-sol** *(m)* basement (3)
**sous-titres** *(mpl)* subtitles
**sous-vêtements** *(mpl)* underwear
**soutenir: se soutenir** to support one another; **soutenu(e)** supported
**soutien-gorge** *(m)* bra
**souvenir** *(m)* memory
**souvenir: se souvenir (de)** to remember (7)
**souvent** often (1)
**souveraineté** *(f)* sovereignty
**spécial(e)** *(mpl* **spéciaux)** special; **effets spéciaux** *(mpl)* special effects (6); **rien de spécial** nothing special (6)
**spécialisation** *(f)* specialization, major
**spécialisé(e)** specialized
**spécialiser: se spécialiser en** to specialize in
**spécialité** *(f)* specialty (4)
**spectacle** *(m)* show
**spectaculaire** spectacular
**spectateur(-trice)** *(mf)* spectator, viewer
**spiritualité** *(f)* spirituality (7)
**sport** *(m)* sport (1); **faire du sport** to play sports (5)
**sportif(-ive)** athletic (1)
**stabilité** *(f)* stability
**stade** *(m)* stadium (1)
**stage** *(m)* internship
**standard** *(m)* switchboard
**station** *(f)* station; **station estivale** *(f)* a summer resort (10); **station-service** *(f)* service station
**statut** *(m)* statute, status
**steak-frites** *(m)* steak and fries (8)
**stimuler** to stimulate
**stratégie** *(f)* strategy
**stress** *(m)* stress (8)
**stressé(e)** stressed (out) (8)
**style** *(m)* style
**stylo** *(m)* pen (P)
**subventions** *(fpl)* subsidies
**succès** *(m)* success
**succursale** *(f)* branch office
**sucer** to suck
**sucre** *(m)* sugar (8)
**sucré(e)** sweet, sugary
**sud** *(m)* south; **Amérique** *(f)* **du Sud** South America (9)
**Suède** *(f)* Sweden
**suffire: il suffit de...** it's enough to . . . **Suffit!** That's enough!
**suffisant(e)** sufficient
**suggérer** to suggest (6)
**Suisse** *(f)* Switzerland (9)
**suisse** Swiss
**suite: toute de suite** right away (6)
**suivant(e)** following (3)
**suivre** to follow (7); **à suivre** to be continued (6); **suivre un cours** to take a course
**sujet** *(m)* subject
**super** great (P)
**superficie** *(f)* area
**supérieur(e)** superior, higher
**supermarché** *(m)* supermarket
**supplément** *(m)* extra charge (10)
**supplémentaire** supplementary
**supporter** to bear, to tolerate, to put up with (7)
**supposer** to suppose, to presume
**suprématie** *(f)* supremacy
**sur** on (1); **sept jours sur sept** seven days out of seven

**sûr(e)** sure; **Bien sûr!** Of course! (5)
**sûrement** surely
**surface: grande surface** *(f)* superstore (8)
**surfer le Net** to surf the Net (2)
**surgelé(e)** frozen (8)
**surgir** to arise, to come up; to appear suddenly, to surge, to begin to grow
**surimpression** *(f)* **d'images** double exposure
**surpasser** to surpass
**surprenant(e)** surprising
**surprendre** to surprise; **surpris(e)** surprised (10)
**surtout** especially, above all (8)
**survêtement** *(m)* jogging suit (5)
**symbiose** *(f)* symbiosis
**sympathique (sympa)** nice (1)
**symptôme** *(m)* symptom (10)
**synagogue** *(f)* synagogue
**synonyme** synonymous
**systématiquement** systematically
**système** *(m)* system (9); **système** *(m)* **de transports en commun** public transportation system (9)

**T**
**tabac** *(m)* tobacco (8); **bureau** *(m)* **de tabac** tobacco shop
**table** *(f)* table (3); **table basse** *(f)* coffee table
**tableau** *(m)* board (P); painting, picture (3), act, scene; **tableau** *(m)* **d'affichage** bulletin board
**tâche** *(f)* task; **tâche domestique** household chore
**taille** *(f)* size (4); **de taille moyenne** medium-sized, of medium height (4); **Quelle taille faites-vous?** What size do you wear? (5)
**tailleur** *(m)* woman's suit
**taire: se taire** to be silent
**talon** *(m)* heel; *****haut talon** *(m)* high heel
**tandis que** whereas, while
**tant (de)** so much, so many; **tant que** as long as
**tante** *(f)* aunt (4)
**tapis** *(m)* rug (3)
**tapisserie** *(f)* tapestry
**tard** late (4); **plus tard** later (4)
**tarte** *(f)* pie (8); **tarte** *(f)* **aux pommes** apple pie (8)
**tartelette** *(f)* **(aux fraises)** (strawberry) tart (8)
**tartine** *(f)* bread and butter (with jam) (8)
**tas** *(m)* pile; **un tas de** a bunch of
**tasse** *(f)* cup
**taxi** *(m)* taxi (4); **en taxi** by taxi (4)
**te** (to, for) you (9), yourself (7); **Ça te dit?** How does that sound to you? (4); **Ça te plaît?** Do you like it? (3); **Je te présente...** I would like to introduce . . . to you.; **s'il te plaît** please; **Te voilà!** There you are!
**technique** technical (1)
**technologie** *(f)* technology
**technologique** technological
**tee-shirt** *(m)* T-shirt (5)
**teinturerie** *(f)* dry cleaner's
**tel(le): tel(le) que** such as (9); **un(e) tel(le)** such a (7)
**télé** *(f)* TV (2)
**télécopie** *(f)* fax
**téléphone** *(m)* telephone (2); **au téléphone** on the telephone (2); **numéro** *(m)* **de téléphone** telephone number (3)
**téléphoner (à)** to phone (3); **se téléphoner** to telephone each other (7)
**téléphonique: appareil** *(m)* **téléphonique** telephone; **carte** *(f)* **téléphonique** telephone card (10)
**télévision (télé)** *(f)* television (2)
**tellement** so much, so (6)
**témoignage** *(m)* testimony, evidence

**température** *(f)* temperature
**temple** *(m)* temple, Protestant church
**temps** *(m)* time (2), weather (5); **de temps en temps** from time to time (4); **emploi** *(m)* **du temps** schedule (P); **en même temps** at the same time; **en tout temps** at all times; **Pendant combien de temps?** For how long? (5); **Quel temps fait-il?** What's the weather like? (5); **temps libre** *(m)* free time (4); **temps verbal** *(m)* tense
**tendance** *(f)* tendency
**tendre** tender
**tendresse** *(f)* tenderness
**tenir** to hold; **Ah tiens!** Hey!; **tenir à** to value; **tenir la maison** to keep house
**tennis** *(m)* tennis (1); **court** *(m)* **de tennis** tennis court
**tentation** *(f)* temptation
**tenter** to attempt
**terme** *(m)* term; **mettre terme à** to put an end to
**terminaison** *(f)* ending
**terminer** to finish
**terrain: sur le terrain** on site
**terrasse** *(f)* terrace (9)
**terre** *(f)* earth; **par terre** on the ground / floor (3); **pomme** *(f)* **de terre** potato (8)
**territoire** *(m)* territory, lands, grounds
**tertiaire: activités tertiaires** *(fpl)* service industries
**test** *(m)* test (7)
**tête** *(f)* head (10); **prendre la tête** to take charge
**thé** *(m)* tea (2)
**théâtre** *(m)* theater (1), drama (1)
**thon** *(m)* tuna (8)
**tiers** *(m)* third; **Tiers Monde** *(m)* Third World
**timbre** *(m)* stamp (10)
**timide** shy, timid (1)
**tiroir** *(m)* drawer
**tisser** to weave; **se tisser** to be woven
**titre** *(m)* title; **à titre exclusif** exclusively; **à titre principal** mainly
**titulaire** *(mf)* holder
**toi** you (P); **chez toi** at your house (2)
**toilettes** *(fpl)* toilet, restroom (3); **faire sa toilette** to wash up (7)
**toit** *(m)* roof
**tomate** *(f)* tomato (8)
**tombe** *(f)* grave
**tomber** to fall; **tomber amoureux(-euse) (de)** to fall in love (with) (6); **tomber malade** to get sick (10)
**ton** *(m)* tone
**ton (ta, tes)** your (3); **tes amis** your friends (1); **ton université** your university (1)
**tort: avoir tort** to be wrong (4)
**tôt** early (4)
**totalité: la totalité de** all of
**toucher** to touch
**toujours** always (2), still
**tour** *(m)* tour, ride (4); **faire un tour** to take a tour, to go for a ride (4)
**tour** *(f)* tower
**tourisme** *(m)* tourism; **office** *(m)* **de tourisme** tourist office (10)
**touriste** *(mf)* tourist; **classe touriste** *(f)* tourist class, coach (9)
**touristique** tourist (9)
**tournée** *(f)* tour
**tourner** to turn (10), to stir to film; **se tourner (vers)** to turn (toward); **tourné(e)** filmed
**tourte** *(f)* pie
**Toussaint** *(f)* All Saints' Day
**tousser** to cough (10)
**tout (toute, tous, toutes)** everything, all (3), whole; **ne... pas du tout** not at all (1); **rien**

**du tout** nothing at all (6); **tous (toutes) les deux** both; **tous les jours** every day (2); **tous les soirs** every evening; **tout à fait** completely; **tout à l'heure** in a little while (P), a while ago; **tout de suite** right away (6); **tout droit** straight (10); **tout d'un coup** all of a sudden (6); **toute la journée** the whole day (2); **tout en** while; **toutes sortes de...** all kinds of . . .; **tout le monde** everybody, everyone; **tout près (de)** right by, very near (3); **tout simplement** quite simply (10)
**toutefois** however
**traditionnel(le)** traditional (8)
**traditionnellement** traditionally
**traducteur(-trice)** *(mf)* translator
**traduire** to translate
**train** *(m)* train (4); **en train** by train (4); **être en train de...** to be in the process of. . .
**traîneau** *(m)* sled
**traîner** to hang around
**trait** *(m)* trait (7)
**traité** *(m)* treaty
**traitement** *(m)* treatment
**tranche** *(f)* slice (8)
**tranquille** tranquil, calm
**transformer: se transformer en** to change into
**transmettre** to transmit; to pass on
**transpercer** to pierce
**transport** *(m)* transportation; **moyen** *(m)* **de transport** means of transportation (4); **système** *(m)* **de transports en commun** public transportation system (9)
**travail** *(m)* *(pl* **travaux)** work; **fête** *(f)* **du travail** Labor Day; **travaux** *(mpl)* **d'aiguille** needlework
**travailler** to work, to study (2); **je travaille** I work (P); **Tu travailles?/Vous travaillez?** Do you work? (P)
**travailleur(-euse)** *(mf)* worker
**travers: à travers** across
**traversée** *(f)* crossing
**traverser** to cross, to go across (10)
**treize** thirteen (P)
**trembler** to tremble
**trentaine** *(f)* thirties
**trente** thirty (P)
**très** very (P)
**tribu** *(f)* tribe
**triste** sad (10)
**trois** three (P)
**troisième** third (3); **troisième âge** *(m)* age of retirement
**trompette** *(f)* trumpet
**trop** too, too much (3); **trop de** too much, too many (6)
**tropical(e)** *(mpl* **tropicaux)** tropical (9)
**trou** *(m)* hole
**trouver** to find (4); **Il/Elle se trouve...** It is located. . . (3)
**truc** *(m)* thing (1); **Ce n'est pas mon truc.** That's not my thing. (1)
**truite** *(f)* trout
**tu** you (P)
**tuba: faire du tuba:** to go snorkeling
**tuberculose** *(f)* tuberculosis
**tuer** to kill
**Tunisie** *(f)* Tunisia
**tunisien(ne)** Tunisian
**Turquie** *(f)* Turkey
**typique** typical (2)
**typiquement** typically
**tyran** *(m)* tyrant

**U**

**un(e)** one, a (1)
**uni(e) (à)** close (to), united, solid-colored; **Nations unies** *(fpl)* United Nations
**unique** only, single, unique
**uniquement** only
**unité** *(f)* unity, unit
**universitaire** university (1)
**université** *(f)* university (P)
**urgence** *(f)* emergency
**usage** *(m)* use
**usine** *(f)* factory
**utile** useful (10)
**utiliser** to use, to utilize

**V**

**vacances** *(fpl)* vacation (4); **en vacances** on vacation (4)
**vacancier** *(m)* vacationer
**vaccination** *(f)* vaccination; **certificat** *(m)* **de vaccination** vaccination certificate
**vache** *(f)* cow
**vague** *(f)* wave
**vaincu(e)** defeated
**vaisselle** *(f)* dishes; **faire la vaisselle** to wash dishes (5); **lave-vaisselle** *(m)* dishwasher
**valeur** *(f)* value; **mettre en valeur** to emphasize
**valise** *(f)* suitcase (9); **faire ses valises** to pack one's bags (9)
**vallée** *(f)* valley
**valoir** to be worth; **il vaut mieux (que)...** it's better (that) . . . (10)
**valse** *(f)* waltz
**valser** to waltz
**vanille** *(f)* vanilla (8)
**vanité** *(f)* vanity (7)
**vaniteux(-euse)** vain
**varappe** *(f)* rock climbing; **faire de la varappe** to go rock climbing
**varicelle** *(f)* chicken pox
**varié(e)** varied
**variété** *(f)* variety
**vaste** vast
**vaut** See **valoir.**
**veau** *(m)* veal
**végétarien(ne)** vegetarian
**véhicule** *(m)* vehicle
**veillée** *(f)* evening together
**veiller** to watch over
**vélo** *(m)* bicycle (3); **en vélo** by bike (4); **faire du vélo** to go bike-riding
**vendeur(-euse)** *(mf)* salesperson (5)
**vendre** to sell (7)
**vendredi** *(m)* Friday (P)
**venir** to come (4); **venir de** (+ *infinitive*) to have just (+ *past participle*); **Viens voir...** Come see . . . (3)
**vent** *(m)* wind; **Il fait du vent.** It's windy. (5)
**vente** *(f)* sale
**ventre** *(m)* stomach, belly (10)
**verbe** *(m)* verb
**verglaçant(e)** icy
**verglas: Il y a du verglas.** It's icy.
**vérifier** to check
**véritable** true, real
**vérité** *(f)* truth
**verre** *(m)* glass (2); **prendre un verre** to have a drink (2)
**vers** *(m)* verse
**vers** toward(s), about, around (2)
**vert(e)** green (3)
**vestige** *(m)* remnant
**vêtements** *(mpl)* clothes (3); **sous-vêtements** *(mpl)* underwear

**vétérinaire** *(m)* veterinarian
**veuf** *(m)* widower (7)
**veuve** *(f)* widow (7)
**vexer** to vex, to upset
**viande** *(f)* meat (8)
**vicieux(-euse)** vicious
**victime** *(f)* victim
**vidéo** *(f)* video (2); **jeu vidéo** *(m)* video game (2)
**vidéocassette** *(f)* video cassette
**vie** *(f)* life (6)
**vieillir** to age, to get old (8)
**viennoiserie** *(f)* baked goods sold at a bakery
**Viêt Nam** *(m)* Vietnam (9)
**vieux / vieil (vieille)** old (1); **Vieux Carré** *(m)* French Quarter (4)
**vif(-ive)** lively, bright; **bleu vif** bright blue
**vigueur: en vigueur** in effect; **reprendre vigueur** to take on a new life
**village** *(m)* village, town
**villageois(e)** *(mf)* villager
**ville** *(f)* city (3); **en ville** in town (3)
**villégiature** *(f)* vacation stay
**vin** *(m)* wine (2)
**vinaigre** *(m)* vinegar
**vingt** twenty (P)
**vingtième** twentieth
**violence** *(f)* violence (7)
**violet(te)** violet (3)
**virus** *(m)* virus (10)
**visa** *(m)* visa
**visage** *(m)* face
**visé(e)** stamped, approved
**visite: rendre visite à** to visit (a person) (7)
**visiter** to visit (1)
**visiteur(-euse)** *(mf)* visitor
**vitamine** *(f)* vitamin (8)
**vite** quickly, fast (7)

**vitesse** *(f)* speed
**vivant(e)** alive
**vivement** greatly
**vivier** *(m)* fish reservoir
**vivoir** *(m)* living room
**vivre** to live
**vocabulaire** *(m)* vocabulary (P)
**vocation** *(f)* calling
**voici** here is, here are (2)
**voilà** there is, there are (2); **Te / Vous voilà!** There you are!
**voile** *(f)* sailing; **faire de la planche à voile** *(f)* to go windsurfing
**voir** to see (1); **aller voir** to go see, to visit (4); **comme tu vois** as you see (3); **se voir** to see each other (7), to find oneself; **Voyons!** Let's see! (5)
**voire** even
**voisin(e)** *(mf)* neighbor (9)
**voiture** *(f)* car (3); **en voiture** by car (4); **voiture** *(f)* **de location** rental car (5)
**voix** *(f)* voice
**vol** *(m)* flight (9)
**volaille** *(f)* poultry (8)
**volcan** *(m)* volcano
**voleur** *(m)* thief (6)
**volley** *(m)* volleyball (2)
**volonté** *(f)* will, wish
**volontiers** gladly, willingly (8)
**vomir** to vomit (10)
**voter** to vote
**vôtre: le/la vôtre** yours
**votre** *(pl* **vos)** your (3); **Ouvrez votre livre.** Open your book. (P)
**vouloir** to want (6); **Je voudrais (bien)...** I would like . . . (2); **Qu'est-ce que ça veut dire?** What does that mean? (P); **Qu'est-ce que vous**

**voudriez faire?** What would you like to do? (2); **Tu voudrais... ?** Would you like . . . ? (2)
**vous** you (P), (to, for) you (9), yourself(-selves) (7); **Je vous présente...** I would like to introduce . . . to you.; **s'il vous plaît** please (P); **vous-même** yourself; **Vous voilà!** There you are!
**voyage** *(m)* trip (4); **agence** *(f)* **de voyages** travel agency (9); **agent** *(m)* **de voyages** travel agent (9); **chèque** *(m)* **de voyage** traveler's check (9); **faire un voyage** to take a trip (5); **voyage** *(m)* **de noces** honeymoon
**voyager** to travel (2)
**voyelle** *(f)* vowel
**vrai(e)** true
**vraiment** really, truly (2)
**vue** *(f)* view (3); **point** *(m)* **de vue** viewpoint

## W

**wallon(ne)** Walloon
**W.-C.** *(mpl)* toilet, restroom (3)
**Web: site** *(m)* website (9)
**week-end** *(m)* weekend (P); **Bon week-end!** Have a good weekend!; **le week-end** on weekends (P)

## Y

**y** there (4); **il y a** there is, there are (1), ago (5)
**yaourt** *(m)* yogurt
**yeux** *(mpl)* (*sing* **œil**) eyes (4)
**Yom Kippour** *(m)* Yom Kippur

## Z

**zapper** to channel surf, to switch back and forth
**zéro** *(m)* zero (P)
**zydeco: musique** *(f)* **zydeco** zydeco music (4)

# Vocabulaire anglais–français

The **Vocabulaire anglais–français** includes all words presented in *Horizons* for active use, as well as others that students may need for more personalized expression. The definitions of active vocabulary words are followed by the number of the chapter where they are first presented. A (P) refers to the **Chapitre préliminaire.** When several translations, separated by commas, are listed before a chapter number, they are all considered active. Since verbs are sometimes introduced lexically in the infinitive before the conjugation of the present indicative is presented, consult the **Index** to find out the chapter where a conjugation is introduced. An *(m)*, *(f)* or *(pl)* following a noun indicates that it is masculine, feminine, or plural. *Inv* means that a word is invariable. An asterisk before a word beginning with an **h** indicates that the **h** is aspirate.

## A

**a** un(e) (P); **a few** quelques (5); **a lot** beaucoup (P)
**able: be able** pouvoir (4)
**about** vers (2), environ (4), de (1); **about it/them** en (8); **About what?** À propos de quoi?; **think about** penser à
**above** au-dessus de; **above all** surtout (8)
**abroad** à l'étranger (9)
**absolutely** absolument
**Acadia** Acadie *(f)*
**accent** accent *(m)* (P); **without an accent** sans accent (P)
**accept** accepter (7)
**accident** accident *(m)*
**accompany** accompagner
**according to** selon
**account** compte *(m)*
**accountant** comptable *(mf)*
**accounting** comptabilité *(f)* (1)
**accustomed to** habitué(e) à
**ache** douleur *(f)*
**ache** avoir mal (à) (10)
**acquaintance: make the acquaintance of** faire la connaissance de
**acquainted: be / get acquainted with** connaître (4)
**across (from)** en face (de) (3); **go across** traverser (10)
**act** jouer *(in movies and theater)* (6); agir
**active** dynamique (1)
**activity** activité *(f)* (2)
**actor** acteur *(m)* (6)
**actress** actrice *(f)* (6)
**actually** effectivement, réellement
**adapt** s'adapter
**add** ajouter
**address** adresse *(f)* (3); **e-mail address** adresse *(f)* mail (3)
**adjective** adjectif *(m)* (1)
**administration building** centre administratif *(m)*
**admire** admirer (9)
**adopted** adopté(e)
**adore** adorer
**adult** adulte *(mf)*
**advance** avance *(f)*; **in advance** à l'avance (9)
**advantage** avantage *(m)*; **take advantage of** profiter de (9)
**adventure** aventure *(f)*; **adventure movie** film *(m)* d'aventures
**advertisement** publicité *(f)*; **classified ad** petite annonce *(f)*
**advertising** publicité *(f)*
**advice** conseils *(mpl)* (8); **give a piece of advice** donner un conseil

**aerobics: do aerobics** faire de l'aérobic (8)
**afraid: be afraid (of)** avoir peur (de) (4)
**Africa** Afrique *(f)* (9)
**African** africain(e)
**after** après (P); **after having done . . .** après avoir fait... ; **day after tomorrow** après-demain
**afternoon** après-midi *(m)* (P); **in the afternoon, afternoons** l'après-midi (P); **It's one o'clock in the afternoon.** Il est une heure de l'après-midi. (P); **this afternoon** cet après-midi (4)
**afterwards** après (P), ensuite (4)
**again** encore (8), de nouveau
**against** contre (10)
**age** âge *(m)*
**age** vieillir (8)
**agency: travel agency** agence *(f)* de voyages (9)
**agent** agent *(m)*; **travel agent** agent *(m)* de voyages *(m)* (9)
**ago** il y a (5); **How long ago?** Il y a combien de temps? (5)
**agree** être d'accord; **Agreed!** D'accord! (2)
**agricultural** agricole
**ahead: straight ahead** tout droit (10)
**AIDS** SIDA *(m)*
**air** air *(m)*
**airplane** avion *(m)* (4); **by airplane** en avion (4)
**airport** aéroport *(m)* (10)
**alarm: alarm clock** réveil *(m)* (7)
**alcohol** alcool *(m)* (8)
**alcoholic drink** boisson alcoolisée *(f)*
**algebra** algèbre *(f)*
**Algeria** Algérie *(f)* (9)
**alive** vivant(e)
**all** tout (toute, tous, toutes) (3); **above all** surtout (8); **all day** toute la journée (2); **all of a sudden** tout d'un coup (6); **all of the time** tout le temps; **all sorts of** toutes sortes de; **all the better** tant mieux; **not at all** ne... pas du tout (1); **nothing at all** rien du tout (6); **That's all.** C'est tout. (8)
**allergy** allergie *(f)* (10)
**allow** permettre (de); **allowed** permis(e)
**almost** presque (2)
**alone** seul(e) (P)
**along** le long de (9); **get along well / badly** s'entendre bien / mal (7)
**already** déjà (5)
**also** aussi (P)
**although** bien que, quoique
**always** toujours (2)
**A.M.** du matin (P)
**amaze** étonner; **amazed** étonné(e) (10)
**America** Amérique *(f)* (9)

**American** américain(e) (P); **American style** à l'américaine (8)
**among** parmi
**amusing** amusant(e) (1)
**an** un(e) (1)
**ancestor** ancêtre *(mf)*
**and** et (P)
**angry** fâché(e); **get angry** se fâcher
**animal** animal *(m)* *(pl* animaux*)* (3)
**animated** animé(e)
**ankle** cheville *(f)*
**anniversary** *(wedding)* anniversaire *(m)* de mariage
**annoying** embêtant(e) (3)
**another** un(e) autre (1); **another glass of...** encore un verre de... ; **another thing** autre chose; **one another** se, nous, vous (7)
**answer** réponse *(f)* (P)
**answer** répondre (à) (6); **Answer the question.** Répondez à la question. (P)
**anthropology** anthropologie *(f)*
**any** du, de la, de l', de, des, en (8)
**anymore: not anymore** ne... plus (8)
**anyone** quelqu'un (6); **(just) anyone** n'importe qui; **not . . . anyone** ne... personne
**anything** quelque chose (2); **(just) anything** n'importe quoi; **not . . . anything** ne... rien (5)
**anyway** quand même
**anywhere: (just) anywhere** n'importe où; **not . . . anywhere** nulle part
**apartment** appartement *(m)* (3); **apartment building** immeuble *(m)* (3)
**appear** paraître
**appearance: physical appearance** aspect physique *(m)* (7)
**appetite** appétit *(m)*
**appetizer** *hors-d'œuvre *(m)* (8)
**apple** pomme *(f)* (8); **apple pie** tarte *(f)* aux pommes (8)
**appointment** rendez-vous *(m)* (6)
**appreciate** apprécier (6)
**appropriate** approprié(e), convenable
**apricot** abricot *(m)*
**April** avril *(m)* (4); **April Fool's Day** les poissons *(mpl)* d'avril
**Arabic** arabe *(m)*
**architect** architecte *(mf)*
**architecture** architecture *(f)*
**Argentina** Argentine *(f)* (9)
**argue (with)** se disputer (avec) (7)
**arm** bras *(m)* (10)
**armchair** fauteuil *(m)* (3)
**around** vers (2), environ (4) autour de

**arrange** ranger (7)
**arranged** rangé(e) (3)
**arrival** arrivée (f) (9); **arrival gate** porte (f) d'arrivée (9)
**arrive** arriver (3)
**art** art (m); **fine arts** beaux-arts (mpl) (1)
**article** article (m) (9)
**artist** artiste (mf); **graphic** artiste dessinateur(-trice) (mf) de publicité
**as** comme (P); **as . . . as** aussi... que (1); **as long as** tant que; **as many . . . (as)** autant de... (que); **as much . . . (as)** autant de... (que); **as soon as** aussitôt que; **as you see** comme tu vois (3)
**ash** cendre (f); **Ash Wednesday** mercredi (m) des Cendres
**ashamed: be ashamed** avoir *honte
**Asia** Asie (f) (9)
**ask (for)** demander (2); **ask a question** poser une question (3)
**asleep: fall asleep** s'endormir (7)
**asparagus** asperge (f)
**aspirin** aspirine (f) (10)
**assembly** assemblage (m)
**associate** associer
**astronomy** astronomie (f)
**at** à (P); **at home** à la maison (P); **at . . . 's house / place** chez... (2)
**athletic** sportif(-ive) (1)
**ATM machine** distributeur de billets (m) (10)
**attend** assister à
**attention** attention (f); **pay attention (to)** faire attention (à) (8)
**attract** attirer
**August** août (m) (4)
**aunt** tante (f) (4)
**Australia** Australie (f) (9)
**automatic: automatic teller machine** distributeur de billets (m) (10)
**autumn** automne (m) (5); **in autumn** en automne (5)
**available** disponible
**avenue** avenue (f) (10)
**average** moyen(ne)
**avoid** éviter (8)
**awaken** se réveiller (7)
**awakening** réveil (m)
**away: go away** partir (4), s'en aller; **put away** rangé(e) (3); **right away** tout de suite (6)

**B**
**baby** bébé (m)
**babysitter** baby-sitter (mf)
**back** dos (m) (10)
**back: bring back** rapporter; **come back** revenir (4); **give back** rendre (7); **go back** rentrer (2), retourner (5); **go back to bed** se recoucher (7); **in the back of** au fond de; **sell back** revendre (7)
**bacon** bacon (m) (8)
**bad** mauvais(e) (1); **It's too bad!** C'est dommage! (7); **really bad** nul(le) (7); **The weather's bad.** Il fait mauvais. (5)
**badly** mal (P), **not badly** pas mal (P)
**bag** sac (m) (5), paquet (m) (8); **pack one's bags** faire ses valises (9)
**baggage** bagages (mpl) (9)
**bakery** boulangerie (f) (8), pâtisserie (f)
**balcony** balcon (m)
**bald** chauve
**ball** balle (f), (inflated) ballon (m)
**banana** banane (f) (8)
**band** orchestre (m) (4)
**bank** banque (f) (10); **bank card** carte bancaire (f) (9)

**banker** banquier (m)
**bar** bar (m) (4)
**baseball** base-ball (m) (2)
**based: based on** basé(e) sur (6)
**basement** sous-sol (m) (3)
**basketball** basket (m) (1)
**bath** bain (m) (7)
**bathe** prendre un bain (7), se baigner
**bathroom** salle (f) de bains (3)
**be** être (1); **be able** pouvoir (4); **be afraid (of)** avoir peur (de) (4); **be ashamed** avoir *honte; **be bored** s'ennuyer (7); **be born** naître, être né(e) (5); **be cold** avoir froid (4); **be familiar with** connaître (4); **be hot** avoir chaud (4); **be hungry** avoir faim (4); **I'm hungry.** J'ai faim. (2); **be interested in** s'intéresser à (7); **be named** s'appeler (7); **be right** avoir raison (4); **be sleepy** avoir sommeil (4); **be thirsty** avoir soif (4); **I'm thirsty.** J'ai soif.(2); **be wrong** avoir tort (4); **be . . . years old** avoir... ans (4); **here is/are** voici (2); **How are you?** Comment allez-vous? (P); **How is it going?** Comment ça va? (P); **I am . . .** Je suis... (P); **isn't it?** n'est-ce pas?, non? (1); **It is located...** Il/Elle se trouve… (3); **It's Monday.** C'est lundi. (P); **My name is . . .** Je m'appelle... (P); **That's . . .** euros. Ça fait... euros. (2); **There are six of us.** Nous sommes six. (4); **there is/are** il y a (1), voilà (2); **The weather's nice / bad / cold / cool / hot / sunny / windy.** Il fait beau / mauvais / froid / frais / chaud / du soleil / du vent. (5); **to be continued** à suivre (6); *you are* tu es/vous êtes (P)
**beach** plage (f) (4)
**beans: green beans** *haricots verts (mpl) (8)
**bear** supporter (7)
**beard** barbe (f) (4)
**beast** animal (m) (6)
**beat** battre
**beautiful** beau (bel, belle, pl beaux, belles) (1)
**beauty** beauté (7)
**because** parce que (P); **because of** à cause de
**become** devenir (4)
**bed** lit (m) (2); **go back to bed** se recoucher (7); **go to bed** se coucher (7); **stay in bed** rester au lit (2)
**bedroom** chambre (f) (3)
**bedspread** couverture (f) (3)
**beef** bœuf (m) (8); **roast beef** rosbif (m) (8)
**beer** bière (f) (2); **draft beer** demi (m) (2)
**before** avant (P); **before (doing)** avant de (faire); **before-dinner drink** apéritif (m) (8)
**beforehand** auparavant
**begin** commencer (2); **The French class begins at...** Le cours de français commence à… (P)
**beginning** début (m); **at the beginning** au début (6)
**behaved: well-behaved** sage (4)
**behind** derrière (3)
**beige** beige (3)
**Belgium** Belgique (f) (9)
**believe (in)** croire (à)
**bell** cloche (f)
**belly** ventre (m) (10)
**belong to** appartenir à, être à
**belongings** effets personnels (mpl) (3), affaires (fpl)
**belt** ceinture (f) (5)
**benefit (work)** bénévole
**beside** à côté de (3)
**besides** de plus, d'ailleurs
**best** (le/la) meilleur(e) (adjective) (1), (le) mieux (adverb)

**better** meilleur(e) (adjective) (1), mieux (adverb) (2); **do better. . .** faire mieux... (8); **it's better, you had better** il vaut mieux (10)
**between** entre (3)
**beverage** boisson (f) (2)
**bicycle** vélo (m) (3)
**bicycle-riding: go bicycle-riding** faire du vélo (5)
**big** grand(e) (1), gros(se) (1)
**bike** vélo (m) (3); **by bike** en vélo (4)
**bikini** bikini (m) (5)
**bilingual** bilingue
**bill** (restaurant) addition (f), (utilities) facture (f); **pay the bill** (at a hotel) régler la note (10)
**billiards** billard (m)
**biology** biologie (f) (1)
**bird** oiseau (m)
**birth** naissance (f); **date of birth** date (f) de naissance
**birthday** anniversaire (m) (4)
**bizarre** bizarre
**black** noir(e) (3)
**blackboard** tableau (m) (P)
**blanket** couverture (f) (3)
**bless** bénir
**blond** blond(e) (4)
**blood** sang (m)
**blouse** chemisier (m) (5)
**blue** bleu(e) (3)
**blueberry** myrtille (f)
**blues** (music) blues (m)
**blush** rougir (8)
**board** tableau (m) (P)
**boat** bateau (m) (4); **by boat** en bateau (4)
**boating: go boating** faire du bateau (5)
**body** corps (m) (7)
**bodybuilding: to do bodybuilding** faire de la musculation (8)
**book** livre (m) (P)
**bookcase** étagère (f) (3)
**bookstore** librairie (f) (1)
**boot** botte (f) (5)
**border** frontière (f)
**bored: be / get bored** s'ennuyer (7)
**boring** ennuyeux(-euse) (1)
**born** né(e) (5), **be born** naître (5), **He/She was born . . .** Il/Elle est né(e)... (5)
**borrow** emprunter
**boss** patron(ne) (mf)
**both** les deux
**bottle** bouteille (f) (8)
**boulevard** boulevard (m) (10)
**bowl** bol (m)
**box** boîte (f), paquet (m) (8)
**boy** garçon (m) (4)
**boyfriend** petit ami (m) (2)
**bra** soutien-gorge (m)
**bracelet** bracelet (m)
**brave** courageux(-euse)
**Brazil** Brésil (m) (9)
**bread** pain (m) (8); **bread-and-butter** tartine (f) (8); **loaf of French bread** baguette (f) (8); **wholegrain bread** pain complet (m) (8)
**break** casser; **break down** (machine) tomber en panne; **break one's arm** se casser le bras
**breakfast** petit déjeuner (m) (5); **to have / eat one's breakfast** prendre son petit déjeuner (5)
**breathe** respirer (10)
**brief** bref (brève)
**briefly** brièvement
**briefs** slip (m)
**bright** (colors) vif(-ive) (5)
**bring** (a thing) apporter, (a person) amener; **bring back** rapporter
**Britain: Great Britain** Grande-Bretagne (f) (9)

**Brittany** Bretagne (f)

**broccoli** brocolis (mpl)

**brother** frère (m) (1); **brother-in-law** beau-frère (m) (4)

**brown** marron (3), brun(e) (4), (hair) châtain (4)

**brunette** brun(e)

**brush (one's teeth)** (se) brosser (les dents) (7)

**Brussels sprouts** choux (mpl) de Bruxelles

**build** construire

**building** bâtiment (m) (1); **administration building** centre administratif (m); **apartment building** immeuble (m) (3)

**burn (oneself)** (se) brûler

**bus** (in city) autobus (m) (3), (between cities) autocar (m) (4); **bus stop** arrêt (m) d'autobus (3)

**business** affaires (fpl); **business course** cours (m) de commerce (1)

**businessman** homme (m) d'affaires (5)

**businesswoman** femme (f) d'affaires (5)

**busy** chargé(e), occupé(e)

**but** mais (P); **nothing but** ne... rien que

**butcher's shop** boucherie (f) (8)

**butter** beurre (m) (8); **bread-and-butter** tartine (f) (8)

**buy** acheter (4)

**by** par; **by bike / boat / bus / car / plane / taxi** en vélo / bateau / autobus (autocar) / voiture / avion / taxi (4); **by chance** par *hasard; **by the way** à propos; **go by…'s house** passer chez… (2); **right by** tout près (de) (3)

**Bye!** Salut!, Ciao!

## C

**cab** taxi (m) (4)

**cabbage** chou (m)

**café** café (m) (1)

**cafeteria** cafétéria (f); **university cafeteria** restau-u (m) (6)

**Cajun** cadien(ne) (4)

**cake** gâteau (m) (8); **chocolate cake** gâteau au chocolat (8)

**calculator** calculatrice (f)

**Caledonia: New Caledonia** Nouvelle-Calédonie (f) (9)

**call** communication (f); appel (m)

**call** téléphoner (3), appeler (6); **Who's calling?** Qui est à l'appareil?

**calm** calme (4), tranquille

**calm down** se calmer

**camera** appareil photo (m)

**campground** camping (m) (5)

**camping** camping (m) (5); **go camping** faire du camping (5)

**campus** campus (m) (1); fac(ulté) (f) (2)

**can** boîte (f) (8)

**can (be able)** pouvoir (4)

**Canada** Canada (m) (9)

**Canadian** canadien(ne) (P)

**canceled** annulé(e)

**candy** bonbon (m)

**canned goods** conserves (fpl) (8)

**cap** casquette (f) (5)

**capital** capitale (f)

**car** voiture (f) (3); **by car** en voiture (4); **rental car** voiture (f) de location (5)

**carafe** carafe (f) (8)

**carbohydrates** féculents (mpl) (8)

**card** carte (f); **bank card** carte bancaire (f) (9); **credit card** carte (f) de crédit (9); **identity card** carte (f) d'identité; **telephone card** carte téléphonique (f) (10)

**care: I don't care.** Ça m'est égal.; **take care of** s'occuper de, (health) (se) soigner

**career** carrière (f)

**careful** soigneux(-euse); **be careful** faire attention (à)

**carefully** soigneusement

**carpenter** charpentier (m)

**carrot** carotte (f) (8)

**carry** porter (4); **carry away** emporter

**cartoon** dessin animé (m)

**cash: pay cash** payer en espèces (10)

**cashier** caissier(-ère) (mf)

**cassette** cassette (f) (3); **video cassette** vidéocassette (f); **videocassette player** magnétoscope (m)

**castle** château (m)

**cat** chat (m) (3)

**cathedral** cathédrale (f)

**Catholic** catholique (P)

**cauliflower** chou-fleur (m)

**cause** cause (f)

**cause** causer

**CD** CD (m) (P), disque compact (m); **CD player** platine laser (f) (3)

**celebrate** célébrer (6), fêter

**celebration** fête (f) (4)

**celery** céleri (m)

**cent** centime (m) (2)

**center** centre (m); **shopping center** centre commercial (m) (4)

**centime** centime (m) (2)

**central** central(e) (mpl centraux)

**Central America** Amérique centrale (f) (9)

**century** siècle (m)

**cereal** céréales (fpl) (8)

**certain** certain(e), sûr(e)

**certainly** certainement

**certificate** certificat (m)

**chair** chaise (f) (3)

**chance: by chance** par *hasard; **have the chance to** avoir l'occasion de

**change** monnaie (f) (2); **Here's your change.** Voici votre monnaie. (2)

**change** changer (de) (6); **change one's mind** changer d'avis

**character** (disposition) caractère (m), (from a story) personnage (m)

**charge: extra charge** supplément (m) (10); **in charge of** chargé(e) de, responsable de

**charge** charger

**cheap** bon marché

**check** chèque (m) (9), (restaurant) addition (f); **traveler's check** chèque (m) de voyage (9)

**cheese** fromage (m) (2); **cheese sandwich** sandwich (m) au fromage (2)

**chemistry** chimie (f) (1)

**cherry** cerise (f) (8)

**chest** poitrine (f); **chest of drawers** commode (f) (3)

**chicken** poulet (m) (8)

**child** enfant (mf) (4)

**childhood** enfance (f)

**Chile** Chili (m) (9)

**chill** frisson (m) (10)

**China** Chine (f) (9)

**Chinese** chinois(e)

**chips** chips (fpl)

**chocolate** chocolat (m) (2); **chocolate cake** gâteau (m) au chocolat (8); **chocolate-filled croissant** pain (m) au chocolat (8)

**choice** choix (m) (8)

**choose (to do)** choisir (de faire) (8)

**chop: pork chop** côte (f) de porc (8)

**chore: household chore** tâche domestique (f)

**Christian** chrétien(ne)

**Christmas** Noël (m); **Merry Christmas!** Joyeux Noël!

**church** église (f) (4), (Protestant) temple (m)

**cinema** cinéma (m) (1); **cinema club** cinéclub (m) (2)

**circumstance** circonstance (f)

**city** ville (f) (3)

**class** cours (m) (P), classe (f) (1); **have class** avoir cours (6); **first class** première classe (f) (9); **tourist class** classe touriste (f) (9); **What is the homework for the next class?** Quels sont les devoirs pour le prochain cours? (P)

**classic** classique (m) (2)

**classical** classique (1)

**classmate** camarade (mf) de classe (1)

**classroom** salle (f) de classe (1)

**clean** propre (3)

**climate** climat (m) (9)

**climb** (tree) grimper, (rocks) escalader

**climbing: go mountain climbing** faire de l'alpinisme; **go rock climbing** faire de la varappe

**clinic** clinique (f)

**clock** horloge (f), **alarm clock** réveil (m) (7)

**close** fermer (2); **Close your book.** Fermez votre livre. (P)

**close to** (location) près de (1); (a friend) uni(e), proche

**closet** placard (m) (3)

**clothes** vêtements (mpl) (3)

**cloud** nuage (m)

**cloudy** nuageux(-euse); **It's cloudy.** Il y a des nuages.

**club** club (m) (5); **cinema club** cinéclub (m) (2); **fitness club** club (m) de gym (1); **nightclub** boîte (f) de nuit (1)

**coach** classe touriste (f) (9)

**coast** côte (f); **Ivory Coast** Côte d'Ivoire (f) (9); **from/of the Ivory Coast** ivoirien(ne)

**coat** manteau (m) (5), pardessus (m)

**code: zip code** code postal (m) (3)

**coffee** café (m) (2); **coffee table** table basse (f)

**coin** pièce (f) de monnaie

**Coke** coca (m) (2)

**cola** coca (m) (2)

**cold** froid(e); **be cold** avoir froid (4); **cold cuts** charcuterie (f) (8); **It's cold.** Il fait froid. (5)

**cold** rhume (m) (10)

**colleague** collègue (mf)

**collect** collectionner

**college: go to college** étudier à l'université

**Colombia** Colombie (f) (9)

**color** couleur (f) (3); **What color is/are . . . ?** De quelle couleur est/sont... ? (3)

**comb one's hair** se peigner (7)

**come** venir (4); **come back** revenir (4); **come down** (from) descendre (de) (5); **come get someone** venir chercher quelqu'un (10); **Come see!** Viens voir! (3)

**comedy** comédie (f) (6)

**comfortable** confortable (3)

**commercial** publicité (f)

**communicate** communiquer (10)

**communication** communication (f)

**compact disc** disque compact (m) (3)

**company** société (f), compagnie (f), entreprise (f)

**compare** comparer (6)

**compatibility** compatibilité (f) (7)

**complain** se plaindre

**complete** complet(-ète) (8); **in complete sentences** en phrases complètes (P)

**completely** tout à fait

**complicated** compliqué(e)

**composition** rédaction *(f)* (9), composition *(f)*
**computer** ordinateur *(m)* (2); **computer science** informatique *(f)* (1); **computer scientist** informaticien(ne) *(mf)*
**concern** concerner
**concert** concert *(m)* (1)
**condition** condition *(f)*
**confidence** confiance *(f)*; **have confidence** avoir confiance (4)
**confused** confus(e)
**congratulations** félicitations *(fpl)*
**connection** *(telephone)* communication *(f)*
**conservative** conservateur(-trice) (7)
**conserve** conserver
**constantly** constamment
**consulate** consulat *(m)*
**contact** contact *(m)*; **contact lenses** lentilles *(fpl)*
**content** content(e) (8)
**continent** continent *(m)* (9)
**continue** continuer (10)
**continued: to be continued** à suivre (6)
**contrary: on the contrary** par contre; au contraire
**control** contrôler (8)
**convenient** commode (3)
**cook** faire la cuisine (5); (faire) cuire
**cooking** cuisine *(f)* (4)
**cool** frais (fraîche); **pretty cool** assez cool (P); **The weather's cool.** Il fait frais. (5)
**copious** copieux(-euse) (8)
**co-renter** colocataire *(mf)* (P)
**corn** maïs *(m)*
**corner** coin *(m)* (3); **on the corner** *(of)* au coin (de) (10)
**corridor** couloir *(m)* (3)
**cost** coûter (5)
**cotton** coton *(m)*
**couch** canapé *(m)* (3)
**cough** tousser (10)
**count** compter (2); **Count from . . . to . . .** Comptez de... à... (P)
**country** campagne *(f)* (3), pays *(m)* (3); **country music** musique country *(f)*; **in the country** à la campagne (3)
**couple** couple *(m)*
**course** cours *(m)* (1); **first course** *(of a meal)* entrée *(f)* (8); **in the course of** au cours de (10); **Of course!** Bien sûr! (5), Évidemment!; **take a course** suivre un cours
**court: tennis court** court *(m)* de tennis
**courtyard** cour *(f)*; **on the courtyard side** côté cour (10)
**cousin** cousin(e) *(mf)* (4)
**cover** couverture *(f)* (3)
**cover** couvrir
**crab** crabe *(m)*
**crazy** fou (folle)
**cream** crème *(f)* (8); **ice cream** glace *(f)* (8)
**create** créer
**credit card** carte *(f)* de crédit (9)
**crime** crime *(m)*, criminalité *(f)*
**criminal** criminel(le) *(mf)*
**criticize** critiquer
**croissant** croissant *(m)* (8); **chocolate-filled croissant** pain *(m)* au chocloat (8)
**cross** traverser (10)
**crustaceans** fruits *(mpl)* de mer 8
**cry** pleurer
**cucumber** concombre *(m)*
**cuisine** cuisine *(f)* (4)
**cultiver** to cultivate (7)
**cultural** culturel(le) (4)
**culture** culture *(f)* (9)
**cup** tasse *(f)*

**cure** guérir
**curly** frisé(e)
**current** actuel(le)
**currently** actuellement
**curtains** rideaux *(mpl)* (3)
**custom** coutume *(f)*
**customs** *(border)* douane *(f)* (9)
**cut: cold cuts** charcuterie *(f)* (8)
**cut (one's finger)** (se) couper (le doigt); **cut class** sécher un cours
**cycling** cyclisme *(m)*

## D

**dad(dy)** papa *(m)*
**daily** quotidien(ne) (7)
**dairy** laitier(-ère) (8)
**dance** danse *(f)*
**dance** danser (2)
**dancer** danseur(-euse) *(mf)*
**danger** danger *(m)*
**dangerous** dangereux(-euse)
**dark** foncé(e); **dark-haired** brun(e) (4); **to be dark** faire noir (6)
**darling** chéri(e)
**date** date *(f)* (4); rendez-vous *(m)*; **What is the date?** Quelle est la date? (4)
**date** sortir avec
**daughter** fille *(f)* (4)
**day** jour *(m)* (P), journée *(f)* (2); **day after tomorrow** après-demain; **day before yesterday** avant-hier; **every day** tous les jours (2); **Father's Day** fête *(f)* des Pères; **Have a good day!** Bonne journée!; **Mother's Day** fête *(f)* des Mères; **the next day** le lendemain *(m)* (6); **the whole day** toute la journée (2); **What day is today?** C'est quel jour, aujourd'hui? (P)
**daycare** crèche *(f)*
**daytime** journée *(f)*
**dead** mort(e) (4)
**death** mort *(f)*
**December** décembre *(m)* (4)
**decide** décider (de) (8)
**decision** décision *(f)*; **make a decision** prendre une décision (7)
**degree** *(temperature)* degré *(m)*, *(university)* diplôme *(m)*
**delay** retard *(m)*
**delicatessen** charcuterie *(f)* (8); **deli meats** charcuterie *(f)* (8)
**delicious** délicieux(-euse) (6)
**delighted** ravi(e); **Delighted to meet you.** Enchanté(e).
**deluxe** de luxe (10)
**demand** exiger
**democracy** démocratie *(f)*
**democratic** démocratique
**Denmark** Danemark *(m)*
**dentist** dentiste *(mf)*
**department** département *(m)*; **department store** grand magasin *(m)*
**departure** départ *(m)* (9); **departure gate** porte *(f)* d'embarquement (9)
**depend (on)** dépendre (de) (5); **That depends.** Ça dépend.
**deposit** déposer
**depressed** déprimé(e)
**depressing** déprimant(e)
**depression** déprime *(f)*
**descend** descendre (5)
**describe** décrire (9)
**description** description *(f)*
**designer fashion** *haute couture *(f)* (5)
**desire** avoir envie de (4), désirer
**desk** bureau *(m)* (3); **front desk** réception *(f)* (10)

**despite** malgré
**dessert** dessert *(m)* (8)
**destroy** détruire
**detest (each other)** (se) détester (7)
**develop** (se) développer
**dictatorship** dictature *(f)*
**dictionary** dictionnaire *(m)*
**die** mourir (5)
**diet** régime *(m)*; **be on a diet** être au régime
**different** différent(e)
**differently** différemment
**difficult** difficile (P)
**difficulty** difficulté *(f)*
**digest** digérer
**dine (out)** dîner (au restaurant) (2)
**dining: dining hall** restaurant universitair *(m)*, restau-u *(m)* (6); **dining room** salle à manger *(f)* (3)
**dinner** dîner *(m)* (8); **before-dinner drink** apéritif *(m)* (10); **have dinner** dîner (2)
**diploma** diplôme *(m)*
**direct** diriger
**direct** direct(e)
**directions** indications *(fpl)* (10); **give directions** indiquer le chemin (10)
**directly** directement
**dirty** sale
**disadvantage** inconvénient *(m)*
**disappointed** déçu(e)
**disc: compact disc** disque compact *(m)*; **compact disc player** platine *(f)* laser (3)
**discover** découvrir
**discuss** discuter (de)
**disguise (oneself)** (se) déguiser
**dish** plat *(m)* (8); **do the dishes** faire la vaisselle (5); **ready-to-serve dish** plat préparé *(m)* (8)
**dishwasher** lave-vaisselle *(m)*
**disorder** désordre *(m)* (3); **in disorder** en désordre (3)
**diversity** diversité *(f)*
**divided** partagé(e) (3)
**diving: scuba diving** plongée sous-marine *(f)*
**divorce** divorcer
**divorced** divorcé(e) (1)
**do** faire (2); **do aerobics** faire de l'aérobic (8); **do better…** faire mieux… (8); **do handiwork** bricoler (2); **Do the homework.** Faites les devoirs. (P); **do weight training** faire de la musculation (8); **Do you . . . ?** Est-ce que vous... ? (1); **I do not…** Je ne… pas (P)
**doctor** médecin *(m)* (10)
**doctorate** doctorat *(m)*
**dog** chien *(m)* (3)
**dollar** dollar *(m)* (3)
**domestic** domestique
**door** porte *(f)* (3); **next door** d'à côté
**dormitory** résidence universitaire *(f)* (1)
**doubt** doute *(m)*; **without doubt** sans doute (5)
**doubt** douter (10)
**down: go / come down** descendre (5)
**downtown** au centre-ville *(m)* (3)
**dozen** douzaine *(f)* (8)
**draft beer** demi *(m)* (2)
**drama** drame *(m)*; **drama course** cours *(m)* de théâtre (1)
**dramatic** dramatique
**draw** dessiner
**drawer** tiroir *(m)*; **chest of drawers** commode *(f)* (3)
**drawing** dessin *(m)*
**dream** rêve *(m)*
**dream (about)** rêver (de) (7)
**dress** robe *(f)* (4)
**dress** habiller; **get dressed** s'habiller (7)

**dresser** commode *(f)* (3)
**drink** boisson *(f)* (2); **before-dinner drink** apéritif *(m)* (8); **have a drink** prendre un verre (2)
**drink** boire (4)
**drive** conduire; **go for a drive** faire un tour en voiture
**drop** laisser tomber
**drums** batterie *(f)* (2)
**dry** sécher; **dry cleaner's** teinturerie *(f)*
**duck** canard *(m)* (8)
**due to** à cause de
**dumb** bête (1)
**during** pendant (7), au cours de (10)
**DVD** DVD *(m)* (2)
**DVD player** lecteur DVD *(m)* (3)

**E**

**each** chaque (3); **each one** chacun(e); **each other** se, vous, nous (7), l'un(e) l'autre
**ear** oreille *(f)*
**early** tôt (4), en avance
**earn** gagner
**earring** boucle *(f)* d'oreille
**earth** terre *(f)*
**easily** facilement (7)
**east** est *(m)*; **Middle East** Moyen-Orient *(m)* (9)
**Easter** Pâques *(fpl)*
**easy** facile (P)
**eat** manger (2); **eat one's breakfast** prendre son petit déjeuner (5); **eat dinner** dîner (2); **eat dinner out** dîner au restaurant (2); **eat lunch** déjeuner (2)
**eccentric** excentrique
**ecological** écologique
**economics** sciences économiques *(fpl)*
**economy** économie *(f)*
**editor** rédacteur(-trice) *(mf)*
**educate** éduquer
**education** éducation *(f)*
**effect** effet *(m)* (6); **special effects** effets spéciaux *(mpl)* (6)
**egg** œuf *(m)* (8); **hard-boiled egg** œuf dur *(m)* (8)
**eggplant** aubergine *(f)*
**Egypt** Égypte *(f)* (9)
**eight** *huit (P)
**eighteen** dix-huit (P)
**eighty** quatre-vingts (2)
**eighth** *huitième (3)
**either . . . or . . .** soit… soit…
**elect** élire
**election** élection *(f)*
**element** élément *(m)*
**elementary school** école primaire/élémentaire *(f)*
**elevated** élevé(e)
**elevator** ascenseur *(m)* (3)
**eleven** onze (P)
**else: What else?** Quoi d'autre?; **What else can I get you?** Qu'est-ce que je peux vous proposer d'autre? (8)
**elsewhere** ailleurs
**e-mail** mail *(m)* (2), courrier électronique *(m)*; **e-mail address** adresse *(f)* mail (3)
**embarrassed** gêné(e)
**embassy** ambassade *(f)*
**embrace (each other)** (s')embrasser (7)
**emotional** sentimental(e) *(mpl* sentimentaux) (7)
**employee** employé(e) *(mf)* (10); **government employee** fonctionnaire *(mf)*
**encounter** rencontre *(f)* (7)
**end** fin *(f)*; **at the end (of)** au bout (de) (3)
**end** finir (8), (se) terminer; **end up doing** finir par faire; **French class ends…** Le cours de français finit… (P)

**energy** énergie *(f)*
**engaged** fiancé(e) (1); **get engaged** se fiancer (7)
**engineer** ingénieur *(m)*
**engineering** études *(fpl)* d'ingénieur, génie *(m)*
**English** anglais *(m)* (P)
**English** anglais(e)
**enjoy: Enjoy your stay!** Bon séjour! (10)
**enough** assez (de) (1)
**enter** entrer (dans) (5)
**enterprise** entreprise *(f)*
**entertainment** distractions *(fpl)* (5)
**enthusiastic** enthousiaste
**entire** entier(-ère)
**environment** environnement *(m)*
**equality** égalité *(f)*
**equals: … plus … equals … .** … et… font… (P)
**errand** course *(f)* (5); **run errands** faire des courses (5)
**especially** surtout (8)
**espresso** expresso *(m)* (2)
**essential** essentiel(le)
**establish** établir
**euro** euro *(m)* (2)
**Europe** Europe *(f)* (9)
**European** européen(ne)
**eve: New Year's Eve party** le réveillon *(m)* du jour de l'an
**even** même; **even though** bien que
**evening** soir *(m)* (P), soirée *(f)* (4); **At ten o'clock in the evening.** À dix heures du soir. (P); **Good evening.** Bonsoir. (P); **in the evening, evenings** le soir (P); **See you this evening.** À ce soir. (2)
**every** tout (toute, tous, toutes) (3), chaque (3); **every day** tous les jours (2); **every evening** tous les soirs
**everybody** tout le monde
**everyone** tout le monde
**everything** tout (3)
**everywhere** partout (3)
**exactly** justement (3), exactement (10)
**exam** examen *(m)* (P)
**example** exemple *(m)*; **for example** par exemple (2)
**excellent** excellent(e) (6)
**except** sauf (2)
**exception** exception *(f)*; **with the exception of** à l'exception de
**exchange money** changer de l'argent (9)
**exciting** passionnant(e)
**excuse** excuser; **Excuse me.** Excusez-moi, Pardon. (P)
**executive** cadre *(m)*
**exercise** exercice *(m)* (P)
**exercise** faire de l'exercice (5)
**exhausted** épuisé(e)
**exhibit** exposition *(f)* (4)
**ex-husband** ex-mari *(m)*
**exotic** exotique (9)
**expensive** cher (chère) (3)
**experience** expérience *(f)*
**explain** expliquer
**express** exprimer
**expression** expression *(f)* (10)
**extra charge** supplément *(m)* (10)
**extracurricular** extra-scolaire
**extraordinary** extraordinaire (9)
**extroverted** extraverti(e) (1)
**ex-wife** ex-femme *(f)*
**eye** œil *(m)* (*pl* yeux) (10); **to have … eyes** avoir les yeux… (4)

**F**

**face** figure *(f)* (7), visage *(m)*

**facing** en face (de) (3)
**fact** fait *(m)*; **in fact** en fait
**fail** échouer (à)
**fair** juste
**fairly** assez (P)
**fairy tale** conte *(m)* de fée (6)
**fall** automne *(m)* (5); **in the fall** en automne (5)
**fall** tomber; **fall asleep** s'endormir (7); **fall in love (with)** tomber amoureux(-euse) (de) (6)
**false** faux (fausse)
**fame** renommée *(f)*
**familiar: be familiar with** connaître (4)
**family** famille *(f)* (P)
**famous** célèbre (4), fameux(-euse)
**far (from)** loin (de) (3); **as far as** jusqu'à (10)
**farm** ferme *(f)*
**fashion** mode *(f)* (5); **designer fashion** *haute-couture *(f)* (5)
**fast** vite (7), rapide (8)
**fast food restaurant** fast-food *(m)* (1)
**fat** matières grasses *(fpl)* (8)
**fat** gros(se) (1); **get fatter** grossir (8)
**father** père *(m)* (4); **father-in-law** beau-père *(m)* (4); **Father's Day** fête *(f)* des Pères
**fatty** gras(se)
**favorite** préféré(e) (3)
**fear** avoir peur (de) (4)
**February** février *(m)* (4)
**feed** donner à manger à (9)
**feel** (se) sentir (8); **feel like** avoir envie de (4)
**feeling** sentiment *(m)* (7)
**ferocious** féroce (6)
**festival** festival *(m)* (4)
**fever** fièvre *(f)*; **have fever** avoir de la fièvre
**few: a few** quelques (5), quelques-un(e)s
**fewer** moins de (8); **fewer … than** moins de… que
**fiancé** fiancé *(m)*
**fiancée** fiancée *(f)*
**field** champ *(m)*
**fifteen** quinze (P)
**fifth** cinquième (3)
**fifty** cinquante (2)
**fight** combattre, se battre; **fight (against)** lutter (contre)
**fill (in)** remplir
**film** film *(m)* (1)
**finally** finalement (6), enfin (7)
**find** trouver (4); **find out information** s'informer (9)
**fine arts** beaux-arts *(mpl)* (1); **It's going fine.** Ça va. (P)
**finger** doigt *(m)* (10)
**finish (doing)** finir (de faire) (8), terminer
**firm** entreprise *(f)*
**first** premier(-ère) (1); **at first** au début; **first course** *(of a meal)* entrée *(f)* (8); **first floor** rez-de-chaussée *(m)* (3); **first name** prénom *(m)* (3); **first of all** d'abord (4); **in first class** en première classe (9); **love at first sight** coup *(m)* de foudre (7)
**fish** poisson *(m)* (8); **fish shop** poissonnerie *(f)* (8)
**fishing** pêche *(f)*; **go fishing** aller à la pêche
**fist** poing *(m)*
**fitness club** club *(m)* de gym (1)
**fitting room** cabine *(f)* d'essayage (5)
**five** cinq (P)
**fixed: at a fixed price** à prix fixe (8)
**flashlight** lampe *(f)* de poche
**flight** vol *(m)* (9)
**floor** étage *(m)* (3); **ground floor** rez-de-chaussée *(m)* (3); **on the floor** par terre (3); **on the second floor** au premier étage (3)

**floral** à fleurs
**florist** fleuriste *(mf)*
**flower** fleur *(f)*
**flu** grippe *(f)* (10)
**fluently** couramment
**foggy: It's foggy.** Il fait du brouillard.
**folk music** folk *(m)*
**folklore** folklore *(m)* (4)
**follow** suivre (7)
**following** suivant(e) (3)
**food** aliments *(mpl)*, nourriture *(f)*
**foot** pied *(m)* (10); **go on foot** aller à pied (4)
**football** football américain *(m)* (1)
**for** pour (P), pendant (5), depuis (7), comme (8); **for example** par exemple (2); **For how long?** Pendant combien de temps? (5); **for the last three days** depuis les trois derniers jours; **go away for the weekend** partir en week-end (5); **look for** chercher (3); **watch out for** faire attention à (8)
**forbidden: It's forbidden to . . .** Il est inderdit de... (10)
**foreign** étranger(-ère) (1)
**foreseen** prévu(e) (9)
**forest** forêt *(f)*
**forget** oublier (8)
**forgive** pardonner
**fork** fourchette *(f)*
**former** ancien(ne)
**formerly** autrefois, jadis
**forty** quarante (2)
**fountain** fontaine *(f)*
**four** quatre (P)
**fourteen** quatorze (P)
**fourth** quatrième (3)
**France** France *(f)* (1)
**frankly** franchement
**free** libre (2), *(price)* gratuit(e); **free time** temps libre *(m)* (4)
**freedom** liberté *(f)*
**French** français *(m)* (P); **French class** cours *(m)* de français (P); **How do you say . . . in French?** Comment dit-on... en français? (P)
**French** français(e) (1); **French fries** frites *(fpl)* (8); **French Polynesia** Polynésie française *(f)* (9); **French Quarter** Vieux Carré *(m)* (4); **French West Indies** Antilles *(fpl)* (9); **loaf of French bread** baguette *(f)* (8)
**French-speaking** francophone
**frequently** fréquemment
**fresh** frais (fraîche) (8)
**Friday** vendredi *(m)* (P)
**friend** ami(e) *(mf)* (P), copain *(m)*, copine *(f)* (6)
**friendly** amical(e) *(mpl* amicaux)
**fries: French fries** frites *(fpl)* (2); **steak and fries** steak-frites (8) *(m)*
**frisbee: to play frisbee** jouer au frisbee (4)
**from** de (P), depuis
**front: front desk** réception *(f)* (10); **in front of** devant (3)
**frozen** surgelé(e) (8)
**fruit** fruit *(m)* (8); **fruit juice** jus *(m)* de fruit (2)
**full** plein(e)
**fun** amusant(e) (1); **Does that sound like fun?** Ça te dit? (4); **have fun (doing)** s'amuser (à faire) (7); **make fun of** se moquer de
**funny** drôle
**furious** furieux(-euse) (10)
**furnishings** meubles *(mpl)* (3)
**furniture** meubles *(mpl)* (3)
**furthermore** en plus (8)
**futon** futon *(m)* (3)
**future** avenir *(m)*

## G

**gain** gagner; **gain weight** prendre du poids
**game** match *(m)* (1), jeu *(m)* (2); **video game** jeu vidéo *(m)* (2)
**garage** garage *(m)*
**garden** jardin *(m)* (5)
**garden** faire du jardinage (5), jardiner
**gardening** jardinage *(m)*
**gate: arrival gate** porte *(f)* d'arrivée (9); **departure gate** porte *(f)* d'embarquement (9);
**general: in general** en général (2)
**generally** généralement
**generous** généreux(-euse)
**gentle** doux(-ce) (6)
**gentleman** monsieur *(m)*; **ladies-gentlemen** messieurs-dames
**geography** géographie *(f)* (9)
**geology** géologie *(f)*
**German** allemand *(m)* (1)
**German** allemand(e)
**Germany** Allemagne *(f)* (9)
**get** obtenir (9), recevoir; **get along** s'entendre (7); **get bored** s'ennuyer (7); **get dressed** s'habiller (7); **get engaged** se fiancer (7); **get fatter** grossir (8); **get lost** se perdre (7); **get married (to)** se marier (avec) (7); **get off** descendre (de) (5); **get older** vieillir (8); **get on** monter (dans) (5); **get ready** se préparer; **get sick** tomber malade (10); **get taller** grandir (8); **get thinner** maigrir (8); **get to know** connaître (4); **get undressed** se déshabiller (7); **get up** se lever (7); **get well** guérir (9); **go/come get someone** aller/venir chercher quelqu'un (10); **What else can I get you?** Qu'est-ce que je peux vous proposer d'autre? (8)
**gift** cadeau *(m)* (10); **gift shop** marchand *(m)* de cadeaux (10)
**girl** (jeune) fille *(f)* (4)
**girlfriend** petite amie *(f)* (2)
**give** donner (2); **give (something) back (to someone)** rendre (quelque chose à quelqu'un) (7); **give directions** indiquer le chemin (10); **Give me your sheet of paper.** Donnez-moi votre feuille de papier. (P)
**glad** content(e)
**gladly** avec plaisir (6), volontiers (8)
**glass** verre *(m)* (2); **a glass of** un verre de (2)
**glasses** lunettes *(fpl)* (4)
**global** global(e) *(mpl* globaux)
**glove** gant *(m)*
**go** aller (2), se rendre (à / chez); **go across** traverser (10); **go away** partir (4), s'en aller; **go back** rentrer (2), retourner (5); **go bike-riding** faire du vélo (5); **go boating** faire du bateau (5); **go by / past** passer (5); **go camping** faire du camping (5); **go down** descendre (5); **go hiking** faire une randonnée (8); **go for a ride** faire un tour (4); **go for a walk** faire une promenade (5); **go get someone** aller chercher quelqu'un (10); **go grocery shopping** faire les courses (7); **go hiking** faire une randonnée (8); **go in** entrer (dans) (5); **go home** rentrer (2); **go jogging** faire du jogging (2); **go on foot** aller à pied (4); **go out** sortir (2); **go rollerblading** faire du roller (6); **go scuba diving** faire de la plongée sous-marine; **go see (a person)** aller voir (4); **go shopping** faire du shopping (2); **go (water-)skiing** faire du ski (nautique) (5); **go to bed** se coucher (7); **Go to the board!** Allez au tableau! (P); **go to the movies** aller au cinéma (2); **go up** monter (5); **go walking** se promener (7), faire de la marche à pied; **go windsurfing** faire de la

planche à voile; **How's it going?** Comment ça va? (P); **It's going fine.** Ça va. (P)
**goal** but *(m)*
**god** dieu *(m)*
**golf** golf *(m)* (2)
**good: canned goods** conserves *(fpl)* (8)
**good** bon(ne) (1), sage (4); **Good evening.** Bonsoir. (P); **Good idea!** Bonne idée! (4); **good in/at** fort(e) en; **Good morning.** Bonjour. (P); **Have a good day!** Bonne journée!; **Have a good weekend!** Bon week-end!; **It's good to...** C'est bien de… (10); **One has a good time!** On s'amuse bien! (4)
**good-bye** au revoir (P)
**government** gouvernement *(m)*; **government worker** fonctionnaire *(mf)*
**gracious** gracieux(–euse) (6)
**grade** note *(f)*
**gram** gramme *(m)* (8)
**grammar** grammaire *(f)*
**grandchildren** petits-enfants *(mpl)*
**granddaughter** petite-fille *(f)* (7)
**grandfather** grand-père *(m)* (4)
**grandma** mamie *(f)* (7)
**grandmother** grand-mère *(f)* (4)
**grandparents** grands-parents *(mpl)* (4)
**grandson** petit-fils *(m)* (7)
**granny** mamie *(f)* (7)
**grape(s)** raisin *(m)* (8)
**grapefruit** pamplemousse *(m)*
**graphic artist** dessinateur(-trice) *(mf)* (de publicité)
**gray** gris(e) (3)
**great** super (P), extra, génial(e) *(mpl* géniaux) (4), formidable (7), magnifique
**Great Britain** Grande-Bretagne *(f)* (9)
**green** vert(e) (4); **green beans** *haricots verts *(mpl)* (4)
**greet** saluer
**grilled** grillé(e) (8)
**grocery: go grocery shopping** faire les courses (8); **grocery store** épicerie *(f)* (8)
**ground** terre *(f)*; **ground floor** rez-de-chaussée *(m)* (3); **on the ground** par terre (3)
**ground: ground meat** bifteck *hâché *(m)*
**group** groupe *(m)* (6)
**grow (up)** grandir (8)
**guess** deviner
**guide** guide *(m)* (9)
**guidebook** guide *(m)* (9)
**guilty** coupable
**guitar** guitare *(f)* (2)
**gym** club *(m)* de gym (1), gymnase *(m)*

## H

**hair** cheveux *(mpl)* (4); **comb one's hair** se peigner (7); **hair stylist** coiffeur(-euse) *(mf)*
**Haiti** Haïti *(m)*
**half** moitié *(f)*
**half** demi(e) (P); **half-brother** demi-frère *(m)*; **half hour** demi-heure *(f)* (7); **half-sister** demi-sœur *(f)*; **It's half past two.** Il est deux heures et demie. (P); **a kilo and a half** un kilo et demi (8)
**hall** couloir *(m)* (3); **dining hall** restaurant universitaire *(m)*, restau-u *(m)* (6); **lecture hall** amphithéâtre *(m)* (1); **residence hall** résidence universitaire *(f)* (1)
**ham** jambon *(m)* (2); **ham sandwich** sandwich au jambon *(m)* (2)
**hamburger** *hamburger *(m)* (8)
**hand** main *(f)* (7); **on the other hand** par contre
**handiwork: do handiwork** bricoler (2)

**handsome** beau/bel (belle) (1)

**hang up** raccrocher

**Hanukkah** *Hanoukka (f)

**happen** se passer (7), arriver; **What happened?** Qu'est-ce qui s'est passé? (7)

**happiness** bonheur (m) (7)

**happy** content(e) (8), heureux(-euse) (7); **Happy Birthday!** Bon anniversaire!

**hard** dur(e); **have a hard time** avoir du mal à

**hard-boiled egg** œuf dur (m) (8)

**hardly** ne... guère

**hard-working** travailleur(-euse)

**hat** chapeau (m) (5)

**hate (each other)** (se) détester (7)

**hatred** *haine (f)

**have** avoir (3); **have a drink** prendre un verre (2); **have one's breakfast** prendre son petit déjeuner (5); **have class** avoir cours (6); **have difficulty doing** avoir du mal à faire; **have dinner** dîner (2); **have fun (doing)** s'amuser (à faire) (7); **have just (done)** venir de (faire); **have lunch** déjeuner (2); **have to** devoir (6)

**hazel eyes** yeux (mpl) couleur noisette

**he** il (1); **he is . . .** c'est..., il est... (1)

**head** tête (f) (10)

**health** santé (f) (8); **health center** infirmerie (f)

**healthy** sain(e) (8)

**hear** entendre (7)

**heart** cœur (m)

**heavy** lourd(e)

**Hebrew** hébreu (m)

**heels: high heels** *hauts talons (mpl)

**height** *hauteur (f), taille (f); **of medium height** de taille moyenne (4)

**hello** bonjour (P), (on the telephone) allô (6)

**help** aider (5); **May I help you?** Je peux vous aider? (5)

**henceforth** désormais

**her** la (5); **to her** lui (9); **with her** avec elle

**her** son (sa, ses) (3)

**here** ici (P); **here is/are** voici (2)

**herself** se (7), elle-même

**Hi!** Salut! (P)

**high** élevé(e), *haut(e); **high fashion** *haute couture (f) (5); **high heels** *hauts talons (mpl); **high school** lycée (m) (6); **high school student** lycéen(ne) (mf) (6)

**hiking: to go hiking** faire une randonnée (8)

**him** le (5); **to him** lui (9); **with him** avec lui (6)

**himself** se (7), lui-même

**his** son (sa, ses) (3)

**historic** historique (9)

**history** histoire (f) (1)

**hobby** passe-temps (m) (2)

**hockey** *hockey (m) (2)

**hold** tenir

**holiday** fête (f) (4); **national holiday** fête nationale (f)

**home: at home** à la maison (P); **come / go home** rentrer (2)

**homework** devoirs (mpl) (P); **Do the homework.** Faites les devoirs. (P)

**honest** honnête

**honey** miel (m), chéri(e)

**honeymoon** lune (f) de miel, voyage (m) de noces

**hope** espérer (3)

**horrible** horrible (6), affreux(-euse)

**horror movie** film (m) d'épouvante (6)

**hors d'oeuvre** *hors-d'œuvre (m) (inv), entrée (f) (8)

**horse** cheval (m) (pl chevaux); **ride a horse** monter à cheval

**horseback: go horseback riding** faire du cheval

**hose: panty hose** collant (m)

**hospital** hôpital (m)

**hostel: youth hostel** auberge (f) de jeunesse (10)

**hot** chaud(e) (2); **be hot** avoir chaud (4); **hot chocolate** chocolat chaud (m) (2); **The weather's hot.** Il fait chaud. (5)

**hotel** hôtel (m) (5); **hotel manager** hôtelier(-ère) (mf) (10)

**hour** heure (f) (P); **half hour** demi-heure (f) (7)

**house** maison (f) (1); **at / to / in my house** chez moi (2); **pass by the house of . . .** passer chez... (2)

**household** ménage (m); **household chore** tâche domestique (f)

**housemate** colocataire (mf) (P)

**housework** ménage (m) (5)

**housing** logement (m) (3)

**how** comment (P); **How are you?** Comment allez-vous? (P); **How does that sound to you?** Ça te dit? (4); **How do you say . . . ?** Comment dit-on... ? (P); **How many** combien (de) (3); **How many are there of you?** Vous êtes combien? (4); **how much** combien (de) (3); **How much is it?** C'est combien?, Ça fait combien? (2); **How much is . . . plus / minus . . . ?** Combien font... et / moins... ? (P); **How old is . . . ?** Quel âge a... ? (4); **How's it going?** Comment ça va? (P); **How's the weather?** Quel temps fait-il? (5); **That takes how long?** Ça prend combien de temps? (4)

**however** pourtant (8)

**human** humain(e)

**humor: sense of humor** sens (m) de l'humour (7)

**hundred: one hundred** cent (2)

**hunger** faim (f)

**hungry: be hungry** avoir faim (4); **I'm hungry.** J'ai faim. (2)

**hunter** chasseur (m)

**hunting** chasse (f); **go hunting** aller à la chasse

**hurry** se dépêcher (de); **hurried** pressé(e)

**hurt: one's... hurt(s)** avoir mal (à)... (10); **hurt (someone)** faire mal (à quelqu'un)

**husband** mari (m) (2)

**I**

**I** je, j' (P)

**ice** glace (f); **ice cream** glace (f) (8)

**ice-skating** patin (m) à glace; **go ice-skating** faire du patin à glace

**icy: It's icy.** Il y a du verglas.

**idea** idée (f) (4)

**idealistic** idéaliste (1)

**identify** identifier

**identity card** carte (f) d'identité

**if** si (5)

**ill** malade (10)

**illness** maladie (f)

**image** image (f)

**immediately** immédiatement, tout de suite

**impatient** impatient(e) (4)

**importance** importance (f) (7)

**important** important(e) (5)

**imprison** emprisonner (6)

**improve** améliorer (8)

**impulsive** impulsif(-ive)

**in** dans (P), **en** (P), chez (+ a person) (7); **go in** entrer (dans) (5); **I live in** (+ city) J'habite à (+ city) (P); **in advance** à l'avance (9); **in bed** au lit (2); **in front of** devant (3); **in love** amoureux(-euse); **in order to** pour (1); **in the country** à la campagne (3); **in the morning** le matin (P); **in your opinion** à votre avis (8)

**include** comprendre (8); **included** compris(e) (10)

**indecision** indécision (f) (7)

**indefinite** indéfini (m)

**independent** indépendant(e)

**India** Inde (f)

**Indies: West Indies** Antilles (fpl) (9)

**indifference** indifférence (f) (7)

**indigestion** indigestion (f) (10)

**Indochina** Indochine (f)

**industry** industrie (f)

**inequality** inégalité (f)

**inexpensive** pas cher(-ère)

**infidelity** infidélité (f) (7)

**inflexibility** inflexibilité (f) (7)

**influence each other** s'influencer

**inform (oneself)** (s')informer (9)

**information** renseignements (mpl) (3); **find out information** s'informer (9)

**inherit** hériter

**in-laws** beaux-parents (mpl)

**insensitivity** insensibilité (f) (7)

**inside** à l'intérieur

**insist** insister (10)

**instant** instant (m)

**instead** plutôt (4)

**institution** institution (f)

**instructions** instructions (fpl)

**intellectual** intellectuel(le) (1)

**intelligent** intelligent(e) (1)

**intend** avoir l'intention de (4)

**interested: be interested in** s'intéresser à (7)

**interesting** intéressant(e) (P)

**international** international(e) (mpl internationaux)

**interpret** interpreter

**interpreter** interprète (mf)

**introduce** présenter; **Let me introduce . . . to you.** Je vous/te présente...

**introverted** introverti(e)

**investigation** enquête (f)

**invitation** invitation (f) (6)

**invite** inviter (à) (2)

**Irak** Iraq (m)

**Iran** Iran (m)

**island** île (f) (9)

**Israel** Israël (m) (9)

**it** ce (P), il (P), elle (1), le, la (5); **How's it going?** Comment ça va? (P); **isn't it?** n'est-ce pas?, non? (1); **it's . . .** c'est... (P); **It's going fine.** Ça va. (8); **of it** en (8)

**Italian** italien (m)

**Italian** italien(ne)

**Italy** Italie (f) (9)

**itinerary** itinéraire (m) (9)

**its** son (sa, ses) (3)

**Ivory Coast** Côte d'Ivoire (f) (9); **from/of the Ivory Coast** ivoirien(ne)

**J**

**jacket** veste (f), blouson (m); **ski jacket** anorak (m) (5); **windbreaker jacket** blouson (m)

**jam** confiture (f) (8)

**January** janvier (m) (4)

**Japan** Japon (m) (9)

**Japanese** japonais (m)

**Japanese** japonais(e)

**jar** pot (m) (8)

**jazz** jazz (m) (1)

**jealous** jaloux(-ouse) (7)

**jealousy** jalousie (f) (7)

**jeans** jean (m) (5)

**jelly** confiture (f) (8)

**jewelry** bijoux (mpl)

**job** poste (m), travail (m)

**jog** faire du jogging (2)
**jogging** jogging (m) (2); **go jogging** faire du jogging (2); **jogging suit** survêtement (m) (5)
**join** rejoindre
**journal** journal (m)
**journalism** journalisme (m)
**journalist** journaliste (mf)
**judge** juge (m)
**juice** jus (m) (2)
**July** juillet (m) (4)
**June** juin (m) (4)
**just** seulement (8), juste (10); **I would just as soon…** J'aimerais autant… (10); **have just (done)** venir de (faire); **just anything** n'importe quoi

## K

**keep** garder
**key** clé (f) (10)
**keyboard** clavier (m)
**kidney** rein (m)
**kilo** kilo (m) (8)
**kilometer** kilomètre (m)
**kind** genre (m); **all kinds of . . .** toutes sortes de…
**kindergarten** école maternelle (f)
**kiosk** kiosque (m) (10)
**kiss** baiser (m), bise (f)
**kiss (each other)** (s')embrasser (7)
**kitchen** cuisine (f) (3)
**knee** genou (m)
**knife** couteau (m)
**knit shirt** polo (m) (5)
**know** (person, place) connaître (4), (how, answers) savoir (9); **get to know** connaître (4); **I don't know.** Je ne sais pas. (P); **known** connu(e); **What do you know about…?** Que savez-vous de…?; **Do you know how to…?** Savez-vous…? (8)
**knowledge** connaissance (f)

## L

**Labor Day** fête du travail (f)
**laboratory: computer lab** laboratoire (m) d'informatique (1); **language lab** laboratoire (m) de langues (1)
**lack of** manque de (m)
**lady** dame (f); **ladies-gentlemen** messieurs-dames; **lady's suit** tailleur (m)
**lake** lac (m)
**lamb** agneau (m)
**lamp** lampe (f) (3)
**landscape** paysage (m) (9)
**language** langue (f) (1); **language lab** laboratoire (m) de langues (1)
**large** grand(e) (1); copieux(-euse) (8)
**last** durer
**last** dernier(-ère) (5)
**late** tard (4), en retard (10); **later plus** tard (4); **See you later.** À tout à l'heure. (P); À plus tard! (2)
**laugh** rire
**laundry** linge (m); **do laundry** faire la lessive (5)
**law** loi (f); (field) droit (m)
**lawyer** avocat(e) (mf)
**lazy** paresseux(-euse) (1)
**learn** apprendre (à) (4); **Learn…** Apprenez… (P)
**leave** quitter (4), partir (de) (4), sortir (de) (6), (something behind) laisser (3), s'en aller; **leave each other** se quitter (7)
**lecture hall** amphithéâtre (m) (1)
**left** gauche (f) (3); **to the left (of)** à gauche (de) (3)
**leg** jambe (f) (10)
**leisure activity** loisir (m)

**lemon** citron (m) (2); **tea with lemon** thé (m) au citron (2)
**lend** prêter
**lense: contact lenses** lentilles (fpl)
**less** moins de (8); **less . . . than** moins... que (1)
**let** laisser; **Let's see!** Voyons! (5)
**letter** lettre (f)
**lettuce** laitue (f) (8)
**level** niveau (m)
**liberal** libéral(e) (mpl libéraux) (7)
**library** bibliothèque (f) (1)
**life** vie (f) (6)
**lift weights** faire de la musculation (8); faire des haltères
**light** (weight) léger(-ère) (8), (color) clair(e)
**like** aimer (2); **Did you like it?** Ça t'a plu? (6); **Does he like it?** Ça lui plaît? (9); **Do you like?** Est-ce que vous aimez? (1); **I like . . .** J'aime… (1); **I like it!** Il/Elle me plaît! (5); **I would like . . .** Je voudrais (bien)… (2); **like each other** s'aimer bien (7); **What would you like?** Vous désirez? (2); **You'll like it!** Ça te/vous plaira! (9); **You would like . . .** Tu voudrais…, Vous voudriez… (2)
**like** comme (1); **What is/are . . . like?** Comment est/sont... ? (1)
**lime** citron vert (m)
**line** ligne (f); **online** en ligne (7)
**lip** lèvre (f)
**liquid** liquide (m) (10)
**listen (to)** écouter (2); **Listen to the question.** Écoutez la question. (P)
**liter** litre (m) (8)
**literature** littérature (f) (1)
**little** peu (de) (8); **a little** un peu (P); **little by little** petit à petit (6)
**little** petit(e) (1)
**live** habiter (2); **Do you live…?** Vous habitez…? (P); **I live in . . .** (+ city) J'habite à... (+ city) (P)
**liver** foie (m)
**living room** salon (m) (3)
**loaf of French bread** baguette (f) (8)
**loafers** mocassins (mpl)
**loan** prêter
**lobster** *homard (m) (8)
**local** local(e) (mpl locaux) (9)
**located** situé(e); **It is located…** Il/Elle se trouve… (3)
**lock** fermer à clé
**lodge: ski lodge** chalet (m) de ski (10)
**lodging** logement (m) (3)
**lonely** seul(e)
**long** long(ue) (4); **a long time** longtemps (5); **as long as** tant que; **How long ?** Combien de temps? (4); **no longer** ne... plus (8)
**look (at)** regarder (2); **look (+ adjective)** avoir l'air (+ adjectif) (4); **look at each other** se regarder (7); **look for** chercher (3); **look like** ressembler à; **look very good on someone** aller très bien à quelqu'un
**lose** perdre (7); **get lost** se perdre (7); **lose weight** perdre du poids
**lot: a lot** beaucoup (P), **a lot of** beaucoup de (1); **not a lot** pas grand-chose
**love** amour (m) (6); **fall in love (with)** tomber amoureux(-euse) (de) (6); **love at first sight** coup (m) de foudre (7); **love story** film (m) d'amour (6); **true love** le grand amour (7)
**love** aimer (7), adorer; **love each other** s'aimer (7)
**luck** chance (f) (5)
**lucky: be lucky** avoir de la chance (9)
**luggage** bagages (mpl)
**lunch** déjeuner (m) (7); **have lunch** déjeuner (2)

**lung** poumon (m)
**luxury** luxe (m)
**lyrics** paroles (fpl)

## M

**machine** machine (f); **automatic teller machine** distributeur de billets (m) (10)
**madam (Mrs.)** madame (Mme) (P)
**magazine** magazine (m) (9)
**magnificent** magnifique
**mail** courrier (m); **e-mail** mail (m) (2), courrier électronique (m); **mail carrier** facteur (m), factrice (f)
**main** principal(e) (mpl principaux) (8)
**major** se spécialiser en
**majority: the majority of the time** la plupart du temps (7)
**make** faire (2); **make (+ adjective)** rendre (+ adjectif); **make a decision** prendre une décision (7); **make money** gagner de l'argent; **make up with each other** se réconcilier (7); **made up of** composé(e) de
**make-up** maquillage (m); **put on make-up** se maquiller (7)
**mall** centre commercial (m) (4)
**mama** maman (f)
**man** homme (m) (1); monsieur (m)
**management** gestion (f)
**mango** mangue (f)
**manual worker** ouvrier(-ère) (mf)
**many** beaucoup (de) (1); **how many** combien (de) (3); **How many are there of you?** Vous êtes combien? (4); **so many** tant (de); **too many** trop (de) (6)
**map** plan (m), carte (f)
**March** mars (m) (4)
**market** marché (m) (8)
**marketing** marketing (m) (1)
**marriage** mariage (m) (7)
**married** marié(e) (1); **get married (to)** se marier (avec) (7)
**marvelous** merveilleux(-euse)
**mathematics** mathématiques (maths) (fpl) (1)
**matter: It doesn't matter to me.** Ça m'est égal.; **What's the matter?** Qu'est-ce qu'il y a?
**May** mai (m) (3)
**may** pouvoir (4); **May I help you?** Je peux vous aider? (5)
**maybe** peut-être (3)
**me** moi (P), me (9); **Give me . . .** Donnez-moi… (P)
**meal** repas (m) (6)
**mean: What does that mean?** Qu'est-ce que ça veut dire? (P)
**mean** méchant(e) (1)
**means** moyen (m); **means of transportation** moyen (m) de transport (4)
**meat** viande (f) (8); **ground meat** bifteck *haché (m); **meat spread** pâté (m) (8)
**medical** médical(e) (mpl médicaux)
**medication** médicament (m) (10)
**medicine** (studies) médecine (f), (medication) médicaments (mpl) (10)
**medium** moyen(ne); **medium-sized** de taille moyenne (4)
**meet** (by design) retrouver (4), (by chance) rencontrer (7), faire connaissance (1), se réunir; **Let's meet at . . .** Rendez-vous à…; **meet each other** se rencontrer, se retrouver (7)
**meeting** réunion (f)
**melon** melon (m)
**member** membre (m)
**memory** souvenir (m), mémoire (f)
**menu** (fixed price) menu (m) (à prix fixe), carte (f) (8)

**merchant** marchand(e) *(mf)* (6)
**Merry Christmas!** Joyeux Noël!
**message** message *(m)*
**Mexico** Mexique *(m)* (9)
**microwave oven** four *(m)* à micro-ondes
**middle** milieu *(m)*; **in the middle of** au milieu de
**Middle East** Moyen-Orient *(m)* (9)
**midnight** minuit *(m)* (P)
**milk** lait *(m)* (8); **coffee with milk** café *(m)* au lait (2)
**milk** laitier(-ère) (8)
**million: one million** un million (de) (3)
**millionaire** millionnaire *(mf)*
**mind** esprit *(m)* (7)
**mine** le mien (la mienne, les miens, les miennes)
**mineral water** eau minérale *(f)* (2)
**minus: How much is . . . minus . . . ?** Combien font... moins... ? (P)
**minute** minute *(f)* (5); **at the last minute** au dernier moment
**mirror** miroir *(m)*
**mischievous** espiègle
**miss** mademoiselle (Mlle) (P)
**mistake** erreur *(f)*; **make a mistake** se tromper
**mister (Mr.)** monsieur (M.) (P)
**mistrust** se méfier de
**modern** moderne (1)
**mom** maman *(f)*
**moment** instant *(m)*, moment *(m)*
**Monday** lundi *(m)* (P)
**money** argent *(m)* (2); **save up money** faire des économies
**monster** monstre *(m)* (6)
**month** mois *(m)* (3); **per month** par mois (3); **this month** ce mois-ci (4)
**mood; in a good/bad mood** de bonne/mauvaise humeur
**more** plus (1), encore (8), plus de (8); **more and more** de plus en plus (8); **more or less** environ (4); **more . . . than** plus... que (1); **no more** ne... plus (8), pas plus (4)
**morning** matin *(m)* (P); **at eight o'clock in the morning** à huit heures du matin (P); **Good morning.** Bonjour. (P); **in the morning, mornings** le matin (P); **morning hours** matinée *(f)* (2)
**Morocco** Maroc *(m)* (9)
**mosque** mosquée *(f)*
**most: most of** la plupart de (7), **the most** le (la) plus
**mother** mère *(f)* (4); **mother-in-law** belle-mère *(f)* (4); **Mother's Day** fête *(f)* des Mères
**mountain** montagne *(f)* (5); **go mountain climbing** faire de l'alpinisme; **go to the mountains** aller à la montagne (5)
**mouth** bouche *(f)* (10)
**move (into)** s'installer (à/dans) (7)
**movement** mouvement *(m)*
**movie** film *(m)* (1); **go to the movies** aller au cinéma (2); **movie theater** cinéma *(m)* (1); **romantic movie** film *(m)* d'amour (6); **show a movie** passer un film (6)
**Mr.** monsieur (M.) (P)
**Mrs.** madame (Mme) (P)
**much** beaucoup (de) (1); **as much . . . (as)** autant de... (que); **how much** combien de (3); **How much is it?** C'est combien?, Ça fait combien? (2); **not much** ne... pas grand-chose; **so much** tellement (6), tant; **too much** trop (3)
**muscular** musclé(e)
**museum** musée *(m)* (4)
**mushroom** champignon *(m)*
**music** musique *(f)* (1); **listen to music** écouter de la musique (2)

**musical** *(movie)* comédie musicale *(f)*
**musical** musicien(ne)
**musician** musicien(ne) *(mf)*
**mussel** moule *(f)* (8)
**must** devoir (6); **he/she must** il/elle doit (3); **one/you must . . .** il faut... (8)
**mustache** moustache *(f)* (4)
**my** mon (ma, mes) (3); **at / in / to my house** chez moi (2); **my best friend** mon meilleur ami *(m)*, ma meilleure amie *(f)* (1); **my friends** mes amis (1); **My name is . . .** Je m'appelle... (P); **with my family** avec ma famille (P)
**myself** me (7), moi-même

## N

**naive** naïf(-ïve)
**name** nom *(m)* (3); **first name** prénom *(m)* (3); **His/Her name is . . .** Il/Elle s'appelle... (4); **My name is . . .** Je m'appelle... (P); **What is . . . 's name?** Comment s'appelle... ? (4); **What's your name?** Tu t'appelles comment? *(familiar)* (P), Comment vous appelez-vous? *(formal)* (P)
**named: be named** s'appeler (7)
**nap** sieste *(f)*; **take a nap** faire la sieste
**nationality** nationalité *(f)* (3)
**native** natal(e)
**natural** naturel(le)
**nature** nature *(f)* (7)
**near** près (de) (1)
**nearly** presque (2)
**necessary** nécessaire (10); **it is necessary to . . .** Il faut... (8), il est nécessaire (de)...(10); **it will be necessary to . . .** il faudra...
**neck** cou *(m)*
**necklace** collier *(m)*
**necktie** cravate *(f)* (5)
**nectarine** nectarine *(f)*
**need** avoir besoin de (4); **I/you/we/you need** Il me/te/nous/vous faut (9); **one needs...** il faut... (8); **What size do you need?** Quelle taille faites-vous? (5)
**needy** nécessiteux *(mpl)*
**neighbor** voisin(e) *(mf)* (9)
**neighborhood** quartier *(m)* (1)
**neither** non plus (3); **neither . . . nor** ne... ni... ni...
**nephew** neveu *(pl* neveux) *(m)* (4)
**nervous** nerveux(-euse); **feel nervous** se sentir mal à l'aise
**never** ne... jamais (2)
**new** nouveau / nouvel (nouvelle) (1); neuf (neuve); **Happy New Year!** Bonne année!; **New Caledonia** Nouvelle-Calédonie *(f)* (9); **New Orleans** La Nouvelle-Orléans (4); **New Year's Eve party** le réveillon *(m)* du jour de l'an
**news** nouvelles *(fpl)*, *(television program)* informations *(fpl)*
**newspaper** journal *(m)* (5)
**next** prochain(e) (4), ensuite (4); **next to** à côté (de) (3); **the next class** le prochain cours (P); **the next day** le lendemain *(m)* (6)
**nice** sympathique (sympa) (1), gentil(le) (1); **The weather's nice.** Il fait beau. (5)
**niece** nièce *(f)* (4)
**night** nuit *(f)* (5); **night stand** table *(f)* de chevet
**nightclub** boîte *(f)* de nuit (1); **to go to a nightclub** aller en boîte (2)
**nightgown** chemise *(f)* de nuit
**nine** neuf (P)
**nineteen** dix-neuf (P)
**ninety** quatre-vingt-dix (2)
**ninth** neuvième (3)

**no** non (P); **no longer** ne... plus (8); **no more** ne... plus (8), pas plus (4); **no one** ne... personne; **No problem!** Pas de problème! (3)
**nobody** ne... personne
**noise** bruit *(m)* (10)
**none** ne... aucun(e)
**non-smoking section** section non-fumeur *(f)*
**noon** midi *(m)* (P)
**nor: neither . . . nor** ne... ni... ni
**normal** normal(e) *(mpl* normaux)
**normally** normalement
**north** nord *(m)*; **North America** Amérique du Nord *(f)* (9)
**Norway** Norvège *(f)*
**nose** nez *(m)* (10)
**not** ne... pas (P); **I do not work.** Je ne travaille pas. (P); **not... anymore** ne... plus (8); **not at all** ne... pas du tout (1); **not bad** pas mal (P); **not one** ne... aucun(e); **not yet** ne... pas encore (5); **Why not?** Pourquoi pas? (2)
**notebook** cahier *(m)* (P)
**nothing** ne... rien (5); **nothing at all** rien du tout (6); **nothing but** ne... rien que; **nothing special** rien de spécial (6)
**notice** remarquer
**noun** nom *(m)* (3)
**nourishment** nourriture *(f)*
**novel** roman *(m)* (9)
**November** novembre *(m)* (4)
**now** maintenant (P)
**nowadays** de nos jours
**nowhere** nulle part
**number** chiffre *(m)* (P), numéro *(m)* (3), nombre *(m)*; **telephone number** numéro *(m)* de téléphone (3)
**numeral** chiffre *(m)* (P)
**numerous** nombreux(-euse)
**nurse** infirmier(-ière) *(mf)*

## O

**obey** obéir (à) (8)
**object** objet *(m)*
**observe** observer
**obtain** obtenir (9)
**obvious** évident(e)
**obviously** évidemment
**ocean** océan *(m)*
**Oceania** Océanie *(f)* (9)
**o'clock: It's . . . o'clock.** Il est... heure(s). (P)
**October** octobre *(m)* (4)
**of** de (1); **Of course!** Bien sûr! (5); Évidemment!; **of it/them** en (8)
**off: get off** descendre (de) (5)
**offer** proposer (8), offrir
**office** bureau *(m)* (1); **post office** bureau *(m)* de poste (10); **tourist office** office *(m)* de tourisme (10)
**official time** l'heure officielle *(f)* (6)
**often** souvent (1)
**oil** huile *(f)*
**okay** d'accord (2); **It's going okay.** Ça va.
**old** vieux/vieil (vieille) (1), âgé(e) (4); **be . . . years old** avoir... ans (4); **get older** vieillir (8); **How old is . . . ?** Quel âge a... ? (4); **oldest** aîné(e)
**omelet** omelette *(f)* (8)
**on** sur (5); **online** en ligne (7); **get on** monter dans (5); **on foot** à pied (4); **on Mondays** le lundi (P); **on page . . .** à la page... (P); **on sale** en solde (5); **on . . . street** dans la rue... (10); **on the corner (of)** au coin (de) (10); **on the courtyard side** côté cour (10); **on the ground/floor** par terre (3); **on the weekend** le week-end (P); **on time** à l'heure (4); **On what**

floor? À quel étage? (3); **put on** mettre (5); **try on** essayer (5)

**once** une fois (6); **all at once** tout d'un coup (6); **once more** encore une fois; **once upon a time** il était une fois (6)

**one** un(e) (P); **on** (4); **no one** ne... personne; **not one** ne... aucun(e); **one another** se, nous vous (7)

**oneself** se (7)

**one-way ticket** aller simple (m) (9)

**onion** oignon (m) (8); **onion soup** soupe (f) à l'oignon (8)

**only** uniquement (6); seulement (8), ne... que; **only child** fille unique (f), fils unique (m)

**open** ouvrir; **Open your book.** Ouvrez votre livre. (P)

**opening time** l'heure d'ouverture (f) (6)

**opinion** avis (m); **in your opinion** à votre avis (8)

**opportunity: have the opportunity to** avoir l'occasion de

**opposite** contraire (m)

**optimistic** optimiste (1)

**or** ou (P)

**orange** orange (f) (8); **orange juice** jus (m) d'orange (2)

**orange** orange (3)

**Orangina** Orangina (m) (2)

**orchestra** orchestre (m) (4)

**order** commander (2), ranger (7)

**order** ordre (m); **in order** en ordre (3); **in order to** pour (1)

**organic products** produits bios (mpl) (8)

**organization** organisation (f)

**origin** origine (f); **of. . . origin** d'origine... (7)

**Orléans: New Orleans** La Nouvelle-Orléans (4)

**other** autre (1); **each other** se, nous vous (7); **on the other hand** par contre; **on the other side (of)** de l'autre côté (de); **sometimes . . . other times** quelquefois... d'autres fois (7)

**ought to** devoir (6)

**our** notre (nos) (3)

**ourselves** nous (7); nous-mêmes

**out: dine out** dîner au restaurant (2); **go out** sortir (2); **Take out a sheet of paper.** Prenez une feuille de papier. (P); **watch out (for)** faire attention (à) (8)

**outdoor** de plein air (4)

**outdoors** en plein air

**outgoing** extraverti(e) (1)

**outing** sortie (f) (6)

**outside** à l'extérieur, dehors, en plein air; **outside of** *hors de

**oven** four (m); **microwave oven** four (m) à micro-ondes

**over** (par-)dessus; **invite friends over** inviter des amis à la maison (2); **over there** là-bas (8)

**overcast: The sky is overcast.** Le ciel est couvert.

**overcoat** manteau (m) (5), pardessus (m)

**owe** devoir (6)

**own** propre

**oyster** huître (f) (8)

## P

**pack one's bags** faire ses valises (f) (9)

**package** paquet (m) (8), colis (m)

**page** page (f) (P)

**pain** douleur (f)

**paint** peindre

**painter** peintre (mf)

**painting** tableau (m) (3), peinture (f)

**pajamas** pyjama (m)

**pal** copain (m), copine (f) (6)

**pale** pâle

**panties** slip (m); **panty hose** collant (m)

**pants** pantalon (m) (5)

**papa** papa (m) (4)

**paper** papier (m); **sheet of paper** feuille (f) de papier (P)

**parade** défilé (m)

**pardon me** pardon (P)

**parents** parents (mpl) (4)

**Parisian** Parisien(ne) (mf) (9)

**park** parc (m) (1)

**parking lot** parking (m) (1)

**part** partie (f)

**participate (in)** participer (à)

**particular: in particular** en particulier

**partner** partenaire (mf) (7)

**part-time** à temps partiel

**party** (social) boum (f), fête (f) (1); (political) parti (m)

**pass** passer (2), (exam) réussir à (8); **pass by the house of . . .** passer chez... (2)

**passenger** passager(-ère) (mf)

**passerby** passant(e) (mf)

**passion** passion (f) (7)

**Passover** la pâque juive (f)

**passport** passeport (m) (9)

**past** passé (m); **in the past** au passé, autrefois

**past** passé(e) (6); **It's a quarter past two.** Il est deux heures et quart. (P)

**pasta** pâtes (fpl)

**pastime** passe-temps (m) (2)

**pastry** pâtisserie (f); **pastry shop** pâtisserie (f)

**pâté** pâté (m) (8)

**patience** patience (f); avoir de la patience **to have patience** (4)

**patient** patient(e) (mf)

**patient** patient(e) (6)

**pay (for)** payer (2); **pay attention (to)** faire attention (à) (8); **pay the bill** régler la note (10)

**peace** paix (f)

**peaceful** tranquille

**peach** pêche (f) (8)

**peanut** cacahouète (f)

**pear** poire (f) (8)

**peas** petits pois (mpl) (8)

**pen** stylo (m) (P)

**pencil** crayon (m) (P)

**people** gens (mpl) (1), on (4); **poor people** les pauvres (mpl); **some people** certains (mpl); **young people** les jeunes (mpl)

**pepper** poivre (m) (8)

**per** par (3)

**percent** pour cent

**perfect** perfectionner

**perfect** parfait(e) (7)

**perfectly** parfaitement (7)

**performer** artiste (mf)

**perhaps** peut-être (3)

**period** période (f), époque (f)

**permit** permettre (de); **permitted** permis(e)

**person** personne (f) (6)

**personal** personnel(le) (3); **personal service** service personnalisé (m) (8)

**personality** personnalité (f) (1)

**personally** personnellement

**Peru** Pérou (m) (9)

**pessimistic** pessimiste (1)

**pharmacist** pharmacien(ne) (mf)

**pharmacy** pharmacie (f) (10)

**philosophy** philosophie (f) (1)

**phone** téléphone (m) (2); **on the phone** au téléphone (2)

**phone** téléphoner (à) (3); **phone each other** se téléphoner (7)

**photo** photo (f) (4)

**physical appearance** aspect physique (m) (7)

**physics** physique (f) (1)

**piano** piano (m) (2)

**picnic** pique-nique (m)

**picture** tableau (m) (3)

**pie** tarte (f) (8); **apple pie** tarte (f) aux pommes (8)

**piece** morceau (m) (8); **piece of advice** conseil (m) (8)

**pierced** percé(e)

**pineapple** ananas (m)

**pink** rose (3)

**pity** pitié (f); **what a pity** c'est dommage (7)

**pizza** pizza (f) (8)

**place** endroit (m) (9), place (f) (10); **at/to/ in . . . 's place** chez... (2); **in it's place** à sa place; **take place** avoir lieu

**place** mettre

**plaid** écossais(e)

**plan** projet (m) (4); **make plans** faire des projets (4)

**plan** organiser; **plan on doing** avoir l'intention de faire (4), compter faire (9); **planned** prévu(e) (9)

**plane** avion (m) (4); **by plane** en avion (4)

**plant** plante (f) (3)

**plastic** plastique (m); **plastic bag** sac (m) en plastique

**plate** assiette (f)

**play** (theater) pièce (f) (4)

**play (a sport)** jouer (à un sport) (2), faire (du sport) (5); **play music** faire de la musique (2); **play (the piano)** jouer (du piano) (2)

**player: CD player** platine laser (f) (3); **DVD player** lecteur DVD (m) (3)

**plaza** place (f) (10)

**pleasant** agréable (1)

**please** plaire à

**please** s'il vous plaît (formal) (P), s'il te plaît (familiar)

**pleased** content(e)

**pleasure** plaisir (m); **It would be a pleasure!** Avec plaisir! (6)

**plum** prune (f)

**plumber** plombier (m)

**plus: How much is . . . plus . . . ?** Combien font... et... ? (P)

**P.M.** de l'après-midi, du soir (P)

**poem** poème (m) (9)

**point out** signaler

**Poland** Pologne (f)

**police** police (f)

**policeman** agent (m) de police

**polite** poli(e)

**political** politique (1); **political science** sciences politiques (fpl) (1)

**politics** politique (f) (7)

**poll** sondage (m)

**pollution** pollution (f)

**Polynesia: French Polynesia** Polynésie française (f) (9)

**pool** billard (m); **swimming pool** piscine (f) (4)

**poor** pauvre

**pop music** musique populaire (f) (1)

**popular** populaire (1)

**population** population (f)

**pork** porc (m) (8); **pork chop** côte (f) de porc (8); **pork roast** rôti (m) de porc

**portrait: self-portrait** autoportrait (m) (P)

**Portuguese** portugais (m)

**possibility** possibilité (f) (4)

**possible** possible

**post office** bureau (m) de poste (10)

**postcard** carte postale (f) (9)

**poster** affiche (f) (3)

**potato** pomme (f) de terre (8)

**poultry** volaille (f) (8)

**pound** livre *(f)* (8)
**poverty** pauvreté *(f)*
**powerful** puissant(e)
**preach** prêcher
**precisely** justement (3)
**prefer** préférer (2), aimer mieux (2); **I prefer . . .** Je préfère... (1)
**preferable** préférable
**pregnant** enceinte (10)
**preparations** préparatifs *(mpl)* (9)
**prepare** préparer (2); **Prepare for the exam.** Préparez l'examen. (P)
**prepared: prepared dish** plat préparé *(m)* (8)
**preschool** école maternelle *(f)*
**prescription** ordonnance *(f)* (10)
**present** cadeau *(m)* (10)
**pretty** joli(e) (1), beau/bel (belle) (1); **pretty cool** assez cool (P)
**prevent** empêcher
**price** prix *(m)*; **at a set price** à prix fixe (8)
**principal** principal(e) *(mpl* principaux) (10)
**private** privé(e) (10)
**probable** probable
**probably** sans doute (8); probablement
**problem** problème *(m)*; **No problem!** Pas de problème! (3)
**process: be in the process of doing** être en train de faire
**product** produit *(m)* (8); **organic products** produits bios *(mpl)* (8)
**profession** profession *(f)* (7), métier *(m)*
**professional** professionnel(le) (7)
**professor** professeur *(m)* (P)
**program** programme *(m)*
**programmer** programmeur(-euse) *(mf)*
**progress** progrès *(m)*; **make progress** faire des progrès
**promise** promettre (de) (6)
**pronunciation** prononciation *(f)*
**protect (oneself) (against)** (se) protéger (contre)
**protein** protéines *(fpl)* (8)
**proud** fier(-ère)
**province** province *(f)* (3)
**prune** pruneau *(m)*
**psychology** psychologie *(f)* (1)
**public: public transportation** transports en commun *(mpl)* (9)
**publish: publishing company** maison *(f)* d'édition
**pullover (sweater)** pull *(m)* (5)
**punish** punir
**purple** violet(te) (3)
**purpose: on purpose** exprès
**purse** sac *(m)* (5)
**put (on)** mettre (5); **put away** rangé(e) (3); **put on make-up** se maquiller (7); **put on weight** prendre du poids; **put up with** supporter (7)

## Q

**qualify** qualifier
**quarter** quart *(m)* (P); **It's a quarter past two.** Il est deux heures et quart. (P)
**question** question *(f)* (P); **ask a question** poser une question (3)
**quick** rapide (8)
**quickly** vite (7)
**quiet** tranquille; **be quiet** se taire
**quite** assez, plutôt; **quite a bit** pas mal de; **quite simply** tout simplement (10)

## R

**rabbit** lapin *(m)*
**radio** radio *(f)* (2)

**rain** pluie *(f)* (5)
**rain** pleuvoir (5); **It's raining. It rains.** Il pleut. (5)
**raincoat** imperméable *(m)* (5)
**raisin** raisin sec *(m)*
**Ramadan** ramadan *(m)*
**rapid** rapide (8)
**rarely** rarement (2)
**raspberry** framboise *(f)*
**rather** plutôt (1), assez (1)
**raw vegetables** crudités *(fpl)* (8)
**rayfish** raie *(f)* (8)
**reach** atteindre
**react (to)** réagir (à)
**read** lire (2); **Read . . .** Lisez... (P)
**ready (to)** prêt(e) (à) (4); **get ready** se préparer; **ready-to-serve dish** plat préparé *(m)* (8)
**real** réel(le), véritable
**realistic** réaliste (1)
**realize** se rendre compte
**really** vraiment (2)
**reason** raison *(f)*; **the reason why I . . .** la raison pour laquelle je...
**reasonable** raisonnable
**receive** recevoir (9)
**recent** récent(e)
**recently** récemment (5)
**recognize (each other)** (se) reconnaître (7)
**recommend** recommander
**reconfirm** reconfirmer
**record** disque *(m)*, *(sports)* record *(m)*
**record** enregistrer
**recorder: video cassette recorder** magnétoscope *(m)*
**recount** raconter (7)
**recycle** recycler
**red** rouge (3), *(hair)* roux (rousse) (4); **red wine** vin rouge (m) (2); **turn red** rougir (8)
**reflect (on)** réfléchir (à) (8)
**refrigerator** réfrigérateur *(m)*
**refuse** refuser (de)
**region** région *(f)* (4)
**regional** régional(e) *(mpl* régionaux) (4)
**register** s'inscrire (3)
**regret** regretter (6)
**regularly** régulièrement (8)
**relationship** relation *(f)* (7), rapport *(m)*
**relatives** parents *(mpl)* (5)
**relax** se reposer (7), se détendre; **relaxed** décontracté(e)
**religion** religion *(f)* (7)
**religious** religieux(-euse)
**remain** rester
**remarried** remarié(e)
**remember** se souvenir (de) (7)
**rent** loyer *(m)* (3)
**rent** louer (4)
**rental car** voiture *(f)* de location (5)
**repeat** répéter (2); **Please repeat.** Répétez s'il vous plaît. (P)
**replace** remplacer
**require** exiger, demander; **required** requis(e), obligatoire
**research** recherche *(f)*; **do research** faire des recherches
**resell** revendre
**resemble** ressembler à
**reservation** réservation *(f)* (9); **make a reservation** faire une réservation (9)
**reserve: nature reserve** parc naturel *(m)*
**reserve** réserver (9)
**residence hall** résidence universitaire *(f)* (1)
**resort: summer resort** station estivale *(f)* (10)
**resources** ressources *(fpl)*
**respond** répondre (6)

**rest: the rest (of)** le reste (de) (7)
**rest** se reposer (7); **rested** reposé(e)
**restaurant** restaurant *(m)* (1); **fast food restaurant** fast-food *(m)* (1); **university restaurant** restau-u *(m)* (6)
**restful** reposant(e)
**restroom** toilettes *(fpl)* (3), W.-C. *(mpl)* (3)
**retired** retraité(e)
**return** retour *(m)* (9)
**return** rentrer (2), retourner (5), **return something to someone** rendre quelque chose à quelqu'un (7)
**review** *(for a test)* réviser
**rice** riz *(m)* (8)
**rich** riche
**ride: go for a ride** faire un tour en voiture (en vélo) (4)
**right** *(direction)* droite *(f)*, *(legal)* droit *(m)*; **to the right of** à droite de (3)
**right** correct(e); **be right** avoir raison (4), **right away** tout de suite (6); **right by** tout près (de) (3); **right there** juste là; right? n'est-ce pas?, non? (1)
**ring** bague *(f)*
**ring** sonner (7)
**river** fleuve *(m)*, rivière *(f)*
**road** chemin *(m)*, route *(f)*
**roast: roast beef** rosbif *(m)* (8); **pork roast** rôti *(m)* de porc
**rock: rock music** rock *(m)* (1); **go rock climbing** faire de la varappe; **hard rock** *hard rock *(m)*
**rollerblade** faire du roller (6)
**rollerblading** roller *(m)*; **go rollerblading** faire du roller (6)
**romantic** romantique; **romantic movie** film *(m)* d'amour (6)
**room** pièce *(f)* (3), salle *(f)*; **classroom** salle *(f)* de classe (1); **dining room** salle à manger *(f)* (3); **fitting room** cabine *(f)* d'essayage (5); **living room** salon *(m)* (3)
**roommate** camarade *(mf)* de chambre (P)
**round-trip ticket** (billet) aller-retour *(m)* (9)
**routine** routine *(f)* (7)
**row** rang *(m)*
**rug** tapis *(m)* (3)
**run** courir (9); **run errands** faire des courses (5); **run into (each other)** (se) rencontrer (7)
**Russia** Russie *(f)* (9)
**Russian** russe *(m)*

## S

**sack** sac *(m)* (5), paquet *(m)* (8)
**sad** triste
**safety** sécurité *(f)*
**sailing: go sailing** faire de la voile
**salad** salade *(f)* (8)
**salami** saucisson *(m)* (8)
**sale: on sale** en solde (5)
**salesclerk** vendeur(-euse) *(mf)* (5)
**salmon** saumon *(m)* (8)
**salt** sel *(m)* (8)
**same** même (1); **all the same** quand même
**sandal** sandale *(f)* (5)
**sandwich** sandwich *(m)* (2); **bread-and-butter sandwich** tartine *(f)* (8); **cheese sandwich** sandwich au fromage *(m)* (2)
**Santa Claus** le père Noël
**satisfied** satisfait(e)
**Saturday** samedi *(m)* (P)
**sauce** sauce *(f)*
**sausage** saucisse *(f)* (8)
**save** sauver; **save up money** faire des économies
**saxophone** saxophone *(m)*

**say** dire (6); **How do you say . . .** in French? Comment dit-on... en français? (P); **They say that . . .** On dit que... (4)

**scallops** coquilles St-Jacques *(fpl)*

**scarf** *(winter)* écharpe *(f)*, *(dressy)* foulard *(m)*

**scenery** paysage *(m)* (9)

**schedule** *(classes)* emploi *(m)* du temps (P), *(train)* horaire *(m)*

**school** école *(f)* (6); **high school** lycée *(m)* (6)

**science** science *(f)* (1); **computer science** informatique *(f)* (1); **political science** sciences politiques *(fpl)* (1); **science fiction** science-fiction *(f)*; **social sciences** sciences humaines *(fpl)* (1)

**scientist** scientifique *(mf)*; **computer scientist** informaticien(ne) *(mf)*

**scuba diving** plongée sous-marine *(f)*

**sculpture** sculpture *(f)*

**sea** mer *(f)* (9)

**season** saison *(f)* (5)

**seat** place *(f)*, siège *(m)*

**seated** assis(e) (9)

**second** seconde *(f)* (5)

**second** deuxième (3), second(e); **in second class** en classe touriste (9)

**secretary** secrétaire *(mf)*

**section** section *(f)*

**security** sécurité *(f)*

**see** voir (1); **as you see** comme tu vois (3); **Let's see!** Voyons! (5); **see each other** se voir (7); **See you in a little while.** À tout à l'heure. (P); **See you later!** À plus tard! (2); **See you soon.** À bientôt. (P); **See you tomorrow.** À demain. (P)

**seem** avoir l'air... (4), sembler; **It seems to me that . . .** Il me semble que...

**self: myself** moi-même; **self-portrait** autoportrait *(m)* (P); **self-service restaurant** self-service *(m)* (8)

**sell** vendre (7); **sell back** revendre (7)

**semester** semestre *(m)* (P)

**send** envoyer (10)

**Senegal** Sénégal *(m)* (9)

**sense of humor** sens *(m)* de l'humour (7)

**sensitive** sensible

**sentence** phrase *(f)* (P); **in complete sentences** en phrases complètes (P)

**sentimental** sentimental(e) *(mpl* sentimentaux) (7)

**separate** séparer; **separated** séparé(e)

**separately** séparément

**September** septembre *(m)* (4)

**serious** sérieux(-euse), grave

**serve** servir (4); **served** servi(e) (10)

**server** serveur *(m)*, serveuse *(f)* (8)

**service** service *(m)* (8); **service station** station-service *(f)*

**set** mettre (8); **set the table** mettre la table; **with a set price** à prix fixe (8)

**settle (in)** s'installer (à/dans) (7)

**seven** sept (P)

**seventeen** dix-sept (P)

**seventh** septième (3)

**seventy** soixante-dix (2)

**several** plusieurs (8)

**sexy** sexy (2)

**shall: Shall we go . . . ?** On va... ? (2); **What shall we do?** Qu'est-ce qu'on fait?

**shame** *hu* honte *(f)*; **It's a shame!** C'est dommage! (7)

**shape** forme *(f)*; **in shape** en forme (8)

**share** partager (3)

**shared** partagé(e) (3)

**shave** se raser (7)

**she** elle (1); **she is . . .** c'est..., elle est... (1)

**sheet of paper** feuille *(f)* de papier (P)

**shelf** étagère *(f)* (3)

**shellfish** fruits *(mpl)* de mer (8)

**shirt** chemise *(f)* (5); **knit shirt** polo (5)

**shiver** frisson *(m)* (10)

**shock** choquer

**shoe** chaussure *(f)* (5); **tennis shoes** baskets *(fpl)* (5)

**shop** magasin *(m)* (4); **butcher's shop** boucherie *(f)* (8); **fish shop** poissonnerie *(f)* (8); **gift shop** marchand *(m)* de cadeaux (10); **pastry shop** pâtisserie *(f)*; **tobacco shop** bureau *(m)* de tabac

**shopkeeper** marchand(e) *(mf)* (6), commerçant(e) *(mf)* (8)

**shopping: go grocery shopping** faire les courses; **go shopping** faire du shopping (2); **shopping center** centre commercial *(m)* (4)

**short** petit(e) (1), court(e) (4)

**shorts** short *(m)* (5)

**shot** piqûre *(f)*; **give a shot** faire une piqûre

**should** devoir (6); **one shouldn't . . .** il ne faut pas (10)

**shoulder** épaule *(f)*; **shoulder-length hair** cheveux mi-longs *(mpl)* (4)

**show** montrer (3), indiquer (3); **show a movie** passer un film (6)

**show time** séance *(f)* (6)

**shower** douche *(f)* (7)

**shrimp** crevette *(f)* (8)

**shy** timide (1)

**shuttle** navette *(f)* (10)

**sick** malade (10); **get sick** tomber malade (10)

**side** côté *(m)*; **on the courtyard side** côté cour (10); **on the other side (of)** de l'autre côté (de)

**sight** vue *(f)*; **love at first sight** coup *(m)* de foudre (7)

**silver** argent *(m)* (2)

**similar to** semblable à, pareil(le) à

**simply** simplement (10); **quite simply** tout simplement (10)

**since** depuis, comme (7), depuis que

**sincere** sincère

**sing** chanter (2)

**singer** chanteur(-euse) *(mf)*

**single** célibataire (1), seul(e)

**sink** *(bathroom)* lavabo *(m)* (10), *(kitchen)* évier *(m)*

**sir** monsieur (M.) (P)

**sister** sœur *(f)* (1); **sister-in-law** belle-sœur *(f)* (4)

**sit (down)** s'asseoir; **Sit down!** Asseyez-vous!

**site** site *(m)* (9)

**situation** situation *(f)*

**six** six (P)

**sixteen** seize (P)

**sixth** sixième (3)

**sixty** soixante (2)

**size** taille *(f)* (4); **medium-sized** de taille moyenne (4)

**skate** *(fish)* raie *(f)* (8); patin *(m)*

**skateboard** faire du skateboard (6)

**skating** patin *(m)*; **go (ice-)skating** faire du patin (à glace)

**skeptical** sceptique

**ski** ski *(m)*; **ski jacket** anorak *(m)* (5); **ski lodge** chalet *(m)* de ski (10)

**ski** faire du ski (5); **water-ski** faire du ski nautique (5)

**skiing** ski *(m)* (5); **water-skiing** ski nautique *(m)* (5)

**skin** peau *(f)*

**skinny** maigre (8)

**skirt** jupe *(f)* (5)

**sleep** dormir (2)

**sleepy: be sleepy** avoir sommeil (4)

**slice** tranche *(f)*, pavé *(m)* (8)

**slightly** légèrement

**slim down** maigrir (8)

**slip** combinaison *(f)*

**slow** lent(e); **slow motion** ralenti *(m)*

**slowly** lentement (8)

**small** petit(e) (1)

**smell** sentir

**smoke** fumée *(f)* (8)

**smoke** fumer (3); **smoked** fumé(e) (8)

**smoking section** section fumeur *(f)*

**snack** collation *(f)*

**snail** escargot *(m)* (8)

**sneeze** éternuer (10)

**snob** snob

**snorkeling: go snorkeling** faire du tuba

**snow** neige *(f)* (5)

**snow** neiger (5)

**so** alors (1), tellement (6), donc (7); **so many, so much** tant (de); tellement (de); **so-so** comme ci comme ça (2); **so that** afin que

**soap** savon *(m)*

**soccer** football *(m)* (1)

**social** social(e) *(mpl* sociaux); **social sciences** sciences humaines *(fpl)* (1); **social worker** assistant(e) social(e) *(mf)*

**society** société *(f)*

**sociology** sociologie *(f)*

**sock** chaussette *(f)* (5)

**sofa** canapé *(m)* (3)

**soft** doux(-ce) (6)

**software** logiciel *(m)*

**sole** sole *(f)*

**solid-colored** uni(e)

**solution** solution *(f)*

**some** des (1), du, de la, de l', en (8), quelques (5), certain(e)s

**somebody** quelqu'un (6)

**someone** quelqu'un (6)

**something** quelque chose (2)

**sometimes** quelquefois (2), parfois

**somewhere** quelque part

**son** fils *(m)* (4)

**song** chanson *(f)*

**soon** bientôt (P); **as soon as** aussitôt que; **I would just as soon…** j'aimerais autant… (10); **See you soon.** À bientôt. (P)

**sorry** désolé(e) (10); **be sorry** être désolé(e) (10), regretter (6)

**sort: all sorts of** toutes sortes de

**sound: How does that sound to you?** Ça te dit? (4)

**soup** soupe *(f)* (8); **onion soup** soupe *(f)* à l'oignon (8)

**south** sud *(m)*; **South Africa** Afrique *(f)* du Sud; **South America** Amérique *(f)* du Sud (9)

**space** espace *(m)*

**Spain** Espagne *(f)* (9)

**Spanish** espagnol *(m)* (P)

**Spanish** espagnol(e)

**speak** parler (2); **Do you speak…?** Vous parlez…? (P); **I speak . . .** Je parle... (P); **speak to each other** se parler (7)

**special** spécial(e) *(mpl* spéciaux) (6)

**specialty** spécialité *(f)* (4)

**speech** discours *(m)*

**speed** vitesse *(f)*

**spend** *(time)* passer (2), *(money)* dépenser

**spider** araignée *(f)*

**spinach** épinards *(mpl)*

**spirituality** spiritualité *(f)* (7)

**spite: in spite of** malgré
**split** partagé(e) (3)
**spoon** cuillère *(f)*
**sport** sport *(m)* (1); **play sports** faire du sport (2); **sports club** club *(m)* de gym (1)
**spot** site *(m)* (9)
**sprain one's ankle** se fouler la cheville
**spring** printemps *(m)* (5); **in spring** au printemps (5)
**square** *(town)* place *(f)* (10)
**stadium** stade *(m)* (1)
**staircase** escalier *(m)* (3)
**stairs** escalier *(m)* (3)
**stamp** timbre *(m)* (10)
**stand: I can't stand . . .** J'ai horreur de...
**star** étoile *(f)*
**start** commencer (2); Le cours de français commence… **French class starts…** (P)
**state** état *(m)* (3); **United States** États-Unis (3) *(mpl)*
**station: radio station** station *(f)* de radio; **service station** station-service *(f)*; **subway station** station *(f)* de métro; **train station** gare *(f)*
**stay** séjour *(m)* (7); **Enjoy your stay!** Bon séjour! (10)
**stay** rester (2), *(at a hotel)* descendre (à) (5)
**steak** bifteck *(m)* (8); **steak and fries** steak-frites *(m)* (8)
**steal** voler
**stepbrother** demi-frère *(m)*
**stepfather** beau-père *(m)* (4)
**stepmother** belle-mère *(f)* (4)
**stepparents** beaux-parents *(mpl)*
**stepsister** demi-sœur *(f)*
**stereo** chaîne hi-fi *(f)* (2)
**still** encore (4), toujours
**stomach** ventre *(m)* (10)
**stop: bus stop** arrêt *(m)* d'autobus (3)
**stop** (s')arrêter (7); **stop by the house of . . .** passer chez... (2); **stopped up** bouché(e)
**store** magasin *(m)* (4); **bookstore** librairie *(f)* (1)
**storm** orage *(m)*
**story** histoire *(f)* (9); conte *(m)* (6)
**stove** cuisinière *(f)*
**straight** tout droit (10)
**straightened up** rangé(e) (3)
**strange** bizarre
**strawberry** fraise *(f)* (8)
**street** rue *(f)* (1); **on . . . Street** dans la rue… (10)
**strength** force *(f)*
**stress** stress *(m)* (8)
**stressed (out)** stressé(e) (8)
**strict** sévère
**striped** rayé(e)
**strong** fort(e) (8)
**struggle (against)** lutter (contre)
**student** étudiant(e) *(mf)* (P); **high school student** lycéen(ne) *(mf)* (6); **student center** centre *(m)* d'étudiants
**studies** études *(fpl)* (1)
**study** étudier (1), préparer les cours (2); **I study . . .** J'étudie... (1); **Study for the exam.** Préparez l'examen. (P); **What are you studying?** Qu'est-ce que vous étudiez? (1)
**stupid** bête (1), stupide
**style** style *(m)*; **American style** à l'américaine (8)
**stylist: hair stylist** coiffeur(-euse) *(mf)*
**suburbs** banlieue *(f)* (3); **in the suburbs** en banlieue (3)
**subway** métro *(m)* (4); **by subway** en métro (4)
**succeed (in)** réussir (à) (8)
**such as** tel(le) que (7)
**sudden: all of a sudden** tout d'un coup (6)

**suddenly** soudain, tout d'un coup (6), soudainement
**suffer** souffrir
**sufficiently** suffisamment
**sugar** sucre *(m)* (8)
**suggest** suggérer (6)
**suggestion** suggestion *(f)*
**suit** *(man's)* costume *(m)* (5), *(woman's)* tailleur *(m)*; **jogging suit** survêtement *(m)* (5)
**suitcase** valise *(f)* (9)
**summer** été *(m)* (5); **in summer** en été (5); **summer resort** station estivale *(f)* (10)
**sun** soleil *(m)*
**sunbathe** prendre un bain de soleil (4)
**Sunday** dimanche *(m)* (P)
**sunglasses** lunettes *(f)* de soleil (5)
**sunny: It's sunny.** Il fait du soleil. (5)
**superior** supérieur(e)
**supermarket** supermarché *(m)* (8)
**superstore** grande surface *(f)* (8)
**supplement** supplément *(m)* (10)
**supplies** provisions *(fpl)*
**sure** sûr(e), certain(e)
**surely** sûrement
**surf** surfer; **surf the Net** surfer sur le Net (2)
**surprise** étonner, surprendre; **surprised** étonné(e), surpris(e) (10)
**surrounded (by)** entouré(e) (de)
**swallow** avaler
**sweater: pullover sweater** pull *(m)* (5)
**sweatshirt** sweat *(m)*
**sweatsuit** survêtement *(m)* (5)
**Sweden** Suède *(f)*
**sweet** doux(-ce) (6)
**sweets** bonbons *(mpl)*
**swim** nager (4), se baigner
**swimming pool** piscine *(f)* (4)
**swimsuit** maillot *(m)* de bain (5)
**Switzerland** Suisse *(f)* (9)
**swollen** enflé(e)
**sword** épée *(f)*
**symptom** symptôme *(m)* (10)
**synagogue** synagogue *(f)*
**system: public transportation system** système *(m)* de transports en commun (9)

## T

**table** table *(f)* (3)
**take** prendre (4), *(something along)* apporter, *(a person)* emmener; **take a course** suivre un cours; **take advantage of** profiter de (9); **take a tour** faire un tour (4); **take a trip** faire un voyage (5); **take a walk** faire une promenade (5); **Take out a sheet of paper.** Prenez une feuille de papier. (P); **take place** avoir lieu
**tale: fairy tale** conte *(m)* de fée (6)
**talent** talent *(m)*
**talented** doué(e)
**talk** parler (2); **talk to each other** se parler (7)
**tall** grand(e) (1)
**tan** bronzer (5); **tanned** bronzé(e)
**tangerine** mandarine *(f)*
**tart** tartelette *(f)* (8)
**taste** goûter (9)
**taxi** taxi *(m)* (4); **by taxi** en taxi (4)
**tea (with lemon)** thé (au citron) *(m)* (2)
**teacher** *(elementary school)* instituteur(-trice) *(mf)*; *(secondary school)* professeur *(m)*
**team** équipe *(f)*
**technical** technique (1)
**technician** technicien(ne) *(mf)*
**technology** technologie *(f)*
**tee shirt** tee-shirt *(m)* (5)
**telephone** téléphone *(m)* (2); **talk on the**

**telephone** parler au téléphone (2); **telephone card** carte téléphonique *(f)* (10); **telephone number** numéro *(m)* de téléphone (3)
**telephone** téléphoner (à) (3); **telephone each other** se téléphoner (7)
**television** télévision (télé) *(f)* (2)
**tell** dire (6), raconter (7)
**teller: automatic teller machine** distributeur de billets *(m)* (10)
**temperature** température *(f)*
**temple** temple *(m)*
**ten** dix (P)
**tennis** tennis *(m)* (1); **tennis court** court *(m)* de tennis; **tennis shoes** baskets *(fpl)* (5)
**tenth** dixième (3)
**terrace** terrasse *(f)* (9)
**test** examen *(m)* (P), test *(m)* (7), contrôle *(m)*
**than: more . . . than** plus... que (1)
**thank (for)** remercier (de) (10); **thank you** merci (bien) (P)
**thanks** merci (bien) (P)
**Thanksgiving** jour *(m)* d'Action de grâce
**that** ça (P), cela (7), ce (cet, cette) (…-là) (3), que (P), qui (7); **I think that . . .** je pense que... (P); **that is . . .** c'est... (1)
**the** le (la, l', les) (1)
**theater** théâtre *(for live performances)* *(m)* (1); movie theater cinéma *(m)* (1)
**theft** vol *(m)*
**their** leur(s) (1)
**them** les (5); **of them** en (8); **to them** leur (9); **with them** avec eux, avec elles
**themselves** se (7), eux-mêmes *(mpl)*, elles-mêmes *(fpl)*
**then** alors (1), ensuite, puis (4), donc (7)
**there** là (8), y (4); **over there** là-bas (8); **right there** juste là; **there is, there are** il y a (1), voilà (2); **There are six of us.** Nous sommes six. (4); **There you are!** Te/Vous voilà.
**therefore** donc (7)
**these** ces (…-ci) (3); **these are . . .** ce sont... (1)
**they** ils, elles, ce (1), on (4)
**thick** gros(se)
**thickness** épaisseur *(f)*
**thief** voleur *(m)* (6)
**thin** mince (1); **get thinner** maigrir (8)
**thing(s)** chose(s) *(f)* (3), truc *(m)* (1), affaires *(fpl)*; **That's not my thing.** Ce n'est pas mon truc. (1)
**think (about)** penser (à) (7), réfléchir (à) (8); **I think that . . .** Je pense que... (P); **What do you think (about it)?** Qu'en penses-tu?, Qu'en pensez-vous?
**third** troisième (3); **Third World** Tiers Monde *(m)*
**thirsty: be thirsty** avoir soif (4); **I'm thirsty.** J'ai soif. (2)
**thirteen** treize (P)
**thirty** trente (P)
**this** ce (cet, cette) (…-ci) (3); **this evening** ce soir (2); **this is . . .** c'est... (1); **this month** ce mois-ci (4); **this semester** ce semestre (P); **this way** par ici (5)
**those** ces (…-là) (3); **those are . . .** ce sont... (1); **those (ones)** ceux (celles) (8)
**thousand: one thousand** mille (3)
**three** trois (P)
**throat** gorge *(f)* (10); **have a sore throat** avoir mal à la gorge
**through** par; **through the window** par la fenêtre (6)
**throw** jeter; **throw up** vomir (10)
**thumb** pouce *(m)*
**Thursday** jeudi *(m)* (P)

**thus** donc (7)

**ticket** billet *(m)* (9), ticket *(m)*; **one-way ticket** aller simple *(m)* (9); **round-trip ticket** billet aller-retour *(m)* (9); **ticket window** guichet *(m)*

**tide** marée *(f)*

**tie** cravate *(f)* (5)

**tight** étroit(e)

**till: a quarter till** moins le quart (P)

**time** *(clock)* heure *(f)* (P), temps *(m)* (2), *(occasion)* fois *(f)* (5); **a long time** longtemps (5); **at that time** à ce moment-là; **At what time?** À quelle heure? (P); **free time** temps libre *(m)* (4); **from time to time** de temps en temps (4); **have a hard time** avoir du mal à; **most of the time** la plupart du temps (7); **official time** l'heure officielle *(f)* (6); **Once upon a time…** Il était une fois… (6); **One has a good time.** On s'amuse bien. (4); **on time** à l'heure (4); **opening time** l'heure d'ouverture *(f)* (6); **show time** séance *(f)* (6); **sometimes … other times** quelquefois… d'autres fois … (7); **time period** époque *(f)*; **What time is it?** Quelle heure est-il? (P)

**timid** timide (1)

**tip** pourboire *(m)*

**tired** fatigué(e) (6)

**tiring** fatiguant(e)

**title** titre *(m)*

**to** à (P); **to go to a club** aller en boîte (2); **to . . .'s house/place** chez… (2)

**toast** pain grillé *(m)* (8)

**toasted** grillé(e) (8)

**tobacco** tabac *(m)* (7); **tobacco shop** bureau *(m)* de tabac

**today** aujourd'hui (P)

**toe** doigt *(m)* de pied (10)

**together** ensemble (2)

**toilet** toilettes *(fpl)* (3), W.-C. *(mpl)* (3)

**tolerate** supporter (7)

**tomato** tomate *(f)* (8)

**tomorrow** demain (P); **the day after tomorrow** après-demain; **tomorrow morning** demain matin (4)

**tonight** ce soir (2); **See you tonight.** À ce soir. (2)

**too** aussi (P), trop (3); **That's too bad!** C'est dommage! (7); **too many** trop (de) (8); **too much** trop (de) (6)

**tooth** dent *(f)* (7)

**tour** tour *(m)*; **take a tour** faire un tour (4)

**tourism** tourisme *(m)*

**tourist** touriste *(mf)*; **tourist class** classe touriste *(f)* (9); **tourist office** office *(m)* de tourisme (10)

**touristic** touristique (9)

**toward(s)** vers (2)

**towel** serviette *(f)*

**town** ville *(f)* (3); **in town** en ville (3)

**toy** jouet *(m)*

**traditional** traditionnel(le) (8)

**traffic** circulation *(f)*

**train** train *(m)* (4); **by train** en train (4); **train station** gare *(f)*

**training: do weight training** faire de la mascu(lation) (8); faire des haltères

**trait** trait *(m)* (7)

**translate** traduire

**translation** traduction *(f)*

**transportation** transport; **means of transportation** moyen *(m)* de transport (4); **public transportation** transports *(mpl)* en commun (9)

**travel: travel agency** agence *(f)* de voyages (9); **travel agent** agent *(m)* de voyages (9)

**travel** voyager (2)

**traveler's check** chèque *(m)* de voyage (9)

**treatment** traitement *(m)*

**tree** arbre *(m)* (1)

**trimester** trimestre *(m)*

**trip** voyage *(m)* (4); **take a trip** faire un voyage (5)

**tropical** tropical(e) *(mpl* tropicaux) (9)

**trouble** difficulté *(f)*; **have trouble** avoir des difficultés, avoir du mal (à)

**trout** truite *(f)*

**truck** camion *(m)*, *(pick-up)* camionnette *(f)*

**true** vrai(e) (8); **true love** le grand amour (7)

**truly** vraiment (3)

**trumpet** trompette *(f)*

**truth** vérité *(f)*

**try (on)** essayer (5)

**T-shirt** tee-shirt *(m)* (5)

**Tuesday** mardi *(m)* (P)

**tuna** thon *(m)* (8)

**Tunisia** Tunisie *(f)*

**Turkey** Turquie *(f)*

**turkey** dinde *(f)*

**turn** tourner (10); **turn in (something to someone)** rendre (quelque chose à quelqu'un) (7); **turn on** mettre (8); **turn red** rougir (8)

**turnover: apple turnover** chausson aux pommes *(m)*

**TV** télé *(f)* (2)

**twelve** douze (P)

**twenty** vingt (P)

**twin** jumeau (jumelle) (1)

**two** deux (P)

**type** genre *(m)*

**typical** typique (2)

**typically** typiquement

## U

**ugly** laid(e) (1)

**umbrella** parapluie *(m)* (5)

**unbearable** insupportable

**unbelievable** incroyable

**uncle** oncle *(m)* (4)

**under** sous (3)

**understand** comprendre (4); **Do you understand?** Vous comprenez? (P); **I understand.** Je comprends. (P); **No, I don't understand.** Non, je ne comprends pas. (P)

**understanding** compréhension *(f)* (7)

**underwear** sous-vêtements *(mpl)*

**undressed: get undressed** se déshabiller (7)

**unfaithfulness** infidélité *(f)* (7)

**unfortunately** malheureusement

**unhappy** malheureux(-euse)

**uniquely** uniquement (6)

**United States** États-Unis *(mpl)* (3)

**university** université *(f)* (P); fac(ulté) *(f)* (2); **university restaurant** restau-u *(m)* (6)

**university** universitaire (1)

**unless** à moins que

**unlikely** peu probable

**unmarried** célibataire (1)

**unpack** défaire ses valises

**unpleasant** désagréable (1)

**until** jusqu'à (2)

**up: get up** se lever (7); **go up** monter (5); **straightened up** rangé(e) (3); **up to** jusqu'à (2); **wake up** se réveiller (7); ; **wash up** faire sa toilette (7)

**us** nous (9)

**use** utiliser (6), employer

**used to** habitué(e) à

**useful** utile (10)

**usually** d'habitude (2)

**utilize** utiliser (6)

## V

**vacation** vacances *(fpl)* (4); **on vacation** en vacances

**vaccination** vaccination *(f)*

**Valentine's Day** Saint-Valentin *(f)*

**vanilla ice cream** glace *(f)* à la vanille (8)

**vanity** vanité *(f)* (7)

**variety** variété *(f)*

**VCR** magnétoscope *(m)*

**veal** veau *(m)*

**vegetable** légume *(m)* (8); **raw vegetables** crudités *(fpl)* (8); **vegetable soup** soupe *(f)* de légumes

**vegetarian** végétarien(ne)

**very** très (P); **very near** tout près (de) (3)

**vest** gilet *(m)*

**veterinarian** vétérinaire *(mf)*

**video** vidéo *(f)*; **video cassette** vidéocassette *(f)*; **video cassette recorder** magnétoscope *(m)*; **video game** jeu vidéo *(m)* (2)

**Vietnam** Viêt Nam *(m)* (9)

**view** vue *(f)* (3)

**vinegar** vinaigre *(m)*

**violence** violence *(f)* (6)

**violent** violent(e)

**violet** violet(te) (3)

**virus** virus *(m)* (10)

**visa** visa *(m)*

**visit** visite *(f)*; **medical visit** consultation *(f)*

**visit** *(place)* visiter (1), *(someone)* rendre visite à (7); **go visit** *(a person)* aller voir (4)

**vitamin** vitamine *(f)* (8)

**vocabulary** vocabulaire *(m)* (P)

**voice** voix *(f)*

**volleyball** volley *(m)* (2)

**volunteer** *(work)* bénévole

**vomit** vomir (10)

**vote** voter

## W

**wait (for)** attendre (7)

**waiter** garçon *(m)* (2), serveur *(m)* (8)

**waitress** serveuse *(f)* (8)

**wake up** (se) réveiller (7)

**walk** promenade *(f)* (5); **go for / take a walk** faire une promenade (5)

**walk** aller à pied (4), marcher (8)

**walking** marche *(f)* à pied; **go walking** se promener (7), faire de la marche à pied

**wall** mur *(m)* (3)

**wallet** portefeuille *(m)* (5)

**want** vouloir (6), avoir envie de (4)

**war** guerre *(f)*

**warmth** chaleur *(f)*

**wash** (se) laver (7); **wash clothes** faire la lessive (5); **wash up** faire sa toilette (7)

**washbasin** lavabo *(m)* (10)

**waste** gaspiller; **waste time** perdre du temps

**watch** montre *(f)* (5)

**watch** regarder (2); **watch out (for)** faire attention (à) (8); **watch over** veiller

**water** eau *(f)* (4)

**watermelon** pastèque *(f)*

**water-skiing** ski nautique *(m)* (5)

**way** façon *(f)* (6); **show the way** indiquer le chemin (10); **this way** par ici (5)

**we** nous (1), on (4); **Shall we go. . . ?** On va… ? (2); **What shall we do?** Qu'est-ce qu'on fait?

**weak** faible

**weakness** faiblesse *(f)*

**wear** porter (4); **I wear a 42.** Je fais du 42. (5); **What size do you wear?** Quelle taille faites-vous? (5)

**weather** temps *(m)* (5); **The weather's bad / cold / cool / hot / nice / sunny / windy.** Il fait mauvais / froid / frais / chaud / beau / du soleil / du vent. (5); **What's the weather like?** Quel temps fait-il? (5)

**Website** site *(m)* Web (9)

**wedding** mariage *(m)*; **wedding anniversary** anniversaire *(m)* de mariage

**Wednesday** mercredi *(m)* (P)

**week** semaine *(f)* (P); **in one/two week(s)** dans huit/quinze jours

**weekend** week-end *(m)* (P); **Have a good weekend!** Bon week-end!; **on weekends** le week-end (P)

**weigh** peser

**weight** poids *(m)*; **do weight training** faire de la musculation (8), faire des haltères; **gain weight** prendre du poids; **lose weight** perdre du poids; **put on weight** prendre du poids

**welcome** bienvenue *(f)*, **You're welcome.** De rien. (P); Je vous en prie. (2) Je t'en prie.

**well** bien (P); **get well** guérir; **well-behaved** sage (4)

**west** ouest *(m)*; **West Indies** Antilles *(fpl)* (9)

**what** qu'est-ce que (1), que (2), comment (P), quel(le) (3), ce que (5), ce qui (7), quoi; **What day is today?** C'est quel jour, aujourd'hui? (P); **What does that mean in English?** Qu'est-ce que ça veut dire en anglais? (P); **What is/are . . . like?** Comment est/sont... ? (1); **What is . . . 's name?** Comment s'appelle... ? (4) **What is your name?** Tu t'appelles comment? *(familiar)* (P); Comment vous appelez-vous? *(formal)* (P); **What luck!** Quelle chance! (5); **What's the weather like?** Quel temps fait-il? (5); **What time is it?** Quelle heure est-il? (P)

**when** quand (2)

**where** où (1); **from where** d'où (1)

**whereas** tandis que

**which** quel(le) (3); que, qui (7); **about/of which** dont (7); **which one** lequel (laquelle) (6)

**while** tandis que, pendant que; **See you in a little while.** À tout à l'heure. (P); **whil**e **on** au cours de (10);

**white** blanc(he) (3); **white wine** vin blanc *(m)* (2)

**who** qui (1)

**whom** qui (2), que (7)

**whole** tout (toute); **the whole day** toute la journée (2)

**wholegrain bread** pain complet *(m)* (8)

**whose** dont (7)

**why** pourquoi (2)

**widespread** répandu(e)

**widow** veuve *(f)* (7)

**widower** veuf *(m)* (7)

**wife** femme *(f)* (2)

**win** gagner (2)

**wind** vent *(m)*

**windbreaker** blouson *(m)*

**window** fenêtre *(f)* (3); **ticket window** guichet *(m)*

**windsurfing: go windsurfing** faire de la planche à voile

**windy: It's windy.** Il fait du vent. (5)

**wine** vin *(m)* (2)

**winter** hiver *(m)* (5); **in winter** en hiver (5)

**with** avec (P); chez (+ *person)* (7); **coffee with milk** café au lait *(m)* (2)

**withdraw** retirer (10)

**without** sans (P); **without doing it** sans le faire

**woman** femme *(f)* (1); **woman's suit** tailleur *(m)*

**wonder** se demander

**wonderful** merveilleux(-euse)

**word** mot *(m)* (P); *(lyrics)* parole *(f)*

**work** travail *(m)*

**work** travailler (2); **Does that work for you?** Ça te/vous convient? (9); **Do you work?** Tu travailles? / Vous travaillez? **I work . . .** Je travaille... (P)

**workbook** cahier *(m)* (P)

**worker** *(manual)* ouvrier(-ère) *(mf)*

**world** monde *(m)*; **Third World** Tiers Monde *(m)*

**world-(wide)** mondial(e) *(mpl* mondiaux) (5)

**worry (about)** (se) préoccuper (de)

**worse** pire

**would: I would like to . . .** Je voudrais (bien)... (2); **What would you like to do?** Qu'est-ce que vous voudriez faire... (2); **You would like . . .** Tu voudrais... (2)

**write** écrire (2); **How is that written?** Ça s'écrit comment? (P); **Write the answer.** Écrivez la réponse. (P)

**writer** écrivain *(m)*

**wrong: be wrong** avoir tort (4); **What's wrong?** Qu'est-ce qui ne va pas? (10)

**Y**

**yard** jardin *(m)*

**year** année *(f)* (4), an *(m)* (5); **be . . . years old** avoir... ans (4); **Happy New Year!** Bonne année!; **New Year's Eve** le réveillon *(m)* du jour de l'an

**yellow** jaune (3)

**yes** oui (P), si (8)

**yesterday** hier (5)

**yet** pourtant, déjà; **not yet** ne... pas encore (5)

**yogurt** yaourt *(m)*

**you** tu, vous (P), te (9); **And you?** Et toi?, Et vous? (P); **See you tomorrow!** À demain! (P); **Thank you!** Merci! (P); **There you are!** Te / Vous voilà!; **with you** avec toi, avec vous

**young** jeune (1)

**your** ton (ta, tes) (3); votre (vos) (3); **Open your book.** Ouvrez votre livre. (P); **What is your name?** Tu t'appelles comment? *(familiar)* (P), Comment vous appelez-vous? *(formal)* (P); **your friends** tes amis (1)

**yourself** te, vous (7); toi-même, vous-même(s)

**youth** jeunesse *(f)* (7); **youth hostel** auberge *(f)* de jeunesse (10)

**Z**

**zero** zéro (P), nul(le)

**zip code** code postal *(m)* (3)

**zucchini** courgette *(f)*

**zydeco: musique zydeco** musique *(f)* zydeco (4)

# Indice

# Credits

**Text Credits:** p. 27 Document France Télécom—Les pages jaunes—édition 1991; **p. 61** Onisep, *L'enseignement supérieur en France, 2003/2004*; **p. 85** Le Trapèze; **p. 95** L'heure du thé; **p. 96** Aux Trois Obus; **p. 126** Université Laval; **p. 127** Brune, no 5, 1992; **p. 132** Adapté de Kate Macrae, *Les couleurs et leurs effets sur la nature humaine*, www.sylkacoordination.com; **p. 168** Bruce Daigrepont, *Cœur des Cajuns*, Bayou Pon Pon, ASCAP-Happy Valley Music, BMI from *Cœur des Cajuns* on Rounder Records (#6026); **p. 206** Adapté de Gérard Mermet, *Francoscopie 2003*, Larousse; **p. 226** *L'officiel des spectacles*, no 2958, mercredi 3 à mardi 9 septembre 2003, Paris, France, p. 15; **p. 231** Courtesy of Yahoo; **p. 255** Courtesy of *Première*, no 245, août 1997; **p. 292** «Tous les matins, je me lève» vu dans *Vogue Hommes*, no 152, septembre 1992; **p. 293** *Rouen Poche*, no 92, du 15 au 21 juillet 1987; **pp. 294-295** «Les Français et l'amour», *Notre Temps*, novembre 2001; «La femme des années 2000», *Madame Figaro*, septembre 2003; «Le regard des hommes sur les femmes», *DS Magazine*, mai 2002; **pp. 308-309** Maraîchers; **p. 336** Jacques Prévert, «Déjeuner du matin» in *Paroles* © Éditions Gallimard; **p. 389** Choubouloute, p. 71; *Trois-Ilets Magazine*

**Photo Credits:** All photographs not otherwise credited are owned by Thomson Learning and Heinle Image Resouce Bank. We have made every effort to trace the ownership of all material and to secure permissions from the copyright holders. In the event of any question arising regarding the use of any material, we will make the necessary corrections for future printings.

**p. 2**: Raoul Dufy, "Nature Morte" 1934. Collection Alice Warder Garrett, Evergreen House Foundation/The Johns Hopkins University, Baltimore, Maryland; **p. 5** br: ©Gontier/The Image Works; **p. 23**: ©Rick Strange/Index Stock Imagery; **p. 25**: ©Owen Franken/CORBIS; **p. 28**: Pablo Picasso "Baie de Cannes" 1958. Musee Picasso, Paris. Giraudon/Art Resource/NY. ©2005 Estate of Pablo Picasso/Artists Rights Society (ARS), New York; **p. 30** b: ©Charles & Josette Lenars/CORBIS; **p. 31** l: ©R. Sidney; **p. 31** r: ©D. Bretzfolder/PhotoEdit; **p. 54** l: ©Jean-Paul Pelissier/Reuters/Landov; **p. 54** r: ©Siochan /Gamma-Presse; **p. 58** tl: ©Beryl Goldberg; **p. 58** bl: ©Paul Almasy/CORBIS; **p. 58** mr: ©Stuart Cohen/The Image Works; **p. 64** t: Henri Matisse, "Nature Morte aux Grenades" 1947. ©2005 Succession H. Matisse/Artists Rights Society (ARS), New York; Musee Matisse, Nice. Giraudon/Art Resource, New York; **p. 64** b: ©Beryl Goldberg; **p. 66** tl, br: ©Beryl Goldberg; **p. 66** tr: ©Jim Zuckerman/CORBIS; **p. 67** tl: Henri Matisse, "Creole Dancer" ©2005 Succession H. Matisse/ Artists Rights Society (ARS), NY. Photo: Gerard Blot, Reunion des Musees Nationaux/Art Resource, NY; **p. 67** m: ©Hideo Haga/HAGA/The Image Works; **p. 67** b: ©Beryl Goldberg; **p. 73** t: © Esther Marshall/Heinle; **p. 90**: ©AbleStock/Index Stock Imagery; **p. 96** tl: ©Maria Taglienti/Index Stock Imagery; **p. 96** br: ©Beryl Goldberg; **p. 97** tl: ©IPA/The Image Works; **p. 97** tr: Nicholas Raducnu/Heinle; **p. 102**: William Raphael "Derriere le Marche Bonsecours" 1866. National Gallery of Canada; **p. 104**: ©Robert Holmes/CORBIS; **p. 105** tl: ©SuperStock; **p. 105** mr: ©Walter Bibikow/Index Stock Imagery; **p. 105** bl: ©David Whitten/Index Stock Imagery; **p. 123**: ©Ulrike Welsch; **p. 130**: ©Andreas von Einsiedel; Elizabeth Whiting & Assoc./CORBIS; **p. 132** t: The Granger Collection, New York; **p. 132** bl: ©AP/Wide World Photos; **p. 133**: © J.A Kraulis/Masterfile; **p. 138** t: Henri Beau, "The Expulsion of the Acadians in 1755" 1900. Musee Acadien de l'Universite de Moncton, Canada. Bridgeman Art Library; **p. 138** b: ©Philip Gould/CORBIS; **p. 140** tl: ©Neil Rabinowitz/CORBIS; **p. 140** tm: ©Reuters/CORBIS; **p. 140** tr, bl: ©Philip Gould/CORBIS; **p. 141** t: ©Nathan Benn/CORBIS; **p. 141** m: ©Owen Franken/CORBIS; **p. 141** b: ©Philip Gould/CORBIS; **p. 155**: © Mark Segal/Index Stock Imagery; **p. 163**: © Diaphor Agency/Index Stock Imagery; **p. 167**: ©Philip Gould/CORBIS; **p. 168** t: The Granger Collection, New York; **p. 168** ml: Andre Mantelet-Martel, "Street Scene, New Orleans," Waterhouse and Dodd, London, UK/Bridgeman Art Library; **p. 168** mr: ©Ewing Galloway/©Index Stock Imagery; **p. 168** b, **p. 169**: ©Bettmann/CORBIS; **p. 174**: Robert Delaunay "La Tour Eiffel" 1910-1911. Basel Kunstmuseum. Giraudon/Art Resource, NY; **p. 176** tl: ©Ulrike Welsch; **p. 176** bl: ©Paul Almasay/CORBIS; **p. 176** br: ©Rhoda Sidney/PhotoEdit; **p.177** l: ©SuperStock, Inc./SuperStock; **p. 181** br: ©Mark Antman/TheImage Works; **p. 187** l: ©Sandro Vannini/CORBIS; **p. 187** m: © Eric Bouret/Gamma; **p. 188**: ©Tom Craig; **p. 195** tl: ©Bill Ross/CORBIS; **p. 195** tr, br: ©Robert Holmes/CORBIS; **p. 195** bl: ©Bachman/The Image Works; **p. 199** tl: ©George Simhoni/Masterfile; **p. 199** ml: ©Horst von Irmer/Index Stock Imagery; **p. 199** mm: ©Robert Holmes/CORBIS; **p. 199** bm: ©Beryl Godlberg; **p. 199** br: ©Bachmann/The Image Works; **p. 204**: ©Robert Harding World Imagery/Alamy; **p. 205** l: ©Beryl Goldberg; **p. 205** r: © Paul Thompson; Eye Ubiquitous/CORBIS; **p. 206** t, b: ©Tom Craig/DIRECTPHOTO.ORG; **p. 207** b: ©SuperStock; **p. 216**: ©Buddy Mays/CORBIS; **p. 217** tl: ©Brenda Tharp/CORBIS; **p. 218** m: ©Ray Juno/ CORBIS; **p. 219** ml: ©Egberhard Otto/Getty Images; **p. 222** t: Henri Rousseau, "Notre Dame" 1909. The Phillips Collection, Washington, DC; **p. 222** b: Constantin Brancusi "Le Baiser." circa 1911. Musee National d'Art Moderne, Paris. Giraudon/Art Resource. ©2005 Artists Rights Society (ARS), New York/ADAGP, Paris; **p. 224** t: ©Mark Antman/The Image Works; **p. 224** br: ©Kindra Clineff/Index Stock Imagery; **p. 225** tl: ©Tom Craig/Index Stock Imagery; **p. 225** bl: ©Directphoto.org/Alamy; **p. 225** br, tr: ©Walter Bibikow/Index Stock Imagery; **p. 246**: ©Hulton Archive; **p. 254** t: ©Tom Craig/DIRECTPHOTO.ORG; **p. 254** b: © UGC/Studio Canal +/The Kobal Collection; **p. 255**: © Vincent Kessler/ Landov; **p. 260**: Camille Pissaro, "Port de Rouen" 1896. Musee d'Orsay, Paris; **p. 262** tr: © Jonkmanns/Laif/Aurora; **p. 262** bl: ©Jack Reznicki; **p. 263** t: © Taxi/Getty Images; **p. 263** bl: © Alain Nogues/ CORBIS Sygma; **p. 273**: ©Index Stock Imagery; **p. 277**: ©Owen Franken/CORBIS; **p. 286** t: ©Royalty Free/CORBIS; **p. 286** b: ©Olivia Baumgartner/ CORBIS Sygma; **p. 291**: ©Henri Cartier Bresson/MAGNUM; **p. 294**: ©PhotoDisc/Getty Images; **p. 300** t: Raoul Dufy, "Les Affiches a Trouville." 1906. Musee National d'Art Moderne. ©2005 Artists Rights Society (ARS), New York/ADAGP, Paris; **p. 300** b: "La Tapisserie de Bayeux," 11th century. Bauex, Musee de la Tapisserie. Erich Lessing/Art Resource, New York; **p. 302** tl: ©SCPhotos/Alamy; **p. 302** mr: ©Lee Snider/The Image Works; **p. 303** tl: ©Brownie Harris; **p. 303** tr: © Diaphor Agency/Index Stock Imagery; **p. 303** br: ©Erich Lessing/Art Resource, NY; **p. 313** t: © Catherine Karnow/ CORBIS; **p. 313** b: ©Tom Craig/Index Stock Imagery; **p. 315**: ©Esther Marshall/Heinle; **p. 317**: ©David R. Frazier, Photolibrary, Inc.; **p. 328** b: © Image State/RF/Alamy; **p. 337** tl: ©Image Source/Alamy; **p. 337** mr: ©C Squared/Getty Images; **p. 337** b: ©Zefa/O.Graf/ Masterfile; **p. 338** t: ©Ulrike Welsch; **p. 338** b: ©Stuart Cohen; **p. 344**: Joseph-Jean Laurent, "Man in Orange Hat" 1970. Milwaukee Art Museum, Gift of Richard and Erna Flagg; **p. 346** tl, br: ©Don Klein/DDB Stock Photo; **p. 347** tl: ©SuperStock; **p. 347** tr: ©Rolf Richardson/Alamy; **p. 347** bl: ©Joe Carini/The Image Works; **p. 347** br: © Christophe Marciniak; **p. 353**: ©Philippe Giraud/CORBIS Sygma; **p. 365**: ©Robert Fried; **p. 366**: ©Tiziana and Gianni Baldizzone/CORBIS; **p. 366** b: ©Phyllis Picardi/Index Stock Imagery; **p. 369** tl: ©Michael Freeman/CORBIS; **p. 372**: ©Peter Hvizdak/The Image Works; **p. 373**: ©Index Stock Imagery; **p. 374** t: ©Sophie Bassouls/CORBIS; **p. 374** b: ©Hulton-Deutsch Collection/CORBIS; **p. 375** tl: ©Robert Fried; **p. 375** tr: ©Heldur Netocny/Panos Pictures; **p. 380** t: Gerard, Valcin, "Coumbite" 1971, Private Collection. Manu Sassoonian / Art Resource, NY; **p. 380** b: ©Robert Fried; **p. 382** tr, bl: ©Robert Fried; **p. 382** br: ©Suzanne Murphy/DDB Stock Photo; **p. 383** tl: ©Marc Garanger/CORBIS; **p. 383** tr, bl, br: ©Robert Fried; **p. 383** ml: ©Walter Bibikow/Index; **p. 387**: ©Walter Bibikow/Index Stock Imagery; **p. 397**: ©Philip Gould/CORBIS; **p. 400**: ©ThinkStock LLC/Index Stock Imagery; **p. 403**: ©Stuart Cohen/The Image Works; **p. 410**: ©Alyx Kellington/CORBIS; **p. 411**: ©Kathleen Marie Rohr/DDB Stock Photo; **p. 421** t: ©Bruce Paton/Panos Pictures; **p. 421** ml: ©David Reed/Panos Pictures; **p. 421** mr: ©Betty Press/Panos Pictures; **p. 421** bl: ©Brian Vikander; **p. 421** br: ©G. Wulfsohn/Panos Pictures; **p. 422** t: ©Robert Grossman/CORBIS Sygma; **p. 422** b: ©Otto Lang/CORBIS; **p. 423** tr: ©CORBIS; **p. 423** ml: ©Chris Lisle/CORBIS; **p. 423** bl: ©Robert van der Hilst/CORBIS; **p. 423** br: ©Chinch Gryniewicz, Ecoscene/CORBIS; **p. 424**: ©Ulrike Welsch; **p. 426**: Pieter Bruegel, "Return of the Hunters" 1565. Kunsthistorisches Museum, Gemaeldegalerie, Vienna. Erich Lessing, Art Resource, NY; **p. 428** tl: ©Morton Beebe/CORBIS; **p. 428** tr: ©S.Vidler/SuperStock; **p. 428** br: ©Royalty-Free/CORBIS; **p. 429**: ©SuperStock; **p. 441**: ©Keren Su/CORBIS

# France

MER DU NORD

Pays-Bas

Allemagne

Grande-Bretagne

Dunkerque

Calais

Belgique

Lille

NORD-PAS-
DE-CALAIS

Valenciennes

Luxembourg

MANCHE

Amiens

Cherbourg

HAUTE-
NORMANDIE

PICARDIE

Reims

Meuse

Metz

LORRAINE

ALSACE

Rhin

Le Havre

Rouen

Seine

Caen

BASSE-
NORMANDIE

Paris

CHAMPAGNE-
ARDENNE

Nancy

Strasbourg

VOSGES

Saint-Malo

Versailles

ILE-DE-
FRANCE

Moselle

Mulhouse

Brest

Fougères

Troyes

Seine

BRETAGNE

Rennes

Le Mans

Orléans

BOURGOGNE

Saône

Besançon

PAYS-DE-LA-LOIRE

Angers

Blois

Chambord

Dijon

FRANCHE-
COMTE

JURA

Suisse

St-Nazaire

Loire

Tours

Chenonceaux

Nantes

Chinon

Azay-le-
Rideau

Bourges

Nevers

Chalon-sur-
Saône

CENTRE

Loire

Poitiers

OCEAN

LIMOUSIN

Vichy

Rhône

Annecy

La Rochelle

Clermont-
Ferrand

Lyon

ATLANTIQUE

POITOU-
CHARENTES

Limoges

Saint Étienne

RHONE-ALPES

Italie

Périgueux

AUVERGNE

Grenoble

ALPES

Bordeaux

MASSIF CENTRAL

Rodez

Rhône

PROVENCE-
ALPES-
COTE-
D'AZUR

Monte-
Carlo

Monaco

AQUITAINE

Garonne

MIDI-PYRENEES

Avignon

Grasse

Nîmes

Tarascon

Aix-en-
Provence

Biarritz

Bayonne

Toulouse

Montpellier

Nice

Pau

Béziers

Toulon

Cannes

PYRENEES

Carcassonne

Narbonne

Marseille

Espagne

Andorre

LANGUEDOC-
ROUSSILLON

Perpignan

MER MEDITERRANEE

0    75 km

CORSE

Ajaccio

**Afrique**

Pays et régions où le français est langue officielle, co-officielle ou administrative

Pays et régions où le français est langue d'enseignement privilégiée

0    500    1000    1500 km

Tunisie
Maroc
Sahara occidental
Algérie
Libye
Égypte
Mauritanie
Sénégal
Dakar
Gambie
Guinée-Bissau
Guinée
Mali
Niger
Tchad
Soudan
République de Djibouti
Sierra Leone
Côte-d'Ivoire
Burkina Faso
Togo
Bénin
Nigeria
Ghāna
Lomé
Lagos
Cotonou
Abidjan
Liberia
Cameroun
République centrafricaine
Ethiopie
Somalie
Guinée-Equatoriale
Bangui
Ouganda
Kenya
São Tomé & Principe
Libreville
Gabon
Congo
République démocratique du Congo
Ruanda
Burundi
Point-Noire
Kinshasa
Luanda
Tanzanie
Seychelles
Comores
Mayotte
Angola
Zambie
Malawi
Maurice
Réunion
Namibie
Zimbabwe
Mozambique
Botswana
Madagascar
Swaziland
Afrique du Sud
Lesotho

N